Inglorious Passages

Inglorious Passages

Noncombat Deaths in the American Civil War

Brian Steel Wills

 University Press of Kansas

© 2017 by the University Press of Kansas
All rights reserved

Published by the University Press of Kansas (Lawrence, Kansas 66045), which was organized by the Kansas Board of Regents and is operated and funded by Emporia State University, Fort Hays State University, Kansas State University, Pittsburg State University, the University of Kansas, and Wichita State University.

Library of Congress Cataloging-in-Publication Data
Names: Wills, Brian Steel, 1959– author.
Title: Inglorious passages : noncombat deaths in the American Civil War / Brian Steel Wills.
Description: Lawrence, Kansas : University Press of Kansas, 2017. | Series: Modern war studies | Includes bibliographical references and index.
Identifiers: LCCN 2017038280 | ISBN 9780700625086 (cloth: alk. paper) | ISBN 9780700625093 (ebook)
Subjects: LCSH: United States—History—Civil War, 1861–1865—Casualties. | United States—History—Civil War, 1861–1865—Social aspects. | Soldiers—United States—Death—History—19th century. | War casualties—United States—History—19th century.
Classification: LCC E468.9 .W58 2017 | DDC 973.7/1—dc23
LC record available at https://lccn.loc.gov/2017038280.

British Library Cataloguing-in-Publication Data is available.

Printed in the United States of America

10 9 8 7 6 5 4 3 2 1

The paper used in this publication is recycled and contains 30 percent postconsumer waste. It is acid free and meets the minimum requirements of the American National Standard for Permanence of Paper for Printed Library Materials Z39.48-1992.

To all who served and sacrificed
their "last full measure,"

And in memory of friends and historians
Wiley Sword, Mike Ballard, and Martin Ryle.

Contents

A photo gallery follows page 168.

Preface and Acknowledgments

Leading military historian John Keegan examined the "face of battle" by focusing on the iconic European engagements of Agincourt (1415), Waterloo (1815), and the Somme (1916). He opened his study with an admission that although he had read and studied about the battlefield extensively, "I have never been in a battle. And I grow increasingly convinced that I have very little idea of what a battle can be like."[1]

That scholar and I share that history. Yet, clearly, Keegan wanted to come to understand better the experience of the battlefield and the degree to which that ordeal evolved over time. He also recognized that even in combat, death came from sources other than enemy weapons. "Accident has always caused a portion of battle's deaths and wounds," he observed. Whether the suffocation of soldiers "beneath the press of bodies at Agincourt" or the accidental discharge of weapons at Waterloo and the Somme, men died who might not otherwise have done so.[2] In discussing the role of accidents in causing fatalities among soldiers, Keegan observed, "In real warfare they are yet more frequent, so much so that, during quiet weeks in the Vietnam campaign, traffic accidents often killed more American soldiers than did the Viet Cong."[3] He offered no statistic as foundation for the assertion, but his point remained clear. Men have perished in wartime outside of the context of hostile fire on the battlefield or under unexpected circumstances on it.

However, the British historian's argument was not the reason I undertook this study. In *The War Hits Home*, published in 2001, I attempted to examine and assess the experience of warfare from 1861 to 1865 in the community in which I was reared: Suffolk, Virginia, in what was then Nansemond County, and the surrounding area. I found that there were powerful and often poignant stories of fatal accidents and encounters and collateral civilian deaths that occurred in that region during the Civil War.[4] I wanted to allow such stories as those to be told

ix

and known, apart from the cold calculations of statistics, even when the causes of those ends reflected no sense of the sacrifices that could be expected from combat. In each case, they represented the harsh realities that the loved ones who had gone off to war were not going to be returning home to renew their lives and rejoin their families once the formal hostilities were ended.

Part of the motivation for this work also came from popular culture. As a young person, one of my most enduring family experiences was watching the motion picture *Shenandoah*, in which Jimmy Stewart's Charlie Anderson attempted desperately and ultimately unsuccessfully to avoid the war raging around him and prevent it from affecting adversely his tight-knit clan in the Shenandoah Valley of Virginia. Although Anderson and his sons never enlisted for armed service, the conflict nevertheless impacted the family when circumstances led to the deaths of several of its members—two killed by roving soldier deserters and another by a startled youthful Confederate picket. After Anderson and his entourage of family members returned from an unsuccessful search for the missing youngest child—"the Boy"—the empty chairs around the table in the Anderson household reflected these unintended and inglorious passages as the remaining members of the clan gathered for their meals.

The Charles Humphreys story that leads this work came later, but it seemed perfectly suited to putting into contemporary words what I wanted to say. The same sentiment was true for civilian victims of the conflict. Some of these individuals perished while caught up in battles that reached their homes or communities or in factories and under other circumstances associated with wartime production and supply. These final encounters happened for each of these people, often in situations they could not have imagined and with a cost that their loved ones were required to endure.

Many individuals and institutions have assisted with the research for this work. The efforts of many colleagues in the profession to edit and produce letters, diaries, and other memoirs have been essential to this project. Likewise, the Library of Congress's excellent website "Chronicling America" has proved indispensable for reaching newspaper sources. Individually, many people have offered assistance in various ways. Wayne Willingham graciously provided examples for use in the volume. Nick Picerno sent a volume of letters and several references for inclusion pertaining to Maine soldiers. Jim Ogden offered numerous examples. Ann Gunnin shared her volume, *Letters to Virtue*, on her kinsman Charles W. Sherman after a talk I presented at a meeting of the Clara Barton Tent in Georgia.

During my semester as Lewis P. Jones Professor of History at Wofford College in Spartanburg, South Carolina, my colleagues were not only extraordinarily gracious but also helpful in allowing me to make my public presentation on this topic and use the materials in the library and archives for research. Thanks especially to colleague and friend Tracy Revels and to Phil Stone in the library for their support.

My own Department of History and Philosophy and the Dean's Office in the College of Humanities and Social Sciences at Kennesaw State University have been likewise supportive. As always, Randy Patton, my colleague, friend, and former officemate from graduate school at the University of Georgia, has been a bulwark. The Center for the Study of the Civil War Era, of which I have had the privilege of serving as director since 2010, has allowed me the freedom to engage in research and writing when I am not undertaking other activities to support the center's programming and operations.

In Wise, Virginia, my wife, Elizabeth, has remained a necessary foundation of support for all the projects I have undertaken, whether this one or those connected with the Center at Kennesaw. My mother, Harriet Wills, in Suffolk, Virginia, will be pleased that our relative Charles Hasker made it into this volume, although he was fortunate to survive his encounter with death while on a trial run of the Confederate submarine *Hunley*, in which so many others did not.

Any work is a matter that depends upon the good offices of many individuals. Although any remaining mistakes remain exclusively my own, I wish to thank Susan Ecklund for her superb copyediting and Kelly Chrisman Jacques and her colleagues at the University Press of Kansas for their parts in shepherding the manuscript through the publication process.

The book's dedication is for the people, soldier and civilian, whose sacrifices have tended to be overlooked or forgotten and for the lives and work of friends and fellow historians the profession has lost recently: Wiley Sword, Mike Ballard, and Martin Ryle. I have worked with each of these fine men in various capacities through many years. In addition to other personal connections, Wiley was an Honorary Advisory Board Member for the Civil War Center at KSU, and Mike worked closely with the Center on a meeting of the Western Theater Historians held in Kennesaw in 2015. Finally, Martin Ryle was a professor of mine at the University of Richmond, and we shared an extraordinary journey (my first) to Europe in 1982 that has remained a cherished part of my memory ever since. From London and Le Grande Place to Geneva, Paris, and Versailles, we had a wonderful time living and learning. Each of these men illustrates that historians are often premier people as well as scholars.

Introduction
"This Inglorious Taking Off"

> This inglorious taking off is hardly what I antici-
> pated in coming out to fight for my country. None
> will know whether I made a brave ending, or *where*
> I met my death.
> *Chaplain Charles Humphreys contemplating a close call*
> *with his mortality, March 1865*

> From these honored dead we take increased devo-
> tion to that cause for which they gave the last full
> measure of devotion—that we here highly resolve
> that these dead shall not have died in vain.
> *Abraham Lincoln, Gettysburg Address*

Charles Humphreys did not die. However, the Union chaplain came as close as he could when trying to cross the rain-swollen North Anna River in Virginia in mid-March 1865. He was part of a contingent of mounted troops maneuvering their way across what would ordinarily have been an easy fording place except for the rising water and pitch darkness. Instead, as he wrote, "The only guide to the ford for each cavalry-man was the horse in front of him, and without suspecting it, this was another instance of the blind leading the blind." Somehow, the chap-lain became unhorsed and nearly drowned. In contemplation of his encounter with eternity, Humphreys recalled:

> I thought of the unheroic homeliness of my being smothered there alone
> in the river's moist shroud as contrasted with the sustaining inspirations in
> meeting death with brave companions on the field of glorious war. I said to
> myself: "This inglorious taking off is hardly what I anticipated in coming out

1

to fight for my country. None will know whether I made a brave ending, or *where* I met my death."[1]

Captain Edward H. Mix of the Sixteenth Connecticut was not as fortunate as his comrade in the clergy. Despite being one of the last of his unit's original officers, he had already faced difficulties with discipline and insubordination and was on his way home aboard a transport in March 1864. A "blow from the boom" struck Mix and propelled him overboard, causing him to drown under the burden of his coat and heavy boots before help could reach him. The unit's historian, who had also served in the regiment, observed that the accident "snatched [him] from the bloody glory of dying in his country's cause, to perish alone and un-cheered—no banner above him but the silent clouds—no sounds around him but the rush of waters." Mix's comrades lamented that the circumstances would not allow them to offer his remains the honors of war.[2]

Soldiers and civilians alike on both sides had made sacrifices, glorious or otherwise, since 1861, when a lanky figure took his place on a stand before a large crowd gathered on the fields of Gettysburg, Pennsylvania, on Thursday, November 19, 1863. Now assembling on the same hallowed ground to witness the dedication of a cemetery, the observers expected to hear the appropriate oratory that marked such occasions. Yet, on this day, the honor of keynote speaker belonged to famed orator Edward Everett, who regaled the audience for some two hours with an address, featuring the expected historical and literary allusions and offering a detailed account of the engagement that had occurred earlier on the ground in July.[3] Then, the tall man rose to add remarks that have since become arguably the most famous words uttered on behalf of national ideals in any conflict and the soldiers who perished defending them:

But, in a larger sense, we can not dedicate, we can not consecrate, we can not hallow this ground. The brave men, living and dead, who struggled here, have consecrated it, far above our poor power to add or detract. The world will little note, nor long remember what we say here, but it can never forget what they did here. It is for us the living, rather, to be dedicated here to the unfinished work which they who fought here have thus far so nobly advanced. It is rather for us to be here dedicated to the great task remaining before us—that from these honored dead we take increased devotion to that cause for which they gave the last full measure of devotion—that we here highly resolve that these dead shall not have died in vain—that this nation, under God, shall have a new birth of freedom—and that government of the people, by the people, for the people, shall not perish from the earth.

When this expression came from the sixteenth president of the United States at the ceremony at Gettysburg, the symbolism reflected therein captured the nature of the republic over which Abraham Lincoln had been presiding during the course of his tumultuous administration. The message also came to represent the essence of the struggle from the Union perspective and cast the conflict in terms and tones sufficiently lofty to explain and justify the loss of life that the North had already endured and would have to be prepared to continue to experience in order for the Union cause to emerge triumphant.[4]

In terms of their relation to the fallen warriors, President Lincoln's words may have seemed most, if not entirely, applicable to those who had lost their lives in combat or as a direct result of it. Yet, such sentiments would subscribe just as meaningfully to the many individuals who had volunteered for service, submitted to conscription, or worked on behalf of the war effort in homes and factories only to make the ultimate sacrifice outside of the context of such battlefields as Gettysburg, Vicksburg, Antietam, Chickamauga, Wilson's Creek, or Pea Ridge. Their loss, in the course of the warfare that engulfed their worlds, was as real to themselves and their family members and friends as if they had perished under the effects of shot and shell, minié ball, saber, or bayonet.

Confederate sacrifice was just as genuine as that made by the Union forces that President Lincoln sought to remember. Already, graves in communities far and wide across the South held the mortal forms of individuals who had borne the final costs as surely as their blue-coated opponents. The region's soil contained the remains of Southern sons and daughters as well as those who had come to oppose them, and the price was no less severe for the absence of appropriate oratory or the fact that so many met their final moments away from the blazing weaponry of their antagonists. Indeed, some of the most poignant passages in letters home and other personal accounts came in response to the fatal impact of diseases and accidents that cut short the promise of so many lives.

The images of war, especially in the minds of the young and the uninitiated, were of banners flying and glory won over the din of battle. One romantic Confederate explained in a letter home just after his state had joined the other Deep South states in secession in April 1861, "Virginia, mindful of the blood that flows in her old veins, mindful of her historic fame, proud of the prestige of her past, has shaken off her lethargic slumbers and under the very heel of the tyrant awakes and arises to glory again." For John Sheffey, the attraction of the pageantry of the moment was irresistible. "With banners waving, and the measured tread of legions of armed men," he wrote, "she marches like a giantess to the conflict, and all her brave sons now like the sons of Old Sparta will remember how glorious a thing it is to die for their country."[5]

Such men were prepared to fall in the headlong charges or under the galling blasts that they expected to mark any major confrontations of the war, with sacrifices to bear stark but noble witness to the price exacted by that conflict upon its participants. Yet, there was no single motivating factor that drove men in blue and gray or butternut to offer their lives in this fashion if required. Some saw meaning primarily in terms of patriotism or liberty. Others looked first to family and home. Many thought in terms of community or neighbors as worthy of demanding their shared sense of duty and commitment. Still more heeded a moral or religious calling for their service in the ranks against a foe that they felt threatened the very fabric of the earthly world they inhabited. Nearly all felt the urge to stand for something greater than themselves, whatever that might be. "Dying well" was not only part of the "civic culture"; it was part of the personal culture for these soldiers, too.[6]

Yet, many would not necessarily die in battle after all, and the staggering casualties of the higher-profile engagements often masked the passing of individuals under what might be considered mundane or even ignoble circumstances. Historian Wiley Sword has noted the ultimate conundrum of the war for so many of the soldiers—having the courage to risk their lives for a greater purpose even as situations beyond their control often emerged that would deny that sacrifice the validity of the context of the battlefield. "To do and die thus," Sword explained, "was also an indelible contribution to the cause in which he had joined."[7]

It was a singular fact that more individuals died in noncombat situations than perished from the actions of hostile forces. A newspaper from Vermont informed its readers in early 1863 of the dramatic statistics associated with fatalities among the men in uniform: "The excess of the mortality due to disease and accident, over that due to wounds in action, is a noticeable fact in the volunteer army of the United States, as in all other armies, *two-thirds* of the deaths of officers and *five-sixths* of those of the men resulting from disease and accident; the remaining one-third and one-sixth, respectively, being caused by wounds received in battle."[8]

For the men in the field the issues were not matters of raw data but intensely personal. In November 1861, a Union soldier from Illinois wrote home, "Tiford fever is Rageing here verry much their had been several Deaths of it." A Confederate explained in August 1862, "T. G. Fremen is Ded and they is Several mor that is Dangerous with fever they hev Been 11 Died with the fever in Co A since we left kinston." A Louisiana officer observed a year later that the sick soldiers he encountered "cannot be kept down in their wretched bunks, but stagger about jabbering and muttering insanities, till they lie down and die in their ragged, dirty uniforms." Captain John W. De Forest could only lament the conditions that had "turned our fine regiment into a sickly, dispirited, undisciplined wreck" and produced "forty-two deaths in forty-two days."[9]

In October 1862, only a month after the single deadliest day of the war near the Maryland village of Sharpsburg, a Northern newspaper presented a resolution to one of the fallen that illustrated the stark realities for so many. Henry P. Smith had not died from the direct wounds received in combat. "The deceased left home two months ago to do his part in sustaining the Government," the notice offered. "He had passed through the terrible battle of Antietam, unharmed, but the exertion and the subsequent hardships and exposures proved too much for his vigorous frame—and an attack of violent disease soon followed." The soldier's mother, who traveled to nurse her son, instead had the sad duty of conveying his remains home with her. "The friends and acquaintances of the young patriot will ever cherish his memory. He is another victim of the slave-holders rebellion."[10]

The surviving warriors also realized the fatal effects of war upon soldiers and civilians outside of the scope of the formalized fighting itself. Not everyone who perished was destined to do so in lines of battle next to their comrades, while serving artillery pieces in batteries or fortifications, or while engaged in mounted or waterborne action against their enemies. Even extracting the devastating effects of disease, the losses in noncombat experiences were staggering and deeply felt on both sides of the Mason and Dixon line. Historian George Rable captured the essence of reality for so many who had taken up a uniform and brandished arms to confront their foes only to fall away from a battlefield that might provide their deaths with that sense of meaning: "Even without engaging the enemy, for many soldiers death had become a familiar companion, a daily reminder of their peril."[11]

The incongruities of the conflict seemed to become magnified in the most troubling manner. Men might die in combat facing the foe, but to meet mortality away from the battlefield seemed especially disconcerting. "An hour ago I was by the graveside of Marcus Dawson, of Co. D," a Union chaplain recorded from outside Harpers Ferry, Virginia. "There upon a point commanding a view of the Shenandoah Valley for miles—lie fourteen men of the 107th [New York], fallen by fever and now at rest." Most troubling, for the clergyman, was the knowledge of the personal role he had played with another victim: "I know nothing of Dawson save that as a Christian I have assisted in burying him. But I saw in the hospital the body of a young man, three days dead, whom I myself enlisted. I have his name in one of my old books, and as I looked upon his blanket shroud, I earnestly tested myself, was I right in telling him to enlist?" Despite whatever doubt he may have encountered, the chaplain concluded that he need not repent for his "pleedings" and "statements of duty."[12]

In their examination of civilians and soldiers in the war, Scott Reynolds Nelson and Carol Sheriff reflected on the impact of death upon the participants and their contemporaries: "The war's carnage tied together the military and civilian realms in ways that extended well beyond the shared anxieties about a good death and well beyond civilian initiatives to contain disease and thwart mortality." For the affected populations at home and in the field who would experience the effects of war, the degree of destruction to life would cause many to "reconsider some of their most fundamental assumptions about the world around them."[13]

Even for those who remained at home, in settings that might have been thought safer and more secure from unexpected harm, the fatal impact of war existed. For many households, the danger was as close as the nearest armed body and as present as the next skirmish or battle. Mayhem presented itself in myriad other forms to citizens on both sides of the divide, in the city streets, the hospital wards, and the manufacturing and industrial centers. In Washington, the press of demand for war production turned sprawling facilities such as the Washington Arsenal and the Navy Yard from storage to production centers, with the attendant dangers as new personnel filled the workshops.[14]

Richmond saw a similar surge as the agencies of the respective governments and the supporting civilian infrastructure geared up for a war of indeterminate size and duration. Historian Emory Thomas noted the expanded role of women in industrial plants as part of the Confederacy's "revolutionary experience" in wartime. "Factory work was another genuine departure from tradition," he explained, noting that the dangers inherent in the work were as real as those found in battle. "In March 1863 a room full of explosives at an ordnance plant in Richmond blew up. The great majority of the sixty-nine dead workers were women and girls." Despite the tragedy, individuals soon cleared the rubble and restarted operations in a facility that remained "staffed with more undaunted females."[15]

Even so, sickness remained the greatest threat. Paul E. Steiner described the phenomenon as "natural biological warfare."[16] James I. "Bud" Robertson Jr. labeled this aspect of the soldier experience "the grimmest reaper."[17] Bell Irvin Wiley, the dean of Civil War soldier life, illustrated the fatal impact of illness on men in both Union and Confederate ranks by entitling a chapter on disease among the Confederate soldiers "The Deadliest Foe."[18] Wiley also observed, "In the Federal forces four persons died of sickness for every one killed in battle, and deaths from disease were twice those resulting from all other known causes."[19] Circumstances could strike men down long before they would have had a chance to experience combat or after they had survived it on earlier occasions.

A Georgian fighting with the Army of Northern Virginia noted the disconcerting fact that illness was ravaging the ranks to a much greater, and alarming, degree than combat. "Our Comp. has lost about 25 [men] with sickness and one with the bullet," Mason Hill Fitzpatrick noted in early August 1862. Disease had taken its toll on his comrades, and in his letter home, with a quiet sense of urgency he retreated to the only solace that he thought the situation offered: "Pray for me."[20]

A surgeon in Kentucky recalled watching men die from the ravages of illness with such demoralizing regularity that he observed, "It was worse than a battle." G. C. Phillips admitted that in the crisis that had arisen, the "drs were all at sea." A decline in critical cases came after Phillips suggested some new measures out of desperation to do something as much as anything else, but when the regiment abandoned its encampment, the surgeon asserted that the men "who suffered and died at Camp Beauregard, were just as brave and patriotic as their comrades and friends" who would fall on the battlefield. Years later, Phillips concluded, "It was no fault of theirs that they did not live to be killed at Shiloh, Vicksburg or Franklin, where so many of the regiment were killed, and whose resting places are marked by headstones and beautiful monuments—erected by loving descendants and friends in memory of their heroism, courage and glorious death."[21]

In the Army of the Potomac statistics bore out the devastation of noncombat deaths on the men in the ranks. The conditions besetting Major Thomas W. Hyde's Seventh Maine prompted him to write home about the *"horrible"* nature of soldier life in Virginia. "We have averaged one death per day ever since we came out," he noted dejectedly. Another soldier explained simply that the prevailing attitude in late 1862 was that if formalized combat did not occur soon, "there will be no army to fight with."[22] Gerald F. Linderman explained that for two Ohio regiments, the losses resulted in critical reductions in the number of effectives available before either had lost "a single soldier killed in action."[23]

In addition to fatal illnesses, misfortune, incompetence, mismanagement, and simple neglect were also often responsible for the conditions that led to the unnecessary deaths of soldiers in noncombat situations. One Union commander complained, "A reckless and ambitious man will risk everything to gain promotion, and in the hazard will throw [away] the lives of thousands of his fellow citizens. Their health, comfort and personal safety are hardly thought of by him, and if thought of are [of] too little consequence to interfere with his own advancement." Alvin Coe Voris of the Sixty-Seventh Ohio Volunteer Infantry concluded that such individuals would be less likely to be held in esteem if people at home became more aware of their behavior: "If they knew more many an officer who has a fair share of fame [today] would sink so low in public estimation as never to be heard of only as an object unworthy [of] the place and responsibilities he holds."[24]

Charles Sherman employed the strongest tone regarding health care for the troops in a letter to his family from his camp in October 1862: "I have known men that has been told that nothing was the Matter with them and before midnight thay was Dead men. That is the Class of Doctors we have with us and if Justice was meated out to one that is with us he whouled be hanging on the first Tree the Boys couled get him to."[25] Certainly, many in the ranks shared a disdain for the surgeons charged with their care, but the price paid by these men, including outside of combat situations, where 9 medical officers perished in accidents and 285 by disease, indicated their sacrifices as well.[26]

Death also made an impact upon the men in the ranks in other unexpected and often unexplained manners. Union chaplain Thomas Van Horne provided examples of officers in the Army of the Cumberland who perished in such ways, including First Lieutenant John P. D. Gibson of the Eighty-Eighth Illinois Infantry, "Killed accidentally at Loudon, Tenn., April 17, 1862"; Assistant Surgeon William Morrow Knox of the Seventy-Eighth Pennsylvania Infantry, "Killed accidentally at Louisville, Ky., April 27, 1862"; First Lieutenant William C. Shelbey of the Tenth Tennessee Infantry, "Killed accidentally, August 26, 1863"; First Lieutenant William Aulbach of the Second Missouri Infantry, "Killed accidentally at St. Louis, Mo., December 31, 1863"; First Lieutenant Alexander M. Boggs of the Twenty-Seventh Illinois Infantry, "Killed accidentally near Atlanta, Ga., July 23, 1864"; First Lieutenant N. Jordan Camp of the Twenty-Third Missouri Infantry, "Killed accidentally, August 4, 1864"; and First Lieutenant Frank M. Flickenger of the Eighty-Fourth Indiana Infantry, "Killed accidentally, March 13, 1865."[27]

Other individuals fought internal demons or found the strain of facing battle more than they felt they could tolerate and chose to end their lives rather than desert their comrades or face criticism from loved ones at home. The great irony for these individuals was that in dying by their own hands they would be spared the agonies of death or maiming on the battlefield. Such notions may have seemed to run counter to Victorian ideals, but they represented the range of explanations that included a desire to retain some measure of control over one's personal fate. They also reflected the degree to which sacrifice was universal among soldiers and civilians, even in the midst of the expected casualties of war. As one correspondent noted rhetorically, and with a palpable sense of resignation after recounting "accidents, or mischances" that had come to his attention in 1863: "Thus you see, that though war has its horrors, the imagination seldom pictures these daily dispensations of Providence which everywhere surround us."[28]

The soldiers themselves recognized that all deaths, regardless of their circumstances, affected comrades in the ranks as well as their loved ones at home. William Pitt Chambers of Mississippi undoubtedly spoke for many when he observed, on April 3, 1863, "I saw a coffin being taken to one of the companies in our rear this afternoon. Some soldier died away from home and most likely without the gentle ministrations of a mother or a sister." Another comrade's fate reminded him that greater ramifications usually came with these deaths. "He leaves a helpless family."[29]

As such experiences illustrated, not every situation allowed for a complete understanding of the circumstances that had claimed the life of a soldier outside of the context of battle. Two brief notices in a newspaper from Port Royal, South Carolina, appearing in May 1863, simply noted the names, units, and causes of death for two such individuals: "Erastus K. Vosburg, Private Co. D, 47th New York Vols., April 29th, chronic diarrhea," and "Daniel Bennet, Private Co. G, 62nd Ohio, April 30, of wounds received by the accidental explosion of a shell."[30] Friends or family members learning of the outcomes from this source would not know the length of Private Vosburg's illness or the nature of the accident that took the life of Private Bennet. Nor would they have whatever comfort might be derived from knowing that these men had died in combat in the face of the enemy.

In addition to providing common annoyances, extremes in weather contributed to the fatal tolls as well. A Confederate soldier recalled of his service, "If the dust and heat were not on hand to annoy, their very able substitutes were: mud, cold, rain, snow, hail and wind took their places." Seasonal tempests that unleashed sudden violent thunderstorms could spawn bolts of lightning that caused those seeking shelter or otherwise exposed at inopportune times and locations to defy the odds of being struck down. Storm-tossed oceans, rough surfs, raging rain-swollen rivers and creeks, or a misstep at a wharf or canal could spell doom for those unlucky enough to encounter them.

Transportation accidents on land and water that ranged from railroad collisions, derailments, and boiler explosions to riding mishaps, drownings, and vehicle incidents also caused their share of deaths among the soldiers. Similarly, civilians who perished in such instances, or when factory explosions or other deadly situations occurred, found their lives compromised outside the context of battle or as collateral casualties in it. People in situations from which they could not extract themselves safely faced as much danger in those circumstances as those engaged in direct combat with their opponents in the field.

Carlton McCarthy, whose memoir of soldier life offered a view of this experience to postwar readers, related many details of the minutiae of that profession, including the story of a deserter pulled from a stream after being shot while swimming across. "And so," he concluded, "while there had been no fighting, there were always incidents to remind the soldier that danger lurked around, and that he could not long avoid his share."[31]

Yet, aside from expressing a sense of the hazards soldiers faced away from the battlefield, McCarthy's description of the fate of the deserter pointed to the ambivalent nature of defining noncombat deaths among uniformed personnel. The outcome for the soldier in question could be attributed to the legitimate shooting of an escapee, an act of malice on the part of the men who had shot him, suicidal action on the part of an individual who surely had an expectation of the risk of being shot, poor luck and timing, or myriad other factors. However, it did not occur as a result of a formalized encounter with an opponent in which one had the opportunity to defend oneself and put his counterpart at the same risk for injury or death.

Many cases of fatalities of men in the ranks allowed for such levels of interpretation. When a conscript died because he refused to submit to service or killed an officer tasked with enforcing the government's policies, both individuals fell in the context of the war outside of the battlefield, in noncombat situations, if not as noncombatants themselves. Men who perished when refusing orders or while engaging in mutinous acts still died, offering themselves no chance for rehabilitation or redemption. Even for those individuals executed as spies or deserters, whose acts involved questions pertaining to the legitimacy of their acts, there were inconsistencies in the application of punishments and degrees of subjectivity that put some before their executioners while sparing others from such final outcomes.

Similarly, soldiers who ceased to be able either to defend themselves or to threaten the lives of others were no longer acting in the capacity of combatants. As captives or prisoners, such individuals were at the mercy of those who held them. Whether in prison facilities or in circumstances that one scholar described as "the atrocity-producing situation," in which attackers lashed out viciously at targets they deemed threatening regardless of their status, individuals perished in the context of warfare away from the traditional lines of engagement.[32]

If those who practiced forms of unconventional or irregular warfare forfeited their rights to be treated as soldiers by virtue of their tactics, the application of measures that resulted in the deaths of those whose standing was unclear or persons after being taken into custody was another matter. As historian Phillip Shaw Paludan has observed, "While guerrillas could be killed if engaged in battle and could be denied the right to become prisoners, once they had been captured they could not be executed without legal proceedings to determine their status as guerrillas and their guilt for killing or destroying. . . . Execution of a prisoner without such a proceeding was murder."[33] In short, noncombat mortality embraced all forms of death—soldier, civilian, and animal—not involving direct and deliberate fire between hostile or enemy forces, but related to the prosecution of, or circumstances surrounding, their engagement in the American Civil War.

Union major general George Thomas understood the cost of warfare as much as anyone and determined a method of honoring and remembering the sacrifices of the men in uniform. He ordered appropriate burial for the soldiers, with a "Mortuary Record" for each that would indicate as much personal information about that individual as possible. If he was dubious of states' rights, ordering "mix 'em up" rather than have the fallen laid out by state designation, Thomas nevertheless understood that society felt the tangible weight of each of those losses.[34]

General Thomas understood the depth of sacrifice these men in uniform had made and were making, but those not engaged in combat themselves endured the same experiences when caught up in the fighting that affected their homes and communities, or when experiencing unsafe conditions related to the war or wartime production. Individuals in those cases paid with their lives. Asymmetrical, or unconventional, warfare added to the dangers by blurring the lines between those who were engaged in it and those who were not. All deaths in these circumstances represented inglorious passages in one sense, but particularly so when based upon vengeance or misidentification. Noncombatants occasionally became combatants for a brief duration at least, when killing someone else out of fear or some other situation that would not likely have existed outside of the context of war.

Historians have begun to appreciate that for the men who served and the families and civilian workers who supported them, noncombat fatalities were as significant as battle deaths in establishing the full force of the American Civil War upon the people compelled to live through it. Tracy Revels has noted, "The ultimate deprivation of the Civil War was the death of a loved one."[35] Barton Myers observed, "Accidental death or wounding was less common than death from illness, but it indicated the variety of hazards soldiers faced away from the battlefield."[36]

Pulitzer Prize–winning author James McPherson offered the accepted numbers for the individuals killed in the Civil War in his book *Battle Cry of Freedom*: "More than 620,000 soldiers lost their lives in four years of conflict—360,000 Yankees and at least 260,000 rebels."[37] However, he recognized that the figures were hardly precise, stressing that "Civil War casualties cannot be known with exactitude because of incomplete or faulty reports."[38]

In an effort to revisit the question of fatalities associated with the conflict, J. David Hacker undertook a fresh examination of the subject by employing "a census-based count" that established "a probable range . . . from 650,000 to 850,000 excess deaths, with a preferred estimate of 750,000."[39] McPherson noted in his commentary provided as an introduction for the Hacker essay in *Civil War History* that he had long considered "the standard estimate of 258,000 Confederate war dead was a significant undercount." The scholar explained that in addition to challenges concerning accurate record keeping, the Confederacy left other deaths unreported: "There were no reported Confederate noncombat deaths from 'miscellaneous' causes—accidents, drownings, causes not stated, et cetera—compared with the nearly twenty-five thousand such deaths recorded for Union armies."[40]

The numbers of deaths for the American Civil War would indeed be staggering and almost incomprehensible for modern generations to process with any meaningful degree of appreciation. For the individuals affected, the quantification became deeply personal, and it mattered little the specific reasons that caused those ends to come or the circumstances under which those last moments unfolded. The people of that generation would have understood well what Sir Thomas More meant when he observed in *Utopia*, "The way to heaven out of all places is of like length and distance."[41]

As James McPherson observed, for the men who served the Union and for whom record keeping made special notice, noncombat fatalities contributed substantially to the toll exacted in lives by the war. For the Federal service these numbers included 2,795 officers and 221,791 men who died of disease; accidental deaths (except drowned), 142 officers and 3,972 men; drowned, 106 officers and 4,838; murdered, 37 officers and 483 men; committed suicide, 26 officers and 365 men; executed by U.S. military authorities, 267 men; perished from sunstroke, 5 officers and 308 men; other causes, 62 officers and 1,972 men; and causes not stated, 28 officers and 12,093 men.[42]

Union army statistics indicated that various maladies affected the soldiers, with devastating results. Out of 1,451,613 cases of acute or chronic diarrhea, 35,127 of these proved fatal. There were fewer cases of acute or chronic dysentery, at 287,522, but they resulted in another 9,431 deaths. Other intestinal illnesses affected 27,248 men and led to 1,476 additional deaths.[43] For these soldiers, according to one study, these types of illnesses "produced more sickness and mortality than any other kind of disease."[44]

Whatever the reason, death came to the soldiery in many forms and exacted meaningful tolls not only on the individuals involved but also on the units in which they had served. These outcomes reduced the effectiveness of service at every level of military organization. For example, the Fourth Arkansas lost a number of its men to accidents in the first full year of the war. Second Sergeant Ben Wheeler, "drowned in Tenn. river," and Richard Austin Jr., "Killed by Accident Dec. 1861," were two fatalities from Company D, while W. B. Summer of Company K was "killed at home, Nov. '61," Obadiah Reid of Company I was "Killed by accident May '62."[45]

The Sixth Virginia Infantry sustained heavy losses in battles such as Malvern Hill (15 killed or mortally wounded), Second Manassas (21), Wilderness and Spotsylvania Court House (17), and the Crater, at Petersburg (23). But the regiment endured a greater number of "Non-Combat Related" fatalities, listed by historian Michael A. Cavanaugh as "Accidents—4 As P.O.W.—16 Suicide—1 Sickness—101 [with a] Grand Total 246 deaths during the war."[46]

One account for a North Carolina brigade (Garland-Iverson-Johnston-Toon) recorded: "20 men met accidental or violent non-battle deaths. Four were murdered, 1 committed suicide, 4 were killed by militia taking up deserters, 6 were killed in accidents, most involving discharge of a weapon, and 6 others were killed by falling trees or in railroad accidents." In addition, three members of the brigade faced charges for murder.[47]

Another North Carolina brigade (Pettigrew-Kirkland-MacRae) suffered the loss of 1,137 men to fatal illnesses.[48] In addition, 21 men perished from causes not associated with disease. Of these latter individuals, 4 men died by weapons that should have been in friendly hands, including their own.[49]

The colorful Louisiana units that came to fight with their comrades in Virginia, sometimes literally, also suffered heavily in both combat and noncombat situations. Among the latter circumstances, the 1st Louisiana Volunteers lost 74 men to disease and 1 to an accident. The 2nd Louisiana tallied 181 deaths to disease and 4 by other means. The 5th Louisiana lost 66 to disease, 2 to mischance, 1 to murder, and 1 to execution. Of the unit's officers, 4 died of disease, and 1 was killed in a duel. The 6th saw 104 soldiers die of disease, 5 killed accidentally, 1 executed for desertion, and 1 drowned. The 7th listed 68 as dying of disease, 2 killed accidentally, 1 murdered, and 1 executed. The 8th Louisiana lost 171 to sickness, 2 to murder, and 1 to accident. The 9th suffered heavily in fatal illness, with 349 dead, while 4 died by other means. The 10th saw 58 men dead of disease, 3 by murder, and 2 killed accidentally. Losses in the 14th Louisiana stood at 85 to disease, 5 killed or mortally wounded in a riot at Grand Junction, Tennessee, 1 perishing accidentally, 1 by execution, and 1 by drowning. The 1st Special Battalion, Louisiana Infantry, had 15 men die of disease, 2 executed, and 1 killed by an unnamed mishap.[50]

The First Regiment Michigan Sharpshooters exacted a toll on their opponents in the bloody fighting that marked the Overland Campaign of 1864. However, the war demanded sacrifices of them as well, on and off the battlefield. In addition to the significant number of men who perished from disease and as prisoners of war, several died of other causes:

William E. Holmes. . . . Co. H—Angola, IN, murdered while at home on
furlough, 23 September 1863.

Samuel Kaquatch. . . . . Co. K—Philadelphia, PA, killed by railroad car,
2 August 1864[.]

Samuel H. Patterson . . . Co. B—Near Petersburg, VA, killed by accidental
explosion of a shell, 5 December 1864[.]

Sash-ko-bon-quot. . . . . Co. K—Camp Douglas, IL, accidentally killed,
27 December 1863.

Abel Shaw . . . . Co. F—Dearborn, MI, died of wounds received
while on guard duty, 5 June 1863.

Henry Smith. . . . . Co. H—Camp Douglas, IL, suicide, 25 September
1863.

Charles A. Vliet. . . . . . Co. C—Camp Douglas, IL, accidentally killed on
the railroad, 8 February 1864.[51]

The Fourth U.S. Cavalry sustained the loss of 68 troopers to battle from deaths
or mortal wounds, with others presumed to have perished that pushed the total
to approximately 112 men. Another 91 men fell to fatal illness. As was the case
with other units on both sides, 3 men died from "unknown" causes and 9 from accidents. The rolls put 4 of the command's deaths to drowning and 3 to "murdered
by citizens," while 1 died of a "skull fracture," and another perished from stab
wounds in a house of ill fame. One wounded trooper killed himself.[52]

For members of U.S. Colored Troops regiments, the figures for men perishing
from various reasons were especially significant when compared with their white
colleagues. William F. Fox's compilation of regimental losses included a table de-
noting "Total Deaths from Disease, Accidents, and Other Causes" that set the official classification of the numbers for these troops at 29,658 from disease, 576 from
accidents and drownings, and 3,621 from all other causes except from battle.[53]

Joseph Glatthaar has found that neglect, buttressed by racism, led to excessive
deaths in these units. For example, pneumonia struck down 5,233 of these men,
producing a mortality rate five times greater than among white volunteers with
the same malady. A lieutenant, posted in Louisiana observed, "The mortality in
our Regt. beats anything I ever saw." He noted that men "frequently drop dead
in the streets, and in two or three instances have been laying dead in the weeds
some distance from camp."[54]

William Fox's listing of regimental losses also provided a wide-ranging view
into the impact of noncombat fatalities in Union ranks, presented initially under
"deaths from all causes" and followed by thorough examinations of the corps and
regiments:

Cause	Officers	Enlisted Men	Aggregate
Died of disease	2,712	197,008	199,720
In Confederate prisons	83	24,783	24,866
Accidents	142	3,972	4,114
Drownings	106	4,838	4,944
Sunstrokes	—	308	313
Murdered	37	483	520
Suicide	26	365	391
Military executions	—	267	267
Executed by the enemy	4	60	64

The deaths from accidents were caused, principally, by the careless use of fire-arms, explosions of ammunition, and railway accidents; in the cavalry service, a large number of accidental deaths resulted from poor horsemanship.

The number of drowned may seem large, but the average is less than three men to a regiment. This loss was occasioned largely by bathing and boating. At times, some regiments would sustain a larger loss while fording rivers, or landing from small boats in the surf.[55]

The compilation did not specify every variation, with Fox creating an all-encompassing category, "causes known but not classified." He explained that this classification included the deaths of 2,034 soldiers "resulting from quarrels, riots, and the like, and which are not definitely reported as murder; from being shot for insubordination, or by provost-guards or sentinels in attempting to escape, or pass the lines; from exhaustion or exposure; [and] killed while depredating upon the property of citizens."[56]

Fox also provided noncombat fatalities in the U.S. Navy, setting the number at 3,000 individuals and explaining, "This includes 71 deaths from accidents; 265 from accidental drowning; 37 scalded; and 95 deaths in Confederate prisons."[57] Additionally, his compendium contained excerpts from muster rolls that pointed to the wide variety of fatal encounters listed officially for the men who wore blue.[58]

Drew Gilpin Faust has written of the importance of the final passage in the journey of life by noting, "Mortality defines the human condition."[59] In assessing Fox's compilation of statistics, she raised the underlying issue to be addressed by his "highly particular—and even peculiar" accounting of the "deaths of hundreds of thousands of individual men." For Faust, "Fox articulated a dilemma that lay at the heart of the effort to understand Civil War death: how to grasp both the significance of a single death and the meaning of hundreds of thousands."[60] For one of President Lincoln's secretaries, the point came home with the death of a lone sentry in Washington at the outset of the war: "In those days a man was of more importance than afterwards."[61]

Reid Mitchell has observed that Americans in the nineteenth century "hoped that they and their loved ones would make 'good deaths.'" Such passages to immortality would provide solace in times of sorrow and comfort to assuage the grief of loss. As Mitchell explained, "All battlefield deaths, all military deaths except those by execution, could be made into 'good deaths.'"[62] President Lincoln's address at Gettysburg would come to serve as the articulation of the meaning of that sacrifice for generations to come.

Yet, many individuals existed in situations where their deaths would occur, as one participant in the Atlanta Campaign described for some comrades on isolated picket posts or skirmish lines, with "no hope of glory before them."[63] If these final passages for soldiers and civilians alike were less glorious in their circumstances, individuals still mourned their losses and strove to accept them, if not come to some sense of understanding regarding them, and had to live with the outcomes they had most dreaded when these kinfolk and community members went off to war.

One participant lamented particularly those who lost their lives in the "closing days of the war." As General Reub Williams explained of such victims, "They had passed through many battles, skirmishes almost innumerable, dashes on picket posts and the constant danger to which the soldier is exposed at all times when the enemy is near. And at the same time they were never safe from the accidents of war, whether the enemy was near or not." The death of one who had enlisted in the opening days of the conflict, yet was "called upon to lay down his life in the very closing days of the long-drawn out struggle as a sacrifice," troubled him most. Williams understood that the loss would fall heaviest on the loved ones who had held out hope for the soldier's safe return.[64]

The conflict affected lethally participants, soldier and civilian, across the broadest spectrum outside of death in action against an armed and organized foe and illustrated the ways in which family members and associates experienced the ultimate sacrifices of comrades and loved ones during the war that ravaged the nation in the mid-nineteenth century. These conditions included fatality in the context of camp or hospital by disease, military instruction, martial ceremony, transportation involving men, animals, or supplies used or being moved for wartime purposes, friendly fire, accidental or collateral deaths in battle, industrial or production mishap, military justice, murder of soldiers in any settings including prison or civilians by individuals in uniform, and the like. With such losses accounted, a greater understanding of the enormous toll of the war on the lives of participants associated with it would be possible.

A depiction of life and death that appeared in the *Corning Journal* of New York on May 30, 1861, as the citizenry who patronized its pages prepared for war, may best summarize the myriad challenges that faced the recruits, in addition to combat: "The casualties of the camp and the field, the hardships that rack the frame and make disease a frequent visitor, the exposures and scanty supplies of food and clothing that render the pestilential air of the malarious regions deadly effective . . . these are the dangers that must cross the path of the gallant volunteers, before they can hope to return to their homes."[65] Just as surely, the deaths that occurred under any of these circumstances produced the brutal sense of finality that stripped the futures of such individuals from them and from those who waited at home in vain for them to return.

1

The First Fatalities

Death in the Early Days of the Civil War

It was undoubtedly a rash act. . . . Yet who can refrain from grief to see them fall in such a way as this—not by the fortunes of war, but by the hand of an assassin?

Charles Coffin on the death of Elmer Ellsworth

The firing on Fort Sumter in Charleston Harbor, South Carolina, and the outbreak of extended hostilities between North and South presented the peoples of both sections with opportunities for service. These, in turn, created the circumstances that called for sacrifices to be made, as often popularly phrased, "on the altar of the nation." Glorification of death on the battlefield offered a sense of immortality to people who already understood the harsh nature of nineteenth-century life. However, combat was not assured to be the only means by which such sacrifices would be made.

So much of what was to come in this bloodiest of American conflicts appeared early in ways that would not portend the scale of death that would hold through much of the war. Yet, from the opening moments of the struggle, individuals were offering "their last full measure," as President Abraham Lincoln later famously expressed at Gettysburg, to their respective causes. Such passages were usually not wrapped in circumstances that would characterize the fallen on fields of honor. They were part of the real-life existence of the volunteers who rushed to the ranks expecting to return shortly to the warm embrace of their kinfolk or civilians who confronted unexpected aspects of warfare emerging around them. These inglorious passages were also concrete realities for their friends and family, denying them the presence of loved ones who would never reclaim their places at their sides.

Perhaps the first fatality that can be attributed to the conflict between the North and South occurred before a war between the states had actually begun. Citizens were already mustering to become soldiers and fulfill their duties in defense of their respective states even as the initial wave of secession in the Deep South states rolled forward. On February 12, 1861, a twenty-four-year-old chaplain accompanying such a unit, Noble Leslie DeVotie, fell from the gangplank as he attempted to board a steamer with Alabama troops bound for Fort Morgan, outside Mobile. The Tuscaloosa native and former pastor of First Baptist Church in Selma could not be rescued, and after three days, his lifeless body surfaced. DeVotie's passage from his earthly domain was hardly as glorious as any he might have envisioned when he set out to inspire others or provide comfort to those who might risk their lives in the warfare threatening to erupt.[1]

On February 1, shortly before the minister's death in Alabama, a secession convention had voted to take Texas out of the Union. Voters would confirm the action in a matter of weeks, but in the interim, Brevet Major General David E. Twiggs stunned his superiors in Washington by ceding control over the Federal facilities in the Lone Star State to the local authorities on February 18. Subsequently, when U.S. troops left Texas on March 20, another unlikely death occurred. First Lieutenant James B. Witherell was attempting to step aboard the coastal steamer *Arizona* from the steamboat *Mustang*. Although the craft were at anchor at the mouth of the Rio Grande during the transfer, the officer failed to navigate his way safely from one vessel to the other, with nearsightedness apparently contributing to the mishap that sent him plunging into the waters below. Even before the war had started, the conflict had, as one scholar described it, the "first POW death," when Witherell failed to surface.[2]

One of the great ironies was that the Confederate bombardment of Fort Sumter that started on April 12, 1861, and ended the following day produced no deaths as shot and shell pounded the masonry walls of the unfinished fort. The first fatalities here occurred only when the direct hostilities had closed, and Private Daniel Hough of the surrendering garrison was part of a crew engaged in firing a salute for the departing Union troops. He introduced a fixed round into a bore that still contained embers from a previous discharge. The black powder made contact with the ignition source, and the resulting premature explosion ripped through the Federal soldier, tearing away his right limb. Hough could not survive the trauma. Nearby rounds also detonated, sending shards of metal and pieces of the damaged masonry through the unfortunate individuals who were too close to avoid the hazard. Of the handful of men struck in this fashion, Private Edward

Galloway was the only other soldier, besides Hough, who remained in mortal danger and died within a few days. Historian W. A. Swanberg noted of the soldier killed most directly in the incident, "In Private Hough the Union had its first dead—the first of many to come."[3]

Clashes between soldiers and civilians in the streets of cities where disputed loyalties existed also led to some of the war's earliest deaths. On April 19, 1861, as men from the Sixth Massachusetts marched through Baltimore en route to Washington, citizens gathered to convey their disgruntlement at the display of martial power. Bricks, paving stones, and other methods of violent expression escalated the situation to a point at which more substantial firing occurred. In the chaos, indiscriminate firing led to inadvertent casualties, including the death of one young boy on a ship in the harbor.[4] When the smoke from the encounter subsided, four soldiers and twelve local residents lay dead, "the first of more than 700,000 combat casualties during the next four years," according to historian James McPherson.[5]

A similar event in St. Louis, Missouri, in May 1861, failed to garner as much attention as the Baltimore episode, but it represented the volatility of relations between martial forces and local citizens in that region. The flash point occurred in the aftermath of the surrender of militia at Camp Jackson on May 10 to Union troops under the command of Nathaniel Lyon. As the nearly 700 captives passed through two lines of their adversaries, civilians gathered to demonstrate support for the prisoners and hurl epithets at the Federals. Union attempts to suppress these expressions only exacerbated the situation. An angry individual fired several shots at Captain Rufus Sexton without effect, halted only by a fatal bayonet thrust from one of the troops. Subsequent firing left some twenty-seven residents dead or mortally wounded, the youngest of these several teenage boys and fourteen-year-old Emma (Emily) Somers.[6] The fatalities in the ranks included William Hollinghast, Conrad Lappe, Bernard Miller, and John Shaukbeer, as well as a mortally wounded Captain Constantin Blandowski of Company F, Third U.S. Volunteers, who died several days later on May 26.[7] As a Home Guard regiment under Charles Stifel passed through town to the arsenal, it took and returned fire, causing the deaths of another dozen people, including two of the soldiers.[8]

Only a month after this outburst, another violent encounter happened in St. Louis when troops marching past the Recorder's Court returned fire from an undetermined source with a volley that riddled the building, leaving police officer Nehemiah M. Pratt and Deputy Marshal Frenzel dead or dying, as well as at least three others in the vicinity.[9] Neighboring Kansas had already been "bleeding" for some time prior to the war period, but Missouri was now experiencing a spate of bloodshed of its own.

Certainly, the most dramatic of the stories of early martyrs in the sectional conflict included the colorful Elmer Ellsworth and the hotel keeper James Jackson, who killed Ellsworth and then died himself. Colonel Ellsworth was as flashy as a commander of Zouaves ought to be. He held himself erect and wore proudly the colorful uniform that distinguished his unit. The sight of a Confederate flag fluttering over a hotel in Virginia across the Potomac from the nation's capital sent him into a towering rage. Resolved to tear the offending banner from its perch, he crossed into the rebellious neighbor state on May 24 and strode confidently toward the Marshall House hotel in Alexandria. He could not know that the proprietor of the property, James T. Jackson, cherished similar zeal, although for his cause and not the Union commander's.

The fates of the two men collided on a stairway as Ellsworth descended with the flag in his hands. Jackson approached the twenty-four-year-old officer with a shotgun leveled at him, pulled the trigger, and blasted the Zouave into oblivion. A soldier accompanying Ellsworth stepped forward to assist, too late to save the colonel, but in time to dispatch his assailant. The Union had its martyr, for whom President Lincoln allowed the honor of letting his remains lie in state in the East Room of the executive mansion.[10] The young Confederacy had a hero as well in the slain hotel keeper.

Ellsworth's death so moved Abraham Lincoln that he composed a note of condolence to the soldier's parents, which read, "In the untimely loss of your noble son, our affliction here, is scarcely less than your own. So much of promised usefulness to one's country, and of bright hope for one's self and friends, have rarely been so suddenly dashed, as in his fall." Lincoln noted their brief, but personal, acquaintance and offered such solace as he could to the grieving father and mother: "In the hope that it may be no intrusion upon the sacredness of your sorrow, I have ventured to address you this tribute to the memory of my young friend, and your brave and early fallen child." The president closed warmly as "sincerely your friend in a common affliction."[11]

Ellsworth's passage prompted unusual outpourings of emotion and response. Marshall House became a destination for individuals hoping to secure mementos of the occasion.[12] One Union soldier recalled traveling to the vicinity. "The house is still standing and a guard is placed there," Newton Colby wrote his father. "I went in and stood where the gallant Zouave fell. The floor and staircase have been entirely cut and hacked by the curious who all get pieces to send away." Colby seemed to condemn the practice but succumbed to temptation himself. "The stairway being down I had to climb up a slanting board to get up to the flag staff—from which once flowed the secession flag which cost Ellsworth's life—but which now bears the stars and stripes. I climbed up the flag staff and with my knife worked off a piece."[13]

Ellsworth's passage at the hands of an angry Southern sympathizer was hardly of the glorious nature he would have imagined for himself. A contemporary remarked in this manner to a comrade in the aftermath of the incident: "Poor fellow . . . it was undoubtedly a rash act, but it only showed the heroic spirit that animates our soldiers, from high to low, in this righteous cause of ours. Yet who can refrain from grief to see them fall in such a way as this—not by the fortunes of war, but by the hand of an assassin?"[14]

Confederate sources were hasty to take issue with Northern characterizations of the colorful Zouave, and equally swift to point out the worthiness of the Virginia hotel keeper's sacrifice. "The blood of the first Martyr has flowed," a Richmond newspaper editorial observed. "A Virginia citizen, defending the flag of his country, has been cut down by the murderous minions of despotic power. But, glorious death!" Besides assuring that all Virginians would hope to emulate the example if given the opportunity to die as Jackson had done, the writer considered the death properly avenged by the slain man's own actions: "He sent the bloated miscreant, who claimed the glory of pulling down the first Confederate flag, to the infernal shades where he belongs, and gave him and his ruffian crew a foretaste at the threshold of what they have to expect from the South, at every step of the long and weary road they have begun to travel." Rejecting any further "words" of reconciliation or "hopes of peace," the editorialist concluded, "We are in war, with depraved, brutal and merciless savages, and our only motto, by day and night, should be—'War to the Knife.'"[15]

The first deaths indeed made impressions on those who recorded them. Charles Haydon, of the Second Michigan Infantry, scribbled in his journal on Sunday, May 5, "We got news yesterday that one man who enlisted in our Co. at Kalamazoo was dead. His name was Henry Carrier—a good stout boy—he was taken sick the day before we started & died soon after." Carrier would not share in the experiences of his comrades in the service to come and establish a bond with them in that respect, but his passing would not go unnoticed. "This is the first death in our Co. & I believe the first in the Regt.," Haydon observed.[16]

In these early days of the conflict, fatal accidents could happen in many fashions and affect diverse individuals. In the *Richmond Daily Dispatch* of April 22, 1861, a notice brought attention to the untimely demise of "Capt. Angus Greenlaun, an old citizen of Memphis, Tenn., [who] was killed on the 17th inst., by the premature discharge of a cannon." Greenlaun had lived a storied existence. A Richmond native, "he, with other galiant spirits, flocked to the standard of [Sam] Houston, and was in most of the battles by which her independence was won." After the war for Texas independence, he had come back to Memphis "and engaged in steamboating."[17] Yet, with all the risks Greenlaun had faced in these other settings, it was not until the opening stages of the American Civil War that he offered the supreme sacrifice.

Another fatal accident occurred in Norfolk, Virginia, in May. This one involved Second Lieutenant Storrs of an Alabama regiment. According to the writer, "Powder," who supplied readers with information from the camps through his letters, "He was (purely accidentally) shot and killed by Mr. Hunt, then on duty as sentinel." Noting that the remains would be sent to Storrs's home, the writer observed, "How sad the occurrence; and what makes it still more so, the deceased had, only two days prior to his leaving home to help us fight our battles against a common foe, been united in the holy bonds of matrimony to one of the South's fairest daughters." However, he was careful to explain that Storrs's death outside the context of the battlefield had meaning for the newly widowed bride and the nation: "May God sustain and enable her to bear this sore affliction, and may she be comforted and derive solace from the fact that he met his death (although accidentally by the hands of a friend) in defending the rights of his beloved country. His bereaved companion, fond relatives and friends may rest assured that they have the deep, heart-felt sympathies of every Virginian."[18]

Virginians were not the only ones to make such sacrifices. The *Western Democrat* of Charlotte, North Carolina, reported the inadvertent death of a native son of that state: "Mr. Daniel Agner, a young man, and a member of the Rowan Artillery, of this place, accidentally shot himself on Monday 13th, with a pistol." It was unclear whether Agner was cleaning his weapon, examining it, or had some other motivation at the time of the incident. According to the account, "He had his pistol out cocking it with the muzzel towards him, when his thumb slipped off the cock causing the explosion. The load lodged in the lower part of the breast. He lived about two hours after the fatal accident happened."[19]

Nor were Confederate forces the only ones to experience such deadly early encounters. On May 10, the *National Republican* of Washington related an incident in which a soldier fell victim to a "most deplorable accident" at "'Camp Cameron,' the headquarters of the New York seventh regiment about eight o'clock yesterday morning." Lavy Keyes, "the son of a prominent auctioneer in New York city," saw an object on the ground in the company street. "It appears that the deceased stooped to pick something up near the place where a number of guns had been stacked, and, as he was in the act of rising, the stack was accidentally struck, and one gun exploded, the load taking effect in the body of Keyes, and killing him almost instantly." The soldier "was only about twenty-two years of age, and was highly esteemed by his comrades, who feel deeply his untimely end."[20]

Another tragic incident occurred at Camp Curtin, near Harrisburg, Pennsylvania, when one of the Union volunteers "was fixing a lock on a loaded rifle [and] it was prematurely discharged." The round "passed directly through the head of a bystander named Geo. Madison, of Shippen, Cameron county, Pa., a member of the Cameron Rifles, killing him almost instantly."[21]

In the Trans-Mississippi, troops gathering there were as susceptible to mishap as in any of the other theaters of operations. Albert Marshall deplored the foolishness exhibited in a situation that arose in Missouri with the Seventh Nebraska: "A lieutenant was carelessly handling his revolver when it went off and wounded two men, one quite badly through the leg and the other mortally. The latter died during the day and was buried this evening." Marshall strenuously condemned the manner in which the loss had taken place, writing, "Such carelessness as this ought to be severely punished."[22]

Early war camp accidents were not the only source of trouble. The heated atmosphere into which individuals entered who asserted their views on the subjects of the day often prompted sharp responses that went beyond rhetoric. In North Texas, on May 25, 1861, two men holding strong Unionist views found themselves confronted by a pair of individuals with opposing secessionist positions. One of the former fell dead and the other wounded as the argument elevated to violence. The two surviving men obtained an acquittal from the local justice of the peace as disputes continued to fester in the region.[23]

Troops on both sides were quickly assembling for service in a war that many thought would not be extensive or costly. Moving these relatively large numbers of men and the resources to sustain them would have proved a daunting challenge under any circumstances, but in wartime these factors became magnified. Unfortunately, human error added to the mix as well, such as when soldiers under Colonel Joseph B. Kershaw reached the busy juncture of Orange County Court House in Virginia in the spring of 1861. These men arrived safely, but while they were awaiting the transfer of other cars, a train out of Manassas Junction barreled down the track, the engineer oblivious to any danger ahead. Later claiming that faulty equipment prevented him from alerting others to an imminent collision, the railroad official exhibited negligence that allowed the engine and cars to careen into the troop train.[24] Despite the tragic loss of life that had occurred, a subsequent newspaper report from Richmond provided a positive assessment of the situation by asserting, "It is fortunate, indeed, that a much larger number were not killed or badly wounded." Nevertheless, at least two of the Confederate soldiers, "Messrs. McMullen and Gentry, volunteers from Green county, Va.," were among the unfortunate fatalities in the incident.[25]

On the same day readers first learned about the wreck at Orange County Court House, the *Richmond Daily Dispatch* reported a single death on the rails: "Julius Sadler, a private in Col. D. H. Hill's 1st Regiment of North Carolina Volunteers, a native of Charlotte, N.C., fell from the cars of the Richmond and York River Railroad on Friday night last, while his regiment was being conveyed to Yorktown, when nine miles from this city, and had his head mashed off, falling directly under the wheels." Unfortunately, no one seemed to be aware of the mishap, and Sadler was only found when the train made the return trip over the same track. The writer thought it worthwhile to draw lessons from the incident: "Accidents of this kind, serious as they are, may reasonably be looked for, but that fact should incite not only soldiers, but railroad employees, to be more guarded in making the hurried journeys the exigencies of the times demands at their hands."[26]

Soldiers and civilians alike were at risk in many ways as troops gathered and the competing nations sought to mobilize the means of waging war. Ramping up war production also increased the chances for fatal incidents. In June 1861, Washington's *Evening Star* told the story of one unfortunate soul who had perished from such a mishap in the city: "Mr. John S. Davis, who was so seriously wounded by the explosion of the magazine of a cap machine, in the Navy Yard, on Monday last, died of his injuries on Saturday evening at his residence in the Navy Yard." Declaring the victim to have been "universally respected," the account offered no additional details.[27]

June also provided the period for a horrific event that nevertheless left the chronicler philosophical about the incident. In a letter published in a Pennsylvania newspaper a man posted at Fort Pickens, Florida, related on June 16, "Yesterday, we lost a man on the Gulf beach, who was taken by a shark, while bathing." The comrade "had only left the water a few moments when the event occurred," or he might have become a victim himself. Still, the situation caused a reflection that suggested a stoic effort at protecting oneself from the harrowing associations. "The loss of a soldier, by accident or disease, seems a melancholy event," the writer explained,

> yet among men who are accustomed to see such things, and are as familiar with death as with any other companion, the event occupies the mind only during the passing hour, and with a "poor fellow, he was a good soldier," or some other expression, he passes from the mind and never again occupies the thoughts, except some circumstance connected with his life, or a similar event, cause him to be recollected for the moment.[28]

In the summer of 1861, water transportation cost the lives of men who would not thus be allowed to reach the front lines to confront their enemies in battle. A "Fire Zouave" named Humboldt from New York was part of a small party attempting to cross "the Eastern Branch in a skiff, which upset in the middle of the stream." The account added, "Two of them saved themselves by swimming ashore, but the third drowned." Similarly, Albert Warren perished when he fell off a vessel on which he was traveling. In the service of his country for only a month, the twenty-five-year-old private drowned on June 5, with hardly time to become acclimated to his new martial life, much less to have any opportunity to experience combat.[29]

At about the same time, while traveling on the cramped steamer *Marion* with his comrades from the Ninth New York Volunteers, George Warren "fell overboard and was drowned." Charles Johnson recalled his friend "Tobe" as "a splendid fellow," who had served his company "as my file-leader during our farewell march through the city."[30] Lucius Barber of the Fifteenth Illinois Volunteer Infantry noted a tragedy as he embarked on the steamer *Alton* heading toward the mouth of the Missouri River: "We then turned our course up that stream. Just as we turned our course, a soldier from Company H fell overboard, and just as assistance was within reach, he sank to rise no more."[31]

The circumstances were less clear for Charles Wright, whose body surfaced after he "drowned at Camp Clay." The nature of the unmarried soldier's death was subject to a coroner's inquest, although the *Cincinnati Daily Press* offered no additional details.[32] The same paper noted another means by which a high-profile noncombat death was inspiring the local populace to remember sacrifices already being made and offer a sense of normalcy in turbulent times. The notice provided information on the presentation of "several tableaux presenting the death of Colonel Ellsworth" and called for supporting the "National [which] is the only theater open in the city at present, and ought therefore, notwithstanding the war times, to be well patronized."[33]

Despite the attempt in Cincinnati to use his untimely death for other purposes, Elmer Ellsworth's violent demise had deprived his command of his leadership, but the Zouaves would not be the only ones to suffer in this way. The stresses and strains for other officers who shouldered the responsibility for preparing their men for the dangers of warfare were enormous under any conditions. In the early days of the conflict, at least one individual apparently found this aspect of his authority too great a burden to endure. Captain Christopher F. Fisher, of the Petersburg Cavalry (or Light Dragoons), had much to contemplate as the allure of militia activities in peacetime gave way to the realities of potential combat in wartime. According to historian Robert J. Driver Jr., "The new leader lost his mind and killed himself after expressing concern about the war and the safety of his men."[34]

As they worked their way from Louisiana, the Zouaves who enlisted to serve the Confederacy left a wake of drunkenness and rowdiness that almost had to be admired for its zeal. Unfortunately, they also lost some of their number as violence in their own ranks occurred. Historian Terry Jones noted, "Along the way one Zouave was shot and killed by a company officer and another was accidentally killed under unknown circumstances."[35]

When they reached Grand Junction, Tennessee, some of the members of the Fourteenth Louisiana managed to secure and smuggle onto their train liquid refreshment. Despite attempts to close the stores and post guards to prevent access to the dangerous intoxicants, enterprising men climbed through the back windows of the establishments anyway, and the men proceeded to celebrate. Officers who sought to quell the disorder and reassert discipline found the task overwhelming. At least one sergeant became an inadvertent victim when Colonel Valery Sulawkowski, commanding the regiment, fired at and killed him under the mistaken impression that he was one of the troublemakers. When the disturbances subsided, seven men lay dead and another nineteen wounded. A newspaper report of the aftermath drew understandable comparisons to other settings in wartime: "The hotel looks like a hospital after a hard fought battle. The dead and wounded are strewn all over the second floor."[36]

The men who enlisted did not expect to perish before they reached the battlefield itself, but even in such situations would not have imagined that if they did, they would face mortal danger from their own comrades. Yet, as in most circumstances associated with combat, especially early in the war, "confusion compounded" may be the best phrase to describe what was taking place in the arena of the battlefield. Popular historian Webb Garrison looked at the results of a Union raid on June 1, 1861, on Fairfax Court House and concluded that the death of Captain John Quincy Marr of the Warrenton Rifles there occurred as "the Civil War's first recorded instance of friendly fire."[37] Certainly, as newly minted citizen soldiers approached unknown dangers, the elements were rife for mistakes to be made as people with trigger-happy reactions and overactive imaginations produced deadly tolls.

Similarly, when Union forces approached Philippi in western Virginia, uncertainty marked the course of their march. In a night attack conducted in rainy conditions on June 3, the Federals managed to surprise their sleeping opponents; however, the same circumstances allowed many of those men to escape and led to another regrettable occurrence. The inability of the raw troops to coordinate their movements contributed to the missed opportunity, and the only individual in the blue ranks to perish died when he shot himself accidentally. The Federals had achieved a victory the press dubbed afterward as the "Philippi races," but the skirmish had led to an unintended fatality.[38]

Elsewhere in Virginia, at Big Bethel, a small engagement with a big name took place on June 10, 1861, in which the same type of confusion reigned. Riding at the front of his column, Union brigadier general Ebenezer Pierce and several staffers appeared only as a body of unidentifiable riders. Expecting the possibility of such circumstances, Union major general Benjamin Butler had ordered that his men take precautions that would include the use of watchwords and armbands when confronting unknown forces. In the firing that followed, Union troops from the Seventh New York under Colonel John Bendix and Third New York under Colonel Frederick Townsend fired at each other, and although some of these combatants emerged unscathed from the poor visibility and inaccurate volleys, members of Pierce's command were not so fortunate. "When we found the supposed enemy advancing," Pierce tried to explain, "I threw out skirmishers, who, to my surprise, I soon found uniting themselves with the supposed enemy, who in a few minutes proved to be friends, and a portion of the forces from Newport News, commanded by Colonel Bendix. The result of this fire upon us was, 2 mortally wounded (1 since dead); 3 dangerously; 4 officers and 12 privates slightly; making a total, 21."[39]

In his initial after-action report on the engagement, General Butler labeled the matter an "almost criminal blunder" that cost the lives of "two men of Townsend's regiment."[40] As the Union commander pondered the incident almost a week later, he added, "I find nothing to add or correct in my former dispatch." The individual responsibility for causing the exchange remained unclear, but Butler felt he had done all he could to prevent such an occurrence: "It was evidently a mistake, and in spite of the precaution that, before any order to fire was to be given in the dark, the watchword 'Boston' should be shouted, and that Colonel Townsend's men should be distinguished by a white badge upon the arm, with which order Colonel Townsend complied." Butler noted the confused nature of the combat that contributed to the mishap: "I make no doubt that the battery would have been taken but for another unfortunate mistake, as reported to me, wherein the colonel of a regiment mistook two companies of his own men, which had been separated from him by a thicket, for a flanking party of the enemy." He concluded testily, "It would seem that the skirmish was lost twice because our officers mistook their friends for their enemies."[41]

Confusion at Fairfax Court House and Big Bethel had cost the lives of soldiers by their own men in some of the earliest instances of "friendly fire." The attempt of some captured Federals to escape led to another incident in northwestern Virginia in 1861. Georgian Irby Scott wrote home in July to explain that firing by the guards of a Virginia unit on the escapees "produced the greatest excitement among the[ir] whole regiment, who thinking they were attacked fired at random and killed eight of their own men and wounded several more."[42]

In early June, disaster struck on the rails for men traveling on the Cincinnati Marietta Railroad. A small newspaper picked up the account of June 6 "of the unfortunate accident" from the *Cincinnati Gazette*. "Five companies, number five hundred men, all fully armed but not uniformed, of the Twenty-second Ohio Regiment," took passage to Chillicothe, Ohio, from which they departed in midafternoon. "The train proceeded at a tolerable speed; between fifteen and eighteen miles per hour," according to surviving witnesses. "When one mile east of Raysville—twenty miles from Chillicothe—the axle of the tender broke, and six cars were precipitated down an embankment, and literally crushed to pieces." One of the cars landed in a creek, with the force of the accident propelling some of the passengers "out the doors—two of which were open in each car, one on either side." Among the fatalities was George W. Ballou, who "fell under the first car as it went down the embankment into the creek, and was killed instantly." The newspaper provided gruesome details of the aftermath. "When his comrades removed the crushing weight from his body, they could scarcely recognize his features. His neck and arms were lacerated, and the flesh all over his body horribly mangled." The account noted that another member of the company was fortunate to survive and pronounced several individuals, including William Sligh, Isaac Dumpla, and Frank Gascon, likely to die from the injuries they had sustained in the accident.[43]

Occasionally men who rode the rails in less conventional manners met untimely ends by the nature of their choice of accommodation. The *Richmond Daily Dispatch* of June 8 contained a brief description that included some speculation concerning the demise of one unfortunate traveler: "Mr. Mark Bantley, a member of the Quitman Guards, of Forsyth county, Ga., was killed a few nights ago on the Pensacola Railroad. It is supposed he fell from the top of the cars and was crushed."[44]

Several days later, the same newspaper reprinted a report from the *Norfolk Herald* of "an accident of a very painful nature" that had taken place "in the camp of the 1st Regiment of Louisiana Volunteers." The incident occurred when "Jas. M. Redford, of Capt. Anderson's Kentucky company, attached to the above Regiment, was accidentally shot while in camp, by private McBride, of the same company, and died in half an hour afterwards."[45]

Perhaps the most unexpected of these deadly occurrences in these early days of war took place when busy soldiers finally had an opportunity to relax. A twenty-year-old printer, now serving as a lieutenant in a Mississippi regiment, went for a sail with another comrade in Florida. Fellow Mississippian William Nelson wrote on June 14, 1861, to tell his own mother of the tragedy that had befallen the officer: "Lieut. Henry of La-Fayette Guards from Oxford, was yesterday drowned while out sailing in making a short turn the sail dipped & he and an Irishman fell out of the boat, the Irishman swam to shore, but Henry was either drowned or taken under by a shark, as his body has not been recovered as yet."[46]

For others, the allure of water and the chance to take advantage of what must have seemed a harmless indulgence also proved fatal. On more than one occasion, a simple desire for cleanliness led to dire results. In June 1861, a Cincinnati newspaper noted the death of a soldier who undoubtedly hoped only to divest himself of the effects of the summer heat and the grime of his profession: "A soldier named McNally, attached to the 'Greenup Invincibles,' from Greenup County, Ky., was drowned in the river, while bathing yesterday."[47] Despite the name attached to his unit and the expectation that any challenge to such a designation would come more likely from enemy fire, a simple and routine task proved deadly for this one member.

Alfred Fisher, a twenty-one-year-old native of New York City, had only been enlisted as a soldier for a month in the Ninety-Ninth New York Volunteers when he met the same fate. While he was stationed with his unit in the Chesapeake Bay region of Virginia, the enticement of the water in the midst of summer heat must have been too great for the urban youth to resist. His record in the regimental history noted simply, "Drowned, June 22, 1861, while bathing at Old Point Comfort, Va."[48]

Uncertainty created dangerous conditions for some of the men learning their duties. The *New York Herald* provided readers with the outlines of a fatal incident in Washington: "First Lieut. David Lewis, of the Metropolitan Rifles, of the District of Columbia Volunteers, was accidentally and fatally shot this morning, at the Chain Bridge, by one of his comrades."[49] The sketch did not indicate particulars regarding the encounter, but the Federal capital remained on edge over the possibility of any imminent threatening movement by Confederate forces from Virginia, and hypervigilance seemed to lead to violent death for a colleague in this instance.

Clumsiness and carelessness also created opportunities for inadvertent deaths. According to one account, "Second Sergeant Charles H. Chapman, of the Slatter (La.) Guards, was accidentally shot and killed by private Philip Sweeny, of the company, at their rendezvous in New Orleans, on the 21st inst." Routine duties could quickly take an unexpected and unintended turn when due diligence failed to occur. In this case, the notice included an explanation of the circumstances:

"It appears that private Sweeny was cleaning his musket, and Sergeant Chapman was standing by conversing with Sweeny and another man. Sweeny, in the act of rising from the seat where he was sitting, dropped his pistol from his belt." When the weapon struck the floor, it "exploded the cap and the ball passed through Sergeant Chapman's wrist and into his left breast, entering the heart. He died almost instantly."[50] For the sergeant, the end had come as swiftly and surely as any he might have experienced in combat, but at the hand of a friend rather than a foe.

As this situation illustrated, fatal mishaps need not occur on a battlefield or because of hostile actions. In the period when citizens were adapting to life as soldiers on a grand scale, unintentional deaths seemed to proliferate. The description of an incident appeared in a July 13, 1861, newspaper account in Washington. The writer noted, "A soldier of one of the New York regiments encamped near the Park was accidentally shot with a revolver, yesterday morning by a companion, and instantly killed."[51] Another inadvertent death was part of the record compiled by Chaplain Thomas Van Horne. This one listed Second Lieutenant Thomas L. Job as "Killed accidentally July 18, 1861," without more explanation.[52] On the same day, the *Richmond Daily Dispatch* noted the death of a man assigned as part of the personal staff for an officer. "Lieut, Kirkpatrick, of the 23rd Regiment, shot his servant (a white soldier named Biddle,) dead, yesterday, by accident."[53]

Joseph Twichell wrote his father in July about an incident that occurred while he remained at Camp Scott on Staten Island, New York, in June 1861. The young man had left seminary to become a chaplain of the Excelsior Brigade. A Protestant among Irish Catholics, Twichell learned about life as well as war in the three years he served with the regiment. Just after the Fourth of July, he explained, "The only unanticipated incident of the day was a powerful one. A man was killed, for trying to break guard." In attempting to leave camp without authorization, the soldier, whom the chaplain described as "a desperate fellow" who "had before been insubordinate," confronted a sentinel. "The guard ran him through with a bayonet, or rather, he rushed upon the point of one," according to what Twichell had learned. An inquiry exonerated "the faithful guard—of the dead man's own regiment" and recommended his promotion. "To me this seems dreadful," the chaplain reflected, "but I suppose it was right and best, and that I shall grow less sensitive on such matters. I have been enough already in this camp to show me that I shall get used to things which before [would] have been [only] night-mares."[54]

Later in the year, a similar occurrence left a member of a Home Guard unit dead at the hands of a soldier at Ellicott's Mills, Maryland. Apparently, Private William H. Knight, of the Independent Patapsco Guards, sought to hone his skills with the bayonet, and Private Simeon Fishbeck, of Company B, Sixtieth

New York, agreed to become a sparring partner. As the men parried with each other, Knight "snapped" his weapon, and Fishbeck responded in kind. Unfortunately, the latter's weapon contained a charge, and the round dropped the guardsman in his tracks. According to one account, the injured man only "survived until the next day."[55]

Alcohol added a volatile factor for some of the men, with fatal effect. The *Richmond Daily Dispatch* reprinted a Memphis newspaper story concerning "two soldiers of Capt. Jackson's regiment of heavy artillery, now stationed at the fort at the foot of Jefferson street, [who] entered a drinking place near the railroad crossing on the Raleigh road." When Owen McCarty saw "that his companion had become helplessly intoxicated," he "took from him for safe keeping twenty-seven dollars he had about him." Unfortunately, several of the fellow patrons noticed the friend's good deed and followed the soldiers as they left the establishment, "went up to them and demanded the money. On being refused by McCarty, one of them with a pistol shot him. The ball struck the heart and death was instantaneous." The robbers then attempted "to take the money from the dead man's pocket" but fled when two mounted soldiers approached. During the subsequent pursuit, "one of the two, Chas. Philips, was arrested. Another of the party, James Barton, was arrested yesterday morning." Word quickly spread of the act, and comrades of the deceased assembled outside of the jail demanding immediate justice for the slain soldier. "Toward noon, symptoms of a riot were apparent, and shouts were uttered of 'bring him out, hang him,' in reference to the one supposed to have fired the fatal shot." Hoping to defuse the volatile situation, a number of "influential citizens mingled with the crowd, recommending that the law should be allowed to take its course." The promise of a speedy prosecution "pacified the crowd, which soon began to diminish, and order was restored."[56]

When accidents or nefarious acts did not take lives, other circumstances could emerge that did. As men in Missouri entered new quarters at Camp Hovey, the "sad news" spread "that Henry Johnson, a fine, intelligent young man who had been left in the hospital at Camp Butler, had committed suicide by drowning himself in the small lake at that place." Albert Marshall found the situation almost incomprehensible. As he wrote, "This sad information seemed too incredible for belief. I saw and had a talk with him just before we came away and he appeared to be in good spirits. He said that he was gaining nicely and would be with us in a few days." The news of his friend's death left Marshall depressed, but under the circumstances, he tried to withhold judgment: "With a big war on hand and his command going to the front, it would seem that a soldier would know that he could have lots of good chances of being killed and to die in an honorable and useful way, and that he need not commit suicide."[57]

Smaller engagements had already produced inadvertent deaths among friendly troops. Larger-scale operations promised to provide greater opportunities for such tragedies. In the confused action that marked the fighting associated with Manassas/Bull Run in the summer of 1861, numerous incidents took place in which men fell under the muzzles of their compatriots. Early on in the July 17 engagement along Sudley Road in the area of Matthews Hill, troops from South Carolina failed to identify properly comrades from Louisiana as the latter moved forward as skirmishers to support them. Two of the members of the colorful Tiger Rifles fell mortally wounded, and only the direct action of Major Chatham Roberdeau Wheat to prevent further firing kept more deaths from occurring.[58]

In the chaotic conditions of battle, troops on both sides found themselves in mortal danger from their own forces. Colonel William B. Franklin reported that when the First Minnesota Regiment moved to protect a threatened battery, fire struck them from the rear. "It was so near the enemy's lines that friends and foes were for a time compounded," he explained afterward.[59] For the men victimized in this manner, the nature of any resulting deaths would be difficult to determine, but the outcome was as certain regardless.

William Tecumseh Sherman also noted the problematic nature of combat in this early engagement. Regarding the Second Wisconsin, the Ohioan observed, "This regiment is uniformed in gray cloth, almost identical with that of the great bulk of the secession army, and when the regiment fell into confusion and retreated toward the road there was an universal cry that they were being fired on by our own men."[60]

Civilians also learned quickly that warfare held no distinctions for those who served and those who did not and yet became victims by proximity. One of the most poignant early stories of the war involved the widowed octogenarian Judith Henry, whose home on Henry House Hill became a focal point for some of the fiercest fighting.[61] Edward Porter Alexander, destined to achieve fame as Robert E. Lee's artillerist, recalled the effects of the day's combat: "The body of poor old Mrs. Henry, very old & bed ridden, lay in her bed struck by one cannon ball & about three musket balls. The house was riddled from every direction."[62] Historian James I. Robertson Jr. noted, "The aged widow suffered the misfortune of being in the wrong place at the wrong time," adding that she had the sad distinction of becoming "the only known civilian to die in the battle."[63]

On the same day as the fighting raged along Bull Run, the First Texas Infantry was moving hurriedly toward the scene of combat from the Confederate capital via the Richmond, Fredericksburg and Potomac Railroad. Heavy rainfall had persisted along the route and compromised the track when it washed away a culvert. The resulting derailment cost the Texas infantry lives.[64]

Soldier humor was one coping mechanism some of the men employed to counteract the demoralizing effects of death. In one instance, a usually jovial colleague appeared distressed about the status of a popular tent mate. The exchange began, "Lieutenant, did you hear about Corporal Lewis?" "No, what is the matter with him?" "He is now in his tent dyeing." The officer hurried to the scene, overcome with emotion at what he expected to find. Relief must have mixed with anger as he opened the tent fly to see the supposedly stricken soldier "sitting before a glass dyeing his new-grown mustache."[65]

Unfortunately, for many of the men who had entered the service of their country, even efforts at humor could not mask the tragedy surrounding them. Winchester, Virginia, was rapidly becoming a rendezvous for the sick and dying. Judith Brockenbrough McGuire saw the full effect of the scourge of illness. On July 18, she confided in her diary, "But Winchester, what shall I say for Winchester that will do it justice? It is now a hospital. The soldiers from the far South have never had measles, and most unfortunately it has broken out among them, and many of them have died of it, notwithstanding the attention of surgeons and nurses."[66]

Shortly after the clash of forces had taken place in Northern Virginia and the blue-clad participants withdrew toward their capital, Washington experienced a different shock. A violent blast rocked the Navy Yard in the city, producing casualties. Accounts in the local newspapers noted the deaths of "two worthy young men" in an explosion in "the rocket house." The first of these, "Francis C. Brown," was twenty-six years old and died "about two hours" after the accident had occurred. "He is a plasterer by trade, and leaves a wife and one child." The second was "John P. Ferguson, a young unmarried man, about 20 years of age, [who] was badly burned, and died about 6 o'clock in the same evening."[67]

For these civilians, even with the recent bloodletting at Manassas/Bull Run to jolt sensitivities for a July 1861 readership not yet inured to the lengthy casualty lists to come, the deaths of individuals like Francis Brown and John Ferguson seemed especially tragic. An influx of women and children that would soon occur to replace the men who had worked in these dangerous environments also meant that their lives would be at greater risk from industrial accidents and mishaps as well as other exposures to the dangers of war and wartime production.[68]

Confederate war clerk John B. Jones sensed the changes in casualty figures likely to happen as fighting swelled between the antagonists. At the beginning of the summer, he confided in his diary the news of some of the engagements that had occurred elsewhere, concluding, "These are the pattering drops that must inevitably be succeeded by a torrent of blood!"[69] If such views confined themselves to the impact of battle, they glossed over the numbers of the slain that were already occurring from other circumstances. Still, many of these individual stories appeared in newspaper accounts or other public forms to shape opinions regarding the conflict and the sacrifices it engendered. It remained to be seen if the noncombat fatalities that captured attention in the early part of 1861 would continue to do so, even as those passages impacted the families, friends, comrades, and loved ones of the soldiers and civilians from whom war was exacting the highest price.

2
The Battle in Camp
Death in the Soldier Encampments

Ther vakens in ranks can be fill with others but in the sirkle of friends at home and a round fiar side tha neve can be fild.
Milton Barrett, Eighteenth Georgia

He died the death of a soldier—died from a fever caused by the exposures of a soldier's life . . . he yielded up his life as a sacrifice upon his country's altar.
Account of the death of Captain V. G. McDaniel

Out of all the lives lost in this way, I never once knew the original idiot to be injured.
Comment by General Francis A. Walker of soldiers pouring powder from shells

The word "camp" has a pleasant sound to it, and yet death visited frequently upon men there as it did in other, seemingly more likely settings. Fatal illness accounted for the vast majority of the men who perished in this environment. Historian Bell Wiley's observation for the troops who converged from all parts of the South to battle a foe in the field applied to the forces in blue as well: "The most destructive enemies of Confederates were not the Yankees but the invisible organisms which filled the camps with sickness."[1] As historian Wiley

36

Sword observed of these volunteers, "They had come to fight opposing soldiers; but the greater enemy, the one they must constantly grapple with in unsanitary camps while often ingesting putrid food and contaminated water, was the ill health so prevalent everywhere."[2] The effects hit especially hard on those at home, as Georgian Dolly Burge remarked in her diary in early 1862. "News came this morning. Bob Wright was brought from Yorktown a corpse," she recorded on May 2. "Another soldier fallen by sickness not the sword."[3]

The uneven quality of care for the men struggling with illness contributed to higher rates of mortality in some locations. When President Lincoln's secretary, William O. Stoddard, embarked upon what he called "my exceedingly curious vacation" to the recently seized coast of North Carolina, he met and befriended a captured Confederate colonel. On a tour of the local grounds that included "two army graveyards," the visitor from Washington inquired, "How is this thing? You didn't lose half as many men as we did in the fighting. Your troops are all acclimated and you ought not to have had so many in hospital. But look at the difference in the death rate, as testified by the graveyards. I can't understand it."

The Confederate officer promised to explain the discrepancy and took Stoddard to Union facilities marked by the placards "Christian Commission," and "Sanitary Commission," where the men received attention and provisions. "'Do you see this?' asked the colonel. 'Well! Our poor fellows had nothing of this kind. No surgeons to speak of. No Christian Commission. No Sanitary Commission. No such supplies.'" He maintained that few of his men ever recovered sufficiently to return to the service, then corrected himself. "'It wasn't quite as bad as that, but when ten of your men come in here, nine of them get back into the ranks again. Ours are out yonder in the graveyard.'"[4]

A Georgia soldier captured in colorful fashion the sense the early recruits felt about the dangers of the service they were now encountering. Milton Barrett of the Eighteenth Georgia explained from his post in Virginia: "Thrue the kind provandents . . . and all wise god i am enjoying good health while many of my Brother solgers has sicken and dide." Guarding prisoners in Richmond, Barrett could see the effects of illness, broadly noting the "sicness that has bin in our regement." He felt deeply the losses in his ranks. "But thirty of our brave boys is gon to return no moar. Three from my company who sleep in the silent room wert tha will wake no moar." For these men, the loss would be felt at home as well: "Ther vakens in ranks can be fill with others but in the sirkle of friends at home and a round fiar side tha neve can be fild. We bered them in the oners of war and mark the place so ther friends may find ther graves."[5]

An encampment in Kentucky named Beauregard accepted its first occupants in October 1861 and was abandoned and burned on February 21, 1862. Nevertheless, in its short existence, the posting represented the last one for many of the men who reached it. One historian noted, "Between twelve and fifteen hundred southern soldiers perished, not from Yankee bullets but from typhoid fever, measles, and cerebrospinal meningitis."[6]

Similar effects occurred in the blue ranks as well. During this period, Colonel Thomas E. Bramlette, commanding at Columbia, Kentucky, explained to Brigadier General George Thomas, "Typhoid fever is striking our men a heavy blow; 233 of my regiment now down, and dying daily." Calling for the command to move at the earliest opportunity, he noted, "While marching we never have any sick; when we stop the men sicken and fall like leaves." Finally, Bramlette observed, "We would rather die in battle than on a bed of fever."[7]

For a Union soldier from Wisconsin, the common feature of camp life in Virginia in the winter of 1861 was death. "Almost every day we are called upon to follow some comrade to the soldier's grave," James Anderson explained. "It is very sad to see a funeral party marching slowly to the mournful wail of the fife or the dismal tap of the muffled drum and think of some poor fellow lying buried in the field."[8]

A South Carolinian despaired to his wife, "We have just done burying P. Wright. He only lived for four days after taking pneumonia." These deaths due to illness left him uncertain. "It seems there is more to be feared than battle."[9] Anxiety remained ever-present for those who knew that their well-being could be compromised fatally at any time. A Union soldier captured this sentiment as he lamented the death of his brother to "brain fever," telling their sister, "It was very hard to see him die so suddenly but here a man can be well and hearty one day and can die the next."[10]

Soldiers who confronted the early deaths of their comrades expressed a mixture of sentiments. Henry Hayward of the Twenty-Eighth Pennsylvania told his sister in August 1861 about the response the men had to the passing of Private James Brown, who had refused "an honerable Discharge" on account of his frail health because he said "he had come with the Company, and he would die with them." When Brown's determination cost him his life, his friends in the ranks offered the family the only tribute they could think to muster when "they raised $76 to send him home."[11]

Marching across parts of Tennessee and Kentucky in the fall of 1861, Texas troops endured circumstances made worse by illness. John Gregg informed W. W. Mackall at headquarters in Hopkinsville that 749 of his men had arrived: "Except a number of sick men on the road our nine companies are all here." However, for some their travels had already ended. "Five of our number died on the way."

Others might well follow. "From exposure to cold and wet on our journey we have more coughs and colds than I ever saw among the same number of men."[12]

An underlying sense of vulnerability resided in the minds of the officers and men who had gone to war to fight an opponent they could see and understand, only to confront one they could not. A lieutenant in the Twenty-Second Virginia observed, "I really believe that the diseases produced by exposure since we left our camp will cause more deaths and produce more suffering than would have resulted from a hard-fought battle."[13] Another Virginian, Captain James K. Edmondson, admitted, "It does not become me to say so, but I am fully impressed with the belief that there is more danger of my falling prey to disease than there is of falling by the bullets of the enemy."[14]

A Union soldier from Maine was no more sanguine concerning the scourge of illness befalling his regiment. "Most of us have lost our courage and expectations of reaching home, or even dying on the battlefield," he remarked resignedly, where he felt that risking his life under those circumstances would offer "a fate less cruel than dying by inches."[15] A Confederate counterpart serving in western Virginia concurred with the sentiment, explaining to his sister, "I have always said that I feared disease in the army more than anything else," before subsequently observing that many comrades were "gone, yes gone where a great many of us will soon go."[16]

From his camp in Washington, D.C., Charles W. Gould of "Company I, 3rd Regiment Excelsior Brigade," of New York wrote his sister on August 19, 1861, "The constant appearance of death seems to take away the fear of it."[17] Turning his focus to the fatal illness that was besetting his unit, he explained a month later that while his health remained "good" and he hoped it would "remain so," others were not so fortunate. "Death comes to us by many a way. . . . Many here to[o] has bit the dust. Ogden Grules is among them. He died in the hospittle in Washington." Gould noted that he hoped to "prepair to meet the Monster Death as he is daily staring us in the face. He is calling many of our friends from among us."[18] As summer gave way to autumn, Charles Gould could not help but notice the mounting toll of illness. He did not expect a battle momentarily, "still there is a great deal of dainger in camp." The effect was significant: "More die from disese than on the battle ground. George Smith the Prenologist is dead."[19]

For so many men away from their homes and families for the first extended period, the correspondence that served as a bond between them also provided the grounds for expressing uncertainty and concern. George H. Randall had enrolled in the Fourth Vermont Infantry as a musician but soon was complaining to his wife of a sore throat and general sickness. Then, perhaps without realizing the alarm it might cause her, he commented, "Probably there are twenty five that will get A discharge and some eight or ten that will die ther was one man buried yesterday."[20]

On November 11, another Vermonter passed word to his mother about the death of a comrade: "Adam Potter of Cornwell and a good boy he was when he was alive but he is gon to his home with[out] any friendes to console him and comfort him in his last hour." Corporal Henry H. Wilder observed stoically, "To morow morn we pay the last respects to him [w]home we did hope but ashort time agoe would get well and goe thorough this War with us and be able to meete his friends again . . . but it was not Gods will and t[h]erfore we cannot have him for a tent mate but it is well as we know for it is Gods will." Still, the soldier knew that the sense of loss he felt was minimal when compared with that of those who were worrying about the fate of their soldier at home: "But sad and lonly as it is with me I cannot feal as bad as his Mother when she gets the sad inteligance."[21]

By February the situation was becoming more personal, as Gould complained, "I would have writen before but have been sick my self."[22] At the end of the month, another letter reached home, but from Gould's comrade Lieutenant J. P. Sandford, who informed the family, "Your Brother Charles was taken sick about two weeks since which proved fatal. He died on Saturday night last and was buried on Monday following with the honors of War. *His disease was Typhoid Fever.*"[23]

Deaths hit closest to the men when they affected the squad or mess. Gerald F. Linderman has noted that "the mess became the focus of comradeship" and in many ways substituted for the sense of family the men had left behind them when they went to war.[24] Union soldier Albert Marshall felt the loss of one comrade intensely. "Of those who died," he observed, "A. M. Brookfield was my most intimate friend. He was in the same squad and room with me." In addition to their personal relationship, Marshall felt stunned by the situation that led to his comrade's demise. "His death was almost as sudden to me as though he had fallen in battle. He had been quite sick but it was thought had fully recovered, and he had returned to quarters from the hospital rejoicing in being again at home, as it were, with us." However, matters turned quickly when Brookfield suffered "a relapse and died in a few short hours. It was a sad event to our little number, his roommates."[25]

John Henry Cowin expressed the same sentiment when he recorded the death of Sam Dorrah from illness: "Thus died one of my best friends and messmates in the army, and nearest neighbor at home." His friend's demise dealt Cowin a terrible blow. "Deeply do I deplore his loss, but can only exclaim God's will be done. He giveth and he taketh away." So many more men were dying that, two days later, Cowin remarked, "In this way we will all soon be gone. Disease will kill many more than the enemy." Nor did it seem that only the weak would perish. In early October, he noted another death: "Wm. H. Willingham died this morning at half past ten o'clock of Typhoid-Pneumonia, after an illness of about two weeks. . . . He is the last person upon whom one would have thought that death would fix his hold. He was one of the largest and healthiest men in the Company. But death makes no distinctions, but seizes upon all alike." Cowin could not shake the sensation and the next day confided, "The death of these two fellow soldiers and friends has cast a gloom over the whole company. . . . We know not upon whom death may lay his icy fingers next as in both these cases, it may be upon those whom we least expect."[26]

Deaths from illness also struck in the remote outposts of the backcountry on the fringes of the major campaign theaters. Kentuckian Edward "Ned" Guerrant's mood turned melancholy as he contemplated wartime realities among his comrades. "Continual association with scenes of suffering, of danger & of death," he wrote, "is tending greatly to render me insensible to grief—or compassion. Death is nothing here, where so many die & all are liable to—at any moment." The young officer felt the cruelty of the situation for the suffering acutely. "I have seen the sick, the dying & the dead all stretched upon their scanty straw pallets in the same room," he noted. "To die in such a place with no familiar face to look upon—no friendly ear to whisper a last request—no loving hand to close our dying eyes & stretch us for the grave—O! this thought is insupportable! But thus the sick soldier died." Subsequently, Guerrant noted, "Two soldiers died in the Hospital (C.H.) today," in tiny, remote "Gladesville" in Wise County, Virginia. "I wonder they don't all die."[27]

Georgian William Stilwell felt a similar sense of oppression to that expressed by his comrade from Kentucky. Telling his wife that sickness was prevailing in the regiment as it camped near Richmond, he remarked, "Elie Norman died in our Company the other day. Out of three brothers Dobbins that lived above McDonough, there is but one left and he is bad sick." The news was also dire for the other men who had gone to war to defend their homes and families. "There have [been] about thirty six men died out of our regiment since we come to Virginia, mostly with measles and a great quantity sick now."[28]

At the end of August 1862, diarist William Chambers reflected on the condition of so many in his unit: "Two more of Company B have died since my last entry. Winston Morris died at home on the 23d inst., and J. R. McPhail at Clinton on the 25th." The tally had continued to grow almost unremittingly. "Two other deaths have not been noted in these pages. Marion Cook died at Miss. Springs on the 1st of August, and W. M. Pace at Monticello on the 7th." These unexpected passages left a foreboding sense of gloom for the surviving comrades. "Thus we have lost by death 14 in all in a little over two months. Seventeen in all have died, including two who never left their homes."[29]

Often, the individuals laid low in this fashion appeared to their associates to be among the least likely to face such an undeserving fate. Second Lieutenant Samuel Summer of the Fifth Vermont Infantry expressed the soldier's perspective concerning the unexpected loss of such comrades in a letter to his parents, observing, "We bearyed one of our men a few days ago by the name of Sco[t]t from Woolcot he died with a feaver was a man of a strong constitution and one of the best soldiers we had."[30]

This theme seemed to prevail. A Minnesotan, writing from Corinth, Mississippi, explained to his father that sickness was thinning the ranks of some of the most promising members: "The best of our non-commissioned officers, Corporal Hanks, died yesterday morning after a long illness. It seems to be a fatality with us that we are continually losing our very best men." Aside from the shock of losing those who seemed to be the strongest among them was the feeling that death might mean personal oblivion: "There was something so sad in our comrade's dying alone so far from home and loved ones, to be buried in these nameless woods,—while the mighty march of events passes on and over his forgotten grave." One consolation was the sense of camaraderie the losses generated among the survivors. "These deaths have had a good effect upon the men," the soldier explained, "making them feel kinder and more brotherly towards each other. We are no longer a mass of discordant elements thrown together and called a Company, with no fellow-feelings for any others outside of our own platoons . . . but we are now bound together by common bereavements and common dangers into one body."[31]

Former schoolteacher Benjamin White left his civilian vocation to become a lieutenant in the Sixth North Carolina. In December 1861, he was already drawing dire conclusions regarding a service only six months old, explaining in a letter on December 3, "It is a fact that the Battlefield is far less to be dreaded than the sickness in Camp and the privations and the hardships we have to undergo." His assessment that "the Army is no place for Boys and sick folks" would be underscored in the months ahead as the regiment lost more and more men to disease.[32]

Sickness continued to take its terrible toll on the Vermonters in their Virginia campsite. Just before Christmas, Private Hiram M. Hunter told his sister of the "painfull sircomstances" that caused him to write: "Seth has departed this life. . . . He had the lung feaver and then the typhorid feaver sat in." Even so, the bereaved comrade offered thoughts of solace that he hoped would provide comfort: "Be of good chear for gods will must be done not ourn."[33]

The impact of the death of a comrade by disease led one soldier to comment in his diary, "I learned last night that one of our men died Oct. 15th at Georgetown Hospital. We learned the fact by way of his Father who wrote to find whether there was any pay due him." Second Lieutenant Charles Haydon thought the lack of knowledge represented by this man's death in particular was the most unnerving aspect of such circumstances: "This dying off without our knowing it is what ought not to be. We expected to see him returning every day for duty."[34]

Others waiting at home had no hope of seeing loved ones before their mortal days had passed. Phebe Arthur learned that her husband, Richard, was desperately ill and wrote to admonish him to "take good care of your self and get well," repeating for emphasis, "be sure and take good care and not take no more cold." Unhappily, as she wrote those loving words, she did not know that he had already succumbed to "Typhoid pneumonia," as a captain in the unit explained to her as the ultimate cause of Richard's death.[35]

For some, there was the nagging sense that such deaths not only were all-pervasive but also illustrated the lives squandered without having had the chance for engaging their opponents in combat. The sounds of musketry prompted one soldier to explain that these emanated not from the battlefield but from being fired over the graves of the fatally ill, who, despite the recognition of their service the salute symbolized, had thus perished "unhonored and unsung." He wrote home, "In several regiments near us about three deaths take place daily."[36]

Atlanta resident Sam Richards watched in dismay as his town began to receive the sick and wounded being transferred there, crowding civilian structures with new occupants. On February 28, 1862, he noted, "Our city is now full of sick soldiers many of the large hotels and public buildings being appropriated as hospitals." Nevertheless, one case in particular caught his attention and demanded his sympathy. As Richards wrote, "One poor fellow died to-day who in coming here passed within 30 miles of his wife and prayed to be put out there that he might go home to die, but the rules of war would not permit so he had to die among strangers. Oh what dreadful misery this horrid war has produced and the end is not yet."[37]

Fatalities from disease were occurring at such levels as to overwhelm systems never designed to handle the numbers they were experiencing. In Washington, the display of deceased soldiers awaiting burial sparked a public outcry against the unavoidable signs of negligence and disregard for human dignity. One historian noted the alteration in attitude as well as appearance wrought by the terrible price of war. "There had been a time when the loss of one young Ellsworth had thrown the capital into mourning," Margaret Leech explained. "Now, from the silver-mounted rosewood of the higher officers to the cheap pine slats of ordinary soldiers, the business of death was plied like any other prosperous trade."[38]

For some entrepreneurs, warfare was indeed turning death into a booming business, but many at home confronted such finalities on a smaller and much more intimate scale. Whether serving as sources of inspiration or caution, notices in newspapers continued to relate the deaths of individuals. When F. E. Estes died "of typhoid pneumonia" on March 31, 1862, at Orange Court House, Virginia, the composition announcing his passage in a Canton, Mississippi, newspaper offered a powerful tribute to the fallen warrior: "Poor boy! He had but just entered upon his military career when God called him away from the turbulent scenes of earth," leaving a "loving mother and sisters" bereaved by his passing.[39]

Union general Robert McAllister expressed his concerns to his wife regarding the fatal illness that was impacting his command at "Camp Advance," outside Richmond, Virginia: "I am sorry to say we have had two deaths in our regiment yesterday—dysintery and typhoid fever." Then he touched on a familiar theme present in soldier correspondence, capturing the contradictory spirit of such sacrifice in a way that reflected a contemporary understanding of deaths that occurred outside the context of the battlefield: "Poor fellows. They came to serve their country and have done it nobly. But here, far from home, with no kind friends to soothe their dying pillow, they pass off the stage of action with no one really to feel their loss here."[40] Another Union soldier from Connecticut noted stoically, "I am put in mind of the Shortness of Life by seeing the Firing Parteys of the 8 Vermont as thay Pass by with the Corps of Some of thair Members. Thay have Buerd quit a number of thair Comrades Since thay have been with us."[41]

Working his way through the Peninsula Campaign in 1862, North Carolinian Benjamin White detailed in a letter to a former student the terrible price that many of his comrades were paying by virtue of poor weather conditions, bad roads, and dismal care for those who fell ill. "So a large number have died One Company had lost seven men two of our Company have died. Haywood Younger and Greely Ray," he wrote from "Camp near Yorktown, April 26th 1862." A month later he was at Richmond, but the situation remained dire. "There has been great mortality in this regiment altogether we have not lost less than 150 by death in camp." The whole period had been a harsh one. "The mortality in our army during the latter part of March and the month of April has been frightful in a few weeks this regiment lost fifty men, most from Measles and Pneumonia. Since the last of March we have lost eight men from our company."[42]

The fall of 1862 was also proving exceptionally deadly for soldiers from Georgia. One fellow wrote to his mother almost plaintively, "Times is bad here and getting worse. . . . They are dying dayly. There has been about 15 died since

Sunday morning Last Thursday there was six that died. Two died in about fifteen minutes between their deaths." Assuring his mother that he remained well, Eli Landers employed a literary allusion to convey his thoughts: "It's like Brutus to see a man die on such places but they can't help theirself." To Landers the deaths were personal. "There has been two of the Lawrenceville County died since we come here. Their names was Cadell and Underwood." Other friends struggled as well, including a comrade who seemed to have recovered. "We have had a very serious time since this time yesterday morning for we have witnessed the death of one of our fellow solgers to wit Thomas Sanders. He died with a relapse of the measels. . . . His relapse was very hasty to death. He only lasted 5 days this last time." Landers had remained by his side. "He was out of his senses all the time" and seemed to want to "skip off all the time. He said he was going home but the poor fellow will return home with his eyes closed."[43]

Fatal illness continued to plague the command as it moved through North Carolina in 1862. "I hate to tell you that we had to witness the death of one of our worthiest soldiers last night named William Dickison," Landers explained. "He died at 4 o'clock. We all mourn the loss of him very much, but there is one thing that I am glad to say, he died in Triumph of Honor. Throughout the company he will ever bear the name of a worthy soldier." There were elements of solace, but Landers could not help but become almost overwhelmed by the situation he and his comrades faced. "It makes me feel bad to see so many of our men dying. It looks like that our regiment has had hard luck but we had no reason to wonder."[44]

Diseases had devastated units when the men first assembled in 1861, but even as the war progressed, fatal illnesses remained part of the life-threatening experiences of the men in the ranks. For many, the conditions in the camps were problematic in terms of limiting, much less eradicating, the dangers they faced in that quarter. Lieutenant Henry Lyon of the Thirty-Fourth New York chronicled the failing health of a compatriot in his diary. On Sunday, July 20, the officer noted, "Pelton who has been sick went to the hospital (Regt.). He was quite sick the rest of the boys doing as well as can be expected. Burial now everyday." His colleague would be numbered among the dead in a matter of days. "W. Pelton died in hospital at 9," Lyon wrote on Tuesday, July 22. "Went to get boards for coffin. Had one of the boys make it and we buried him in P.M." The men did the best they could by their fallen comrade. "Services performed by chaplain. A good grave was dug and a board bears his name."[45] Finally, Lyon explained in a letter to his brother as he struggled with the realities of sickness and death, "Pelton, you will hear by the time this reaches you, has died in the Hospital here. Poor fellow—it seems worse to us than it would if he had fallen on the field of Battle."[46]

To be sure, illness could strike at any time, but not all of the death associated with disease occurred directly. In August 1862, Lieutenant William A. Summerow of the Fifty-Second North Carolina entered a hospital in Petersburg, Virginia, to combat a case of typhoid fever. Whatever his prognosis might have been, in a fit of delirium he left his bed suddenly and plunged to his death from an upper-level window.[47] At the same time, another North Carolinian exhibited similar behavior after experiencing what one witness labeled a "sudden fit of desperation." Nineteen-year-old John Roland was convalescing at the Second North Carolina Hospital after participating in the fighting of the Seven Days Campaign. Without warning, he produced a knife and wielded it wildly against a doctor and attendants before turning it on himself in gruesome fashion. Even then, no one could prevent Roland from crashing through a window onto the ground below, where the impact and his other injuries contributed to his death.[48]

Similarly, while remaining at a hospital in a converted "old abandoned cotton mill, located on the bank of the Shenandoah River," New Yorker Rice Bull recorded being awakened by the sound of shattering glass. He explained, "I sprang up and saw a man with his head out of the window struggling to throw himself out." Although managing to bring the stricken man back into the room, Bull could not stay the damage already done. "He was badly cut by the glass and bled freely. He never regained consciousness and died before morning. There was little sleep for anyone that night." Bull would remark of the distressing atmosphere, "We were almost surrounded by dying men."[49]

Occasionally, the cases were stranger than they seemed at first glance. Like so many, Orson W. Olds died of typhoid fever in Washington on November 11, 1862. However, he had gone to the hospital for a very different reason. "Young Olds—son of Carl," Daniel Holt referenced for his wife in a letter nine days later. "He died at Georgetown after receiving what I considered at the time a slight injury from falling from a tree. So uncertain is life." The doctor used the same occasion to note the impact of such deaths on the regimental leadership itself, writing, "Some companies are commanded by non-commissioned officers and some by Second Lieutenants. Thirteen have died since leaving Camp Schuyler in Hermiker county."[50]

In Virginia, where the slaughter of Fredericksburg represented the waste that many in the public and in the ranks began to associate with a war that seemed to hold no prospect for concluding, the ravages of illness continued to have a deleterious effect on morale. A Connecticut soldier lamented to his mother that if she could "see the poor fellows dying around you [here], worn out by marches and disease and see the misery brought upon us by this awful war, then you would be still more anxious to have the war ended."[51]

A New Hampshire corporal who had missed the killing fields of Fredericksburg nevertheless remained struggling for his life against a more relentless, and remorseless, foe. As he lay dying from illness, only a few days after the main fighting had subsided, the soldier was only able to gain sufficient strength to take a last look at an image of the beloved wife and eight-month-old twin children that he would be leaving behind.[52]

Surgeon Daniel M. Holt characterized the sense of foreboding that settled over the Army of the Potomac in early 1863 when he wrote his wife, "The health of the regiment is bad. Death's upon our track, and almost every day sees its victim taken to the grave." The rate of those succumbing to disease must have seemed like the unrelenting beat of the muffled drum of the burial march. "Yesterday two, and to-day two more were consigned to their last resting place, and still the avenger presses harder and harder claiming as his victim the best and fairest of the men."[53]

Kentuckian Ned Guerrant noted almost clinically from his camp on the border region of Virginia, Tennessee, and his home state, "Long ways from any place," of the sudden death of a comrade: "One of Col. Slemps soldiers died of this new malady this morning." The eighteen-year-old "young man" had only "entered service two weeks ago in perfect health, [but] died after five days illness." Explaining the symptoms in graphic detail as the would-be warrior declined so rapidly in condition, the staff officer concluded that the once-vibrant youth had received a final visit from "*Death's Dread Minister.*"[54]

Billy Gray had been an eighteen-year-old farmworker when he enlisted and almost immediately began battling illness. By 1863, he was struggling with remaining in the ranks at all. Going absent without leave in May, he stayed free through the summer months but by October returned to face court-martial and received a sentence of "40 days hard labor." When Gray complained of the harshness of his treatment, the roll notation indicated, "He ought to thank Heaven . . . for if all the evidence had been brought against him . . . the Court could [not] have gotten around inflicting the penalty of death." In any case, whatever reasons had prompted his earlier flirtations with desertion, Gray could not escape the certainties of the dangers soldiers faced, even when not engaged in battle. In mid-1864, after a stint in Richmond to serve his sentence, William C. Gray ended up back in a hospital in Salisbury, North Carolina, dying of chronic diarrhea on July 7.[55]

Winchester, Washington, Richmond, and Atlanta had experienced early on in the conflict the impact of the tremendous influx of sick soldiers in their midst. Likewise, other cities in which troops congregated also became centers of pestilence. Campaign and siege conditions had already turned Vicksburg, Mississippi, into a vast camp of affliction for soldiers and residents but continued to plague the troops still stationed there. On September 11, 1863, the *Alexandria Gazette*, in Virginia, recorded, "A large number of the army, both officers and men, are afflicted with the diseases incident to that locality. Many deaths occur daily, so much so, as to require whole cargoes of coffins to be shipped there."[56]

Meanwhile, in the Trans-Mississippi, conditions were so unwelcoming for the troops garrisoning or passing through Helena, Arkansas, that some of them referred to the town as "Hell-in-Arkansas." The quartermaster of a Wisconsin cavalry regiment that would suffer 75 of a total of 284 deaths from disease attributed the high mortality rate in the river town to "warm weather and poisonous spring water" before asserting that while some were discharged and others recovered, "many died and most of them were buried there on the hill side with military honors."[57]

Disease continued to be a great killer of the men who left home to serve their respective causes, but who would not fall in combat. In July 1863, Ohioan Andrew Rose wrote his parents from his posting in Tennessee to share grim tidings: "Christopher Dimick was ded that makes 3 of the Dover boys that has died out of 42 and one killed. that is about the way there is more dies by sickness than gets killed."[58] The sense of loss remained palpable for their comrades and loved ones, even as people came to grips with the nature of such deaths. A piece in a West Virginia newspaper in October 1863 captured the contradictions of those lamenting the loss of soldiers outside of the context of battle when it provided readers with the account of the death of Captain V. G. McDaniel following an extended illness: "Doubtless his proud, though undemonstrative spirit, longed to meet the great conqueror—Death—on the battlefield and that his last lingering gaze might decry the discomfiture of the severed ranks of ingrate rebels against his cherished, his beneficent country; yet, in the inscrutable workings of a mysterious Providence, his ardent desires were never to be realized." Even so, the writer explained sympathetically, "Death cheated him [only] in part; for he died the death of a soldier—died from a fever caused by the exposures of a soldier's life . . . he yielded up his life as a sacrifice upon his country's altar."[59]

The men in the ranks suffered the greater portion of deaths to disease, but a handful of general officers from both sides fell prey to illnesses that cost them their lives. A Georgian who had resettled in Texas and hailed from Waco, Allison Nelson had a long and colorful career before assuming command of a Texas regiment in the Civil War. Unfortunately, the ink on his promotion to brigadier general in September 1861 had barely had a chance to dry when he became ill with a persistent fever. By October 7, the former filibusterer, militiaman, and Texas Ranger was dead.[60]

Frederick W. Lander had been a civil engineer, an explorer, and a railroad surveyor before he became a Union brigadier general in 1861. However, he suffered from a persistent "congestive chill" while serving in the field, which prompted him to request relief from his duties. Unfortunately for Lander, complications that included pneumonia led to his death on March 2, 1862.[61]

Georgian John S. Bowen had attended the University of Georgia before entering West Point and embarking on a career in the Old Army or Regular Army. He was among the men captured by Nathaniel Lyon at Camp Jackson, Missouri, in 1861, before becoming a Confederate officer and rising through the ranks. Promoted to major general, he endured the grueling fighting for Vicksburg in the summer of 1863, only to perish from the effects of dysentery at Raymond, Mississippi, on July 13, as a paroled prisoner of war.[62]

Major general and native Kentuckian John Buford performed admirably for the Federals, with particular note at the opening phase of the battle of Gettysburg. Family ties to a cousin who served as a general officer in the Confederate armed forces did not prevent or mitigate his dedication to defending the Union, but another factor limited his long-term effectiveness. While serving in Virginia in the aftermath of the summer campaigning, Buford fell victim to typhoid fever. Struggling to regain his health, he lost that final engagement, dying on December 16, 1863.[63]

Brigadier General Daniel Phineas Woodbury had remained with the Union despite marrying into a Southern family. A West Pointer, he had served with distinction and assisted with numerous engineering projects before the war. His final duty came in Florida, where yellow fever caused his death on August 15, 1864.[64] Woodbury's Alabama-born comrade Major General David Birney experienced the debilitating effects of disease when he contracted "a virulent species of malaria." Despite convalescing at his home in Philadelphia, the officer, who had served actively since the Peninsula Campaign, could not survive his illness. He lost his last battle on October 18, 1864.[65]

General Thomas E. G. Ransom had served in various capacities and suffered wounds before operating effectively under Ulysses Grant in Mississippi in 1863. Recovering from another wound received in the Red River Campaign, he took a command in the Atlanta Campaign before perishing from the effects of typhoid fever on October 28, 1864.[66] Regardless of his failing health, Ransom insisted, "I will stay with my command until I am carried away in my coffin." Then, when informed of his condition as the end approached, his response reflected stoicism and fortitude: "I am not afraid to die. I have met death too often to be afraid of it now."[67] From Atlanta, Georgia, Thomas Christie, an artillerist who had served under the officer, observed to his father, "We hear with sorrow of the death of

General Ransom during the recent movement. He was a most worthy young officer. When he died he was in command of our Corps."[68]

Death could indeed come in many forms other than from the effects of disease
for commissioned and noncommissioned officers and privates alike. The adjutant
of the Twenty-Third New York explained the causes for some of those who had
died in the earliest days of the conflict. Although several of the men William
Haight discussed were victims of disease or other circumstances, he noted that
another perished "poisoned by eating wild fruit."[69] Similarly, William Fox noted
that "A. Lohman," of Company A, Eighth New York, "died of poison while on
picket, by drinking from a bottle found at a deserted house."[70] A poisoning of
another type of consumption appeared to have occurred at Camp Curtain, in
Harrisburg, Pennsylvania, in August 1862. As troops arrived in the locality, discipline in terms of access broke down. One of the individuals who apparently
took advantage of the opportunity was a woman who brought pies with her for
sale. Seven individuals who purchased and consumed the pies were supposed to
have died from them, and when found out, the civilian admitted to harboring
secessionist views.[71] A few months earlier, John Long, of Company E, Fourth
Kentucky Cavalry, perished from the effects of an undetermined "poison" while
located at his camp in Wartrace, Tennessee.[72]

The stresses and strains of warfare and command also manifested themselves in
many, and occasionally fatal, ways. Individuals with inherent or preexisting factors
could find that the service exposed or enhanced such vulnerabilities. However
long Charles Emery of the Ninety-Ninth New York Volunteers may have lived had
he not gone to war, or the degree to which his circumstances contributed to his
end, the record nevertheless indicated that the Boston native "died of apoplexy,
August 29, 1863, in his tent, Gloucester Point, Va."[73] Similarly, the historian of
the Twenty-Fourth Wisconsin Infantry noted the death of First Assistant Surgeon
Charles Mueller, "who succumbed to apoplexy, or stroke, at age thirty-seven," although overconsumption of alcohol likely contributed to his demise.[74]

Humans susceptible to extremes in their physical and mental health conditions were unlikely to find the elements of wartime service beneficial. Suicide
remained the manner in which some of them dealt with the demons that haunted
them. Diane Miller Sommerville examined suicides among Confederate soldiers
as corollaries of war and determined that evolving attitudes allowed other white
Southerners to process these deaths. "Although soldier suicides might not be
heralded as heroic in the classical tradition," she concluded, "they nevertheless
were viewed as tragic and honorable."[75]

For some men, the battlefield presented circumstances that left them few alternatives to taking their own lives. Studying the Union soldier in battle, historian

Earl Hess observed that in some 400 Federal cases suicide became "a tragic and extreme way for a soldier to escape the horrors of the battlefield." Some of the men who sought this method of escape carried into war underlying circumstances "of mental and emotional problems stemming from their civilian lives, but others did so for war-related reasons." In instances on the battlefield where death was certain or conditions so grim, some soldiers seem to have taken matters into their own hands as a last measure of control regarding the timing and nature of their final moments.[76] However, individual deaths occurring in this fashion meant that these men had sacrificed their lives to the war as surely as those who fell in the formalized engagements of the conflict from direct enemy fire.[77]

On the day after Christmas in 1861, Confederate brigadier general Philip St. George Cocke was enduring declining health as he rested at his home, Bellmead, in Powhatan, Virginia. The general had led troops at Manassas, but the prospect for future service was dim. Although Cocke was only fifty-two, perhaps the weight of his illnesses and the likelihood that he could not return to leadership in the ranks were too much for him. Family members would discover his body in the yard of the home with a pistol at his side from which he had produced the fatal wound to his temple.[78] Another Confederate wrote his father from Richmond to tell him the news: "We have just heard of the suicide of General Phil St. George Cocke in his own house and in the presence of his family, he placed [a] pistol at his head and shot himself." Then, Greenlee Davidson offered an explanation for the troubling story: "His mind has been unhinged ever since the commencement of the Secession Movement."[79]

The situation in which Thomas D. Stringer of the Sixth Virginia Infantry met his fate was not known, but the prewar tailor who had enlisted in Norfolk as a corporal in April 1861 had a checkered wartime career. Reduced to private by October, he apparently failed to restore his equilibrium with the coming of a new year. His service record simply indicated "committed suicide in Norfolk, 1/16/62."[80]

A New Yorker who had joined the Ninety-Ninth New York Volunteers the previous May at age twenty-six apparently could not reconcile himself to life as a soldier. At the end of November, he was posted with his command at Fort Monroe, in Virginia, when he "shot himself."[81] An Ohio diarist noted the fate of another comrade on June 13: "A 2nd Kentucky man was buried to-day. He purposely shot himself last night."[82]

A Confederate who had joined the service after the initial waves of patriotic enthusiasm had passed seemed inordinately overwhelmed by the duty that held him in the ranks. A comrade noted that the soldier had "left a child 11 days at home" and experienced other setbacks that left him spiraling out of any sense of self-control. Rather than face these depressing conditions, he drowned himself. "He was troubled generally," Private Harden Cochrane concluded.[83]

Captain Charles H. Shepley of the Nineteenth Illinois Infantry had no specific explanation advanced for the soldier's demise, and therefore his death might be attributed to carelessness, pure accident, or choice: "Died; March 23, 1862, from accident with his revolver."[84] On April 14, 1862, a Union diarist noted the passing of a comrade and recorded a cause that could have been a statement of facts concerning an unintended act or a description of a self-inflicted wound. Rufus Kinsley observed, "One of the Mass. 31st killed by the accidental discharge of a pistol."[85]

Mental health was as critical a component of the lives of soldiers as their physical well-being. The degree to which a genuine sense of "homesickness" or "blues" contributed to underlying vulnerabilities among some of the men in arms was present in the minds of those who witnessed the decline of comrades they could not attribute solely to other factors. One Union general explained the phenomenon effectively: "Ask any doctor who served in regiments and hospitals, and he will tell you that many soldiers, fresh from the farm of their parents . . . died from the effects of homesickness outright, and in many other cases it laid the foundation of diseases that ended in death." Reub Williams cited the example of Charles F. Davis to substantiate his contention, noting that he was "twenty-three and was engaged to be married" when he joined the service and progressed from "listless, then rather peevish," before entering the regimental hospital, from which he never left alive. Williams concluded, "Homesickness had too strong a hold upon him," adding, "His was not the only case of deadly homesickness, which came under my observation, by any means."[86] Another soldier wrote of the malady in February 1863: "Tell John to cheer up and not allow the 'blues' to take hold of him. I am of the opinion that they have killed more men than the sword."[87]

Traditional weapons need not be required for the final acts of desperate individuals. A forty-year-old married farmer from Connecticut who had left home to take up arms in defense of home and country had to endure the separation and the difficult conditions of camp and march as a soldier. On August 25, he apparently used medicine to relieve the deeper level of pain he felt oppressing him. A colleague noted in a diary entry that the fellow had "committed suicide by taking opium."[88]

For at least one tortured soul, unrequited love would so overwhelm him that he would never have the opportunity to challenge another for the affections of the one he had loved and apparently lost. A Camden, South Carolina, newspaper reprinted a notice from the *Charleston Mercury*, which told the tale of a local tragedy: "Third Lieut. Jarret of the 23d S.C.V., committed suicide yesterday forenoon, about 11 o'clock in Society-street, near East Bay, by shooting himself with a pistol through the head, causing instant death." The distraught soldier was supposed to have been the victim of "a disappointment in a love matter [which] led to the commission of the fatal act."[89] Unhappily, the lovelorn soldier did not view matters in the manner of a colleague, who wrote in his diary, "There are nowadays a great many ingenious & philosophical ways of killing men. No one need die for love unless he prefers that way."[90]

Although having served in the Mexican-American War, as a Union brigadier general in the Civil War, Francis Engle Patterson had a somewhat checkered career. Plagued by illness and charged with carrying out an unauthorized retreat while located near Catlett's Station on the Orange and Alexandria Railroad, he was subject to an investigation into the affair when "found dead in his tent . . . killed by the accidental discharge of his own pistol," on November 22, 1862.[91] Subsequently, a newspaper account from Michigan offered a more benign, if incongruous, explanation for the general's demise: "Gen Patterson's death was caused by the accidental discharge of a pistol which he kept under his pillow, while in the act of changing it from one hand to the other on awakening."[92]

Francis Patterson's passing in these circumstances allowed for several possible explanations and pointed to the difficulty of determining with exactitude on every occasion an accurate cause of death. Was he the victim of an accident, his own negligence, or a suicide? Fellow Union general Robert McAllister provided little clarity, while relating what could be known: "We have just got the news of the death of Genl. Patterson. He shot himself through the heart last night."[93]

Sudden and unexplained deaths vexed the soldiery affected by the act. From his camp, "Near Woodstock V.A.," Captain William Wells of Company C, First Vermont Cavalry, wrote to his brother Charles, on April 5, 1862. Hot days and cool nights, with work details and occasional skirmishing, were the order of the day. However, one incident involving Colonel Jonas P. Holliday disturbed Captain Wells and became the centerpiece of some of his correspondence with his sibling: "To day as the Regt had mooved about one or two miles this way word came forward that the Col. was wounded & had sent for the Surgeon." After dispensing with some duties, Colonel Holliday then "rode down from the Road to the [Shenandoah] River about 5 or 6 Rods from the Road there dismounted hitched his horse took out a Revolver and *shot* himself & fell into the River. he shot himself in the middle of his forehead." Staff members found their colonel "floating away from shore . . . [and] pulled him out." Miraculously, the officer remained alive, but in such a condition as not to survive for long. Wells was obviously distressed, lamenting, "I do not know what the Cause of his committing such an act was. we shall miss him very much."[94]

Charles H. Carr of the Forty-First Virginia Infantry had already battled a difficult adversary while at Camp Winder Hospital in Richmond with a case of dysentery in May and June 1862. Then he contracted typhoid fever and entered the Confederate General Hospital in Farmville, Virginia. He may well have been struggling with delirium when he reached for a weapon as he lay in the ward. The record indicated only that he "committed suicide there 6/62 with [a] revolver."[95] For Carr, the war and his seemingly incessant fight with illness were at an end.

Taking matters into one's own hands was one option men faced when the alternatives were capture and imprisonment or worse. A badly wounded soldier had to recognize that giving himself up to the mercy of the opponents he had been fighting was to take on unknown risks that might prove detrimental in the extreme. While numerous examples would exist of extraordinary compassion for a fallen foe, the demonization of the enemy and the fear of uncertainty could serve as counterweights. Kentuckian Ned Guerrant likely did not know the circumstances for a comrade following a firefight in which he suffered a wound, including the severity of that injury, but Guerrant felt confident enough to assign a motive to the soldier's final act. "Eight Southern men killed in M't Sterling," he wrote on August 17, 1862. "One of them after fighting—killed himself to prevent being captured."[96]

The circumstances were less clear for a distraught member of the First Michigan Sharpshooters. Private Henry Smith of Company H had been an older enlistee, at age forty-two, but he left nothing to explain one of his subsequent actions. Upon relief from guard duty late on September 25, 1863, Smith walked away to a location where he could not be disturbed or dissuaded and shot himself. A comrade applied the label "deranged" to explain an act that could not help but disturb those who knew the man and now were left to mourn his loss under such circumstances.[97]

In early March 1863, Halbert Paine was in the midst of an operation near Brashear City, Louisiana, when he interrupted the description of the movement of his command to note an individual tragedy, writing, "Lieut. Robert Swiney, 8th New Hampshire became suddenly insane and killed himself with his revolver." Picking up the narrative of his unit's operations, Paine offered no additional explanation for the suicide of the officer or his reason for attributing the act to the man's startling shift in mental health.[98]

On August 19, 1863, Charles Sherman wrote his "Wife & Chirldren & Parents" from Berwick Bay:

A Sad day this as been. Our Second Leautenant Allen of Ledyard, one of the kindest hearted men and a Braver one thair is not in this lower Worled, tryed to take is own Life. He has been Sick for some time but has tryed to keep up. . . . At last one of the men found him with his Jackknife open and his Thorat Cut and it apeared that he had tried to open the Vaines in his arm, but thay do not appear to have bled much. Thair is little hope of is recovey. It is very unfortunate that we did not find him Earler in the day.[99]

Ten days later, Sherman noted that the situation had terminated badly for the officer he had mentioned earlier: "I have writen you about our Second Leautenant Stanton Allen Cuting his throat while laboring under a fit of Insanity. We did what we couled for him but we couled not save him. He has gon from us to that other Worled. We must not Judge him for we know not how soon our turn may come to try that unseeing Path."[100]

Another incident appeared in the January 28, 1864, *Alexandria Gazette*. The notice offered a brief statement regarding an incident involving an otherwise unidentified man: "The soldier, who jumped from the fourth story of the Mansion House, last week, while laboring under delirium, died of his injuries on Saturday morning last."[101] Whether attributable to a man whose state of mind was rational if distraught, or to one subject to a bout of illness that had rendered rationality less operative, the end nevertheless came dramatically for this troubled individual.

A member of the Forty-Fourth New York had obtained a furlough for a period in 1864, when his permitted time at home in Utica, New York, reached an end. While it is impossible to know what tormented Private Edwin Wilbur about returning to the ranks, he chose not to do so, but also did not want to desert his comrades. Rather than face the dilemma, Wilbur selected suicide as his only option and perished by his own hand on February 5.[102]

Another individual who met his end in an uncertain manner was a Mississippi noncommissioned officer. On February 24, 1864, a comrade recorded, "Sergt. B. F. Devlin of Company G died suddenly yesterday afternoon. He was for several months commissary sergeant for the regiment." As the men in his unit "marched out to dress parade they left him sitting in his cabin. When they returned he was dead." William Pitt Chambers did not assign a cause for this sudden change in circumstances for his distressed brother in arms.[103]

The *Soldiers' Journal*, produced at the "Rendezvous of Distribution," in Virginia, offered the sad tale of "A DISTRESSING SUICIDE," in the July 13, 1864, edition. "On Wednesday last the Veteran Reserve Camp connected with this post was startled with the announcement that a member of Company F, of the command, named William Pitman, had committed suicide." Taking the context of the event "from a gentleman who was present at the time the deed was committed," the writer noted the likely explanation that the soldier "had been laboring under a temporary aberration of mind, induced, as was generally supposed, by an unfavorable condition of domestic affairs at home." Unable to secure a furlough to attend to the matter, Pitman seemed equally powerless to overcome his depression. "On the morning of the day alluded to above," the account proceeded, "he exhibited the usual symptoms of insanity, walking the floor of the barrack as if in deep meditation, until 10 o'clock, A.M., when halting suddenly he drew from his pocket a Colt's pocket-revolver, and before the men about him became aware of his intentions, deliberately placed the muzzle of the pistol between his eyes, and fired, the ball passing through his brain, causing instant death."[104]

For Private J. Q. Taylor, Company A, 11th North Carolina, the war provided the context for an unfortunate distinction. Although there was no explanation for his action, he became the sole member of his brigade identified as having taken his own life by shooting himself intentionally on October 24, 1864.[105]

Despite the frequency of such occurrences and the poignancy of those whose lives ended in this fashion, other activities associated with what must have seemed to outsiders as the ordinary routine in the military also took their tolls on the men in uniform. These final passages resulted from numerous causes that ranged from carelessness to misfortune.

Confederate Irby Scott noted several situations among comrades in the early days of the war in Virginia: "There was one of the same regiment shot himself accidentally yesterday morning he died from the wound, also another shot his hand off today." These types of incidents led the soldier to conclude, "I had rather they were not so close to us." He was just as grateful that such misfortune had not yet befallen his unit. "We have not had the first accident since we left Georgia."[106]

Other units were less fortunate than Scott's was initially. In the late summer of 1861, a Raleigh, North Carolina, newspaper presented the latest news on army deaths that had "recently occurred in our Camps in Virginia, among the soldiers." Although offering no causes for the majority of the men listed, the account did so for a soldier named "stalling of Franklin, who accidentally shot himself through the head," on July 23 at Yorktown.[107]

The *Richmond Daily Dispatch* cited an incident from "The Knoxville (Tenn.) Register, of the 29th ult." At Cumberland Gap, "N. P. Jackson accidentally shot himself through the heart a few nights since." An attorney before the war had commenced, "Mr. Jackson, who was acting as Assistant Quartermaster at Cumberland Ford, had gone to bed with a pistol upon his person, which, by some unexplained accident, during the night, became discharged, the ball piercing his heart and producing instant death." The odd occurrence had cost the unit "a young man of much promise and ability."[108]

Absentmindedness or carelessness proved to be the bane of a soldier's existence in these earliest days of warfare. In September 1861, a member of the Tenth Pennsylvania Reserves was serving on guard duty when he dropped his weapon, and a round smashed into his head, "killing him almost instantly." At approximately the same time, one of the Seventh Pennsylvania Reserves managed to fire a pistol shot that struck him in the head.[109]

In the raucous atmosphere of camp, especially in remote regions where heavier fighting did not often occur, men could take out their aggressions in other ways. In February 1862, Kentuckian Edward O. Guerrant noted, "There were three fights in camp today demonstrating that they are emphatically fighting 'bhoys.'" No serious outcomes resulted from these altercations, but the staffer added that in the lax atmosphere, "One of Captain Shawhan's men accidentally shot & killed himself."[110]

A Union soldier, Samuel McIlvaine, recorded a mishap at the end of March 1862. "Another unfortunate accident happened in camp today," he began. "One of the men in Company K of our regiment accidentally shot himself through the breast with his pistol, which fell out of his belt or pocket while stooping for something, and striking on the rock with muzzle up, went off." While the man did not die outright from the situation, McIlvaine concluded, "he will hardly live."[111]

Samuel Kenyon, who had enrolled in Company I, Forty-Fourth Regiment New York Volunteer Infantry, in September 1861 at the age of twenty-four, was with his comrades in Virginia in the early summer of 1862 when he mishandled his weapon, with devastating results. According to his record, this situation led to his being "accidentally wounded by a pistol shot in camp at Gaines Mill, Va.," and he "died June 12, '62 in the same camp."[112]

Iowan Silas Haven recorded a strange incident in his diary on June 21, 1863, while he was serving in Moscow, Tennessee: "One of our men from Company H shot himself yesterday morning and had to have his big toe took off close up to his body." Haven knew the fellow and seemed to think little of the incident from the first indications. By the end of that day's entry, however, the situation had taken a decided turn for the worst. As Haven wrote, "John Book, the man that shot himself, died today. It seems that all the men that got shot in the 27th shoot themselves. It takes a great while for men to learn how to handle a gun."[113]

The *Nashville Daily Union* recorded a similar incident on November 27, 1863: "On Thursday night last, about seven o'clock, Mr. Ira A. Polley, member of Co. E, 14th Michigan, accidentally shot and killed himself, the ball entering his right side below the ribs and passing through the heart."[114] The account did not specify the circumstances that took the soldier from the ranks so unexpectedly.

Private John Hughes was the unfortunate victim of an accident during a drill. According to one account, on the day of the incident, the Allegany County Regiment had been engaged in the standard, but onerous, activity: "The men were ordered to take a brief rest, when the deceased thoughtlessly leaned his head upon the muzzle of his gun, with his foot placed upon the hammer of the lock, no doubt raising it, and allowing it to fall." The writer spared no detail of the results, noting, "The piece instantly went off, driving the contents, a ball and two buckshot through his head, which was most horribly mangled, scattering his brains for a number of yards, over his fellow-soldiers." Interestingly, given the carelessness exhibited, the writer concluded, "What is remarkable about this sad affair is, that the cap, it is said, had been removed from the tube," and thus should have rendered the weapon harmless.[115]

An eighteen-year-old private with the "One Hundred and Fiftieth regiment, Penn. Volunteers, (Buck tails,)" but assigned temporarily as a guard at the "Old Capitol with the One Hundred and Thirty fifth Penn. Regiment," met his end when mishandling his musket and shooting himself accidentally. "The charge entered near his chin and passed out through the top of his head," according to one account. Hiram Waddle "expired almost instantly."[116] Another report indicated that when the private was in the act of bringing the weapon "to an order arms violently, the hammer fell and the load was discharged."[117]

Sadly, such tragedies did not subside as the major hostilities drew to a close in early 1865. Even while the formalized fighting was coming to an end, Union chaplain Thomas Van Horne recorded, "First Lieut. James P. Scott, R.Q.M." of the Second Michigan Cavalry suffered a fatal incident. "Shot himself accidentally at Cleveland, Tenn., May 15, 1865."[118]

Carelessness or mishaps with weapons were not always to blame for the fatal accidents that befell men while engaged in seemingly benign activities. For one young man the desire to look the part of a soldier cost him his life. When eighteen-year-old farmer William Ford learned that he and his comrades in the 11th Missouri Infantry would be acquiring new uniforms, he wanted to be sure that the new clothing was in the best possible order. On September 4, 1861, the farmer-turned-soldier decided to wash the garments but failed to return from his mission when he drowned in the process.[119]

Unfortunately, for too many, the desire for improved hygiene, comfort, or simple recreation was responsible for deaths when it involved water. In August 1861, a Joliet, Illinois, newspaper reported that a "young man of this city, named F. R. Whiting," had perished "while bathing in the river at Cairo, on the 16th ult., [after he] was seized with a cramp and was drowned before help could come to his relief."[120]

A similar fate befell "Rezin House, of Capt. Washburn's Company, 25th Regiment, whose body could not be recovered until the following day." The short notice offered few details, but correspondence published in another section of the newspaper on the same day provided a fuller sense of House's final moments. In the letter, "Jere" explained, "At Fetterman [Virginia], Capt. Washburn lost one of his men by drowning." The writer noted that House was known to be "somewhat addicted to drinking. He was believed to have been intoxicated, and went into the river, with some others to bathe." Unfortunately for the soldier, as he "attempted to swim across," he was unable to reach the opposite bank and "when about two thirds of the distance, sank to rise no more."[121] Rezin House may have contributed to his demise, but some of his comrades chose to remember him. In a subsequent letter, "Jere" noted that owing to the "distance" from camp of the recovery of the man's remains, "he was not buried with the honors of war to which he was entitled." Nevertheless, the squad was tasked with locating him and offered the fallen warrior their own tribute. "Jere" explained:

> I fired a salute over his grave with my revolver, and Alex Sinclair and myself cut his name, the place of his late residence, and the time and manner of his death upon an oak board at his grave. This was the last of the first man lost in this war from a Monroe county company. Reeze was a resolute man, and in an action would have been a useful and reliable man. Let him rest in peace.[122]

Confederate units shared these lethal conditions with their counterparts in Federal service. While on detached duty from the Fiftieth Virginia, First Sergeant William E. Heninger, of Company C, must have thought to ameliorate the effects of the summer heat when he decided to dip into the local waters. Instead, the forty-five-year-old farmer from Tazewell County, Virginia, "drowned in New River near the mouth of Wolfe Creek whilst bathing."[123]

At thirty-four years of age, William McDonald of Boston had already passed in years the ages of many of his new comrades when he joined the Ninety-Ninth New York in June. Unhappily for him, his life's experience was no guarantee against misfortune. On September 28, he sought to cool off or wash away the summer grime when, according to the regimental record, he drowned at Hampton Roads.[124]

On April 6, 1862, Rufus Kinsley noted in his diary, "Six of the Maine boys were drowned while bathing."[125] Two days later, another Union soldier, Patrick Dwyer, drowned in Mill Creek near Fortress Monroe, Virginia. Twenty years old when he enlisted, the New York City native had been in the service for only a year when he met this untimely and inglorious end to his martial career.[126]

Lucius Barber, a member of the Fifteenth Illinois, joined his comrades in taking advantage of any opportunity to shed their uniforms for a plunge in the area waters. On August 20, 1862, he noted that such excursions had become a routine for the men: "Every morning before the sun rose I used to get up and go down to the river and bathe, and hundreds did the same. A good many waited until the heat of the day and then they would stay in the water for hours." When sickness seemed to beset the men who lingered too long, the commanders sought to exert greater control by attempting to limit the activity. "Col. Turner issued an order regulating the hours of bathing," Barber recalled, "but the boys paid little attention to it and several were drowned."[127]

In the heat of summer, the number of fatalities in the area of Fredericksburg became significant enough to attract the interest of the *Richmond Daily Dispatch*, which undoubtedly hoped to highlight the dangers Union soldiers faced in fighting against the Confederacy. On July 1, 1862, the paper recorded, "Homer C. Little, of the Sixth Wisconsin regiment, was drowned on the 20th instant, while bathing near the pontoon bridge at Fredericksburg. This is the third soldier drowned in the Rappahannock, near the bridge, since the arrival of General [Rufus] King's division."[128]

With the arrival of spring and the warmer weather that accompanied it, once again some soldiers sought to rid themselves of their accumulated grime. Even if water temperatures were not yet summerlike, Sebastian Rothwinkler of Wisconsin must have thought the occasion worth venturing. Unfortunately, the soldier who went in for a bath did not return from it. Comrade Gilbert Claflin noted in a May 11 letter what had occurred the day before: "Yesterday one of the boys belonging to our regiment Company F was drowned when out bathing. The cramp took him, and his body has not been found."[129]

Captain Daniel Meader of the Fourth Tennessee Cavalry (U.S.) also lost his life while engaging in the same activity. The record indicated simply: "Drowned bathing, August 8, 1863."[130] Approximately a month later, the desire for cleanliness claimed another individual. William Bluffton Miller of the Seventy-Fifth Indiana Infantry recorded the event in his diary entry of September 1: "There was a man by the name of Robert Cummings of Company 'I' drowned in the river while batheing this evening." Miller noted that the soldier was not alone: "There was five hundred men in the river but assistance did not reach him in time to save him. He drounded near the middle of the river."[131]

Union diarist Benjamin McIntyre added the death of a comrade in Brownsville, Texas, to his February 26, 1864, entry: "A Soldier of the 91st Ill. was drowned while bathing in the Rio Grande."[132] For Joseph Ambrose of the First

North Carolina Union Infantry, there was no explanation beyond having "accidentally drowned at New Bern, North Carolina in May 1864."[133]

In the summer of 1864, John M. Gould of Maine noted the passing of comrades with the baleful conclusion, "Death faces us on every side." His comment, recorded on June 18, stemmed in part from the severe effects of disease upon his own regiment but on at least one other factor as well. As described by Gould, "The same day a man of the 114th N.Y., whose regiment was camped next to us, was drowned while bathing in the river, and all the experts at swimming from both regiments, dived for his body."[134]

Water proved a deadly feature for Texans serving east of the Mississippi River in early 1864 when one of them secured a skiff to use, with a comrade, for the purpose of fishing. Unfortunately, for Private Harvey Gregg and his partner, the waters of the Black Warrior River in Alabama posed a greater risk to their safety than the men might have imagined. A whirlpool swamped the vessel, and the men drowned when they plunged so unexpectedly into the waters.[135]

These soldier/fishermen were likely sober when they perished, but one of the banes of every commander's existence was the presence of one or another variation of spirituous drink and a tendency among those who could obtain it toward overindulgence. Historian James I. Robertson Jr. noted succinctly, "Fatalities from drunkenness were not uncommon."[136] The affliction impacted officers as well as noncoms and privates. "Col. Dewey of the 23d Iowa is *dead*," Sergeant Boyd of the Fifteenth Iowa observed. "Old Whiskey at last laid him *out* as it is laying out many a thousand other men in this Army." The malady was having a deleterious effect on Boyd's morale as well, with the diarist concluding, "It is killing more than the Confederates are killing."[137]

Another member of an Alabama company perished during an incident directly related to excessive consumption of alcohol. John Cowin noted in his diary at the end of October 1861, "Dr. [John T.] Jenkins who was struck on the head is reported to be dying. His skull was fractured by the blow. It all resulted I believe from the effects of whiskey." As expected, by the next afternoon, the injured man had died.[138]

In Arkansas, the new year of 1862 was barely open when word came to members of a Texas cavalry regiment of a tragedy at a nearby post. On January 16, James Bates confided in his diary, "While waiting for our dinners the lady received the news that her husband had been killed at Ft. Smith a few days ago by falling down a flight of stairs while drunk." The Texan could not avoid moralizing, "Poor woman, the blow was hard enough without her sorrow being ten fold more bitter knowing how he died." Then Bates drew the larger lesson: "This war will give an aching heart to many a wife widowed and children made orphans—but near despair must be the bitter grief of those who mourn some loved one dead & a drunkard."[139]

The *Cleveland Morning Leader* brought a story to the attention of its readers that featured the ill effects of drinking to excess. The report was of the body of a soldier found drowned after having been "missing for nearly a month." An inquest found that the Cleveland native's demise was "accidental," but the writer thought the cause of death attributable to another cause: "He was laboring under a mania a potu (or madness from drinking)."[140]

Death away from the field of battle seemed to stalk the command to which Chaplain Joseph Twichell was attached. As Twichell recounted, "One of our men, Louis McFee of Co. H.," had returned from a march and engagement with the enemy in Virginia, exhausted by the experience. As a balm, he "procured some vile whisky and drank it to excess. He was wild-drunk all Saturday afternoon—fell into a stupor at about 10 o'clock P.M., and was found dead in his tent the next morning at 9." The official cause of death seemed less convincing to the men who knew the situation best. "Apoplexy of the brain, the doctors said—murder and suicide, every body else. It was awful, *horrible*," Twichell concluded, and the minister used the burial service to provide his views to the men regarding the need for them to focus on their spiritual well-being. "The occasion was one calculated to inspire the preacher and hold the audience. I had the advantage of breathless attention, and I have good reason to believe that by God's help, my words were not in vain."[141]

Alvin Coe Voris, stationed in Suffolk, Virginia, in October 1862, experienced the ill effects when some of the troops there acquired homemade alcohol. "Cider whiskey called 'Apple Jack' did more work than the enemy," he noted. "The 13th Ind had one man killed by a comrade, had his head broken by a blow from a gun. The assailant broke the stock of his musket on his head, he struck so hard."[142] Earlier the officer had grappled with this antagonist while the men moved through Washington City for deployment in Virginia. Voris managed to control the rowdiest of his drunken soldiery and prevent tragedy with the help of the persuasion of his "*apostles*" (pistols) and some other strong-arm tactics, but he noted that another unit had suffered from the malady he had avoided with his command: "The 4th Ohio lost 3 men."[143]

Officers and men stationed in the vicinity of Port Hudson, Mississippi, found the usual diversions to wile away the time honing their martial preparations. For some, these included more than improving defenses, drill, or fatigue duty. Despite the prohibitions he imposed to bring order and discipline to his command, Major General Franklin Gardner met with mischief in the form of the consumption of spirituous drink. For at least one soldier, the craft by which he secured liquor in contravention to the restrictions resulted, according to historian Lawrence Hewitt, in his having "literally drank himself to death."[144]

Occasionally the long-term effects of alcoholism proved fatal. Colonel R. H. Gray of the Twenty-Second North Carolina finally lost his battle with that demon on March 16, 1863.[145] A few days later, his commanding officer, William Dorsey Pender, wrote home to tell his own wife of the depressing news. "He was a fine soldier and a nice gentleman," Pender told Fanny, before revealing his regrets in the matter. "If his officers had let me know of his condition I could have stopped his drinking in time probably to have saved him." Of course, the degree to which he could have altered the course for a man determined to proceed was questionable speculation for the superior officer. Still, Pender lamented the loss of a friend and associate, whose departure had come "without even the satisfaction that his death accomplished anything except to show how soon one can kill themselves with whisky."[146]

In November 1863, one of the men in the 129th Illinois explained the impact of overconsumption of alcohol on a comrade. The fellow "died day before yesterday," having gotten "into a row and got stabed so that he died two days after." The rowdy warrior was hardly a poor specimen from the writer's perspective. "He was a tip top solder only he could get on a spree once in a while." Unhappily, this time the "spree" had not been without its cost to the "solder" and the cause he had served.[147]

The strains of war could add to the breakdown of individuals, with fatal consequences. In the vicinity of Brandy Station, Virginia, Chaplain Joseph Twichell told of a regrettable decline in the condition of a comrade who had turned increasingly to the bottle for relief. On May 1, 1864, the minister explained in a letter home:

> During the afternoon of [last Tuesday], Patrick McCarty of co. F., after a short but severe illness aggravated by previous dissipation, died in the regimental hospital. The poor boy (for he was scarcely 20 years old) had been drunk nearly all winter, procuring liquor, by his natural acuteness and address, when no one else could get it—rushing to ruin—crazy after the cause of his wretchedness, yet at times touched with horror at what he was doing.

Although he attempted to renounce his drinking, a furlough provided temptations too great to avoid, and McCarty sealed his doom when he "came back bloated and shaking with incipient delirium tremens, fell sick with typhoid pneumonia and died as an old man whose constitution is enfeebled by age—the most pitiable instance of life thrown away I ever witnessed."[148]

Men who faced shot and shell in battle understood the dangers that existed from the horrific effects of enemy fire. Yet, fire of a different nature could impact lives as well, even at a distance from the battlefield. Three men perished when the barracks at Camp Sigel in Milwaukee, Wisconsin, burned in January 1863. Coming as it did while the men slept, even those who managed to escape with their lives lost everything else in the way of personal effects. Most tragically, according to one account, one soldier "lived quite a length of time after the fire, but was shockingly burned." When conscious, he had begged his comrades to kill him rather than have him continue to endure the agony until he finally succumbed to his extensive injuries.[149]

A year later, in January 1864, at Camp Butler near Springfield, Illinois, flames ravaged the officers' quarters and destroyed the quartermaster's stores and the buildings. Two officers also lost their lives in the conflagration. A newspaper account noted, "Capt. Dimon and Lieut. Bennett of the 38th Illinois cavalry, were burned to death." Others suffered injury from burns to their faces and extremities.[150]

"Policing" a camp applied to efforts to maintain cleanliness and good order among the tents or other structures that constituted the bivouac. Sanitation was critical to discipline and health for the soldiers. Such work kept details occupied in cleaning the company "streets," but it could pose unwitting dangers. While at Dalton, Georgia, in the spring of 1864, Confederate Sam Watkins recorded the fatal circumstances associated with this seemingly innocuous duty. "In sweeping the streets and cleaning up, an old tree had been set on fire, and had been smoking and burning for several days, and nobody seemed to notice it," he explained in setting the scene. Subsequently, at a revival session, ten men knelt "at the mourners' bench," in close proximity, "when the burning tree, without any warning, fell with a crash right across the ten mourners, crushing and killing them instantly."[151] These men belonged to Benjamin Franklin Cheatham's command; six of them perished at the scene, while four others died subsequently from the effects they had suffered.[152]

Mortal dangers could come from any quarter, even when the men were not in the immediate vicinity of enemy forces. Although the exact circumstances were not always clear, such deaths occurred as the soldiers moved through heavily timbered regions of the South. Jacob Thomas was located in the vicinity of Wild Cat Mountain, Kentucky, when he perished "by the falling of a tree," on November 17, 1861.[153] Similarly, William Haight, adjutant of the Twenty-Third New York, noted that one of the men in his unit died when "killed by the falling tree."[154]

Another account involving troops stationed in the burgeoning defenses outside Washington exposed such conditions. On August 24, 1861, from "Arlington

Heights, Va.," a participant recalled that in addition to the works, the men were engaged in other duties: "Chopping out roads and falling trees to obstruct the passage of an army occupy some of our time." Although he did not relate the incident directly to this activity, Newton Colby noted, "A week [ago] today we buried a young man out of Capt. Summer Bartow's Co. C, who died from injuries received from a falling tree while chopping. His name was Pease." The situation had an impact on the freshly minted soldier, who observed, "It was the first death in the Regiment and the measured cadences of the funeral march and reversed arms were sad sights and sounds to us."[155]

While encamped in the field in early 1862, a Warrenton, Virginia, native named Sinclair, esteemed by those who knew him "as a good soldier, zealous patriot and a man of moral worth," met his end suddenly in the night. An account in a Mississippi newspaper reported, "He was killed, March 25th, by a tree falling upon his head while asleep in his tent. *Requiescat in pace*."[156]

Soldiers found the rigors of camp life challenging, but few could imagine that the basic requirements of duty outside of the battlefield would exact the greatest sacrifice from some of them, too. Working on entrenchments could save the lives of those who employed them for use in the face of enemy assault. Nevertheless, the construction of such fortifications was not without potentially deadly consequences. At Suffolk, Virginia, Henry Ingalls of the Sixth Massachusetts recorded the strenuous efforts he and his comrades undertook to perfect the defenses that surrounded the town. "We work 1 hour and [have] 1 hour off," he noted.[157] However, as a team of approximately forty men labored in clearing trees in front of one of the Union forts, he witnessed one of these fall on a comrade. According to Ingalls, "It struck him across the neck and he was killed instantly." The victim, Dennis McCarthy, was only twenty-two years old at the time of his death.[158] Another individual also had a fatal encounter while laboring in the Federal works at Suffolk. On September 28, 1862, Ingalls noted, "A man in Co. G was killed while chopping a tree falling on him; he survived but a few hours."[159]

With the approach of inclement wintry weather, the troops in the armies often settled into what might be termed more permanent quarters. For the men who would otherwise be subjected to the worst of winter's blasts, the construction of stouter housing was an essential element. Yet, death stalked these men just as surely in such camps as it had done earlier elsewhere. The Third Texas Cavalry had the benefit of an especially active and inventive quartermaster in Captain Hannibal Harris. Whereas most units had to make do with limited tools for fashioning their structures, Harris secured a saw that could supply cut boards for the command's use. His work, including meticulous attention to site and construction, continued apace until he ventured too close to the saw, had an article of clothing enmeshed in the teeth, and suffered injuries sufficient to cause his death in a matter of days.[160]

In December 1863, soldiers in the Fiftieth Virginia underwent the necessary task of felling trees for their winter quarters. One such detail was at work when two of the tree trunks fell simultaneously. Focused on his work and yet cognizant of the danger, Private Henry Lindsey, of Company I, moved away from one tree, but stepped inadvertently into the path of the other. A fellow soldier, and kinsman by marriage, informed the widow, "The tree struck him on the shoulder and mashed him into the ground, mashing his head all to pieces and breaking his thigh." Perhaps trusting that by offering the graphic description it would serve as some solace to indicate that the victim had not suffered in a lingering manner in the accident, Wesley Smith felt it imperative to add quickly, "He never knew what hurt him."[161]

On January 23, 1863, the *Richmond Daily Dispatch* offered the sad tale of a similar fatal accident: "Lieut. D'Arey W. Paul, of Petersburg, Va commanding company K, 10th Virginia regiment, was killed in his tent, near Fredericksburg, Va., on Tuesday morning last, by the falling of a tree which had been cut down by . . . his men. He was sleeping at the time, and was instantly crushed to death by the limbs of the [tree]."[162]

In the Mississippi River region, a network of watercourses, swamps, and forests presented obstacles and occasionally provided deadly circumstances for unsuspecting troops to endure. In early 1863, such an incident occurred when, according to a historian of the fighting on the Yazoo River, "a giant elm tree fell upon the tents of the 47th Indiana on the river above Fort Pemberton, killing four soldiers outright and fatally wounding two others."[163]

In the summer of 1864, as Union troops advanced toward Atlanta, skirmishing and fighting frequently gave way to the preparation of defensive lines there. If positions remained in a location for any length of time, fatigue parties would range ahead to clear fields of fire and use timber to shore up the extensive earthwork fortifications being formed. A Kentucky newspaper did not provide enough detail to determine if the incident was related to this type of activity or to inclement weather that might have contributed to a weakening of supportive soil when it reported, "We learn that Adjutant Joe Dudley of the Sixteenth Kentucky, was killed by a tree falling on him in Fulton county, Ga." Another comrade had been fortunate when he "made a narrow escape at the same time."[164]

In another instance, a soldier recalled creating "strong fortifications of heavy timber chopped down in the darkness of night when we could scarcely see to strike two licks in the same place with our axes," and only the cries of compatriots would indicate when a tree was set to fall. Although most scrambled to safety, "one man in the 102d Illinois was killed by a tree falling on him."[165]

Men who ought to be learning to mitigate the dangers of warfare often found themselves victimized by their own curiosity and experimentation. Chaplain Joseph Twichell of the New York Excelsior Brigade was in camp in Maryland, along the Potomac River, when shells from across the waterway fell nearby. The exercise would have been innocent enough had it not been for the way in which some of the soldiers reacted to the situation. "The third Regiment met a sad accident with one of these secession projectiles," Twichell recorded in October. "It was fired across and fell near the river bank not far from camp. Failing to explode, the guard picked it up and brought it to their quarters." The officers present "inspected" the item, "extracted" the fuse, and "laid" it "away out of sight." Men of lesser rank, who had not had the privilege of a close look at the piece of ordnance, could not overcome a desire to see it for themselves. "Some of the men got hold of it, and like fools were playing with it." Pouring powder out of the round and dousing the shell with water was supposed to render it "entirely harmless, but subsequently on a cigar's being applied to the fuse hole, it exploded, killing two men dead and wounding several others, one of whom, at least, has since died."[166]

Petersburg, Virginia, provided the venue for a bizarre incident that led to fatality for one of the men serving in the Forty-Fifth Georgia there. Siege warfare provided unwelcome diversions in the forms of shelling and sharpshooting that forced occupants of the enormous trench lines on both sides to take precautions. Even so, men were not always as careful as they should have been when the explosive ordnance was no longer arcing over their heads. Confederate Mason Hill Fitzpatrick noted one incident in a letter home on October 16, 1864: "One of Co. F, Marcus Jackson of our Regt. was taking the powder out of a shell two days ago, and it exploded and killed him." Fitzpatrick did not relate if he thought the purpose was to render the round inert or offer another potential explanation, but he observed that the effect was definitive: "It tore him up wretchedly. He lived [but] about 5 hours."[167]

Union general Francis A. Walker was particularly harsh in his assessment of the parties responsible for such accidents, noting, "I have known several cases of soldiers opening shells, pouring out all the powder (they always pour out all the powder), and then dropping in a coal or a match to see if there were any powder left." Even so, the victims were not always the ones who initiated the act. "Out of all the lives lost in this way," Walker observed, "I never once knew the original idiot to be injured."[168]

Life in the camps could be tedious and routine, but there always seemed to be room for questionable behavior that could lead to unanticipated fatal results. William Henry King of the Twenty-Eighth Louisiana Infantry noted two instances of artillery shells producing fatal results after they had been fired. In the first case, he learned from the contents of a comrade's letter that the initial Union shelling of a salt works "did no harm." Then, genuine harm occurred: "One shell was found unexploded, & Albert Spurlin & his mess appropriated it to the use of a fire log. It exploded, wounded Spurlin mortally, & Drew Malone slightly."[169]

The reaction to a St. Patrick's Day incident may have represented best the sense some of the soldiers had for the fatal mischief that could arise in camp and symbolized the dangers that existed in such settings. On March 17, 1863, William Henry King explained that whatever else discretion might dictate, the presence of an artillery shell had proved too great a temptation for members of a Louisiana mounted unit to ignore: "Two men belonging to the La. Cavalry attached to this division, in playing some tricks with a shell, it exploded, killing one, & wounding two others." His conclusion fit many of the situations that arose for so many of the soldiers who did not survive their periods in camp: "'Tis passing strange that men have no more prudence."[170]

3

"The Rhythm of the Rails"
Fatalities in Rail Transportation

And the rhythm of the rails is all they feel.
Arlo Guthrie, "City of New Orleans"

I want to go home.
Final diary entry of Private Samuel Melvin, critically injured in a railroad accident, September 1864

Fatalities in transportation systems of modern America are all-too-familiar phenomena, particularly during holiday periods when large numbers of people cram into their vehicles, board airplanes or trains, and travel over extensive distances to visit with friends and family. Civil War soldiers suffered tragedies as well when moving over vast distances, particularly when traveling on dilapidated and deteriorating rail lines. Death could come suddenly to men as they crossed the land they had joined the service to defend, often piled inside or atop boxcars that were not meant to accommodate passengers but were pressed into service for that purpose.

Deadly railway accidents plagued travelers in both the North and the South during the Civil War, as well as costing the lives of men who would never have the opportunity to face their foes on the battlefield or taking the lives of those who had already survived harrowing combat encounters. These accidents could come from train wrecks or boiler explosions, but they also occurred when men failed to anticipate ordinary dangers or take simple precautions. Not all of the fatal accidents occurred because of poor rail conditions, adverse weather, or human error on the part of operators. Some of these incidents happened because of the carelessness of the individuals themselves. Two members of the Eleventh Pennsylvania Reserves perished on their way to Camp Curtin when they failed to clear a low bridge while riding atop the railcars.[1]

The *Richmond Daily Dispatch* carried another such account, taken from a Tennessee newspaper, of a victim whose choice of rail accommodation also proved deadly from the same cause: "We learn that on Tuesday last, a Mr. Waldrup, a member of the Lynnville volunteer company, which was then enroute for Nashville, was killed by his head coming in contact with a bridge." Although the writer of the original piece did not divulge the source of his information, he concluded that the victim in this instance "was on top of the cars and totally unconscious of the approaching danger until the fatal collision had been made.— Pulaski (Tenn.) Citizen, Dec. 18."[2]

When some of the Louisiana Tigers climbed on top of the train on which they were traveling or tried to find places between the cars, they cursed anyone who sought to inform them of their potential risks. Such prudence seemed especially lacking when the results proved fatal. Perhaps not unexpectedly, as historian Terry Jones explained, "One was killed when the train passed under a low bridge, and three others on the couplings were crushed to death when the train lurched suddenly."[3]

Josh Callaway barely had a chance to catch his breath after a long and exhausting trip from Saltillo, Mississippi, to Montgomery, Alabama, conducted in large part by rail. However, on the morning of August 6, 1862, he was able to "snatch a moment" to write his wife: "We left Saltillo last Thursday at 3 o'clock P.M. on a box car without seats. There was another company in the same car so that we were very much crowded; most of us having to stand up." As the trip progressed, several of the men "climbed on top to sleep but about midnight it set in to raining and ran us back inside and we stood on our feet the balance of the night." Aside from the inconvenience, Callaway survived the experience; others in his command did not. As he wrote, "The Regt. has lost five men since we left Saltillo. One died very suddenly on the cars last Friday." Hard luck had also befallen others: "The cars ran over one yesterday, making four killed. One fell off the cars yesterday while running fast. I suppose he will die."[4]

Other soldiers paid a similar price for what must have appeared to be the convenience of avoiding the overcrowded cars jammed with humanity. In September 1863, a Union sergeant from Pennsylvania noted, "Henry Lake fell asleep, fell off, [was] run over, and killed." The next day, a doctor observed that "8 men from our

Corps by carelessness in riding on top of [the] cars have been swept off by bridges and killed." A few days later a New Yorker wrote home of "8 men killed by getting nocked off of the cars."[5]

The situation must have appeared to be almost epidemic, prompting one officer to bring the matter to the attention of the Union secretary of war, Edwin Stanton. On October 1, 1863, Major General Carl Schurz pleaded special circumstances in connection to delayed transportation. Train schedules suffered in the midst of an atmosphere of confusion and mismanagement. "On the morning after our departure," Schurz explained, "I learned that several men belonging to my command had met with severe accidents on the trains ahead of mine, two men being killed and a good many left behind; all this in consequence of a lack of system and order on board the cars."[6]

Major General Joseph Hooker insisted that nothing his subordinate had done to assert order on the rails had delayed movements in the field. He seemed less certain that fatal incidents could be prevented: "The accidents referred to as having happened on the way were caused by the men falling off the tops of the cars while under way, a luxury they would indulge in whether their officers were with them or not; at all events no orders to the contrary checked it."[7]

As the war progressed, soldiers who sought to make their travel by rail less onerous could allow it to turn more dangerous instead. A Richmond newspaper pointed out the inherent dangers for its readers by reporting, "Serg't E. C. Jones, of Co. H. 15th Va. regiment, was killed on the Richmond and Petersburg railroad Wednesday evening. He had gotten on top of the cars to ride, and as the train passed under a bridge near Petersburg, he received a blow on the head from the bridge timber, which caused his death in a few hours. He was from Richmond, and was a most estimable young man."[8]

A notice that appeared in Washington's *Evening Star* of February 5, 1864, read, "Yesterday, as the down passenger train from the front was leaving Fairfax Station, William Miller, a private of the 2nd New York regiment, was thrown from the platform of one of the cars, and falling upon the track the train passed over him, killing him instantly." Nothing detailed the reason for Miller's fatal plunge.[9] A comrade of Miller's from another New York regiment perished later in the year. Charles Clements was on his way home when tragedy struck. As he traveled by train, the soldier from Company E, 179th New York, put himself in an unspecified but precarious position when he died on November 14, 1864, by "falling from the cars while on furlough."[10]

Even for men who exercised reasonable care, dangers existed. One account noted the effect from a malfunction aboard a train transporting pieces of heavy ordnance: "About three miles from Columbia an axle on the first train snapped and two cars in the rear went off the track. One of the cannons came off its mooring, struck Pvt. John Collins, and killed him."[11]

Mere proximity to activity on the rail lines could lead to tragedy. The *National Republican* in Washington reported on December 3, 1861, "On Saturday afternoon, a private named Deney, belonging to Captain Clark's company District volunteers, now guarding the railroad between this city and Beltsville, was accidentally killed, by a train of cars passing over him, near Bladensburg, on the Washington Branch railroad."[12] There was no additional information to clarify the exact circumstances for the unfortunate victim.

Also unclear was the reason for the senseless death in February 1862 of a soldier in northwestern Virginia. Apparently, according to the *Daily Intelligencer* of Wheeling, William Grosehort, "of Captain Shockey's company, 6th Virginia Regiment," chose a most inopportune place and time to rest. "On the evening of the 21st, an engine was running out [of] the Northwestern Road from Parkersburg," the account began. "The engineer suddenly heard a scream, and felt that the engine was clogged. Upon getting down, he discovered the mangled remains of poor Grosehort. The unfortunate man is supposed to have been lying upon the track."[13]

In March 1863, as the Eighth Virginia Infantry traveled in North Carolina, First Lieutenant James W. Pierce of Company B met with an untimely end. The man who had enlisted in 1861 and endured a bout of disease in late 1862 did not survive the trip. Although the absence of specific information left others with no explanation for his final circumstances, Pierce was "killed on the Wilmington & Weldon R.R. 3/10/63 by being run over by the cars."[14]

Even when trains were in the process of uncoupling cars, or making other adjustments in the rail yards and depots, lapses in judgment could prove fatal. News of the death of "a soldier belonging to the 14th Georgia regiment . . . killed at Gordonsville by the Central cars running over him" made the newspapers in both Richmond and Staunton. According to the account, "He was attempting to cross the track, and in stepping from the platform of the depot to the road, his foot became entangled in some way, and he fell. Before he could recover himself the cars were upon him crushing and mangling him in a horrible manner." The unfortunate victim "had been in a Richmond hospital for some time, but had been discharged" and was on his way to rejoin his regiment, "with high hopes of serving his country usefully, when death in its most instantaneous form numbered him among its victims."[15]

The August 18, 1863, edition of Wheeling, West Virginia's *Daily Intelligencer* described an incident that occurred when an engineer attempted to correct an unintentional decoupling of cars: "A soldier belonging to Col. Bemis' regiment of Pennsylvania three months militia, was killed near Wellsville night before last while coming down the P. and C. railroad on the cars." The situation developed when the official realized that the engine and the baggage car had become separated and "suddenly checked up" the train. "The consequence was a collision between the two pieces of the train," resulting in the death of the soldier and injury to several others.[16]

The *Evening Star* of Washington conveyed the news of a fatal accident on August 27, 1863: "Last evening as the small engine at the Depot was regulating the cars upon the track, Barney McClusky, of Co. C, 1st Delaware regiment, was caught while stepping across, and knocked down, the wheels of the engine fracturing one leg at the knee, and cutting the other off at the ankle. He was taken immediately to Judiciary Square Hospital, where he died in a few hours."[17]

Union sergeant Stephen Flaherty noted one incident in a letter home from Missouri, which he attributed to the influence of whiskey: "One of the soldiers had climbed upon the tender, and, an instant after the engine was detached from the train both being in rapid motion—attempted to spring over the increasing space between the tender and the first car in the rear.—He failed to reach the car and fell just ahead of it." Cries immediately arose of "man killed," and Flaherty took in at a glance that "the rail beneath our car steps as we passed out we observed that it was covered with gore." Whether curiosity had gotten the best of him or the location of his departure from the train car offered the view, the sergeant major found the horrific tableau enthralling. "Beneath the car just ahead, was the mangled trunk of a man's body, almost in a nude state," from the manner in which it had been dragged. "Ten or fifteen feet from it lay the head of the man." The soldier who experienced the effects of combat on his comrades found that he could not endure the "sickening sight and . . . I turned hastily from it then."[18]

On May 12, 1864, an Ohio newspaper described the fatal injury of "John McIntyre, from Delaware county, [who] was run over by a locomotive and a passenger car at the depot yesterday afternoon, and so terribly mangled that no hopes are entertained of his recovery." Although the precise nature of the accident did not accompany the account, the writer felt sufficiently informed to assert, "He appeared to be intoxicated, and although warned off the track, again returned to it just as [the engine] was passing, the wheels of which ran over his arms and legs, crushing them in a horrible manner." The severe damage required amputation of one of the limbs, "but at last accounts the chances were that he would not survive until morning."[19]

Chaplain Van Horne's accounting of soldiers in his command demonstrated that officers were not immune to death on the rails:

Captain Ezekiah H. Tatem of the Sixth Ohio Infantry. Killed by railroad accident, July 19, 1862. Twenty-second Michigan Infantry, Captain Henry Carlton. Killed on railroad, June 6, 1863; First Michigan Mechanics and Engineers, Captain James W. Sligh. Died by railroad accident, November 15, 1863; Twenty-ninth Pennsylvania Infantry, Second Lieut. William Harrington. Killed by railroad accident, March 4, 1864; Assistant Surgeon Sherman C. Ferson. Killed by railroad accident, October 7, 1864.[20]

Eagerness to end a long trip caused one Union officer to confront his own inglorious passage. By one account, Major Otis A. Whitehead died from a round discharged by a pistol he was carrying in his pocket "while he was in the act of jumping from the cars at the station . . . killing him instantly." The writer noted that the native of New York City "leaves a wife, who is now stopping at the Louisville Hotel, to mourn his untimely end." Colleagues expressed admiration for the paymaster as "a very efficient officer, and [one who] enjoyed the love and esteem of all who knew him."[21]

In October 1863, a member of the Twenty-Eighth Pennsylvania Volunteer Infantry was able to write a letter to his father from a camp along the Duck River in Tennessee after a "long and fearfull journey" by rail. Apparently, Ambrose Hayward wanted to relate an experience that had come perilously close to costing him his life when a train collision occurred. Miraculously, no one seemed to have perished from this incident, but as the trip continued, this situation did not last. "We had come thus far with but few serious accidents having occurred," Hayward continued, "but here, rum flowed free and the effects of it showed itself upon the men. many of the brave Soldiers who for 2 years have withstood hardships & escaped the enemys bullets became perfectly reckless for their lives. they would reel backwards & forwards on the top of the Car or climb up the sides when at full speed." It was probably inevitable that a mishap would occur. "I saw one man struck in the head by a bridge. another fell between the cars, the wheels passing over both thighs." This latter moment was particularly impactful to the witness, who explained, "At the time the later accident occured I was standing in the door. I heard the cars as the[y] jumped over him. when our car came to him it was awfull to feel the shock of the car and to see him laying upon the track, watching the wheels as they rolled towards him." Hayward speculated that the canteen the man carried around his neck "was full of whiskey," but noted, "There were a number more killed upon the train."[22] Hayward related the same information in a truncated fashion to his brother two days later, noting, "There was many a fatal accident occured on our journey and rum was the cause of it all. I saw one poor fellow struck by a bridge another was run over both his thighs."[23]

Another victim of a fatal accident had survived adventures at sea only to perish while riding on a train over land. The *Richmond Daily Dispatch* of November 27, 1863, reported, "Capt. James Dude, who has made several daring raids upon the enemy's shipping in the Gulf, was run over by the cars on the Mobile and Ohio railroad, on the 19th, and killed." Captain Dude "had just returned from an expedition after the enemy's vessels, and captured a schooner called the Norma within a mile and a half of Fort McRea, near Pensacola." Initially slipping past the Union blockaders, the officer found any hope for final escape also hindered. The newspaper account elaborated, "Being hotly pursued by one of the Federal gunboats, he beached and burnt the vessel, and brought the Captain and crew to Mobile." The forced respite from his duties allowed Dude to visit with friends locally for "a few days" before "he started home to see his family, when the lamentable accident occurred."[24]

Regular patrols and guards on trains became standard precautions against threats of attacks by Confederate guerrillas, bushwhackers, or raiding cavalry, but they put men in uniform in danger from unexpected sources. Union sergeant Leander Stillwell of the Sixty-First Illinois Infantry described the role and its significance: "Every foot of the railroad had to be vigilantly watched to prevent its being torn up by bands of guerrillas or disaffected citizens. One man with a crow-bar, or even an old ax, could remove a rail at a culvert, or some point on a high grade, and cause a disastrous wreck." The patrols on the tracks and guards on the trains also became targets themselves. Even so, Stillwell asserted, "I liked this railroad guard duty."[25]

Three soldiers carrying out such routine duties would not have concurred with this optimistic assessment when they met their ends in a collision of trains south of Nashville in August 1863. The men, identified in an Ohio newspaper as "Levi Conwell, Obediah Conwell and —— Wright, of the county, and soldiers in the 52d Ohio," were aboard "one of the trains as guards."[26] If the reasonable fear was danger from opposing parties, the actions taken to mitigate those concerns also created genuine threats to men's lives because of the mode of transportation they were taking.

Ironies occasionally surfaced as individuals undertook practices that placed them in critical situations they may otherwise have avoided. One victim of a rail accident was Frank M. Dennis, the first surgeon assigned to a train "specifically intended for ambulance use by the Army of Tennessee," according to historian Glenna Schroeder-Lein.[27]

Travel on the roadways could cost the lives of individuals, but the number of victims was often greater when disaster struck while troops journeyed together by train. The large-scale movement of men and matériel by rail was likely to produce fatalities simply because of the increased volume on the tracks of the Union and the Confederacy. Rail systems across the country had already experienced significant numbers of accidents, with the United States leading the world in that category before the war, despite concerted attempts to reduce those numbers.[28] Adding wartime conditions to the situation could not help but increase the likelihood that accidents and associated deaths would rise as well.

On November 7, 1862, Rufus Kinsley recorded another incident arising from the negligence of men who should have recognized the risks of their actions. "An ammunition train that left here this morning, to supply our boys up the road, was blown up at Lafourche, killing 15 men and one negro woman," Kinsley explained. "Two lieutenants of the 8th New Hampshire, sat smoking in a car that contained two tons of powder, and a large quantity of shells and balls, besides infantry cartridges, when the explosion took place. Six cars were demolished, and the engine and tender scattered to the four winds of heaven." The effect was not inconsequential for his unit: "Three of our Reg. killed and Lieut. Nason, of our Co., slightly wounded."[29]

From "Camp Thibodaux," Charles W. Sherman of the 12th Connecticut Infantry wrote home on November 8, 1862, noting briefly an incident that had occurred nearby: "Thair was Tirable Acident on this Rail Road that we have opend from New Orleans to this Place. A Car Load of Aminition exploded Killing 11 men Wounding 10 more." Although the tragedy had cost the lives of comrades, the impact for the soldier was not limited to the human toll exacted. Sherman concluded practically concerning the matter, "The Amitition was for this Brigade."[30]

Accidents on the rails were responsible for many deaths, but in the age of steam, defective, overworked, or poorly tended boilers became man-killers, too. An unusual circumstance occurred in December 1861 near the camps of the Sixtieth New York. As the sentries paced their rounds on the night of the eleventh just before midnight, the sounds of an explosion and a shrill whistling noise filled the air. The corporal of the guard reported an object landing nearby and returned from an investigation with a piece of locomotive boiler flue still hot from the blast. As the men approached the wrecked engine, they found one individual severely injured and the engineer thrown from the cab. The unit's chaplain noted, "The fireman remained at the tender, but was so badly scalded that he survived but a few hours."[31]

In the summer of 1863, the explosion of a locomotive "at Nicholasville, [Ky.,]" left carnage among the ranks of several regiments. On June 8, the *Daily Green Mountain Freeman* noted that of those killed in the incident, "three belonged to the 35th Mass., one to the 21st Mass., and one to the 7th R.I."[32] The following day, the paper provided the names of the casualties from the incident, including "9th New Hampshire, N. D. Blackmer, mortally wounded," and the dead Rhode Islander, "name Bentley."[33]

A more thorough rendition of the affair came to the readers of the *New York Herald* from roving correspondent James C. Fitzpatrick, who had been at the scene, "seated upon the platform of the second car, reading a newspaper and enjoying my customary post prandial pipe, when the explosion took place." The physical damage had been extreme, with the engine "or rather what had been the engine . . . [left] a snarled and crumpled mass of metal." The force of the explosion had hurled pieces of the train widely. "The front part of the locomotive, with the smoke stack, lense and cowcatcher, was blown about one hundred feet away, and lay on the side of the road. Immediately beneath the engine a hole was blown into the ground, the ties torn up and the rails twisted out of shape." Most of the casualties came from "two cars immediately alongside the locomotive [which] were shattered, and the soldiers in them either killed or wounded." Fitzpatrick provided a listing of these individuals that included the slain soldiers: "William Bentley, Seventh Rhode Island, head shattered and neck broken. John Leverett, Thirty-fifth Massachusetts, head mangled; died four hours after the accident. E. W. Gage, Co. K, Ninth New Hampshire, skull broken; died two hours after the explosion."[34]

On July 8, 1863, the *Richmond Daily Dispatch* carried a detailed account of a similar mishap in central Virginia that produced "serious results": "The locomotive explosion, on the Petersburg road, last Monday afternoon . . . [caused] the death of four individuals." The train "was running up Falling Creek grade, on its way to Richmond," when the fatal eruption occurred. "The explosion was caused by the blowing out of the crown of the fire box, which is now supposed to have been cracked for some time." The defect left the engine vulnerable for a catastrophic failure when extreme pressures exerted themselves on it, as occurred here. "By the force of the concussion," the narration continued, "the locomotive seems to have been lifted from the track, carried a distance of twenty feet, turned entirely around, reversing [course], and then upset in a ditch." The track itself suffered extensive damage. "Some of the rails were bent almost double." Unfortunately, signs of trouble had existed prior to the disaster. The account noted, "A friend of the engineer says he was very much depressed for several days before the fatal accident, and remarked that he did not like to see the steam and water escaping by the clay bolts in his engine."

Fatalities had resulted. "Mr. Hugh Barus, the engineer, died from the scalding he received in half an hour after the explosion; and his fireman, Jim Trent, (a negro,) died soon after." In addition to the civilian deaths, "One of the soldiers killed was a member of the 2d Georgia regiment; the other was a marine from on board the steamer Atlanta." Others suffered injuries, but the casualty figures could have been worse. "Most of the coaches were filled with ladies, sent from the North by flag of truce, and paroled Confederate prisoners, and it is really wonderful that so few were injured."[35]

As the war progressed, troops moving across significant distances, on overworked rails, and with exhausted crews were bound to confront disaster. The *Cleveland Morning Leader* offered its readers a cautionary set of statistics in March 1863, under the ominous heading, "Deaths by Railroad Accidents." Although many of the fatalities did not involve soldiers, others did. "According to approximate reports," the account began, "there were 123 deaths by railroad accidents in Ohio during the last year. Of these, 55 were employees of railroads, and 18 were passengers, 16 being soldiers." The tally included wrecks, collisions, and other forms of misfortune on or along the rails. "Of all the killed, 59 met their deaths by walking on the track, 11 by striking bridges, 10 fell off trains, 4 by getting on trains while in motion, and 3 by getting off." The writer thought the lesson of many of these situations worth emphasizing: "More than half the deaths thus clearly resulted from personal carelessness."[36]

Derailments were among the most dramatic examples of these rail mishaps. On August 15, 1861, the *Richmond Daily Dispatch* reported the outcome of such a fatal railway incident in southwest Virginia: "On Saturday last, one of the trains on the Virginia and Tennessee Railroad, which was loaded with troops, ran off the track near Marion, in Smythe county, resulting in the killing and wounding of several of the volunteers. The following is a list of the casualties: Of the Palmetto Guards, A. J. Bond was killed; F. Winckle and S. Burton were dangerously injured." Others from the units involved were fortunate to escape with only slight injuries.[37]

A second fatal incident occurred when a bridge near Huron, Indiana, collapsed under the weight of a passing train. The men on board belonged to Colonel J. B. Turchin's Nineteenth Illinois Regiment, with "over one hundred soldiers" thought to be killed or injured. The report offered an assessment from an operator on the line that gave readers some details of the accident: "Bridge No. 48 broken in two. It let four cars down into the bed of the creek, and one on top of them. . . . There are about one hundred men wounded and ten or fifteen killed." That individual speculated, "It is thought the bridge was weakened by some malicious persons," but, while this was certainly plausible, he offered no substantiating evidence to support this conclusion.[38]

Subsequently, a Michigan newspaper added more information on the rail disaster for interested readers. The writer noted, "The accident on the Ohio and Mississippi Railroad proves worse than at first reported." Explaining that numerous cars plummeted into the creek, he continued, "These cars contained 250 men. . . . Captain Howard, of company I, was killed. Up to this time about 30 dead have been taken out, and more are under the wreck." Still thought to be the result of sabotage, the wreck, as much as it could be reckoned, claimed the lives of the following:

> Co. E—Martin Kelly. Co. F—C. H. Valentine, J. W. S. Babbitt. Co. G— C. H. Cutting, David Noble, G. M. Bradstone. Co. I—Capt. B. B. Howard, Corporals Samuel Clark, Jerry Ingram and A. Painter, William Frost, L. Carroll, Isaac Coleman, Henry Conners, John Brown, Joseph Smith, McConnelly, Robert Bruce, H. C. Burroughs, William Hanwick, Antoine Raffner, Peter Fowler, William Ringer, John Douglas, Henry Hunt, and four others, names not yet ascertained.[39]

The early part of 1862 also proved to be a deadly time for travel by rail for other passengers. Among the larger-scale events that took place was one with the dateline "Poughkeepsie, March 15," when a train left the rails unexpectedly. "The down train, with the Ninety-fourth regiment on board, met with an accident. Five cars were thrown into the water near Tivoli, by a broken rail." Casualties in the accident fell most heavily on the troops being transported but included at least one citizen as well. "Four men, belonging to company G, from Cape Vincent, were killed, and ten injured. A civilian was also killed." The newspaper provided a list of the deceased that included another tragic twist: "Samuel Glazier and Barton Glazier (father and son)," as well as "Nelson Forton[,] John Sharman [and] Master Driscol, civilian."[40]

In a diary entry from his camp in Meridian, Mississippi, William Pitt Chambers recorded the news of an incident on the Mobile and Ohio Railroad on April 25, 1862: "A serious accident occurred on the M. and O.R.R. eight miles below here this morning, by which six soldiers were killed and about 15 others seriously injured."[41] A Camden, South Carolina, newspaper explained that the train bound for Corinth, Mississippi, from Mobile, Alabama, "ran off the track a few miles above Enterprise, Miss., killing six men, among them five soldiers of the Nineteenth South Carolina Regiment. About twenty were wounded."[42] Then, during the summer of 1862, as troops transferred to Kentucky for operations there, a train wreck occurred on the track between Mobile and Montgomery, causing the deaths of another six men from the Sixth Tennessee.[43] The shifting of soldiers from other posts to a concentration point at Corinth illustrated both the benefits and the dangers involved in the utilization of the Confederacy's interior lines of communication and transportation.

Rail lines in southwest Virginia also remained busy with the movement of men and supplies along the Virginia and Tennessee Railroad, which kept portions of the Confederacy connected to the important salt and lead works at Saltville and Wytheville. Confederate staffer Edward O. Guerrant was traveling along a portion of that line near the Glade Spring Depot in August 1862, when he provided an offhand comment about the dangers of rail travel in the region. "Cars run off the track yesterday," he wrote on August 15. "Killed two men & injured others." He did not mention if those who perished were soldiers or railroad workers, but the deadly nature of derailments was prevalent nonetheless.[44]

Men learned quickly to inure themselves to the destruction they witnessed on battlefields. Because transportation tragedies were not uncommon, they could produce similar reactions among some of the individuals exposed to them. On September 5, 1862, Rufus Kinsley and his comrades "were thrown from the track" in an accident that left "one man killed, 12 badly wounded, and half a dozen cars smashed fine enough for 'oven wood.'" However, what disturbed the soldier most was that on the following day he remembered seeing four men sitting by the wreck "wholly absorbed in a game of Eucher, while men more *human* were pulling the dead and wounded from the ruins."[45]

More men perished in transportation accidents in September. On September 10, an Ohio newspaper noted the particulars of "Another Railroad Disaster." The account related some details: "A special train conveying the 98th Illinois Regiment, Colonel Funkhouser, enroute to Louisville, was thrown from the track at Bridgeport, Illinois, on the Ohio and Mississippi Railroad, about 9 o'clock last night, causing the instant death of five soldiers, and severely wounding thirty or forty more."[46]

Leander Stillwell had recently received promotion to sergeant in the Sixty-First Illinois Infantry. He recalled a close encounter with accidental death that occurred as he and his comrades boarded trains in Mississippi: "Well, in our time, the old regiment was hauled over the country many times on trains, the extent of our travels in that manner aggregating hundreds and hundreds of miles," he observed. "And such a thing as even ordinary passenger coaches for the use of enlisted men was unheard of." Stillwell recounted that on the afternoon of September 24, he experienced the "only railroad accident I ever happened to be in." A rush for one of the coaches filled it before the sergeant and his "chum" could get inside but also prevented them from being in the accident that followed almost immediately when the car left the track and "plunged into a cattle guard," or deep depression. "Well, the front end of the car went down into that hole, and then the killing began. They stopped the train very quickly, the entire event couldn't have lasted more than half a minute, but that flat car was torn to splinters, three soldiers on it were killed dead, being frightfully crushed and mangled, and several more badly injured." The sergeant noted that had the train been traveling at full speed, "there is simply no telling how many would then have been killed and wounded."[47]

On October 21, 1862, the newspaper in Staunton, Virginia, related the details of an accident that occurred "about 6 miles west of Charlottesville, when five cars, filled with soldiers, and the tender, were precipitated over an embankment about twenty feet." The cars lay in heaps, "shattered and broken to pieces, one turned bottom upwards," and the occupants strewn about. "By this accident five soldiers and two servants were instantly killed and about seventy wounded—some four or five mortally." The account provided information on the killed and seriously wounded, noting among the former "James H. Barnes, 18th Ga. regiment, Geo. Griffin, of Hampton's Legion, Lipscomb's cavalry, S.C., Serg't J. E. Corley, regiment not known . . . George Owen, 45th Ga. regiment . . . [and] One, name not known, apparently about 30 years of age, large beard." Identities for at least some of the victims came from correspondence found on their persons, and Owen had "many letters" in his possession that he was carrying "for members of the 45th regiment."[48]

Another horrendous accident occurred in February 1862 when a freight train left Meridian, Mississippi, bound for Vicksburg, and approached a span that was supposed to cross the Chunky River. Unfortunately, heavy rains had compromised the structure, and by one account, "it gave way precipitating the engine and four cars into the river." The toll was heavy for the passengers, many of whom were soldiers heading for duty at Vicksburg. The southwest Virginia newspaper carrying the story picked up from a counterpart in Mobile informed its readers, "A large number of passengers were on the train, and from fifty to one hundred were drowned." Although less important to the loved ones of those who perished, the account continued, "The bridge cannot be repaired until the river falls."[49]

Writing after the war about the role of Choctaws as Confederate soldiers, S. G. Spann recounted the efforts some of them made to rescue their comrades in distress. He recalled that only "the hindmost car" failed to navigate the bridge before the span "had swerved out of plumb" sufficiently to send the car careening "into the raging waters with nearly one hundred soldiers." Others began immediately to work at retrieving their comrades from the depths. Spann noted, "Ninety-six bodies were brought out upon a prominent strip of land above the water line." But all was not as dire as it seemed. "Twenty-two were resuscitated and returned to their commands." Unfortunately, the remainder could not be saved and had to be buried by the rail line that had cost them their lives.[50]

In March 1863, the *Nashville Daily Union* printed a letter from a local doctor who explained that after a train wreck a family living nearby demonstrated extraordinary humanity and compassion to the victims. The accident had occurred some twelve miles from Nashville, but at too great a distance for the badly injured to be transported there safely in their battered conditions. Two women from the household took the men into their home, tending to them as best as circumstances would permit. H. W. Frillman noted, "One of the men died yesterday, the 6th inst. His name was Sam Patten, 8th Indiana Bat. of Artillery. He was permitted, by the kindness of Mrs. Davis, to be buried in her family burial ground." The injured men had requested that the doctor compose a letter to demonstrate their gratitude toward the attempts the civilian noncombatants had made "to alleviate the sufferings of the wounded."[51]

At the same time, an account of "persons who were killed or drowned by the accident which occurred on the Southern Railroad eighteen miles west of Meridian," at the end of February, appeared in the *Staunton (Va.) Spectator.* Among the soldier fatalities were "Young, C. C. Thompson, William Towles, A. A. Hill, all of the 27th Alabama Regiment," and "Major J. S. Lily, of the 12th Mississippi Regiment." A lack of discipline had led to the increased risk to the men's lives. The account noted, "The engine and several cars were under water, and it is supposed that between sixty and seventy persons were lost—mostly soldiers, who, it is said, broke open the cars and got aboard before the train left Meridian, though they had been warned by the officers of the road of the dangers attending the trip."[52]

On April 10, 1863, a fatal mishap occurred when a Norfolk and Petersburg locomotive disappeared through an open draw on a bridge spanning the South Fork of the Elizabeth River. Damage to the engine and several cars represented the physical cost of the human error that caused the disaster, but Captain J. B. Bowdisa, who was serving as the commissary of subsistence while stationed at Suffolk, Virginia, also perished aboard the train when it plummeted into the waters below.[53]

One private in a Vermont cavalry command wrote his brother from "Dismounted Camp Md.," on October 26, 1863, to update him on his status. Admitting that he had been "verry unlucky with horses lately," Charles Chapin was traveling by train when a different form of misfortune occurred. "We had gone about three miles when we run off the track," he explained to Wilbur, "eight of the cars tiped over four smashed all to pieces." He had been riding on the roof of one of the cars that managed to remain on the rails, although that night—"it was raining and black as tar"—conditions that undoubtedly added to the chaos and confusion in the aftermath of the accident. "We immediately got down to assist those unfortunate ones which were under the broken mass the groans and cries I shall never forget we worked nearly all night." Fortunately, the toll among the men was not as severe as might be expected ("only one killed I believe"), although the carnage among the animals was much heavier. Chapin quickly shrugged off the harrowing experience, observing that the remainder of the survivors had reached Washington and the routine resumed for the dismounted warrior, although he lamented that in the excitement of the rail accident he had lost one of "a pr. of rebel spurrs" he had intended to send his brother, while he had been "helping the poor fellows out from under the cars."[54]

Manassas Gap Railroad was the scene of a fatal accident in November 1863, a few miles from the junction that had provided a name for two significant Civil War engagements. The circumstances involved cattle cars converted for use in bringing off broken-down cavalry mounts for rehabilitation. Some "one hundred and twenty-six soldiers [detailed] as a guard" rode the train as it careened through the darkness and encountered a curve "at the height of speed" that exerted excessive pressure and "tore the rails from the old and rotten ties." A number of the cars derailed. "The soldiers placed for the trip on the rounded roofs, were shaken and thrown off right and left, as the cars thumped over the displaced ties and rails and fell under the moving train, or went down the embankment with the wreck." The reporter observed, "Seventy-five of them were maimed, some of whom have since died," but provided no specifics as to names, ages or companies, beyond their association with "[Judson] Kilpatrick's cavalry."[55]

Men moving from the Murfreesboro, Tennessee, area after Braxton Bragg's engagement there with William S. Rosecrans had already experienced one of the bitterest engagements of the war thus far, but they would be called upon to endure new challenges during the transfer. The train carrying a number of these soldiers in the direction of Chattanooga left the rails some two miles east of the town of Stevenson, Alabama. While the toll of seven killed was not as extensive as in other rail accidents, these men still gave their lives as surely as their comrades had in the fighting around Stones River.[56] Similarly, a train headed for Chattanooga with 300 occupants arrived after a grueling journey with at least three men dead in the cars, another expiring at the depot while awaiting transportation, and yet another perishing while being taken to the hospital.[57]

On January 16, 1864, a Columbus, Ohio, newspaper shared the news of a fatal incident on the rails out of Pennsylvania: "Philadelphia, Jan. 14—An accident happened to the train, which left Pittsburg for this city, on the Pennsylvania Railroad, early Tuesday morning, at a station west of the mountains." In the course of the journey, a "rail broke, and one of the cars was precipitated down an embankment. A Michigan soldier and Pennsylvania soldier were killed, and several injured."[58]

Another account appeared the next day that provided additional context. "The past few days have been quite prolific of railroad accidents in this neighborhood, and the loss of several lives has been the result," it began. "On Tuesday last, the Express east was thrown from the track near Lockport by the breaking of a rail, by which mishap . . . a member of the First Michigan Cavalry named C. Shaw [was] killed."[59] The Pennsylvania victim remained unidentified as a confirmed fatality or by name or unit.

About midday on Saturday, October 15, 1864, an effort to transport patients from one facility to another by rail led to tragedy on the Shore Line Railroad. The account noted that a train, which "consisted [of] six passenger cars, containing two hundred and seventy-five sick and wounded soldiers" being moved from New Haven, Connecticut, to Reedville, Massachusetts, derailed in spectacular fashion. "When about four miles east of the Connecticut River, and while passing through a deep rock cut, known as 'Rocky Ledge,' a broken rail threw the entire train from the track and dashed the cars into the solid rock ledge on either side." One of the passenger cars flipped in the air and ended up perpendicular across the track, "forming a complete arch some twenty feet high." Several cars were "smashed to such an extent that it would be impossible for a spectator to ascertain the number [of cars] that was in the train except by counting the wheels."

The violence of the accident hurled the passengers from their berths and caused the deaths and serious injuries of many. "Nine of the soldiers were taken from the ruins dead," according to the news report. "One of the killed was jammed between a car and the rocks in such a manner that it was night before the body could be extricated, the cars being a perfect wreck."

A follow-up dispatch in the same newspaper provided the names of the soldier victims, as well as a brakeman, Horace Beebe:

L. V. Phillips, 32d Massachusetts regiment.
Edward W. Dalton, 10th New Hampshire reg't.
N. W. Doyle, recently from the Chesnut street hospital, Philadelphia.
William Muffit, Co. E, 6th Connecticut regiment.
Thomas Johnson, 59th Mass. Regiment.
Richard A. Young, Veteran Reserve Corps.
Montgomery Green, 2d Connecticut Artillery.[60]

A second account offered additional description and detail: "Saturday morning a special shore line train of six cars left at 8 A.M. with 400 soldiers on board. They were heading for Reidville, Massachusetts, and were one mile south of East Lynne. They were thrown from the track at Rocky Neck. Three cars were dashed into atoms and two badly smashed." For all of the physical damage, the impact on the riders was bound to be severe. "Seven soldiers and one brakeman were killed instantly. Nine soldiers and two brakemen were severely mutilated." The configuration of the geographic features along the tracks contributed to the destruction. "The rock on each side of the cars seemed to crush in on them like an anvil. The bodies were terribly crushed and hardly recognizable." Despite the carnage, a stoic survivor observed that he and his comrades had "learned to bear the hardships in the Virginia battlefield and were not going to knock under now."[61]

Sadly, late-war incidents continued to produce victims who would not live to see the outcome of the conflict. This fate awaited Quartermaster Sergeant George W. McCracken as he traveled in East Tennessee at the end of March 1865. Emerson Opdycke was part of a caravan of "five sections of thirteen cars each" that left Chattanooga early in the morning. "Three miles this side of Cleveland Tenn., a brake came loose and six cars were thrown from the track. The Q.M. Sergeant of the 88th Ill. was killed and four others injured."[62]

Confederate railroads became notorious for the dilapidation into which they fell from overuse and poor maintenance, but the rail systems of the North suffered as well from wartime demands. Historian Thomas Weber has noted for these overworked systems, "As the war dragged on, the railroad plant began to deteriorate. The railroads had so much business they could not shop their rolling stock for any but the most essential repairs, and maintenance of track and of motive power was likewise neglected." Higher costs for "materials and labor led many railroads to postpone major repairs until better times." With those days still to come, the numbers reflected the harsh realities. Weber explained, "In 1861, 63 accidents killed 101 and injured 459; by 1864 there were 140 accidents, killing 404, injuring 1,846.[63]

As devastating as such incidents were, the victims came from events involving single trains. The effects increased when the circumstances involved multiple sets of locomotives and boxcars with many more passengers. On September 1, 1861, a horrific accident occurred in southwest Virginia involving two trains, "with 1,100 troops, one company of eighty-two from Mobile, Alabama, and the balance from New Orleans, mashed up at the bridge west of Abingdon depot, killing one and wounding twenty odd." The diarist who recorded the incident added, "The soldier scalded in the mash up died last night."[64] From Louisiana, the *Shreveport Daily News* offered some additional information, forwarded by "an engineer" concerning "a serious accident," that had occurred near Abingdon. The writer noted, "The Askew Guards Capt. Brady, belonging to the 4th Louisiana regiment, had 1 killed and 13 wounded. Names not yet known."[65]

The most specific information regarding the accident came in subsequent publications. The *New Orleans Daily Crescent* provided information from an Abingdon newspaper, informing its readers: "A train of cars loaded with Louisiana troops

(Col. McGinnis' regiment) was ascending the grade on the opposite side of the creek; and just east of the bridge the collision took place. The locomotive buried itself in the rear car one-third of its length, knocking in the front of the boiler, tearing away the smoke-stack, and otherwise damaging the engine." The physical damage had been extensive, and the writer noted, "So complete was the wreck" of the first car on the train following "that it seems miraculous" that the toll was not heavier. As it was, "One man was instantly killed in this car." Of those impacted the account noted, "Donohough, killed. Harvey Givins, scalded; and since dead."[66]

On September 17, the *Richmond Enquirer* listed the fatalities in the accident as "'Askew Guards'—Dunnahoo, killed; Wm. J. Moffat, seriously injured in the back, and died on the 8th inst." And from the "Grirot Rifles": "Harvey Givins, badly scalded, and died next day." Others sustained injuries of various sorts, and the writer credited the bravery of one member of the Askew Guards for working to prevent "many from being scalded and burnt to death."[67] Three days later, the same publication noted the passing of "Mr. Moffatt, one of the soldiers who was injured by the accident on the Tennessee railroad, near Abingdon, on the 1st inst., [who] died on Sunday night, inst." The writer explained that Moffatt, while now a member of "the Askew Guards, from New Orleans, was a printer, and had been, heretofore connected with the 'Delta' office."[68]

The *Lewistown Gazette* of Pennsylvania provided an account of an incident on September 25: "A fatal accident occurred on the Northern Central Railroad on Saturday night, about five miles from Baltimore. Two trains, the first with eighteen, the other with eleven cars attached, were conveying the 49th Pennsylvania regiment, Col. Wm. H. Irwin, to Baltimore, en route for Washington, when . . . the rear train ran into the front and killed two soldiers instantly." The paper noted, "The two killed were three months' men, who had served out their time, and had re-enlisted for the war. Their names were John Fulton, aged 20 years, and Daniel Parker, aged 24 years." A coroner's inquest found the cause of the accident to be "neglect in suffering two trains to run at different rates of speed—the first train only making 10 or 12 miles an hour, while the rear was going at the rate of 15 or 16, and thus caused the collision."[69]

Confederate general John B. Gordon survived a train accident in the spring of 1862, as his troops and others shifted to resist the movement of Union general George B. McClellan on the Virginia Peninsula. Gordon recalled, "The long trains packed with living Confederate freight were hurried along with the utmost possible speed. As the crowded train upon which I sat rushed under full head of steam down grade on this single track, it was met by another train of empty cars flying with great speed in the opposite direction." The officer explained that the encounter produced a "fearful collision" with "harrowing results." The incident had a powerful impact on Gordon: "Nearly every car on the densely packed train was telescoped and torn in pieces; and men, knapsacks, arms [weapons], and shivered seats were hurled to the front and piled in horrid mass against the crushed timbers and ironwork." He marveled that anyone could have survived the catastrophe and was grateful that his wife, traveling with him, remained unscathed. As might be expected in the emergency, the officer quickly became involved in the work of recovery. As he recalled, "I superintended the cutting away of debris to rescue the maimed and remove the dead."[70]

In September 1862, a soldier noted that a train carrying troops near Philadelphia produced fatalities when it wrecked. "During the next two or three hours we rescued out of the wreckage the mangled remains and corpses of more than thirty victims of the collision," he explained. The matter became instantly more problematic when a third train hit the rear of one of the disabled set of cars. "I speak of this to show how dangerous the railroad service of that time was," the soldier noted.[71]

In November 1862, a train accident cost the life of the son of Colonel H. J. B. Clark of North Carolina. The *Newbern Weekly Progress* noted the mishap that had occurred at the end of the previous month "on the Raleigh and Gaston Railroad, near Forestville, by which several persons lost their lives," including Lieutenant Clark, "and others seriously injured."[72] An elaboration of the accident in the paper explained the circumstances by which the trains collided with a force that propelled one engine on top of the other, "dashing the passengers violently to the back of the car and through the shattered sides and windows."[73]

The wrecks themselves could be tragic, with the deaths of some a matter of the misfortune of being in the wrong place at the time the ill-fated moment arrived. Michael Sullivan of the Eighth Indiana was one such unlucky soul when he stepped out onto the smoking platform of his train as the collision took place that caused his demise.[74]

May 1863 brought the news of an additional transportation disaster in North Carolina when two trains collided into each other near Halifax on the Wilmington and Weldon line. A Charlotte newspaper noted that the accident "resulted in the death of one man and the wounding [of] five others, two of whom it is thought cannot survive." According to information from the scene, the writer explained, "The name of the man killed was Allen Temple, a member of Pettigrew's brigade, as was also the men who were wounded."[75]

In Georgia, a fatal occurrence happened north of Cartersville on September 16, 1863, when two uncoordinated trains "met on a curve going full speed." The resulting crash sent men and railroad equipment hurtling, although one individual remained trapped, agonizingly "caught between the tender and the engine by the thigh." All efforts to untangle him from the wreck proved futile as he "burned and screamed and begged to be cut loose for some three hours before life was extinguished." The toll among the troops on both trains stood at fourteen to eighteen dead. A South Carolina newspaper observed, "Everyone standing on the platforms was killed." Others among the forty to sixty-eight injured were more fortunate. "I like to been killed . . . myself," one relieved survivor explained. "I got loose by some meanes and run up a steep bank before I knew I was hert."[76]

Other victims of rail disasters suffered horrendous fates, as the train carriages in which they had been traveling quietly one minute became roaring infernos the next. On March 13, 1864, the *New York Herald* described the case of a "terrific collision" in Alabama that turned quickly to the worst case for those still trapped in the wreckage: "The train was set on fire from the stove and the broken lamps. Three ladies from Huntsville and a soldier belonging to a Minnesota regiment perished in the burning car."[77]

The regimental history of the Fourth Minnesota offered more detail. A timeline for the disaster put the train at the depot in Stevenson, Alabama, at 9:00 P.M., with a departure for Nashville an hour later. The train stopped at Anderson Station, some eleven miles away, to take on water when another train plowed "into it from behind, about 11:00 P.M." The force of the collision "telescoped" two cars and set three passenger cars on fire, leading to the loss of life.[78]

Good intentions improperly executed led to a rail disaster in Georgia in 1864. William R. Stilwell noted the accident in a letter to an uncle while traveling through his home state as William T. Sherman's forces struck south of Atlanta at Jonesboro. John Bell Hood had filled a train with wounded to be evacuated and then sent it away on the Macon and Western Railroad with no notification. The results were predictable. "We had a collision between Milner Station and Barnesville," Stilwell explained of the situation that developed south of Atlanta. "A great many are killed and wounded. The most awful time I ever saw. Thank God I am alive, I jumped off the train, hurt my leg and skinned my face but slightly." Thirty-one individuals were less fortunate, dying in the affair, with others badly injured. "Oh, God, what an awful time," the soldier reiterated, "while I write hundreds of mangled forms lie groaning and howling around me."[79]

Stilwell had asked the uncle to relate word of his safety to his wife so that if she learned of the accident she would not be worried. Finally, on September 6, he could tell her himself from Virginia. "I arrived here this morning after a long and tiresome trip. I am in good health," he started before shifting the subject. "I got skinned and bruised up smartly by the collision of the cars at Barnesville, Georgia." Estimating the toll as lower than it had been, he nevertheless felt deeply affected, writing, "I have never seen such a sight in my life, twenty-six persons were killed and many wounded. I was riding on top of the cars because I could not get inside. I jumped off and got hurt some but I am all right now, and thank God that I got off so light."[80]

In this instance, a failure of communication that included improper notification by Hood's staff to rail authorities contributed directly to the situation. An official with the Macon and Western concluded pointedly of the incident, "Had the orders given from this office been regarded, the collision would not have occurred."[81]

A postwar "summary of the late railway accidents in the North" looked back at late 1864 and the dire predictions of a "terrible era of railroad massacres which seems at last to have arrived." Cataloging "the dreadful record of the last year," the newspaper account included the October 15 Shore Line accident, as well as additional ones that involved soldier fatalities:

OCTOBER 24.—Two trains came into collision on the Baltimore and Ohio Railroad. The engineer, fireman and one soldier were instantly killed; fifteen persons wounded.

OCTOBER 29.—Collision on the Chattanooga and Atlanta Railroad. Five soldiers killed and fifteen wounded.[82]

The deaths of soldiers away from the dangers of the battlefield seemed especially tragic, but prisoners being transferred or returning home after enduring long periods of captivity presented stories that were even more poignant. One of the worst of these accidents in terms of numbers involved occurred during the movement of Confederate prisoners of war from Point Lookout, Maryland, to a new camp opened in Elmira, New York, in July 1864. The 833 captives were the fourth set of men being forwarded to their new accommodations, and 128 Union officers and men had charge over them during the transfer. Part of the operation involved a voyage by steamer that proceeded without incident, but in the shift from the vessel to the train several prisoners managed to escape, delaying the departure by more than an hour while Union troops located and recovered them.

Once under way, the caravan progressed as swiftly as steam power, the terrain, and the groaning cars and tracks would allow. Then, as the locomotive, tender, and seventeen railcars ambled along the rails near the little Pennsylvania town of Shohola, tragedy struck in midafternoon on July 15 when they collided at a sharp curve with a fifty-car coal train heading for them on a single track that was supposed to be clear. Miscommunication and inattention by a telegraph operator who was apparently experiencing the continuing aftereffects of a night of drinking led to the circumstances that followed.[83]

At the scene of the wreck, there was momentary silence before everything descended into chaos. The impact of the collision forced the locomotives into a posture that reminded one survivor of the stance of giant contending wrestlers.[84] Between the buckling cars and the violence of the encounter, the unwitting passengers, prisoners, and guards alike had found themselves tossed and battered. Shards of metal, shattered wood, and smashed glass filled the air like the missiles these men might have faced on any battlefield. A witness described the aftermath in gruesome detail, noting the appearance of "headless trunks" and "mangled" bodies sandwiched between the wrecked cars, with some of the unfortunate victims "impaled on iron rods and splintered beams." Writer Jack Jackson noted the particular impact on a Confederate regiment that easily might have occurred in combat: "Thirteen soldiers of the 51st North Carolina Infantry lost their lives in a few seconds, making the disaster one of the war's costliest moments for that unit."[85] Historian Robert Hoffsommer observed of the carnage, "The impact telescoped the leading prison car into a space of little more than six feet; all four guards [usually placed two at the front and two in the rear of each car] and all but one of the 38 prisoners were killed, most of them horribly mangled."[86]

As this account indicated, the Confederate prisoners suffered the brunt of the damage, but they were not the only victims. Union guards perished when the cars behind them crushed into them. One Federal sentinel was hurled onto the top of the train tender in such a manner as to be found sitting upright with his weapon remaining firmly in his grasp as if still at his post. Engineer Walter Ingram of the prisoner train suffered an excruciatingly slow death pressed against the hot boiler by a load of wood that would-be rescuers tried to remove as rapidly as possible while he pleaded with them to stay clear in case of an explosion. His compatriot, Fireman William Tuttle, was already dead from the impact of the crash.[87]

Local citizens, including farmer John Vogt and his family, worked to assist the survivors and recover the dead, covering some of the most horrifically shattered bodies with whatever was available to shield onlookers from witnessing the full impact of the carnage.[88] Despite being thrown violently in the collision, Union guard Frank Evans survived. Shaken by the experience, he recalled, "Taken all in all, that wreck was a scene of horror such as few, even in the thick of battle, are ever doomed to be a witness of."[89] A newspaper writer described the situation in similar terms:

Sadly familiar as the last three years have rendered the country and the public with tales of blood, scenes of slaughter, and the accumulated horrors of the battle-field, we are not yet so used to them as to feel unmoved when, on a smaller scale, some fearful railroad catastrophe brings them to us face to face amid the quiet of civil life.[90]

Because of the summer conditions, those who could do so helped to construct a ditch and makeshift coffins to bury the dead alongside the track as quickly as possible. Some of the badly injured joined their comrades in death before the task was complete. The human death toll for the wreck stood at fifty-one prisoners, nineteen guards, and several of the crew members of the two trains. In a brutal twist to the tragedy, the man responsible for the accident through his own negligence did not miss the opportunity to attend a dance that evening, although he vanished the next day and was never again seen in the community.[91]

Prisoners at the Confederacy's notorious Camp Sumter, otherwise known as Andersonville, endured unimaginable hardships and difficulties. Men died in various ways as disease and despair took their toll. Nevertheless, some individuals survived their captivity only to perish when transportation accidents occurred. As Union prisoners of war were being transferred from Camp Sumter to Camp Lawton in 1864, many of those men suffered from weakened constitutions and ongoing illnesses. Whether this was the case for one man, or he simply proved unlucky, on the morning of November 4, a prisoner "made a misstep and broke his neck" as he slipped "between the car and the platform" while trying to descend from the train.[92]

A Vermont newspaper described an accident that left men mangled and dead, including an individual recently released from a notorious Confederate facility in Richmond: "Most of those who were killed by the recent railroad collision near Lafayette, Indiana, were returned soldiers. One of them had been in Libby prison over a year." The account noted the greater impact of these unexpected losses on those who were waiting for them anxiously at home: "Many of them were expecting to be married soon, and the letters and photographs of their intended wives were found upon their persons. About thirty were killed."[93]

Only a few months earlier, in September 1864, a short time after the fall of Atlanta to the powerful combination of Union forces under William T. Sherman, Confederate general John Henry Winder sought to remove as many prisoners from Andersonville as possible so as to secure them from liberation by Federal troops. Locomotives took the prisoners away, but the strain proved too much for the poorly maintained lines, and the final string of cars derailed before it had proceeded many miles from the camp. Amid the wreckage were a number of prisoners and guards, crushed as the vehicles left the track. Others sat dazed and bewildered nearby under guard until they could be returned to Andersonville the

next day. Private Samuel Melvin was among the soldiers who found the experience more grueling than his emaciated frame could accept. He would be unable
to leave the prison hospital, a belated victim of the accident and the conditions
that had rendered him too weak to survive it. In what would become the final
entry of his diary, Melvin observed poignantly the message of so many soldiers, "I
want to go home."[94]

4
Not Fooling with Mother Nature
Death from Natural Occurrences or "Acts of God"

One of our Tenn. boys was killed by a tree falling on him in a storm while on picket guard night before last. He belonged to the 9th Tenn Maney's Brigade.
U. G. Owen in a letter to his wife, 1864

For the first time in many years I cried like a child. . . . Had they been shot down in the fury of battle I should not have lamented them so much, for the price of Liberty is the blood of the brave.
Lieutenant John Sheffey after watching comrades drown in a botched crossing

He was almost home, and his great anxiety to reach home, made him venture to ford the river, which was at the time very high and rapid, and he lost his life in the attempt.
Account of Artidore Bear, who died while trying to reach his home near Waynesboro, Virginia, March 1862

There is nothing quite like a summer thunderstorm in the Deep South. The lightning cracks in amazing displays of nature's pyrotechnics, and the thunder claps with impressive roars. Placid waters become surging torrents. Winds and

93

slashing rains, swelling creeks, and rampaging rivers quickly present dangers to animals and human beings that rival those they would experience on any battle-field. In his listing of regimental losses, William Fox noted that among those who died under these circumstances was John Hoffman, of Company F, Fifty-Sixth New York.[1]

While the chances of perishing from a lightning strike were not significant, those chances did exist, as some of the men in the field learned. Rufus Kinsley noted in his journal, "April 12, 1862. Awful thunder storm all last night. 4 men of the 31st Mass. killed by lightning."[2] Halbert Paine experienced the same weather. "A violent storm occurred at night, with thunder, lightning, wind and rain," he noted in a diary entry on April 11. He differed from his comrade only by observing that one fewer man had died. "In the 31st Massachusetts regiment three men were killed and seven wounded by lightning."[3]

Lightning continued to strike with fatal effect in May 1862. A severe storm took place at the end of the month that a member of the Forty-Fourth New York remembered vividly: "During the afternoon occurred a terrific thunder storm, during which lightning struck the tent of Quartermaster Sergeant Howlett and Sergeant Major Weber, instantly killing the former, rendering the latter insensible and igniting and exploding a box of cartridges." Fortunately, the ammunition did not seem to produce additional casualties, but Henry C. Howlett's fate demonstrated the powerful and deadly punch a sudden Southern thunderstorm could produce.[4]

Lightning created more deadly havoc in Virginia in the following month. In the early hours of June 3, a "terrific discharge of the electric fluid" flashed across the sky, as one New Yorker observed. When a bolt reached ground in the bivouac of Battery E, First New York Light Artillery, the impact was severe. Some twenty individuals felt the effects, including unconsciousness for a few. Corporal James Bryant was less fortunate, dying instantly.[5]

On June 16, 1862, Confederate marine Henry Lea Graves recorded in a letter home the aftereffects of another storm-related incident that occurred at his camp at Drewry's Bluff, Virginia: "One of the same crew was killed yesterday by a stroke of lightening. I saw the body this morning and a horrible looking sight it was." Then, quickly assessing his reaction, Graves added, "Such sights do not affect me as they once did." The alterations war had brought on him troubled the soldier to the extent that he felt the need to explain himself: "I can not describe the change nor do I know when it took place, yet I know that there is a change, for I look on the carcass of a man now with pretty much such feelings as I would do were it a horse or hog."[6]

From Montgomery, Alabama, Josh Callaway informed his wife of the difficulties the men had faced coming from Mississippi over a long and difficult trip by rail. Unfortunately, some of his mates had experienced fatal encounters in the cars, but two others fell victim to natural phenomena. "Two were killed by lightning last Monday," Callaway wrote on Wednesday, August 6, 1862, without providing greater detail about the location or circumstances of the event.[7]

In the aftermath of the vicious fighting that marked the Second Manassas Campaign, Union forces under Philip Kearny undertook a rearguard defense of John Pope's forces as they retreated. The engagement occurred in a violent thunderstorm, with driving rain and lightning impacting the men on the field and contributing to the death of General Kearny, who was "killed when he rode into a Confederate regiment in the confusion resulting from the storm," according to historian Robert Krick.[8]

Charles Sherman and his comrades had to endure deadly weather conditions in Louisiana in 1863. Writing to his parents "around April 22," he explained, "When we came hear this day, we have being having Rain with thunder & Lighting. Two Poor Fellows of the 75th New York that was on Picket Duty in front of our Camp was struck. One as Died from the effects of the shock." The disturbing state of affairs for these men reminded all that hostile fire was not the only source of danger to them. "When it dose thunder and Lighten it is very sevear," Sherman observed, "and we are not safe."[9]

A Dayton, Ohio, news account told readers about a "soldier killed by lightning" in the summer of 1863. Without much elaboration or detail, the July 20 reference explained, "A man named Moore, a member of Co. B, 24th Iowa, was killed by lightning on the 13th inst."[10]

At some point in the summer of 1863, Mississippian Frank Montgomery recorded the death of a comrade due to the effects of a thunderstorm. While at camp near Bandon, Mississippi, the cavalryman noted, "I witnessed one day a death by lightning." Men from "Captain Turner's Pontotoc company had its quarters under a spreading oak just in front of the abandoned dwelling in which I had my quarters, when a thunder storm came up and a bolt struck the tree. There were at the time three or four men under the tree, all were shocked, but one young High, a brave soldier, was killed." A surgeon attempted to revive the stricken warrior, "but life was extinct."[11]

While serving on the Atlanta Campaign in Georgia, T. W. Connelly noted the impact of adverse weather conditions on his command. On July 17, 1864, after the men of the Seventieth Ohio had settled into their camps near the Chattahoochee River, Connelly recorded, "During the night, a terrific thunder storm came up, when we were completely drenched by the rain." Unfortunately, he added, "Some three or four were reported killed by lightning."[12]

At Shelbyville, Tennessee, the colorful postwar diarist Sam Watkins related the story of his experiences alongside his comrade Berry Morgan. In conditions that Watkins could only describe as having been like a "tornado," the men found themselves being battered. Like their other comrades who scrambled for cover from the pelting rains and high winds, Morgan and Watkins located "an old shed" in which to seek shelter as the storm swirled around them. "I could hear nothing for the blinding rain and flying dirt and bricks and other rubbish," Watkins remembered vividly. Then, in a matter of minutes, the worst was over. "When it was passed, I turned to look at 'poor Berry,'" the soldier-writer explained. "Poor fellow! his head was crushed in by a brickbat, his breast crushed in by another, and I think his arm was broken, and he was otherwise mutilated." The "handsome boy" had fallen victim to the vicissitudes of Mother Nature.[13]

William Pitt Chambers experienced the turbulent effects of nature when he and his comrades operated in the region north of Vicksburg. As he recalled, "On Saturday night there was a violent storm of wind and rain. The ground we occupied was heavily timbered, and this timber had been deadened some years before and was ready to fall." Chambers was fortunate to avoid serious mishap himself, "but we learned subsequently that several men were killed by falling timber on the east side of the Yazoo River."[14]

The *Memphis Daily Appeal* of April 1, 1863, included a letter from a correspondent named "Nestor," who was writing from Vicksburg. "Among other casualties, occasioned by the storm," he explained, "was the killing of eleven soldiers by falling trees." He also could not be certain that the toll might not rise. "It is not likely that this number embraces the whole, as others may have occurred that have not come to my knowledge."[15]

The threat in the vicinity of Vicksburg continued into the summer. General Reub Williams recorded an incident in July when the skies darkened suddenly and rain and wind pounded the men. He observed, "I can truthfully say that neither before nor since have I witnessed a more fearful storm than the one that prevailed that night." Unfortunately, many of the less ambulatory men had been gathered on a ridgeline in what would have been normally "a beautiful pine grove." In this instance, beauty gave way to more sinister conditions, and Williams learned, "A pine tree had been blown over by the wind and fell across several of the tents killing several men outright and wounding some twenty-five others." Williams suffered the loss of a friend, "Major Parrott, of Lagrange Indiana," but he realized the realities of the profession. "Such, however, was the life of a soldier! There is safety nowhere in wartimes, and thousands of men met their death by accident, instead of being killed in the forefront of battle."[16]

In a letter to "My beloved wife," from "Chatham's Div. Hospital 3 miles Nor of Atl. Ga., July 16, 1864," Confederate doctor U. G. Owen observed, "One of our Tenn. boys was killed by a tree falling on him in a storm while on picket guard night before last. He belonged to the 9th Tenn Maney's Brigade."[17] A member of the Fifty-Seventh North Carolina perished when a falling tree crushed him in 1864.[18]

Union troops suffered similarly. Chaplain Thomas Van Horne listed "First Lieut. Martin L. Linninger," Seventy-Ninth Illinois Infantry, as "Killed by fall of tree, November 19, 1862."[19] In the winter of 1864–1865, such dangers continued to exist for the men of both sides. John L. Collins recalled a tragedy when he and his comrades settled under a spacious oak. "It was a dark and drizzly night," he remembered. "Under these conditions down came this old oak." Collins managed to avoid the threat, but others were not so fortunate. "It fell squarely across the bodies of Col. Sykes, Capt. Perry, and Sergt. Owen. The two latter evidently never knew what struck them." A servant survived, as did the colonel, whose "moanings soon aroused the camp." Men rushed to free the victims. "Capt. Perry and Sergt. Owen were laid out in the silent embrace of death. Col. Sykes was entirely conscious of all the surroundings." The stricken officer had only a short time to live and made final statements for his family members, while also observing "that he would not mind it if he had fallen like his brother," in battle.[20]

Heavy squalls could prove brutal, but the pelting, steady rains brought greater risks as they swelled water tables to dangerous levels. A member of the First Minnesota recorded particularly vicious weather on February 27, 1862: "The storm continued all day with a very high wind, so that but little could be done in crossing men or materiel. Several mishaps had occurred, and one man was drowned."[21]

The tremendous outburst of inclement weather that buffeted Tybee Island, Georgia, on a June day in 1862 had an unexpected impact afterward for the Forty-Eighth New York when it deposited a trove of beer and wine that the men quickly salvaged for their use. Nicknamed "Perry's Saints" after the peacetime avocation of their colonel, James M. Perry, who had been a minister, the men who indulged nevertheless did so with gusto. The whole affair proved horribly unnerving for the former preacher, who suffered a fatal attack in his tent the following day, undoubtedly brought on by the stress of the unsavory event made possible by the bounty bestowed by the storm-tossed waters.[22]

Natural obstructions created by heavy rainfall and unstable soil conditions also caused havoc for travel by rail. In one instance, Washington's *Evening Star* provided a story of the transportation dangers posed in such situations. "Mobile, Aug. 9—Last night a soldier train ran into a landslide, between Pollard and Montgomery, and killed 12 and wounded 57 of the 1st Mississippi battalion of artillery."[23]

So many men died due to weather-related issues away from the battlefield, but others also perished because of such conditions during engagements with the enemy. In the tremendous fighting that marked the Battle of Chancellorsville, the combatants engaged not only each other but also the elements in the struggle for survival. On May 5, a Confederate participant noted in his diary that the "rain fell in torrents." A Union counterpart observed grimly that wounded comrades "lay sprawled in the mud and filth" in several inches of water in some places that he heard had claimed the lives of at least two men who drowned as they huddled next to a cabin. "They were lying close under the eaves and were unable to move when they were covered by the water that fell from the roof."[24]

Soldiers who had endured brutal fighting occasionally became unwitting victims of nature once the combat had subsided. In one instance, as wounded men clung to life in the trenches at hard-fought Spotsylvania Court House, in May 1864, steady rainfall filled the low-lying areas and drowned some of them.[25]

Men who escaped the shot, shell, and minié balls in the trenches of Petersburg, Virginia, could not always foresee or prepare sufficiently for the dangers presented by ordinary weather phenomena. Thus, in the summer of 1864, a torrential rain set in with sufficient volume to bring disaster to unwitting Union troops. The *Lewistown Gazette* of Pennsylvania told readers of an incident in which "the water suddenly entered a deep gully used by our troops for shelter from the enemy, causing the loss of a few lives by drowning, principally colored soldiers."[26] Without a unit designation, it could not be certain if these were some of the troops who had survived the carnage of the fighting at the Battle of the Crater in July, only to face deadly natural conditions a month later, but the likelihood that one could perish while trying to remain safe from enemy shot and shell demonstrated the vagaries of life and death in the trenches.

For members of the Army of the James, holding positions outside Richmond and Petersburg presented more than the anticipated threats to life. A raging rainstorm in August produced swells that one historian noted were "nine feet deep in places, sweeping everything from their path, including breastworks, tents, wagons, stacked rifles," and other items. Many of the men were fortunate to scramble to higher ground, although over twenty members of one regiment were "unable to climb out of their pits" and were "swept away and drowned in the mud-stained waters."[27]

Steady rainfall at numerous periods during the conflict plagued the men who marched on surfaces the water had inundated and transformed into significant obstacles to their efficient progress and dangers to their persons. Those same heavy rains created dangerous obstacles of normally placid creeks and rivers. As early as August 1861, rain-swollen waters claimed victims campaigning in western Virginia, when Confederates attempting to cross the Gauley River lost control of a flatboat serving as a ferry, sending four men to their deaths. According to one reckoning, three of the victims, "Hugh Scott, Jno. Jones, and Geo. Bear, were Smyth Dragoons." Lieutenant John Sheffey of the same unit noted, "The river was much swollen, and, as the poor fellows went down the boiling stream, among the rocks, and into the furious rapids, the scene was sad and fearful beyond description." Sheffey admitted unashamedly that the incident shook him badly. As he later explained, "For the first time in many years I cried like a child" as he had watched his friends swept to their doom. Even the "excitement" of a subsequent engagement could not clear his mind. "I have tried to forget the horror of that hour," he wrote, "but I can never cease to grieve over the untimely fate of the poor fellows to whom I had become so much attached. Had they been shot down in the fury of battle I should not have lamented them so much, for the price of Liberty is the blood of the brave."[28]

In September 1861, First Lieutenant George K. Hogg, of Company K, Third Pennsylvania Cavalry, drowned when "an old flatboat" pressed into service for ferrying troops across the Patuxent River floundered. "It was a sad ending of a brave young life. He had seen less than one month service, having been mustered in on August 19," the unit's historian recorded of "the first death of an officer in the regiment."[29] The colonel of the First Massachusetts included reference to the deceased officer in his communications: "In relation to the lamented death of Lieutenant Hogg, I learn that the accident was caused by the unseaworthy condition of the boat, which gave way under the weight of the men and horses on board."[30]

A similar accident occurred in the Trans-Mississippi later in the war. Union soldier Albert Marshall noted that his unit had crossed Big Bayou and Saluria Bayou without accident, albeit on "very poor ferry boats." Others were less fortunate: "The troops in our advance had a sad accident yesterday. While they were crossing one of the ferries heavily loaded with soldiers sunk in the deepest part of the water. About forty men were lost." Marshall indicated, "Twenty-five of those who met this sad fate were members of the Sixty-ninth Indiana Volunteers. The others were some of the colored troops who were working the ferry." He concluded of the incident, "Such a serious loss of life in such a manner is far sadder than to see our comrades fall in battle."[31]

Troops who had to cross raging rivers found the challenges severe, if not deadly. Citing a dateline of "Winchester, Va., April 17" in 1862, the *Sun* of New York conveyed the "Sad Disaster" of a capsizing boat that was carrying troops from the 75th Pennsylvania, while attempting to traverse the Shenandoah River. The account put the estimated number of persons lost at "between 40 and 50 men and several officers."[32] William Fox set the regimental loss at "2 officers and 51 men, drowned by the swamping of a scow."[33] Similarly, the Sixty-Ninth Indiana suffered significant losses when a boat sank in Matagorda Bay in an accident that cost the lives by drowning of two officers and twenty men.[34]

Real danger also remained in negotiating the many waterways the troops encountered as they crossed areas where roads were mere paths and fords the only means of moving from point to point over creeks and rivers. Colorful Georgian Milton Barrett wrote his siblings from his "Camps on the banks of the Shannado [River]" to let them know how miserable the river crossing had been for the men: "We have had rain in abounce. . . . We waided the river last night. it was up to our arms and it was with much difacult that we keep our provishons and powder dry. several of the boys fel down and got ther rashons and powder wet."[35]

Crossing major rivers or streams, especially when heavy rainfall had turned them into heaving caldrons of churning floodwaters, could prove fatal. Private Ambrose R. Henderson, a farmer before the war and a member of Company F, Fiftieth Virginia, was not so fortunate when he faced such a water barrier in Virginia. He was only eighteen years old when he "drowned in the New River near the Narrows" on July 5, 1862. The muster roll indicated that Henderson had been detailed earlier as a teamster but did not specify if he remained in that role at the time of his death, or the exact nature of his drowning.[36]

The White River in Missouri proved a particular nemesis if entries from the diary of Benjamin F. McIntyre can be used as a gauge. On January 3, 1863, he noted, "Another day south of White River," before telling of a misfortune in crossing it. "Several of the 1st Iowa Cavalry attempted to Swim the stream this morning and in doing so James Robertson of Koekuk lost his life. His body has not been recovered."[37]

Yet, this situation failed to match a disaster that occurred on March 1. "This day has passed us by leaving a most painful incident for us to record," McIntyre wrote. Observing the use of a ferry line that he felt provided little security for loaded flatboats, he professed to have "shuddered at the thought of how frail a link connected them from accident and death." Then, the unthinkable happened as a loaded boat became unmanageable and sank. "The river presented a Scene I do not again wish to witness—Men and mules struggling in the water for life, many clinging to the Sunken boat—the water was icy cold & the current setting from the shore required a superhuman effort to reach it. While we as gazers on could render no assistance & be only witness of their death Struggle." Some of the men came agonizingly close to shore before giving out, "raising their hands above their heads and you could see the agony on their face and hear the cry—O cannot you save me—then sunk to rise no more."

The veteran remained traumatized by the events that had unfolded before him. As he recorded in his diary, "I have seen death in many forms—have seen my companions fall at my Side in battle and without a feeling of sorrow passed on to revenge them—I have seen those expire who have been wounded. . . . But to die as our companions have today—to sacrifice all for the sake of their country and then to find Such a grave."[38]

McIntyre wrote subsequent entries as new circumstances forced him to relive the tragedy. On March 16: "Another drowned man was found today in the river about half a mile below this place. It proved to be one of those who lost his life Mar 1st by the accident of the ferry."[39] Then, again, on April 15: "Another body of a man who perished in the catastrophe of March 1st was found today."[40] It was as if the river was slowly returning the souls lost to it as somber reminders of the mortality of the men who had dared to challenge it.

Union troops passing through East Tennessee had the benefit of large elements of friendly individuals who remained loyal to assist or welcome them, but they were also susceptible to the natural dangers that awaited. In one case, soldiers came to grief while attempting to cross when "one of the boats capsized and one captain and thirty-two men of the 27th New Jersey regiment . . . were drowned." Historian B. F. Thompson added, "The men were encumbered with knapsacks and unable to swim, and were swept down stream by the rapid current and sank beneath the waters before aid could reach them."[41] Another account of the affair attributed the disaster to the breaking of one of two ropes being used to pull the boat across the river.[42]

The same region cost more men their lives in similar fashion when Kentucky-born Colonel William P. Sanders conducted a raid there in June. On June 18, members of the expedition got separated as they reached the swollen Clinch River. Members of the rear guard plunged into the waters and immediately encountered difficulties as submerged rocks presented additional obstacles. Among those who perished were First Sergeant Amos H. Holden, whose commission as lieutenant had reached camp in his absence, Corporal Edwin F. Hunt, and Privates Thomas H. Kilby, George C. Wood, and Thomas T. White. Colonel Sanders's response to the report that the men had died was cold, but practical. According to the messenger, "He remarked that it was unfortunate, but could not be helped."[43] Two months later, Sergeant Lucius C. Niles would meet the same fate, listed in the regimental history of the 112th Illinois as "Drowned in Emery River, near Kingston, Tenn., Aug. 31 '63."[44]

Even for individuals who encountered water courses with which they would have felt familiar because of their earlier experiences, real dangers existed. Perhaps most troubling were the tales of soldiers who had been bound for their homes when tragedy befell them. Artidore Bear was on his way back after a year serving in the saddle for the Confederacy when he reached a crossing of the South River near his native Waynesboro, Virginia. Hoping, as one account described, "to see the 'good old folks at home,'" he took the risk of attempting to cross the last water barrier that remained in his way. "He was almost home," the writer observed, "and his great anxiety to reach home, made him venture to ford the river, which was at the time very high and rapid, and he lost his life in the attempt."[45] Shortly afterward, a Federal soldier experienced the same outcome while attempting to reach his home. Edgar C. Shepard, of Company H, Fifth New York Cavalry, "drowned April 22, 1863, while en route home on furlough."[46]

Often military operations required the participants to face such risks as columns moved across landscapes dotted with rivers and streams. In the midst of a raid in the latter part of 1863 against the Virginia and Tennessee Railroad, Union troops found it necessary to plunge their mounts into a river as Confederate forces moved against them, resulting in the "loss of 4 men drowned."[47] In the same operation, the after-action report noted, "14th Pennsylvania Cavalry 6 privates drowned" and "Gibson's battalion 1 private drowned."[48]

Heavy periods of rain and the intense heat and humidity of the Deep South plagued the soldiers marching toward or defending Atlanta in the summer of 1864. William T. Sherman was no great advocate of cavalry, but he thought that extended raids could disrupt Confederate supply networks and communications while he dealt with the larger forces interposed between his command and the city. In August, Judson Kilpatrick was one of the men tasked with accomplishing this mission as he took his troopers south of Atlanta. As his men approached rain-swollen Cotton Indian Creek, the column confronted a dangerous obstacle. Historian David Evans explained, "Ordinarily a quiet country stream about twenty-feet wide and two-and-a-half-feet deep, the recent rains had swelled it to a raging torrent, three times its normal size." Kilpatrick led the way, then supervised and assisted as the rest followed. Private Francis M. Jones was one of the last to make the effort. Riding a mule after having lost his mount in action at Lovejoy's Station, he coaxed the animal into the water. However, when the mule balked in the middle of the crossing, Jones fell into the current and failed to surface. No one was in a position to assist, and he was lost. Other accounts added to the total of men potentially drowned in the operation, but Evans was only able to corroborate Jones's death.[49]

Troops moving through the rain-soaked landscape of Virginia in late 1864 experienced similar fatal misfortune. Theodore Lyman, aide-de-camp to General George Gordon Meade in the Army of the Potomac, recorded a mishap in his diary entry of December 9: "Though the day was very cold & windy, the infantry took to the water, and forced the passage, losing 32 men of whom two or three were drowned."[50]

In February 1865, the cavalry of George Armstrong Custer was moving through the Valley of Virginia when the troops found it necessary to cross the rain-swollen Shenandoah River. Colonel Francis T. Sherman of the Eighty-Eighth Illinois recorded, on February 28, the engineering prowess of his men, while illustrating that mortal dangers remained nevertheless: "Two miles south [we] threw [a] pontoon bridge over the Shenandoah River in one hour & 10 minutes. Custer lost one man drowned in fording."[51]

Marching through all types of conditions was the mainstay of the foot soldier's experience in the war. If moving at night, the men faced uncertain footing or the presence of obstacles that could prove dangerous. Navigating difficult conditions plagued wheeled conveyances from supply wagons and ambulances to artillery pieces. Mishaps with these heavy vehicles meant the possibility of fatalities for drivers, riders, and anyone passing in the vicinity.

On September 17, 1862, Sharpsburg or Antietam became the single bloodiest day in American history as the combatants traded fierce blasts of musketry and artillery volleys across the rolling landscape. Yet, in the aftermath of that enormous bloodletting, men continued to perish under different circumstances while Robert E. Lee sought to disengage his Army of Northern Virginia from Maryland soil. As the Confederates worked toward crossings on the Potomac River on the night of September 18, darkness and confusion marked the painful progress. A chaplain from one of the North Carolina commands noted the chaos as vehicles collided wherever weariness or inattention held sway. "Ram! Jam!" the minister noted in his diary. "Wagons and ambulances turned over!" Then, without specific reference as to whether the individual was an occupant or someone trudging along nearby, he added, "One man was killed by the overturning of an ambulance."[52]

When the weather turned extreme, threats could pose dangers to the men in the ranks and produce deadly consequences. Operations near Yorktown, Virginia, in 1862, Burnside's Mud March in Virginia and the Tullahoma Campaign, in Tennessee, in 1863, and the Atlanta Campaign in Georgia, in 1864, saw frequent and severe downpours that affected movement by turning roads quickly into quagmires, washed away bridges, and inundated low-lying areas. At the iconic site of the first major confrontation between the opposing forces, heavy rainfall saturated the region around Manassas and created a torrent of Bull Run. "I have often heard persons talk of and I have read of stormy nights, of rain falling in torrents and the wind blowing hurricanes," one Confederate recorded in his diary, "but last night was ahead of all that I ever heard or read of." The next day, he was part of a command required to address the damage. "The railroad bridge across Bull Run has washed away and the creek is all over the country, so there is another job of work for our regiment." Unfortunately, in the course of the morning, fatal accidents occurred. "Two members of the 12th Mississippi regiment were drowned, one of them attempted to cross but the current being too strong carried him under and he was drowned. Another fell from the bridge and was drowned." Alabamian John Cowin speculated that alcohol might also have had something to do with the latter soldier's death.[53]

Road systems in the rural South did not require much in the way of external elements to become treacherous, but they could become particularly harmful for the men and animals that slogged along them when subjected to copious amounts of rainfall. A Union surgeon captured the spirit of the men in January 1863 when he observed in a letter to his wife, "The weather is quite warm and pleasant for the season of the year, but mud!! ah-me!—that's the rub! It is this we fear the most—more than rebel bullets or shells."[54]

A Minnesotan colorfully described the situation as the men endured the extremes of the "sunny South." He explained, "The cold was not so severe and snows not so deep as in Minnesota, but the mud was deeper." He felt that his description could not do the situation ample justice, since this element "was something that had to be experienced to be properly sensed. It was a revelation to us from the North. We did not know that just mud could be so deep, so sticky, and so nasty."[55]

A Cleveland newspaper picked up an account titled "The Mud of Yorktown" that had originally appeared in the Philadelphia Inquirer. In this instance, a Union general purportedly "saw a soldier drowned in the road, along which he was running a telegraph line." The writer did not offer corroboration of the incident but employed it to add a curious feature he considered relevant: "We have often seen men in the mud up to their knapsacks, which have been the means of saving many a life by acting as a kind of buoy or life preserver." Unfortunately, for the unnamed victim, any equipment he may have had on his person at the time apparently failed to prevent his demise.[56]

For one soldier, at least, the conditions he faced on the wet Virginia roads near Falmouth were too onerous to overcome psychologically. As the Iron Brigade marched, one of the members of the vaunted unit collapsed from illness and exhaustion. Officers prodded the soldier to return to his feet and rejoin the ranks, but the distraught warrior considered his options, placed his rifle against his chest and fired. He simply could not bring himself to endure more. Virginia mud had seemed to claim another life.[57]

Through much of the 1864 Overland Campaign in Virginia, soldiers on both sides recounted the overwhelming aspect of the liquid that inundated the roads over which they moved or the lines they created for defensive purposes. Surviving marches over roads turned to streams left many with an understandable sense of foreboding that the troops often tried to mask with morbid expressions of humor. Some accounts described men who waited by deep mud holes to watch others plunge into them, and camp rumor persisted that more than one unfortunate had actually suffocated or drowned in the muck.[58]

Mud became an almost universal nemesis for the men throughout the regions in which they campaigned, but heat or sunstroke felled them just as readily as they attempted to carry out their martial duties. Union surgeon Daniel M. Holt recalled the impact that seeing men felled by the effects of the sun had on him initially: "It was something new to me to see men fall as if shot and die almost as quickly, from sun stroke. A moment previous to falling he would be marching on as if nothing unusual was to pay, when a stagger and fall, and in some instances death, followed each other in a few moments time."[59]

In correspondence with his wife, Alfred Hough included a brief reference to the tremendous toll marching had taken on his comrades in Alabama in June 1862. "I saw something of the terrible realities of a hard march," he explained, noting that a rider had dropped back "and asked for our doctor who rode back with him." Hough soon learned the purpose of the errand. "When we reached the top of the hill as I passed by I saw a poor fellow lying under a tree just dead! The doctor had not reached him in time." He overheard the surgeon reading from a paper on the dead man's person that gave his name as "N. O. Hack" and advised, "If I am killed write to my mother." Hough, who found the sentiment heart-wrenching, noted in his letter, "We passed many that I don't think will ever get much farther, in fact I have heard of a number that died on that day."[60]

Lucius Barber of the Fifteenth Illinois Volunteer Infantry observed the dire effects of sun and heat upon the men as they trod along the dusty roads of West Tennessee in July 1862: "The heat was intense and water very scarce, and the dust suffocated us. The 19th of July was the hottest day we had yet experienced." Men quickly began to drop out of the columns, some to rest, others to rise no more. According to Barber, "The army moved very slowly, resting ten minutes every half hour, in the shade, when we could find it, but notwithstanding, scores of men would drop down, some dying instantly, other[s] so far gone as not to be able to move." Barber, who admitted his own high level of distress during this phase of the operation, noted simply, "It was a common sight that day to see dead soldiers by the roadside."[61]

During the same period, while posted in Memphis, Tennessee, an Ohio soldier wrote to explain the detrimental effects of the conditions on some of his comrades. "I was informed that 5 or 6 men died out of our Brig. on our way Saturday, 2 of whom were of the 70, 2 of the 48 Ohio," Sam Evans observed. "They were overdone by heat or sun struck." He had survived the ordeal, but it had shaken him as well. "This kind of soldering tries a man's mettle."[62] In a subsequent letter, he added details for his grandmother: "Three of the 70 Regiment died by sun stroke. 3 of co. F have died since we left Corinth. Oliver Gray Wilson M. Elles, Wm. Faughn."[63]

As Confederate forces under Robert E. Lee moved in the direction of Maryland in the fall of 1862, unseasonably warm conditions greeted them and contributed to heavy straggling along portions of the line of march. On September 5, one of the distressed soldiers wrote, "It has been an awfully hard march. Two men died in one day from sun stroke." Conditions improved concerning the temperatures, but too late for the stricken men.[64]

The following summer the sweltering heat returned to plague the soldiers who marched and fought through it. Wisconsin troops found the conditions almost unendurable as some of the men trudging along gave way to them. James S. Anderson confided in his diary in mid-June 1863, "This is the most severe march I ever was on, the day was hot and sultry, and nine men of our Brigade dropped dead from exhaustion."[65]

The summer of 1863 indeed proved grueling for troops waging war in the South. James A. Wright of the First Minnesota Regiment recorded the effects of the conditions in Virginia and drew a comparison to Daniel in the Bible in the process: "The mid-June sun was shining with intense rays from a clear sky and from about as near directly overhead as it gets in that latitude—making a sultry, summer afternoon. The calorific rays seemed to scorch and blister and burn, as if trying to rival a 'fiery furnace.'" For the men struggling through the conditions, the situation bordered on unbearable. "It was one of the most heart-breaking marches of our experience, and many men wilted in the scorching heat and dust like mown grass. There were many prostrations—men staggering from the ranks and falling as if shot. There were a number of cases of fatal sunstroke, and some dying almost as quickly as if struck by a bullet in a vital part." Ambulances filled "with helpless men," and stragglers who managed to survive continued to appear through the evening and into night.[66]

Similarly, Southern troops suffered as they marched through Maryland and into Pennsylvania. From Chambersburg, Eli Landers of Georgia noted for family members at home, "We have had a long hard march since I wrote you last and some very hot weather. It was very severe on us soldiers." The weather had since moderated somewhat, and the men suffered less as a result, "but during them hot days there was hundreds of our boys fainted and fell in the road and many of them died but I have been able to keep up all the way."[67] Another Federal on that grueling march noted, "Two of my men were barefooted—their feet swollen so badly they could not get their shoes on, but these men came into camp that night, one to meet his death the next day."[68]

Men performing their duties outside the Southern states or away from lines of march also remained at risk. When members of the Sixteenth Connecticut participated in what became known as the "Blackberry Raid" outside Portsmouth, Virginia, the men suffered tremendously. An officer explained in a letter home, "We saw no fighting, but had a very hard time in other respects. I have had several men ruined for life by the heat." Another participant observed glumly, "Marched 20 miles. Lots fell out. About a dozen fell dead."[69]

In New York, tremendous heat left numbers of persons stricken, from traditional laborers and ordinary citizens to men in uniform. On August 4, 1863, the *New York Herald* listed several victims, including "John Meddlecatt, a discharged volunteer, who served two years," and an "unknown soldier, wearing the uniform of Hawkins' Zouaves," who was found "prostrated at the corner of Frankfort and William streets."[70]

Another account from August 1863 offered the news that an unnamed soldier stationed at Fortress Monroe, in Tidewater, Virginia, fell victim to "sunstroke" during the searing heat that locals pronounced as severe as any the region had experienced.[71] A different Union veteran fell to the effects of sun and heat on the coast of South Carolina. The comprehensive listing of casualties appearing in the *New South* of Port Royal included "Thos Cummings, E, 97th Penna, 20th sun stroke."[72]

At the same time, as they moved through the area of Orange Court House, Virginia, Confederate troops staggered along the roadways under what one of them termed "the hottest sun that I ever felt." That soldier survived the grueling experience, but other comrades were not as fortunate. He recorded, "The men were constantly dropping out from overheat, and one or two died from the effects."[73]

Soldiers serving in Georgia during the Atlanta Campaign faced such dangers. George W. Ide of Company G, Twenty-Fifth Wisconsin, was near Dallas when he fell to the effects of the sun on June 2, 1864.[74] At the Battle of Ezra Church, fought subsequently on a searing late summer day outside Atlanta, the combatants experienced the demands of temperature as well as enemy fire. The conditions proved so intense that at least one individual succumbed while trying to aid in the resupply of ammunition to his comrades on the front lines. Reub Williams recalled the "very large and rugged man" stricken fatally as he hoisted a box of 1,000 cartridges onto his shoulder from a nearby wagon. The fellow collapsed under the 100 pounds of weight he bore in the intense heat of the day.[75] Similarly, on July 28 in Georgia, John McMillen, of Company B, Seventieth Ohio, "died instantly" from the effects of the heat.[76]

August conditions in Virginia were equally brutal. During the movements associated with the fighting at Second Deep Bottom or Fussell's Mill, Union troops experienced heat that felled some of their number along the line of march as surely as enemy fire. General Francis A. Walker noted that his troops "literally passed between men lying on both sides" of the road leading from a landing, "dead from sunstroke." He explained the impact vividly: "The rays of the August sun smote the heads of the weary soldiers with blows as palpable as if they had been given with a club."[77]

The opposite extreme of the heat and storms of summer was the bitter cold and freezing precipitation of winter. One of the members of the Eighth Louisiana, whose activities as a unit had already gained a reputation in Virginia for excessiveness, chose an inopportune time for indulging in libation. In November 1861, he passed out after a drinking binge and froze to death in the snow.[78] Just over a year later, the same situation cost the life of a member of the Eighth Louisiana.[79]

Wintry conditions may not have caused the death of one Union soldier directly, but when the fellow wandered away from camp in early 1862, he did not return to his mates after a fatal plunge. From Camp Butler, Illinois, surgeon James A. Black of the Forty-Ninth Illinois Volunteer Infantry noted in his diary on January 22, "A men fell through the Railroad bridge over Sangamon river last night onto the ice and [was] killed. supposed to be drunk don't know him."[80]

For some men in the Thirty-Eighth New York Regiment, the fatal situation occurred when they sought to combat the cold with their own heat source. "Two members of Company F, who had been acting as cooks in the regiment, were in the habit of taking a pan of hot coals every night into the tent where they sleep," according to a report in the *New York Herald* that appeared on February 5, 1862. "Last night, the tent being closed tight, the snow having filled up all the chinks, there was no opportunity for the gas to escape. The consequence was that this morning one of the men, John Scott, was found suffocated to death, and the other, John McNeill, almost insensible." Expecting a burial with full military honors, the writer noted, "This is the first death that has occurred in the regiment since July last. . . . Soldiers should remember that pure air is at all times essential, not only to life, but to health."[81]

All forms of weather extremes could prove deadly, but those appearing in the winter undoubtedly produced the most common examples of exaggeration with regard to allegedly fatal consequences for the men who faced them. In early January 1864, the *Weekly National Intelligencer* of Washington drew from the Chicago newspapers to provide accurate assessments and allay concerns relating to fatalities caused by freezing temperatures: "There was a report current in the city that six men had frozen to death at Camp Fry. There is no truth in it. There was much suffering among the men, of course, but no deaths." The account also passed along news of the demise of "forty prisoners" who had supposedly "frozen to death at Camp Douglas." Dismissing the quantity of deceased Confederates as exaggerated, the writer had to admit, "The number was subsequently reduced to eight," before he cast doubt on that reduced tally as well.[82]

Nevertheless, like some of their Confederate counterparts, prisoners of war perished from exposure to the extreme elements. The U.S. Sanitary Commission noted the deaths of fourteen men in one cold night at Belle Island in Richmond.[83] Similarly, Union captive John Ransom maintained that some thirty of his comrades had succumbed to the adverse conditions that beset them in their relatively exposed positions.[84]

Some of the excess in reporting deaths associated with cold conditions came in the form of camp rumor passed on and compounded. Soldiers subjected to uncomfortable, if not deadly, situations regularly needed little prodding to assume the worst when word filtered down of some extraordinary event that was said to have taken place with their comrades. Likewise, newspapers contributed with sensationalized accounts, and the authors of not a few postwar memoirs could not resist the dramatic impact on the reader of stories that featured extreme elements. If, as historian Robert Krick has maintained, "the contemporary mythical tales continue to appear to this day, elaborated by time and often enshrined as demonstrable truth," circumstances existed that reflected the fact that the potential danger of extreme cold weather conditions to life was genuine.[85]

During the winter of 1862, when the news came that a soldier had been found frozen to death, an initial assumption seemed to be that he simply failed to obtain sufficient means for surviving the cold. But in a letter to his daughter, dated February 21, Robert McAllister explained, "As to that man who was said to have frozen in the stable, it now appears he died in consequence of having drunk too much liquor."[86] While the consumption of large amounts of alcohol might seem to be useful in helping to ward off the blasts of winter, this soldier had demonstrated that it actually contributed to his demise.

Men posted in Virginia in January 1862 witnessed snow, sleet, and cold conditions. Georgians took advantage of the situation to test their skills for improvised sledding or skating in the icy conditions. "We had fun snowballing and sliding downhill on planks since it snowed. Some of the boys go skating on a neighboring mill pond," one observed. Then the novel activity turned deadly for a participant. "Unfortunately, one poor fellow broke through the other day and was drowned."[87]

While posted at Fredericksburg, Virginia, in December 1862, Spencer Bonsall of the Eighty-First Pennsylvania confided his thoughts in a journal. Among his first impressions was the severity of the meteorological conditions. "The weather is very cold, and the ice near the shore is thick enough to bear the weight of several men who are sliding on it," he noted on December 7. "The whole country is covered with ice and snow, and everything looks dreary enough."[88] When not huddled in their tents, men gathered around fires to stave off the cold, but on the next day, Bonsall observed, "Several men have frozen to death in their tents during the last two nights."[89]

For security purposes, stationary forces required that pickets or vedettes remain outside of the camps. These men endured conditions away from the relative protection of their tents or winter quarters and found the hours on such duty dull and oppressive, if not dangerous and deadly. The threat occasionally came from guerrillas or bushwhackers who prowled the fringes of the main forces looking to make their own brand of contribution to the war effort by targeting isolated individuals, but also from the extremes of weather that could take their toll on the exposed men.

During the difficult winter of 1863–1864, Confederate general James Longstreet spent time in what his side might easily have deemed the purgatory of heavily Unionist East Tennessee. "Lee's War Horse" had failed to drive Ambrose E. Burnside from strong positions at Knoxville and had drifted in the direction of southwest Virginia. Historian Benjamin Cooling noted of the shivering soldiery, "With temperatures well below zero almost every night, pickets froze to death at their posts."[90]

Perhaps the most famous illustration of this type of phenomenon came from the writing of the soldier-author Sam Watkins. His book "Co. Aytch" contained the dramatic account of some eleven men with responsibility for guarding a portion of the line as pickets. "Some were sitting down and some were laying down," Watkins remembered, "but each and every one was as cold and as hard frozen as the icicles that hung from their hands and faces and clothing—dead!" He recalled that two of the men occupied more advanced positions from their comrades. He found them "standing with their guns in their hands, as cold and as hard frozen as a monument of marble—standing sentinel with loaded guns in their frozen hands!"[91]

Not unlike Watkins's postwar memoirs, sensational headlines during wartime brought the fates of some of the soldiers who served in distant locales to their readers. In December 1862, an Ohio newspaper reported, "Soldiers Frozen to Death" before relating, "Six of our pickets of the Army of the Potomac froze to death Saturday night, [while] seven died from the effects of cold at camp Murry near Alexandria."[92]

A harrowing tale of conditions for soldiers in Virginia told of the challenges the men faced in obtaining appropriate garb to resist the brutality of winter weather. Citing an account from the *Hartford Times* of Connecticut, the *Dayton Daily Empire* provided its readers a "private letter from a soldier in Burnside's army, to his mother in this city from Falmouth a day or two previous to the disastrous battle of Fredericksburg," in which the man described the arrival at "the dead house [of] twelve dead bodies of our soldiers, who had been frozen to death while on guard duty!" The victims had insufficient clothing to ward off the bitter cold. "The mercury on two nights sunk to 13 and 14 degrees, and ice six inches thick floated in the river. Their shoes were in many instances almost worthless, being Massachusetts contract shoes, with soles glued on."[93]

At the same place and time, a Union general wrote to tell his wife how concerned he was over the health of his command. "We are having quite a number of deaths—typhoid fever and colds settling on the lungs," Robert McAllister observed. "These winter campaigns are very hard on the men. Shelter tents and cold storms do not agree well and will kill a grate many men."[94]

The early part of 1864 proved particularly harsh for men in arms exposed to the elements. On January 5, a West Virginia paper conveyed the dismal tidings: "Three Federal soldiers were frozen to death at Camp Nelson [in Kentucky] on Saturday night."[95] Another report with a dateline from Springfield, Illinois, January 2, 1864, which emanated from a Pennsylvania newspaper published more than a week later, asserted, "We are completely snowed in. The weather is bitter cold. Several soldiers have frozen to death at Camp Yates."[96]

An Evansville, Indiana, paper noted that the steamer *Belle Memphis* had arrived in Memphis, Tennessee, "having the bodies of five men of the 52d Indiana, who were frozen to death above Fort Pillow."[97] Men from another Indiana unit, as well as at least ten African Americans posted at Island Number 10, "were frozen to death" or suffered life-threatening frostbite and hypothermia. A party from Company B of the Second Indiana found itself stranded on a sandbar after "the skiff which contained them became unmanageable." Two escaped to seek help, but of the remaining seven so exposed to the conditions, "three of them were discovered frozen to death on the bar. The names were Second Lieutenant

Edwin Alexander and privates N. W. Falkenberg and Wm. Taylor." Two others died, despite being found by a local resident who brought them into his house.[98]

As almost a generic notice, the *Nashville Daily Union* inserted a line in the general reporting of the war, "Five men were frozen to death during the late cold spell."[99] At about the same time, reports appeared of the deaths of four soldiers due to freezing, although there were indications of other contributing factors as well: "One or two of these unfortunate men who were frozen to death, I regret to announce, were in a state of intoxication bordering on insensibility, and to this fact alone may be attributed their terrible fate."[100]

Wintry conditions created dangers for prisoners of war as well as for men in the field. Historian John Lundberg noted the situation for some of the Confederate captives placed at Camp Douglas, Illinois, after the fall of Vicksburg, "With almost no protection from the bitter winds and snow off Lake Michigan, hundreds of Texans died within the first month of incarceration. In that first month the temperature dipped to 40 degrees below zero, and in one night forty prisoners froze to death." The circumstances for their officers were difficult as well. When 308 of them boarded cars to be transferred from Alton, Illinois, to Camp Chase in Ohio, they endured frigid conditions. "That night," Lundberg observed, "Lieutenant William F. Rogers of Company F, 15th Texas, froze to death."[101]

As a prisoner at Belle Isle in Richmond, John Ransom kept a diary that noted the depressing condition of the captives held there. On November 24, 1863, his entry opened chillingly on several counts: "Very cold weather. Four or five men chilled to death last night."[102] On December 1, he added to the tally of weather-related fatalities: "A man froze to death last night where I slept."[103] Death from the frigid conditions occurred with alarming regularity.[104]

In January 1864, the *Evansville (Ind.) Daily Journal* noted the deaths of two soldiers at Camp Chase, as well as numerous cases of frostbite on the extremities of comrades who survived. For some Confederate captives, the conditions were equally life-threatening. According to the newspaper account, "Four rebel prisoners were frozen to death while asleep on the cars at Jeffersonville."[105]

At Point Lookout Prison, Maryland, dismal weather contributed not only to the general misery of the captives being held there but also to some of their deaths. George Peyton of the 13th Virginia recorded in his diary on December 12, 1864: "Snowed last night and blew up clear and cold. Wind blew hard all night. Two men froze to death."[106] Another prisoner noted the nature of the conditions that frequently plagued the facility and its inhabitants: "In the winter, a high tide and an easterly gale would flood the whole surface of the pen, *and freeze as it flooded.*"[107]

For men who sought to divert their attention from combat, wintry recreation could prove as deadly, especially if the participants allowed their passions to lead them astray. Historian Bell Wiley noted a mishap involving some of Joseph Johnston's men sheltering for the winter of 1863–1864 in north Georgia: "Another soldier reported that two men were killed in snow fights near Dalton, Georgia."[108]

Other natural conditions often prevailed that put the lives of men at risk even when they were not experiencing extremes in temperatures. For the men who worked their way through the vast countryside and passed through swamps and dense forests during the months that rendered active campaigning more effective, there were other, often unseen, dangers. Joseph Wallpole, a farmer who had enlisted in the Southampton Greys at the small hamlet of Jerusalem, Virginia, in the spring of 1861, found himself in a Richmond hospital before the end of the next year. In the course of his soldierly duties he had encountered a foe that struck as suddenly as an enemy combatant. The diagnosis was "moris serpentis" or the "bite of a serpent," and although no record appears extant that identified the type of reptile that inflicted the wound, a subsequent infection first cost the soldier his leg to amputation, and then his life, on November 15, 1862.[109]

In the wilds of the Western Theater, along the Yazoo, the soldiers faced hazards from more than Confederate weaponry. On June 22, 1863, Wesley Gould informed his sister, Hannah, "This is the roughest country I ever saw. I have read a good deal about the forests of Miss. but this goes beyond my expectations. It is here that you find reptiles of all descriptions. You can hardly [take a] step without stepping on a snake. Rattlesnakes are very numerous here."[110]

Charles B. Haydon continued a diary he had kept since the beginning of his enlistment. Now, in Mississippi, he also had new and different kinds of entries to make, and while it is likely that some of his comments reflected hyperbole and camp gossip, they also shed light on the natural dangers that existed for the soldiery engaged in keeping John C. Pemberton's Confederates ensnarled in Vicksburg. On June 27, he observed, "The country is not so bad after all as I was first led to believe. There are not so many snakes or other infernal machines [Confederate torpedoes or mines] as was represented. The alligators eat some soldiers but if the soldiers would keep out of the river they would not be eaten."[111] Another of Grant's men, assigned to the works on Snyder's Bluff, outside Vicksburg, noted glumly, "Almost every day we heard of some soldier dying from the bite of a rattler."[112]

In eastern Virginia, cold weather had a decided effect on more than the men who endured it. Millett Thompson of the 13th New Hampshire Infantry explained that while camped near Suffolk, Virginia, he and his comrades had encountered many unwelcome visitors. On March 22, 1863, he observed that during a period of harsh weather, "The snakes entered many of the tents for shelter, when the storm commenced."[113] A "snake or two" could also be found in the well supplying the men with water, and in early April he noted, "It is not an unusual thing here now for a soldier, on rising in the morning, to shake out of his blanket a full-grown snake, a copperhead or moccasin. These cool nights cause the snakes to desire warm bedfellows."[114]

Men engaged in warfare encountered many natural hazards, but on rare occasions the desire to enjoy the wonders of the world around them, particularly when those images were new to them, could increase the risks to their lives unknowingly. Figures such as Ulysses S. Grant and George H. Thomas could not resist the temptation to climb Lookout Mountain, where wartime photographs captured their images. These well-known personalities avoided serious mishaps, but others, in different locations, were not so fortunate. It is impossible to say if intoxication was involved or simply the desire to take in the vistas offered to him when Private John Flarety of the Second Massachusetts cavalry climbed atop a bluff outside Washington, D.C. He may only have wanted a better view of the Potomac River or the environs of the capital city ringed by extensive fortifications designed to keep Confederate opponents at bay. In any case, a Washington newspaper reported that the cavalryman lost his footing and "fell from a precipice near Fort Ethan Allen, (across the river) and received injuries that resulted in his death in a short time."[115]

For men who survived their encounters with nature's extremes, there were the equally terrifying moments when natural elements contributed to man-made situations to bring about deadly results. Most distressing among this type of wartime experience were the moments when men incapacitated by wounds or injuries watched as flames broke out and crept toward them. Compassion and humanity often prevailed to prevent these gruesome deaths, as it did at Kennesaw Mountain when Colonel William H. Martin of the First and Fifteenth (Consolidated) Arkansas called for a cessation of hostilities to aid fallen Federals from being consumed in the brushfire that had stirred up outside his works. The fire had begun to reach some of the men when Martin reacted. "Boys, this is butchery," he yelled and convinced the soldiers of both sides in the vicinity to halt their shooting and scramble to rescue the wounded.[116]

Similar situations occurred at the Battle of the Wilderness and elsewhere. A Union participant in the war recalled such cruel circumstances in the aftermath of one engagement. "The ugly feature of this strip of ground was that it was thickly covered with pine needles, which had caught fire," Reub Williams remembered later. "This material burns rapidly so it was not at all strange that we came across quite a number of the bodies of the enemy, who having first been wounded, had burned to death by the on sweeping flames that flashed across this battle-field." Williams cited as evidence the conditions of some of the deceased, who presented the signs of trying to protect themselves from the approaching conflagration. He concluded succinctly, "Certainly and surely a 'foughten field' is a horrible place to view."[117]

Warfare presented many expected dangers to the soldiers who joined their respective ranks to battle their foes in arms. Yet, when it came to natural phenomena, threats to life could come in many other forms, too. Wind, rain, storms, snow, frozen temperatures and precipitation, swampy conditions and myriad creatures in the wild were among the elements that soldiers often encountered with potentially fatal consequences. Men would find that nature could be cruel and, when adverse circumstances arose, that their lives could be lost as surely as they would be on the fields of Shiloh or Stones River, Pea Ridge or Perryville, Antietam or Fredericksburg, Chancellorsville or Gettysburg, Vicksburg or Missionary Ridge, and Kennesaw Mountain or Franklin and Nashville.

5
Slipshod Soldiering
Fatal Mounted Accidents and Deaths Associated with Animals and Mascots

All night I lay down feeling more sad than I have
for many days. God knows the future.
Reaction to the death of Chaplain George Knox
when his horse fell on him

That proud dashing form is cold and stiff in death,
the light in those eagle eyes is gone out, and the
splendid mind has ceased to exist so far as we are
concerned.
Account of the death of Confederate general
William Baldwin in an equestrian accident

A generic phrase often applied to young people growing up has its roots in the playful term "horsin' around." "Jine the cavalry" became the popular mantra for anyone who thought such troops would experience the war as a lark. Best exemplified by dashing figures like James Ewell Brown "Jeb" Stuart, John Hunt Morgan, and George Armstrong Custer, the mounted service of the Confederacy especially, but to a lesser degree of the Union, represented the romantic view conjured up by images of glorious saber charges and jaunts across the countryside. Yet, during the American Civil War, the cavalry arm also took considerable grief from those who were not in it, and there was the widespread belief among those who trod the ground that one never saw a "dead man with spurs on."[1]

Of course, what was not taken into account, or if it was, got dismissed quickly, were the long hours in the saddle that came with the raids and scouting expeditions conducted under grueling conditions. Saddle sores and boils were hardly glamorous, and mounted duty could be as deadly dull, and plain deadly, as any service in the field. Accidents often accounted for such noncombat fatalities. Unfortunately, one's life was not just at risk from the sabers and carbines of opponents but from the act of riding itself. Men and their mounts were not always compatible with each other, and poor weather conditions and equipment failures added to the danger, too. Prominent figures were not immune to such troubles. The war would have taken a very different course had riding mishaps that happened to Ulysses S. Grant and Robert E. Lee proved fatal.[2]

Recruits did not always come to their new line of work with sufficient experience in the saddle. Southerners were likely to have more exposure to riding than many of their Northern counterparts. As one scholar observed, "The Northerner, even if he came from the country, was more likely to be familiar with a horse as a farm animal and beast of burden than as a mount." However, the purpose of training and drill was to breed the sense of confidence in the saddle that would allow the trooper to retain his proper focus on his primary mission of waging war successfully. "A trooper who was properly less afraid of the enemy than he was of his mount . . . was a liability, not an asset," as historian Jack Coggins explained.[3]

Proximity to animals of all types offered the chance for dangerous encounters even in the midst of routine duties. Early October 1861 brought the news of a fatality to the readership of a newspaper in the nation's capital. This instance involved the mortal injury of "one of the teamsters employed at the Government stables near the Observatory" when he "was kicked in the forehead by an unruly horse, which caused a fracture of the skull, resulting in his death yesterday morning."[4]

The more likely fatal event was liable to occur with a fall from a horse and could affect everyone from a general's staff and entourage to mounted officers or cavalrymen in the field. For one individual, associated with Union general George B. McClellan, bad luck and ill timing doomed him:

About half past eight o'clock last evening, a colored man, named David Dodson, (one of General McClellan's servants,) while riding along F street on a fine charger at full speed, attempted to turn a corner very short, when he was thrown from the saddle. While in the act of falling, he made a grasp for the saddle, but missed it, and his head was thrown violently against the ground, breaking his neck.

Bystanders summoned medical attention for the victim, "but before it had reached him, life was extinct."[5]

On October 13, 1861, the *Nashville Union and American* explained that a Confederate officer, "Col. Lyon, of the Eighth Arkansas," had suffered a fatal riding accident when his horse "fell through the trestle work at the Tennessee river bridge, killing the colonel."[6] Actually commanding the Sixth Arkansas, Richard Lyon "was killed October 10, 1861, by his horse falling over a precipice with him, while superintending the crossing of his regiment over the Tennessee river."[7]

More than a week later, the editors of the *National Republican* entered reports on two mounted fatalities. According to this account, "On Monday afternoon, about three o'clock, as Major Lewis, of the twelfth (Syracuse) New York regiment, was returning from a ride on horseback to his wife's boarding house, (Mrs. Frederick's,) on Capitol Hill, he was thrown, or fell from, his horse and dislocated his neck. He lived only a few minutes." The tragic event happened when the officer was attempting to meld his soldierly duties with his domestic obligations. "On leaving his wife in the morning, he had promised to come and dine with her, and was on his return to her when the accident occurred." The same source provided a brief description of another fatal mounted incident: "At about the same time, a soldier named Wilson, attached to the cavalry company which arrived here on Sunday, and was quartered on Capitol Hill, was thrown from his horse in the vicinity of his quarters, and killed."[8]

Military reviews were part of the martial pageantry as well as an opportunity for inspection for superiors and civilian guests alike. Grand reviews represented the largest scale of this activity, with high-ranking military and political figures usually in attendance. In the aftermath of being appointed to replace Lieutenant General Winfield Scott as commander of the Army of the United States, George B. McClellan held such an event in November 1861, which turned tragic when some of the officers involved disregarded basic safety precautions. An Alexandria newspaper reported the outcome: "Near the close of the grand review, Col. Taylor, of the New York 33d, accompanied by the surgeon of the regiment, while riding at high speed over the review grounds, ran into a private with their horses. The blow killed the soldier almost instantly." The writer noted that the collision unhorsed the surgeon as well, causing him to be "so badly injured that he died within an hour." General McClellan ordered the colonel held, as the responsible officer, "into close custody," for the reckless incident.[9]

A Union chaplain also experienced more than the indignity of being thrown when he participated in a review of troops on October 31, 1864. John Mead Gould captured the incident and his own personal angst in a vivid journal entry that began innocuously enough: "October 31—Pleasant. The 2nd Division is in the 6th Corps and in camp near Strasburg were reviewed today. Gen'l Emory invited his Division and Brigade commanders to accompany him." One of these officers passed the invitation along to Chaplain George Knox. As described by Gould, "The horse he rides is not a very good animal and Captain Turner very generously lent him his. The Capt. had been trying to use the army bit in his horse's mouth and as usual had made the [animal's] mouth sore and the horse very sensitive." Apparently limited in equestrian skills, Knox did not realize the situation, and although he used a standard bit and bridle, "when he mounted and pulled the rein the animal reared." Gould speculated, "This induced the Chaplain probably to pull still more. At all events the horse reared too far for his balance." As the animal tumbled over, so did the rider. "Mr. Knox fell off and struck on his head, the back part of it, and the horse then fell with his whole weight upon him." The impact of both blows was significant. "Thus the injury to the brain and the rupture of the major artery of the left leg, each would have caused death."

Initially, Chaplain Knox survived the fall, but the damage was too great. He lay in "the most intense pain from the wound in the leg which seemed to drown the pain in the head. The Doctor gave him numerous doses of morphine," but this treatment seemed to have "no visible effect." The stricken man appeared to stabilize enough that Gould felt confident in leaving his side to return to his own quarters. He had barely reached them when word arrived, "Mr. Knox is dead." Gould explained, "I could hardly believe it even after I saw the corpse." Words spoken so recently between them took on enhanced meaning now that the minister was gone. "At night I lay down feeling more sad than I have for many days. God knows the future," the soldier observed. "For myself I have no courage to think of it."[10] The next day, men from the command sold the minister's "private effects" for about sixty dollars, then "raised in the reg't. enough to bring this amount up to $480. So we feel that the widow can have a little something to start her life of sorrow on."[11]

With the first Christmas of the war away from home on the minds of so many, Colonel Thomas L. Cooper, of the Eighth Georgia, was riding when his horse threw him from the saddle and he died instantly. The thirty-year-old officer had lost a brother from wounds suffered at Manassas in September and was the oldest son of a prominent Bartow County, Georgia, family. Cooper had attended Franklin College in Athens and practiced law until the outbreak of hostilities led to a captaincy in the Atlanta Greys. Subsequent promotions came his way, but he had only recently risen to command of the regiment when the fatal accident occurred.[12]

Another unfortunate soldier suffered a mishap while attempting to ride his horse. A Richmond newspaper quoted "the Carrsville, Isle-of-Wight, correspondent of the Petersburg Express, dated January 2d," who said, "A promising lad, the son of Mr. H. Batton of this county, was a few days since instantly killed by the accidental discharge of a pestel whilst mounting his horse." The accident struck the Batton household particularly hard. "Mr. B. peculiarly merits the sympathies of his friends in his multiplied bereavements having lost within the past few weeks an older son, a member of the Stanchfield Artillery and an interesting little daughter."[13]

On March 10, 1862, a Richmond newspaper picked up the story of another fatal riding accident for a surgeon attached to a Confederate unit. The account did not specify if the horse referenced was newly broken for riding, skittish in nature, or affected by some activity that frightened it, but the result was catastrophic for the would-be rider. The writer noted, "Norfolk, March 9. Dr. Swann, of the Wise Legion, of Petersburg, was killed to-day in attempting to mount his horse. He was thrown and dragged, fracturing his skull. He died in four hours."[14]

The circumstances were not always clear when individual riders left their saddles and perished from their falls. Nevertheless, frightened animals could lead to fatal results as occurred in separate incidents in Tennessee and southwest Virginia in the spring of 1862. On May 11, a Union soldier, Samuel McIlvaine, included in his diary a circumstance he labeled as a "rather singular death . . . in Company I of our regiment this morning." Early in the morning, "before day, two or three loose horses came rushing through the quarters & among the sleeping men, passing near where this man, H. Osborne, lay." Although he was supposed to have roused with the rest of his comrades at the time of the startling intrusion, when the men returned to their slumbers before awakening for their traditional morning routine, "this man was found dead." McIlvaine did not offer a position as to what might have happened between the initial disturbance and morning call, but Osborne's death was clearly perplexing to his surviving comrades.[15]

On May 19, 1862, while in Virginia, Edward Guerrant, a staff officer from Kentucky who served with Confederate general Humphrey Marshall early in the war, recorded a strange sequence of events in his diary: "Tonight the horses of the Battalion Cavalry—stampeded & run over a great many of the men—injuring some of them severely—& exploding a gun which killed Brady of Holliday's company." The staffer did not identify the type of weapon that fired the deadly projectile but concluded, "A terrible accident. Some of the horses run away & were never heard of."[16]

In the summer of 1862, Minnesotan James Wright recalled "a tragic-comic incident in the brigade camp" that occurred when mounted men exhibited "attacks of 'speed mania,'" as they raced to the river to water their horses. "Horseflesh was considered valuable," he explained, "and it was considered dangerous and detrimental to race the horses in hot weather." An angry General Willis A. Gorman had taken steps to restrict the practice, and a sentry with orders to arrest practitioners quickly got his opportunity when an officer and an orderly galloped past. The soldier called for the men to halt. The officer "looked surprised, saluted, but did not slacken his gait—and the sentry promptly brought his rifle to his shoulder. There was a flash, a bang, and the horse and rider rolled in the road. The sentry's bullet had gone through the horse, passing within a few inches of the officer's leg, killing the horse and tumbling his rider in the road in front of him." Only the general's personal intervention prevented the incensed officer from shooting the guard. "I never heard the sentry was punished or put to any trouble or inconvenience," Wright observed, but added, "There was no more racing through the camps during the few days more we remained there."[17] A year later, a Union diarist noted the continuation of the practice, which he termed "an awful specimen of the degradation incident to Army Life." Samuel Cormany observed that this instance of horse racing cost the lives of "3 Men killed and 4 horses."[18]

On August 30, 1862, an account appeared in a Port Royal, South Carolina, newspaper of a fatal riding accident involving "Corporal Edwin F. Hickok, of Co. K, 6th Connecticut Regiment, belonging to the mounted guard, and acting as courier between Seabrook's and Hilton Head." It was unclear if Hickok was carrying dispatches or acting in some other capacity at the time, but he met with a terrible mishap while riding. Instead of arriving and returning safely from his trip, the Connecticut Yankee "was found dead yesterday morning on the road near Drayton's plantation." An investigation revealed that "the unfortunate man had been thrown from his horse, and his neck was dislocated by the fall."[19]

Another riding mishap occurred in late 1862, as reported in a South Carolina newspaper on November 26. "On the night of the 6th instant, at the camp within a few miles of Staunton, Va., Lieut. Crawford, of Chester District. S.C., was thrown from his horse and dragged, (his foot hanging in the stirrup,) and was so severely injured that he died the next day. He belonged to Col. Black's South Carolina cavalry."[20]

For all of the disparagement many foot soldiers felt for their mounted comrades, there was more than a passing interest in entering their ranks. Unhappily, one Confederate infantryman who had served with the Forty-Sixth Tennessee and escaped capture when Island Number 10 fell to Federal forces was not so fortunate when he subsequently joined the cavalry. The colorfully named Green Prince "was Killed by being thrown from his horse."[21]

Holidays and other special events seemed to bring out a propensity for speed in some of the men who had animals with that attribute they wanted to showcase. A story in the *Daily National Republican* of Washington gave readers the account of an unusual and deadly riding accident that occurred during races associated with such a celebration. "Thomas Mooney, quartermaster of the Ninth Massachusetts regiment, who was one of the party that met in the hurdle race in the army—got up by Gen. Meager's brigade, on St. Patrick's day—had died of his injuries," the writer noted. "Mr. Mooney was riding at great speed on the hurdle course, when he met, mid-way, Surgeon Faxon, of the Thirty-second New York regiment, who was riding swiftly." Realizing that a collision was imminent, the riders turned their mounts "simultaneously to avoid each other, but unfortunately in the same direction, and then [the horses] came together with a shock that killed them so instantaneously that they never stirred afterward." The men involved survived the experience with injuries.[22] Assistant surgeon Charles Johnson, of the Tenth Tennessee Infantry, was not as lucky as his New York counterpart. In his *History of the Army of the Cumberland*, Chaplain Thomas Van Horne explained that the doctor was "killed by a fall from his horse, April 15, 1863."[23]

The volatile Trans-Mississippi region, which had bred the violence of "Bleeding Kansas" before the war and vitriolic border civil war since, saw the massing of a force under the notorious William Clarke Quantrill in the summer of 1863. Quantrill felt he had scores to settle with the inhabitants of Lawrence, Kansas, and rode with the notion of wreaking vengeance upon them. In the earliest hours of August 21, a man who lived some miles outside of the town took it upon himself to ride and warn the citizens that a raiding force was headed their way. Unfortunately, in the darkness of the hours before dawn, while hurrying at full gallop, the animal stumbled, and both the rider and his horse perished from the fall before completing the mission. Quantrill and his raiders reached the sleepy town and began the systematic killing of its citizens and burning of its structures, unimpeded by local forces that had not received any advance notice of their coming.[24]

On October 4, 1863, Kentuckian Ned Guerrant recorded the death of a comrade in an artillery unit: "L't Jas. Schoolfield in comd. of Williams' Battery informed me of the death of poor 'Bud' Peters who was a member of his battery." Marion "Bud" Peters "was drowned yesterday while crossing the Chucky river. His horse stumbled & threw him off where the water was not more than two feet deep, but it was so swift, he couldn't stand up, & never rose but once, after he went down." Guerrant mourned a lost friend, felled in a situation that would have seemed unimaginable to a veteran. "Farewell poor 'Bud'! We drop a soldiers tear over your untimely grave, & hope a better home awaits you."[25]

Later in the month, a newspaper correspondent in South Carolina reported the mysterious passing of a Confederate staff officer in Charleston. "On Wednesday morning last," the writer explained in his open letter of October 18, "Capt. Wm. H. Wagner, of General Ripley's staff, was found dead near the corner of King and

Broad-St. about day-light by a negro, who reported the fact to the guard house." The circumstances of the death were uncertain enough to warrant an investigation. "A Jury of inquest was impannelled, who brought in a verdict, that he came to his death by being thrown from his horse." It was not clear if any other factor, such as alcohol or excessive speed, was involved, but the fatal riding accident was not the only tragedy to impact this family. The same letter continued, "A brother of the deceased, not long since, was killed by the bursting of a cannon."[26]

Only two months later, on December 22, 1863, a colorful Union brigadier general died when his horse crushed him in a fall. Michael Corcoran was already a controversial figure even before the Civil War, when he won notoriety for his response to a visit by the Prince of Wales and during the early days of the conflict for his treatment as a hostage by Confederate forces after being captured at First Bull Run. Corcoran was riding with his friend and Irish compatriot Thomas Meagher when his mount slipped on the icy surface of the ground near the division's winter quarters at Fairfax Court House in Virginia.[27] The two men had planned to bring their wives to camp for Christmas and were traveling back from the depot where they had met them when the accident occurred. Meagher's shock at the sudden turn of events from holiday celebration to preparations for a funeral for his friend left an indelible impression. As he recalled, "There, in that very room which I had occupied for several days as his guest . . . he lay cold and white in death, with the hands which were once so warm in their grasp, and so lavish in their gifts crossed upon his breast."[28]

On February 19, 1864, a Confederate brigadier general, William E. Baldwin, suffered a fatal plunge from the saddle when one of his stirrups failed, causing him to strike his right shoulder so violently as to produce his death in a short period after his fall.[29] One soldier noted the impact of the general's demise on the men in his regiment: "There is a gloom over our camp today. *Gen. Baldwin is dead!* That proud dashing form is cold and stiff in death, the light in those eagle eyes is gone out, and the splendid mind has ceased to exist so far as we are concerned."[30]

Union colonel Joshua B. Howell's martial connections included family service in the Revolution and the War of 1812 and early war assignments along the East Coast, but this all ended for him when his mount fell on September 12, 1864. Just turned fifty-eight, Howell was one of the older men in the ranks, but the game and badly injured officer lingered for two days before succumbing to the damage he had sustained in the accident. He would not know of his promotion seven months later to brigadier general.[31]

Horses were not always directly involved in fatal accidents by their own actions but could be participants when circumstances went awry. A South Carolina newspaper noted such a situation in July 1862: "We regret to learn that on

Friday morning, whilst the Dixie Rangers were under inspection by Col. Walker, at Green Pond Station, Charleston and Savannah Railroad, a fatal accident occurred, resulting in the death of a member of that company." During "an inspection of arms," the mounted officer was examining the men in the ranks when "private Laurence Kavanaugh's carbine being loaded, although the cap was removed, the piece became somehow entangled in the rein and was discharged, the ball passing through the head of private T. W. Clagett, and killing him instantly."[32] An exercise meant to increase the soldiers' proficiency had ended in the death of one of the men by a mounted comrade's weapon.

Almost a year later, a similar accident occurred when a member of the Third Pennsylvania Cavalry assembled "for a retreat parade," following a stint on other duty. The unit's regimental historian related "a sad accident" that had occurred in Company C on June 4, 1863: "While the officer in command was inspecting the sabres of the rear rank, a sharp report was heard, and Private Eli Hartenstein fell dead in his place." The trooper had unwittingly begun the startling turn of events when "only a few minutes before the bugle call" he had "returned from picket duty but had not drawn the cartridge from his carbine." The incident occurred as he "was unslinging and bringing it to 'order arms,'" when the weapon apparently fell from his grasp and "the concussion of the piece on striking the ground exploded it, sending the bullet from under his chin out of the top of his head, killing him instantly." The sense of loss was heavy in the command for an individual who was known as "an exceptionally good man and a true soldier, and was beloved by all his comrades."[33]

Life could prove precarious even for the groom of the mounts of a general officer, serving in his capacity well away from the sphere of active hostile operations. But for the man attending the horses of Union general Orlando B. Willcox, an accident would prove his undoing. In a letter home from Newport News, Virginia, on February 13, 1863, the general announced, "This has been a sad day to me. Arndt, my devoted groom, injured himself on board the transport by a strain producing a severe hernia from which he is not likely to recover. I fear he cannot survive many days even." The general was not so much being pessimistic as realistic, writing, "He inquires for Roebuck [the general's horse], takes hold of my hand, squeezes it & calls me his dear General. He has some idea of his danger. Gangrene has set in."[34]

Willcox had praised Arndt for his work in keeping the general's mounts "in splendid condition," but he could now do little to alleviate the pain of the suffering man, much less prevent the inevitable as his servant's condition deteriorated.[35] Reporting on February 17, "Poor Arndt is very low," the general noted dejectedly, "It will be a great blow to me to lose him."[36] He brought the servant's favorite horse to the bedside for the ailing man to see him, and "he was wild with flattering delight."[37] However, General Willcox could do little more than revive his groomsman's spirits momentarily by the gesture. Finally, on March 1, the officer observed of "poor Arndt" that he had lost his battle with his injury and "we buried him with all the honors of war yesterday near my head quarters."[38]

Horses could prove deadly for their riders, but other working animals were often problematic as well. One historian observed, "Though of uncertain temperament and not as steady under fire as his half-brother, the horse, the pack mule with a case of small-arms ammunition strapped to each side was a familiar sight on many battlefields."[39] Indeed, mules were a mainstay for the armies of both sides in all areas of transportation. They brought loads of ammunition and other supplies and equipment to the forces that required these resources to campaign successfully, hauling as much as "250 to 300 pounds 20 miles a day" as pack animals, according to one authority.[40] Raiding forces frequently targeted the animals when slashing into opposing wagon trains, shooting or sabering the mule hitches in their traces to disable the vehicles and allow for them to be captured or destroyed.[41] In one instance, Union major general Andrew Jackson Smith recorded the loss of "27 mules killed," as Confederate cavalry descended on a portion of his column in the summer of 1864.[42]

The men who routinely worked with the teams that pulled wagons, ambulances, and other vehicles were often notorious for their colorful language and temperaments that matched their charges. Yet, as cantankerous as army mules were known to be, they could also be dangerous to the health and safety of those handlers. The exact nature of the encounter was not recorded in this case, but one such individual, Private Lorenzo Brown of the 112th Illinois Infantry, died near Waynesboro, Kentucky, on August 23, 1864, when one of his mules kicked him.[43]

Life-threatening outcomes could happen from an ill-timed fall or unlucky blow, but the men who rode and handled animals and equipment regularly accepted such risks. Even so, fatal accidents could occur at any moment involving the animals or the conveyances for even the most seasoned personnel. As one of the functions in wartime of the *Western Reserve Chronicle* of Warren, Ohio, the newspaper sought to keep its readers informed of the activities in the field of area units. On December 18, 1861, it passed along the latest information from one regiment, noting the death of one of the noncombatant laborers associated with the command: "A teamster named Jacob Clark, from New Lisbon; fell from his wagon, the wheels passed over him and killed him."[44]

Early in 1862, the *Richmond Daily Dispatch* noted an unfortunate accident for another teamster: "Rudolph Arnstein, wagon master, was accidentally killed at the Burnt Ordinary, in James City county, Va., on Saturday, the 11th of the present month, while conveying a train from Richmond to Yorktown." Without offering an explanation, the writer observed, "He jumped from a wagon in motion, and fell, one wagon wheel passing over his chest, and causing his almost instantaneous death." The account pointed out that the deceased individual's belongings, including "some money and effects found in his possession," would be held for safekeeping until they could be passed along properly to his next of kin.[45]

From his post at Murfreesboro, Tennessee, surgeon John Bennitt of the Nineteenth Michigan related to his wife in September 1863 the price of the war, even at his location distant from the primary fields of action: "A lieutenant—was run over & killed a few miles north of here—He came here for me to bury."[46] Bennitt did not specify whether the accident had occurred by virtue of a wheeled vehicle or by an animal that had gotten out of control, but real dangers remained as people operated in the presence of heavy equipment and the teams of animals that moved them forward.

As the armies grew in size and sophistication, the dangers increased for those working the teams that supplied them. In 1864, a chaplain's report from the rendezvous of distribution camp in Virginia included the notice of the death of another teamster. At the end of a listing of men felled by disease for a week in April, Chaplain William J. Potter added, "April 15—James Smith, citizen teamster, Philadelphia, Pa. Died of injuries received in being run over by a wagon."[47]

The Civil War took a terrible toll on people. It also decimated the animals caught up in it. A conflict that depended upon the transfer of enormous stores of supplies and other resources over vast distances meant the employment of extraordinary numbers of various types of beasts of burden. The requirements for these animals to operate under all types of conditions exacted a price from these creatures that the soldiers themselves often witnessed and that commanding officers had to take into account in drawing up and executing military operations and meeting logistical demands. Poor weather and roads were more than inconveniences; they were the means by which animals as well as people could break down or die.

By virtue of its location, Washington became a gathering point for the animals needed to support military forces in the Eastern Theater of the war. "In the corrals which occupied the vacant lots near the Observatory, thousands of horses and mules were packed together," according to historian Margaret Leech. When fire broke out suddenly, some 200 of these animals perished in the flames, while others had to be destroyed because of injuries they sustained while fleeing through the streets. "The next morning," Leech observed of the catastrophe, "scorched and blackened horses were lying all about the streets. There was a dead horse in the southern enclosure of the Treasury."[48]

An account in the *Evening Star* was particularly graphic about the deaths of the animals and the degree to which people had struggled to save them. "Many of the horses were smothered by the smoke," the description in the newspaper confirmed as one cause of death, "but the most of those destroyed were literally burned at the stake." More of the animals might have perished had humans not taken immediate and drastic action. According to the account, "The scene was awful in the extreme, as the flames spread and soldiers and citizens, with knives and axes, cut the halters of the frightened animals, and sent them scampering in every direction." Yet, for all these exertions, the newspaper writer speculated, "About two hundred horses [were] literally burnt to a crisp" by the searing conflagration.[49]

From his camp in Annapolis, Maryland, a Vermont cavalryman described the impact of the war on his unit's horses. As the regiment bivouacked in Washington, poor weather ravaged the animals that had already endured the perils of travel. "Our horses while there were Picketed out exposed to storm which togeather with a long and fatigue[ing] ride caused many deaths," Private William H. Daniels observed. "(I think 29)."[50]

During the movement of his Ohio troops from Washington to the Chesapeake Bay in June 1862, Colonel Alvin Voris experienced an accident that he recalled to his wife that "precipitated" some of his men "into the bay." The same event sent animals plunging into the waters as well, and Voris had the sad duty to communicate the loss of his cherished mount. "Fanny has gone to revel with *old sea horse* & act as palfrey for the mermaids," he tried to explain gently. "She was a fine animal, kind, gay, and an excellent saddle horse, was the finest in the Regt." Employing another watery allusion to soften the blow, perhaps as much to himself as to the recipient of his correspondence, Voris observed, "Well may she have a fine time in the princely stables of Old Neptune." Finally, he added an indication that the loss of the animal would affect more than himself: "Say nothing to Eddie about it, as I will get him another horse when I get home to stay."[51] Like so many of her human compatriots in these unlikeliest of circumstances, Fanny would not be returning home when the war was finally over.

As Colonel Voris experienced, moving men and animals from point to point exposed them to the dangers of transporting them over those vast distances. When an expedition traveled along the length of the Atlantic coast and into the Gulf of Mexico to reach its destination, the journey was long, grueling, and exceedingly dangerous. A member of the Eighth Vermont remembered stormy conditions that swelled the seas and battered the vessels and their living cargoes. "After twenty-six days at sea," he explained, "without further ill-fortune than the discomfort of the heavy seas and the loss of one hundred and thirty horses, the force arrived at Ship Island on April 5, 1862, and at once landed."[52]

Conditions in the area of Fredericksburg turned particularly difficult for the animals in a Virginia battery as the harshness of winter set in for 1862–1863. The men and horses endured "rain, snow and the coldest kind of weather" and a heavy snowfall on the night of February 21–22 that resulted in the deaths of several of the animals from exposure to these numbing elements.[53]

Panicked animals could cause problems as well, especially when confined in close quarters with human beings crammed aboard steamers or other transports. One Union soldier wrote home to tell of an instance when the mules on his vessel became frightened. The danger on the craft itself must have seemed to outweigh other considerations when "the men that were nerest the Paddle box jumped off into the River." Charles Sherman noted that the captain took immediate measures to recover the swimmers: "A Boat was lowerd and 4 picked up and thair is two missing. One of them the Ordly Sargent of Camp and Named Thomson, a fine fellow. He had just got Promoted." The soldier explained that matters might actually have been worse than they were in the chaotic and deadly moment. "It was very Lucky the Boat was at Anchord," he observed. "If we had been goin every one of them whouled have been Drowned as the Boat whouled have Sucked them under."[54]

Animals served other purposes for the men in the field as well. To function, soldiers in the armies had to eat, but occasionally the consequences of providing such provender as beef on the hoof came at a premature cost to the cattle. On January 22, 1863, hospital steward Spencer Bonsall complained of the effects from a substantial herd of cattle corralled near his posting in Virginia, "In the space between our encampment and the shore, there are about 3,500 head of cattle belonging to the U.S. They are intended for the army, to be manufactured into fresh beef, and are to us a great nuisance, as they keep the whole place in a perfect quagmire and interfere with our passage from the camp to the landing." However, the cattle were not immune to danger outside of potential cook-pots. According to Bonsall, "In unloading cattle today from the boat, which on account of the tide could not approach the shore, 52 head were drowned by their being made to jump overboard and swim."[55]

When the steamer *Ruth* developed difficulty from a fire on a run from St. Louis, Missouri, to Helena, Arkansas, the toll did not just fall upon the humans being transported aboard the vessel. A news account of the tragedy tallied the additional costs: "The boat had on board 99 head of beef cattle, [and] 122 mules," among other supplies destined for the troops in U.S. Grant's army, "all of which was lost."[56]

Another collision on the inland waterways produced apparent fatalities among both the human and nonhuman passengers in August 1863. Silas Haven of the

Twenty-Seventh Iowa wrote his wife from Helena, Arkansas, to say that although his unit arrived safely, "the boat that the 49th IL was on [was] run into night before last and sunk. Five men jumped overboard and was drowned." In addition, he observed, "The regiment lost all their mules, guns ammunition and camp baggage."[57] The next day, as the situation became clearer, Haven modified his initial report of gloomy news by noting, "The 49th IL came in today. They did not lose any men but all their wagons, part of their mules, some guns and a lot of baggage."[58] A surgeon with the Illinois unit noted the accident in his diary: "The Courrier Colided with the Str Des Arch and sunk the former at 3 A.M. We lost Several mules, and considerable other property including tents company records etc."[59]

A Union cavalry private from Vermont recorded a rail accident that accounted for the loss of a number of horses. In a letter to his brother, Charles Chapin described the event and his efforts to extract his comrades from the wreckage. Although a number of them endured various injuries, and at least one died, by his reckoning, the animals suffered most. "The poor horses fared harder still being in the cars while the men were on top," he explained, before adding, "53 of them were killed besides as many more went hobbling about some on two feet some on three."[60]

Union cavalry general Judson Kilpatrick became known as "Kilcavalry," although he could hardly be held responsible for an incident that involved transporting his disabled mounts by rail in late 1863.[61] In that situation, a seventeen-car train was converted from carrying cattle to haul "126 condemned horses," to the rear, along with a detail of soldier guards. In the course of entering a curve too fast, the rails gave way, and part of the train left the track and hurtled down an embankment "as far back as the ninth car down the steep." Many of the humans involved became casualties, but the animals suffered, too. Regarding the mounts that had seen sufficient service to break them down and require them to retire from the field for rest and recuperation, the reporter observed, "Fifty horses were killed or crippled so as to be useless."[62]

Just over a week after this accident, a deliberate act on the part of an unthinking soldier cost an artillery crew serving a heavy battery in Charleston, South Carolina, one of its team. On November 18, Major Edward Manigault noted, "About 10 O'clock one of Capt. Beals' Men, Co. C, 22 Batallion Georgia Artillery, in violation of Standing Orders, shot at a Crane in the middle of the Camp at Battery Haskell, and killed a horse belonging to Captn. Gregg's Battery, Co. 'C' S.C. Siege Train." The unnamed assailant "was immediately arrested and Charges preferred against him."[63]

Other animals in the same command perished when their diets proved insufficient. "One horse belonging to Co. 'A' Siege Train died this morning and one

Mule belonging to Co. 'B' Siege Train," Manigault noted on the day following the accidental shooting in camp. "Both appeared to die of Cholic superinduced perhaps by the inferior Corn furnished to the Animals and the want of fodder."[64]

Adequate care was critical for the health of the horses upon which the opposing armies depended. Failing to allow mounts to cool properly after riding them for extended periods before giving them water could cause debility, if not death. Attention to diet was also essential. As one Union officer observed, "Poor forage, sudden changes of forage, and overfeeding, produced almost as much sickness and physical disability as no forage at all."[65]

Unfortunately, when things went wrong, there was often little that the men could do to mitigate matters. With regard to applying remedies, some efforts proved as disastrous as the afflictions they sought to cure. When the Third Pennsylvania Cavalry suffered a case of "one hundred and ten broken-down quadrupeds on the picket line, neglected and played out," the unit turned to one of its members to restore the animals to fitness. Onetime farmer Elias G. Eyster concocted a mixture in the form of pills, administered to the sick animals with every expectation that the crisis was past. Instead, first one and then others of the horses succumbed, with "a myriad of buzzards" soon circling overhead. The astonished Eyster explained that his method had worked for the English cavalry, and that only the weakest of the animals had given way. As a demonstration of his confidence, he approached one of the horses that seemed spritelier than the rest and gave him a slap on the hindquarters. "There is a horse ready for duty now," he asserted. Instead, the mount "jumped forward, kicked his heels high, fell on his side, gave a terrible resounding groan, a few convulsive kicks, and was dead." The lieutenant sought to defend the "Vets," as the men had dubbed Eyster and his companions, to the incensed major, insisting, "They are good soldiers, but poor doctors." The unit soon received replacements, and the erstwhile veterinarians returned to their normal duties.[66]

Poor diet and overwork produced startling reductions in the animals the armies required to remain functional to the fullest degree of efficiency. Union officer Alfred Hough, stationed in Chattanooga in late 1863, noted in a letter to his wife, "Our animals are all dead or used up, and another supply must be had before we leave the railroad and river" for active campaigning.[67] In early 1864, the effect was more sensorial than martial. From the same posting, he told her, "If it were not for the dead mules lying around town, I could enjoy riding around, for it is really beautiful here naturally."[68]

Campaigning in every theater was hard on men and animals, especially in adverse weather conditions. In April 1864, snow hit the backcountry of Virginia, complicating the movement of cavalry in the region. Confederate staffer Ned Guerrant noted, "Snowed this morning like Lapland. AWFUL!! WEATHER." But his focus was also elsewhere: "R.R. killed & crippled seven horses of 4th K'y. Cav. last night. Some 40 are missing this morning. The balance of the brigade moved on to Saltville this morning."[69]

In Judson Kilpatrick's mounted operations around Atlanta in August 1864, a water crossing proved especially deadly for the pack mules that accompanied his column. At least one soldier had already become a victim when the animals burdened with carrying loads of supplies entered the stream. One participant offered a grim description: "As soon as they reached the swift current they would roll over and down the stream they went, generally all we could see was four legs sticking up out of the water kicking vigorously."[70]

No animals in the major armies required accidents or freak events to lead to their deaths. The battlefield became a terrible killing ground for services that depended on these animals for moving artillery pieces, as well as in the cavalry. However, when the campaigns were over, the dying for these creatures did not subside. The Army of Tennessee experienced critical shortages throughout its history not only from battlefield losses but also from transportation demands. After the disastrous defeat at Nashville in December 1864, an officer assessed that besides losing so many guns in the engagement, the army had suffered even more because "so great a number of horses were killed or starved on the retreat that all companies cannot be furnished, and as a result many batteries will have to be consolidated."[71]

Animals could prove exasperating and dangerous, but they could also display an extraordinary sense of loyalty, even at great risk to themselves. When escapees killed a guard at a prison in Richmond, a newspaper carried the account of a canine's affection for the slain man:

A crowd of soldiers on duty at the prison were soon collected around the scene of this lamentable disaster; but here a singular incident occurred the large dog, (belonging to Capt. Alexander, the commandant of the prison,) whom doubtless all have seen and admired who have ever visited the Castle, took a position alongside the dead body, and would permit no one to approach until the proper officers came up and relieved him of his charge.

The animal seemed to recognize a duty and "followed the corpse into the building, seemingly determined to keep watchful guard over the remains until the last." The writer observed, "This exhibition of affection for the deceased soldier was truly touching, and indeed remarkable." Private Sutton Byrd of the Fifty-Third North Carolina had received an honor guard of a different type in this last tribute to him by the devoted canine.[72]

Animals that served as mascots for units could provide inspiration, but they shared the same dangers as the humans with whom they were associated. When members of the Fourth Minnesota were involved in a fiery accident in Alabama in March 1864, the adjutant of the unit described the circumstances, before noting that not all the fatalities involved people: "George the mascot of Company K was burned up."[73]

A terrible fate also awaited an animal attached to a Union unit patrolling the waters. A young seaman, Charles Mervine, wrote in his journal at the beginning of September 1864 about a troubling shipboard incident during blockade duty: "At 3:15 A.M. this morning Anthony Dougherty came on deck in a state of insanity and after creating a great excitement and killing our favorite cat, he was secured after some trouble and put in double irons." Mervine did not elaborate on why his mate targeted the animal, or on what the feline might have symbolized for the troubled sailor, but despite the dramatic outburst, life and duty were meant to continue unabated. "Pleasant day," he concluded immediately after describing the episode.[74]

For some of these companions and mascots of the individual soldiers and units in the field, service could be as exacting as for the humans involved. In one of the war's earliest engagements at Wilson's Creek or Oak Hills, in August 1861, the casualties were not confined to the men who participated. According to a regimental historian, troops from the Third Louisiana had adopted "a large dark-and-tan colored dog" that had joined them on the march, and the animal quickly became "a universal pet." Because of his tendency to lead the column, the men dubbed him "Sergeant." W. H. Tunnard recalled that as the battle unfolded, the dog remained at the forefront: "Amid the storm of leaden bullets and the fierce rattle of musketry in the first close, deadly and obstinate engagement with the enemy 'Sergeant' charged through the bushes, leaping over logs and obstacles, barking furiously all the time. He seemed to enjoy the fight exceedingly." The actions of their pet animated the men but caused at least one of them to call out a warning for the animal: "Get out of that Sergeant, you d——d fool, you'll be killed." Tunnard observed that almost immediately "a fatal ball struck him, and with a long piteous whine, he rolled on the ground never to rise." The soldier-historian concluded rather incongruously, "The intelligent animal fell among the prostrate forms of many who had fed and caressed him, the victim of his own fearless temerity."[75]

When Captain Werner Von Bachelle fell at Antietam, the "fine Newfoundland dog, which had been trained to perform military salutes and many other remarkable things," remained by his side as he had done in every other circumstance. Forced to abandon the soldier with the ebb and flow of battle, the men returned to the ground to see that "the dog stayed with his master, and was found on the morning of the 19th of September lying dead upon his body." The demonstration of loyalty was not lost on the soldiers. "We buried him with his master. So far as we knew, no family or friends mourned for poor Bachelle, and it is probable he was joined in death by his most devoted friend on earth."[76]

The 11th Pennsylvania received a terrier puppy in camp just after the war had begun. The dog, named "Sallie," became the unit's mascot and learned the military routine readily. She saw action in major engagements from Cedar Mountain to Gettysburg, where she remained on watch over the bodies of some of the fallen human comrades. President Abraham Lincoln doffed his famous stovepipe hat during an inspection when he spotted the faithful canine. Wounded at Spotsylvania, Sallie never faltered from her role until February 5, 1865, when the 11th Pennsylvania charged into the thick of the fighting at Hatcher's Run. Sallie was still with the men when a round struck her head and she died instantly. The surviving men who found her gently buried her in the field where she had fallen, as distraught over her loss as that of any other colleague.[77]

The Confederate equivalent was the Second Maryland Battalion's canine mascot, "Grace." Like Sallie, Grace proceeded into battle with her unit and perished there.[78] Another Southern mascot had a significant distinction from the rest. "Old Douglas" of the Forty-Third Mississippi was a camel, which served as an unusual pack animal for the command. Old Douglas was at Vicksburg when a Union soldier took aim and ended his martial career.[79]

As farmers, teamsters, or anyone else who worked with them could attest outside of the context of war, animals were often unpredictable, creating hazards and causing deaths among the people in whose company they operated. Their loyalty could be equally commendable. However, in all events, such creatures paid as terrible a price in the conflict as their human companions. Whether they became the victims of combat, accident, or malice, even the most innocent animals faced the same uncertainties and dangers. Few circumstances illustrated this better than occurred as Union soldiers moved through Columbia, South Carolina, in 1865. One Union soldier displayed incredible cruelty by killing a puppy as a child played with it outside her home, while another demonstrated equal compassion by consoling the child and helping to bury the slain pet.[80]

6

Not So Friendly Fire
Death at the Hands of
Compatriots, by Accident,
in Personal Confrontations,
or in Affairs of Honor

A great many serious accidents occur from the careless use of firearms, and many limbs and lives have been lost from the bullets of friends, as well as foes.
Spencer Bonsall, Falmouth, Virginia, February 25, 1863

Poor Tobe, he was a good soldier and had passed through many battles and skirmishes, and it seemed hard that he should thus fall at the hands of a friend.
Samuel Sprott on the death of a friend by a comrade

He was young and strong—6 ft and 2 in. high and so straight that they called him Ram-rod—full of plans as any man alive—expecting in time to become the Quartermaster and to go home from the wars in honor if not glory—and there he lies cold.
Death of Quartermaster Sergeant Michael Cowell
by accidental discharge of a sentry's weapon

Many situations combined on Civil War battlefields to give various meanings to the concept the "fog of war." Especially in the earliest phases of the conflict, the uniforms of the combatants contributed to the confusion of battle and the uncertainties that led to misidentification of individuals and troop formations. As such, men lost their lives in ways that seemed to have been not only unnecessary but also avoidable. Compounding these deaths were the ones that came from incidents of mutiny or violence in the guise of defending personal honor or over other perceived grievances.[1]

Friendly fire casualties existed from the outset, with examples prevalent in 1861 in small engagements like Big Bethel and larger ones like First Manassas. Albert Sidney Johnston at Shiloh and Thomas Jonathan "Stonewall" Jackson at Chancellorsville were among the more significant losses from unintended friendly sources. Men also perished when their comrades demonstrated unusual behavior or proved negligent, careless, or incompetent in their handling of the implements of war. Battlefields were understandably hazardous, but one's demise at what should have proved to be friendly hands was hardly uncommon. After a close call with death or injury by a stray shot from friendly sources, Union hospital steward Spencer Bonsall concluded of the incident, "A great many serious accidents occur from the careless use of firearms, and many limbs and lives have been lost from the bullets of friends, as well as foes."[2]

Mishaps in the confusion of battle never subsided as long as hostilities remained in effect, and soldiers perished at the hands of comrades throughout the conflict. The chaos of combat contributed to situations in which men perished at the hands of their friends as forces deployed across unfamiliar and disputed ground. Dr. J. Weist of Ohio described in vivid fashion his view of a battle that included a gruesome moment where one fallen soldier "has been crushed by the wheel of a passing cannon."[3] According to historian Gordon Rhea, at the bitter fighting around Spotsylvania Court House in Virginia in 1864, in at least one instance as artillery pieces moved, "The guns' wheels crushed the dead and wounded into the mud."[4]

The swift movement or sudden appearance of troops in proximity to an opposing force could produce unintended deaths and wounds among friendly forces. Mistaken identity cost the life of at least one Confederate by his own comrades in Virginia. Dragoon lieutenant John Sheffey recorded in his diary at the end of September 1861, "One of our scouts was killed yesterday by another of our own men—under the belief that he was one of the enemy." In the fluid environment of the early stages of the war, he added, "Such occurrences were not rare. I was myself upon a scout while we were returning from Gauley—and was in imminent peril from the same cause."[5] Then, in November, such uncertain circumstances led to tragedy when Georgia troops fired on their Virginia cavalry comrades in a case of mistaken identity.[6]

At least two members of Louisiana units in Virginia lost their lives at the hands of comrades who mistook them for Union troops on the picket lines in the dark. An unnamed sergeant and Lieutenant Alfred Scanlon of the Tenth Louisiana died in separate, although similar, circumstances as they attempted to inspect the posts under their authority.[7]

Destined to lead the Fifty-Fourth Massachusetts to glory against Fort Wagner in South Carolina, Robert Gould Shaw was in Virginia with another command in the spring of 1862. He noted a "friendly fire" incident in a letter home on March 9: "Night before last there was a great alarm and a Maryland (Union) regiment fired into a body of our own cavalry killing three horses & one man. It was a very unfortunate thing and it doesn't seem to be decided, who was most to blame—the Marylanders or the Michigan Cavalry."[8]

Confusion over the proper identification of potential targets was an ever-present danger on the Civil War battlefield, especially early in the war. On March 18, 1862, Wesley Gould wrote his sister in part to commiserate with her over the death of their brother Charles to disease. Then he added a description of an incident among his comrades in South Carolina. "Last week there were three of our companies out a scouting," he explained. "They were out at night. They met unexpectedly, and it being so dark they could not tell each other, so Co. H fired a volley of musket balls into Co. K killing the captain and one of the corporals instantly and wounding 7 more. One has since died."[9]

The expedition in which this mishap occurred had been designed for the capture of Confederate pickets in an area that the reporting officer described as "on the mainland at the plantation of a Mr. Mattis," based on intelligence provided by runaway slaves according to an after-action report. Lieutenant Colonel James A. Beaver explained that he divided the approaching parties into three parts and moved at night to surprise the Southern sentinels. Unfortunately for the participants, misidentification led to fire from one of the attacking columns, "resulting in the death of Captain Rambo and Corporal Reighand of Company K, of the forty-first Regiment Pennsylvania Volunteers, and the wounding of several others, privates in the same company, one of whom has since died from the effects of his wound."[10]

On May 23, 1862, the Newbern Weekly Progress in North Carolina reported, "A fatal accident occurred in the 2d., Maryland regiment, last Friday night. It seems that a German soldier of Company I, crossed the lines, unseen in the darkness, after eight o'clock, and on his return, was challenged by the sentry." Whether a language barrier contributed to the circumstances or the soldier simply did not hear and understand the challenge, deadly uncertainty remained. According to the account, "Failing to make any reply, the sentinel shot him and the man died of his wounds the next day."[11]

Minnesotan James Wright recalled a different incident in Virginia in the summer of 1862 that involved his regiment and members of the Nineteenth Massachusetts. "We did not dream of it then, but another tragedy was to be added to the already too long list of accidents connected with military movements at night—and that, too, at a moment when the greatest danger seemed to be over," he recalled. In a moonlit night, as firing suddenly developed, the road on which the Minnesotans were moving seemed to come alive. According to Wright, "Our training as soldiers and the instinct of self-preservation all prompted us to resistance, and—without waiting for orders—we fired—some at the passing horsemen and some up the road, from which direction most of the bullets were coming." The firing stopped. "The whole affair had scarcely exceeded a minute in duration." The real impact quickly became clear. "But in that brief interval," Wright recalled, "brave men who had periled their lives together in defense of their country suffered deaths and wounds at the hands of each other. A number of men had been hit." For the Minnesotans, the "loss of the regiment had been two killed and nine wounded." A New York command had also been involved, "supposing they were the enemy." Wright concluded, "It was an unfortunate, pitiable affair, but none of the participants are really to blame for their part in it. It was simply a mistake, when everyone was trying to do the best they could and really did the proper and common-sense thing as they understood the situation. The loss of the Nineteenth and of the cavalry was about the same as our regiment."[12]

John B. Woodward recorded the story of an individual who had a decidedly different encounter as a rail guard in what he described as a "melancholy accident." On August 14, 1862, he noted the "death of Corporal Holt of E Company" because of "gross carelessness," as a "member of picket guard No. 2, posted on the railroad." Holt and his comrades had just been relieved "and were coming into camp, marching down the track," when the men of "guard No. 1" approached along a different path. The officer in charge of that detachment of the Fourth New York Volunteers did not want the men to return with loaded muskets and commanded them to face the tracks "and they discharged their pieces by volley." Unfortunately, rather than firing harmlessly, the rounds struck the corporal fatally. "The escape of the others is simply miraculous," Woodward observed, but added, "As usual in such cases the victim was one of the very best soldiers in the regiment."[13] Another Union soldier captured the sentiment earlier with the observation, "Our line of pickets are quite reckless in their sports and freaks when on duty.

Firing frequently contrary to orders, and venturing from their posts in which case they are liable to shoot each other, and be shot at by friends of other regiments."[14]

Picket fire was responsible for another death in Tennessee, in the summer of 1862. While posted at Bethel, surgeon James Black noted the severe wounding of a comrade. "Serg't Wm. G. McKinney was Shot accidentally this morning at 3.0'clock, and his *thigh broken*, by James Davis Co. 'K,, 49 Ills Inft. while on Picket," the doctor wrote on July 7. Approximately a week later, Black was optimistic. "I got a Pass and went to Jackson Tenn. to see Serg't McKinney," he noted on July 16. "He is apparently doing well some hopes entertained of his recovery." Then, a turn for the worse left the ailing soldier in mortal danger, and on August 11 the surgeon posted the entry, "Srg't Wm. G. McKinney died at Jackson, Tenn. to-day."[15]

While moving through the region in early January 1863, Edward Guerrant happened upon a group of local residents "performing the last obsequies to the mortal remains of a dead soldier—a young man—a Kentuckian. Killed in the road nearby—by one of our own pickets—Wynn. Who was that unfortunate boy—Jason Mark of Montgomery Co., K'y." Guerrant's inquiries led him to conclude, "It is thought he was asleep on his horse & didn't hear the sentinel when he challenged, & unconscious, rode in at the gate of Death. Farewell, poor boy."[16]

Often circumstances arose that created the context for the reactions of soldiers charged with protecting their campmates. In May 1863, at Folly Island, South Carolina, the actions of Southern guerrillas in harassing Union pickets led to a tragedy when a captain in the Sixty-Second Ohio approached nervous sentries on the following evening. In the uncertainty of the moment, one of the men fired at the figure, and Captain Bazell Rogers "was shot dead by one of his own men taking him for a rebel."[17]

On January 28, 1864, Brigadier General Thomas E. G. Ransom reported the results of a reconnaissance that had taken place on Matagorda Peninsula a few days earlier. The expedition had experienced one unfortunate incident. As Ransom described it, "I regret to be obliged to report the death of Capt. Charles R. March, of the Thirteenth Maine Infantry, who died on the 23d instant of a wound in the head, received from a shot fired by a sailor of the steamer Sciota, who had landed with Colonel Hesseltine's regiment to get a beef." Major General Napoleon J. T. Dana, commanding the Union forces in Texas, forwarded the relatively routine communication, citing an "entirely successful" operation that had occurred "without loss or accident," before adding incongruously, "except the sad death of Capt. Charles R. March."[18]

Mistakes, miscalculations, and misfires resulted in unintended deaths among friendly forces from the outset of the conflict, but when artillery shot and shell fell on such targets, the results were often devastating and always unforgetta-ble. At the Battle of Wilson's Creek or Oak Hills, in August 1861, Confeder-ate attackers captured several Union cannon, but fire meant to assist them had a different effect. W. H. Tunnard of the Third Louisiana explained, "Here fell Capt. Hinson, of Company B, and his brother-in-law, Mr. Whitstone, killed by an unfortunate shot from one of our own batteries, under charge of Capt. Reed, which unknown to the regiment, had been pouring a heavy and destructive fire upon these guns."[19]

Circumstances continued to exist in which individuals died inadvertently from rounds meant to be expended against their opponents. In a poignant letter to the widow of a comrade, Lieutenant A. T. Martin expressed his condolences and per-sonal sense of loss. "It becomes my sad and painful duty to inform you of the death of your beloved consort, Andrew Devilbliss, who was killed in the attack on this place October 30, 1864," Martin explained from Florence, Alabama. Although the sense of loss was no less great than it might have been otherwise, Devilbliss had not died at the hands of the enemy. Instead, "He was wounded mortally by one of our own shells and expired almost immediately. His last words were 'Lieu-tenant, write to my wife.'" Martin testified as to the slain man's character and esteem, noting where his gravesite could be found before closing, "Sympathizing with you in your affliction and knowing a just God will console you in distress, I am very resp'y, Lt. A. T. Martin."[20]

In the chaotic combat that marked the Knoxville Campaign of 1863, soldiers found themselves the unwitting victims of their own fire. During the early phases of an assault on Fort Sanders by James Longstreet's Confederates, one of the Union artillery shells burst prematurely, killing one Federal comrade and wound-ing another.[21] Union troops also fell victim to their own actions in the summer of 1864 as David Hunter retreated from the vicinity of Lynchburg, Virginia, while conducting a raid. Alabamian Joel Calvin McDiarmid noted in a diary entry on June 21 that as the Confederates pursued, they came across evidence of efforts to destroy supplies that cost some of the retreating men their lives: "They set fire to some ordnance wagons that had barrels of powder in them, which exploded while some of their men were passing, killing six or eight men." McDiarmid observed almost clinically of the scene, "We saw their mangled forms lying on the roadside. Some of them had their legs and arms torn off and thrown fifty yards from their bodies."[22]

In the horrific fighting that later marked the battle of Franklin, Tennessee, in John Bell Hood's 1864 Campaign, friendly fire accounted for a portion of the casualties there as well. During the assault on the Union defensive positions of John Schofield, a participant recalled, "Lieut. Frank H. Hale, of Co. H, succeeded in scaling the works and crawled about twenty feet inside the Federal lines to the frame house . . . stood in the yard of the Carter house, where he was killed, filled with bullets from the guns of his own regiment."[23]

The most high-profile instances of the phenomenon involved the highest-ranking members of the military or their staff members. Friendly fire almost certainly cost the life of Albert Sidney Johnston as he attempted to direct the Confederate advance against the Union forces at Shiloh on April 6, 1862. Having led men across a landscape dotted by Union camps, woods, fields, and ravines, he remained on his horse, Fire-eater, in the vicinity of Sarah Bell's peach orchard, when the fatal round struck. Johnston had suffered a wound in the leg from a pre-war duel that deadened his ability to sense the injury and, although he carried a tourniquet on his person, failed to detect the need to use it. Swaying in the saddle when Tennessee governor Isham Harris, acting as a volunteer aide, approached, he responded to an inquiry as to his being wounded, "Yes, and I fear seriously." Captain W. L. Wickham and Harris helped the stricken general from his horse and took him into a ravine to avoid additional fire. Already ashen and in shock, Johnston was now unresponsive. Colonel William Preston, the general's former brother-in-law, arrived from his role in the fighting and asked, "Johnston, do you know me?" However, there was no sense that Johnston understood. Shortly, he ceased to breathe, and the Confederacy had lost its highest-ranking general killed during a battle.[24]

In determining the nature and source of Johnston's fatal wounding, historian Wiley Sword observed, "Certainly the movements of a general on horseback are not precisely definable, and it is impossible to say with certainty where Johnston was positioned when he was struck. From the direction of the charge, the weapons carried," and the position of the Confederate forces, "it seems probable that a stray ball fired by one of his own men during the attack inflicted the fatal wound."[25]

Albert Sidney Johnston's death had far-reaching implications, as did that resulting from the most famous instance of friendly fire, which came at the close of the first day of fighting at Chancellorsville. Following a spectacular flanking march that ended in a furious assault late in the day on May 2, 1863, Thomas J. "Stonewall" Jackson's men drove back Union troops under Oliver O. Howard. The Confederate commander sought to determine the status of conditions to his front and rode from his lines in the gathering darkness to reconnoiter. As he approached a portion of the Southern lines whose defenders were unaware of his presence to their front, the riders attracted first sporadic, and then sustained, fire. Jackson took rounds to his right hand and left wrist and arm. The last proved the most destructive to the stalwart warrior.

Somehow, Jackson survived the fusillade and the enormous fire that both sides now opened on the scene. Pulling him to the rear, the men who carried their injured leader could do nothing to alleviate his anguish. Finally, Jackson reached an ambulance, and although continuing agonies awaited, he moved off from the field and immediate danger. Surgeon Hunter McGuire tended his superior, but early in the morning of May 3, it became apparent that for Jackson to have any chance for survival, the shattered limb had to be removed. Jackson endured the amputation and began to show signs of improvement, but sepsis proved a more difficult opponent to overcome than any other he had faced in combat. In an increasingly weakened condition, "Lee's Right Arm" succumbed on May 10.[26]

Almost a year later, at the Battle of the Wilderness, Confederate general James Longstreet, "Lee's War Horse," nearly suffered the same fate at the hands of friendly units. Micah Jenkins was not so fortunate to escape, as were other members of the party. In the swirl and confusion of battle, Jenkins took a round in the head from which he ultimately perished. Captain Alfred E. Doby and Private Benjamin B. White died at the scene. Joseph Kershaw had tried to suppress the fire by calling out "They are friends," and then yelling, "F-r-i-e-n-d-s!" His efforts proved too late, for the damage had already been done.[27]

Soldiers did not have to be near fighting to have similar instances occur. The challenges of the earliest days of the conflict produced fatal accidents sustained as training for war unfolded. Instruction and drills meant to save lives could cost them instead. In one situation, occurring in October 1861, a Washington newspaper noted, "A. H. Stewart, a soldier of the seventh New Jersey regiment, was accidentally killed, while on guard, Wednesday, at the camp on Meridian Hill. His sergeant was instructing him in some of the details of his duty when his musket was accidentally discharged, the ball entering his body, and causing his speedy death."[28]

Other accidents resulted from drills gone awry. At bayonet practice, one Union soldier caught the hammer of his musket on his clothing, causing the weapon to discharge. The round struck a sergeant in his upper torso. The victim had endured two wounds at Bull Run, but his long-term health was less certain at the hands of a comrade. The account noted, "He lies in a precarious condition, but being of a strong constitution the surgeons think he will ultimately recover." The unwitting assailant, who had survived a battle wound of his own, "had seen the result of his carelessness (in drilling with a loaded gun)" and reported to his commander's tent, insisting, "'O, Captain, for God's sake shoot me; I don't want to live a minute, I've killed poor Cummings.'" Unfortunately, his assessment proved accurate, with the wounded sergeant dying the following month.[29]

Sometimes soldiers simply engaged in behavior that would be perplexing to any sober observer. The deaths that resulted from these incidents were as senseless as they were wasteful of personnel who would otherwise be able, theoretically, to continue their service. When curiosity morphed with a lack of prudence, the outcomes might appear to be obvious in hindsight but were clearly lost on those who engaged in those questionable practices. Others became the victims of completely unintended and inadvertent circumstances they could not have foreseen and thus had no reasonable opportunity of avoiding.

In the early war period, even as men trained to become soldiers, horseplay accounted for some of the inadvertent deaths that occurred. One such instance took place in the fall of 1861 when a lighthearted encounter turned deadly in the area of Fort Caswell, on the coast of North Carolina. The "melancholy accident" happened as "a young man named Lee" neared a guard post. According to a newspaper account, "It would seem that Mr. Lee got shot and instantly killed by a gun in the hands of another member of the company named Westbrook." The latter had just been relieved of his duty, with what was supposed to be an uncapped weapon that also remained loaded. Seeing his friend approach, Westbrook "playfully halted him and raising his gun pulled the trigger; not of course expecting it to go off without the cap, but it did, and the ball entered Lee's chest, killing him almost instantly." The unwitting assailant "was immediately placed under arrest."[30]

In December 1861, the *Richmond Daily Dispatch* reported an account from a Columbia, South Carolina, newspaper on the twenty-fifth that featured a situation that arose from unfortunate and preventable circumstances: "A fatal accident occurred at the headquarters of the Rebel Guards yesterday afternoon. It appears that two of the members, named Wm. Starling and Warren Cooper, were scuffling playfully, when a gun in the hands of Cooper was accidentally fired, striking Starling in the left Breast and killing him instantly."[31]

Eighteen hundred sixty-two was less than two weeks old when Private James H. Gronto, a farmer from Princess Anne County when he enlisted in a Virginia regiment, died by the accidental discharge of a musket in his home state.[32] A newspaper account offered additional details: "An accident which resulted in the death of a volunteer, occurred at the Guard House, in this city, on Saturday afternoon, about two o'clock." According to the *Richmond Daily Dispatch*, "James H. Gontor, a member of Company F, Sixth Virginia Regiment and W. H. Rainey, a member of the same command, were sky-larking, it appears, when a pistol in the hand of the latter, was accidentally discharged, the contents of which entered the head of Mr. Gontor, inst above the right eye, and passed obliquely over the left, tearing out his brain and killing him immediately, at Norfolk."[33]

On October 20, 1862, another "fatal accident from the careless use of fire-arms" made the news in the Confederate capital. "A member of the town guard of Manchester, commanded by Captain Mosby, was instantly killed, at an early hour yesterday morning by a fellow soldier." The writer explained, "One of the men, who had just come off guard duty, entered the barrack where a number of his comrades were sleeping," with his weapon still in his hands. One of the men awoke, and the guard "pointed his musket" in his direction. The comrade called for him to put the weapon down, but this demand "only made him more assidu-ous in showing that no possible danger could result from his procedure." As fate would have it, "the musket exploded, and the ball entering the head of the half sleeping soldier blew the entire top of his skull off. The originator of the accident was taken in custody."[34]

A death resulting from rambunctiousness between comrades happened in Virginia in November of the same year. Edward King Wightman of the Sixth New York explained the matter "of a little incident" to his brother. The situation involved members of "a German regiment, the 103rd N.Y.V., who in common with all their countrymen are quick tempered and almost ungovernable, nothing being more justly ranked among daily occurrences than Dutch Fights—officers and men alike partaking in them." While returning from dress parade, Wightman noticed a crowd gathered by a tent and found the men making a "post-mortem examination of a German just killed 'by a friend.'" The incident involved two comrades, "bantering each other on their respective delinquencies in the bayonet exercise, [who] had adjourned to a quiet part of the wood, and there, after a short trial of skill and a few passes, the foot of one had slipped over a rolling stone, and the heart of the other was pierced with cold steel." The question of culpability quickly settled with "a regimental funeral, and the death was, of course, pro-nounced 'accidental.'"[35]

In late 1862, Sergeant Major Stephen F. Flerharty wrote from his "Camp 'Lost River' near Bowling Green" to relate the tale of a foolish and fatal encounter. "To-day a member of the 108th Ohio, in camp here, was accidentally shot through the head and instantly killed," he explained on November 10. "A comrade sport-ively cocked his gun, aimed it at him—supposing it unloaded—pulled the trigger, and the poor fellow fell dead at his feet." The shock of the incident gave way to rumination: "It was a sad accident, and the wretched survivor has learned a lesson in blood which should have been the legacy of common sense."[36]

Even in the latter stages of the conflict, tragedy could unfold when individ-uals became complacent in their duties. In the winter of 1864, on what he re-membered was "a beautiful moonlight night," Samuel Sprott heard a shot on the picket line. "I had heard such a cry too often not to know what it meant," he observed, but he did not learn until he reached the location that one Confederate had shot another inadvertently. Two friends, John Praytor and J. P. Vann, were pacing their lines when a third person arrived, and Praytor remarked, "Now if he was a Yankee I could get him," while aiming in Vann's direction. When a shot suddenly rang out and Vann dropped, the extent of the tragedy reached its height. "No one was more surprised than Praytor," Sprott related, "he and Vann were perfectly friendly at the time and, in fact, there had never been any trouble between them." Nevertheless, the soldier had received a fatal shot and died the next day. "Poor Tobe," Sprott noted of the slain warrior, "he was a good soldier and had passed through many battles and skirmishes, and it seemed hard that he should thus fall at the hands of a friend."[37]

Alcohol was a frequent component in deadly situations arising between would-be friends. Men prone to excess when enjoying libations presented threats to others that increased the risks for themselves. Hard-drinking Michael Farrell of the Fourth Kentucky Cavalry was already known as a "dangerous drunk" when he took occasion to wield a stolen sword and approached Lieutenant Sylvester Raplee in a threatening manner. Raplee tried the improvised expedient of tossing a rock at Farrell, but the gesture failed to stop him, and the officer resorted to his sidearm in the extremity. Others considered the officer's actions justifiable under the circumstances.[38]

When Edward O. Guerrant received confirmation of the death of the son of the general on whose staff he had served, he almost immediately knew the cause. "How sorry I am to learn of the death of Capt. Jno. Marshall, son of General Humphrey Marshall, who was killed in a personal difficulty with one Lt. Roberts in Castle Woods" in southwest Virginia, Guerrant wrote on February 16, 1865. "Without a serious difficulty, or grave altercation between them, with no adequate cause, (if any cause could be adequate to produce so dreadful a result) for the perpetration of such a crime, Roberts drew a pistol after some hasty wor[d]s between them & shot him through the bowels. This about Friday evening, which resulted in his death about sunrise on last Saturday morning, 11h." However, the Kentuckian felt confident that heated language was not alone to blame. "Another triumph of 'the Still,' another victim on the crowded, bloody altar of Bacchus. A sacrifice to the bad habit of intemperance, & dissipation this gallant young officer, fond son, & promising man has offered up his life in the very pride of his manhood, the very flower of his strength & his years. Alas poor John! You deserved a better fate!"[39]

Several incidents illustrate the most bizarre of the wartime deaths not attributable to a battlefield engagement. One took place in a boxing match that ended badly. Private Meridith D. Stamper was sparring with Private H. D. Wagoner from the Twenty-Sixth North Carolina in April 1862 when a blow cost Wagoner's life.[40] Another occurred on October 7 of the same year and involved a fatal encounter tinged by the presence of spirituous drink. According to an account in a Virginia newspaper, "About 12 o'clock yesterday two members of Capt. Whitingham's artillery battery, encamped in the vicinity of the Central Fair Grounds, named Patrick Fagan and James Morrissey, while slightly under the influence of liquor, began a dispute, which ended in Fagan, who is a strong and hearty man, striking Morrissey, who was a feeble old man, a violent blow on the side of the neck with his fist." The impact was decisive. "Morrissey instantly fell dead. This astounding result of a single blow with the fist seemed to overcome Fagan with horror, who stood in stupefied amazement until taken into custody by some of his comrades, who conveyed him to Castle Thunder, where he is now a prisoner."[41]

When not engaged in dangerous pugilistic adventures, the men in the ranks could indulge in other doubtful activities. Andrew Evans wrote his brother Sam to convey news from home: "Elliot Eubanks, was brought home dead Friday last. He was a member of the 7th O Cavalry stationed at Harrodsburg, Ky. and lost his life by fooling with a shell." The unfortunate soldier had not fallen prey to any utilitarian effort gone wrong but to a misguided prank. "He threw it into the fire to scare somebody, & it killed him and hurt some others." Andrew drew a lesson from the incident, declaring it "a clear warning loaded shells should not be tampered with."[42]

Similarly, in a camp in Virginia, some of the members of the First New York Dragoons engaged in the habit of tossing rounds of ammunition into fires as others stood nearby to watch their reactions. What must have appeared to be harmless pranks turned deadly as Sergeant Peter Gunther leaned over one blaze to light the tobacco in his pipe, "when some one jokingly threw in a cartridge, which, exploding drove the ball through his head," according to the regiment's historian. Reverend James R. Bowen concluded of the incident, "This put an end to a foolish practice that had to some extent prevailed."[43]

Likewise, card games and other seemingly innocent diversions could provide the circumstances for fatal encounters among would-be comrades. In April 1862, two men from Company A, Sixtieth New York, were engaged in a game when one accused the other of cheating and threatened to shoot him. According to the chaplain who recorded the incident, the soldiers were actually friends, and the threat was made lightheartedly. However, when Elderkin Rose carried the playful moment further, jest turned to tragedy when he waved an old pistol he thought was unloaded and the discharge struck Wallace Smith fatally in the chest. The mortified assailant was inconsolable about the death of his comrade.[44] Another such situation involved the discovery of eight soldiers gathered away from camp without passes and playing dominoes on the evening of December 3, 1864. When Edward Underhill attempted to arrest the men, some of them took an opportunity to make a dash for one of the doors. Calling for the men to halt, the frustrated officer drew his service revolver, fired, and killed Private John Redman as he tried to run away.[45]

Any soldiers who wandered off in search of sustenance or recreation outside of the confines of their camps or fortifications could put their lives at risk from roving guerrillas or bushwhackers. However, in the case of some of the men posted at Holly Springs, Mississippi, in the summer of 1864, the danger came from a closer and less likely source. On August 28, 1864, Dr. James Black recorded in his diary one such instance: "Two men killed by our own men shooting at hogs. one of them belonged to the 58th Ills."[46]

Urban centers presented different, but no less lethal threats. On January 15, 1862, the *Richmond Daily Dispatch* reprinted an account of another odd fatality from "Norfolk, Jan. 14," which read, "A gentleman by the name of Ray, belonging to the 7th Louisiana regiment, fell from a window in the third story of the Atlantic Hotel, last night, and died in a few minutes."[47] What he had been doing in such a precarious and dangerous position remained a mystery.

The same situation occurred with another soldier in Richmond. On October 20, one of the city's newspapers told its readers, "Yesterday, about half-past 2 o'clock, a soldier named Charles Cluts, belonging to the 7th North Carolina, fell from one of the rear windows of the barrack on Franklin street, and striking (after a descent of 20 feet) on a door which was open below lodged on it." The impact of the blow was significant, with Cluts "taken off quite dead having no doubt broken his back, besides sustaining other injuries."[48]

Perhaps one of the strangest events of the war took place in the camps of the Sixth Virginia Infantry at the end of 1863. Robberies had plagued William Mahone's command to the extent that officers took extraordinary steps to secure their property. Apparently not receiving permission to post traditional sentries for the duty, the regiment chose instead to use a youthful African American armed with a musket loaded with peas. When Private John W. Hudson of the Sixteenth Virginia approached the lad, the fellow fired at him. Even this might have been survivable, but the guard remained persistent in his duty and clubbed Hudson in the head. The soldier's death led to an outburst of his comrades against the assailant. Only personal intervention by General Mahone prevented further mayhem or loss of life from occurring as a result of the incident.[49]

Accidents plagued individuals and deprived them of the opportunity to continue the fight against their traditional enemies, although they could also lead to expressions of grim humor. In one case, a soldier lying severely wounded by an accidental discharge of a firearm recovered his senses enough to make a request of the surgeon attending him. A historian of the First Minnesota Infantry explained, "One day he said, 'Doctor, will you stop those fellows from playing that tune?'" The music the band had been practicing within earshot was the "Dead March." The zealous musicians had obviously intended nothing deliberately callous, the medical officer explained. "They thought it was to be their first chance for a military funeral."[50]

In some instances, enough information did not exist to determine the exact nature of a fatality by those who heard about it from afar. Writing to his mother from "Camp Magnolia" on August 2, 1861, William C. Nelson provided a picture of his current circumstances and added a notice of those who had perished. Several of these friends were reported to have been killed at Manassas, but the disturbing news was of a comrade "killed accidentally two days after the battle."[51]

Nelson did not know much about the soldier, including his identity, but the man to whom he referred was eighteen-year-old Thomas Tucker, one of two brothers who had attended the University of Mississippi just prior to the war, enlisted, and then suffered a wound at First Manassas. His death occurred when he was killed "by an accidental discharge of an officer's gun on July 23, 1861."[52]

The Confederate Seventh Tennessee Infantry suffered the first of two early deaths due to special circumstances. Records indicated that a prewar clerk, Private William J. Bruce, was "accidentally killed by gunshot," on August 17. Then, on November 23, the roster of the regiment listed former teacher Private Harrison S. Clark as "accidentally killed," without additional elaboration as to the nature of the situation that had led to his untimely demise.[53]

Such accidents seemed to plague the developing citizen-soldiers. Anxious to confront their enemies in battle in the area of Harpers Ferry, the men of the Twenty-Eighth Pennsylvania answered the long roll for what turned out to be a false alarm. In a letter to his brother on August 8, 1861, Ambrose Henry Hayward explained that the word came down, "thus relieving the minds of our gallant 28th from the thoughts of meeting the Rebels" and necessitating a "change" to an "attack upon salt pork and Hard Crackers as it was past the time" to eat. Unfortunately, not all was lighthearted, for the chaos of the moment proved deadly for one of the soldiers. Hayward explained, "During the excitement a member of Company I was caping his rifel when it went of and the ball passed through the head of one of his owne Company killing him instantly."[54]

Another comrade reported on the incident in more detail. Corporal William Roberts noted the "excitement" and "one very sad occurrence." Private James McGoldrick "was standing in front of the tent & some fool was playing with a loaded rifle, right in front of him, when the trigger fell on the cap, & the load was discharged right into his temple coming out the back of his head. He fell a corpse without uttering a groan."[55]

In October 1861, a soldier from "one of the Pennsylvania regiments" had just retired from sentry duty and entered his tent, when a comrade "outside of the tent, in fitting a cap on his musket, accidentally let the hammer fall, and the piece discharged, with fatal effect." The shot hit the victim "through the breast, and [he] died almost instantly."[56]

Ill tidings continued to emanate from Washington as the spate of accidents and unfortunate incidents continued. On October 10 the tale of "Tarman Roff, a native of New Jersey, and a member of company B, second regiment of Fire Zouaves," appeared in a Richmond newspaper. Roff "was accidentally shot at Camp McClellan, in Maryland, on Monday last, and died the following morning. He was in his tent and a comrade in an adjoining tent threw down a musket, which, being at full cock, was discharged. It was loaded with a ball and three buckshot, and one of the latter entered the right groin of Roff and ruptured the intestines, causing his death."[57]

A month later, the martial career of Corporal Francis Muncy came to an abrupt end when he was "accidentally shot" at Camp Dickerson. The twenty-two-year-old prewar farmer from Lee County, Virginia, had traveled to Wytheville, Virginia, to enlist.[58] After a cavalry officer perished at the hands of a comrade in Frederick, Maryland, on November 13, an account in the *National Republican* of Washington shared the news with readers: "Lieut. Annon, of Capt. Horner's cavalry of the Home Brigade, was instantly killed this afternoon, at 5 o'clock, at the barracks, by the accidental discharge of a carbine in the hands of a private soldier." The men seemed to be "conversing together," while the private was twiddling with his weapon by "moving the gun-hammer with his foot,(!)," the writer noted, adding his own editorial sense of incredulity to the moment, "when it slipped, and the load entered the unfortunate officer's forehead."[59]

In the distant Trans-Mississippi, the year ended with the unintentional death of a Confederate cavalryman. James C. Bates recorded in his diary entry for "Mon. Dec. 30th 1861 This morning one of Whitfield's Battalion was killed by an accidental discharge of a six shooter." Whether purely accidental or the result of carelessness, it had been fortunate that others did not suffer similar fates. "On yesterday two of his men were wounded in like manner," he added.[60]

Georgia cavalryman William Gaston Delony related a tragic incident to his wife from his camp in Virginia in March 1862: "I have a poor fellow in Camp dying hour by hour from a gun shot wound. One of his comrades was examining a new pistol which he did not understand. It went off in his hands and four balls entered his shoulder & arm. 3 of the balls cannot be found & the Surgeon thinks he is bleeding internally slowly to death." Delony's description of his fallen associate reflected the sense that the victims of such accidents were often among the best members in the unit: "He is a fine young fellow by the name of Tucker Barrett from Lumpkin Co.—a good soldier & a clever man."[61]

An incident in March 1862 caused Chaplain Joseph Twichell to ponder questions of mortality and immortality. As Twichell wrote, "Last Tuesday night, Quartermaster's Sergeant [Michael C.] Cowell—a young man—24 years old—son of a most respectable Irish physician in New York—received a mortal wound by the accidental discharge of a sentinel's musket just as he was in the act of giving the countersign." As part of his duties, the chaplain ministered to the wounded warrior and friend as he "lingered in great agony for twenty-six hours" before succumbing. "The death of Mr. Cowell as well as the manner of it threw an unusual gloom over the regiment," Twichell explained. The Protestant minister agonized over the degree to which he could provide comfort to a dying man, while remaining true to the need for the individual to embrace his eternal fate honestly. "I knew Cowell well. His tent was next to mine and our intercourse was frequent and always agreeable." The chaplain thought highly of his compatriot and regretted the circumstances that had cut short the man's life. "Poor fellow! He was young and strong—6 ft and 2 in. high and so straight that they called him Ram-rod—full of plans as any man alive—expecting in time to become the Quartermaster and to go home from the wars in honor if not glory—and there he lies cold."[62]

Another shooting mishap took place as Maine troops moved through the Shenandoah Valley in June 1862. Diarist John M. Gould noted at the end of the month, "The most melancholy event of the week occurred this morning while resting. Orderly Serg't. Frank H. Pratt of Co. K (Lewiston) was accidentally shot by some ones kicking a guns hammer, which exploded the gun sending the bullet under the cheek and coming out over the right eye killing him instantly." The disturbing event was made more so for Gould because of his acquaintance with the victim. As Gould remarked in his journal, "He was a fine fellow, smart and of rather good education and appearance. I have had considerable intercourse with him while Serg't. Major and to see him lying there with the life blood pouring from the two wounds was more sickening than anything I have seen during the war."[63]

New Yorker Charles Johnson related another incident in his diary on September 1, 1862: "Charles W. Haltzman was accidentally shot while on his post on guard this morning." The event was all the more regrettable because of steps supposedly taken to avoid such situations. "A member of our own Company was the unfortunate cause of the accident, he being in the act of taking the cap from his piece *for greater safety* when it was discharged into poor Haltzman's head."

Johnson rushed to the scene "and was in time to see the poor boy where he had fallen, with his head in a dark pool of blood, presenting a ghastly picture." Haltz-man had asked his friend a few days earlier to make a sketch of him, and Johnson observed, "I am very sorry I did not do so then, as it might have been of some comfort to his poor mother."[64]

New Yorker Peter Weinstein, who had been nineteen at the time of his en-listment, died "by accident" on May 12, 1863, at Falmouth, Virginia.[65] Although the precise nature of this incident did not appear in the description on the rolls, or whether it had occurred because of his own actions or those of another, the circumstances nevertheless illustrated the fact that as the war progressed, men continued to perish under unusual conditions.

On June 2, 1863, a Staunton, Virginia, newspaper presented a story of another tragedy to its readership: "An accident occurred on the 25th ult., on the road leading from Dayton to Bridgewater, Rockingham county, which caused the in-stantaneous death of a member of Witcher's Battalion, named—FINLEY. A musket in the hands of a comrade, was accidentally discharged, the ball, striking Finley's gun, glanced off, entering his breast and passing upward, produced death."[66] Later in the month, an Indiana newspaper noted, "James A. Reynolds, of the 46th Ind. Reg . . . was killed a few days since in front of Vicksburg, by the accidental discharge of a gun in the hands of a comrade."[67]

For one individual, facing the dangers of battle in Mississippi, the worst threat came not from opposing shot and shell or bullets but from his own weapon. Z. A. Easterling was moving forward with his comrades when, as one of them recorded, "a sad accident occurred." William Pitt Chambers noted that the soldier was "weak from his recent illness" and quickly became "utterly exhausted" from the exertions of "our forced march." He stopped to rest beneath a tree, but when firing started again, "he took his gun by the muzzle to draw it to him. The ham-mer struck the tree, the cap exploded and the whole charge struck his right arm, literally tearing it to fragments from the wrist to above the elbow. Never will I forget the horror-stricken face as he cried, 'Oh! Pitt, I have ruined my arm!'"[68]

Taken to the rear, Easterling found not only that his active military career was over but that his life was in danger. A list of those who had died in Company B included the notation, "Private Z. A. Easterling died at home Sept. 23, 1864, from the effects of a self-inflicted accidental wound."[69] However, Chambers sub-sequently learned that it was not the hospital stay that had led to his comrade's demise. While on furlough in 1864, he visited with Easterling's mother and be-came aware of his friend's fate. "Not till that afternoon had I learned that her son and my former messmate was dead. The arm was amputated, he recovered, went home and became able to handle tools with his left hand. He cut his knee with an ax in September. The wound inflamed, became gangrenous and killed him." The somber reality set in for the survivor, who wrote, "Thus, only I am left of our mess as we constituted it at Vicksburg in May 1862."[70]

The *New-York Daily Tribune* carried the story of another death that was "the direct result of carelessness." In this instance, "A member of the 23d Brooklyn Regiment, engaged in priming his piece, with the muzzle pointed toward the 28th Brooklyn Regiment, carelessly exploded it, wounding privates Peterman (fatally in the bowels) and Getz (slightly in the arm) of Co. I of the 28th." According to a witness who was fortunate not to become a victim himself, "The ball whistled past low enough to startle some of us, and noticing the confusion in the 28th, I walked up to discover the cause, and saw the poor fellow lying there with the blood slowly welling from a wound in his bowels." The destruction was evident: "The ball had entered his back and passed entirely through the body, coming out of the bowels just above the left groin." The tragic loss impacted more than the victim's army comrades. "He was a resident of Williamsburgh, and leaves a wife and six children."[71]

While stationed with his unit defending Vicksburg, Mississippi, in the summer of 1862, William Pitt Chambers noted a confrontation with a Federal landing party that resulted in several deaths among the Union ranks, and one Confederate under uncertain circumstances: "Our loss was one man accidentally killed."[72] That the man had not perished by enemy fire was evident in Chambers's description of the unfortunate outcome for his comrade.

Private John J. Rainey of Company A, Fifth Virginia Cavalry, had enlisted in 1861 and reenlisted in Company C in 1862 at the age of nineteen. The young trooper became a grizzled veteran and remained in the saddle for the next two years. Under circumstances not clearly delineated, he died from an "accidental pistol wound to [the] left side 4/15/1864 on 4/16/1864."[73] Then in early summer, James K. P. Clayton of the Third Virginia Infantry met his end. The record indicated that the man who had enlisted as an eighteen-year-old at Jerusalem, Virginia, perished three years later in the neighboring state: "Accidentally killed himself at Greensboro, N.C., June 12, 1864."[74]

A newspaper report from Port Royal, South Carolina, on March 31, 1864, noted: "A sad accident occurred at Yellow Bluff yesterday." The situation developed while a "scouting party was out." One member of the squad "was running, with his pistol in his hand, he fell, and the weapon was discharged. The ball passed through the heart of Lieut. D. H. Jones, Company I, 55th Massachusetts Colored Volunteers, killing him instantly."[75]

On October 21, 1864, a touching obituary appeared in the *Alexandria Gazette*, in which a sister mourned the loss of her young soldier brother. Unfortunately, the circumstances had not been that enemy fire struck him down, but rather that he suffered the fatal injury from friendly hands. "Departed this life on the 19th, THOMAS H. TRUSLOW, in the 20th year of his age.—He came to his death by the explosion of a gun in the hands of a comrade, and his last words were, where is my mother dear, and the home he loved so well." The anguished sibling added simply, "He leaves an affectionate mother, two sisters and one brother to mourn their erreparable loss."[76]

Even as soldiers prepared to enter battle with their opponents, the circumstances could turn quickly. Iowan Silas Haven recounted an incident during the Red River Campaign in 1864: "We had a sad accident happen in our company just before we was ordered to charge. We were all laying down, and a gun went off and shot one of our men through the breast, but we are in hopes he will recover."[77] Haven remained optimistic two days later: "Our man that was shot accidentally is getting well. He was shot through the breast. It went in on the left of his backbone and come out near his throat. He was laying down at the time. The same ball cut another man a close call."[78] Unhappily, Jacob Beck did not actually continue to improve, dying on the same day that the letter was written, March 20, 1864.[79]

While participating in William T. Sherman's "March to the Sea," Jesse Campbell met with an unfortunate mishap. His commander, Captain Alfred Benson, related the sad news to the victim's father: "Your son Jesse D. Campbell is no more." On December 7, they had been marching and "had gone a little in advance of the Regt." The soldier had spotted a field of potatoes and was "sitting by the side of the road waiting for the Regt." with a comrade "when Campbell whose gun was leaning against the fence reached out to draw it toward him when the hammer caught upon the ground or in some weeds, and the load was discharged in his right breast killing him instantly."[80]

Pulling guard duty could also be dangerous. Historian Lonnie Speer noted, "Guards also killed themselves accidentally or each other at several prison sites including Richmond, Salisbury, Washington City, St. Louis, Alton, Elmira, and Point Lookout."[81] One Confederate captive from North Carolina related an incident at the latter that involved two sentries, "fooling with their guns [in] what they called playing bayonets." The tragic outcome for these men came when one shot the other. Bartlett Yancey Malone of the Sixth North Carolina noted the pleas of the one toward his fallen comrade: "Jim, Jim get up from there, you're not hurt, you're [only] trying to fool me."[82]

For Carlton McCarthy, an experience at "Fort Clifton," on the Appomattox River, near Petersburg, served to illustrate "every-day life on the lines." In this case, those detailed to duty worked on the first floor, while the others rested above them in the two-story structure. "One night, when the upper floor was covered with sleeping men," McCarthy recalled, "an improvised infantryman who had been relieved from duty walked in, and preparatory to taking his stand at the fire, threw his musket carelessly in the corner." The weapon discharged, and the sergeant of the guard immediately took steps to determine if any damage had been done. A hasty roll call left one name unanswered, and when the men went to where "Pryor" was supposed to be sleeping, he was still there. Getting no response to their entreaties, they examined their comrade and found him to be dead. "The ball had passed through his heart, and he had passed without a groan or a sigh from deep sleep to death. The man who was killed and the man who was sleeping by his side under the same blanket, were members of the Second Company Richmond Howitzers." The unwitting assailant was also an artillerist from another unit, pressed into service as a guard.[83]

The prisoners themselves could turn on each other with fatal results. The most well-known incidents involved the "raiders" in Andersonville, who plagued their comrades until some of them answered on the gallows for their crimes.[84] But arguments and personal disputes over matters that ranged from food and blankets to opposing political views led to violence and death for some of the participants.[85]

The deaths of such vulnerable men at the hands of comrades was particularly deplorable, but for their compatriots in the field, even happy occasions presented unexpected dangers when would-be moments of celebration changed for the worse with little or no warning. A report from April 15, 1862, told the story of a "singular and fatal accident." Quoting from an April 9 edition of the *Knoxville Register*, the *Richmond Daily Dispatch* informed readers of "a lamentable accident which occurred at Athens, Tenn, a few days ago, as follows: Lieut. J. T. Havis, of Captain Chambers's company, Bradford's regiment, stepped into the express car at Athens on his way to join his regiment at London. Upon the arrival of the up train the news of our victory near Corinth reached Athens, when a simultaneous cheering and shouting commenced." Lieutenant Havis did not want to miss the opportunity to join in on the festivities. "He having a double-barrel shot gun in his hand, put it through the window to fire. He being left-handed, held the gun some little distance from his face and pulled the trigger." When the "first barrel missed fire," the officer was unphased, and "trying the other, both barrels went off simultaneously, causing such a heavy rebound that the butt of the gun striking him in the face, literally tore his hand to pieces, killing him instantly."[86]

As the misguided celebrations for the fall of Corinth continued on one side, the frustrations of defeat and retreat swelled on the other. As artillery was shifted over indifferent roads and bridges that occasionally collapsed under the weight of the teams, tensions among the cannoneers mounted. Drinking and fighting marked the path for some of them, and a member of the Jefferson Artillery died when he got into a row with a comrade from the Washington Artillery of New Orleans.[87]

In February 1863, the visit of General Benjamin Butler to the Baltimore area resulted in what the writer of a *New York Times* piece labeled as "a most melancholy accident . . . which cast quite a gloom over the party." Butler and Major General Robert Schenck, with the latter's staff and a "Committee of Reception," toured various fortifications protecting the city, including the famed Fort McHenry. At Fort Marshall, the firing of a salute in the visitors' honor was to take place. According to the *Times*, "Just as the General and his party had passed along the ramparts, out of range of the gun, the gunner, supposing that the whole party had passed, fired a thirty-two pounder." The occasion turned instantly to tragedy. Among those lingering too long in an exposed position was Commander Maxwell Woodhull, USN, who fell victim to the charge in a gruesome and fatal fashion, having "received the whole charge, which blew the flesh from his lower limbs and caused his death in a few moments. His body was blown [over] the ramparts to the distance of thirty feet."[88] This was an inglorious passage for an individual who had served his nation and for whom President Lincoln expressed personal regret at his loss.[89]

In the artillery batteries of both sides, routine drills and other activities could also turn deadly in an instant. On June 2, 1862, a Kansas newspaper informed its readers, "Last evening while firing a salute at Camp Union, from the large pivot gun. It was prematurely discharged, killing one of the gunners a Mr. Kelley, of Independence, and also blowing off the thumb of the man at the vent hole." Duties meant to safeguard against accidents if carried out properly failed to do so in this instance. "It seems that the gun had been insufficiently swabbed out, and Kelley was in the act of driving home the cartridge, when the intense heat caused the thumber to open the vent, when the gun was instantly discharged, literally tearing away the entire right arm and the left hand, and carrying away all the left side of his face." The damage was extensive. "There was a wound in the right breast like that made by a pistol ball. The body was otherwise bruised and torn in a most shocking manner."[90]

Another salute gone awry took place in Arkansas in July 1863. Writing from Helena, S. W. Haven explained to his brother, "We celebrated the fourth on the eighth and fired salutes in honor of the taking of Vicksburg." The scene quickly turned from celebratory to horrific. As recounted by Haven, "We had a very bad accident the other morning. We was ordered to fire a salute of thirty-six guns; the last shot was fired by No. 6 gun." Apparently, all went according to the drill book until the person responsible for preventing air from entering the vent at the breech failed in his duty. "When William Davis was ramming it down, the gun went off and killed him." The effects on the injured number one man from the blast were significant. "He was terribly burnt, both hands torn to pieces and one shoulder. It throwed him about 10 feet. He did not come to his senses at all, lived 2 hours, did not move, only breath hard; the first occurred we have had in our battery." Haven remained shaken by the death, ending his letter: "Can't stop to write any more, so good bye."[91]

Poor decisions, coupled with the presence of heavy ordnance, could lead to disastrous and deadly results. Following the battle of Belmont, Missouri, in which Confederate forces defeated Union troops under Ulysses S. Grant, the defenders located across the Mississippi River at Columbus, Kentucky, sought permission from Major Alexander P. Stewart to clear the giant artillery piece Lady Polk of its last charge by firing the gun.[92] Stewart thought the less dramatic but tried method of extracting the round with an implement was preferable and opposed the request. Undeterred, the crew members approached Stewart's superior, Major General Leonidas Polk, who had arrived to inspect the scene of the recent battle and offered praise to the crew for the huge cannon's role in the fighting. The former Episcopal bishop, now turned soldier, saw no harm in firing the piece. A demonstration would enable him to see the weapon's capabilities for himself and delight the assembled parties. Thus, the process went forward and the charge detonated. Black powder smoke obscured the effect initially, but it quickly became clear that the Lady Polk had burst, sending fragments into the men serving the piece and the observers who had gathered to witness the firing demonstration. Eleven individuals perished as a result of the incident, although Polk managed miraculously to survive it.[93] An account in the *Staunton Spectator* noted the deaths of two officers and seven privates: "The names of the officers who were victims to the sad casualty are Lieut. Snowden, of the Confederate States Infantry, and Capt. Keiter, of the Artillery."[94]

A Maryland newspaper carried the account of a similar, although less deadly, incident in its December 5, 1862, edition: "On Friday last at the trial of some new guns belonging to Alexander's Battery, stationed near Williamsport, one of the guns, from some cause, bursted, killing one and wounding several persons who were near it."[95] If the purpose of the "trial" was to test the soundness of the tubes, the resulting effect proved more deadly to friends than to foes.

Although making no specific time reference, W. S. Basinger of the Savannah Volunteer Guards recalled a six-inch rifled tube that seemed to defy attempts to seat charges properly: "Frequent examinations with the best means at hand failed to disclose the cause of this." Rather than being retired or sent for refitting, the cannon in question "was afterwards removed to Fort Bartow, at Causton's Bluff.

The first time it was fired there, it burst, killing and wounding a number of persons." A subsequent investigation "disclosed that the casting was imperfect; and that, if it had been fired at the enemy's ships as intended, on the occasion above mentioned, it would probably have burst then, with disastrous results."[96] Presumably, the reference to disaster meant with regards to failing to repel the Union vessels rather than avoiding the casualties to the crew that happened anyway.

Vicksburg proved a deadly place to be for combatants, but not always from the expected sources. On June 23, 1863, William Christie wrote his brother while outside the city serving with a battery of artillery that was attempting to help induce the defenders into surrender:

> There are a few Deaths from secesh Bullets every week, and occasionally one from the Premature Bursting of a shell, from our own guns, we are so near the Rebs we cant hurt any of our own men. But one of the eleventh Ill. infantry was I fear mortally wounded yesterday By a fraction of shell from the first Missouri's Battery Co. C: his Bowels were torn and both his lungs visable.

Christie thought he recognized a culprit for this type of incident besides proximity: "We find [that] most of the St. Louis shell spherical case, are not trustworthy. I Believe there are a number of secesh workmen in that Arsenal, that Deliberately make a Bad job of there work, so that there Southern brethren may not Be hurt."[97]

On August 29, 1863, a notice reprinted from the *Washington Republican* denoted a misfire in South Carolina: "After being fired seven times, the 300-pounder Parrott gun, used by [Quincy] Gilmore against Sumter, became disabled by the premature discharge of a shell, which burst off the nozzle and, we regret to add, killed a captain and several of the gunners." As was often the case in such circumstances, the precise nature of the accident was unclear: "Whether this explosion occurred while putting the shell into the gun or while it was in the act of making its speedy exit from the nozzle, is not stated."[98]

In the period in which Braxton Bragg's Confederates held the Federals in check at Chattanooga, Tennessee, Southern gunners on Lookout Mountain occasionally lobbed shells toward their blue-coated opponents. Michael V. Sheridan recorded the unintended effects on three privates who sought to experiment with an unexploded piece of ordnance. "Such of the twenty-pounder, octagonal shells as failed to explode—and more than a few did fail—were a great curiosity to our men, what with their strange shape and the cluster of percussion-caps set in the shell's point," he noted. Had the devices performed as expected, any casualties attributed to them would be understandably combat related. However, in the case that the Union officer witnessed, the men involved brought tragedy upon themselves through their own actions. "One day a shell fell quite near where I was standing, and it did not burst," Sheridan continued. "Presently three privates came along and one of them carried the shell over in front of a tree and laid it down, and he himself got behind the tree, reached around it, and, before I knew what he was about, he brought down a hatchet—smash—upon the percussion caps." Predictably, the supposed dud became a live round. "It tore off the arm of the man behind the tree and instantly killed his two comrades." Displaying a soldier's morbid sense of humor, Sheridan speculated that the badly injured soldier, provided he managed to survive his convalescence, in later years would claim the loss of the limb happened while he was under enemy fire "storming Missionary Ridge."[99]

The circumstances were similar for an individual in Atlanta as William T. Sherman's forces shelled the city in the summer of 1864. According to one report on July 31, a misguided sense of utility, rather than curiosity, prevailed: "On Sunday, a militia man picked up a 24-pounder fuse shell, which fell near where he was stationed, without exploding, and was pecking away on it with a rock, to get the powder out, when it bursted, killing him instantly."[100]

On October 3, 1864, a Richmond newspaper told of another unfortunate incident:

About half-past 2 o'clock Saturday morning, the pickets in front of Captain William J. Dabney's battery, on the track road, fired off their guns, ran in and reported the enemy were upon them, which caused much confusion. Private John B. Allen, of this city, had charge of the magazine, and went in to prepare shells for the guns. The first shell, a twenty-four pound spherical case, exploded when he cut the fuse, killing him instantly, dreadfully mangling his body and mortally wounding private George Brown, who was holding a lantern for Allen to see how [to] cut the fuse.[101]

In the chaotic conditions surrounding the fighting at Port Hudson, a different threat emerged due to the geography there. In a letter home, Charles Sherman explained the risk he and his comrades faced from fire by Union tubes: "After getting through the Cane field, the 12th was ordered to Lay Down in front to support 3 Batterys and if thair is a Disagreeabl Place to any man, it is to take the fier from both sides. We had men killed by shell from our guns."[102] Subsequently, he observed, "Thair is being large number of men hurt by shell from our own guns. The fact about it, this place is a hard Nut and it takes in a large Extent of ground and the Woods Plague us."[103] Such dangers did not subside. As Sherman later wrote, "We Lost lots of men by our own Shells Bursting as soon as thay left the Canon and the Peices fliying among the men that were Suporting the Battery."[104]

Nothing could be more demoralizing than experiencing the effects of fire meant for one's opponents. Theodore Lyman, who served on George Meade's staff, observed, "In spite of the great advances, much remains to be done in the fuses of shells; not a battle is fought that some of our men are not killed by shells exploding short and hitting our troops instead of the enemy's, beyond." He thought he could attribute the unhappy phenomenon to a couple of possible explanations: "Sometimes it is the fuse that is imperfect, sometimes the artillerists lose their heads and make wrong estimates of distance. From these blunders very valuable officers have lost their lives."[105] Of course, either reason would provide little solace to the men on whom the friendly metal rained or to the loved ones who would be left to mourn their losses.

Experiencing warfare firsthand proved no guarantee against foolish acts that could have deadly consequences. Members of the First Michigan Sharpshooters had already seen a great deal when they settled into a new camp at the end of 1864. Unfortunately, one experience remained, prompted when one of the men located a toy cannon and decided to use it for impromptu salutes. Locating a number of unexploded cannonballs as a source of powder, several of the men gathered the loose granules as they worked on their project. An ignition source of some kind brought about an explosion, and both Henry Patterson of Company B and William Burns of Company G suffered severe damage. Patterson's wounds were so extensive that, despite medical care, the twenty-year-old soldier died from them. Even so, explicit orders had to come from headquarters noting punishment for "any enlisted man detected burning powder in any way except in the discharge of his duties," while the men were forbidden "to extract powder from shell[s] that have not been exploded."[106]

Artillerist Charles Bright survived the Battle of Gettysburg, only to fall to the consequences of a tragic accident. Just after the fatal event, one of his comrades wrote to convey news of the "sad fate of my highly esteemed and loved friend Charley Bright . . . [who had] met with his death on Friday last 10th under the following circumstances." Apparently, one of the artillery pieces that had been engaged in the battle contained a round that "through the neglect of the officers had not been removed and on the morning of the accident Charley and 3 others got under the caissons a short distance in the rear and directly opposite the guns for the purpose of getting in the shade or taking a sleep the morning was dreadful warm." While the men rested in supposed safety, orders to pack ammunition led a corporal to a set of friction primers whose utility he questioned because of their exposure to the elements. Taking the primers to the weapon to see if they remained functional, "he very unfortunately went to this gun not Knowing it was loaded it immediately went off cutting through the axle of the caisson and causing the shell to burst right in among where they were lying tearing Charley in a dreadful manner the accident hapened at halfpast ten oclock and he died in about one hour and a half afterwards." The passing of Bright, who was popular in the unit, in this manner "caused a gloom and darkness over the whole company And the corporal that accidently fired the gun off is almost crazy about it." The soldier's death deeply affected the writer, who labeled it "a sad affair, Charley was the best friend I had since I came here and with his friend's I deeply mourn his loss." The friend remained at Bright's side "from the time the accident hapened until he breathed his last. He died easy concidering his wounds."[107]

When not becoming the victims of accident or other mishaps, the men in uniform also risked death for the sake of honor. In the earliest days of the war, August heat and strong emotions proved a volatile mix for would-be Confederate warriors. On August 3, 1861, Southern diarist Mary Chesnut labeled a near collision of "Southern lads" over a disputed camping ground for their troops an example of "thrilling with fiery ardor"; she concluded, "The red-hot Southern martial spirit is in the air." She also referenced a volatile exchange between Georgians and South Carolinians over gifts intended for President Davis's wife, Varina. The next day, Chesnut explained, "[Arthur B.] Davis, a Georgian, killed [Captain Charles H.] Axson, a Carolinian, on the cars, in a quarrel which grew out of watermelons."[108]

The *Richmond Daily Dispatch* carried an account of the incident it described as "lamentable." Axson was indeed "bringing with him some watermelons and fine tropical fruits as a present to distinguished friends in Richmond," when the Georgian took exception and damaged the items. Subsequently, Davis approached the officer and insisted that he had acted under the influence of alcohol and was sorry. Cooler heads seemed to prevail, but another misunderstanding arose when, once more drinking, Davis brandished a weapon. Axson attempted to hold Davis to prevent the firearm from discharging accidentally. The latter exited the car briefly but returned to insist that the person who had manhandled him identify himself. When the South Carolina captain came forward, the Georgian fired, striking him fatally in the chest.[109]

A subsequent account from "disinterested eye-witnesses" noted "*both* parties were inebriated" during the incident, and that while an effort was made to secure Davis for proper disposition, "a posse of armed men" forced his release, "took Mr. Davis a half mile out of town, and there brutally murdered him; shooting him, and on his falling, one of the party ran up and stabbed him." The writer took particular pains to stress the Georgian's reputation and social status: "He was connected with (and never disgraced his connection), the most honorable families in Georgia, being a grandson of ex-Gov. [William] Schley."[110] A third version, presented by a South Carolina doctor who insisted he saw "the whole affair, from Alpha to Omega," offered the extent and nature of the confrontation that began when a drunken Davis destroyed six melons and declared he would pay for them with "a brace of splendid pistols and an Arkansas tooth-pick." A subsequent reconciliation appeared to settle the matter, but additional alcohol consumption led to the final event as Davis shot an unarmed Axson and continued to boast about the matter afterward until he left the train at Weldon, North Carolina.[111]

Killings associated with questions of honor were not limited to Southerners. As historian Lorien Foote explained, "Few northern men dueled, but they would fight and kill for honor." One example was Bernard J. McMahon. During his service in the Mexican-American War and at other prewar posts, he received insults from comrades with whom he later served in the Civil War, with the most egregious assaults on his honor coming from Captain Andrew McManus of the Sixty-Ninth Pennsylvania. Through an extended process of interaction between them, the two men moved toward a violent denouement on the night of May 27, 1863, when McMahon shot down his antagonist. McMahon faced charges and a guilty verdict for murder from a court-martial but ultimately received a pardon from President Lincoln in September.[112]

New Yorker Henry Lyon thought his days of soldiering were following a relatively quiet pattern. "Our Camp life and Picket duty goes on in the same routine," he wrote home in October 1861, before adding, "broken occasionally by some event more or less exciting which gradually subsides and leaves us in the same channel as before." As an example, Lyon related one of these "exciting" moments: "While our Co. were on Picket two men in Co. B. had a little row while drunk or particularly so when one stabbed the other ripping his bowels open in two places, making frightful gashes in fact letting his inwards out." The injured man "lingered from about 9 o'clock at night until next morning when he died." The commander turned the assailant over to the "Civilian authorities," although Lyon thought soldiers should be "punished here in the Reg. I think it could have been the better way."[113]

At the end of 1861, Virginia cavalryman Robert T. Hubard Jr. wrote his brother with the latest information he had from the front. While much of this news was of a benign nature, Hubard related a tragedy that involved members of a Louisiana unit and the sense of honor that prevailed among them that required redress when challenged. "A duel in the 5th Louisiana a few days since resulted most fatally," he explained. "The firing was simultaneous, both parties were shot in the groin and died in a few hours." The circumstances particularly impressed the cavalryman, who noted, "It is the only instance I ever knew of both parties being shot in the same place at the first fire." Then, almost as an afterthought, he added, "A day or two after another duel in the same regiment resulted in the death of one party."[114]

Duels among Louisianans had been common. Captain Alex White of the Tigers took offense to a characterization of his men by an officer on General Richard S. Ewell's staff. Heated words turned the matter into an affair of honor. The aggrieved parties selected rifles for their weapons and stepped off on the dueling plain, with deadly results for the aide. White's shot "bored through just above the hips," and the staffer "died in great agony." In a bitter twist, the soldiers Captain White had risked his life for and taken another to defend their reputations subsequently tore through the streets of Lynchburg, Virginia, in a drunken spree.[115]

On October 18, 1862, a staff officer from Kentucky recorded a tragic encounter in his diary: "Maj James Sudduth shot & killed Bowman of Miller's Bath Company & was afterwards shot by Bowman, Hop Bickley & L't Miller,—and will die shot through the head." The reason for the confrontation was not evident from the diary entry, but returning fire against his assailant was undoubtedly the final act Riley Bowman could muster. It was also clear that Ned Guerrant thought highly of his fallen comrade: "Poor Bowman! He was a good, & brave soldier. Yesterday, I saw him in health & strength. Today how cold, how lifeless!! 'Soldier rest, thy warfare is o'er.'"[116]

In the summer of 1863, Robert E. Hearn of the Fourth Tennessee Cavalry reported the death of one comrade and the severe wounding of another in an encounter that took place away from the battlefield. Writing home from "Near Chattanooga July 9th/63," he covered his own health and state of the command before slipping in the incident: "Mr. Seddeth and Bracket got into a difficulty and shot each other. Bracket died on the spot and Seddeth is thought to get well, but he is shot through the right lung." The dead man, Anson S. Brackett, had enlisted in the regiment on January 3, 1862.[117]

Groups of individuals who remained in close proximity to each other and shared a mutual disdain could create volatile situations that turned deadly. One of these instances occurred in August 1863, when soldiers stationed in Washington confronted some civilians. The *Alexandria Gazette* related the event in its edition of August 7: "A serious affray occurred between five young men and a party of teamsters on the public grounds south of the President's house, in Washington, on Wednesday, originating in the conduct of two women, who came along and took off the hat of one of the young men, and carried it among the teamsters." The trivial but humiliating act stirred the passions of the soldiers and led to shots being exchanged between the groups as taunting turned to violence. The newspaper account added, "Two brothers, named Wm. and George Hensley of the party of five, received such wounds as will probably cause their death[s], the teamsters, some twenty in number at one time firing pistols freely; another young man named Edward Thompson, was seriously cut on the head with a stone."[118]

By the end of winter 1864–1865, events suggested that the conflict was close to reaching a conclusion. Yet, even in such circumstances, personal difficulties between comrades could lead to deadly encounters. In one such instance, J. C. Clifton, of Company C, Twelfth Tennessee Cavalry, became embroiled in a disagreement with an associate on February 7, 1865. The situation escalated among the friends-turned-antagonists, with tragic consequences. The rolls for his unit listed the Union cavalryman as "killed in a fight with one of his own company."[119]

Mutinous moments were occasionally fatal ones for those involved in either their perpetuation or their quashing. The intensity of emotions and the proximity of weapons could prove a deadly combination. Captain Charles G. Stone of the Seventeenth New York had to deal with a growing threat from angry men held in confinement that accelerated when one of the internees, named O'Keefe, threatened a guard. Stone responded by ordering the man to sit before him, but the soldier refused, and the officer gave him a peremptory order to obey or be shot. Apparently, not believing the captain would follow through on his threat, O'Keefe remained defiant, and Stone killed him.[120] Although fatalities associated with such encounters did not occur often and usually resulted in the deaths of the troublemakers when they did, officers could become victims as well.[121] Captain Charles A. Clark of the Twenty-Fifth Illinois Infantry died when he confronted some of his men. Chaplain Van Horne noted of his fellow Cumberlander, "Killed in quelling mutiny, November 25, 1863."[122]

Occasionally, general officers also found themselves embroiled in personal matters or confrontations that led to unexpected fatalities. In some cases, these incidents were famous, or infamous, as parables of the impropriety of angering spouses. Perhaps the most celebrated case of amour gone awry happened in May 1863, when Dr. James Peters confronted Earl Van Dorn at the general's headquarters in Spring Hill, Tennessee. The flamboyant officer had developed an affection for Peters's wife, Jesse. Despite warnings from aides that trouble might ensue, Van Dorn insisted that he had done nothing for which anyone need be concerned and that, in any event, he enjoyed her company. What Dr. Peters thought of the general's intentions might have been a matter the soldier should have considered more deeply, but the relationship continued regardless of any consequences.

Finally, on May 7, Dr. Peters rode to the Nathaniel Cheairs house that served as Van Dorn's headquarters and strode to the top floor. Entering the room, the doctor prepared to face the officer he considered guilty of impropriety, if not actual infidelity, with his wife. Accounts varied as to how the confrontation transpired, particularly in terms of an ambush-style execution from behind, but that Peters had killed the alleged paramour was clear.[123]

Private soldiers were also not above involving themselves in fatal attractions of a sort. One Illinois soldier, Lucius W. Barber, recorded a situation in May 1864 that pitted two comrades as competitors for the affections of the same woman. Terming the event a "tragical occurrence," he observed, "The foolish men agreed to settle the matter, privately, by fighting a duel with their rifles." Unfortunately, the prowess the men had achieved in the use of their weapons worked against them here. "At the first fire both fell dead," Barber observed, before offering the example as "a warning" to females "never to have more than one sweetheart."[124]

Perhaps most unforgivable, given their level of command responsibility, were the deaths that resulted from personal grievances between officers who wore the same uniforms and were supposedly fighting for the same cause against a common foe. These moments occurred in many situations, elevated by heated emotions, occasionally stimulated by drink, and usually exacerbated by conflicting personalities. The scions of important families were not immune to circumstances where honor and violence collided. Such was the case when an incident that started with a good-natured debate mixed with alcohol and hot tempers. The conversation between Alfred Rhett and his brother and their drinking companion Arnoldus Vanderhorst turned to opinions over the quality of West Pointers versus those who had not attended the U.S. Military Academy. Vanderhorst invoked the name of Colonel William Ransom Calhoun, a relative of the iconic South Carolinian John C. Calhoun. Harboring a grudge toward the West Pointer, Alfred disparaged the officer to his friend, and Vanderhorst took exception. Unwilling to prevent the dispute from spiraling out of control, the principals met on the dueling plain, ostensibly to settle the matter. Neither antagonist struck the other, but rather than call the issue closed, Colonel Calhoun issued a challenge of his own to the hotheaded Alfred Rhett. On September 5, those two men met on the grounds of the Charleston Oaks Club with a decidedly different outcome. Rhett's shot struck Calhoun, and within a short time the wound proved fatal.[125]

Mary Chesnut may have anticipated the event with her description of an earlier incident that had involved Calhoun. In August of the previous year, she noted that Ransom Calhoun was one of those "foolish, rash, harebrained Southern lads [that] have been within an ace of a fight for their camping ground with a Maryland company. That is too Irish, to be so ready to fight anybody, friend or foe."[126]

One of the more famous such incidents occurred in the Union ranks when Brigadier General Jefferson C. Davis took exception to the treatment and tone of William "Bull" Nelson toward him, in Louisville, Kentucky, in 1862. Nelson's style was admittedly provocative and profane. Those who knew him best understood that these qualities were hardly the sum of a man who could be extraordinarily engaging when not angered. Yet, Nelson often was brusque when another person earned his disdain and easily enraged at almost any pretext.

The situation reached the final stages on September 29, 1862, at the Galt House hotel. Incensed at enduring what he considered intolerable treatment at the hands of General Nelson, Jefferson Davis sought an apology from the former sailor. Nelson declined, insisting of Davis, "Go away you God Damned puppy, I don't want anything to do with you!" Tempers rose along with the rhetoric as Davis tossed a wadded-up hotel visiting card into his antagonist's face and Nelson struck the officer with additional verbal insults to underscore his disregard.

The outraged Nelson stomped off, leaving the astonished bystanders to speculate as to what would happen next. A friend offered Davis a revolver, warning that the trigger was easy to engage and that he should "be careful." Then, as the six-foot four-inch Nelson emerged on the landing of the staircase, the much smaller Davis demanded that he stop. When Nelson continued toward him, Davis blurted, "General Nelson, take care of yourself," and his weapon discharged. The 300-pound officer fell forward, realizing that he had been hit and declaring to a friend, "I am murdered." Subsequently, friends and associates of Nelson threatened to hang Davis, but others thought that officer's actions, while extreme, were justified under the circumstances. An active campaign in Kentucky against Confederate general Braxton Bragg allowed the anger to dissipate and the matter to fade in intensity.[127]

In Suffolk, Virginia, where Union forces faced Confederates under General James Longstreet in April 1863, tensions built and personalities clashed among the defenders.[128] Lieutenant Colonel Edgar A. Kimball arrived in the area with the Ninth New York to augment the defense of the town. A veteran of the Mexican-American War who had already seen service at Roanoke Island and Antietam, Kimball possessed unquestioned courage. But his judgment, and an apparent willingness to indulge in the consumption of spirits while enjoying the convivial company of friends, proved less advantageous elements in his character.

Kimball had already marched his command under trying circumstances for a grueling thirty-mile trek from Portsmouth in inclement weather when he spent the evening renewing acquaintances. In the early morning hours of April 13, he departed for his own camp when he noticed a group of riders approaching. The Confederates were already in the vicinity of the Union lines, and there was always the possibility that this was a mounted detachment scouting them. He called for the riders to halt and demanded the appropriate countersign be given.

The leader of the approaching contingent of horsemen was Michael Corcoran, a mercurial Irish Union general who had already achieved notoriety by being held and threatened with summary punishment by the Confederates after First Manassas. Corcoran had never met Kimball and was unclear who it was that now so abruptly challenged him. He contended afterward that he demanded a name and authority for the peremptory action, only to receive the reply "that it was none of my —— business." Corcoran's version of the incident reflected the temperament of the men as well as the uncertain nature of the circumstances:

> I expostulated with him on such conduct, and told him to remember that he was not on duty, and had no right to be there and stop me from proceeding, and that he must let me pass. I asked him if he knew who he was talking to, and then gave him my name and rank, telling [him] my business there, but it was of no avail. He answered: "I do not care —— who you are."

In the composed manner of reflection, Corcoran maintained that he merely wished to proceed with his business and offered no overt resistance initially to the treatment to which he felt he was unjustifiably being subjected: "He thereupon put himself in a determined attitude to prevent my progress, and brandishing his sword in one hand, and having his other on a pistol, as I then supposed, made a movement toward me with the evident design of using them, making an impolite statement that I should not pass. It was at this point that I used my weapon."

Corcoran's round smashed into Kimball's neck, severing an artery but not preventing the stricken soldier from exclaiming, "Damn you, fire again!" Despite this show of bravado, the officer was indeed mortally wounded.[129]

Kimball's death, especially under such dubious circumstances, prompted strong reactions. Edward King Wightman informed his brother of the incident, citing the proximity of the opposing forces and the demand for strict security measures. "Gen. Corcoran and staff attempted to pass a sentinel without the countersign," he explained, "and Kimball, who happened to be near, backed the soldier." The general's fire found its mark, but "the lion-hearted old man was up again in a moment, and with his sword drawn, contemptuously calling upon Corcoran to 'fire again.'" Wightman was convinced that whatever the protests to the contrary might be, the general had fired with inexcusable deliberation. "He knew [it was] Kimball when he fired."[130]

Corcoran's behavior may have spurred, if not exacerbated, the situation, but other accounts introduced the presence of heavy drinking by Kimball as a factor as well. Wightman described the colonel as "a little tight" on the occasion, and another individual, George W. Griggs, later employed the same terminology regarding the state of Kimball's sobriety. "While in a state of intoxication," Griggs recalled years later, Kimball "ran from his tent, seized (Michael) Corcoran's horse by the bridle, drew and flourished his sword, and demanded of the general the countersign." One of the proprietors of a popular "drinking house" in Suffolk at the time, the man observed plainly, "Griggs & Nolen sold Kimball the whiskey that caused his death."[131]

The incident created a highly charged atmosphere for the men of Kimball's regiment. "The boys raved rather than talked," a soldier explained, "and many would have gone through the whole legion for the blood of the assassin."[132] Only timely intervention by Union general George Washington Getty prevented retaliatory violence and allowed calm to be restored in the ranks.[133]

Armed confrontation among supposed comrades was not confined to such situations. One of the most tempestuous personalities of the war, Confederate cavalry raider Nathan Bedford Forrest, nearly engaged in duels with several superiors, including the ill-fated Earl Van Dorn. Yet, in the aftermath of a successful defense against a Union raid in Alabama by Colonel Abel Streight, Forrest came perilously close to losing his life to a disgruntled subordinate, Lieutenant Andrew Wills Gould.

Gould had participated in the operation that pursued Streight's force across northern Alabama but had lost a section of artillery pieces when the Union commander staged an ambush. Forrest's chief artillerist, John Morton, insisted, "Gould thought it best to abandon them," since the horses he might have used to extract the cannon were dead or dying and tangled badly in the traces. Forrest could hardly see the matter in the same light and detected cowardice in his unfortunate subordinate's behavior.

At the conclusion of the raid, Forrest determined to transfer Gould to another command, a step that Gould could not accept without besmirching his honor. Consequently, the officer "sought an interview with General Forrest" to clear the record. Morton knew both men, recognized the volatility of the situation, and hoped to defuse it in the interests of the officers and the service. Unfortunately, he had not been able to intervene before Gould approached Forrest's headquarters at the Masonic Building in Columbia, Tennessee, on the afternoon of June 13, 1863.[134]

A private conversation turned heated, and, with four young boys serving as witnesses, the comrades became antagonists. One of the boys heard Gould say "it's false," or "that's all false," to Forrest's allegations, and Forrest drew out a penknife with which he had been whittling earlier, while watching Gould intently. The lieutenant struggled with an unseen object in the long duster he wore, but before he could remove the pistol, Forrest struck. A bullet from the weapon hit the Confederate general in the side but did not prevent him from thrusting the knife into Gould. The lieutenant staggered from the hall, across the street, and into a tailor's shop.[135]

"No damned man shall kill me and live!" Forrest bellowed as he heard the preliminary diagnosis that he had suffered a possibly fatal wound. Reaching a horse and saddle in the street, he grabbed a couple of pistols and proceeded to seek out his assailant. Gould was in the process of being examined himself when Forrest appeared. The latter fired and believed that he had avenged his death.[136]

A further examination offered Forrest the assurance that there appeared to be no perforation of any vital areas, and thus he was in no mortal danger from his wound. The doctors offered to remove the bullet, but the cavalryman's bluster returned. "It's nothing but a damned little pistol ball!" he replied and then directed the men to find Gould and remove him to a better location for his care.[137]

In an improbable moment of reconciliation, General Forrest was supposed to have visited Lieutenant Gould at his bedside and received a dispensation for the act. "General, I shall not be here long, and I was not willing to go away without seeing you in person and saying to you how thankful I am that I am the one who is to die and that you are spared to the country," Gould explained generously. "What I did, I did in a moment of rashness, and I want your forgiveness." Forrest assured the feeble officer that he forgave him, regretting only that the wound was apparently going to prove fatal.[138]

Nathan Bedford Forrest had been spared, but a duel cost the life of Confederate brigadier general Lucius M. Walker at the hands of his comrade John S. Marmaduke. Questions of courage and cowardice in earlier fighting at Helena and Reed's Bridge, Arkansas, led to an exchange of communications that accelerated into a challenge made and accepted. The final scene played out at sunrise, on September 6, 1863, with both men and their seconds meeting in a duel designed to settle the matter honorably. The duelists missed with their initial shots, but a second struck Walker in his lower side, compromising a kidney and impacting the spine. As paralysis spread, the injured officer knew that he had been mortally wounded, and a surgeon arrived to confirm that diagnosis. Although Walker survived until the next day, his injury proved fatal.[139]

In 1864, Lieutenant Colonel Thomas Vimont of the Seventh Kentucky Cavalry took exception to a subordinate officer whom he insisted had sought a transfer "for a position in the rebel army," or in one of the U.S. Colored Troops regiments being formed. The lieutenant's mentor, Major William W. Bradley, insisted that the allegation of seeking a place in the Confederate army in particular was false and defamatory and required retraction. Vimont refused to rescind his statements, and when the men met subsequently, tempers rose with an accompanying level of obscenities. The lieutenant colonel made a gesture for his weapon, while continuing to hurl invectives, when Major Bradley fired, mortally wounding his antagonist. Witnesses praised Bradley's restraint to the provocations and attributed Vimont's behavior to intoxication; a subsequent hearing cleared the officer of a murder charge.[140]

Near the end of the war, honor aggrieved remained a factor for at least two Confederates. On April 6, 1865, as Ulysses Grant closed on Robert E. Lee at Appomattox, a confrontation took place in Texas between Colonel George W. Baylor and Major General John A. Wharton. The situation escalated from a verbal exchange to physical threats and assertions of falsehood that Baylor maintained impelled him to shoot and kill the unarmed Wharton as a justifiable matter of respect.[141] Commenting on the nature of such deadly altercations as those that claimed the lives of Wharton and Walker earlier, historian Lawrence Lee Hewitt observed wryly, "Rather than a dumping ground, the Trans-Mississippi became a graveyard," for these generals.[142]

Men who perished at the hands of their friends and comrades, or by circumstances that ought otherwise not to have proved threatening to their lives, joined their compatriots who died from other noncombat-related incidents. Most demoralizing were the cases in which these deaths came deliberately from men who should have been allies rather than antagonists. In each of the cases, loved ones would feel these losses as keenly as if the men had fallen on the battlefield, but the nature of these passages must have made them more difficult to comprehend or reconcile.

Abraham Lincoln's address at the dedication of the cemetery at Gettysburg became symbolic of the losses that soldiers would suffer on the battlefields, but it also underscored in its sentiments the similar sacrifices outside of direct hostile action made by so many soldiers and civilians. (Library of Congress)

A stylized envelope featuring the tableau of Francis Brownell avenging the death of Colonel Elmer Ellsworth at the hands of civilian James Jackson. (Library of Congress)

Weather proved to be especially troubling for Civil War soldiers, with mud as their particular nemesis. Heavy downpours, storms, and lightning were responsible for numerous deaths. (Library of Congress)

Private Sampson Altman Jr. belonged to the Twenty-Ninth Georgia Volunteers organized in Big Shanty, Georgia, today Kennesaw. Disease cut his career short, as it did for so many on both sides of the conflict. (Library of Congress)

Civil War camp life provided the setting for many fatal circumstances for the men who inhabited the camps, including mishaps in the construction of quarters and personal interactions gone awry. (National Archives)

Learning the craft of soldiering and mishaps at drill meant the end of many martial careers, often before these victims encountered their first opponents in battle. (Library of Congress)

The seemingly simple and harmless activity of bathing could cost men their lives as unexpected conditions, such as cramps or strong currents, put them at risk. (Library of Congress)

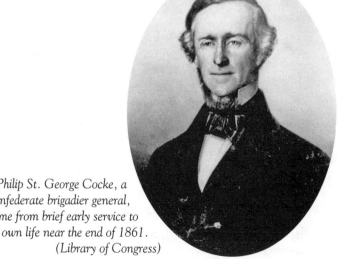

Philip St. George Cocke, a troubled Confederate brigadier general, came home from brief early service to take his own life near the end of 1861. (Library of Congress)

Brigadier General John Buford was one of the Union heroes of Gettysburg, but he proved no match for the ravages of disease, perishing from the effects of typhoid fever on December 16, 1863. (Library of Congress)

Accidents on the rails often cost the lives of men who had survived combat, including prisoners of war being transferred to camps for internment. (Library of Congress)

The ruins of Judith Henry's house at Manassas and the site of her death from the fire that surrounded it in July 1861. (Library of Congress)

Despite the benefits of movement over vast distances, train wrecks—through collisions, derailments, or other mishaps—killed soldiers and civilians alike in wartime. (National Archives)

Snow dark against distant sky - quite dark
in shadow and evergreen.   very hazy and
colorless distance

Nature could prove to be a vicious adversary for the men in the ranks. Although wintry conditions were often sensationalized, they caused more than discomfort for some of the soldiers who had to endure them. (Library of Congress)

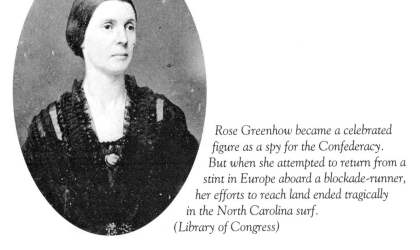

Rose Greenhow became a celebrated figure as a spy for the Confederacy. But when she attempted to return from a stint in Europe aboard a blockade-runner, her efforts to reach land ended tragically in the North Carolina surf. (Library of Congress)

Travel could be inordinately dangerous to soldiers in the war, especially when they encountered rain-swollen rivers. Any misstep could, and occasionally did, prove fatal. (Library of Congress)

Death on the waters came in many forms, from accidental drownings and scaldings to mishaps and miscalculations. A premature explosion on the USS Westfield *outside Galveston, Texas, in January 1864, cost a number of lives among the officers and crew who were trying to prevent the ship's intact capture. (Library of Congress)*

OPPOSITE: *Albert Sidney Johnston (second row, left), Thomas J. "Stonewall" Jackson (second row, right), and Earl Van Dorn (top row, second from left) were among the higher-ranking Confederate generals to die in the war. Johnston fell to likely friendly fire at Shiloh in 1862, as did Jackson at Chancellorsville in 1863, while Van Dorn perished from the gun of an angry husband in Spring Hill, Tennessee, in 1863. (Library of Congress)*

W. O. B. Branch

Earl Van Dorn

J. H. Morgan

W. Barksdale

A. S. Johnston

J. E. B. Stuart

Stonewall Jackson

J. S. Bowen

Zollicoffer

L. Tilghman

A. J. Jenkins

Ben M. Cullough

Leonidas Polk

G. J. Rains

Confederate Dead

At some point on the night of May 29–30, 1863, Lieutenant John S. Hunt of the Fourth U.S. Artillery fell from the steamer on which he was a passenger and drowned in a river in Virginia. (Photograph courtesy of Nicholas Picerno)

W. J. BAKER'S
Photographic Studio,
12 Tibbitts Block,
Utica, N. Y.

Additional copies of this Picture can be obtained at the above establishment.

John S. Hunt, 1st Lt. 4th U.S. Arty.

Walked overboard in his sleep the night of May 29½–30th 1864, while enroute with his Battery, "I" 4th U.S. Arty., from Bermuda Hundred, James River, to White House Landing Pamunkey River. Va., and was drowned. He was a superior officer.

The reverse side of the above image, with an account of Hunt's mishap.

Brigadier General William E. Baldwin of the Fourteenth Mississippi died when his stirrup broke and he fell from his horse on February 19, 1864. (Library of Congress)

General Charles F. Smith lost his life as a result of an accident he experienced at Shiloh—he injured his leg while exiting a small craft in which he was traveling. He died while attempting to convalesce at Ulysses Grant's headquarters in the Cherry Mansion in nearby Savannah, Tennessee. (Library of Congress)

Michael Corcoran's killing of Colonel Edgar Kimball at Suffolk, Virginia, nearly sparked a mutiny. The Irish-born Union general would later die from the effects of a fall from his horse. (Library of Congress)

Occasionally workers such as these men became unwitting victims when mishaps occurred while they were handling deadly cargoes. (National Archives)

Factory explosions and fires caused many civilian deaths during the war. Washington, Philadelphia, Richmond, and Charleston were among the cities whose residents suffered from such wartime misfortunes. (Library of Congress)

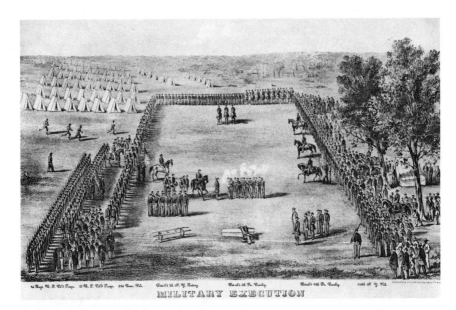

MILITARY EXECUTION

Military executions demonstrated the risks of desertion or served as the ends of justice, yet they left those at home with losses no less real for their circumstances. (Library of Congress)

The destruction of the steamboat Sultana marked a tragic end for many, including recently released Union prisoners of war. The death toll represented a greater number than perished later on the Titanic. (Library of Congress)

7

"As Neere to Heaven by Sea"
Fatalities on the High Seas and Inland Water Courses

We are as neere to heaven by sea as by land.
English explorer Sir Humphrey Gilbert before drowning off Nova Scotia

How uncertain is life. How near is death.
Reaction to the drowning of Private Joseph Wolf

Somehow it looked hard and cruel that after over three years' faithful service they were fated at last to lose their lives by drowning in the cold waters of the Cumberland, and be devoured by catfish and snapping turtles,—but such are among the chances in the life of a soldier.
Leander Stillwell, Sixty-First Illinois Infantry

In the midst of stormy weather, sixteenth-century English explorer Sir Humphrey Gilbert was supposed to have expressed himself stoically and heroically to individuals on a nearby craft just before his ship, *Squirrel*, disappeared beneath the churning waters off the coast of Nova Scotia. In September 1583, a member of the expedition recorded, "The Generall sitting abaft with a booke in his hande, cried out unto us in the [*Golden*] *Hinde* (so oft as we did aproch within hearing), 'We are as neere to heaven by sea as by land.'"[1] Naval duty in the American Civil

War likewise could be tremendously hazardous, whether one's service came in the brown water navies of the inland waterways or the blue water navies of the oceans and seas of the world.

Following a harrowing experience moving from Washington down the Potomac River and into the Chesapeake Bay by steamer, one Union officer concluded that the government should be held culpable for the misfortunes of his men, even if the newspapers neglected to uncover these matters for their readership. Alvin Voris observed: "I discover however that the papers are verry cautious not to say anything about the reckless cruelty of Uncle Samuel in putting his faithful soldiers on board of rotten unseaworthy tubs, in which merchant men would not risk their pork for a voyage down the bay."[2]

Soldiers seemed to be cognizant of the dangers in this form of transportation. Indianan Samuel McIlvaine shared his concerns in a catalog of potentially fatal mishaps as he traveled by steamer with his comrades in February 1862: "It was now I got my first *good* view of the noble Ohio, flowing in all its majesty. . . . Ah, noble old river! could thee but speak, what tales of horror thou couldst unfold; of blood, of murder, of steamboat collisions, of bursting boilers, of burnings, scaldings and drowning men and women and children."[3]

Passengers were not the only ones at risk. Those who worked on the craft faced the chances of mortality as well. Historian George Burkhardt noted the hazards confronting the men who served aboard vessels of all types in the conflict. Routine operations could turn deadly in an instant with one misstep or miscalculation. As he explained, "With no safety harness, men plunged to their deaths from masts, yards, and rigging or fell overboard to drown." Heavy ordnance could burst or roll, endangering their crews, and faulty equipment or carelessness took their toll as well.[4]

Perhaps the most bizarre incident reported for the individuals who served the vessels of the opposing forces in the conflict came from Captain Charles Henry Davis, who noted, "A man was killed in the mortar fleet this morning in a curious way. He had a cylinder of loose powder over his shoulder and a lighted cigar in his mouth." Although he probably did not need to elaborate, Davis added, "His head was blown off." No other details appeared to be necessary, but the officer concluded of the incident and the victim, "These mortar men are said to be very careless."[5]

Captain Davis may have been unduly harsh in singling out his misguided comrade on the river craft, because a counterpart on land experienced a similar mishap. From the river town of Paducah, Kentucky, Sam Evans wrote home to relate a tragic occurrence: "There was a soldier killed by the explosion of a box of cannon cartridges, secesh cartridges taken at Clarksville. He was smoking a cigar and some of the fire fell into the box." Although the perpetrator had proved unlucky, others nearby were more fortunate. Evans concluded, "If the powder had not been damp quite a number would have been killed."[6]

Transportation by water often produced fatalities at alarming rates, especially where weather and geography combined to exacerbate threatening conditions. Navigational hazards were especially notorious in North Carolina's Outer Banks, where shipwrecks had occurred from the times when Spanish galleons and numerous pirates roamed the region. Moving large numbers of troops provided the circumstances for men to face death even before they could encounter the opponents they were traveling to confront. Chaplain Thomas Van Horne listed several victims of Federal movements in the area, including twenty-four-year-old Private John R. Auten and twenty-three-year-old Thomas Golding, who drowned on November 1, 1861, at Hatteras Inlet, North Carolina. Twenty-two-year-old Sergeant John McClinchy suffered the same fate at approximately the same time as his comrades. McClinchy had risen in rank from corporal only a few months before he became a victim of the surf on the North Carolina coast. All three men had enlisted on May 4, 1861, to fight for their country but would perish in its defense far from the grounds of any traditional battlefield.[7]

The *Memphis Daily Appeal* of December 14, 1861, noted the loss of several individuals when their vessel apparently swamped in the waters along the Gulf Coast: "Lieut. Wm. Casey and Sergeant W. L. Thompson, of the Tuscumbia 'Franklin Blues,' and privates Hugh Henary and J. J. Gilchrist, were drowned a few days since, in Mobile bay." Explaining that the men were posted at Fort Morgan, the writer observed that in the course of a return trip from nearby Fort Gaines, "it is supposed that their boat capsized: the boat being found bottom upward on the beach is the only clue to their fate," although individuals subsequently recovered the remains of Sergeant Thompson.[8]

In an expedition being mounted by troops under Union general Ambrose Burnside against the Confederate defenders of the coast of North Carolina in early 1862, disaster seemed to plague some of the men as they attempted to navigate dangerous conditions. At the beginning of the operation a steamer collided with a small craft conveying troops, costing the life of one soldier. Then, off Hatteras, another boat bringing men to shore swamped in the surf, leading to the drowning deaths of Colonel Joseph W. Allen and chief surgeon Frederick S. Waller of the Ninth New Jersey. Both men struggled for a time to remain afloat, but heavy clothing and accoutrements prevented their survival. An unfortunate residual effect of the doctor's death was the loss of a number of soldiers in the regiment to disease before his replacement could arrive.[9]

Similarly, Frederick Phisterer compiled an "Honor Roll" of those who died from New York. His numbers included "308 drowned and 37 scalded to death" from circumstances "not incident to battle."[10] In the ranks of the fallen among the field officers, he noted, "Second Lieutenant James De Ponthieu Wilkes [134th Infantry] died October 6, 1862; drowned at sea off Hatteras, N.C.; and Second Lieutenant James McMahon [2nd Cavalry], drowned at sea December 22, 1864." Phisterer added naval personnel to the list. Gunner Vernard Duycker was part of the crew that captured the blockade-runner *Mary Clinton*, but he perished while trying to bring the ship into port on June 26, 1861. Acting second assistant engineer Thomas drowned on August 5, 1864, as did acting master's mate John Woodman on October 27, 1864, and acting ensign William Dunne on December 28, 1864.[11]

Already struck by the drowning of an officer in late 1861, the Third Pennsylvania Cavalry experienced further loss early the next year when several members fell victim to mishap while being transported by water. The regimental historian noted the "unfortunate accident," which took place on March 24: "Privates Joseph Baeltow, Batholomew Gahagen, and David Leonard were drowned at Alexandria, Va. after the embarkation of their companies on that day." Apparently, the men were walking together on the deck in the evening when the trouble occurred. "In the darkness they stepped overboard and were not missed until their bodies were found floating in the morning."[12]

On the Atlantic coast, circumstances occurring in mid-May 1863 brought news of the unexpected death of a Union sailor near Port Royal, South Carolina. "In this Harbor, on the night of the 16th of May," according to a notice appearing at the end of the month in the local *New South*, "J. G. Bills, Gunner, U.S.N., . . . was drowned by the capsizing of a boat." The accident exacted sympathy from comrades, who experienced "an irreparable loss" and were left to "mourn his untimely end."[13]

Uncertainties existed in the Trans-Mississippi as well. News from an expedition under Nathaniel Banks at the end of 1862 brought word to eastern readers of a tragedy that had taken place in maneuvers in that distant theater of operations. Picking up a report from the *New York Herald*, the *Evansville (Ind.) Daily Journal* noted, "The expedition landed safely on the Texas shore of the Rio Grande, after losing one or two vessels in a norther, but no lives." Yet, having survived the tempest, the danger to the men had not subsided. "Seven soldiers were drowned, however, while disembarking."[14]

The following year, troops from the Fifteenth Maine had another dangerous encounter while landing "on the Texas shore," near the mouth of the Rio Grande. On November 18, 1863, the *Nashville Daily Union* shared a story with its readers that explained, "A high surf was running, and four boats were capsized and seven soldiers and two sailors drowned." An attempt to save some of the endangered men met a challenge when the vessel rescuing them experienced resistance from Mexican forces, who refused to allow the craft to land on Mexican soil, "and the boat was compelled to cross the river to the Texas side." Fortunately for the beleaguered participants, hostile Confederate fire did not further complicate matters. "During the whole time not an armed rebel was seen."[15]

Outside Fort Fisher, the formidable earthwork that protected Wilmington, North Carolina, risks apart from the direct fighting seemed to abound. Edward Wightman kept his brother informed of the progress they were making in attacking the position, but his letters at the end of the year contained references to the rough waters and the impact on the small craft carrying soldiers. On December 26, 1864, he observed, "Many boats were swamped and dashed in pieces on the sands." The result, he feared, was that "many may be drowned, and even if successful, all the poor fellows will be drenched."[16] Two days later, Wightman participated in extracting some of the men from the vicinity of the fort and assessed the results as not nearly as dire as he had feared. As he explained, "Early in the afternoon the last man had embarked, only two of our men and one rebel prisoner having been drowned in the operation."[17]

While participating in operations against Fort Fisher, Union naval officer William B. Cushing saw the indirect toll that war could inflict upon his comrades in arms. He recalled, "In the intermediate time, between the assault and the surrender, the tide had risen and drowned many of our wounded who fell upon the beach; and swept off into the remorseless ocean the hero clay of many a gallant sailor. How few realize at what a cost our Nation's unity has been *purchased!*"[18] To be sure, these men had suffered wounds in battle that debilitated them, but they perished under circumstances other than those of direct combat and with injuries that need not otherwise necessarily have proved fatal. Their deaths came as a natural phenomenon; the waters often viewed as the primordial stuff of existence engulfed them.

Death could come collectively, but often it touched the lives of singular individuals who had the misfortune of dying while being transported on America's inland waterways. A soldier in the 11th Missouri Infantry experienced a tragic moment that cost him his life and served as the regiment's first fatality. On August 24, 1861, as the unit was being moved, English-born Samuel Brown fell into the Mississippi River and could not be saved.[19] Then, on December 21, the *Cincinnati Daily Press* conveyed the story of Jacob Winter, of the Twenty-Eighth Ohio, who "fell overboard" from the *Collier* while the vessel was carrying him "on her trip down [the river]."[20]

While posted at Green Island, the Savannah Volunteer Guards were fortunate to avoid deaths from the illnesses striking so many of their comrades elsewhere in the fledgling Confederacy. However, they were not able to prevent misfortune from happening to them entirely. W. S. Basinger recorded that in the first winter of the war one man met an untimely end: "The only member lost on the island was private James S. Griggs of Company B, who fell into the river and was drowned while endeavoring to recover a boat which had broken adrift. Generally esteemed and beloved as he was, his death was much lamented by all."[21]

Such dangers came to soldiers and civilians of all classes, including political leaders. Louis Powell Harvey had been governor of Wisconsin for only a short time when the Battle of Shiloh brought home to him the terrible price war was exacting from his constituents. The governor was not content to remain in the statehouse and watch the conflict unfold from afar. He felt compelled to travel to the scene and visit with those who had sustained wounds, as well as to honor the fallen. Unfortunately, on April 19, 1862, the weather was not cooperative for this portion of the Wisconsin politician's journey, and while attempting to cross from one steamer to another in the midst of stormy conditions, Harvey lost his footing and plunged into the churning waters of the Tennessee. The strenuous attempts to save him proved fruitless; the governor disappeared from view, only to have his body found downstream two weeks later.

At about the same time, an accident related to water transportation also contributed to the death of a Union general who had demonstrated skill and stood high in the estimation of fellow West Pointers and comrades in blue Ulysses S. Grant and William T. Sherman. Charles Ferguson Smith had performed well at Fort Donelson, in February 1862, conducting a counterattack against the defenders of the works that caused consternation among the Confederate leadership there. Promoted to major general, Smith was entering a vessel when he scraped his leg. Developing an infection that a severe bout of dysentery complicated, the stalwart officer could not recover and died in his bed in Grant's headquarters in the Cherry Mansion, at Savannah, Tennessee, on April 25, 1862.[22]

Although the deaths of high-ranking officials or those involving larger numbers of troops caught the easiest attention, solitary fatalities occurred frequently and carried the poignancy of individual lives lost. Chaplain Thomas Van Horne's identification of fallen warriors in the Army of the Cumberland included two men who perished on the waters in the early years of the war. Twenty-five years old at the time of his enlistment in May 1861, Private Albert Warren fell off a transport in New York Harbor a month later and drowned.[23] Twenty-nine-year-old Private John Walan met a similar fate near Aquia Creek, Virginia, on August 13, 1862.[24]

The Daily Evansville (Ind.) Journal of Indiana told readers of a "soldier belonging to the 7th Illinois cavalry [who] fell overboard from the General Anderson at

Paducah, on her downward trip, and was drowned."[25] Similarly, while moving by transport with his battery from Bermuda Hundred on the James River to White House Landing on the Pamunkey River in Virginia, Lieutenant John S. Hunt of the Fourth U.S. Artillery met with a bizarre end, when he "walked overboard in his ship the night of May 29th 1864." Whether deprived of adequate rest and unlucky in his footing or simply sleepwalking, the man, described as "a superior officer," was "drowned" in the incident.[26]

A Richmond newspaper carried another poignant story of an individual who met his end in one of the South's waterways:

> The Montgomery Mail records the following fatal accident. Mr. Linebaugh was on his way to General Hood's army to act as correspondent of the Richmond press, a position to which he had recently been appointed: Dr. John H. Linebaugh, a distinguished scholar and writer, of Alabama, was recently drowned in the Alabama river while attempting to leap from a steamer to the shore. The vessel upon which he was a passenger ran into the bank, and the passengers becoming alarmed, a number attempted to reach the shore; among them, Mr. Linebaugh, who was the only one drowned.[27]

The latter part of 1864 saw another drowning when New Yorker George Arvin fell overboard from the transport *North America* on December 22.[28]

A similar incident occurred to another individual a few months later. While on temporary furlough, Joseph Wolf, "a private of Co. G., 4th Va. Vol. Infantry, from Jackson county, West Va.," was traveling on the steamer *Silver Cloud No. 2* when he went overboard. A West Virginia newspaper summarized the ironic nature of the incident for its readership: "He had passed through all the dangers and the hardships of the service unharmed and re-enlisted for another term—but just as he was ready to enjoy a little season of rest, and while almost in sight of home he was drowned. And when all danger seemed past then he died." A veteran of the assault on Missionary Ridge and other engagements, Wolf was apparently trying to "draw up some water from the river" when he lost his balance. The writer could only lament, "How uncertain is life. How near is death."[29]

As an older veteran at approximately age forty-seven, Vermonter Charles Tillison was on his way home after becoming "sick in May 1864." The fellow who had enlisted in 1862 "as private in Co. E, 2d Vt.," had become so ill that he was dispatched to the hospital facilities at sprawling City Point, Virginia, for shipment "north on a hospital ship." The record did not state if he had become disoriented or was out of his head, but he would never reach Vermont alive. "On the way, he apparently fell overboard and drowned."[30] Perhaps ominously, Charles had written his son from "Camp Near Brandy Stashin" to send him a package containing "eny thing that is licker." He instructed the boy to take special care in his packaging: "If yo send the Box bee cafule And pack it so it wont wratle for they are gitin [v]ery strick." Tillison seemed to anticipate reselling the contraband items for a tidy profit. "And if I can git it heare it will bring me [a] good too hundred dolars the minet I git it."[31]

Another unfortunate Union soldier was on a steamer traveling from Saint Louis, Missouri, to Smithland, Kentucky, when he experienced a fatal mishap. After reaching their destination, a comrade recorded in his diary on November 28, 1864, "one of Co. 'E,' fell overboard last night, drunk, and was drowned & lost." Dr. James Black seemed to suggest that the man's absence had gone unnoticed until the vessel docked in Kentucky.[32]

Sergeant John M. Gould of Maine recorded the deaths of several men who drowned in units from his state. Private George W. Simpson of Company E in the Tenth Maine perished at Harpers Ferry, Virginia, on May 3, 1862, although no specific cause for the mishap appeared. In May, two years later, the same outcome happened for Private John J. Brown at Alexandria, Virginia. For privates Lyman B. Lovejoy (Company F) and Calvin B. Burnell (Company G) of the Twenty-Ninth Maine, the explanation for their deaths was drowning as a result of "steamer sunk by collision," on May 27, 1864.[33]

Similar fatal mishaps continued to occur in the early part of 1865. In the first week of January, as the steamer *John H. Dickey* made its way from Vicksburg for New Orleans carrying members of the 161st New York to their new assignments, the vessel collided with another, the *John Raine*. A chaplain with the regiment recalled how in a moment the voyage went from routine to chaotic as a sudden jolt and the sounds of cracking timbers betokened disaster. Men struggled to assess the situation amid the wreckage and columns of steam. "In their fright, many of the men leaped into the water to swim ashore, but three were drowned in the attempt," William E. Jones explained. Of the numerous wounded and injured, two others "died a few days afterward."[34]

Occasionally, death on the inland waters occurred through negligence or incompetence. In the case of a nine-car freight train being moved by water aboard a steamer near Perryville, Maryland, "a brakeman failed to put on the brakes," and the cars "ran overboard off the steamer Maryland." The accident might have proved comical had it entailed only embarrassment for the crew member, except for the somber added note, "One soldier was drowned."[35]

Chaplain Van Horne's faithful listing of soldiers associated with the Army of the Cumberland included the following officers who died under unclear circumstances that involved their proximity to watercourses in the South: First Lieutenant Courtland W. King of the 1st Kentucky Infantry, "Drowned in Bear Creek, Ala., June 15, 1862"; Second Lieutenant William S. Hamilton of the 71st Ohio Infantry, "Drowned, August 19, 1862"; Captain Thomas J. London of the 13th Ohio Infantry, "Drowned in Mississippi River, September 29, 1863"; Second Lieutenant John A. McKee of the 74th Ohio Infantry, "Drowned, February 1, 1864 at Cincinnati, Ohio"; First Lieutenant C. P. Hunter of the 134th New York Infantry, "Accidentally drowned in North Anna River, March 11, 1864"; Second Lieutenant Joseph W. Cartwright of the 12th Kentucky Cavalry, "Drowned at Burkesville, June 22, 1864"; and Captain Seneca P. Goulding of the Seventh Kentucky Cavalry, "Drowned at Benton, Ala., April 10, 1865."[36]

Occasionally, operations meant to deny opponents important military resources could go awry, with fatal results. On January 1, 1863, when the Union vessel *Westfield* ran aground off Galveston, it could not be refloated. A crew went aboard to set explosives that would destroy the ship rather than let it fall into enemy hands. Unfortunately, Commander William B. Renshaw and the men who accompanied him perished when the detonation occurred prematurely. An assistant engineer with the Union forces captured the dramatic moment in a subsequent report: "It was now about 8 o'clock. Captain Renshaw ordered the Saxon and Mary Boardman to come near the Westfield and take off the crew, as he intended to blow her up." The bulk of the crew left, with the exception of "Captain Renshaw, Lieutenant [Charles W.] Zimmerman, two other officers, and the crew of the captain's gig, who remained until the last to fire the vessel." With these preparations complete, "The fire was applied, Captain Renshaw was descending the ladder, and all the rest were in the boat, when (at 8:45) the after magazine prematurely exploded, and they were all blown up with the vessel."[37] Chief engineer William R. Greene was among the officers killed in the incident, which another report set at four officers and six men in addition to Renshaw.[38] The fleet surgeon, J. M. Foltz, provided the fullest accounting of the lost team, which he identified as missing:

1. William B. Renshaw   Commander
2. Charles W. Zimmerman   Lieutenant
3. W. R. Greene   Acting assistant engineer
4. John Callahan   Gunner's mate
5. Samuel P. King   Quarter gunner
6. W. Esson   Coxswain
7. Rodolphus C. Hibbard   Seaman
8. Henry Bethke   do
9. Peter Johnson   do

10. Mathew McDonald	Ordinary Seaman
11. Hugh McCabe	Second-class fireman
12. William Reeves	do
13. George E. Cox	do[39]

Naval operations against the Confederate defenders on the Mississippi River brought personnel into traditional dangers from opposing ordnance but also created the conditions for some participants to perish in other ways. While Federal ships confronted the garrisons holding Forts St. Philip and Jackson en route to New Orleans, one of two men died when he fell from the masthead of the *Katahdin*.[40] Edward Butler recalled the burial rites being read for two men: "One was [said] over a mere boy, who, with the ship rolling heavily, had lost his hold upon the rigging, and in his fall became impaled through the head upon a belaying pin in the rail along the ship's waist, causing instant death."[41]

A year later, in March 1863, several of the Union vessels threatening Port Hudson sustained substantial damage, and the threats to the crews included the usually horrific wounds as metal tore through superstructures and into soft flesh. Yet, at least one unfortunate individual perished when in the midst of the heavy combat he fell from the *Hartford* into the river. Lieutenant Edward Terry, aboard a nearby vessel, could discern the cries for help and called out, "Man overboard, throw him a rope," but the marine drifted away in the current before the assistance could reach him.[42]

Although they were not under enemy fire at the time, a similar situation occurred the next year with another pair of Union vessels. The *Peosta* was one of several tin-clad gunboats plying the western waters in operations against the Confederates. It often teamed with the *Paw Paw*, and when that vessel experienced difficulty, the *Peosta* moved up to render aid. Unfortunately, during the January 10, 1864, effort, two of the crew fell overboard and drowned before they could be rescued.[43]

J. W. Bell of the U.S. Navy provided an account of the death of a colleague to the editors of the *Western Reserve Chronicle* in early February 1864. In a short notice he explained, "James P. Williams, Acting Quartermaster on board U.S. Flag Ship Peosta, and formerly of Warren, O., came to his death on the evening of the 6th of February, by falling overboard while in the act of drawing a pail of water from the river." The shocking situation did not go undetected, for when the officer "called for help," the commander of the vessel ordered boats to be lowered immediately, "but the current being very strong, he sank down to a watery grave before they could give him any assistance." Bell described Williams as "a fine young man of about 19 years of age" and noted that he "was loved by all who knew him. He leaves many dear friends to mourn his death."[44]

In Texas, an accident involving the transportation of troops proved fatal at the end of July 1864. Two steamers had arrived to provide the means of transferring members of the Twentieth Wisconsin and the Ninety-Fourth Illinois. In his diary, Benjamin McIntyre provided an account of what happened next. "The boats were lying side by side in the stream," he noted. "The two regiments were ordered upon them at an early hour—it was very dark and no lights were placed on the boats so that the troops could desern their way distinctly over piles of freight of every variety." The use of two vessels for two different regiments complicated matters as well. "The 20th Wisc. Reg. were to take the outside boat—necessitating them of course to pass over the inside one. The river was full banks, the current very swift. Each man had his Knapsack strapped to his back and of course also a full set of equipments besides his cartridge box containing forty rounds." The situation would not have been out of the ordinary had the men been ensured of proper lighting or guidance. Instead, as the writer explained, "One of the soldiers of the 20th thus equipped in passing over boxes, coils of rope, barrels, wood, tents etc. made a misstep and fell into the river." The fellow managed to keep himself afloat for a few minutes, but a yawl launched to retrieve him only "got within a few feet of the drowning man when he sank." McIntyre considered the death more than a mere accident, maintaining, "A single lantern upon the bow of the Steamer would have Spared this melancholy accident." As it was, he felt the matter was likely not to remain in the forefront of people's minds for very long.[45]

Charles Sherman had the misfortune of witnessing the evidence of numerous water-related fatalities in his service on the Gulf coast in 1862. In one case, he noted, "The morning that we got to Fort Jackson I was on gard on the quarter Deck to keep the men from intruding on to the Oficers. Looking toward the North American thay was taking Troops from her to put in Fort Philips. One of the men fell into the Stream, knapsack, Belts and all." The crew of the vessel responded almost instantaneously. "Thay droped a boat in duble quick. It was not a mineut before thay was rowing after him and we couled see them Grasp the knapsack that was floating and lift that into the Boat but no man." The effort at rescuing the soldier represented a concerted application of resources. "Thay had 3 boats down then and thay looked for him some little time, but found him not and it is very Deep and when he struck the water the knapsack flipped him over is head and the undercurrent kept him down and carried him downstream." Unfortunately, the situation was not unique. "There was 5 drowned at Ship Iland he same way. They were in swimming and the undertow carried them out till thay were drowned and then Flung them Back dead."[46]

On June 14, Sherman provided another instance of a water-related fatality: "We Lost one of our men by Drownding Last night. He was a good swimer." The soldier concluded of the conditions, "The Missippi is a Dangrous Stream. It is full of Eadeys and the under Curent is so Strong that it is Daingrous to Drop your self under has you Can in most Streams. The Body has not been found and Probley will never be."[47]

In August, he wrote once more of a comrade's death: "Thair was a Leautenant of one of the Batterys Drowned Wensday of this Week. His Body was not found till today, Sadurday. He got into one of the Eadeys or Worlpools that the Mississippi is toubled with." Repeating his earlier thoughts on the inherent dangers, Sherman added, "Thair is no hope of anyone if thay Fall into the Curent or is Sucked down in the Pooll formed by the Curent meeting one another on the Sides of the Stream. The Watter runs up and then Down."[48]

Even as the war progressed, Charles Sherman recorded additional deaths that surely must have sounded very familiar to the recipients of his correspondence. On July 8, 1864, from New Orleans, he wrote to his wife, "Chirldren," and parents to relate a collective update that included a difficult scene: "As we was going up to Morganza Bend, we met a Dead Soldier floting face dowan wards in the Watter with is Knapsack on. He must have fell overboard from some Boat and he may stay in the River any length of time, for human life is not thought much of in theas times."[49]

Would the same fate await William Johnson as he boarded a transport to return to his hometown of New York City on a furlough? He must have felt fortunate to have the chance to see his loved ones once more after facing the dangers of wartime service. Nevertheless, a warm return to the embrace of loved ones for the man who had enlisted at age twenty-seven, at the end of 1861, was not meant to be. In circumstances not delineated in any detail in his regimental listing, he would be recorded as follows: "Died March 19, 1864 on his way home on Transport Ellen S. Terry."[50]

Refugees from slavery often experienced harrowing circumstances to realize their freedom. Blockading vessels could appear as likely sources of succor for fugitives in the regions they patrolled. The commander of USS *Governor Buckingham*, stationed off the coast of North Carolina, submitted a report in February 1864 that outlined the attempt of a party that included women and children to reach his vessel. As the craft came alongside, the heavy swells swamped the boat and threw the occupants into the water. The Federal blockader managed to rescue four men, two women, and three children, but W. G. Saltonstall reported,

"One of the latter was dead when brought on board. They escaped on Sunday night from Shallotte Inlet."[51]

Whether slaves or free, African American noncombatants took risks as refugees or when serving as guides for Union units. On the watercourses that crisscrossed the South, some of these individuals took on important roles as river pilots for Federal vessels. In March 1862, one man was engaged in this vital task when he fell into the hands of local Confederate forces in Florida. Wounded in the firefight, the captive became an object lesson in the eyes of his captors, who executed him to discourage similar activities among his peers.[52]

Even with the help of local pilots, accidents continued to plague the busy water routes. While his regiment traveled from Paducah, Kentucky, toward Nashville, Tennessee, to reinforce George Thomas as he awaited the approach of John Bell Hood's army, Leander Stillwell of the Sixty-First Illinois Infantry recalled two tragic incidents. Stillwell and his comrades were aboard the "little stern-wheel steamboat 'Rosa D'" and had joined with the "Masonic Gem" to make the journey in tandem. Perhaps for security or stability, the two vessels remained lashed together for the larger portion of the trip. But, Stillwell explained, "In going up the Cumberland the regiment lost two men by drowning; Henry Miner, of Co. D, and Perry Crochett, of Co. G." No one had seen Miner after a glimpse of him "on the lower deck of the boat," but at some point, he vanished, leaving only a kepi on the deck. "It was supposed that in some manner he missed his footing and fell between the boats, and was at once sucked under by the current and drowned."

Crochett's fate was less uncertain. He "stumbled and fell into the river in the day time, from the after part of the hurricane deck of the boat. He was perhaps stunned by the fall, for he just sank like a stone." Again, nothing could be found by the skiff dispatched to rescue him except his "little wool hat [which] was floating around on the top of the waves, but poor Perry was never seen again." Stillwell did not know if the body of either soldier ever surfaced, but he lamented their losses, especially under the circumstances. "Miner and Crochett were both young men, about my own age," he explained, "and had been good and brave soldiers. Somehow it looked hard and cruel that after over three years' faithful service they were fated at last to lose their lives by drowning in the cold waters of the Cumberland, and be devoured by catfish and snapping turtles,—but such are among the chances in the life of a soldier."[53]

Cities with canals, rivers, and other courses could also pose risks to the unwary or unlucky. At the end of January 1863, the following notice appeared in Richmond of an investigation into two mysterious drowning deaths in the waterways of the city: "Inquest—Acting Coroner Richard D. Sanxay yesterday held an inquest over the remains of the two Federal soldiers who were drowned by falling into the James River and Kanawha canal, on the morning of Tuesday, as they were journeying from the Libby Prison to the Petersburg Depot, in this city." The investigation determined "that the bridge spanning the canal" had collapsed without warning after having been in continual use "for six years and upwards." The writer concluded, "Abundant evidence was on hand that it had been used on all occasions, without fear of the result, up to the late fatal accident."

In addition to the inquiry into the deaths of "Daniel LaRuke and George Ephart, of Company K, 30th Indiana regiment," the two Federal soldiers who lost their lives on the occasion, an effort was made to find out how an "unknown stranger" came to his death. "This latter, as was said on yesterday, resembled a Georgia soldier from his uniform, and had been in the water for several weeks." Based upon the evidence, the author of the article concluded, "So far as the Federal soldiers were concerned, [the inquiry] came to the conclusion that their death was caused by the breaking of the bridge and their subsequent falling into the canal by reason thereof." For the "unknown stranger" the circumstances were less clear but pointed to the victim having "accidentally" fallen into the canal and drowned as a result.

Misfortune seemed to be the hallmark of the investigation. The writer added, "While the inquest was progressing, another body was fished out of the canal, which proved to be that of F. Padican, of the 18th Mississippi regiment. It was ordered to be buried without the formality of an inquest. Three other Federal soldiers yet remain to be accounted."[54]

On December 3, 1863, the *Gallipolis Journal* of Ohio offered its readers a cautionary tale: "Another soldier was drowned at the wharf-boat on last Friday night. His name or Regiment we have not been able to learn. It seems that he walked overboard in the dark, and being encumbered with his overcoat, knapsack, etc., sunk almost immediately. It is high time some more stringent police regulations were adopted at the wharf, especially at night." Unfortunately, this type of incident was not new or uncommon for this location. "Six or seven soldiers have been drowned at our wharf, nearly all of whom might have been saved, had the proper precautionary measures been used."[55]

Inquests and inquiries might determine negligence or willfulness when individuals perished in local waters. But even among seasoned crewmen, situations that might be relatively routine could become deadly. In late 1861, a twenty-nine-year-old New Yorker named Russell Johnson became the victim of an accident that involved the attempt by one vessel to employ a line or cable to tow another. The entry for Johnson noted simply, "Killed, Oct. 4, 1861, by breaking of a hawser."[56]

These dangers continued to exist as personnel carried out such seemingly ordinary operations during the war. The sandbars at the mouth of the Mississippi River posed an obstacle for larger craft as the Union fleet gathered to threaten New Orleans from the Gulf in March 1862. The suspension of the dredging of the channels had allowed silt to accumulate and compelled the use of tugs to pull the vessels across that could not pass under their own power. In the course of one of these efforts, two men perished when a hawser parted.[57]

In 1864, the same fatal circumstances befell another man as reported in a Port Royal, South Carolina, newspaper: "John Ross, a deck hand on the steamer *Fulton* had both legs broken below the knee by the parting of a hawser, attached to a steam-tug. He was carefully conveyed to the General Hospital, and died from the effects of his wounds Wednesday morning last." Ross's death hit especially hard at home, although his comrades made an effort to assist his bereaved loved ones. "He leaves a large family in New York,—for whom a liberal subscription was made by the officers and crew."[58]

In December 1863, John Dahlgren forwarded ill tidings from a Union vessel plying the waters of Florida. The accident had occurred aboard the USS *Seneca* at the end of November and involved an individual the commander described as "an excellent man." Michael Hogan, an "ordinary seaman," was "heaving the lead in the main chains" when a "parting of the breastband" caused him to fall overboard. Efforts immediately got under way to rescue him, but these failed to locate Hogan, and he was presumed to have drowned.[59]

Likewise, open or moving machine parts on the war craft of the Civil War could produce fatalities as well, even outside of the context of combat. While serving duty on the Nansemond River near Suffolk, Virginia, in 1863, a service member experienced deadly misfortune. As reported in the *New York Times* in April of that year, "John Healy was killed on board the *Mount Washington* last evening, by getting caught by the crank of the engine."[60]

As the deaths of some of these men indicated, routine duties were not without their risks. Mooring vessels or securing them from an anchorage entailed potentially fatal situations. In late December, such a tragedy struck a crew member in Mississippi. An account of the campaigning noted that the gunboat *Tyler* was attempting to get under way after receiving coal when the accident occurred. According to historian Myron J. Smith Jr., "As her hook was being drawn out of the mud, Seaman Daniel C. Bice slipped and fell overboard, hitting his head on the anchor toe and disappeared. His body was not recovered."[61]

Once under way, vessels and their crews could be in as much danger from the stresses and strains on the engine mechanisms meant to propel them. On

March 18, 1862, the *Western Democrat* of Charlotte, North Carolina, informed its readers, "Yesterday, Sunday morning, while the old steamer Johnson, ferry-boat plying between Beaufort and Fort Macon and the Morehead City Railroad wharf, was lying at the Fort wharf awaiting for passengers and freight on her way to connect with the up train, her boiler bursted, killing one man, a Mr. Parsons, member of Capt. Guion's company, and wounding three others."[62]

A lesser, although still fatal, disaster occurred on the waters in the new year. According to the February 17, 1863, edition of the *Alexandria Gazette*, "In New York, last Saturday, an explosion of a steam pipe occurred on board the Whitney iron battery Keokuk, by which four men lost their lives."[63]

Tragedy struck in New York Harbor on April 15, 1864, when the Union gunboat *Chenango* suffered a boiler explosion. Newspapers across the North carried the news of the sensation, with the headline in the *New York Herald* trumpeting, "Appalling Disaster in the Harbor" on April 16 and offering "Additional Details of the Shocking Catastrophe" the following day. Before heading to Fortress Monroe in Virginia, the vessel was making adjustments "for the purpose of correcting her compasses." According to the account, "When opposite Fort Hamilton, at a quarter past four P.M., her port boiler suddenly exploded, blowing up the decks and severely scalding all connected with the engineering department—thirty-three in all."[64]

On April 17, the newspaper offered readers an "Accurate List of the Casualties" and noted "Nineteen of the Sufferers Dead and Twelve Others in a Hopeless Condition." Describing the graphic nature of some of the injuries, the writer also provided details on the roles of the individuals involved:

> The following is a list of those who died on board previous to being removed to the Marine Hospital—
> Name . . . Rate.
> 1—John Maber . . . Coalheaver.
> 2—John Murphy . . . 1st class fireman.
> 3—James Smith . . . Gunner's mate.

> The following persons died after being removed to the Marine Hospital. We give their names in order of death, with the hour of the occurrence of each—
> Name . . . Rate . . . Time.
> 1—Henry Livingston . . . Coalheaver. . . . . . 9:30 P.M.
> 2—John White. . . . . . Third Asst. Engineer . 10:20 P.M.

3—Jos. A. Conway
 or Wm. Bone . . . First class firemen . . 12 M.
4—Bernard Boyle. . . . First class firemen . . 12:50 A.M.
5—Archibald Fleming . . Second class firemen . .1:30 A.M.
6—Frank P. Root. . . . Second Asst. Engineer . 1:30 A.M.
7—Albert Skedaway . . . Second Asst. Engineer . 3 A.M.
8—Mitchell Rody. . . . Coalheaver. . . . . . 3:50 A.M.
9—John M. Smith. . . . First class boy. . . . 4 A.M.
10—J. A. Cahill. . . . Act'g Chief Engineer . 4:10 A.M.
11—Geo. Wilson. . . . Seaman. . . . . 6:45 A.M.
12—Jos. Lyons. . . . . Ship's Cook. . . . . . 8 A.M.
13—Martin Mitchell . . Landsman. . . . . . . 8 A.M.
14—John Rody. . . . . Landsman. . . . . . . 9:50 A.M.
15—Wheeler Sherman . . Coxswain. . . . . . . 11 A.M.
16—Jas. I. Macombay . . —— . . . . . . 1:55 P.M.

Nineteen had died up to five o'clock yesterday afternoon.

The *Herald* account also provided more specific information on the backgrounds of some of the officers involved. Noting the Virginia birth of first assistant engineer and acting chief Joseph Cahill, the writer explained, "He took an active part in suppressing the rebellion, and never faltered in his attachment to the flag of his country. In a moment, without warning, this promising officer was taken from us, beloved and regretted." For John White, acting third assistant engineer, "He leaves a family to mourn his loss." Similarly, Frank P. Root, acting second assistant engineer, "leaves a wife and three small children unprovided for in Brooklyn. He was a fine gentleman, and very much respected by all who knew him."[65]

The following month, the *New York Herald* attempted to focus optimistically on the naval disaster that had cost so many men their lives: "It is a beautiful provision of Providence that out of their very disasters mankind learn lessons of wisdom. Many a great evil has been overcome, many a great wrong made right, many an habitual error corrected, through the influence of these accidents and misfortunes which every day overtake the human race, and for a time overwhelm them with gloom and sorrow." For the writer, a situation that had caused "unspeakable anguish in many families" had also prompted investigations by which "a very extraordinary light has been thrown upon the manner in which the boilers and machinery of many of the government's vessels are constructed, and by the aid of this exposure it is to be hoped and expected that a radical reform will be immediately commenced in the entire system of constructing these important portions of our steam vessels-at-war."[66]

Even with the possibility of reform as a salve for the losses sustained, flaws in operating systems continued to be marked by tragedy. Another serious accident took place aboard the USS *Tulip* when an explosion destroyed that vessel and killed forty-nine men on November 11, 1864.[67] The *Evening Star* provided a harrowing version of the incident "whereby," it asserted, "over sixty lives were lost." Traversing the Potomac River, the gunboat, "attached to the Potomac Flotilla," experienced distress "at 6 o'clock and 20 minutes, [when] the boilers exploded with a terrific crash, rending the upper portion of the vessel to atoms, scalding the officers and crew and throwing them in all directions." The men charged with the responsibility for the craft were among the victims. "Captain [William H.] Smith, the pilot, James Jackson, Master's Mate Hammond, and the quartermaster were on the bridge over the boilers, and must have been blown to atoms. The only trace left of Captain Smith was his hat." A couple of the initial ten survivors picked up subsequently died from their injuries, with several others expected to do likewise, while the rest of the men onboard were assumed to have perished.[68] An officer on another vessel reported locating the wreck and recovering some of the personal effects of the crew members, then added in a postscript, "I should have mentioned that the cutter referred to above was entirely stove, and that I found some of the ribs and knees of the Tulip on shore, showing that the vessel was completely blown to pieces."[69]

On January 27, 1865, the steamer *Eclipse* suffered a catastrophic boiler explosion while plying western waters that caused the deaths of twenty-nine members of the Ninth Indiana Battery.[70] The commander of the post at Paducah, Kentucky, reported that the vessel "blew up at Johnsonville at 6 A.M. this day" and set the number of men killed at ten. Some sixty-eight injured men, "more or less," had come under his responsibility, and Brigadier General Solomon Meredith pledged to the governor of Indiana in a wire, "I am doing all I can for them."[71]

The inability of all waterborne craft to avoid other vessels, particularly in the narrow passageways of southern watercourses, produced additional fatalities. While traveling aboard the steamer *Burton* on May 17, 1862, Wisconsin native Halbert Paine recorded an accident involving two craft on the busy western waterways: "The *Ceres*, having the 6th Michigan aboard, collided with the *Kineo*, and in the collision a soldier lost both his legs; and afterwards died."[72] Later in the summer, he noted a second incident, in which a steamer bearing wounded men and the body of General Thomas Williams from Baton Rouge, collided with another vessel and sank in which "many of the wounded were lost."[73]

The impact of such collisions could be felt individually or collectively, but it did not escape even those who had not witnessed or experienced them directly. From his post in Mississippi, New Englander Charles Sherman reported the grim realities: "Thair is quite a number of Bodys Floting in the River at this time has one of our Gun Boats run into a Steamer that had over a Hundred of our Wounded on Board that was Wounded in the Late Battle up to Baton Rouge."[74]

A water transportation accident on August 13, 1862, resulted in casualties that reminded one newspaperman of a battlefield encounter. The report summarized the impact of the collision of two troop transports, the *West Point* and the *George Peabody*, with the loss of some seventy-five men, consisting of "gallant soldiers, who, having recovered from sickness, were en route here to rejoin their comrades." The severe loss of life among the men caused the author of the piece to observe, "It would be a very sharp battle in which seventy soldiers were killed, yet that number here ingloriously perished."[75]

The dangers of traversing narrow waterways, laced with both natural and manmade obstacles, in the area north of Vicksburg were sufficient to command the attentions of the officers who led their men through them, but at least one became so incensed by the conditions that he protested to his superiors. "It would be simply murdering my men," Brigadier General Clifton B. Fisk explained, "to crowd them, as it would be necessary to do." The avowed abolitionist believed the situation was not unlike those that enslaved persons had experienced in the worst days of the Atlantic slave trade: "Nearly two hundred new-made [graves] at Helena contain the bodies of men of my command who were murdered outright by crowding them into dirty, rotten transports, as closely as slaves in the 'middle passage.'" Fisk was not through venting his anger or demonstrating the degree to which he felt the service was culpable. "The company from the Twenty-ninth Iowa, on the *Luella*, lost all their arms and clothing by the sinking of that staunch vessel, and one of my best officers, Lieutenant [Lucius B.] Nash, will doubtless die from injuries received thereby."[76]

Historian Myron Smith noted another accident in the region that occurred when a "launch from the *Volunteer*, with an officer from (Brigadier General Leonard F.) Ross's staff, a clerk and two 46th Indiana soldiers, was sent ashore on an errand." During its return, the vessel missed its rendezvous with the *Volunteer* and was run over and swamped inadvertently by the *Ida May*. The account noted that some of the occupants of the floundering craft were more fortunate than others: "All four men were thrown into the water, with two sucked under the transport, only one of whom surfaced to be rescued with the first two."[77]

A collision on the Red River between the USS *Conestoga* and the ram *General Price* resulted in the loss of the former. According to his report of the incident,

Rear Admiral David D. Porter assigned fault for the accident on the pilot of the ram, "while passing her at night . . . [and] not paying proper attention to the signals, which were properly made by the pilot of the *Conestoga*." Porter noted, "So great was the blow that the *Conestoga* sunk in four minutes, the *Price* having cut into her engines and sunk her immediately. The vessel will, I fear, be a total loss, as nothing but the tops of the wheelhouses are to be seen, and the water is now very low." Fortunately, the human toll was not as great as the financial or physical loss. "All the officers and crew escaped in the boats (except two of the latter, who were drowned), notwithstanding the short notice they had" for reacting to the emergency, "which speaks well for the disciple of the ship."[78] The commander of the *Conestoga* repeated the praise for the crew under the difficult circumstances and reiterated the loss of "two seamen, James Brennan and Thomas Robinson, the latter of the *Lexington*."[79]

Fire could prove to be as unnerving for men confined to wooden vessels as for those facing fire of a different sort from an opposing force hurling metal at them. Under the latter circumstances, there was at least the option of returning the rounds in defense. However, for the former, once flames erupted and spread, there was often little one could do to combat the danger and avoid perishing under the most gruesome circumstances. Such dangers could erupt quickly as with the Confederate vessel *Natchez*, which was hauling cotton when flames broke out. The crew could not extinguish the blaze, and five slaves and three whites died in the incident.[80]

In August 1863, a newspaper account detailed a tragic accident that involved the "splendid new steamer Ruth, valued at $100,000," when the boat burned "opposite the foot of Island No. 1," in the Mississippi River. Heading toward Helena, Arkansas, from St. Louis, Missouri, the vessel contained "eight Paymasters and their clerks, with $2,600,000 in greenbacks to pay off Grant's army." Although some civilians traveling or working onboard perished, the greater number of deaths occurred for the men in uniform. "Thirty-one soldiers of company H, Ninth Wisconsin, Lieut. Courier, one corporal and four privates are lost." The danger did not cease for the men who managed to work themselves clear of the wreck initially. "Three men were killed by a stage plank falling on them while in the water; all together there were about thirty lives lost."[81]

A terrific explosion occurred at Vicksburg, Mississippi, in September 1863, as a mixed team of civilians and soldiers loaded ammunition on a steamer. Although the death toll among the workers was severe, the impact on soldiers detailed for assisting with the operation was also significant. The accidental dropping of a box of percussion ordnance initiated the blast. A newspaper account set the estimated number of soldier fatalities in the incident at "twenty-five" out of some 100 to 200 men involved.[82]

Accidents with gunnery on the vessels could also end in unintended fatalities. A standard protocol could turn deadly, as the members of the crew of the USS *Mohican* would attest. In the act of firing a salute upon entering the port of Bahia, a premature explosion cost the life of one man and left another badly wounded.[83]

On August 13, 1864, Washington's *Evening Star* related an unusual accident that cost one Union sailor his life: "This morning, while the gunners at the experimental battery were practicing with a small piece against a target, one of the balls went through, striking Master's Mate Thos. Bowers, on the Teaser, which was lying within range. The wound inflicted is a serious one in the head, and although he is still living, there are but little hopes of his recovery." Although the vessel was ostensibly located out of range, its position left its occupants at unintended risk. "It seems that the ball, in passing through the target, glanced to one side."[84]

A Richmond newspaper reprinted the "particulars of a melancholy accident" that had originally appeared in the *New Orleans Picayune* in November 1861:

> On Wednesday night (the 15th), between 10 and 11 o'clock, as Orderly Sergeant James Sherrin, of Pelican Guards, Company B, now on board the Confederate States Ship steam Red Rover, was making the usual rounds to the different posts, he entered into a conversation with private James O Rourke, a friend of his, on Post No. 6, and asked to examine his rifle. While he was handing it over, the trigger being accidentally on a full cock, the rifle was discharged, and the full charge entered Sherrin's right arm, between the elbow and shoulder, and penetrated the right breast.

Comrades immediately summoned medical assistance, "but the physician, Dr. Hegewinzh, upon examination, pronounced the wounds mortal, and Father Burke, of the Jesuit's Church, being called, administered to the unfortunate Sergeant the consoling rites of his church." Taken to the "Charity Hospital by his fellow-soldiers," Sherrin nevertheless succumbed to his injuries and "expired shortly after."[85]

In another instance of a bizarre accident, the June 21, 1864, edition of the *Evening Star* reported, "On Wednesday last, J. Burger, a first-class boy on the gunboat Anacostia, was on shore down the river, and the hammer of his rifle caught in the brush, by which it went off, and the ball entered his right side, passing through both lungs and out the left shoulder." Burger clung to life initially after being "brought out to his vessel, where his wound was dressed, but he died on Friday."[86]

Less lamented was Captain Walter G. Dunn of the 109th Pennsylvania, who perished in a boat accident late in the war, but the mishap may very well have prevented some of the men in his command from resorting to what would become known in a later conflict as "fragging," or intentional homicide meant to appear as accidental or enemy induced. One of Dunn's men described him as "a tyrant to the men since he has been in command of the Regt, and had he lived and shewed himself after our boys got home, in all probability he would have been killed, for he was brutal almost beyond Endurance."[87] Certainly, the captain was fortunate that some of his men had not already acted upon the desire for retribution in camp or battle, where an accident might appear as a matter of course during warfare.

Death came to another unfortunate individual in the East on April 25: "On Friday night a fatal accident occurred on board the Dragon, of the Potomac Flotilla, which was lying off the Wycomico River. Acting Master's Mate Stephen M. Casey, while in the act of stooping, let his pistol fall out of the frog, when it fell on a step and exploded, the ball entering his right breast, and passing upwards, caused his death in a few minutes." The Washington *Evening Star* piece offered the following additional information about the victim: "The deceased was a young man of about 27, and had been attached to the flotilla for about six months."[88]

Charleston Harbor, South Carolina, provided an example of circumstances gone awry at the end of August 1863 with the sinking of the steamer *Sumter*. An after-action report by Major Robert De Treville at Fort Moultrie indicated that "a low, black steamer" approached the city, "coming in from the direction of the enemy's fleet." Not being able to identify the vessel, he decided to take no chances. "As soon as she was in easy range, I ordered fire opened, and she apparently, stopped her course." Major De Treville waited for the crew to signal the fort if the ship was friendly as was supposed to be the established procedure, but when nothing transpired, the fort fired another "4 or 5 shots," until a small light appeared. The mysterious standoff continued until a small craft finally came ashore. "This morning the steamer is plainly seen off Morris Island, sunk, and I am reliably informed that 2 men of the Twentieth South Carolina Volunteers were killed."

De Treville condemned the circumstances that led to "so unfortunate an occurrence." He added, "Not a word of warning was given to any one of the batteries that a steamer laden with our own men would be coming in at that hour from the very direction from which we momentarily expected the approach of an enemy." As bad as the situation was for the vessel and the two men lost, the officer believed matters could have been worse. "Had this fort opened with all its guns, the result would have been, indeed, disastrous. As it is, we have cause of congratulation that the neglect of the officer in charge of the boat to use the necessary precautions has resulted in so small a loss."[89]

Quartermaster major Motte A. Pringle, in whose service the *Sumter* was operating, offered an alternative version that exonerated the officers and crew of the stricken vessel of any culpability for the incident. Having landed his supplies and taken on board the contingent of soldiers, Pringle faced a crucial decision. As he reported, "I found that the tide had fallen so low as to render it impossible for me to bring the steamer over the flats between Forts Sumter and Johnson. It remained for me either to keep the boat at Cumming's Point till daylight, and run the risk of being shelled by the enemy, or to pursue the course outside of Fort Sumter." Pringle saw the circumstance as routine. "Little dreaming of being fired into by our friends, I of course adopted the latter alternative." Once the firing began, he insisted that he caused a whistle to be blown "and myself waved the best lantern (an oil one), I could find, toward the fort." He explained that his actions should have had the proper effect in saving the vessel and occupants from additional friendly fire. "I am credibly informed that all the signals which I have enumerated were distinctly heard, or seen, by many officers and men on the island, and also the screams of the men begging, 'for God's sake,' not to shoot, were heard." Pringle observed that the shot that caused the fatalities came after his efforts to end the firing, "so that if our signals had been respected as soon as observed, no damage would have been done."[90]

Charleston Harbor was also the scene of a series of fatal occurrences for the Confederacy's revolutionary submersible craft, *H. L. Hunley*. Developed in the private sector in Mobile, Alabama, the submarine came under government control and shifted to the South Carolina coast, where it would be expected to challenge the Union blockading vessels. Before it could undertake that effort, two accidents, on August 29 and October 15, 1863, cost the lives of most of the crew members, including the inventor, Horace L. Hunley.

In the first incident, an accident caused the craft to dive when not prepared, and only Lieutenants John A. Payne and Charles H. Hasker and two others succeeded in extricating themselves. Hasker went down with the vessel when the hatch cover caught his leg, but he managed to free himself and swim to the surface. The remainder of the crew perished. "Poor fellows," one soldier concluded of the men trapped in the odd-shaped iron craft, "they were five in one coffin."[91] Another man wrote home of the impact of the tragedy for him and his comrades: "It has cast quite a gloom over us. Strange, isn't it, that while we hear with indifference of men being killed all around us, the drowning of one should effect us so."[92]

One of the contemporaries recalled the state of the *Hunley* after being raised from the second fatal plunge in the waters of Charleston Harbor: "When the hatch covers were lifted considerable air and gas escaped. Captain Hunley's body was forward, with his head in the forward hatchway, his right hand on top of his head." Mr. Thomas Park was located in the "after hatchway," in the same contortion caused apparently as the men struggled to work free from the sinking vessel. "The other bodies were floating in the water. Hunley and Parks were undoubtedly asphyxiated, the others drowned."[93]

In the North, trials for underwater craft led to the death of Major Edward B. Hunt, tasked with developing a one-man submersible. On October 2, the *New York Times* contained an account of the incident: "Maj. HUNT had, it is well known, been engaged for many months in the construction of a new submarine battery of his own invention, which promised to give the most important results. Yesterday, it is stated, that in making experiments on the vessel a shell burst, and the gas evoked so affected him that he fell down into the hold, producing concussion of the brain." Hunt survived the incident initially but sustained sufficient trauma that after moving to the Naval Hospital, he "died during the day." The writer offered a compelling tribute to the fallen officer: "He died, although not on the battle-field, yet in harness, devoted, with all his powers of soul, mind and heart to the service of his country."[94]

A subsequent notice of the funeral of the fallen officer attributed the fatal accident to "the premature explosion of a shell with which he was experimenting." It also included a copy of "General Orders, No. 31," issued from headquarters in New York, that noted Hunt's death as "the result of an accident, while engaged in the prosecution of investigations incident to his profession, and immediately connected with the war in which we are now engaged."[95]

Tampering with or encountering Confederate devices designed to sink or disable vessels could prove deadly for Union personnel regardless of their branch of service. According to former U.S. lieutenant colonel William Fox, who compiled an account of regimental deaths in the war, the 132nd New York experienced significant losses when "an accidental explosion of torpedoes" occurred on May 26, 1864. The blast left thirty-one men dead.[96] In the aftermath of the fighting at Mobile Bay in 1864, U.S. Marine Josiah Gregg captured the routines and dangers of duty there. "An accident occurred on shore this P.M." he wrote of some of the troops encamped nearby on August 25. "A lot of men were handling some torpedoes when one exploded, killing and wounding several." He explained that the next day some of the men brought on his vessel for treatment succumbed to their injuries as well: "Four of the wounded men died last night" and were buried "with the usual services."[97]

Moving through the difficult terrain to the north of Vicksburg, Mississippi, presented many challenges to vessels and the crews who manned them. In addition to the threat of artillery batteries or, more ominously, the Confederate underwater torpedoes or mines, there were the natural obstacles of narrow, winding passages, unseen shoals, and other obstructions to overcome. A scholar of the campaign identified at least two instances in which crew members became victims of the natural growth that characterized the Yazoo River environment. In one case, a black crewman named Coffee, lying in sick bay, was crushed "when a huge limb, broken off by the persistence of our smokestacks, came down end-wise on the deck, and passing through, administered the death blow."[98] Similarly, "A giant limb fell upon the top deck of [the] Lioness, killing a deckhand."[99]

When human error or accidents did not lead to fatalities on board the vessels of North and South, adverse weather conditions could lead to the same result. From his posting at Ship Island, Mississippi, Rufus Kinsley noted in a letter to his sister at the end of December 1863 the death of a comrade: "He was on one of the gun boats in a heavy storm, two weeks ago yesterday, and was lost overboard. His body washed ashore to-day." Kinsley could not resist the chance for a lesson: "Didn't your geography [books] tell large stories about storms on the Gulf of Mexico?"[100]

Blockade duty entailed dangers for both those who attempted to enforce and those who sought to elude the closure of Confederate ports. In early January 1862, storms slammed the Outer Banks of North Carolina, jostling Union naval vessels and threatening crew members. On land, New Yorker Charles Johnson noted the "fearful time" his colleagues aboard the ships were experiencing, although he seemed distressed that the squalls prevented smaller craft from being able to "come ashore with our mail." Even so, the foot soldier recognized the danger and, while sheltered somewhat himself, "learned that the whole fleet had been threatened with destruction, and that an officer and two men were drowned in a desperate attempt to reach the shore in a small boat."[101]

In the same volatile waters, the Monitor, which had earlier achieved legendary status when it engaged the Confederate ironclad Virginia in a historical encounter in Hampton Roads in March 1862, came to grief. The "cheesebox on a raft," as some called it, had accomplished its task of safeguarding the blockade of the Chesapeake Bay, but by late in the year it was needed elsewhere. Secure enough in relatively stable waters, the Monitor was not particularly seaworthy, especially when those seas were the storm-driven tempests of the Outer Banks. Yet, in late 1862, that was the region into which the Monitor traveled with fatal results. Heavy swells quickly overwhelmed the vessel in ways that Confederate shot and shell had not accomplished easily. The Monitor swamped, carrying sixteen crewmen to the bottom on December 30.[102]

Laden with a heavy load of ammunition in rough water, the USS Weehawken suffered a similar catastrophic event on December 6, 1863, when it sank accidentally, taking the lives of four officers and more than twenty men. The USS *Philadelphia* reported saving nine officers and forty-one men when it answered the distress messages, but noted, "one of whom died before getting on board."[103] An inquiry into the incident created a flurry of communications among officials in the navy.[104] The results were nevertheless inconsequential to those who perished, listed in the course of the investigation, where known, along with their duties:

List of the *Weehawken*'s officers supposed to be lost.
    Henry W. Merian, third assistant engineer.
    Augustus Mitchell, third assistant engineer.
    George W. McGowan, acting third assistant engineer.
    Charles Spongberg, acting third assistant engineer.
List of men's names who are supposed to be lost from the *Weehawken*.
    1. Thomas Piper, quartermaster.
    2. James Scallon.
    3. John Buckley.
    4. John Kerrigan, landsman.
    5. John Carpenter, landsman.
    6. Joseph Grogan, second-class boy.
    7. Chas. F. Davis, first-class fireman.
    8. John Williams, landsman.
    9. Chas. H. Willson, seaman.
    10. Wm. H. Williamson, officers' cook.
    11. Christian Anderson, ship's cook.
    12. John Rutledge, third-class boy.
    13. Ralph Anderson.
    14. Edward Goghan.
    15. Edward Mullen, second-class fireman.
    16. Michael Cline, coal heaver.
    17. James Lennon.
    18. Thomas Mee, first-class fireman.
    19. Robert Nugent, coal heaver.
    20. Thomas Donovan, ordinary seaman.
    21. William G. Pike, ordinary seaman.
    22. George M. Leighton, first-class fireman.
    23. Henry Sumner, second-class fireman.
    24. Thomas Stathers, first-class fireman.
    25. Thomas Donlin, landsman.

26. Stephen C. Newman, first-class fireman.

27. Not ascertained.[105]

Cape Hatteras continued to prove dangerous for ships and deadly for crews in the waning stages of the war. A captured and converted steamer, USS *General Lyon* caught fire and sank in those treacherous waters on March 31, 1865, costing the lives of 11 officers and 195 men belonging to the Fifty-Sixth Illinois. This death toll contributed to the regiment's standing among other comparable units from the state with the highest total of fatalities among officers and enlisted personnel from noncombat causes.[106]

Drowning and accidents accounted for many of the deaths of the personnel who walked the decks of vessels in the war, but even in the midst of combat, bursting cannon or premature explosions in their own arsenals produced horrific and psychologically challenging fatalities. One participant concluded, "It is a good deal worse to have a gun explode, than to have the men wounded by the enemy's shot, for they lose confidence."[107]

While engaging Confederate defenders on the upper Mississippi River, the Union crews serving heavy rifled pieces experienced a catastrophic failure. On March 18, 1862, A. M. Pennock explained from Cairo, Illinois, "A rifled gun burst on board the *St. Louis* and killed 2 men outright, wounding mortally 2 more, and wounded 10 others."[108] In his report, Andrew Foote noted specifically, "Killed (by bursting of rifle gun),—James Jackson, seaman, Chicago, Ill.; P. S. Goth, seaman, Maine," as well as the others who had suffered wounds, several listed as "severely."[109]

Admiral David Dixon Porter noted the alarming frequency of premature explosions from the Parrott rifled guns: "One burst on board the 'Ticonderoga,' killing six of the crew and wounding seven others; another burst on board the 'Yantic,' killing one officer and two men; another on board the 'Juanita,' killing two officers, and killing and wounding ten other persons; another on board the 'Mackinaw,' killing one officer and wounding five men." Understandably, Porter concluded, "The bursting of these guns much disconcerted the crews of the vessels, and gave them great distrust of the Parrott 100-pounder."[110] Even so, Union forces continued to employ the weapon. When the Federals assailed the defenses of Fort Fisher in early 1865, the crews brought all tubes to bear, and the resulting shipboard accidents killed or maimed many of them.[111]

Troops defending against such assaults often suffered similar mishaps. The hard-pressed Confederate garrison attempting to hold Fort Henry in February 1862 against a concerted Union bombardment endured brutal conditions from their own weapons as well as those of the enemy. Accidents involving the cannon shredded the crews, demoralized the survivors, and limited the effectiveness of the fort's fire. The most glaring instance was the destruction of the twenty-four-pounder rifle that had inflicted significant damage on the Union fleet before bursting.[112]

Life on the blockade line could be precarious as well to those trying to penetrate it. A month prior to the loss of the *Monitor*, the *Wilmington (N.C.) Journal* reprinted a report from the *Daily Journal* on November 18 of the deaths of ten crew members of a vessel trying to slip past the blockade to reach that city. "Heavy firing was heard here yesterday forenoon," the account noted. "We learn that the blockaders had run a schooner near Moore's Inlet, on the Sound, and a brig ashore near Fort Fisher." The loss of life came from the "brig . . . Fanny Lewis." After her grounding, the writer explained, "We regret to learn that Captain Gardener, his mate and eight of his crew were drowned in trying to reach the shore."[113]

Such fates remained for others as well. When the renowned Confederate spy Rose Greenhow desperately wanted to return to the South from a period overseas in Europe, the Union blockade of the Confederate coastline was the last barrier to cross. Unfortunately, as she made her way toward the shore of North Carolina, the small craft in which she was traveling swamped in the surf. Weighted down by her clothing and a belt containing gold pieces, Greenhow floundered and drowned.[114]

Patrolling for blockade-runners presented many challenges. In ports of call, pent-up energies and alcohol frequently blended into a volatile mix that in one instance on the island of St. Thomas led to at least three deaths among English sailors with whom the Union blockaders brawled.[115] In other cases aboard those vessels, anger turned to targets based on different antagonisms. White crew members on the *Nansemond* killed two black compatriots, and Samuel Leslie, coxswain on the *Lackawana*, became so enraged that he crushed the skull of an African American seaman, James Johnson. Justice in the first case seemed to be had when officers hanged the white perpetrators of the murders that had taken place on the *Nansemond*.[116]

The duty involved other dramatic moments such as that captured by young Charles Mervine on January 17. "At 2 A.M. I being on watch, we discovered a burning vessel at sea, which proved to be the Rebel Str 'Huntress,'" he explained. "She had a cargo of cotton and having a high pressure of steam on she took fire in running the Blockade." The unsuccessful effort was costly in more than the goods consumed in the flames. "Some of her Crew were lost."[117]

An eventful period continued for the seaman, faithfully recorded in his "Jottings." In June, Mervine and his mates had to "bury one of our Shipmates who was killed by the falling of a Launch." Richard Carroll's remains were consigned to the sea as the crew assembled for the solemn ceremony.[118] Then, in September, Edmund Burke perished "when the Ring stopper parted and is supposed to have struck him, he going overboard and sinking beneath the surface never to rise again, and we going at fast speed at the time, he was no doubt struck by the [paddle] wheel causing instant death, as he was not seen after he fell." Mervine, who noted that the ship lowered a boat to conduct a search "in vain," for Burke, concluded with the thought, "Hoping he has gone to a better world, where troubles are at an end."[119]

On October 15, 1863, Roswell Lamson sat down to write his Katie with a heavy heart, and yet mixed emotions. Proud to serve on the waters—he had once told her that "sailors are the vainest people in the world"—he was pleased to have captured the *Howquah* as it tried to run the blockade off the coast of North Carolina. Still, he admitted, "I am very sad to-night . . . I must give you a short account of the incidents of to-day which commenced so hopefully, continued so exciting and ended so tragically." Chasing the *Howquah*, Lamson's USS *Nansemond* had performed almost flawlessly in narrowly avoiding shoals and pressing her quarry. "None but those who have experienced it can know the excitement of a chase at sea," he observed. But, as the *Howquah* finally "stopped" and "began to blow off steam," the task of boarding and securing the vessel became the next necessary part of the process.

The duty fell to the executive officer, Benjamin Porter, but "Mr. [Samuel T.] Strude, 3 Ast. Engineer requested to go, and while Mr. Porter was attending to some duty forward he got into the port quarter boat with his three firemen." Strude had recently worked with another captured steamer and was a logical addition for the assignment. "The boat was as usual hanging at the davits from cranes from which our boats hang ready to drop in to the water," Lamson explained, "and three of the crew were in her ready to lower when we stopped. Mr. Strude and his men had no sooner got in them [when] the additional weight proved too much for the davits, the after one of which though iron snapped short off and the seven persons in the boat were precipitated into the water." The incident might have proved survivable for all, but "Mr. Strude and a seaman named Terry were struck by the falling boat and the iron crane and never rose." Rescuing the others after hearing an alarm raised, Lamson noted dejectedly, "We watched a long time hoping the two missing men would come up, but the blue waters had closed over them forever." He concluded, "It was startling to see the change in the faces of all from high exultation and pride in the achievement of our vessel to deep sorrow for those [of] our comrades who had so suddenly lost their lives in the moment when they expected to be rewarded for their exertions during the day."[120]

Traveling with his battery mates by steamer, Thomas Christie continued his correspondence with family, but noted from "opposite the mouth of the Yazoo [River]," in January 1863, that the trip had not been uneventful. "This voyage was much pleasanter than the one we made last year up the Tennessee," he began optimistically. "A part of the First Kansas were on the ship with us. I am sorry to say that some of them and some of our men were drunk a good part of the time, and there was much quarrelling and fighting." Except for any bruised bodies or egos, the situation might have been acceptable, but in the course of the tussling, "some drunken men fell overboard and were drowned." Christie concluded understandably, "Drunkenness is one of the worst things in the world."[121]

Excess in the consumption of spirituous drink was hardly confined to rowdy volunteers being transported by water. Men in both the brown and blue water navies found temptations difficult to overcome and lost a number of comrades in that fashion. Cairo, Illinois, seemed to be among the worst locations for imbibing crew members to overindulge, with a number dying from what amounted to alcohol poisoning. The worst outburst took place on April 22, 1862, when the consumption of the contents of five barrels of whiskey contributed to the deaths of sixty men to various causes.[122]

Alcohol plagued the blockaders, too. If crews captured blockade-runners, among the treasures they sought were any caches of intoxicants that might be stowed on board. In one instance, after preventing a vessel and its alcoholic contents from escaping their clutches, a boarding party from the steamer *Florida* experienced a breakdown in discipline requiring forcible restraint that led one officer to employ his saber, and a marine to shoot and kill a drunken man.[123]

A combination of mishaps plagued Confederate operations on the water in the spring of 1865. William Chambers noted in his diary on March 25 about the efforts to move forces in Alabama: "As we neared the landing at Blakely a soldier of Cockrell's brigade, while in a state of intoxication, fell overboard and was drowned." However, the problems were not over for these troops. "An hour or two later two boats collided on the river and one of them was instantly sunk." In addition to the supplies squandered, "several lives were lost," as Chambers understood it. "The collision was the result of sheer carelessness, it would seem, for it was a beautiful starlit night and the boats could easily be seen for several hundred yards."[124]

Service for the men who sought to disrupt Union commerce or those tasked with preventing blockade-running could offer unusual circumstances that would prove fatal. In November 1864, Confederate secretary of the navy Stephen Mallory announced the death of "Passed Midshipman William B. Sinclair." Sinclair had come over to a captured vessel to secure it as a prize for the *Florida*. In the process of the operation, "his boat swamped, and he, the only one of the crew lost, perished in rescuing a seaman who could not swim."[125] For a member of the force patrolling the coastline off Texas, securing the wreck of the blockade-running side-wheel steamer *Denbigh* proved deadly. Captain B. F. Sands observed of the incident on May 24, 1865, "I regret to report that Luke Robins, seaman, of the *Seminole*, was instantly killed by the accidental discharge of his own gun, while leaving the wreck."[126]

Disease had devastated the ranks of many men on land; it would not spare those who served on the waters or at sea. Naval service entailed exposure to sicknesses that ranged from communicable and commonplace to tropical and exotic. Complaints of subjection to the elements and the resulting dire effects among crew members were not without foundation. In an examination of personnel in the Confederate naval service, historian William N. Still Jr. noted, "An abstract from quarterly reports of sick from January 1 to October 1, 1863, revealed 6,122 cases treated and 59 deaths."[127]

For some of these men, the illnesses added complications to other conditions, as it did for Union rear admiral Andrew Hull Foote. He had seen service in the western waters, enduring a severe injury at Fort Donelson, before being tapped to lead a flotilla that was expected to assault Charleston, South Carolina. Internal discord caused Secretary of the Navy Gideon Welles angst as he sought to placate egos without sacrificing a focus on the proposed campaign. Some of this sorted out when Admiral John A. Dahlgren traveled to New York to discuss matters with an ailing Foote and left with an arrangement whereby he would command the ironclads, Foote the flotilla, and Major General Quincy A. Gilmore, the troops connected to the operation.

"Then," as historian Craig Symonds observed, "fate played a hand." Foote's condition deteriorated, and he was confined to bed suffering from extreme headaches and liver failure. Sharing a long-standing friendship with the officer, Secretary Welles feared the worst and deemed the dire situation "a great calamity to the nation." Dahlgren returned to Foote's bedside for what amounted to the naval officer's final blessing, and by the next day, Admiral Andrew Foote was dead.[128]

In Virginia, the members of the James River Squadron, including the training vessel *Patrick Henry*, were enduring difficulties as severe as their comrades on shipboard duty at sea. "The annual report for the Office of Medicine and Surgery revealed 464 men were admitted to the Richmond Naval Hospital between July and September 1864," according to historian John Coski, "though only 13 died." Despite this low mortality rate, Coski concluded, "No other station in the Confederate navy suffered as severely from disease."[129]

Shipboard deaths were common for crews exposed to illnesses or other risks associated with the locations they visited. In the quest for Confederate vessels to subdue that would culminate in the sinking of the feared CSS *Alabama*, the USS *Kearsarge* lost several crew members to disease, ranging from the March 1862 death of Sabine De Santo to pneumonia to that of twenty-one-year-old Mark W. Emery and shipmate Clement Boener to fever in 1863. However, the most gruesome death for a crew member came in July 1862; when Edward Tibbetts was enjoying a swim with a comrade in the waters off Algeciras, Spain, a shark attacked him and killed him before he could be saved.[130]

Deaths from disease on the oceangoing vessels could be as harrowing to the men serving at sea as those experienced in combat, even for those who appeared to be otherwise unaffected. When Commander Stephen D. Trenchard of the USS *Rhode Island* issued a report from his mooring in Hampton Roads, Virginia, on September 6, 1862, he noted the deaths of several individuals from illness, including acting master John Whitmore and an army agent, Edgar Burnett, as well as the death of a third man from typhoid fever. Then, he explained, "I regret further to inform the Department of the loss of David A. Menter, coal heaver, who jumped overboard on the 5th of August," in a fit of anxiety or as an apparent suicide. Trenchard added, "Every means was taken to rescue him, but he sank before the boats could reach him."[131]

Edward Conroy, acting volunteer lieutenant for the U.S. supply ship steamer *Union*, duly filed his report from New York on June 30, 1864, which read: "Eighteen hours after leaving Key West a case of yellow fever was reported to me by the surgeon. . . . I am sorry to state that acting assistant paymaster Asa C. Winter died on board on the morning of the 28th June." Tragedy continued to stalk the vessel. "On the 29th instant Michael Ford (machinist), from Key West, died. I did not consider it prudent to keep the bodies, and therefore buried them at sea with all due respect."[132]

A particularly tragic tale befell the crew of *J. S. Chambers*, on blockade duty off Florida in 1864. Acting master's mate John F. Van Nest wrote a series of letters home that detailed the deteriorating conditions for officers and crew. He began on July 8 with a description of the service they had focused on efforts to interdict illicit cotton shipments, then shifted innocently, but ominously, to another topic: "The weather is very warm and makes me feel very uncomfortable and millions of Mosquitoes, and they almost eat me up and I can scarcely sleep at night for them. I hope that I shall not have to spend another summer down on this coast for it will use me up for I can not stand this weather."[133]

Van Nest continued to chronicle the situation as the schooner moved "Off Indian River, Sunday, Aug. 7th, 1864." He noted, "The last few days have been terrible on board this vessel, between twenty-five and thirty men down sick with some kind of fever." The ship's surgeon insisted "it is not the yellow fever," but men quickly began expiring from it nonetheless. "The Pursuer Steward died with it on Friday morning, a Seaman at night, and another at 6 A.M. Saturday morning. They are sick but a few days."[134]

The raging illness spread rapidly, adding regularly to the toll and to the anxiety of the remaining healthy crew members to avoid it. Van Nest managed to remain well, although on Wednesday, August 10, he noted, "Two more of the men died this morning and I think more will die. . . . It is hard to see men die and still this vessel lies here on the Blockade."[135]

The situation remained precarious as more men perished and others got sick, including the captain and most of the officers. Suffering from the shortage of officers capable of maintaining their duties aboard the *J. S. Chambers* and worn down by the toll taken among his comrades, a worried Van Nest explained to his brother that he was unsure "if I will be permitted to go clear or not." In a postscript on Saturday, August 13, he added hopefully, "We are bound for home. If I live I will see you soon. Tell father."[136]

No letters followed from the beleaguered seaman, but a report by an officer who had assumed command when the captain died, noted, "At 6 P.M. on the 18th instant, Acting Master's Mate J. F. Van Nest in, it is supposed, a fit of derangement jumped overboard and was drowned in spite of every effort made to save him."[137] Far from the context of combat, the war had nevertheless claimed another life.

For some troubled souls like Van Nest, death must have seemed preferable to the conditions they faced. A scholar of the Yazoo River campaign observed that a deadly situation occurred when "a quarter-gunner was found dead down in the boat's shot locker . . . his throat cut and with a stab wound in his chest." Myron Smith explained, "Several times earlier the man had threatened to kill himself," but his mates prevented him from acting rashly. "This time, with no one near enough to him to intervene, he succeeded."[138]

Blockade duty seemed to be especially challenging, with long periods of boredom and moments of dramatic action, interspersed with need for constant vigilance. Under the strains of cramped quarters, poor diet, long hours, and illness, men sometimes snapped. One sailor tried to cut his throat to relieve himself of "trouble," while another took the drastic step of stripping off his coat, announcing "Good bye to all," and throwing himself in front of his vessel's paddlewheel.[139]

Another incident took place in the waning days of the existence of the Confederacy's James River Squadron. Famed Confederate admiral Raphael Semmes had transferred to command in Virginia and noted that the situation he had inherited was daunting. A sailor stationed aboard the ironclad *Virginia II* must have concluded similarly and "committed suicide" rather than continue in it.[140]

For troops heading away from incarceration in Confederate prison camps, the opportunity to return to the embrace of loved ones and the security of home occasionally met with insurmountable challenges. In one instance, the steamer *Massachusetts* encountered disaster at the mouth of the Potomac River when it approached the *Black Diamond*. At approximately 10 P.M. on the night of April 27, the vessels collided, sending men hurtling through the air or jumping into the water. Those who could do so clung to debris in a desperate struggle to survive. Many of them never had this chance for rescue, with estimates ranging from fifty to sixty-five lives lost. The Sixteenth Connecticut saw eight men stricken from its rolls in the accident, including Sergeant Samuel G. Grosvenor, Harold S. Loomis, and Charles S. Robinson of Company B; William T. Loomis and musician George W. Carter of Company D; George N. Champlin of Company I; and Edward Smith of Company K.[141] One survivor reflected on "the bad luck as usual" that seemed to overshadow the unit and concluded, "The whole event was of a pathetic character and sent sorrow into home after home in Connecticut."[142]

An even greater tragedy awaited the Union prisoners of war who had endured their ordeals in captivity at Andersonville and Cahaba prisons only to board the steamer *Sultana* for the trip home in April 1865. Worn, weary, and anxious to put their war experiences behind them, the men scampered onto the vessel in such numbers that the craft became dangerously overloaded. Straining against the weight and the tide, *Sultana* pushed past Memphis when a horrific explosion of the boilers sent steam, woodwork, and people flying through the darkness. Some died from the scalding steam, others from the force of the explosion, but many of the men fell into the rain-swollen torrent to be washed away and drowned. Although the official number of those who perished stood at 1,238 (1,101 soldiers and 137 passengers and crew), other estimates raised the toll to more than 1,700. In any event, the violation of promised salvation from captivity to a long-awaited reunion with loved ones ended for so many in numbers that surpassed even those who later perished aboard the RMS *Titanic*.[143]

Although the *Sultana* disaster occurred while the last of the hostile forces remained in the field, the celebrated Confederate commerce raider *Shenandoah* did not experience its first deaths until long after the guns had fallen silent in the mainland of North America. The vessel had been cruising distant waters in search of Northern whalers to destroy or bond as prizes of war when word reached Captain James Waddell through a neutral vessel that Robert E. Lee had surrendered and Abraham Lincoln had died at the hands of John Wilkes Booth.[144]

Waddell had been aware that the fortunes of his nation were dimming before he embarked on his latest mission, but as long as the government under whose flag he operated remained in existence or unless he received contrary official orders, he would be expected to continue to carry out his mission. The combat-oriented phase lasted until August 2, 1865, when the *Shenandoah* approached a British vessel from which confirmation came of the collapse of the Confederacy. Waddell immediately ordered the disarmament of the ship and crew and the cessation of its martial activities.[145]

The war was over, in one sense, for the *Shenandoah*, but the raider remained well away from a port of call to which it could be brought and turned over for disposition. Captain Waddell resolved to make his way to "a European port," a journey of some "17,000 miles," by his calculation, that represented "a long gantlet to run and escape."[146] Unfortunately, it was during this extended period that the vessel experienced fatalities among its crew.

As late as October 1865, Midshipman John T. Mason remarked optimistically, "I should like to see the cruise finishing without our losing a man." But, Marine sergeant George Canning and fellow seaman William Bill were already desperately ill. Bill was the first to go, passing away on October 26 and buried at sea in a ceremony marred by a noble attempt to prevent Canning from knowing the fate of his deceased shipmate. Then, after rallying briefly, the marine sergeant succumbed in the early evening of October 30.[147] The deaths of these men occurred while the *Shenandoah* remained a Confederate vessel, but the close of the conflict represented the last set of circumstances under which men who were serving in these capacities actively perished in it.

8

Industrial and Storage Mishaps
Death from Industrial or Production-Related Accidents

The scene was most appalling. Dead bodies were lying in heaps as they had fallen.
Aftermath of factory explosion in Pittsburgh, Pennsylvania

Of the occupants of the building, boys, girls and young ladies—not one escaped.
Account of industrial accident from
Staunton, Virginia, newspaper

Those who occupied themselves in this dangerous business seemed to be lamentably careless.
Sallie Putnam after a laboratory explosion in Richmond

Both the United States and the Confederate States had to mobilize massive numbers of troops for war. But, more important, the contestants in this most modern of conflicts had to develop a manufacturing base to generate supplies and resources to maintain those military forces adequately in the field. To be effective, the armies and navies had to have the necessary equipment, from arms and uniforms to accoutrements and ammunition, to wage war on a grand scale. Mass production was necessary and the labor force to sustain it critical. Circumstances required states to take steps to supplement or replace a national system. In Texas, for example, residents and their leaders came to the realization that they would have to fend for themselves when it came to protection and resource production, even when the labor required conflicted with the need for numbers in the ranks.[1]

Richmond saw a tremendous influx of civilians and war-related industries. Tredegar Iron Works quickly surpassed its 1861 workforce population by almost three times, employing some 2,500 individuals in a wide variety of areas.[2] In the Northern economy, as two modern historians have explained, "mobilization was extraordinary, if measured by the proportion of citizens who became wrapped up in some aspect of the war effort."[3] The conditions under which many individuals performed crucial services in support of their respective causes also led to deaths by explosion, fire, and other industrial or production-related accidents. Although many noncombatants would find numerous ways in which to experience the brunt of warfare involuntarily in war zones, others entered the workforce or felt warfare in different and potentially deadly forms away from the battlefields.

Perhaps the most significant symbolic industrial accident in America occurred long after the war with the Triangle Shirtwaist Factory fire in 1911. The loss of life in that tragedy helped to galvanize a nation attempting to come to grips with the unbridled expressions of capitalism and progressive instincts regarding worker safety and corporate responsibility. Yet, such an incident was hardly unknown in the period of the American Civil War itself. Industrial mishaps that caused fatalities among the workforce were occurring from the earliest stages of the conflict and lasted throughout it.

Historians Scott Nelson and Carol Sheriff assessed the impact of the war on civilian populations serving in war-related production as well as on the soldiers in the field, writing, "Alongside poor wages and long hours, workers encountered ever more dangerous working conditions. Agricultural and industrial work had always come with physical, even life-threatening risks, but wartime manufacturing took those risks to an extreme." With the pressure to produce the necessary munitions of war at a pace and on a scale previously unknown and the introduction of employees that included those who were new to their working environments, trouble was bound to occur. "Countless accidents resulted from inexperienced workers trying their hands at unfamiliar tasks," the historians observed. "More than thirty explosions occurred at munition factories, often resulting in scenes no less grisly than those found on battlefields, though here most of the victims were women."[4]

Yet, for the dangers so many of these workers would face, there was a disparity in wages that did not compensate, literally or figuratively, for the risks they took daily. Seamstresses working for the Clothing Bureau in wartime Richmond could expect to make more than their counterparts in the inherently dangerous environment of the arsenals. Sewing cartridges for the soldiers in the field would garner one dollar a day, while an individual producing a shirt for that same soldier would receive the same pay per item. This could be especially galling when class was factored into the equation, where persons of more privileged circles took jobs that would prove less hazardous at better pay.[5]

Frequently, deadly industrial accidents garnered close attention from a readership that had grown used to learning from the newspapers about disasters. Although often detailed, the genealogy of the victims, more than the saturation of death accounts in the popular press, may have accounted for a more generic announcement in the latter part of 1861 concerning a fatal accident filed under the innocent-sounding headline "Percussion Caps," which boasted of production in the city of Washington "at the rate of 250,000 per day," before moving to the sadder news: "Two Germans have been killed by the explosion of the fulminating powder."[6]

On November 7, 1861, the *Cincinnati Daily Press* reported an incident that had taken place in Philadelphia the previous day: "Yesterday afternoon two workmen were killed and one seriously injured by the blowing up of a building at the Bridesburg Arsenal containing fulminating powder."[7] Two days later, a news report appeared of an accident at the Watervliet Arsenal in New York. A short notation mentioned only that "four men were fatally injured" in that blast.[8]

Richmond native Sallie Putnam noted several incidents that led to deaths among civilian workers in the Confederate capital. Without providing much detail concerning the circumstances, she recorded several examples: "A celebrated artist laid aside his palette and pencil, and occupied himself with experiments in fulminating powder, but carelessly neglecting proper caution, lost his life by an explosion." Another individual carried incaution to a greater degree with the same outcome: "An excellent chemist, who would have been invaluable to the government, thoughtlessly smoked a cigar in his laboratory, as he was preparing a powerful detonating compound, and was blown to pieces by an explosion that occurred from a spark from the cigar." The force of that blast was enormous. "His mangled body was found, in parts, many yards from the scene, and the building in which he operated was completely shattered."

Putnam's catalog of mishaps continued: "Very early in the war, another gentleman, after a series of successful experiments, lost his life in an explosion that effectually destroyed the building in which he was operating, and injured several persons in the vicinity." She might have noted that it was well that none of these situations seemed to lead to greater numbers of deaths given their occurrences in the crowded urban environment of Richmond.[9]

Reports of such incidents could be quite graphic. In the case of a "Terrible Explosion in Philadelphia" that rocked a munitions factory on March 30, 1862, the *New York Herald* writer opened with a scathing assessment of the owner's culpability for the disaster before describing the effects of his negligence: "A pyrotechnist named Jackson, who has made three or four hair breadth escapes, and narrowly escaped with his life last summer, had established a manufactory for army cartridges, and had secured a heavy government order, to fulfill which he had employed upwards of seventy hands and worked vigorously, but it is thought carelessly."

He maintained that the poor storage of powder created the necessary conditions for the blast, and the failure of the factory to provide adequate "arrangements for extinguishing fires" proved catastrophic by allowing the flames to "burst out in the ruins, and it is believed, burned to death, many of the stunned and bleeding victims of the explosion." When authorities hastened to the scene, they found crowds of onlookers already gathered to view gruesome images that seared into the consciousness of the witnesses. "The scenes were poignant and terrible in the extreme," the writer explained. "I picked up a bit of a skull, with the hair adhering to it, more than a block (an eighth of a mile) from the place, and a whole human head, afterward recognized as that of John Mehaffey, was found in an open lot." Police were recovering remains of all types. "Some of the workmen were so literally and thoroughly blown apart that only the remotest fragments of their boots remain." Among the dead and mortally wounded workers were "Edward Jackson, dead. John Mehaffey, dead. Horace L. Sloman, fatally burned. Joseph Mirkis, fatally burned. Washington Black, beyond recovery." Others were thought likely to succumb to their injuries.[10]

Likewise, a Washington newspaper offered gory details in a piece titled "Terrible Explosion at Jackson's Pyrotechnic Factory, Philadelphia." This account noted that the victims included a son of the owner, and at least four others killed outright by the blast. "The head of one victim was blown nearly two [city] squares," the writer observed with unadulterated sensationalism, "and the fragments of humanity are scattered about the ruins, presenting a most shocking sight." Others lay in various states of recovery, many "seriously injured," while several remained unaccounted for in the aftermath. "One of the men missing is supposed to have been blown to atoms," and a number of the victims were thought likely not to be able to recover from their wounds.[11]

Some of the accounts provided readers with additional specifics concerning the circumstances of the incident and the identities of some of the victims. A newspaper in Vermont passed along the information that the owner of the facility "had a government contract for filling cartridges, and employed fifty girls and twenty four men." Naming Edward Jackson and John "Mehoffey" as two of the "boys" who could be "recognized," the report once more resorted to the sensational elements of the story that would have seemed more appropriate to the description of the aftermath of a battle: "The heads of three persons, numbers of arms, and other fragments of bodies were found in the neighborhood."[12]

Fatal mishaps occurred in Confederate facilities as well. In May 1862, the *Memphis Daily Appeal* carried the news originally provided in a Columbus, Mississippi, newspaper of a "terrible accident" that had occurred when Thomas Barnes lost his life while working in a "small building" that served as the site "for the manufacture of fulminating powder." Apparently, while working alone, Barnes became the victim of an ignition of the material and "was found horribly mangled, both arms having been blowed off, and his head and side badly lacerated." Although the injured man clung to life initially, he was "insensible, and died in a few minutes."[13]

Indianapolis, Indiana, became the scene of another destructive blast on June 2, 1862, when a "pistol cartridge factor, near this city, exploded." Although several people incurred injuries, one fatality resulted.[14] Then, newspaper headlines in late 1862, blared the tragic tale of a "horrific explosion" and a tremendous "loss of life," when a conflagration ripped through the U.S. Arsenal at Pittsburgh, Pennsylvania, also known as the Alleghany Arsenal, at approximately 2:00 P.M. on September 17. The structure in which the eruption occurred housed some 176 young boys and girls and caused the deaths of "75 or 80" of them. Descriptions in the news accounts provided graphic illustration of the dangers inherent in working in close proximity with explosives. "Those who could not escape in turn were burned up," one account disclosed. "The scene was most appalling. Dead bodies were lying in heaps as they had fallen." The images were almost as searing as the flames that had consumed the victims. "Some places," the writer observed, "where the heat was intense, whitened bones could be seen through smoke and flame. In other places large masses of blackened flesh were visible."

Numbers for the dead were difficult to place with exactitude, given the nature of the destruction to the bodies of some of the deceased in the age before forensic science and DNA tests could confirm the losses that only fragments could attest. "Up to the present time," the writer noted, "sixty-three bodies have been taken from the ruins." However, just as perplexing at this stage for the anxious readership as the challenges for properly identifying those killed was the reason for the incident: "The cause of the explosion is not known. It is admitted by all to be accidental."[15] Another account provided an additional clue: "The cause of the explosion is said to have been the accidental falling of a shell."[16]

Rare instances occurred in which a prominent individual became the fatality in an accidental explosion. In October 1862, the *Daily Dayton Express* reported, "Gen. C. T. James, the inventor of the James Projectile wounded yesterday by the explosion of a shell by carelessness, died here at 8 o'clock this morning." Apparently, in the course of a demonstration at Sag Harbor, Long Island, a worker who was attempting to remove a cap from one of the projectiles with a pair of pliers caused the ignition, resulting in his own death and the mortal wounding of Charles Tillinghast James.[17] The inventor's products had already proven effective in the field, serving as part of the artillery bombardment that caused the surrender of the substantially built masonry Fort Pulaski, in Georgia, on April 11, 1862.

In November 1862, a Raleigh, North Carolina, newspaper provided a brief description of the destruction of "a cartridge factory at Jackson, Miss." on November 5. The blast was thought to have resulted in the deaths of no fewer than "30 boys, girls and young ladies, who were engaged in the factory."[18] More detail emerged from a Staunton, Virginia, account of the effects of the explosion of unknown origin that ripped through powder accumulated for use in cartridges, causing "a fearful concussion." Sadly, the blast shook more than nerves, as the toll among the employees affirmed the extent of the "dreadful calamity." "Of the occupants of the building," the notice offered, "boys, girls and young ladies—not one escaped." Estimating the number of victims at thirty souls, the writer confessed, "In the confusion and excitement prevailing, it is impossible to learn the number certainly," speculating that the death toll might easily "overreach that number."[19]

As the conflict progressed, the production of the devices for firing the weapons of war continued to cause fatalities away from the battlefields as well as on them. January 1863 brought fresh tragedy to New York City when an explosion occurred at the "percussion cap factory of E. Roberts & Co., in Seventy-first street . . . whereby Moses Vanderbeck lost his life."[20] In Washington, another incident happened at about the same time. "An explosion occurred at the Washington Arsenal yesterday," the *Alexandria Gazette* related on January 31, "killing one man and severely injuring several others."[21] Following up a few days later, the paper offered an explanation: "The terrific explosion which took place at the Washington arsenal . . . was caused by an attempt, upon the part of one of the workmen, to extract a fuse from a loaded shell."[22]

The *Raftsman's Journal* of Clearfield, Pennsylvania, had the benefit of time and additional reports to provide detailed information on February 11 concerning the earlier incident in the nation's capital. "At about half past two o'clock, on January 31st, an explosion took place in one of the large store-houses of the Washington arsenal, by which one man was killed outright and several others severely injured—two of whom cannot possibly recover." The account noted that the principal explosive material consisted of "a lot of spherical case ammunition [that] had been sent to the Arsenal from the Army of the Potomac, they having been found useless, on account of defective fuses, and a number of workmen were engaged in removing the fuses preparatory to the insertion of new ones of a better quality." The writer noted, "To facilitate the work, two benches had been put up about the centre of the building, having holes cut in them in which the ammunition was placed, and the fuses were then removed by wrench." In addition to the tedium of the work, there was the danger of complacency, "One of the workers, having worn the fuse on which he was operating down so that the wrench would not take hold, attempted to cut it out with a 'cold chisel.'" A resulting spark "ignited the fuse, and the shell exploded," causing "seven or eight other shells lying near—some being in the hands of the workmen" to ignite as well, and these "exploded also, with a terrific crash, the pieces and balls flying in all directions. One man was instantly killed, and three others so severely injured that life is despaired of."

The damage to lives and property was substantial as the "pieces of the shell and balls flew in all directions, many of them going through the floor above, and the force of the explosion lifted a portion of the same floor." The principal structure involved, "known as Storehouse No. 2," was thought to contain as many as "36,500 rounds of field, 6,500,000 do. [ditto] of small-arm, and about 380,000 rounds of pistol ammunition, which, had it exploded, would have shaken the whole city, and probably killed several hundred people."[23] As it was, the situation provided dramatic evidence that facilities considered relatively safe one moment could become raging infernos the next.

On March 13, 1863, a terrible explosion shook the businesses and residences of the Confederate capital. War clerk John B. Jones observed, "To-day a great calamity occurred in this city. In a large room of one of the government laboratories an explosion took place, killing instantly five or six persons, and wounding, it is feared fatally, some thirty others. Most of them were little indigent girls!"[24]

Diarist Judith Brockenbrough McGuire noted, "Richmond was greatly shocked on Friday, by the blowing up of the Laboratory, in which women, girls, and boys were employed making cartridges; ten women and girls were killed on the spot, and many more will probably die from their wounds. May God have mercy upon them!"[25] Sallie Putnam was less charitable, noting, "Those who occupied themselves in this dangerous business seemed to be lamentably careless." She called such incidents "some of the freaks of death, in its carnival held in Richmond during the war."[26]

News would filter out as the number of fatalities grew. Many victims had perished outright, and others died over the next days from their injuries. At least one individual, Mary Burley, was thought to have drowned when she rushed into the James River in a state of panic to escape the conflagration. Had a bystander not subdued another young girl running toward an unaffected building with her clothes on fire, the toll would have been worse by her certain demise. However, as it stood, according to one scholar's assessment, "at least forty-five of the sixty-eight explosion casualties died."[27]

As word spread across the media sources of the day, news of the traumatic event reached a wide audience. Turner Vaughan, of the Fourth Alabama Infantry, began his March 14 diary entry with the usual regimental news, but quickly added, "A Terrible explosion took place at the Government Laboratory yesterday, accompanied with a serious loss of life."[28] A week after the accident took place in the Confederate capital, the *Abingdon Virginian* reported on it for its southwest Virginia readership. "Between Forty and Fifty Females Killed and Wounded," it explained on March 20. "On yesterday forenoon, between eleven and twelve o'clock, an explosion occurred in Department No. 6 of the Confederate States Laboratory, involving a frightful loss of life and limb to some forty or fifty persons, almost all of whom were females." Noting that "all breechloading and pistol ammunition is prepared" in the affected facility, the writer took pains to remark how difficult the origin of the accident was to explain. "The greatest care has hitherto been observed in keeping the stock of ammunition safely confined." Nevertheless, the force of the blast was tremendous, "tearing down half the building, and killing, wounding and throwing in the air or upon the floor the operatives who were engaged in their labor." The impact had also been jarring to the community, with the victims, "chifly females of different ages, from twelve to sixty years." He added pointedly of a toll that remained incomplete, "Ten were killed by the explosion at the time of its occurrence and others are reported to have died during the day, while it is not expected that half of the survivors will recover."[29]

Josiah Gorgas, chief of ordnance for the Confederacy, did not record the incident in his journal until more than a week later. On Saturday, March 21, he noted: "A fearful accident occurred at our Laboratory here on Friday the 13th of March, by which 69 were killed and wounded of whom 62 were females chiefly girls & children." In almost clinical terms, he explained, "Only four were killed outright, burnt from the burns received in the burning of their clothes the number of dead will probably reach 50." Then, Gorgas let some emotion show when he added an assessment based on his belief in the potential for having avoided the disaster that caused so much devastation: "It is terrible to think of—that so much suffering should arise from causes possibly within our control."

The observation the Confederate official was making stemmed from the source of the explosion. He observed, "The accident was caused by the ignition of a friction primer in the hands of a grown girl by the name of Mary Ryan." Mary did not perish immediately and was able to give an account of what had happened before her death several days later. "The primer stuck on the varnishing board," Gorgas explained, "and she struck the board three times very hard on the table to drive out the primer. She says she was immediately blown up to the ceiling and on coming down was again blown up." The secondary explosions occurred because of the proximity to exposed gunpowder that ordinarily would not be located in the same vicinity. "Cartridges were being broken up temporarily on account of repairs in the shop they usually worked in."[30]

David L. Burton provided a comprehensive list of the victims of the Brown's Island laboratory explosion in a *Civil War Times* article in 1982. The most high-profile fatality was Reverend John H. Woodcock, aged sixty-three, who "was in charge of the room in which the explosion occurred" and who survived initially only to die shortly after. In addition to Woodcock and Mary Ryan, aged eighteen,

other explosion victims buried in Hollywood [Cemetery] are Mary Blessingham, 23; Eliza Willis, 10; Elizabeth Young, 33; Mary Archer, 12; Sarah Haney, age unknown; Annie Peddicord, age unknown; Marannie Garnett, 13; Barbara A. Jackson, 16; Sarah Marshall, 67; Robert S. Chaple, 15; Elizabeth S. Moore, 15; Delia Clemens, 20; and Sarah Foster, 14. Total victims in Hollywood, 15.

In Shockoe, another of Richmond's historic cemeteries, are buried these explosion victims: Alice Johnson, 12; Mary E. Valentine, 14; Margaret Drustly, 16; Wilhemina Defenback, 15; Mary Zerhum, 12; Anne E. Bolton, 14; Nannie Horan, 14; Virginia A. Mayer, 12; Virginia E. Page, 13; Mary Ellen Wallace, 12; Emma Virginia Blankenship, 15; Margaret Alexander, 15; Caroline Zeitenheimer, 16; and Martha Clemmons, 25. Total victims there, 14, and possibly more.

In Oakwood Cemetery in Richmond is buried James G. Currie, a young boy killed in the explosion.

Besides these, newspapers reported that the following persons were killed or injured fatally in the explosion: Mary O'Brian, Martha Burley (whose body was found in the James River), Martha Daly, Mrs. Ann Dodson, Julia A. Brannan, Mary Bowlin, Catherine McCarthy, Mary Zinginham, Mary Whitehurst, Maria Brien, Ella Smith, Anne Davis, Mary Cushing, Louisa Ricely, Ellen Sullivan, and Mary O'Conners.[31]

The laboratory blast in Richmond was the most high-profile industrial disaster for the South but by no means the only one remaining for the Confederacy to endure. On May 28, 1863, the *Wilmington (N.C.) Journal* carried the account of an explosion that tore through a powder mill.[32] In April 1864, a black fireman who worked at the Naval Iron Works in Columbus, Georgia, died after being tossed and scalded by a boiler explosion.[33]

In the North, deadly incidents of this type continued to occur as well. Diarist and illustrator Alfred Bellard detailed a fatal event in Washington in June 1864. "On the 17th a sad accident happened at the arsenal by which 17 young ladies lost their lives by being burnt to death, while many others were injured, caused by an explosion that blew up and burnt some of the buildings." Noting that funerals followed two days later, Bellard added, "The procession to the cemetery preceeded by a brass band was composed of the Sons of Temperance and the girls who worked at the arsenal. The President and other officials and friends of the deceased followed, and then the hearses and ambulances containing the bodies enclosed in handsome coffins, brought up the rear."[34] The somber spectacle was a reminder that the cost of war was not limited to the battlefield or the soldiers who had enlisted in their country's service, but would be borne by even the youngest of citizens.

The summer of 1863 saw additional mishaps as production lines worked to supply the armies in the field with the means of waging war. A Charlotte newspaper reported a fatal explosion in a powder mill at the end of May 1863, in which "four men were instantly killed, viz: Jno N Lee, Jr, Geo Hutchinson, Christopher Ounce, and Charles Klepelburge, the Superintendent, and John Ochler was so badly injured that he died Saturday night." Ochler managed to tell some of those attending him the nature of the tragedy before he died. Noting these last words from the victim, the writer observed, "He states that one of the men commenced knocking the caked powder off the stones with a copper hammer, (which is the usual mode of cleaning them,) when the explosion occurred." Recently set under contract with the state, the "North Carolina Powder Manufacturing Company" facility "was a new one, and was just getting fairly under way in making powder." Approximately 700 pounds of powder were on-site when the event took place. "The Mill was, of course, blown to pieces, and the bodies of the unfortunate men thrown to a considerable distance in the air, mutilating them in a shocking manner." People as far as a dozen miles from the plant felt the shock of the blast that ripped through the early morning, "just after sunrise."[35]

An article titled "A Calamity" in the *Camden (S.C.) Confederate* of June 5, 1863, described another incident: "The Powder mill located about fourteen miles from Charlotte, on the Catawba river, was blown up on Saturday morning about five o'clock." The blast killed "five of the operatives," but the writer asserted that for the time being a cause could not be identified. In the context of the harsh realities of wartime production given the loss of life attendant to the disaster, the piece focused on the physical properties in concluding, "The mill house is entirely destroyed, but the principal portion of the machinery is uninjured."[36] The implication seemed to be that people—the affected workers in this case—could be replaced.

In both North and South, large-scale production for every form of weaponry put the workers involved into jeopardy. Washington's *Evening Star* carried news of a mishap in Indianapolis on June 2 involving the production of rounds for small arms: "The pistol cartridge factory, near this city, exploded to-day." The toll was not as great as in other situations, but the incident left a genuine impact nevertheless. According to the newspaper account, "One person was killed and several wounded severely."[37]

The *Alexandria Gazette* informed readers in June of a "terrible explosion" that had occurred in Hoboken, New Jersey, "in the machine-shop connected with Steven's monster battery." The writer of the piece explained, "There were a number of shells and a quantity of powder in the building, and no less than five distinct explosions occurred." The effects were devastating in terms of property destroyed and horrific with regard to at least one individual: "A clerk named Arnold, in the employ of Thompson & Co., brokers, had his head blown off. All the outbuildings connected with the establishment were totally destroyed, together with the dwellings occupied by the keeper of the yard."[38]

In August, the *Alexandria Gazette* provided a brief notice of another incident in the city of Washington: "There was an explosion at the Washington Arsenal on Friday evening, by which two workmen were so severely injured as to have since died."[39] These deaths would extend the list of the individuals whose lives were a sacrifice for maintaining the level of resources required by the armies and navies to sustain the war effort.

Later that fall, the account of a witness as told to the *Louisville Journal* appeared in the *Evansville (Ind.) Daily Journal*. In this instance, the fatal blast came not from faulty production or flawed protocols but from the "accidental discharge of purcussion shells, which were being loaded into an ammunition wagon." The individual who was "carrying the box let it fall, when the explosion occurred, scattering the fragments of burning fuses into piles of loaded shells scattered over the ground."[40]

A story titled "The Late Accident at Springfield" described an incident that occurred in March 1864: "Eight persons have already died from the effects of the injuries received in the cartridge factory explosion."[41] Two days after that report, the *Soldier's Journal*, emanating from the "Rendezvous of Distribution," in Virginia, remarked, "A fearful explosion in a cartridge factory in the city of

Springfield, Mass., on Wednesday, the 16th inst., by which sixteen persons were injured, five of them fatally." It noted, in a pattern seen too often before, "The sufferers are nearly all women and girls, of whom about forty were employed in the building."[42]

Sadly, some of the victims had lingered in agony for a period after the disaster. Under the headline "Another Victim," the *Burlington Free Press* in Vermont noted the loss of one of the individuals who had survived the blast initially but could not overcome her injuries: "Bridget O'Neil of Montpelier died at Springfield, Mass., March 25th, being the eighth victim of the explosion in the cartridge factory."[43]

George Washington Rains, the leading figure for the Confederacy's production of gunpowder, was acutely aware of the volatility of his working material, even away from the battlefield. For the Confederate Powder Works at Augusta, Georgia, he took extraordinary steps to minimize the impacts of mishaps and maximize efficient production. Nevertheless, all vulnerabilities could not be avoided, and one explosion proved as deadly as it was dramatic, when a temporary wooden structure dedicated "for granulation" of the powder disintegrated in a flash. "There were seven men within the structure, a sentinel outside, and a boy with a mule in a shed adjoining," Rains recalled in a postwar address, before adding the result to the human beings present in clinical fashion. "The bodies of the seven men and the boy and the debris were carried up with the ascending column, and by its revolving action, reduced mainly to small fragments and dispersed; the sentinel was killed by the shock, but his body was not otherwise disturbed."[44]

Fatal accidents could occur in other, no less gruesome, manners as well. The *Richmond Daily Dispatch* of May 6, 1864, reported, "On Wednesday afternoon, at the Tredegar Works, a negro man, who was attempting to hang a belt, was caught by the wheel and whirled around, striking the [wheel] every revolution, until life was extinct." Even more horrifically, "His [body] was thrown off against a spike, and hung on the piece of iron, which entered the back of his head." When an individual tried to extricate the body, another fatality was only narrowly averted as that man "was struck by his whirling body, knocked out of the [place] and severely injured."[45]

Less than a week later, one man lost his life in an industrial accident, according to the *New York Herald* of May 12: "An explosion in the percussion cap manufactory of Dr. E. Golmark, in Carroll street, near Third avenue, on Tuesday afternoon, resulting in the death of Mr. Desler Hintz, who was employed in the establishment and engaged at the time, as supposed, in mixing fulminating powders." The exact cause remained a mystery, as Hintz was the only person present at the time of the accident.[46]

One of the worst accidents at the Washington Arsenal took place in June, resulting in the deaths of eighteen victims. The *Washington Evening Star*'s second edition blared the dramatic headlines on June 17, 1864: "Frightful Explosion at the Arsenal. A Large Number of the Female Employees Killed or Frightfully Wounded. Eighteen Dead Bodies Taken Out of the Ruins Already." This account set the time of the disaster at "ten minutes of twelve o'clock to-day." Noting that while "one hundred and eight girls were at work in the main laboratory making cartridges for small arms, a quantity of fire works, which had been placed off the outside of the building, became ignited, and a piece of fuse flying into one of the rooms, in which were seated about twenty-nine young women, set the cartridges on fire, and caused an instantaneous explosion." Because of the existing partitions, many of the women who might have become fatalities "escaped by jumping from the windows and running through the doors pell mell; but those in the room fronting on the east, did not fare so well, and it is feared that nearly all of them were killed by the explosion or burnt to death."[47]

In a show of compassion, Secretary of War Edwin Stanton instructed the commander of the U.S. Arsenal to meet all the needs of the victims and their families: "The funeral and all the expenses by the recent catastrophe at the Arsenal will be paid by the Department." He insisted, "You will not spare any means to express the respect and sympathy of the Government for the deceased and their surviving friends."[48] Several newspapers reported on the outpouring of sympathy and the large attendance at the funeral, including the presence of President Lincoln and Secretary Stanton.[49]

In 1865, deadly industrial accidents remained a factor. On February 22, Washington's *Evening Star* reported to its readers about an incident at the Naval Yard. "Yesterday, about 11 o'clock, a sad accident occurred in the machinist's department, whereby a workman named Edward Biggs lost his life. He was engaged in oiling the gearing of the machinery, standing on a ladder, and a portion of his clothing catching on the shaft, he was drawn rapidly around it several times, each time some portion of his body striking a beam." The effects were catastrophic. "The machinery was stopped as soon as possible, when it was found that he had been horribly mangled, both legs broken, as also one arm, beside having his body bruised and his head fractured in several places." Removed to "the dispensary of the yard," Biggs received immediate attention, including the amputation of his "right leg above the knee." Subsequently taken to his home, the stricken worker "died about 12 o'clock last night, retaining his senses until within an hour of his death." The thirty-eight-year-old "plasterer by trade" had only worked "in the machine shop but about three weeks." Just as with many of the soldiers in the ranks, the loss would reverberate at home. The writer noted,

"He leaves a family of a wife and four children, who were entirely dependent upon him for support."[50]

The storage, movement, or disposal of dangerous materials could be as deadly to human life as that occurring in industrial facilities. At the end of July 1863, the *Daily National Republican* noted:

> About 4 o'clock yesterday afternoon a fatal accident occurred at the Washington Arsenal. A German, a laborer in one of the machine shops, was unloading a Government car filled with muskets picked up on the late battlefields, when one of them accidentally exploded, killing him instantly. The ball entered the right side and passed through the body. The German was a discharged soldier, having faithfully served in the Peninsular campaigns.[51]

Soldier and civilian deaths continued to come from what might be considered routine duties. On September 19, 1863, several months after the ending of the siege of Vicksburg and the surrender of the remaining Confederate defenders under John Pemberton, new fatalities occurred during an attempt to remove the mounds of ordnance stored in the region for use elsewhere. A team of African American workers, soldiers assigned to assist with the task, and the crew of the steamer *City of Madison* experienced the furious effect of black powder explosives. One newspaper termed the incident, "One of the most frightful accidents, fatal in loss of a large number of human lives and the destruction of an immense amount of property, valued at several hundred thousand dollars, which has ever happened on the Mississippi river."[52]

Another account of the accident noted it took place while the "steamer was loading with ordnance stores." The amount of combustible material slated for transfer was considerable: "Seven thousand six hundred and twenty rounds of artillery ammunition, two and a half million rounds of infantry ammunition, and about two hundred packages of powder, making in all over four hundred tons of explosive material, had already been placed aboard." Unfortunately, in the final stages of the loading operation, "one of the deck hands let fall a box of percussion shell, which instantly exploded."

The initial blast might have been survivable, except for the fact that the resultant fire set off additional rounds in a series of explosions that rocked the vessel. For the most vulnerable persons, the eighteen men working in the hold, there was virtually no chance to avoid or survive the conflagration. Only the second mate and a supervising officer, as well as one of the workers, were in position to escape "as soon as the box fell, and before the discharge of the shell had become general." The rest of the "eighteen souls" working below were not so fortunate.

The blast propelled some of the victims from the vessel. Searchers did not find at least three of these individuals until an hour after the incident, the explosion having thrown them "on the roof of the texas [deck] of the Walsh." The writer of the account offered readers a graphic description: "Two of these were dead, while the body of the third at the time of discovery was cooking, the flesh in pieces having been burnt black. The poor fellow was still alive, with both legs and arms broken, and suffering the terrible torture of being burnt to death, the flames from his clothes having communicated to his body." Fortunately, the badly maimed individual "lived but a few minutes afterwards."[53]

Union artillerist William Christie happened to be in the vicinity when the accident occurred. He wrote to a brother to reference deaths in the unit from disease and explained:

But the Death of a fellow soldier, is a thing not calculated to shock us very much as long as it is in the field or Hospital. But when the lives of a number of men and some women is taken unexpectedly, and in the most shocking manner that a number Perished yesterday; it makes even the most thought-less of us feel afraid, or something akin to fear, at least it does me.

Christie had been assigned to bring fodder for the animals from the nearby levee to the unit's location when he witnessed the accident from afar. As he later described it in a letter to his brother, "Before we got our hay, and about noon as we were leaving the Levee, I saw a great cloud of smoke flame and steam, and a loud prolonged roar as if a great gun had Burst." Hastening to the scene, he was stunned by what came into view. "What a sight when I got to the Boat, or where she had Been, there she lay or what was left of her." In addition to the destruction was the evidence of many lives lost, from soldiers detailed to assist to civilian workers. "Besides the deck hands, one hundred Negroes were in the hold, stowing away the loading, and in fact I suppose there were over a hundred lives lost. . . . After what I seen I cannot write about it with any other feelings than those of horror."[54]

At the end of September 1863, the wires again carried news of a disaster for the Federals regarding the storage of combustible material. On the afternoon of the thirtieth, J. D. Van Duzer informed Brigadier General John A. Garfield, "The ammunition stored at Bridgeport blew up this P.M., having been fired by the careless handling of a box of percussion shell." He noted the initial explosion as having occurred "at 11 A.M. and explosions only ceased entirely at 2 P.M." Colonel R. F. Smith's first report indicated there were "20 men killed and wounded, of whom 6 were killed at once."[55] The next day, October 1, Smith dispelled the rumors of enemy firing associated with the explosions and provided a tally of the casualties: "No cannonading here. Ammunition stored on hill exploded; 7 killed and about 12 wounded."[56]

Such incidents were terrible indeed, but occasionally what appeared to be accidents later came to be understood as not accidental after all. This was the case concerning a tremendous blast that tore through part of the enormous shipping, storage, and transportation complex that constituted the port of City Point, Virginia, at the confluence of the James and Appomattox Rivers. Built on the grounds of the Eppes Plantation, City Point quickly turned into one of the busiest facilities of its type in the world as the people connected with it strove to maintain the supply lines supporting Ulysses S. Grant and the Union forces besieging Petersburg, Virginia.

Shortly before noon on August 9, 1864, an explosion rocked the area, turning wharves and warehouses into kindling and killing and wounding a number of workers and military personnel. Grant immediately wired what he knew to Henry Halleck: "Five minutes ago an ordnance boat exploded, carrying lumber, grape, canister, and all kinds of shot over this point. Every part of the yard used as my headquarters is filled with splinters and fragments of shell." He could not ascertain casualties as a whole but set his own among his staff as "Colonel [Orville E.] Babcock is slightly wounded in the hand and 1 mounted orderly is killed and 2 or 3 wounded and several horses killed." He speculated that the "damage at the wharf must be considerable both in life and property" and promised to provide additional information as he obtained it. "As soon as the smoke clears away I will ascertain and telegraph you," he explained.[57]

In addition to causing damage costing some $2 million, the blast cost the lives of 33 black laborers on the docks, two enlisted men, and two civilian clerks. A vendor working the area died when struck by a saddle that had been stored on one of the vessels containing discarded cavalry equipment. The total of those killed came to 46, with another 126 injured by the blast and flying debris.[58] Meade staffer Theodore Lyman explained that various generals at Grant's headquarters reported, "It perfectly rained shells, shot, bullets, pieces of timber, and *saddles* (of these latter there was a barge load near by). Two dragoons were killed, close to them, and a twelve-pounder solid shot went smash into a mess-chest in the tent."[59]

Thought by Federal officials to have been the result of a terrible accident, the City Point explosion actually resulted from the planting by Confederate agents of a "horological torpedo," or improvised explosive device. Operative John Maxwell, with civilian R. K. Dillard as a local guide, managed to bring the device onto a barge and prepare it for detonation. After they departed and waited approximately an hour, the blast took place, with a concussion that Maxwell and

Dillard felt even at some distance from the scene.[60] It would not be until Richmond fell in 1865 that the documentation emerged detailing the operation as part of the Confederacy's Secret Service activities.[61]

Laborers continued to bear a terrible burden in the waning days of the war. As the territory of the Confederate States of America shrank under the weight of Union incursions, the impressive industrial base that had been painstakingly constructed also became subject to deterioration. Poor conditions and brutal inflation threatened the workers' health and melted their wages. Mortality soared in areas where shortages accelerated, especially among the very young. Historian Harold Wilson noted that at "ten mills along the Savannah River," where the community of workers supporting the facilities numbered "5,417 persons in 1864, 18 of the 450 children employed there died." These youngest persons ranged from ten to fifteen years old, while their compatriots in the next increment to twenty years in age lost 16 of 621 in that year. The morbid reality in one Augusta facility was the need to have on hand sufficient numbers of coffins to meet the demands of the greatest sacrifices being made by the smallest people. Wilson concluded, "Life on the home front was often as exacting as that in the lines."[62]

Little could be as disconcerting or deadly as the unexpected explosion of a powder magazine. At Fort Lyon, near Alexandria, Virginia, a sudden blast shattered the day's routine activities on June 9, 1863. Washington's *Evening Star* provided the general outline of events, noting graphically, "The bodies of the killed were greatly mutilated: a portion of one body being blown nearly half a mile. So also were shells, huge pieces of timber, etc., blown a great distance, some of the former exploding."[63] Another account offered additional details: "At about two o'clock some men were examining artillery ammunition at the northern entrance to the fort, when, from some unknown cause, one of the shells exploded, igniting several others which also exploded, and immediately afterwards the magazine blew up, causing a tremendous concussion and reducing the fort almost to a wreck." Displacing several pieces of artillery, destroying barracks, and "resulting in the instant killing of all those in and about the magazine, some twenty-two in number, and wounding seventeen more in the fort," the blast had occurred when the post commander deemed the stored ordnance "in bad condition" and ordered it "to be taken out into the air." The results were horrific. "The bodies of the killed were dreadfully mutilated and torn. Shell of all sizes and weights were thrown in all directions—many of them for miles." Among the dead were "one lieutenant, two sergeants, and twenty men."[64]

Three days after the explosion, an Alexandria newspaper provided additional details that suggested the men in the magazine were not engaged only in "examining" the shells but also in "airing, and refilling them," when the accident occurred. This account also noted that two more men had died from the effects of the blast, but it gave several examples by which soldiers and civilians, including family members of some of the officers, located near the detonation managed to emerge unscathed.[65] The human losses, according to official reports from Alexandria, were "between 20 and 30 men killed, and quite as many were severely wounded."[66] A second report noted that no one was inside the magazine at the time of the explosion. "Those outside engaged filling shells. Casualties, 20 deaths, 14 wounded."[67]

The following month, the explosion of a quantity of gunpowder being stored at Lebanon, Kentucky, was responsible for the mortal wounding of at least two soldiers posted there. The historian of the 112th Regiment of Illinois Volunteer Infantry included the record of the deaths of Henry J. Roberts and William Herridge. Both men suffered their injuries in the blast that occurred on July 9, 1863, with Roberts dying three days later and Herridge succumbing to his wounds on July 15.[68]

In mid-September 1863, Edward Manigault recorded such an instance in his journal while stationed on the South Carolina coast protecting Charleston: "At 11:05 A.M. the Magazine at Battery Cheves blew up, killing 1 Lieutenant & four Men and wounding two others." In this case, the tragedy might have been averted, as Manigault speculated: "The accident is supposed to have originated from the explosion of a Shell from which the Sergeant of the Magazine was extracting a fuze in order to substitute a longer one for it. The Magazine was completely destroyed." Nevertheless, as might be expected of an artillerist, he added, "None of the Guns [were] injured or dismounted."[69]

A Kansas newspaper editorialized on the nature of accidental calamities: "Several weeks ago there was a tremendous explosion of the newly invented batch of torpedoes, which a detail of Union soldiers had been ordered to take out of a freight car. Many lives were lost, and gross carelessness—amounting to lunacy—which led to the catastrophe, was the subject of severe comment in more than a million of printed sheets." Unfortunately, for all of the publicity the incident had garnered, the writer was not convinced appropriate lessons had been learned and instead commented, "Since then there have been no less than four murderous explosions in arsenals and magazines arising from the same sort of blind recklessness. One would think that the first act of imbecility had been looked upon as an example to be followed rather than as a fault to be avoided. What a self-sufficient, headstrong, unteachable species we are in many things." Expanding the list to larger social matters, the writer concluded glumly, "It is said that we 'live and learn,' but, if the adage is intended to apply to matters that concern the happiness and safety of the human family, it would seem to be a fallacy."[70]

Carelessness remained a fatal factor even as the war wound to a close. At Fort Fisher, outside Wilmington, North Carolina, in the early morning hours of January 16, Union troops celebrating their recent victory proved imprudent in their activities in and about one of the main powder magazines located inside the fort. At least one Union officer had admonished men entering the magazine to exercise more care, and another was trying to determine why no guard was posted to prevent a mishap, when one occurred. Colonel Samuel M. Zent of the 13th Indiana was attempting to address the issue when a devastating blast hurled matter through the air and sent anyone in the vicinity sprawling. The soldier and another officer from the 169th New York with whom Colonel Zent had been talking perished in the explosion, while a portion of the works managed to buffer the effects on Zent himself.[71]

Confederate colonel William Lamb recalled the incident as affecting Union and Confederate soldiers alike: "The next morning after sunrise a frightful explosion occurred in my reserve magazine, killing and wounding several hundred of the enemy and some of my own wounded officers and men."[72] Union major general Alfred Terry reported the mishap as being responsible for "killing and wounding about 130 men."[73] The list of Union officers killed in the incident included Captain Daniel Ferguson and Second Lieutenant Hugh D. McGregor of the 169th New York Infantry.[74]

Onboard the USS *Gettysburg*, Roswell Lamson explained to his fiancée, Kate, in a personal letter that several of his comrades were also among the casualties:

As you have no doubt learned from the papers Paymaster Gillette and Act. Ensign Laighton of the Gettysburg are killed by the explosion of the magazine in Fort Fisher. I sent an officer home in charge of their remains the next day. This accident [cast] more gloom and sadness over the vessel, and fleet than the death of all those who fell in the battle.[75]

A court of inquiry met to consider the "cause of the explosion of the powder magazine" several days later, securing testimony and rendering its "findings." In addition to the absence of guards for the cache of explosives, the most damning of these conclusions included the following: "III. That soldiers, sailors, and marines were running about with lights in the fort, entering bombproofs with these lights, intoxicated and discharging fire-arms. IV. That persons were seen with lights searching for plunder in the main magazine some ten or fifteen minutes previous to the explosion." The adjudicators then offered as their final disposition regarding the incident: "The opinion of the court, therefore, is that the explosion was the result of carelessness on the part of persons to them unknown."[76]

A month later, as the troops under William T. Sherman marched through South Carolina, another accident involving the storage and removal of ammunition cost the lives of some of the Federal soldiers involved. Young diarist Emma LeConte described the sensation in her entry for Sunday, February 19, 1865: "While we stood by the front window the house was shaken by a terrible explosion." Initially she thought the culprit might be a gas leak, but she remembered there had been no gas for several days. Word filtered in that Union efforts to "excavate" buried shells had resulted in "one going off accidentally [which] exploded the rest, killing [and] wounding a great many Yankees."[77] General Sherman noted the incident as an attempt to dispose of ammunition by dumping it into the Saluda River, "causing a very serious accident by the bursting of a percussion-shell, as it struck another on the margin of the water." He explained, "The flame followed back a train of powder which had sifted out, reached the wagons, still partially loaded, and exploded them, killing sixteen men and destroying several wagons and teams of mules."[78]

Even as the last of the Confederate industrial complex and the support infrastructure collapsed as Union armies closed the remaining production centers, dangers existed.[79] Union general Reub Williams noted the threat emanating from the effort to remove military stores in Columbia, South Carolina, when the men charged with executing those tasks failed to employ due caution. "While engaged in destroying the arsenal and removing the shells it contained, a terrible accident occurred by the carelessly handled shells," he recalled. In addition to significant property damage, Williams explained, "The result was a Captain and a number of enlisted men were killed." The incident provided the Union officer with another moment for introspection as he contemplated the lives lost under such circumstances: "A soldier takes his chance in losing his life in the roar and crash of battle, and anticipates death in that way, but he never counts on being killed by accident."[80] In any event, such accidental conflagrations represented some of the last ways in which the weapons of war, even those meant to be stored for safer disposition at quieter times, continued to exact a terrible price from the soldiers working in close proximity to them.

Modern warfare had demanded the full commitment of the respective societies to the production of war material. Citizens found employment opportunities in unprecedented numbers to meet these demands. Unfortunately, for too many of them, the work environment proved deadly. When coupled with other fatalities among workers and the soldiers who assisted or supervised them in the transportation and storage of such volatile components, it was inevitable that the costs in lives from this conflict would rise. As people were learning regularly, individuals did not have to perish on the battlefield to become casualties of war themselves.

9
Collateral Casualties
Deaths of Civilians

Men are shot and hung every few days on the most
trivial of pretexts. It has become so common that it
excites no remark.
Resident of Missouri on wartime violence there

It was particularly sad to see the little boy running
on before, waving a flag of truce, while his father
followed, driving a team in which lay the body of
his wife.
Aftermath of the death of Judith Kilby Smith
at Suffolk, Virginia

Such is life; we are all passing away.
Union officer commenting on the death
of a Southern civilian

Let me tell you spherical case and shell don't discriminate between those who are combatants and
those that are not.
Union soldier outside Vicksburg, Mississippi

Citizens had died in factory accidents and accidents related to war production
since the beginning of the conflict, but more of them would perish in other ways
as well. In his study of civilians and warfare, Hugo Slim noted, "The idea that
there are certain groups of people who should be protected from the killing and

wounding of war and from the worst effects of its impoverishment and disruption is an ancient and enduring one." This argument has developed along with the notion that although they existed in the context of combat, such individuals should be "set apart" from it wherever possible and provided a special status from those waging war. "Civilian is the word," Slim has insisted, "we now rely on to cradle and preserve the ancient idea that mercy, restraint and protection should have a place in war." Yet, regarding attitudes concerning noncombatants, no society has unanimously agreed upon their status or legitimate fates once the missiles of war had been unleashed.[1]

Violence had already plagued citizens before formalized warfare began, particularly in the region known as "Bleeding Kansas." One means of determining the nature of the government of the territory was to drive out or eliminate opponents. However, the volatile area that spanned Kansas and Missouri remained so after the guns roared at Charleston, South Carolina, in April 1861. By the end of 1862, the lament of a resident of Missouri captured the state of uncertainty and death that pertained when she observed, "Men are shot or hung every few days on the most trivial of pretexts. It has become so common that it excites no remark."[2]

For ordinary citizens, regardless of their affiliations or sentiments, life could be precarious. In the scene of the most public sacrifice from the Texas War for Independence, there were new images to sear in people's minds when, according to one scholar, "The trees around the Alamo Plaza were often weighted down by swinging corpses." In addition, a slave woman who had left San Antonio as a teamster asserted that her desire to leave the area as quickly as possible was the result of there being "too much hanging and murdering for me," including having seen a man hanged outside her door.[3]

The cruel bloodshed of Kansas-Missouri, along the Tennessee/Virginia/Kentucky border, or in parts of Texas represented some of the harshest cases of violence against civilians, but people residing in other areas were not immune to the war's bitter intrusions into their lives. In North Carolina, brutal slayings and merciless persecutions on both sides took place almost routinely, targeting individuals and their families for harboring opposing views or in retaliation for real or alleged offenses.[4] In one example, the community of Shelton Laurel experienced the flagrant killings of thirteen Unionist citizens by Confederate troops from the same area based largely on conditions that reflected local antagonisms, exacerbated by wartime shortages, socioeconomic differences, sectional partisanship, and the volatile personalities of some of the participants.[5]

Indisputably, civilians have suffered in every war, and they would find no refuge during the American Civil War either. For noncombatants caught in the context of war, it became increasingly of little interest which side the soldiers who were approaching your home represented. There was a minute chance that whatever those roving units found worth requisitioning would remain behind, whatever the result might be for the family so affected by their now empty larders. On a different scale, the tales of such woe abounded in connection with major military operations from late 1862 onward, particularly as logistical demands increased and traditional lines of supply became compromised or overstretched. The most popularly touted episodes involved William T. Sherman's "March to the Sea" across Georgia and the impact of Union activities in the Shenandoah Valley of Virginia in 1864, but devastation frequently accompanied Union armies tasked with decimating the Confederacy's war-making capabilities and food resources. Practitioners from David Hunter to Philip H. Sheridan understood the applications for the torch, and the "hard hand of war" became a common experience wherever Union armies moved.[6]

Union major general Henry Halleck expressed support for Sherman's actions in Atlanta after the city's fall, as "justified by the laws and usages of war." He felt that "severe rules of war" had become necessary, although he still termed Hunter's destruction of private property as "barbarous."[7] Retaliation by Confederates against the citizens and property of Chambersburg, Pennsylvania, as an answer to what they understood of Hunter's depredations also illustrated the degree to which the conflict could affect Northern civilians and prompted additional acts of reprisal toward Southern noncombatants as well.[8]

In Texas in 1861 and 1862, vicious assaults by Native Americans on settlers in outlying areas led to ruthless retaliatory strikes in which participants did not always differentiate between guilty and innocent parties. Deaths and mutilations stirred passions, especially when children became victims or the circumstances were brutal concerning the treatment of the bodies of the dead or dying. Sensational reports kept such incidents in the forefront and generated support for brutal responses in places as far away as Houston and Galveston.[9]

Civilians in Texas continued to face old dangers as attention turned elsewhere with the unfolding of the new war being waged largely east of the Mississippi. Settlers and travelers who did not exercise sufficient precaution became victims. William Youngblood was engaged in splitting rails for his ranch when he lost his life to a roving band of warriors, as did John Killen and Samuel Kuykendall, the latter when he attempted to pursue and corral one of his oxen that had strayed. The wife of farmer John Brown died when set upon while crossing to a neighboring ranch. Passengers traveling by wagon felt the brunt of this war, with one family losing most of its members, including women and children, to death or capture from a raiding party. Likewise, cattlemen and others fell to attacks as they passed through the region.[10]

In Florida, where the vote for secession had been overwhelmingly in favor of the measure, the cost of war began to be felt among the civilian population from an early period as Confederate priorities turned elsewhere. Chaotic evacuations and Federal incursions produced consternation and casualties. Confederate defenders and Union occupiers found diseases, especially yellow fever, offering fatal challenges. Zealousness could not always compensate for dangers. Among those lost was a young lad from Pensacola who perished from an accidental discharge from a firearm in a militia drill.[11]

For families forced to flee as refugees from the conflict, the war could have a searing impact. Virginian Judith McGuire, herself forced from point to point, captured the essence of the struggle for all such individuals in relating the death of a beloved niece in the winter of 1862–1863: "She reached Georgetown, Kentucky, which was her summer home; her mother was telegraphed for, and reached her just three days before she breathed her last. Dear H[arriet]! another victim of the war; as much so as was her brother, who received his mortal wound at Dranesville, or her brother-in-law, who was shot through the heart at Pea Ridge."[12]

Refugees faced myriad dangers that only increased as the fluid nature of warfare developed and opportunists struck wherever the vacuum of law and order prevailed. As he made his way through the rugged terrain of north Georgia, painter William Ray might have appreciated the natural beauty he encountered before more deadly circumstances arose to deprive him of his possessions and his life. It may or may not have been exclusively because he harbored Unionist sentiments, but when nefarious characters descended to rob Ray, they also shot and killed him.[13]

Vermonter George Randall had explained to his wife the degree to which sickness had impacted his comrades, but he noted that illness hit others as well, observing to her, "And to day one of our ladyes is to be sent home a corpse." By way of explanation, he offered the fact that the person who had died was one of two women married to men in the regiment and present in the camp. Describing both as "good women," he added, "The company that she belong[ed] to feel her loss very much."[14]

Civilian visitors elsewhere also fell victim by virtue of the exposure to the conditions prevailing among the men they had come to see. From Fort Brown, Texas, Union diarist Benjamin McIntyre noted the death of the wife of the surgeon of the Twentieth Wisconsin shortly after she had arrived at the post, "although everything was done that probably could have been for her even at her own home human exertion effected nothing in staying the fatal destroyer of earths populace." The death of "Mrs. Peake" left a lasting impression on the soldier, who wrote, "She was about 30 years of age, of fine appearance and commanded the esteem of all who had formed her acquaintance. Her early death will call up saddened memories while contemplating the incidents connected with it."[15]

Antagonisms festering between loyal Confederates and those deemed disloyal and dangerous among the Unionist population in many parts of the South continued to produce the underlying conditions for violence and death. German immigrants near Fredericksburg, Texas, became concerned enough about deteriorating conditions in their community to organize a Union Loyal League. In turn, this action prompted officials in Austin to mobilize forces to check such Unionist activities. Individual encounters resulted in the deaths of sympathizers on both sides, until a military-style operation set out at the end of August 1862 to squelch any potential insurgency. This mixed force of militiamen and soldiers pursued a caravan of German Unionists heading for Mexico, ending in a bloody shoot-out near the Nueces River. While some of the quarry fled in the confusion of a poorly planned and executed attempt by the Confederates to surround the Union encampment, a stiff resistance left both sides with substantial casualties, including the shooting of some of the Union prisoners after the fighting had ceased.[16]

In October 1862, the violence that had plagued north Texas since before the war played out in wholesale hangings of Unionists or suspected Unionists at Gainesville, Texas. Individual men in the area had already perished when differing positions on the question of loyalty occurred. Saloon owner Jim McCall died when he ridiculed two men for displaying pocketknives as their choice of weapons in the coming confrontations with potential opponents. The slain man's friends took the pair from jail, lynched them, and displayed their bodies in retaliation.[17] By the fall of that year, the scale for vigilante justice rose as a citizen's court convened and superintended over the deaths of at least forty-four men by execution. Local official James G. Bourland saw the drastic measures as crucial in suppressing dangerous levels of dissent in Texas toward the Confederacy. Subsequently, others died while ostensibly "trying to escape custody" or under other questionable circumstances.[18]

A section of Mississippi experienced similar chaos and killing as dissent grew against the Confederacy's war measures, particularly with regard to attempts to implement and enforce conscription. The "Free State of Jones" emerged as so significant a threat in some circles that Confederate troops had to intervene to put down opposition.[19] In March 1864, Lieutenant General Leonidas Polk reported the "weakness and inefficiency by the agents of the Bureau of Conscription" and noted that "conscripts and deserters have banded together in Jones County, and others contiguous, to the number of several hundred; have killed the officer in charge of the work of conscription and dispersed and captured his supporting force."[20] Subsequently, the general had better news, praising these efforts in a short communication: "The expedition I caused to be made under Colonel Maury against the traitors and murderers of Jones and other counties in Southern Mississippi has succeeded in killing and capturing a number of their ringleaders and breaking up their bands." Suggesting that he had achieved a "salutary effect . . . upon that infected district," Polk seemed to believe he had resolved the matter of murderous disaffection in this region at least.[21]

In the North, bitterness between those who supported the Federal war effort and those who opposed it also occasionally burst into violent expressions on the local level. When Copperheads, or Peace Democrats, clashed with furloughed Union soldiers on March 28, 1864, in Coles County, Illinois, the confrontation left nine dead and twelve wounded.[22] The officer in charge of the troops, Colonel G. M. Mitchell, described the situation as commencing when an assembled force of citizens, "whose object in drilling was only known to themselves," opened fire on the command, causing the death of Private Oliver Sallee, Company C, Fifty-Fourth Illinois. Before dying, Sallee managed to kill one of his assailants, Nelson Wells, the "so-called captain" of the citizen's force. Fire quickly "became general," with others being killed or wounded, including Major Shuball York, surgeon of the Fifty-Fourth Illinois. In addition to the armed participants in the melee, a stray shot penetrated "the residence of John Jenkins, citizen, wounding him and since causing his death."[23] Terming the matter "a serious disturbance," Major General Samuel P. Heintzelman, commanding in the affected department, promised to reinforce the "veteran regiment" already located there if the need arose.[24]

Those persons residing in regions subject to the incursions of cavalry raiders or plagued by the infestation of guerrillas or lawless elements faced deadly threats that could materialize at any moment. Wesley Gould noted these circumstances to his sister from a camp in Kentucky in May 1863: "You folks at the North do not know the horrors of this war. You can all stay at home without the least fear of being molested, but if you could hear some of the reffugees from Tennessee that have come to us for protection tell their tale of woe it would freeze the blood in your veins." Cataloging the travails, he observed, "If the people offer aney resistance they are shot down like Dumb Brutes."[25]

A Connecticut Yankee took a similar stand regarding the greater portion of the Northern populace, although his frame of reference was on the effects of the war on the Southern civilians he had encountered in Louisiana and Mississippi:

If you couled see the great Distress that is hear in the once Welthy Planter's Home, as well as those of the Poorer Class, you couled realize the great Curse War is. You to home in the North have not felt the first Eavils of this

War. I know that the Fire on many a Hearth Stone has gone out forever with us, but hear every Womon that you see in goin through a Town is in Mourning. Whare we have Lost one, they have lost five; not in Battle all to gather, but to exposure and Desese.[26]

Union colonel Samuel Hicks, commanding the troops garrisoning Paducah, Kentucky, filed a report in February 1864, which cataloged the dangers civilians faced in his proximity: "The guerrillas entered Mayfield, killed J. B. Happy, a good Union man, took Parson Dugger prisoner, put him in heavy bonds, robbed three stores (all belonging to Union men), took all the goods they wanted, and destroyed the rest, and then left."[27]

The constant challenge in areas of high unconventional activity was the ability to suppress or combat it and the confusion that existed between those who genuinely engaged in such behavior and those who did not. In too many cases, the opportunity to settle scores or take advantage of the chaotic conditions allowed individuals to act under the veneer of battling guerrillas and bushwhackers regardless of genuine motivation. In the course of the war in regions like southwest Virginia, especially along the Kentucky and Tennessee borders, following accepted rules and procedures was often a luxury that participants could not afford. Frequently, individuals acted under the impulse of anticipating danger, as when a Dickenson County native shot and killed a deserter under the assumption that he might pose a threat to the family.[28]

For others, the apprehension proved all too real. Unionist Scott County, Virginia, resident Hiram Marcum spent much of his time sleeping away from his residence rather than risk remaining in it if Confederate patrols should appear. His sixteen-year-old daughter, Julia, bore the brunt of such a visit when she confronted soldiers looking for her father. Frustrated in their effort, most of the party left, but one remained and began menacing her. In the melee that followed, she sustained horrific wounds, but the spirited Julia Marcum fended the man off with an ax until her father could dispatch him with a gun.[29]

Conditions became so severe that Union general Stephen Burbridge disseminated General Orders No. 59 from his headquarters in Lexington, Kentucky, noting the "rapid increase in this district of lawless bands of armed men engaged in . . . plundering and murdering peaceful Union citizens," among other infractions. His solution was to invoke "stern retaliatory measures" that included the edict, "Whenever an unarmed Union citizen is murdered four guerrillas will be selected from the prisoners in the hands of the military authorities and publicly shot to death in the most convenient place near the scene of [the] outrage."[30] As if to underscore his intentions, Burbridge inquired of the commander at Munfordville,

Kentucky, "Have the men been shot that I ordered? If not, then have them shot at once."[31]

Unlike their neighbors in rural or isolated regions, Unionists residing in urban centers of the Confederacy often had to remain largely silent to avoid retributive measures. In Atlanta, Georgia, fears of latent threats from a "Union Circle" focused attention on individuals deemed dangerous. One of these men, a dry goods merchant of Irish descent, drew sufficient concern to warrant his arrest. Unfortunately, his protestations that "everything dear to me, and all I have or own are in and of the Confederate States" were not enough to prevent him from being attacked while in custody and subsequently succumbing to his injuries.[32]

Northern civilians found less reason to expect the enemy on their doorsteps, but when Confederates reached Northern communities, even with strictures against the destruction of private property or the molestation of noncombatants in place, deaths were bound to occur. Even so, while Sharpsburg or Antietam provided the single bloodiest day in the Civil War for the combatants, and dangers for noncombatants obviously existed, the heavy fighting only accounted for at most one civilian fatality.[33] At Gettysburg, where the fighting endured over three days, entered the streets, and took place around the community, civilian deaths were not widespread. Ginnie or "Jennie" Wade became the most iconic symbol of a Northern citizen struck down during the war, felled as she was kneading dough in her kitchen by a round that penetrated two doors before reaching her heart and killing her instantly.[34]

Far more sinister in regions exposed to combat or billeting, for at least a period of time, large numbers of troops was the lingering presence of diseases that spread from the camps and field hospitals into the wider community.[35] In one instance, Sister Mary Lucy Dosh of Saint Mary Academy in Paducah, Kentucky, stepped forward to assist treating the sick soldiers who inundated the town before contracting typhoid fever and dying herself on December 29, 1861. Only twenty-two years old, she was "held in such grateful esteem and affection, that her body, escorted by an officer and a detail of soldiers, was taken to the U.S. gunboat *Peacock* on a caisson," with an honor guard at her burial that consisted of six Union and six Confederate officers who had been her patients.[36]

Winchester, Virginia, experienced tragedy of another type and scale as the sickness brought in by the soldiers hospitalized there spread with fatal effect upon the civilian population, especially among the young, the elderly, and the infirm. One diarist noted a doctor's assessment that scarlet fever was "raging like wildfire" and taking victims from seemingly every household.[37]

Soldiers who left the ranks to recover from severe illnesses at home could also be responsible for threatening the lives of the people who tended them or were otherwise exposed to them. Historian William Marvel observed, "The migration of so many men from disease-ridden armies back to their isolated rural communities inevitably introduced little plagues that ravaged certain hamlets."[38] Communicable diseases found fertile ground in the tight-knit, family-oriented local societies that welcomed home furloughed or recuperating soldiers who also unwittingly brought their afflictions with them. A farmer from Maine, who watched his neighbors grapple with increasing bouts of illness, observed frankly in his diary, "I can hardly realize that so many have died."[39]

The specter of death through illness also affected the families of those who supervised the war effort in the field. William T. Sherman confided to his wife, Ellen, his belief that bringing their son to be near him in Mississippi may have contributed to the youngster's death to disease. The couple's eldest son, Willy, died of typhoid fever on October 3, 1863. Sherman was plagued by the notion that his actions created the deadly circumstances for his son. "Consistent with a sense of duty to my profession and office, I could not leave my post," he explained to a subordinate and friend,

> and sent for my family to come to me in that fatal climate, and in that sickly period of the year, and behold the result! The child who bore my name, and in whose future I reposed with more confidence than I did in my own plans of life, now floats a mere corpse, seeking a grave in a distant land, with a weeping mother, brother, and sisters clustered about him.[40]

To the grieving mother he explained, "Sleeping—waking—everywheres I see Poor Little Willy. . . . Though I know we did all human beings could do to arrest the ebbing tide of Life, still I will always deplore my want of judgment in taking my family to so fatal a climate at so critical period of the year."[41] "Cump" Sherman's anguish continued over the next days. On October 10, he lamented to Ellen, "The moment I begin to think of you & the children, Poor Willy appears before me as plain as life." He could not shake the despair and guilt he felt, asking, "Why should I ever have taken them to that dread Climate? It nearly kills me to think of it. Why was I not killed at Vicksburg and left Willy to grow up to care for you?"[42]

Not even presidents were immune to personal tragedies. Abraham Lincoln also suffered personal loss in the death of a child. While Union arms achieved success in the field at Forts Henry and Donelson in Tennessee, young Willie Lincoln's life ebbed from him in Washington. If the presence of large numbers of troops in the capital provided a sense of security, they also affected negatively the quality of the water sources, including that which supplied the White House.

Mary Todd Lincoln's constant solicitations could not stay the outcome, which arrived on the evening of February 20, 1862, when the young man drew his last breath. Even a normally composed President Lincoln could not contain his shock and grief, and Mary became a bedridden recluse.[43]

Although not to disease, Jefferson Davis also lost a son while serving his nation. Joseph Evan Davis succumbed to injuries sustained from a fall at the Confederate White House in Richmond. In the increasing heat of a warm April 30, 1864, with the windows of the residence open to allow the flow of any breeze, President Davis was in his office and Varina Davis was hosting visitors, including her sister, Margaret, when a servant suddenly appeared. Barely five years old at the time, Joe had wandered out onto the second-floor portico and begun to climb the railing when he slipped and fell to the brick sidewalk below. Unresponsive but still breathing, the boy suffered trauma to his upper extremities that proved too extensive for him to overcome. Within a matter of minutes, the young lad who loved to cajole his father into nightly prayers was gone.

The Davises were inconsolable. Varina could not contain her grief, and only the steely determination that marked the brokenhearted father allowed him to retain his composure. "Not mine, oh, Lord, but, thine," he could be heard to say repeatedly in the midst of the despair that engulfed him as he tried to offer what comfort he could to his grief-stricken spouse. Even an urgent dispatch from General Lee only momentarily turned Davis's attention aside from the intensely personal mission he had undertaken. "I must have this day for my little child," he observed to himself as much as to those surrounding him and turned once more to the tragic duty of a bereaved father. For the remainder of that darkest of nights, Jefferson Davis could be heard pacing the floor of his residence as the events of the day continued to manifest themselves. Richmond would share in the tragedy the next day as children gathered flowers and boughs to place on the young man's grave in the city's Hollywood Cemetery. Monday required President Davis to return his focus to the war, but the loss of this beloved child would remain with him forever.[44] In the following September, Jefferson Davis ordered the structure from which Joe had fallen, as Confederate war clerk John B. Jones explained, to be "pulled down."[45]

For civilians, the last mortal moments could come as they did for Judith Henry, in a place where the paths of combatants and noncombatants intersected, through no particular fault of their own. Others created the conditions from which their deaths emanated through their own actions. While marching to Maryland in the summer of 1862, a Union soldier related an incident that, if true, represented an egregious act on the part of a noncombatant: "The morning we were in Winchester a little drummer boy was walking along under a window and an old Secesh woman caught him by his hair and with her revolver blew out his brains." Retribution was swift and sure: "The next morning a ball passed through her head and she hung there across the window case." Although it was unclear if Private Henry Smith had actually witnessed any of what he was purporting had taken place or was merely passing along camp rumor, the stories illustrated the delicate balance between the martial and the civilian worlds, as well as the ways in which circumstances could compromise the boundaries that were supposed to separate them.[46]

It should not, then, have been shocking to know that as the opposing forces flowed through the city streets, the lines of distinction between the civilian and the martial would become blurred, as when some local citizens harassed Federal troops as they retreated from Stonewall Jackson's advances in 1862. Some of these soldiers became victims of the aroused citizenry, and at least one recorded seeing return fire from the troops with effect on a woman who had shot at them. He explained that he "could see the blood spurt from her breast as the ball struck her, and she fell instantly."[47]

Attitudes toward the treatment of civilians altered as the war progressed but seemed to differ by service as well. Historian Michael J. Bennett noted that Union sailors often recoiled at the brutish and cruel behavior of their soldier comrades toward the locals they encountered. One Union sailor told his mother of an instance of an elderly gentleman who perished in the flames of his residence. "As rough and careless as sailors are," he asserted, "I'll take my oath not one of them would treat women & children as these same dear, dirty volunteers."[48]

Clashes between civilians and soldiers occurred often. Some of these stemmed from issues that could just as easily have arisen in peacetime. As the First Texas Cavalry moved in the direction of Louisiana, unit surgeon John L. White had a violent confrontation with a resident of Hallettsville, Texas, named Smoothers. According to one account, the doctor "shot and killed" the man. Private William Kuykendall concluded of the incident, "A gambling spree the night before led to the killing." Efforts to compel White to answer charges in civilian court fell apart when the regimental commander, Colonel Augustus Buchel, declined to turn him over.[49]

In another incident, in the latter part of 1863, a Confederate soldier halted two travelers on a road leading from Cumberland Gap to Jonesville, in Lee County, Virginia. What initially may have been a stop for verification of identity, if not an opportunity for robbing the men, turned violent, since one of the riders had substantial sums of money on his person. In the altercation that resulted, Francis Bishop, the married civilian father of twelve children, lost his life, while the soldier endured a nearly fatal beating from Bishop's companion and brother-in-law.[50]

The presence of alcohol tinged some of the incidents involving soldier and noncombatant interactions. In one instance, Private William Bates of Company H, First Minnesota, imbibed too freely. Aiming his weapon at an African American cook serving the regiment, the soldier fired a round, striking the man fatally. Subsequently asserting that he did not know the musket was loaded, Bates had a fine of twelve dollars and a fifteen-day stint in the guardhouse levied against him for his actions.[51]

Alcohol was related directly to the death of a civilian in the environs of Washington, in 1863. The *Daily National Republican* reprinted a notice from a neighboring newspaper regarding "Mrs. P. Webster, the old lady who was accidentally shot by one of the First District of Columbia regiment on Tuesday night last, [who] died this morning of her wounds." The tragedy would have been great enough had not other elements compounded it. The writer concluded of the regrettable incident, "This handling of fire arms by intoxicated soldiers is a dangerous business, particularly when shot at random."[52]

The November 12, 1861, edition of the *Richmond Daily Dispatch* provided an example of other dangers to civilians associated with the movement of military forces and supplies:

> To-day a serious accident occurred at the railroad depot in this place. As the Orange and Alexandria train was backing down the track, a negro man belonging to Mrs. Macon drove his team across the track, when he was killed and his wagon mashed up the mules and horses were borne down but not killed. The team was returning from the West, where it had been impressed to aid in transporting provisions for the army.[53]

Another teamster was present when a locomotive boiler exploded in Nicholasville, Kentucky, hurling fragments of metal and spewing scalding steam broadly. For William Cooper, from Covington, Kentucky, the circumstances could not have been worse. He happened to be walking in close proximity, and the shattering blast had a devastating effect upon him. *New York Herald* correspondent James C. Fitzpatrick was also nearby and did not spare his readers the searing detail of the physical destruction wrought on the civilian driver:

> The clothes were torn from his body, with the exception of a fragment of his shirt, which remained attached at the shoulder; his legs were broken in several places, so that they resembled a mass of jelly; his head and hip were perforated with two holes . . . and the lower part of his body was frightfully scalded. When found he was buried head down into a pool of muddy water,

where he had been buried by the force of the explosion. Notwithstanding the terrible nature of his injuries he lingered some two hours, during which time he frequently implored the soldiers standing around him to put an end to his sufferings by a shot from their muskets.

The threat to life from the vicissitudes of war came in many forms. Death could occur when the intent was quite different, as when South Carolina slaveholders or their representatives loaded some 500 slaves onto a train for safekeeping by sending them away from areas exposed to Federal invasion. The owners believed that by removing the slaves "from the thieving Yankees, who were laying waste and robbing the country of every thing they could wherever they went," they were sparing their charges from such abuse. However, in a tragic twist, two of the cars on which these people were traveling "became disconnected and were left behind" on the tracks. "Before the fact was discovered, about 11 o'clock P.M., they were run into by the down passenger train, which was following." The collision caused the cars to become "fearfully crushed and twelve negroes [were] killed—several having been scalded to death by the hot steam from the broken engine."[54]

Tragedies occurred in the most unlikely settings but would not have taken place except for the presence of soldiers or their weapons. Such a situation happened at Fredericksburg, Virginia, in January 1863. Although apparently detailed for protection, one soldier standing guard over a residence allowed carelessness to exact a devastating price among the occupants of the home. A Union surgeon told his wife that he had been summoned "to see a young lady who was shot by her young brother." Apparently, the lad had been watching the sentry and decided to engage in some harmless role-playing of his own. "It was purely accidental," Daniel Holt explained, "the boy took a loaded gun of a guard who was placed at the home, and telling her that he was going to shoot her, drew up and lodged a ball in her body, just below the heart. She cannot survive." The doctor observed that the sibling was "nearly frantic with grief and remorse, and I think he has learned a lesson never to be forgotten—that is to be careful how he handles loaded guns." Dr. Holt was not content with making this point but thought it could be extended, arguing that the same lesson "would be well for our men to learn also;—they are exceedingly green and clumsy and hardly a time when they go out on picket but someone comes in minus a finger, hand or arm."[55] In Mobile, Alabama, it was the creation of earthworks for wartime purposes that provided the context for tragedy when a young girl slipped from a parapet into a trench filled with water and drowned.[56]

Collateral casualties continued to be most likely to occur when warring forces crossed the properties of citizens or used their homes, barns, or other structures for military purposes during engagements. The placement of sharpshooters or batteries in the vicinity could draw fire that would not discriminate if civilians were also present. In these instances, noncombatants could be as likely to experience fatal encounters, even when the shots fired at them were inadvertent or accidental.

In April 1863, Army of Northern Virginia veterans under James Longstreet closed on the small Tidewater town of Suffolk, Virginia. Ringed by a formidable array of earthworks and rifle pits, the community remained in Union hands. Fighting on the thirteenth proved unlucky for at least one family caught in the area between the opposing lines. As projectiles hit their home, the family of George W. Smith, including seven children, remained in the basement. The fire quickly became so pervasive as to impel the Smiths to leave the home and seek protection in an adjacent woods. Unfortunately, while carrying a six-month-old infant in her arms, the mother, Judith Kilby Smith, suffered a wound that killed her instantly.[57] A Union cavalryman offered the heartrending tableau of the reaction of one of the children as the husband and father brought Judith Smith into the town: "It was particularly sad to see the little boy running on before, waving a flag of truce, while his father followed, driving a team in which lay the body of his wife."[58]

One family, living along the path of the war at Centreville, Virginia, north of Manassas, suffered the loss of its patriarch. Although there was no direct link to fighting for the fifty-seven-year-old doctor with decidedly pro-Southern leanings who died suddenly, a Union officer who had come to know the family observed quietly, "Such is life; we are all passing away."[59]

Among the most heart-wrenching stories of the war was one that involved Eva C. Roland as she traveled on a train along the Raleigh and Gaston Railroad in November 1862. The widow of a soldier who had recently died, she had originally journeyed to see her sick husband to help nurse him back to health. Instead, in the company of her father-in-law, Thomas Roland, she was returning to North Carolina with the fallen warrior's remains when the train on which they were traveling collided with another. Thomas perished in the accident, and she was "terribly mangled," leading to an amputation of a leg. Throughout her painful ordeal, Eva Roland impressed those around her with her courage and piety, but the war had exacted a terrible toll on her and her family.[60]

Eva Roland demonstrated an unmatched fortitude in the face of unimaginable tragedy. But others experienced conditions that tested their abilities to meet the crisis and in some cases were unable to overcome them. Historian David Silkenat uncovered several examples of civilians who found that the conflict could "exact a psychological toll on those on the home front." Temperance Sirls and Alexander Ridings hanged themselves, and James Little drowned himself in a well on his property, for reasons that others attributed to the effects of the war or fears concerning loved ones serving in it. Whatever such desperate measures exhibited or masked about the individuals involved, they represented the degree to which the war could impact civilian noncombatants as well as the soldiers who risked their lives on the battlefield.[61]

Death on the rails could be sudden and vicious under any conditions, but when a train collision took place in Alabama in the spring of 1862, the circumstances for some of the civilian passengers and those who witnessed their death struggles were beyond comprehension. Alonzo Brown, adjutant of the Fourth Minnesota, which lost at least one member from its ranks, recalled the horrific image that came amid the flaming wreckage: "We could see the women running around in the burning cars. In all seven were killed or burned to death."[62]

A troubling episode of a different sort occurred concerning a young person from Petersburg, Virginia, in 1863. German Eanes had followed a difficult path since enlisting in the Forty-First Virginia Infantry in May 1861, claiming that he had been born in 1842. Son of a "master carpenter," who had worked in the shops of the South Side Railroad, Eanes struggled to establish his equilibrium on his own before finding himself under arrest in December. Early in the new year he was on punishment detail but initially was exempted from service due to his being "underage." When subsequently conscripted, he fell ill and in November received a discharge. Unfortunately, trouble did not abate for the young would-be soldier, for he engaged in a fight with another lad in 1863 and killed his adversary with a blow from a stone in the streets of Petersburg. The youth with sociopathic tendencies became something of a cautionary tale for the negative effects of war on the sense of order and traditional family structure.[63]

Unfortunately, for some civilians, the implements of war and the residual danger that they represented remained long after fighting had subsided, accounting for unintended deaths. The *Alexandria (Va.) Gazette* noted in the months after the bloodiest single day of combat in the war, September 17, 1862, that ordnance from that engagement was still claiming victims. In its May 7, 1863, edition, the paper offered a sobering story for any misguided individuals who might reside in communities that had experienced heavy combat: "Mr. Jonathan Keplurger, a well known citizen of Sharpsburg, Md., was killed recently by the explosion of a shell picked up on the Antietam battlefield."[64] What the gentleman had intended to do with the piece of ordnance was not identified, but if he desired to remove it or render it harmless, he would have been better served to leave the shell alone. As it was, Keplurger's efforts had clearly gone wrong.

By the summer of 1863, the Western Theater was demonstrating itself to be the chief scene of movement in the war. The ebb and flow of operations in the

Eastern Theater and the distance of the Trans-Mississippi were working against these areas in ways that emphasis on controlling the Mississippi River did not. Ulysses S. Grant had attempted an overland push toward the fortified city of Vicksburg that had bogged down with successful Confederate cavalry raids by Earl Van Dorn against the forward Union supply base at Holly Springs, Mississippi, and Nathan Bedford Forrest against the supporting rail network in West Tennessee. Failing with other strategic endeavors, Grant finally turned to a dramatic movement to cross the great river below the city and pushed inland toward the Mississippi capital of Jackson. At the same time, Federal troops closed on the defenders of Port Hudson, below Vicksburg.

When General Van Dorn's Confederates appeared suddenly and unexpectedly at Holly Springs, the noise stirred curiosity as well as consternation, but it also produced an unintended tragedy. A Union general related what he termed "one of the saddest incidents I saw during the entire war." Reub Williams and the quartermaster of the post "stepped out on the portico . . . to obtain a better view of what was going on, when [a] bright little girl, with curly hair and handsome as a picture, pushed her beautiful face right between us, and she, too gazed up the street." No one seemed to anticipate the danger until it was too late. Williams explained, "As she peeped uptown, she received a bullet almost squarely in the forehead. I felt her little hand clutch my coat and only when she pulled on it so heavily, did I know that she had been hit." The officer took her inside, but there was nothing to be done for the child, and he was left with the image of unimaginable grief. "I shall never forget the scene when mother and father knew that their little one was a victim of Van Dorn's raid."[65]

Heavy Union shelling from the river at Vicksburg had already produced panic among some noncombatants. Robert Patrick included one instance in his diary in which a frightened African American "broke off towards the woods through the darkness, and not being able to see before him he ran over a stump and broke his neck." On another occasion, a number of people visiting with their soldier loved ones became unnerved by the artillery rounds that descended near them. "There were several women who had come down to see their husbands in the camp," the writer explained. "They tried to get away and not knowing the geography of the country, they fell into a stream of water and a woman and child were drowned."[66]

In the meantime, dispensing with efforts by John Pemberton and Joseph Johnston to prevent, or at least slow, his advance, Ulysses Grant moved on relentlessly, capturing Jackson and shattering Confederate forces at Champion Hill and Big Black River before moving against Vicksburg itself. Attempts to blast his way into the citadel failed with the repulse of direct assaults in May, and the Union commander resorted to the slower and steadier method of siege approaches.

At the same time, a Union soldier from Minnesota, but now outside Vicksburg, watching black workers and white soldiers hoisting crates of ammunition drew lessons on the changes war had wrought on slavery and the Southern planters who once benefited from it: "There fine carraiges are used for ambulances: and there People are slain. sons and Brother: Fathers and children are mangled on the same field of Death. and now since we have invested this city, even there women and children are slain, for let me tell you spherical case, and shell don't discriminate between those who are combatants and those that are not." His conclusion for those at home was simple: "Let every one of you be thankful you are not in a Besieged city night and Day."[67]

Field fortifications and siege works on the scale seen at Vicksburg required intensive labor. For the beleaguered Confederates, whose manpower was already stretched thin to man the existing defenses, civilians had to be impressed. Among the efforts by the Federals to overcome these earthworks were tunnels or mines that would enable explosives to be placed beneath Confederate positions for detonation. In an attempt to thwart these measures, the Southerners resorted to countermining operations for which they employed African American laborers. On the afternoon of July 1, two tons of black powder sent a plume of earth, men, and equipment skyward, producing a thirty-foot-deep crater and killing an unknown number of the black workers.[68]

Vicksburg's citizens quickly learned the harsh realities of being confined in a city under fire and forced, increasingly, to seek refuge in makeshift bombproofs. Even before a siege developed, Union shelling had produced at least one civilian death, when one of the immense rounds the Federal gunboats hurled into the town beheaded Patience Gamble. At the height of the operations, a street vendor perished in gruesome fashion from a shell burst, and a woman who had been assisting in a nearby hospital suffered decapitation as she tried to navigate her way back home. Her distraught daughter died only a few weeks after the incident, ostensibly from the shock of losing her mother in such a brutal fashion. An unknown number of civilians perished by Union shelling while participating in a funeral procession for several soldiers killed earlier in the same manner.[69]

By the time General Grant developed his systematic approaches to the defenses, many of the citizens had become dwellers in the caves carved out of the loess soil that honeycombed the hillsides and offered at least the pretense of protection from Union shot and shell. Even so, frustration with being confined forced some to accept the risk to their lives of exposure. As Vicksburg historian Terrence Winschel explained, "Civilians soon realized that they were not immune to the death of the battlefield. Although figures vary as to the total of civilian casualties, the harsh reality was that innocent men, women, and children died victims of war."[70]

Sadly, Vicksburg offered some distinct examples of children and young people becoming victims to the shot and shell fired at the defenders. One of these rounds hit while an infant lay in the supposed safe haven of one of the city's ubiquitous caves. A resident sharing a similar dwelling heard the effects of the Union ordnance that had landed where the victim was resting and later recalled, "A mortar shell came rushing through the air, and fell with much force, entering the earth above the sleeping child—oh! most horrible sight to the mother—crushing in the upper part of the little sleeping head, and taking away the young innocent life."[71]

In another case, an African American child happened upon a shell while playing. Thinking the orb an instrument for amusement, the young person began "rolling and turning it" and in the process "innocently pounded the fuse." What had been meant as a device for exploding the shell over the heads of enemy soldiers had an unintended but devastating effect on a noncombatant, with the result that after "the white smoke floated away," all that was left were "the mangled remains of a life that to the mother's heart had possessed all of beauty and joy."[72]

A teenage boy, volunteering to bring water to a section of the Confederate defenses that required exposure when approaching them, perished by a marksman on the other side. The soldiers in those same trenches were not immune to death from sources other than sharpshooters, shelling, and mine explosions. Historian Michael Ballard noted, "Some ill Confederates who refused to leave the trenches died at their post without suffering wounds; they succumbed to siege conditions."[73]

Inadvertently, the successful conclusion of the siege by the Union forces on July 4 also led to unexpected dangers for other civilians. Six days later, the *Cleveland Morning Leader* reported on a fatal accident at Shelby, where exuberant citizens paid a stern price for their expressions of delight over the recent martial developments: "Last evening (Wednesday) some of the citizens of Shelby got up a celebration in honor of the fall of the famous rebel stronghold, Vicksburg. While the cannon was being fired, it exploded, injuring four or five persons, some of them probably in a fatal [manner]."[74]

Charleston, South Carolina, had been under Union guns with effect on civilians to the extent that Major Henry Bryan, assistant inspector general, filed a report on January 6, 1864, that covered the period August 21 through December 31, 1863. Meticulous and thorough, it included information "on the bombardment of Charleston by the Abolition army," with sections on "damage to property," "damage to life," "number of shots," "proportion of shells which burst," and "what part of the city most frequently struck." Given the sensitivity in the public mind on such an incendiary subject, Major Bryan's overall human assessment could not completely avoid emotion: "The casualties have been remarkably few, and fallen almost entirely upon the civilians who clung to their homes. The whole result has so far been utterly inadequate to the labors and boasts of the besieging forces."

In the section devoted to "damage to life," Major Bryan focused on specific cases:

> Five deaths have resulted from the bombardment, viz. Mrs. Hawthorne, No. 70 Church street, wounded by shell in right side, and died six weeks after; Miss Plane, corner Meeting and Market, left foot crushed by shell, and died in six days; Mr. William Knighton, corner Meeting and Market, right leg taken off, and died in four days; Mr. John Doscher, of German Fire Company, wounded at fire of December 25, and since died; Rebecca, slave of Mr. Lindsay, No. 5 Beaufain street, killed instantly by shell.[75]

Colonel Alfred Rhett added details in another report concerning the Christmas Day bombardment, commending the firemen who responded: "A shell burst very near the engine, but the men continued working and rendered good service." Rhett also noted the effects of the firing on the victims: "Mr. Knighton, a man eighty-three years old, right leg shot off below the knee by a shell."[76]

Later in the same year, a newspaper correspondent forwarded a letter from Charleston for his readers in Yorkville that outlined "several accidents, or mischances occurring here since my last." The first of these described the fates of two "little white boys" and "a negro" who "were instantly killed by the explosion of a shell with which they were tampering to get the powder out—they were dreadfully mutilated."[77]

Similarly, several fatalities resulted from the juxtaposition of childhood curiosity and the implements of war. Two young boys from Gettysburg perished when shells filled with powder they were trying to extract exploded instead.[78] A Port Royal, South Carolina, report noted an "explosion" that had taken place "near Gen. RIPLEY's headquarters, on Southern wharf. A pile of 'Yankee fifteen-inch shells' was lying near the door, when some 'small and thoughtless boys' ran a heated wire into one of them, and the whole pile at once became 'effective;' three persons were killed."[79]

The *Richmond Daily Dispatch* of July 7, 1864, noted, "On Sunday last, while Samuel Farmer, a son of Mrs. Martha W. Farmer, of Richmond, and John Mosby, son of John S. Mosby, of Henrico county, were at play near the house of the latter, about eight miles from this city, they found some shells in the woods, and in trying to open one it exploded, mangling their limbs in an awful manner." The writer explained that "the noise of the explosion attracted some of the neighbors to the spot," but every effort to provide relief proved "of no avail." The boys "died in a few hours after the accident."[80]

Union naval activities against the Confederate defenses at Port Hudson, Mississippi, produced impressive pyrotechnics that garnered the attention of military personnel on both sides. Unfortunately, for civilians caught in the maelstrom, the impacts were more terrifying. For families of some of the officers in the garrison, the blasts caused panic that sent some of them fleeing from the more obvious danger zones into hazards equally threatening. In their rush for safety, at least one of the women and a child plunged into local Little Sandy Creek and drowned. Elsewhere, an African American who was working in a noncombat role as a cook or teamster found the ordeal so great that in his panic to escape he hit his head on a projection from a cabin and broke his neck. Although these deaths were inadvertent results of a bombardment meant to affect the defenders, the fortifications offered these soldiers protections not afforded to the civilians.[81]

The destruction of a steamer on the Mississippi River in the month after the fall of Vicksburg cost some of the soldiers present their lives. However, the price did not fall on the men in uniform alone. Several individuals working on the craft when it burned and sank suffered fatalities among their number as well. An account from August 15, 1863, noted, "Ten negro deck hands, chambermaid, and a colored woman cabin passenger, [were] lost."[82]

Operations in East Tennessee in 1863 between Union and Confederate forces put the citizens of Knoxville at risk. Dr. James Harvey Baker died at the hands of Union troops when he armed himself to help defend the town but never succeeded in leaving the grounds of his home. Mistaking Baker for a Confederate skirmisher or bushwhacker, the Federals pursued him into his house and fired rounds that mortally wounded him through a locked door.[83]

In the subsequent advance of James Longstreet against Ambrose Burnside in the fall, a round felled a black teamster who was maneuvering one of the Union artillery pieces into position on the approaches to Knoxville. In the town itself, only one civilian, a child, was reported to have perished by a round that struck her as she stood in the doorway of her home.[84] Another civilian, described in a regimental history as "a colored waitman of Lieut. Joe D. Beatie, of Company L," in the First Kentucky Cavalry, drowned while the unit crossed the nearby Holston River in September 1863.[85]

Lucius Barber of the Fifteenth Illinois was back in the area that Ulysses Grant had fought his way through to Vicksburg in early 1864 when he and his comrades clashed with Confederate cavalry. The Federals put their opponents to flight, but in the aftermath, Barber saw the effects of a "very melancholy incident." The Confederates had set a line a short distance "beyond a dwelling house where lived a widow with three small children." When the firing occurred, she "came to the door to see what was going on when a ball struck her, killing her instantly." The Union soldier recalled that when the Federals approached the cabin, "they found her form rigid in death, lying in a pool of her own life's blood." Even more poignantly, "Her little children were clinging frantically to her, not realizing that she was dead." Given the confusion of the fighting, Barber may have been right when he asserted, "I do not know from which side the shot was fired that killed her."[86]

Narrow escapes for civilians under fire did not always translate well for the soldiers themselves. General Francis A. Walker recorded an incident that occurred when a portion of an artillery battery set up near a house in central Virginia. The artillerists removed the limber chest and set it apart from the cannon, but in the course of the firing, "a negro woman, crazy with fright, walked out of the kitchen with a shovelful of hot ashes, which she emptied into the chest." Although ammunition chests normally remained closed during action to avoid sparks and embers from reaching the contents, the addled civilian created the hazard the cannoneers hoped to avoid by opening it to dispose of the ashes. The general noted of the mishap, "Two men were killed and others wounded by the explosion that resulted, the cause of the mischief escaping unharmed." Walker thought the ability of the unwitting instigator to avoid death or injury typical, commenting, "In the army it always *was* the fool doing the mischief that got off safe."[87]

Piercing the fog of war in a fluid situation could produce unintended fatalities among those caught in the middle of already dangerous situations. When Confederate raiders struck the Baltimore and Ohio Railroad near Bloomington, Federal forces responded to suppress the threat. A Maryland newspaper provided readers with the tragic elements associated with the deployment of "a Union battery [which] came up and sent several shells after the retreating guerrillas. One exploded in a house on a hill-side, supposed to be occupied by the rebels, [but] which was filled with children who had gathered there for safety." The regrettable circumstance proved fatal for some of the refugees. "Sad to relate," the writer observed solemnly, "two of the children were killed and five wounded by the explosion."[88]

Escaped slaves experienced many of the dangers of life in wartime in contraband camps as impressed workers. Union major George L. Stearns noted the loss of some 800 conscripted black workers who had worked on Nashville's Fort Negley without the benefit of salary for their efforts. These fatalities represented almost 30 percent of the 2,768 workers employed in the enterprise.[89] Others accepted the potential for retaliation for aiding the enemy while serving as guides for Union units. In Florida, zealous members of the Oklawaha Rangers hanged a slave whom they thought guilty of assisting the Federals while conducting local operations in the region of the St. Johns River.[90]

Although the Oklawaha Rangers acted on their own volition in the cause of the Confederacy, the Union War Department attempted to codify rules relating to wartime engagement. Federal war policy crafted by Francis Lieber and distributed as "General Orders, No. 99," in the spring of 1863, addressed such sensitive areas of contact between combatant and noncombatant elements. Lieber's "Instructions for the Government of Armies of the United States in the Field" included a mix of protections and threats for civilians. Operative in this situation were "[No.] 95. If a citizen of a hostile and invaded district voluntarily serves as a guide to the enemy, or offers to do so, he is deemed a war-traitor and shall suffer death" and "[No.] 97. Guides, when it is clearly proved that they have misled intentionally, may be put to death."[91]

Whatever their race, when locals directed columns in pursuit of guerrillas, their necessary proximity to the front also put their lives at hazard. In Kentucky, in 1864, a Unionist citizen named Hood was leading Union troops on a mission when he was struck by fire coming from assailants secreted in the underbrush along the road. The incident illustrated the peril such individuals faced as they sought to make their own contributions to the war effort.[92]

Despite such risks, the men and women who volunteered also faced retribution over questions of their possible duplicity from the very forces they had agreed to lead. In one case, when "asked if the river was fordable," the local resident "stated it was perfectly safe, which led to the drowning of our men." Angry and dubious of the civilian's real motives and intentions toward them, the soldiers responded immediately and decisively: "The citizen was at once thrown in and was drowned."[93]

When Martin Robinson attempted to assist Ulric Dahlgren's Union raiders in their advance on Richmond in 1864 in concert with troops approaching the city on another front under Judson Kilpatrick, he encountered a life-threatening situation he could not have anticipated. The two Federal commanders approached the Confederate capital from different directions and expected to coordinate their efforts in entering the city and capturing or killing key individuals of the Southern political structure, while releasing Union captives from prisoner of war facilities located there.[94]

With the James River as a barrier into Richmond for his column, Dahlgren needed a local resident with knowledge of the terrain to provide a fordable crossing point. A former slave and skilled craftsman who lived in the area, Robinson appeared to be perfectly suited for the vital task. Sent forward by the provost marshal, he carried a positive reference: "At the last moment I have found the man you want; well acquainted with the James River from Richmond up."[95]

Unfortunately, when the raiders neared the crossing point, they found that the river was running too high and could not detect that an acceptable access point actually existed. Thinking the guide guilty of willful deception, a frustrated and angry Dahlgren took the man's bridle and fashioned a noose from which Robinson soon dangled for his alleged faithlessness.[96]

Attempts at escape had marked the institution of slavery from its earliest years, creating the need for an "underground railroad" of support. In the earliest stages of the war, poignant tales emerged of failed attempts to find a path to freedom, including one from abolitionist Laura S. Haviland. She had traveled from Michigan to Columbus, Kentucky, where she witnessed a funeral procession. The individual being laid to rest was a slave who had tried to run away from his servitude in Missouri with family members. As the party rowed a boat for freedom, the master fired at them to compel them to stop and struck the young man. Union surgeons in Columbus worked to save him but could not. Haviland noted that the bereaved mother grieved that the man she had "nussed" with her own son— "They was both babies together"—had been responsible for his death.[97]

Others seeking freedom hoped to find refuge with advancing Federal forces, especially in the aftermath of the Emancipation Proclamation. Yet, even after undertaking the risks inherent in making the effort to escape, there was no guarantee of a welcome reception. Perhaps the most heart-wrenching case occurred at the end of William T. Sherman's "March to the Sea," near Savannah, Georgia. After the troops of General Jefferson C. Davis crossed a pontoon bridge over Ebenezer Creek, outside the city, he ordered the structure removed before the black refugees following his command could follow. Knowing that any chance for avoiding whatever Confederate force might be coming up from behind them, some of the panicked individuals surged into the water to take their chances and drowned.[98] The army thus demonstrated, as one historian has asserted, "an eager appropriation of black men's muscle power and a simultaneous denigration of the lives of black people who were deemed useless to the troops."[99] Sherman had made no secret that he considered such refugees to be impediments to effective military operations, but he considered his general's actions fully justified. "Of course that cock-and-bull story of my turning back negroes that [Joseph] Wheeler might kill them is all humbug," Sherman related to Henry Halleck on January 12. "I turned nobody back." Nevertheless, if actions had to be taken, they were military necessities. As Sherman explained, Davis "took up his pontoon bridge, not because he wanted to leave them, but because he wanted his bridge" for future operations.[100]

Becoming caught between opposing forces could mean raising the suspicions of both sides. A hapless civilian from Stewart County, Tennessee, who sought refuge when a firefight broke out between Union troops and local guerrillas perished instead. A Union officer asserted that his men had fired at the figure fleeing toward them because they were uncertain of his status: "My men supposing him to be one of the rebels, [shot him] as he attempted to escape."[101]

Like those persons who lived under fire in Charleston, South Carolina, the people of Atlanta, Georgia, endured extensive bombardment as part of the military operations that impacted their community. Stephen Davis has examined the voluminous and often contradictory record involving the exposure of Atlanta citizens to Union shelling. He concluded, "The Northern cannonade had killed or wounded a number of civilians uncounted then and uncountable now, save for our guess that perhaps two dozen men, women and children were slain (including casualties caused by shell explosions after the Yankees had ceased firing [from unexploded ordnance]), and at least several score more wounded."[102]

Davis was able to dispel some of the myths associated with Sherman's barrage of the city, including the death of an unnamed child as the first fatality and questions concerning the mortal wounding of free black barber Solomon Luckie.[103] However, the fates of others were less unclear. Among the most gruesome of these happened to a Union-sympathizing resident and businessman, Joseph F. Warner, and his young daughter, Elizabeth. Warner was superintendent of the city gas works in Atlanta and was under suspicion over questions concerning his loyalty to the Confederacy. Union shelling took no such matters into account when, on the night of August 3, a twenty-pound round penetrated the Warner home with devastating effect. Accounts indicated that the shell killed the sleeping child instantly and severed the legs of her father. A report from the *New York Tribune* provided gory details and the poignant cry from Warner to a servant, "Michael get a light quick, for I am killed by a shell." As the dust subsided, the illumination confirmed the horrific scene even as other artillery rounds continued to fall in the vicinity. Coherent, despite the shock of his injuries and the fate of his daughter, Warner managed to make his last wishes known before expiring himself.[104]

In the long siege of Petersburg, Virginia, Union bombardment resulted in an increase in the refugee population, the destruction of homes and businesses, and the disruption of daily life, but not significantly in the number of civilian fatalities. Historian A. Wilson Greene noted that he could account for the deaths of nine noncombatants from Union shelling, "all but two of those occurring in late June or early July [1864]," although the Federal forces were within range of the city until its evacuation in April 1865.[105] The first civilian death came on June 23, with another following three days later and two more at the end of the month. Greene noted, "One woman was struck in the head near Blandford [Church] on June 24, 'breaking the skull and leaving the brains protruding.'" The firing in the area became so intense that daytime burial services had to be suspended.[106] Altogether 625 structures in the city suffered damage, and the architect of the Confederate defensive line, Charles Dimmock, observed in July, "Most of the houses about me had been struck . . . & a man killed in my back yard." Two more Petersburg civilians died near the Old Market on August 27.[107]

Even for those persons not exposed to enemy fire, mortality stalked civilians and workers in many ways. Disaffection with the prosecution of the war or the policies the Lincoln administration implemented to support it could produce civilian deaths as well. Among the most notorious of the outbursts on the home front were the New York Draft Riots of July 1863. Soldiers and civilians alike fell in the bloody encounters that raged over the issues of conscription, exemption, and race.[108] In a flurry of communications, Union officials first tried to assess the situation and then respond to it. Major General John E. Wool set the initial numbers of killed and wounded at approximately sixty but in subsequent reports hesitated to give precise figures. "You will perceive that I have not mentioned the killed and wounded, and for the reason that I have not been able to obtain a correct account of the number," he explained to Secretary of War Edwin Stanton on July 20.[109] One tally accounted for some of the dead: "It is proper to remark that the cavalry on Wednesday morning dispersed the mob with howitzers in West Twenty-second street, when 28 rioters were known to be killed, besides the wounded. Colonel Mott lost 7 killed and 20 wounded."[110]

Even as the opposing armies reached the climactic moments of their duels with each other, loss of life among those who remained in close proximity to war resources continued. William T. Sherman had pushed in his "March to the Sea" to Savannah, Georgia, presenting the city to President Lincoln as a Christmas gift. However, the absence of Confederate defenders did not end the danger to local residents. On the night of January 28, 1865, the city became the scene of a devastating inferno that destroyed property and imperiled lives. According to one account, "For five hours three thousand shells rained down, igniting a raging fire that consumed an estimated 125 wooden tenements inhabited by hundreds of poor people, black and white."[111] A Northern newspaper speculated that the flames may have been "the work of a rebel incendiary," but whatever the origins, they caused widespread destruction. "The arsenal was totally consumed, and a large number of shells, that had been stored there by the rebels, exploded, doing a great deal of damage. It is reported that about twenty persons were burned to death or killed by the explosion of the shells."[112]

Another tremendous explosion occurred in Mobile, Alabama, on the afternoon of May 25, 1865, when a warehouse filled with ordnance erupted. One Union officer described the blast as "resulting not only in the destruction of a considerable portion of the upper part of the city, but in great loss of life."[113] Another explained that at least some of the fatalities included service personnel. He reported, "I regret that two of our men were killed during the afternoon," although he commended one soldier for risking his life to carry another injured person to safety.[114]

From Mobile, Assistant Adjutant General Alfred Fredberg provided a more thorough assessment of the incident to a fellow officer: "We have just passed through a most terrible night, but the danger is, thank God, over. It was a terrible calamity—beyond description. Acres of ground were covered with flames." Noting the destruction that included "several steamers [that] were torn to pieces," he concluded, "The loss of life is terrible."[115]

Reports from Mobile indicated a dire situation and the likely source. "There were at the time four hired men, ordnance employés, and thirty colored soldiers, with a commissioned officer in charge," the depot officer explained. "There was a guard in the building and a private watchman who have always done their duty faithfully." The extra personnel were on hand to see that the transfer would be handled properly, and Captain William Beebe had no reason to think that anything other than a tragic accident had occurred.[116] The acting assistant inspector general, James Patton, reported, "At 3 P.M. to-day a terrible explosion of twenty tons of captured powder shook the foundations of the city, followed immediately by a heavy rumbling explosion of shells and fixed ammunition and a shower of shot, shell, grape, and canister, and pieces of stone and brick." The destruction was widespread, including a substantial area of ruins "from which dead and wounded are being removed." Patton dismissed the speculation of responsibility for the incident as belonging to "an incendiary" or agent, citing the extensive casualties among paroled Confederate prisoners. He placed the human cost at "probably 500" but admitted that any accurate assessment of those numbers or the property damage "cannot yet be estimated properly."[117]

A series of communications passed between General Gordon Granger in Mobile and General Edward R. S. Canby in New Orleans, with information that the latter passed up the chain of command to Washington. Canby explained, "The Marshall warehouse at Mobile, used as a temporary ordnance depot, was blown up yesterday afternoon, causing a considerable destruction of life and property. The cause of the explosion is not yet known, but as it occurred when a train of captured ordnance stores from Meridian was being unloaded, it is probably due to the explosion of a percussion-shell."[118] In a gesture of compassion to the battered citizens, Canby ordered Granger, "Issue rations to the families of all who were dependent on persons who have been killed or disabled."[119]

In June, the *New York Herald* provided the most extensive accounting of the disaster originating from the *Mobile News* of May 28: "The truth of the matter as regards the cause of the accident will never be known; for, of course, every one in or near the building was instantly killed." Among the other fatalities were several individuals on steamers moored nearby. "We saw the bodies of Mr. Mc-Mahon, who was in charge of the carpenter work of Captain Ford, A.Q.M., and of the purser of the steamer Laura . . . who was killed while sitting at his desk." In addition, "John Kavanagh, a paroled Confederate soldier, was killed instantly on board the steamer Kate Dale by the concussion alone. Not a mark was visible upon his body when taken up a few minutes later." Others were less fortunate, even in death. "A number of the bodies recovered are so burned and mutilated that recognition is impossible." The article included an extensive list of the dead and injured, placing the number of the former at "fully two hundred."[120] A subsequent notice set the toll even higher and proclaimed, "Dead bodies are being recovered every day."[121]

Unhappily, the Mobile disaster happened just as the largest of the Confederate forces signaled the intention to lay down arms in the Trans-Mississippi. But prior to that, among the last persons to die in Virginia, at about the time Robert E. Lee's Army of Northern Virginia ceased to exist as an organized entity, were two African Americans. One, Joe Parkman, was a slave musician attached to the Savannah Volunteer Guards when the unit transferred to Virginia. Parkman had demonstrated his preferences at Petersburg, when he resisted calls to desert by Union black troops who saw him. At the time of Lee's surrender, he found a bottle containing a liquid that had been left on the grounds of a camp. Drinking the contents led to "an attack of illness which made it necessary to leave him at a house nearby, where, it is understood, he died." The writer, who had been in the unit, observed, "There was never a man more devoted to the Guards than he. And, faithful to the last, he died in their service."[122]

The other individual, an African American servant named Hannah, was in the home of her master, Dr. Samuel H. Coleman, when an artillery round penetrated the structure early on April 9, 1865. Mortally wounded in the arm, she had remained in the house because of illness when the rest of the occupants had relocated elsewhere on the previous day. Accordingly, as historian Patrick Schroeder has noted, "The deadly shell took the only noncombatant's life during the fighting at Appomattox Court House."[123]

Hostilities were supposed to be at an end as the Confederate defenders evacuated Charleston, South Carolina. True to form for such circumstances, the retreating forces worked to ensure that as little of military value remained behind as possible, including destroying three ironclads and a shipyard, as well as the torching of cotton. Before Union forces could enter the city to secure it, tragedy struck when several boys found some of the remaining gunpowder and tossed small amounts of it into a raging fire of cotton bales. Unfortunately, as the young people scooped the grains for amusement, the trail of powder acted as a fuse, and in the early morning hours of February 18, the accumulation of explosives erupted. By one account, "A tremendous explosion and fire ripped through the depot, maiming, burning, and killing several hundred poor whites and blacks who were there seeking food."[124]

Civilians could not elude the powerful elements of warfare. As individuals or families caught in the swirl of battle or as ordinary citizens undertaking their usual activities, they often encountered situations that produced direct threats to their lives. People in the border regions suffered from the appearance of organized and irregular forces whose interactions with them ranged from disruptive to lethal. At other times, displacement caused circumstances that added to the effects of malnutrition and disease in communities that increased mortality among them as well. If noncombatants hoped to avoid such dangerous intrusions in their lives, they were operating under false premises, particularly as warfare took a harsher turn as it progressed.

10

Not Cheating
the Hangman
Deaths at the Bar of Justice,
for Desertion, or as
Prisoners of War

It matters not with many of these people whether
a life is taken in manly open fight upon the battlefield or within the limits of a closely guarded
prison.
Charles Mattocks on the killing of prisoners of war

He came home to die.
Inscription on tombstone of returned prisoner
Wallace Woodford

The nature of warfare brought every form of human experience to the forefront
at one point or another. War exposes every type of personality and magnifies
every aspect of character. Soldiers must kill, but that killing must also be con-
trolled, kept within acceptable boundaries. Historian John Keegan has observed,
"Man has long sought to restrain war by laws, laws defining both when war is or
is not permissible . . . and what is permissible in war."[1] For men fighting in the
American Civil War as with any conflict, the boundaries could become blurred
or ignored, the choices complicated by many factors, and the rules of engagement
not always clear. In such cases, death could come to soldiers away from the battle-

field as punishment for transgressions or in other circumstances that would cost them their lives as surely as those who perished under enemy fire, depriving their families and friends at home of their safe return.

Historian Bell Wiley noted the circumstances under which some men met a final fate from antisocial acts carried out in uniform. In describing instances of insubordination, he added the phenomenon that in a later war generation would be described as "fragging." "Some officers were killed in these encounters, and a few were probably shot down in battle by aggrieved men of their commands," he explained. "Certainly a number of soldiers on both sides vowed to 'get even' with hated superiors on the field of combat, and it seems reasonable to assume that at least some of them carried out the threat."[2]

Executions brought final justice in many cases, although, as Wiley observed, "The number of men who forfeited their lives for offenses committed during the Civil War cannot be ascertained." For the Federals, the number of men executed stood as follows:[3]

Desertion	141
Murder (including two instances of murder and desertion)	72
Rape (including two instances of rape and some other crime)	23
Mutiny	20
Spying	3
Theft or pillage	4
Other (multiple offenses)	4
Total	267

Nefarious acts did not require a wartime context to occur, but murder and mayhem were especially regrettable when men in uniform were involved. Thomas Kelly, of Company H, Fifth Ohio, was listed on his rolls as "murdered by a comrade," without additional explanation or elaboration.[4] On August 3, 1861, Baltimore's *Daily Exchange* provided the notice of one soldier who died at the hands of another: "William Boyle, the member of the New York 3d regiment, Scott Life Guard, who was stabbed on Thursday evening last by a fellow soldier named James Dolan, died at the Lombard Street Infirmary on Saturday morning." Absent were any details of the fatal confrontation or the disposition of the assailant.[5]

Trouble on the border of Tennessee and Virginia in the autumn of 1861 prompted the assignment of Lieutenant Alexander H. Vaughn of Company H, Eleventh Tennessee Infantry, as provost marshal for Tazewell, Tennessee. Unfortunately, the post would prove challenging in more ways than the Confederate officer's commanders had intended when, during the attempt to make an arrest, Vaughn perished at the hands of some of the suspects he was supposed to apprehend.[6]

Such justice occurred in Texas in the fall of 1861 when two cavalrymen paid for their personal transgressions with their lives. In the first case, the regimental adjutant, James K. Bell, became suspect for "abolitionism & bigamy—the latter being pretty strongly proven against him," when the men in his command "*en masse* took him out & hung him & gave his outfit [saddle, bridle, and other equipment] to a poor boy" in the unit who could not afford the cost of such items himself. Approximately two weeks later, W. L. Essy of Company D suffered the same fate after being "detected in the act of committing a rape upon a married woman in the vicinity of the Camp."[7]

Punishment was more formal and official when General Richard Taylor ordered two Louisiana Tigers to stand before a firing squad for leading a gang that assaulted an officer at a guardhouse holding some of their comrades. Following the rejection of appeals for clemency, on the morning of December 9, Michael O'Brien and Dennis Corcoran took their places to answer for their crimes. Soldiers stood behind the executioners chosen from the condemned men's command, in the event that they should falter in their duties. But, at the appropriate moment, the shots rang out and the two men fell dead, although in a last illustration of indignity, armed Tigers had to disperse with the bayonet souvenir hunters who "combed the death site for pieces of posts and other relics."[8] Present as a witness, North Carolinian Alfred Belo observed of the incident, "It was hard to realize that it was a real execution, so theatrical were the surroundings. This was the first military execution I saw in the army of Northern Virginia."[9] Taylor later termed the event similarly and argued that the extreme "punishment, so closely following [the] offense, produced a marked effect."[10]

Deadly dangers continued to lurk in many quarters for soldiers who did not exercise proper judgment or awareness. Buried in a series of notices in the Alexandria, Virginia, newspaper *Local News* was a single sentence that provided little tangible information but could serve as a warning against indulgent behavior. On December 12, 1861, the writer of the piece observed, "A soldier was murdered in a house of ill fame in Washington, on Tuesday night."[11]

In a raucous New Orleans, Connecticut soldier Charles W. Sherman wrote his parents of a similar incident, although he was less precise in identifying the type of establishment involved: "The 9th Connecticut is all Irsh and thay Landed a Day after us and thay was soon Drunk. Thay Lost one man; he went into some Place and got his Abdomen Cut so he died." Unfortunately, for two other individuals, the temptation to indulge was apparently too great for them to adhere to their duties. "Thay have 2 to be Shot fore leaving his Beat and Geting liquor when he was on gard."[12]

From Indianapolis, Indiana, Lieutenant Colonel Newton Colby wrote that his father could see from his letter that he remained in command at the post "and will understand that I am pretty busy." Colby offered as an example: "I have just returned from a long walk—taken for the purpose of investigating into the facts connected with the murder of one of the men last night in a house of ill fame—He was shot and instantly killed by a person connected with the house." He doubted the capacity of the local authorities, whose loyalty he questioned, adding that he believed they "care not much for the death of a soldier—I have ordered a strict investigation by the Provost Marshal to ascertain if the poor fellow had [met with] fowl play. I am of the opinion that *at least*—he was needlessly killed—although he perhaps did enough to give color to the defense set up by his slayer that it was in self-defense." The most troubling aspect of the situation for Colby was its repetitive nature. As he explained, "This is the second or third instance since I have been here of soldiers meeting their death in these houses of prostitution—and I wish I could hit upon some plan to prevent both such things as the houses and these occurrences."[13]

Assessing the circumstances and justification for taking extreme action in the name of discipline could be a matter of open interpretation. At least one soldier pondered both before determining, "I would do as Lieut. Col. Burke of the 37th did to one of his men if I could not be obeyed in any other way. . . . He ordered a man twice to fall into the ranks. The second time the man openly refused & the Col. shot him through the head in less than 5 seconds. I saw him when he fell." The killing seemed justified to the junior officer, who concluded, "He was never called to account & should not have been."[14]

In the early part of January 1862, Private Michael Lanahan of the Second Infantry, U.S. Army, ascended a scaffold in Washington for the murder of his sergeant. This final act took place publicly, marked by the official pomp of the solemn occasion. The condemned man's last words supposedly were "Good-bye, soldiers, good-bye," while the troops, officials, and members of the public watched the ceremony unfold. According to one account, in the aftermath of the event, "Curiosity hunters divided the rope, and chipped pieces from the scaffold."[15]

Another officer could not avoid personal difficulties with his men. Alfred T. Obenchain had been a Texas state senator before commanding some of the troops who patrolled the region of the state along the northwest frontier. Apparently prone to behavior that tested the patience of his independent-minded subordinates, Obenchain pushed two of the privates to the extreme of killing him in August 1862.[16]

From his camp in northern Virginia, Chaplain Joseph Twichell related the story of an incident with fatal consequences. "I have forgotten to mention a tragedy that was enacted here last week," he observed to his father. "One night, under the influence of liquor and instigated by another, likewise half intoxicated, a soldier loaded his musket, walked to his tent door and deliberately shot a member of the same company for no cause whatsoever, inflicting a wound which proved fatal in sixteen hours." Twichell added that both the "murderer and the accomplice" were under arrest. "It is altogether probable that both will be sentenced to death."[17]

The circumstances were not clear regarding the death of John Hogan beyond his demise. Twenty years old when he enlisted on November 19, 1861, the New York City native was in Norfolk, Virginia, in the spring of the next year when an incident occurred that led to his killing. The record noted simply, "Shot by a negro and died May 28, 1862."[18] The context for another victim in uniform was more straightforward. That soldier perished when a fifteen-year-old from Atlanta took exception to the refusal of the man to pay a wager he had made and the incensed youth smashed him with a rock.[19]

Another individual, Private John McMahon, of Company F, Ninety-Ninth New York Volunteers, sealed his own fate when he killed one of the men sent to arrest him for a homicide. A *New York Herald* report emanating from Fortress Monroe, Virginia, on June 13, 1862, told readers that McMahon "was hung today for wilful murder at the Rip-Raps according to sentence of the Court Martial." The prisoner had offered "no mitigating facts" in his case when he "calmly and deliberately shot Private Michael Dolan, of the same company and regiment, at the same time using the words, 'May God have mercy on your soul.'" According to the report, McMahon "refused to make any explanation" or provide any motive for the act before he would hear similar words spoken for himself.[20]

On October 18, U.S. consul Horatio J. Sprague forwarded intelligence from his post at Gibraltar on an incident that involved the Confederate vessel *Sumter*. Apparently facing charges of "stealing," Second Officer Joseph Hester determined that his best course would be to assassinate his superior. Consequently, on the evening of October 15, after William Andrews had retired to his quarters, Hester "deliberately shot" him "with a revolver, while the latter was lying in his berth." Andrews "expired almost immediately, three shots from the revolver having been fired into his body." Of course, Hester now faced arrest and punishment for homicide in addition to charges of theft.[21]

From the November 17, 1862, edition of the *Alexandria (Va.) Gazette*, readers learned of a deadly encounter among the men encamped nearby. According to the newspaper account, "Last Saturday night, a quarrel arose between two soldiers in the camp of recruits, about two miles out of Alexandria, when one of them was killed by a knife or bayonet in the hands of the other." The perpetrator "was promptly arrested; his name is Hugh M. McKilips, a recruit for the 2d regiment Pennsylvania cavalry." The account offered no reason for the altercation or the presence of influencing agents, but it was clear that another man who had intended to enlist to fight his opponents in battle would never have the occasion to fulfill that destiny.[22]

Similarly, the *Nashville Daily Union* presented its readers with a distressing tale from Louisville, Kentucky, in the opening weeks of 1863. Under the headline "Homicide," the account featured the mortal wounding of "Private James A. Gibson, of company B, 1st Tennessee cavalry . . . in an affray" that cost him his life. "The wounds were inflicted by Arthur Morris and Wm. Lavelle, the latter a member of company F, 72d Indiana infantry." Arrested under a warrant for murder, the assailants faced "an examination" of their involvement in the incident, although no details emerged in this instance to shed light on motivation or circumstances for the Union cavalryman's death.[23]

The end of siege operations and the period of occupation at Vicksburg did not relieve the local citizens from exposure to hostile elements in their midst, although contentious attitudes exacerbated tense situations that led to some of the violence. When white farmer John H. Bobb found African American soldiers on his property, he responded vociferously. During his effort to chase the men off, the soldiers turned on Bobb and killed him. Calls for justice came from various quarters, but no arrests or punishment for the incident followed.[24] Even so, Major General Henry Slocum used the situation as an opportunity to remind the officers in his command of their obligations. In General Orders No. 7, issued from his headquarters in Vicksburg, Slocum emphasized "the importance of maintaining discipline and preventing all marauding and pillaging on the part of the soldiers. . . . The recent murder of a citizen by colored soldiers in open day in the streets of this city should arouse the attention of every officer serving with these troops to the absolute necessity of preventing the soldiers from attempting a redress of their own grievances."[25]

Another violent incident occurred late in the war in Vicksburg that led to a different result for the alleged perpetrators. When a group of black troops entered a local home looking for valuables in April 1865, the residents, J. R. Cook and his wife, Minerva, suffered wounds in the encounter. The injuries proved fatal for Minerva, but not before she offered descriptions of her assailants. Subsequent investigation led to the arrest and condemnation of a dozen men. Nine of these individuals met their ends on the gallows, hanged before their assembled commands, on May 26, 1865. A witness to the ceremony thought some of the men were likely to be innocent and hoped never to have to endure such a spectacle again.[26] Confederate general Richard Taylor had surrendered the forces in the department twenty-two days earlier.

Occasionally, soldiers exhibited greater desires to avoid detention at any cost rather than submit themselves to it. The Sixth Virginia seemed to have developed an unfortunate pattern. Aaron Jones wrote a letter home in April 1862 when threatened with arrest. According to the letter, "They Talked like puting Me in [the] Gurd house The other day becose I would not drill under one Man that was drill Master but I told Him rite plain I wouldnot drill under him. And I dintent. I would a died first."[27] A comrade, Private James C. Barnes of Company H, was in the custody of the Provost Guard in Petersburg, Virginia, when he died on March 23, 1862. Although the exact circumstances of the death were not disclosed, the mechanic-turned-soldier had been listed as absent without leave and was returned to the ranks by an individual who received thirty dollars for helping to detect and detain the deserter.[28]

Another soldier from the Sixth Virginia perished on July 27, 1863. William Patton, a prewar laborer, enlisted as a private but had been detailed as a "baggage guard" in Richmond, earlier in the year. In whatever capacity he now served, Patton was reported as "killed by provost guard, Culpeper C.H., reas. unkn."[29] Another private, this one in the Twenty-Third North Carolina, employed extreme measures when he took exception to an order given him by his sergeant. The soldier became "so enraged that he struck the sergeant with a wooden club killing him."[30]

In another remote corner of the Eastern Theater, a Confederate staff officer from Kentucky noted an unusual occurrence that seemed to have stirred his comrades. "The whole camp full of bustle & excitement," Edward Guerrant wrote in his diary on May 15, 1862. "A soldier trying to escape from the Guard last night—killed *himself* by running into a post."[31] Guerrant did not provide further information on the circumstances of the arrest or his feelings regarding the ultimate outcome for the unlucky fugitive.

Unfortunately, a series of woeful circumstances plagued a Confederate, ultimately resulting fatally for him. The *Richmond Daily Dispatch* of August 12, 1862, noted, "Serg't J. Walton, a member of co. G, 7th Georgia battalion, who was shot not long ago while attempting to escape from a military prison in this city, was not a deserter, but was on his way to join his company, which had been sent to Jackson." The progression of errors that led to the deadly result began when Walton failed to carry with him any authorization for his absence. According to the article, "He had been off on furlough, but not having the proper papers with him, was arrested and placed in the prison." Apparently not willing to wait for confirmation and exoneration, or concerned that none would be forthcoming, the sergeant made "an ill advised attempt to escape from which he was killed."[32]

As Union war policy transitioned from protection of civilian property to a more "hard war" approach, attitudes evolved concerning the requisitioning of private resources. On November 20, 1862, from his camp near Fredericksburg, Virginia, Edward Wightman explained to his brother the outcome for one person in the ranks who had broken army discipline: "On Wednesday one of the 89th [New York Infantry] (Provost Guard) killed a New Hampshire man for sheep stealing."[33] The nature of the comment suggested that the soldier had not been brought before any formal panel for adjudication of his alleged offense.

For all the times that depredations against civilian property went unpunished, there were moments of immediate justice for such activities that occurred in the field. On December 5, 1862, the *Maryland Free Press*, a Hagerstown paper, presented a cautionary tale to its readership: "On Wednesday of last week a soldier, named Sheppard, belonging to the Maryland 7th . . . was shot and instantly killed by Mr. David Manahan, residing near Clear-spring." In an understated tone, the writer noted, "It appears that Sheppard was trespassing upon Manahan's poultry department to a degree not relished by him; when, upon remonstrating with Sheppard, the latter first dispatched Manahan's dog, and then attempted the same operation on Manahan by shooting at him, fortunately, however, not with the same result." Managing to dodge the rounds, the farmer dashed into his house, "seized a loaded gun and fired at Sheppard, tearing off half his head, and producing instant death." Manahan turned himself over "to the proper authorities," but the circumstances caused the grand jury not to charge him with any crime.[34]

The justice system was less sympathetic in a Richmond, Virginia, case, with that grand jury electing to return an indictment in November 1862, duly recorded in the *Daily Dispatch*: "James M. Armour, for the murder of a soldier on Canal street, several months since, while acting as a pretended provost guard."[35] There was no explanation as to why Armour was adopting the pose or if the man he killed suspected the ruse and resisted arrest.

On March 13, 1863, more reports from Richmond highlighted the "excitement" stirred in the city by several events, including "the murder of a Louisiana volunteer, about 10 o'clock to-day. A member of company F, Clarborn Guard, 2nd Louisiana Regiment, by the name of James Sheridan, was murdered by a member of the same company, named Willson by stabbing him in the collar-bone." There was no reason given for the altercation, but the wounded Sheridan "expired about five minutes after he was stabbed." Subsequently "found ensconced . . . in a free woman's house in Pocahontas, about two hundred yards from the place the man was murdered," the perpetrator was taken into custody and "conveyed to jail."[36]

Another account from a Washington newspaper reported the arrest of a Confederate for slaying a comrade. Under the sensational headline "Murder in the Rebel Army," the writer offered no additional context before noting, "C. M. Hawkins, Palmetto artillery, has been confined in Castle Thunder [in Richmond, Virginia] for killing a brother soldier."[37]

Events could be just as troubling away from the Confederate capital, in the isolated fastness of the border region between Virginia and Kentucky. Willie M. Woods had become a casualty of the fighting at Perryville, but when his comrades left him with a family in London, Kentucky, a party of Unionists appeared. Forcibly removing Woods from his bed, the men hanged the hapless soldier in an incident repeated against other convalescing soldiers.[38]

In another instance, a member of the Ninetieth Ohio Volunteer Infantry noted the differential in time between the killing of a comrade and the rendering of justice for the culprit in that case: "5th [June 1863].—Division drill this evening. There was a man hung at Murfreesboro to-day, for murdering one of our soldiers last summer."[39] He did not account for the discrepancy or offer any comment on the sense that a delay had meant that the victim's homicide had not received timely satisfaction.

A Pennsylvania newspaper offered the account of a body floating in the river. The March 26, 1864, edition informed readers of the perplexing tale of a likely murder: "On Wednesday of last week, a man in the U.S. uniform was found dead in the eddy of the Susquehanna." Evidence at the scene provided tantalizing clues in the case that could lead to the deduction of something sinister: "The head was badly bruised and the breast had marks of violence. From the fact of the nose being uninjured it was inferred that he had not fallen upon his face, but had met with foul play and been thrown in the river." Nor was this person the only potential victim. "On Monday morning another body of a U.S. soldier was found drowned in the same eddy."[40]

Tensions occasionally arose on both sides over personal disputes or other matters that led to extreme events. For at least one officer in the Union army, these may have included racial motivations. On August 8, the *Daily Ohio Statesman* offered its readers a cryptic sketch of an incident that had happened three days earlier: "This P.M. Lieut. Fox 2d U.S. Colored Regiment, deliberately murdered a negro soldier, and is under arrest."[41]

A diarist from Norfolk, Virginia, noted the outcome of an unusual circumstance, stoked by the alteration in racial order, which had occurred in that town on June 17, 1863: "Doct Wright who killed the yankee lieutenant, is undergoing his trial. Poor fellow." The local physician had watched as a company of black troops under a white officer passed him in the street. Overcome by the image that challenged his notion of acceptable social order, David M. Wright called out that the officer was a "coward." Lieutenant Alanson L. Sanborn stepped over to order the doctor's arrest for his utterance when Wright drew a pistol and fired at him. Sanborn stumbled into a nearby store but succumbed to his wounds. Taken into custody, Wright received a conviction for the killing. The sentence would be carried out on October 23, 1863, with a hanging on the racetrack of the fairgrounds in Norfolk.[42]

At the last hours, the condemned man's wife sought to have an interview with President Lincoln on the matter, but his response was not calculated to please her. "It would be useless for Mrs. Doctor Wright to come here," Lincoln explained to Major General John G. Foster at Fort Monroe on October 17. "The subject is a very painful one, but the case is settled."[43] After exhausting questions related to the doctor's sanity, the matter came to an end on the gallows in the town where the incident had occurred earlier that year. "Dr. Wright was executed this morning at Norfolk, according to orders," General Foster dutifully reported to General Halleck in Washington. "Everything passed off very orderly."[44]

On August 25, 1863, James A. Greer promised to make an inquiry into the actions of Major George W. McKee, provost marshal in Natchez, Mississippi, relating to "the death of Acting Master R. A. Turner, late commander of the *U.S.S. Curlew*."[45] The inquiry absolved McKee of any responsibility in his comrade's death.[46]

A different review saved Captain Daniel Link of the First Maryland Cavalry from a charge of murder in the death of John Clute, when the latter tried to force his way into a guarded storehouse in West Virginia in December 1864. Angry at the restriction, Clute reacted strongly, verbally denouncing the officer and challenging him to a fight. Shooting the soldier with his revolver, the officer received a guilty verdict that Union major general Winfield Scott Hancock subsequently overturned as justified under the circumstances.[47]

Another victim of extracurricular activities found brief mention in the diary of a Confederate staff officer who learned of the incident during his travels through southwest Virginia. Edward Guerrant observed on May 24, 1864, "While here the body of an escaped Yankee from Saltville was taken to burial. Tried to steal a horse, last night, & a couple of boys on guard at their father's stable, shot & killed him."[48]

Circumstances were not always clear for noncombat fatalities in the ranks. The *Alexandria Gazette*'s brief notice on October 1, 1862, of one of two deaths caused "by the discharge of loaded pistols," read, "A captain in one of the regiments near Washington, yesterday, killed a soldier, in self-defence."[49]

Another situation involved New York City native John Dowd. Only nineteen at the time of his enlistment in July 1861, Dowd seemed to court trouble for himself. Incarcerated in Norfolk, Virginia, by August 1863, for an unknown misdemeanor, he determined to make a break for freedom, which ended badly for him. The record for the soldier showed, "Killed by provost guard bayonet."[50]

In the same month in Nashville, Tennessee, a Union soldier faced the gallows for the murders of a private and a lieutenant in his company, the Eighty-Second Indiana, as well as an uncle while at home on leave. Whether the killings filled the perpetrator with remorse or he simply reacted to the reality of his own fate, a witness described the condemned as praying "all the time" in the company of a chaplain. When the time came for justice to be met, the witness recalled, "I heard his neck crack." At the same time, the soldier who watched the proceedings observed, "I never want to see another man hanged."[51]

The assailant the Michigan soldier had seen die on the gallows was not the only one to face summary punishment for crimes, real or alleged, in Nashville. Personnel at the penitentiary remained active in 1864, with numerous individuals walking their final steps, particularly after being found guilty on charges of bushwhacking or murder.[52] Guerrilla activity continued to be an area in which those who participated often met summary justice before ever being brought to trial or capital justice after a military commission had issued its ruling.

On October 23, 1863, a Richmond newspaper proclaimed:

> Murder of a soldier.—On Thursday morning, between the hours of two and three o'clock, four men succeeded in effecting their escape from Castle Thunder. A previous attempt of the same parties having been discovered and frustrated by the vigilance of the officers, they were confined in the condemned cell, before which a guard is kept continually walking to and fro, and which, from its position in the very centre of the prison, was deemed the most secure place in the building.

Despite these precautions, the account noted, "Obtaining, by some means, the necessary tools, they cut through the floor into the commissary's room beneath, descending into which they secured the arms placed there for safe-keeping; then in a body rushing out into the room used for the reception of visitors, they overthrew the sentinel on guard inside the door, who, being disabled by the fall, could not further arrest their flight." The writer explained that when the fugitives made for the door

> they next encountered the sentinel in front of the prison, on Cary street; he happening to be immediately in their path, one of the number rushed upon him, and placing the muzzle of his gun close to the head of the guard, who in vain attempted to stop their egress, discharged the piece, the whole load

entering the lower portion of the head, inflicting a frightful wound, and of course causing instant death.

By now alerted to the situation, the other guards fired several shots "in rapid succession at the fleeing murderers, but with what effect is not known."

In addition to the details of the matter, the *Daily Dispatch* article provided readers with the identities of the principals in the drama: "The name of the deceased was Sutton Byrd, a private in company C, 53d North Carolina regiment. The names of the parties who committed this cold-blooded murder are E. D. Boone, Edward Carney, Thos. Cole, and John A. Chipman." Boone had a history as "a noted ruffian, having made several escapes from different places, and was closely confined a few days ago for an attempted escape. The others were of a like desperate character, being confined upon serious charges." These men had tried to escape unsuccessfully before. "Several recent attempts to break out by the last named parties had been discovered and frustrated by the officers." The guard's father had arrived to take "the remains to his home" and received an escort through the city to the depot, but not before pausing to take a touching moment of farewell for his deceased son. "When the lid of the coffin was about being placed on, the poor old father knelt down, and glueing his lips to the cold ones of his murdered boy, remained for some moments apparently in prayer."[53]

That this incident occurred where it did was noteworthy. Castle Thunder was notorious for rigid discipline with regard to security. Guards seemed so ready to fire at any prisoner indiscreet enough to approach the windows that when one of their own entered one of the upper-story cells and ventured over to the window to take in the view, a comrade shot and killed him.[54] However, the Confederate facility was not unique. Sentries at Camp Chase, Ohio, Old Capitol Prison, in Washington, and Fort Delaware likewise engaged in the practice of shooting prisoners under similar circumstances.[55]

On August 25, 1862, a Richmond newspaper noted an incident that might have been humorous had it not been for its tragic consequences: "About one o'clock, yesterday afternoon, a soldier named James Cary, belonging to Company C, Wheat's battalion, jumped out of a third story window in [the] rear of the Columbian Hotel, intending to alight upon an adjacent shed, but missed his object, and fell to the ground, a distance of about forty feet." According to the writer of the *Richmond Daily Dispatch* account, the act was no mere stunt but stemmed from a fracas that had involved Cary and some of his comrades:

From what could be ascertained relative to the affair, it seems that he had been engaged in a fight with some of his room mates, and in order to escape arrest by the police, who had been sent for, sought to make his exit from the hotel by the above-mentioned route. He was picked up in a dying condition and was taken to the Baskerville Hospital, on Cary street. He survived only about half an hour.[56]

In the meantime, in the Twenty-Sixth Indiana, Private Moses Hughes died at the hands of his comrade John Campbell at Pilot Knob, Missouri, on May 27, 1863. Although unspecified in the record, Campbell seemed to have received punishment for the incident that involved his detention. Then, on October 4 of the following year, the prisoner contrived to set himself free and deserted "while under arrest for murder."[57]

Samuel Keene, a former riverboat pilot who was now serving as master's mate on the *Beaufort*, went into Richmond on February 2, 1864, for the purpose of returning a member of the crew who was absent without leave. Undoubtedly true to his mission, Keene was apparently also susceptible to the access he had to bars in the city and, according to one report, "indulged too freely in spirituous liquors." His behavior under the influence compelled his arrest and return to the vessel, but unfortunately for the sailor, his adventures were not over. Keene managed to leave his ship and return to the city during the night, making the attempt to arrest a fellow imbiber who "in no manner [was] connected to the steamer." The ensuing confrontation led to the master's mate fleeing the police and in a final encounter being shot fatally when he drew his cutlass and waved it at them.[58]

The circumstances were clear for one man's death in the national capital, although the identity of the victim slain in the District of Columbia in the latter part of 1864 seemed to be unknown for a brief period of time. In the *Alexandria (Va.) Gazette*, an account appeared on October 25, which read, "The soldier who was found murdered in Washington, near Pennsylvania avenue, on Friday, has been recognized, and proves to be Patrick Maloney, of the 14th Massachusetts heavy artillery, stationed at Branch Hospital."[59]

The unsavory actions of a member of Company M, Second New Jersey Cavalry, resulted in an execution in Memphis, Tennessee, on June 10, 1864, for "rape and robbery."[60] Another unnamed soldier perished in Georgia under less than stellar circumstances. A brief notice reprinted at the beginning of April 1865 in a South Carolina newspaper lamented, "Robbery and store breaking is getting to be of frequent occurrence in Macon." As described under the headline "Progressing," theft was not the only situation present in the uncertain environment of a war transitioning awkwardly into peace. According to the notice, "The body of a murdered soldier was found near Talbotton, Ga., a few days since. The skull had been smashed in with an axe." Unhappily, in the days before forensic science or other forms of identification that could offer the chance for notifying loved ones of the fate of their soldier, the victim's remains would be of no assistance in this case. "The body could not be recognized as it had been much torn by dogs."[61]

Men stationed in ports, or at least in close proximity to cities and towns, experienced their share of deadly circumstances that required legal authorities to resolve. "When sailors, and even the elite midshipmen, did get into Richmond, the result was often predictable," historian John Coski observed, adding that the men "on liberty" in the Confederate capital "often proved beyond control."[62]

Perhaps typical of this situation, James Kelley, stationed aboard the training vessel *Patrick Henry*, endured the theft of "a gold ring and $200 Confederate money on the night of February 15, 1864." Nevertheless, the loss of these valuables paled in comparison to what happened to him the following night when he was killed in what the *Richmond Daily Dispatch* termed "murder of a sailor." The account noted:

A seaman, named James Kelley, one of the crew of the s[team]ship Patrick Henry, lying in James river, near Drewry's Bluff, was murdered yesterday morning, about 7 o'clock, at the house of two white women of easy virtue, named Emma Brown and Maggie Jones, located on 24th, between Ma[in] and Cary sts. The deceased received two stabs in the left breast from a small bowie or sheath knife, either one of which was sufficient to have ultimately caused his death.

Lingering for some time after being "removed to the C. S. Marine Hospital," Kelley died, and a jury "returned as their verdict that he came to his death from stabs received at the hands of some person to them unknown."[63]

Having been wounded in battle, Private Alfred Bellard spent 1864 in Washington as a provost marshal's guard. In June, he recorded an unusual incident while serving in that capacity, writing, "On the night of the 4th one of our squads had a little shooting scrape on 11th Street. Lieut. Tyrell of our company was on duty at the theatre, when an officer came along drunk, and refused to show his pass." Attempting to defuse the situation, Tyrell ordered the officer to report to the provost in the morning, "but as he became abusive, the Sergt. was ordered to take him to the guard house." The lieutenant followed as the men moved forward when "the officer pulled out a revolver, and turning round fired a shot a[t] Tyrell and put a ball in his neck." Return fire struck the officer repeatedly before the assailant could be disarmed. "The end of the matter was that Tyrell was promoted to 1st Lieut. of Co. 1st Regt. V.R.C. while his antagonist died and was buried."[64]

In a practical sense, there was little difference between murder in the back streets of a city and the exercise of killing defenseless individuals, even as retaliation for other deaths. Excesses in warfare prompted reactions on the part of those who felt victimized that added to an already bitter war. "Bleeding Kansas" had preceded the Civil War, and border warfare remained emblematic of hatred and mercilessness. Death at Plymouth, North Carolina; Poison Springs, Arkansas; Fort Pillow, Tennessee; and in the aftermath of the Crater at Petersburg, Virginia, illustrated on larger scales the degree to which legitimate warfare could devolve into something more sinister.[65] Although to a lesser extent, the events that entangled members of the Union forces associated with George Armstrong Custer and the Rangers of John Singleton Mosby in 1864 demonstrated a ruthlessness that marked both.

Actions and perceptions in the Valley of Virginia helped to spiral emotions to new and worsening levels of retaliation and revenge. Union troops looked upon Mosby's Rangers as little more than the bushwhacking guerrillas that both sides detested—capable, if not actually guilty, of excess and brutality. When some of these men entered Front Royal, Virginia, on September 23, 1864, they were more than prepared to respond in kind. Unfortunately for him, seventeen-year-old Henry Rhodes picked a poor time to make the fateful decision to borrow a horse to join the Rangers in a raid on a Federal supply wagon train. Meeting stiffer resistance than they had expected, the Southern horsemen disengaged and scattered, but Rhodes was one of a number who could not escape. A placard left on one of the corpses conveyed the vow, "This will be the fate of Mosby and all his men."[66]

The actions of these unconventional elements left the troops defending the border regions with the sense that little recourse was left to them but to employ extreme measures to counter such depredations. Individuals accused of this type of activity often met with summary punishment that reflected the emotions of the circumstances as much as any genuine appeal to justice. In Kentucky, in the summer of 1864, a guerrilla named Waters met his fate at the hands of a firing squad, first defiantly, then in a less than dignified display that left a negative impression on those watching the proceedings. "How humiliating for a man to commit such crimes and then cannot face the music," one Union witness explained. When another young man stood in the same circumstances several days later, the same soldier recalled that despite his youth, this "prisoner" demonstrated himself to be "daring and brave to the last degree." Private Hawley Needham of the 134th Illinois concluded, "His bearing was worthy of one who was to die in a better cause."[67]

In early 1864, Henry Chambers of the Forty-Ninth North Carolina jotted a story of Civil War justice in his diary. On a cold and windy day in February that mirrored the circumstances, the Confederate officer marched out with the regiment to witness a sentence carried out for a man from another North Carolina regiment. "The melancholy ceremony was soon over and we returned to camp," he recorded. "He had twice deserted, and had killed one of his own company who, with some others, were attempting to arrest him."[68]

The men who enrolled for the war expected their decisions to expose them to risks on the battlefield, but they could not anticipate all the challenges that their service would bring. As pressures mounted from loved ones at home, the onerous nature of military life became more apparent, or other issues intruded in their martial careers, doubts and questions often arose. For some, the reason for which they had joined the fight no longer seemed sufficient to hold them in the ranks.

Leaving the ranks without the benefit of authorization became an attractive enough choice for some to make, despite the risks they ran in doing so. Military justice in such contexts could be cruel, with the irony that some offenses would warrant summary punishment at the hands of one's comrades, while others did not. Proximity to homes and loved ones occasionally presented temptations too great to avoid. One regimental historian noted of the early war deployment of the Twentieth Tennessee on provost duty, "but so many of the men lived in and around Franklin, that soon the regiment was short in numbers, the boys quietly took 'French leave' to visit their homes." Rather than condemning the practice or expressing the concern that it might become chronic, the writer observed, "They were not blamed at all, especially as they all returned in a few days."[69] "French leave" might appear to be an indulgence to which soldiers were entitled when they had the intention to rejoin their comrades rather than stay permanently absent from them.

Although executions for desertion may have seemed draconian to those outside the service, especially for individuals whose circumstances included pressures from distressed family members or homesickness, the practice could hardly be allowed to persist without response. On occasion a timely reprieve could even win praise for a commander's willingness to display clemency by staying a death sentence for lesser punishments or allowing the culprit to rejoin his unit. However, as cases mounted, such dispensations were hardly guaranteed.

Whether through moral suasion or sterner measures, both sides sought methods to combat desertion from the earliest days of the conflict. The death by firing squad of William H. Johnson in December 1861 marked what one historian termed the "first execution in the Army of the Potomac," but such deaths remained rare in the early stages of the war.[70] In his examination of desertion in the Confederate ranks, Mark Weitz posited, "From December 1861 until the end of the war the Confederacy executed only 229 men—204 by firing squad and 25 by hanging—a punishment generally reserved for those caught deserting to the enemy."[71]

President Lincoln's assertion that soldiers falling in the war represented sacrifice worthy of reflection and admiration would not seem to apply to those who forfeited their lives through their own less than noble actions. Yet, for such individuals, the broadest judgment also did not always fit each circumstance in the same way. Editors Michael Flannery and Katherine Oomens had to experience this level of examination and assessment when the record indicated that their subject, Spencer Bonsall, had dropped from the rolls as a deserter. "The army's curt and summary dismissal of Bonsall as a deserter belies more revealing dynamics at play," they insisted, noting that "some 278,000" men had left the Union ranks without authorization, "most for a variety of personal reasons ranging from family troubles to a general distaste for military order."[72] Flannery and Oomens maintained that Bonsall's experience reflected the degree to which "by and large men contributed to the war effort as ability and circumstance allowed." The soldier himself had condemned malingerers and cowards. He had also witnessed and experienced war and its effects firsthand before leaving the ranks. Flannery and Oomens concluded, "Desertion is invested with a host of deprecatory meanings that fall away in the face of subjective context. In other words, it is easy to blame deserters until one knows a deserter's story."[73] Similarly, the loss of life resulting from summary punishment for desertion remained as real to those at home as it did for soldiers who perished in the field.

The impact of shooting deserters as an object lesson was not lost on Stonewall Jackson. The Old Testament warrior in gray was untroubled by the kinds of "subtle abstractions and differential niceties of the common or civil law," according to one staffer. When the matter came to hard reality, his response to calls for clemency for several deserters from Colonel James A. Walker of the Tenth Virginia demonstrated his hard-core position by the stern admonition, "Sir! Men who desert their comrades in war *deserve* to be shot!—and *officers* who intercede for them *deserve* to be *hung!*" Jackson had the men brought out before the command and executed as he had prescribed with individuals from the offending companies serving as the firing squads. Old Jack's position had been unequivocal toward Jonathan G. Rogers and Preston Layman for their transgressions, despite the fact that one of the men would be leaving behind seven children.[74]

At about the same time Stonewall Jackson insisted that wayward soldiers be brought to the harshest account for the crime of desertion, a Union soldier from Connecticut was concluding very differently in a letter to his wife and children from New Orleans. On August 30, 1862, Private Charles W. Sherman of the

12th Connecticut explained his views succinctly but clearly, "I whould rather the Rebles whould Shoot our men than [we] Shoot them ourselves."[75]

A situation that proved especially disturbing for a chaplain in a New York brigade occurred when he tried to minister to soldiers facing execution for desertion. "I have been to see the prisoners," Joseph Twichell noted in a letter to his father, "but none of them appear to appreciate their situation. Even to tell them of it and urge the appropriate preparation seems to produce little effect." He expected that the gravity of the circumstance might yet reach the men, "but I am filled with horror at their present state. A dark page of our regimental history seems about to be written. How can I bear it? I try to think [as] little as possible about it."[76]

In Pine Bluff, Arkansas, the measures being taken to dissuade further desertion included two executions. One soldier thought the object lessons had achieved the desired result but clearly held sympathy for the men who paid with their lives for their indiscretions. "They both resided in the City of Houston," Lieutenant T. J. Rounsaville of the 13th Texas Cavalry wrote, "& one of them with a wife and three little children to moan his loss, also one was executed yesterday for the same offence, a young man some 20 years [of] age," who had been taken from the hospital and "looked very thin & meager, was an object of pitty."[77]

Another pitiable case, at least according to diarist Cyrena Bailey Stone, involved troops shot for desertion under the authority of Braxton Bragg. As she wrote, "His soldiers were often shot down by his orders, for the slightest offense. One was put to death for stealing a chicken." However, the situation that disturbed her the most concerned a husband who "obtained leave of absence to go home and attend to a sick wife." When she died, he remained for a few days to "care for the motherless children" before returning to his command. Met by guards who arrested him for desertion, the soldier was nevertheless "ordered to be shot at once." On the day of his execution, one comrade "began to bandage his eyes," but "he would [not] allow it—saying it was not necessary—he was a man, and had met death too often on the battle field to shrink from it now. So he folded his arms across his breast & was shot down by his comrades."[78] Even in the case of extenuating circumstances, there was no escape for this soldier or others like him who felt compelled to choose the bonds and demands of family over their duties in the field.

Whatever their basis, for some of the men who witnessed or carried them out, these executions represented justice fulfilled rather than an onerous duty to be avoided or disdained. A soldier from the Fifty-Fifth North Carolina wrote home after the hard campaigning of the summer of 1863 to tell his wife he expected "hundreds of deserters will now be shot." He concluded firmly, "It seems very hard, but the cause demands it."[79]

Pennsylvania volunteer George W. Fleegen had the unpleasant experience of witnessing the execution of five men from the 118th Pennsylvania pronounced guilty of desertion and sentenced to be shot. Writing from his "Camp near Rappahannock Station, Va.," to a cousin, Fleegen described the atmosphere and outcome of the procedure before pronouncing, "Stern justice was satisfied." He believed that the distasteful but necessary object lesson lay with the men who had transgressed rather than with an inhumane system: "The heaviest penalty man can pay was paid. It was indeed a hard sight and it is sad to think such severe measures must be resorted to but I believe the necessity of the times demand such measures." For the soldier, the requirement came as a result of a pattern that demanded to be checked in the interests of the service. "Deserting has got[ten] to be a thing too common and examples must be made."[80]

For others these desertions and the deaths of soldiers connected to them were signs of the injustice of a war that made unequal demands on the participants, particularly when the homes and families they had gone to war to defend were at risk.[81] In the Confederacy, tenuous links of some to their obligations in the service could come into question. As historian Mark Weitz noted, "each soldier's willingness to place himself and his efforts where the nation felt they were most needed was easily undermined if the Confederacy's sense of priority differed from that of its soldiers."[82]

Whatever the cause, the executions of those unfortunate enough to be caught, or chosen as examples when they returned, cast a pall over everyone who witnessed them. A soldier in the Ninetieth Ohio wrote more in his diary about the shooting of "a man from the 1st Kentucky . . . for 'bounty jumping' and desertion" than he ordinarily committed to paper. After describing the event, he concluded, "This created more gloom" than "a hundred natural deaths, or deaths in battle."[83]

Some of the individuals executed for desertion did not have the opportunity to experience any form of official review or process. Commanding the Fifty-Fourth Massachusetts, Robert Gould Shaw described in a letter to his mother such an incident that involved the Kansas commander James M. Montgomery: "His men being near their homes have deserted rapidly since we returned from St. Simon's. He sent word by their wives & others to the deserters that those who returned of their own free will should be pardoned—that those, whom he caught, he would shoot." When one of Shaw's sergeants apprehended a fugitive who had not returned of his own volition, Montgomery intervened personally, interrogating the man and sentencing him on the spot to be shot. The whole process occurred within an hour and a half, before "at 9:30 he was taken out and shot." Shaw concluded, "There was no Court-Martial—and the case was not referred to a superior officer."[84]

Even for units of long-standing service, desertion remained a reality that everyone faced. The Sixteenth Virginia Infantry had seen hard service in the Maryland and Gettysburg campaigns before another difficult year in 1864. But that year opened with death in another manner when Private James W. Wilkinson and another comrade faced a firing squad on January 10. Wilkinson had entered the service by conscription in April 1862 and had taken leave of his unit by July for the remainder of that year and the better part of the next.[85]

Just over another week had passed when Private George W. Capps suffered the same penalty for being absent from the command without leave. Capps had enlisted in 1861 and spent time in Charlottesville General Hospital before departing the ranks without permission in the summer of 1863. His record indicated that he returned to the command, but his previous travails and indiscretions failed to impress the authorities, and he was "executed by sentence of court martial, Jan. 20, 1864."[86]

In the early part of 1865, as major campaigning reached a critical point, individuals who might have been allowed to see their misdemeanors treated less firmly earlier in the war were not so fortunate at this stage. Union general Robert McAllister recounted a case for his wife and family from Hatcher's Run, near Petersburg, Virginia, as Ulysses Grant attempted to close his siege of the city and Robert E. Lee's Army of Northern Virginia: "Tomorrow we are to witness the execution of one of those poor miserable deserters. I hope it will have the effect of preventing others from committing the like crime." For the officer who had once lamented the noncombat deaths of comrades by illness, this type of inglorious passage carried little sympathy or room for indulgence. McAllister observed, "What a miserable death—to die the death of a traitor, false to his solom oath, false to his country, false to all that is high and holy, false to his friends and all that is near and dear to man on earth."[87]

Robert E. Lee became troubled intensely by the nature of the desertions that existed under his command in the spring of 1864. He addressed the matter candidly with President Davis and cited one incident in particular to illustrate the dilemma. This case involved Private Jacob Shomore, of Company B, Fifty-Second Virginia. Lee was sympathetic, but he understood the larger implications and possible ramifications when he explained:

The fact that prvt. Shomore had been a good soldier previous to his desertion, is insisted upon, as it frequently has been in like cases, as a ground of mitigation, and were he alone concerned, I would be disposed to give weight to it. But I am satisfied that it would be impolitic and unjust to the rest of the army to allow previous good conduct alone to atone for an offence most pernicious to the service, and most dangerous as an example.

General Lee had constantly sought the most just outcome of his deliberations, without jeopardizing the effectiveness of the army. "In reviewing Court Martial cases," he explained, "it has been my habit to give the accused the benefit of all extenuating circumstances that could be allowed to operate in their favor without injury to the service."

Lee felt that rigid discipline had accomplished positive results, albeit at a terrible cost for the individuals involved. As he observed, "The military executions that took place to such an extent last autumn, had a very beneficial influence, but in my judgment, many of them would have been avoided had the infliction of punishment in such cases uniformly followed the commission of the offence." However, there was no doubt in his mind that the actions of some had a greater impact than upon themselves alone. "Desertions and absence without leave not only weaken the army by the number of offenders not reclaimed, but by the guards that must be kept over those who are arrested."[88]

Kentuckian Ned Guerrant would have less reason to look at such circumstances as rigidly when he recorded an order for the execution of a deserter in March 1865. Henry Bishop, who "has always borne a good name heretofore, been a faithful soldier, and was 'persuaded' (to use his own expression) to the fatal course by a more vicious uncle," became an object lesson for stemming desertion.[89] Within a matter of days, Bishop faced execution before his comrades after the commander rejected calls for clemency. "The first execution I ever witnessed," Guerrant asserted. "He cried for mercy, to God, until he fell pierced with four balls thro' the heart," while the beguiling relative who had misled the soldier stood silent, spared by his nephew's last-minute exoneration of any responsibility for his actions in leading him astray.[90]

Desertion carried the obvious risk of facing execution if caught by the party from which one was leaving without permission; but reaching one's destination could prove dangerous as well. The *Daily Confederate* of Raleigh, North Carolina, conveyed the tale of one case involving a pitiable figure who learned the harsh lesson that no good deed would go unpunished: "A man named Bill Jones, who ran away from Richmond some months ago, to escape conscription," had fled to Union-occupied Tidewater Virginia. Unhappily for him, according to the account, "On reaching Norfolk, [he] was pointed out as one of those who raised the first secession flag in Virginia, and was immediately arrested, tried and ordered to be hung by Beast Butler."[91]

For some of those tasked with capturing fugitives and bringing them to justice, the situations they encountered presented mortal dangers, too. Although his muster entry did not specify the date of the incident or the exact nature of the circumstances, First Sergeant Granville Kinder of Company E, Fiftieth Virginia, fell to his death at High Bridge in Southside Virginia, "while in charge of deserters and recruits."[92]

The exact nature of Kinder's fatal plunge from the bridge in Virginia was not indicated, but as his experience illustrated, engaging in the act of recruiting could produce deadly situations for those tasked with such assignments. A Confederate officer located in Unionist East Tennessee confronted a group of people determined not only to stop his endeavors but also to make an example of him. Consequently, they dragged him from his home and killed him while his family witnessed the ordeal. Word quickly spread that the same fate could await any person with Confederate sympathies who operated in the region.[93]

In Mississippi, violence flared between those who sought to avoid conscription and those who wanted to apprehend them. As was the case for Sergeant Kinder, for some of those tasked with the unenviable duty of securing these men, the dangers were quite real. Major Amos McLemore operated in the Jones County area looking for resisters and deserters. On October 5, 1863, while in the company of several other Confederate officers, someone struck him with a fatal shot.[94]

Conscript officers were not the only targets for the fatal ire of those who dissented from Confederate government policies. Agents who undertook to collect proceeds from the "tax in kind," being levied as a way of transferring a percentage of the resources in private hands for the public good, found themselves putting their lives at risk. Reports indicated that at least two collectors had been "ambushed, shot, and killed dead."[95] A Confederate officer responsible for overseeing quartermaster activities in the region complained to his superiors about the disorder in his jurisdiction that thwarted collection efforts and "in many cases exiling the good and loyal citizens or shooting them in cold blood on their own door sills."[96]

Homicide and capital punishment existed for the men in the ranks, but death rates in the Civil War prisons were horrific by any account. Some of the conditions in Northern camps were only marginally better than in their Southern counterparts. Camps and the personnel associated with them on both sides were notorious for their cruelty. Often the deaths resulted from poor sanitation or debilitating conditions, but occasionally they resulted from callousness or accident or occurred at the hands of trigger-happy guards.

Although the conflict turned harsher as it progressed, there were already indications of the tensions between the men in blue and those who wore gray or butternut. These feelings occasionally escalated when men on one side exhibited inordinately foolish behavior toward men on the other side when they took the roles of prisoner of war and guard. In one instance in later 1861, a Georgian recorded an incident that involved a normally placid comrade. James Lemon's friend "A.N." was usually "a most quiet and reserved fellow and had a characteristic of which I had long been aware, and that was he had a 'long fuse' but when that fuse was used up, the 'report' was a fearful thing to behold." Unfortunately, for a group of indiscreet Union prisoners, the lesson came home when one of them deigned to disparage the guard's mother. "Well upon hearing these scurrilous remarks," Lemon explained, "A.N. raised his piece and in a twinkling shot the Yank through the heart." Lemon had not witnessed the incident directly but arrived on the scene in the immediate aftermath and received a full accounting. The soldier "was disciplined but not harshly" for responding to the taunt as he had done, "as all who witnessed the incident testified that A.N. had taken more shameful abuse than any man should be made to endure and if any man deserved to die, it was that foul-mouthed Yankee from New York."[97]

Death could also come without malice and produce genuine regret from the responsible parties. In October 1863, word appeared in print of a "terrible accident in Nashville," involving "about 600 Confederate prisoners," located on the "upper or fifth story" of a building "known as the Maxwell House, which is used as a barracks for our soldiers." The disaster occurred when the men heard "the signal for breakfast" and headed collectively for the stairs that would take them to the distribution line. As the article described it:

> The rush was so sudden and their weight so great that the stairs gave way with a loud crash, and one hundred of the prisoners were suddenly precipitated, with a perfect avalanche of broken and scattering timbers, through two sets of flooring to the third floor, where they landed one quivering mass of bleeding, mangled humanity. Two (whose names we have been unable to learn) were instantly killed, and the whole of them were frightfully disfigured, having their legs, arms or heads broken.

The story contained a glimmer of hope in that so few men had actually died. Ambulances "were hurried to the spot, and the misguided and suffering Confederates, who had braved the dangers of many a hard fought battle to be maimed for life by an accident, were taken to the prison hospital." Here, the writer noted, they received the same care the surgeons would have provided their opponents, and the injured had the additional ministrations of local "secesh ladies" to assist them. A final irony was that for several of the men, the help lent by civilian refugees from other parts of the South, including Georgia and Texas, who had arrived in Nashville, allowed them to be reunited with family members. The writer exonerated the "present efficient commander of the barracks, Captain Lakin of the 89th Ohio," from any blame, noting that he had warned the prisoners "against crowding around the stairways."[98]

A much smaller-scale incident with a similar response occurred while Union prisoners of war were undertaking routine duties near a facility in Salisbury, North Carolina. A Raleigh newspaper reprinted an account that explained the circumstances: "A yankee prisoner was accidentally shot yesterday morning on a wood train of the Western [Rail]Road. He was one of thirty who had been permitted to go up the road to load a train with wood for the use of the prison." Unfortunately, while engaged in this work, one of the guards supervising the effort, "in entering the cars with his gun, accidentally struck the cock against something causing a discharge of the piece. The lead entered the breast of a prisoner, killing him instantly."[99] Salisbury would have an even higher mortality rate among its inmates than Andersonville, although never achieving that level of notoriety.[100] Even so, the writer did not relate the story with any degree of satisfaction but instead stressed, "It was a sad incident, and even in these times when human life is fearfully cheap, cast a gloom over those present who witnessed it."[101]

Tragically, death for prisoners of war was too common, but the killing of confined individuals by guards for infractions that might seem arbitrary was certainly unnecessary. Such stories permeated the tales of captives on both sides, with occasional investigations to determine the validity of the actions taken. Such a flurry of communications occurred in December 1863 in connection with the death of prisoners who exacerbated the situation by disobeying orders from the guards. William L. Pope, private, Ninth Tennessee Cavalry, Company A, perished on the night of November 5, after defying an order from a guard in an act a superior deemed had produced a beneficial effect on the other prisoners.[102] John Lakin, commanding at the exchange barracks in Nashville, Tennessee, had to provide explanations for two shooting cases. The first involved Sergeant William McClelland, Company F, Fifty-Eighth Alabama, killed when ordered "twice to get back on the inside; he (meaning McClelland) shook his head; the guard then shot him dead." The second concerned T. J. Smith, private, Company B, Fifth Georgia, who "came to the window and got up into the window, and the sentinel ordered him away three times, and he paid no attention to the command, and the guard shot him (meaning T. J. Smith, private, Company B, Fifth Georgia), causing his death."[103]

Major Edgar Burroughs of the Fifth Virginia Cavalry had both an unusual pedigree and an end to his military career in the Civil War. A Methodist minister and farmer from Back Bay, Virginia, Burroughs had served as a delegate to the Virginia Secession Convention before the war and enlisted as a first lieutenant. Quickly elevated to the captaincy, he later received authorization to raise a unit of partisan rangers to operate in the area of Norfolk, Virginia. Captured in November 1863, the former minister fell mortally wounded to a shot from a prison guard on January 27, 1864.[104]

At the time of his death, Burroughs was suffering from a bout of smallpox. His brother, a lieutenant of artillery, protested the death to Secretary of War James Seddon, considering it a deliberate killing that demanded that "some steps be taken to retaliate for this wanton act, and stop the murder of our gallant men in future."[105] Robert Ould, the Confederate agent of exchange, endorsed the document with a statement from Union general Benjamin Butler insisting that he had investigated the matter and determined that "Major B. was shot at the window, while he was attempting to escape, and after he had been ordered by the sentinel to retire. He further says that he believes Major B. was in delirium at the time."[106]

The death of one Confederate prisoner of war sparked an intense debate among various entities in March 1864. Sergeant Edwin Young felt sufficiently provoked by the behavior of an L. R. Peyton, variously labeled as a private and a captain, that he fired at and killed him. Initially, Edward R. S. Canby insisted that the sergeant be held for murder for a death he deemed "entirely unjustifiable." However, the response was an insistence that prisoners must obey orders under any circumstances. E. A. Hitchcock maintained, "It is of vital importance that guards over prisoners of war should be protected in the execution of their duty."[107]

Caleb Coplan, a Union soldier from Ohio captured at Chickamauga, found himself at Camp Sumter, where he spotted an item just beyond the "dead-line" and paid with his life while reaching for it. Historian William Marvel noted that Coplan represented "the first man killed at the dead line."[108] In addition to the Ohioan, Marvel noted that deaths at the hands of guards at Andersonville included "George 'Albert,' May 3; Thomas Herbert, May 15; James Babb, July 4; Otis Knight, July 22; William Unversagt, July 27; . . . Maurice Printibill, September 5; August Lohmaer, November 30; and Christian Konold, January 1, 1865," in addition to two unknown individuals, one of whom "crossed the dead line August 25 as a means of committing suicide."[109]

As a prisoner of war, Confederate captain Jonas Alexander Lipps of the Fiftieth Virginia Infantry experienced a bizarre encounter of his own with a guard after being captured in the fighting at Spotsylvania Court House on May 12, 1864. The Russell County, Virginia, native had enlisted as a farm hand from Wise County, at age nineteen and became an officer in the unit when it organized in Wytheville. He survived the capture of Fort Donelson when he became separated from the main body and made his way across country to friendly units. Not so fortunate two years later, Lipps faced a Union guard who "'without any provocation' attempted to bayonet him." The blade penetrated "through the fleshy part of his left arm between elbow and shoulder," but the six-foot, 180-pound prisoner reached out and "grabbed the gun near the bayonet, shoved the Federal back enough to draw the bayonet out of his arm [and] turned the bayonet on the Federal and stuck it through him, killing him." The officer apparently suffered no repercussions from the incident, but Lipps moved from one prison camp to another for the remainder of the war, including a stint at Hilton Head, South Carolina, where he became one of the "Immortal 600," held for a time under Union fire. Ultimately transferred back to Fort Delaware in March 1865, the stalwart Confederate would live only another month before dying of scurvy on April 6, at age twenty-four.[110]

Similarly, Maine prisoner Charles Mattocks spent much of 1864 in one Confederate facility or another and recorded a couple of incidents of brutality that may or may not have been deliberate, but nevertheless cost the lives of at least two comrades. The first of these occurred in Macon, Georgia, in June and without a doubt, in Mattocks's mind, were purposeful. On Sunday, June 12, he observed, "Last night at about 8 o'clock we had a cold-blooded murder in the prison yard. One of our officers was at the spring, or brook rather, washing, and was on the point of returning to his quarters, when the sentinel outside the palisade deliberately shot him." The victim was a lieutenant, O. Gerson, of the Forty-Fifth New York, felled by a teenage Confederate sentinel despite being some feet away from the dead line. Gerson lingered for a time but perished from the rounds of buck and ball that had hit him. "It seems almost impossible that the sentinel could have thought him trying to escape," his Maine comrade noted, "as he deliberately fired upon him without any challenge or warning whatever."[111]

Subsequently, Mattocks learned that rather than being punished for his actions, the young perpetrator of the killing of Lieutenant Gerson was supposed to have been rewarded. "The soldier who murdered one of our officers has received a sort of Confederate justice," he observed. "He has been promoted to Sergeant and furloughed for 30 days." Mattocks speculated that the guard "must be quite a hero at home when it becomes known that he has killed one Yankee." More to the point of his frustration, he added, "It matters not with many of these people whether a life is taken in manly open fight upon the battlefield or within the limits of a closely guarded prison."[112]

Another incident occurred in October, after Mattocks transferred to a facility in Charleston, South Carolina. He recorded in his journal, "A Lt. Young, of the 4th Penn. Cav. was killed two or three evenings ago, while sitting at his camp fire, by the accidental discharge of a musket in the hands of a careless sentry."[113] What the soldier from Maine attributed to accident, from the information he had obtained, was actually closer to the killing that had so incensed him earlier in the year. Another captive noted that the guard fired after a prisoner approached too near the dead line. "The man aimed at escaped unharmed," but the victim, "quietly sitting on the ground, received the bullet in his breast and died in a few hours."[114]

Inadvertent death came to a Richmond prison in December 1864, as well. "Yesterday morning, while Colonel Spencer, brigade officer of the day of General P. T. Moore's command, was inspecting the guard at the Libby prison, a gun exploded, causing the death of one of the Yankee prisoners," according to the *Richmond Daily Dispatch*. The report indicated the unintentional nature of the killing in this instance:

> The Colonel had the gun in his hand inspecting it, and in examining the lock the hammer slipped from his thumb and exploded the cap driving both the ramrod and bullet through the flour of the guard-house above, where the prisoners are confined. The bullet and a portion of the ramrod lodged in the lower position of the prisoner's body, inflicting a wound which caused his death in a few hours afterwards.[115]

Although similar in prevalence and type to those that befell soldiers in camp and in the field, accidents did not result in the largest numbers of deaths for the prisoners. Illness plagued facilities in both North and South, with shortages exacerbating conditions. Confined at Johnson's Island, Ohio, John Dooley of the First Virginia Infantry watched fellow Confederate officers die with alarming regularity. On November 7, 1863, even as he attended a rehearsal for a theatrical production entitled "Battle of Gettysburg," he recorded, "Another funeral from hospital today." Admitting, "don't know the gentleman's name," Dooley explained that the man would be buried "in a small space outside the enclosure (about distant 400 yards) set aside for the Confederate deceased."[116] The Irish American Southern soldier would feel the deaths of other comrades more intently, including that of "Lieut Baya" from Florida, of whom he wrote, "Oh how sad to die thus, far from his friends and the land of his birth, among strangers . . . oh death, could you not wait till the poor boy had returned to the fond ones he loved?"[117]

From the early prisons created from buildings pressed into service to house captives to the stockades and camps that emerged as the war continued, death due to illness was an ever-present phenomenon. A compilation of the Confederate internees who perished at Camp Douglas, Illinois, numbered 4,454 names, including 39 civilians being held there.[118] At Elmira, New York, the death rates were astounding. One scholar observed that of 12,122 Confederate prisoners located there, 2,950 perished, including two dozen civilians; at 24.3 percent, this constituted "the highest death rate of any prison in the North."[119]

Information compiled for the War Department on U.S. military prisons from 1862 through 1865 provided the raw data, but the numbers could not reflect the individual stories of the prisoners. Even so, the statistics for the captives who died were daunting for many of the facilities in the comprehensive listing appearing in the *Official Records*,[120] as shown on pages 296–297.

Historian Lonnie Speer selected the case of Solomon Cook, "a strong, able-bodied soldier who had survived more than a year of fighting bravely and fiercely on the battlefield," as symbolic of those who could not survive their stints in prison camps after being captured. Cook's was one of 30,218 Confederate prisoner deaths; the Union total stood at 25,796. Despite the propaganda that tended to connect to this volatile issue, Speer concluded, "Neither side was more at fault than the other."[121]

Death continued to stalk many of those weakened by the conditions of their captivity. For men, North or South, who had waited through seemingly interminable rumors of exchange and release, hope and health waxed and waned. When the surviving prisoners finally departed for their homes, some would not arrive and others who did had no real hope of recovery. One twenty-two-year-old released captive from Connecticut lasted less than a week after his return. The eventual tombstone erected over the remains of Wallace Woodford included the unequivocal declaration, "He came home to die."[122] Comrade Sidney H. Hayden obtained his release on December 16, hoping to work his way properly through the system. Worn and anxious to return home, he observed of his Andersonville experience in a letter on February 21, 1865, "*Honor, is a poor thing to live on.*" He was able to reach Connecticut and obtained another furlough in March, but in his weakened condition he could not fight typhoid fever successfully. He died of the malady on April 4, 1865.[123]

Henry Wirz, the Confederate commandant of the notorious Andersonville Prison, was only the most famous of the people who met judgment at the end of a rope because of his role in the Civil War. During the conflict, drumhead courts-martial held in the field during ongoing operations were more prevalent than rare. Another notorious figure was the Confederate guerrilla Champ Ferguson. Prone to take "time by the forelock" as he reasoned with regard to killing those first who might prove a danger to his own well-being, Ferguson was ruthless in his actions. These tendencies had a direct impact on his own demise as Federal forces reacted differently toward him than to others who might have expected to receive similar treatment.[124]

PRISON	DIED	PRISON	DIED
July, 1862		*November, 1863*	
Camp Butler, Ill.	41	Camp Douglas, Ill.	100
Camp Douglas, Ill.	146	Camp Morton, Ind.	68
Camp Morton, Ind.	21	Fort Delaware, Del.	156
Fort Delaware, Del.	20	Point Lookout, Md.	119
August, 1862		*December, 1863*	
Camp Butler, Ill.	25	Alton, Ill.	70
Camp Douglas, Ill.	117	Camp Douglas, Ill.	57
Camp Morton, Ind.	26	Camp Morton, Ind.	91
Fort Delaware, Del.	13	Fort Delaware, Del.	82
		Point Lookout, Md.	158
February, 1863			
Alton, Ill.	132	*January, 1864*	
Camp Butler, Ill.	103	Alton, Ill.	84
Camp Douglas, Ill.	387	Camp Morton, Ind.	104
		Fort Delaware, Del.	78
June, 1863		Point Lookout, Md.	138
Fort Delaware, Del.	66	Rock Island, Ill.	231
July, 1863		*February, 1864*	
Fort Delaware, Del.	111	Alton, Ill.	54
		Camp Douglas, Ill.	54
August, 1863		Camp Morton, Ind.	69
Fort Delaware, Del.	169	Point Lookout, Md.	128
		Rock Island, Ill.	346
September, 1863			
Alton, Ill.	75	*March, 1864*	
Fort Delaware, Del.	327	Alton, Ill.	51
		Camp Douglas, Ill.	66
October, 1863		Camp Morton, Ind.	62
Fort Delaware, Del.	377	Point Lookout, Md.	82
		Rock Island, Ill.	283

PRISON	DIED	PRISON	DIED
April, 1864		*January, 1865*	
Fort Delaware, Del.	74	Alton, Ill.	122
Rock Island, Ill.	246	Camp Chase, Ohio	293
July, 1864		Camp Douglas, Ill.	308
Fort Delaware, Del.	110	Camp Morton, Ind.	117
Point Lookout, Md.	204	Elmira, N.Y.	285
		Point Lookout, Md.	161
August, 1864		Rock Island, Ill.	279
Elmira, N.Y.	115	Ship Island, Miss.	601
Point Lookout, Md.	211		
Rock Island, Ill.	114	*February, 1865*	
		Camp Chase, Ohio	499
September, 1864		Camp Douglas, Ill.	243
Elmira, N.Y.	385	Camp Morton, Ind.	133
Point Lookout, Md.	110	Elmira, N.Y.	426
		Fort Delaware, Del.	93
October, 1864		Point Lookout, Md.	233
Camp Chase, Ohio	113		
Camp Douglas, Ill.	109	*April, 1865*	
Elmira, N.Y.	276	Camp Chase, Ohio	132
Point Lookout, Md.	111	Camp Douglas, Ill.	86
		Elmira, N.Y.	267
November, 1864		Fort Delaware, Del.	106
Camp Chase, Ohio	146	Point Lookout, Md.	203
Camp Douglas, Ill.	217		
Elmira, N.Y.	207	*May, 1865*	
		Camp Chase, Ohio	80
December, 1864		Camp Douglas, Ill.	63
Camp Chase, Ohio	153	Elmira, N.Y.	131
Camp Douglas, Ill.	323	Hart's Island, N.Y.	112
Elmira, N.Y.	269	Point Lookout, Md.	324
Point Lookout, Md.	86		
Ship Island, Miss.	70	*June, 1865*	
		Point Lookout, Md.	256

Wirz to a greater extent, and Ferguson to a lesser one, became prime examples of justice meted out beyond a battlefield or war zone, but many individuals came to their ends in connection with the most basic desires of human beings caught up in warfare. Those who fell asleep at their posts, attempted unsuccessfully to desert, or became victims of local groups or dragnets ferreting out deserters or bushwhackers suffered as supremely as others who fell under the hail of shot and shell.

No less a figure than Abraham Lincoln came to see the sad plight of person after person who had run afoul of the military system and stood condemned to summary punishment. His letters contained multiple examples of those he ordered spared from death in this most inglorious manner. Others were not so fortunate. For them, mistakes or missteps of this nature were fatal and redemption a matter for another sphere.

Confederate brigadier general John H. Winder may well have done what Wirz and Ferguson could not: cheat the hangman. A graduate of West Point and a veteran of the Old Army, the Maryland native joined the Confederacy after resigning his commission. As provost marshal of Richmond, he had authority over prisoners of war and deserters. In November 1864, Winder accepted the assignment as commissary general for all Union captives east of the Mississippi River. His implementation of draconian measures in the Confederate capital and his subsequent role with Federal prisoners won him widespread unpopularity. Yet, the officer undertook his duties conscientiously and sought to ameliorate as much suffering as was possible in the struggling Confederacy. The task proved especially daunting in the face of mounting shortages, advancing Union armies, and the policy against prisoner exchange.[125] Winder's biographer, Arch Fredric Blakey, described the general in these last days as "completely used up."[126] On February 6, 1865, while on an inspection tour of a prison facility at Florence, South Carolina, the officer fell dead of an apparent heart attack.[127]

Not everyone who perished in the American Civil War did so under honorable circumstances. Whether the victims of murder or cold-blooded killings themselves, or the perpetrators of infractions that led them to the gallows or the execution posts, some of the individuals who had enlisted to serve failed to survive the war. Even so, friends, associates, or loved ones often remained behind to lament their passing and to offer testimony to the price the conflict could exact from those who participated in it.

Conclusion
"There Is No Glory in It"

I think I would have preferred sudden death from
a cannon shot, to a lingering illness, which would
inevitably result in a dissolution of body and soul.
Confederate soldier Robert Patrick

Father, I am sick of reading in the papers of "the
glory" of war. The truth is, there is no glory in it;
Everything about it is simply horrible.
Union artillerist William Christie

The American Civil War exacted a terrible toll among its participants. Many of
the men who went to war and the civilians who remained at home felt the impact
of deaths from the conflict that would be palpable for generations. Those who
perished in battle could be thought to have offered their lives as a meaningful
sacrifice for defending the Union, the Confederacy, or a specific state, eradicating slavery, upholding constitutional principles, or supporting states' rights. For
others, the reason and purpose were less clear. These individuals lost their lives in
circumstances that defied conventional theories of worthiness or left those who
remained behind with little to assuage their grief.

Historians have elevated the estimates for the total number of deaths associated with the Civil War but could never compensate for the dearth of records
that has made a precise accounting so problematic. The vast number of unknown
markers on the grave sites of Union and Confederate cemeteries has continued to
bear stark, silent witness to the lack of information with which every generation
during or since the conflict has had to contend.

In the Civil War, fatal illnesses claimed the lives of more men than the weaponry of their opponents in combat. The timing of such deaths was particularly

tragic. As one scholar noted of the men who took up arms, "Many made the ultimate sacrifice for their convictions long before they fired their first shot at an enemy."[1] Others succumbed after facing those opponents and surviving their battlefield ordeals. In either case, the fortitude present on the battlefield did not always apply to noncombat situations. "Courage might protect the soldier in battle," Gerald Linderman asserted, "but it offered him little in illness."[2] Nevertheless, the valor exhibited in confronting the unseen foe cannot be discounted. As Wiley Sword has explained, "For every soldier who, instead of fighting the enemy, lay prone in a cot or on the ground enduring from moment to moment, hour to hour, the agonizing pain of sickness, it was an agony of courage in the most morbid sense." Whether the individual retained the faculties to understand his circumstances or faced the end in the haze of impending death, these sacrifices were as real as any other. "Yet, if there was no glory in dying of disease," Sword observed, "there remained the awareness of effort in the purpose of venturing one's life for the common good."[3]

Even so, ambivalence continued to exist for those who were left to reconcile such deaths with the expectation of falling in battle. When he learned that a friend had succumbed to illness, Confederate Robert Patrick remarked, "He died at Tuskegee, Alabama, of consumption, the disease having been brought on by exposure during the siege of Vicksburg. Poor fellow! He had escaped all the shells and balls to linger a few months and die in an obscure village." Patrick used the situation for a moment of hard introspection. "I think I would have preferred sudden death from a cannon shot, to a lingering illness, which would inevitably result in a dissolution of body and soul."[4]

Soldiers who died from disease might yet obtain a level of nobility for their stoicism in the face of death. But those who perished in accidents or other mishaps, at the hands of friendly forces or by their own hands, in transportation or industrial accidents or simply by being at the wrong place at the wrong time, failed to offer even that sense of meaning to their surviving comrades, friends, and families. Nevertheless, for each of them, their friends, and their loved ones, the loss was as real and significant. Their lives mattered.

Individuals and institutions that sought to extol the virtues of the sacrifice of life in the war did so for numerous reasons. In 1863, an obituary in a Virginia newspaper employed state pride to elevate the death of Captain Henry F. Spahr. The writer noted that the soldier had "joined Jeffrey's Holloway Battery, believing his country needed his services," and performed admirably in the ranks until "stricken with disease." Convalescence at Emory and Henry Hospital had not allowed sufficient recovery, and Spahr "was finally sent home," where even parental care could not prevent the son's demise. The author of the obituary concluded, "Thus has Virginia added another to her long list of sacrifices upon the altar of liberty."[5] The rhetoric did not mask the fact that a beloved individual had perished far from the battlefield.

Of course, the men in the ranks understood the realities of the price of wartime service. Union artillerist William Christie may have captured the point best when he wrote home from Vicksburg, Mississippi: "Father, I am sick of reading in the papers of 'the glory' of war. The truth is, there is no glory in it; Everything about it is simply horrible." For the soldier, the battlefield itself was enough to convey that horror, even while fighting for a worthy cause, but he understood other ways that death intruded in the humanity struggling through the conflict and asked, "Is there glory in the cry of the mother as she sees her child's head swept off by a cannonball? Is there glory in the weeping of widows and orphans? Is there glory in the burning cities and the desolated homes that War leaves behind him?"[6] Perhaps Christie's greatest legacy, and that of the many like him who wrote letters, kept diaries or journals, or made observations in newspapers, was to preserve the stories of the ultimate sacrifices of individuals, soldier and civilian, away from direct engagement with their armed opponents in battle.

Veterans continued to suffer in many ways for years following the close of combat in 1865, from wounds, injuries, and illnesses sustained during the conflict. Those conditions were often responsible for lives shortened by their effects. For some of these individuals, the trauma of their experiences was among the underlying factors in suicides.[7] Sergeant Andrew W. Little, a member of the Ninth New Jersey Volunteer Infantry, survived the war in which he had borne hardships and viewed horrors, including the decapitation of friends and the immolation of wounded enemies who had tried to burn a bridge his command wanted to cross. He came home plagued by these wartime visions and took his own life within a few months of his return.[8] Likewise, wartime antagonisms did not subside simply because formal hostilities had ended. In a real sense, these veterans' deaths were also wartime deaths, and when they emanated from causes other than direct hostile fire, they could be added to the inglorious passages of the Civil War.

Soldiers feared that the sacrifices they and their comrades witnessed or experienced would leave them as obscure shadows of lives lived and lost. During an expedition, Second Lieutenant Benjamin F. McIntyre of the Nineteenth Iowa Infantry observed of the demise of a compatriot from Wisconsin:

> He will soon be forgotten and the incidents attending his death be lost amoung the things of the past so far as his regiment is concerned, and the country will forget such a man ever existed—Yet far distant in the Badger State near a little glassy lake are hearts who will preserve his memory green

. . . [of] him who today would be amoung us had ordinary precaution been taken and usual care exercised.[9]

A pro-Union Atlanta citizen seemed to sense the importance of this in the summer of 1863 when he learned that the man who had formerly served as a Sunday school superintendent and a captain in the Forty-Second Georgia had survived the siege of Vicksburg, only to die a short time later, "in the hands of the enemy," from disease. Sam Richards lamented the passing of Captain Thomas W. Davis from the effects of war as surely as if the soldier had perished in battle. At the funeral service, he recorded the officiating minister as offering a "sermon for Capt Davis from the text, 'He being dead, yet speaketh.' It is sad to think how many noble men have lost their lives during the two years that this wicked war has been waged against us by the people of the North."[10] Of course, individuals in pulpits in the North and families and associates across the land would express similar sentiments for their "lost lives" and the call for all of the dead, in whatever circumstances they had sacrificed those lives, to have their now-silenced voices heard.

Appendix

Fatal Accidents to Troops from Indiana, 1861–1865

Smith, John, B, 8th (3 Mons.) — Killed by cars at ——, Ohio.

Petro, Charles, C, 6th (3 Yrs.) — Killed, accidentally, Nolin, Ky., Sep. 26, 1861.

Cochran, John, D, 6th — Accidentally killed at Louisville, May 8, '62.

Stutton, Lewis, F, 6th — Killed accidentally, Dec. 1, '62.

Lloyd, John A., F, 6th — Killed accidentally in skirmish, at Kennesaw, June 18, '64.

Craig, Joseph A., I, 7th (3 Yrs.) — Killed accid'ly near Baltimore, July 22, '63.

Jennings, John A., B, 8th (3 Yrs.) — Drowned, Saluria Bayou, Texas, Mar. 13, '64.

Trout, William, Cpl. E, 8th — Drowned at St. Louis, June 17, '63.

Carney, George, F, 8th — Died April 18, '61; accidental wounds.

Ginney, Dennis, H, 8th — Supposed drowned Helena, Ark., Sep. 16, '62.

Massey, Wilford H., I, 8th — Drowned at Matagorda Bay, March 13, '64.

Baker, William, K, 8th — Committed suicide at Syracuse, Mo., Oct. 20, '61.

Williamson, James K., A, 9th (3 Yrs.) — Died at Nashville, July 29, '64; sunstroke.

Truell, Andrew J., B, 9th — Capt'd Chicm'ga; killed Indianapolis by Pro. Guard.

Driscal, James, C, 9th — Drowned in the Ohio River, Jan. 18, '63.

Widoner, William H., C, 10th (3 Yrs.) — Killed at Bardstown, Oct. 7th, '61; accidental.

Seldmiller, Valentine, E, 10th — Died of poison, Bridgeport, Ala., Sep. 5, '63.

Wenkler, Henry, E, 10th — Drowned, Battle Creek, Tenn., Sep. 2, '63.

Cox, David J., Cpl., K, 10th — Killed accidentally on R.R., Sep. 14, '64.

Reed, Samuel A., C, 11th (3 Yrs.) — Drowned in Tenn. River near Crump's Landing, March 30, '62.

Cochran, James, Cpl., D, 11th — Drowned, Oct. 5, '61.

Barner, Henry, K, 11th — Drowned, Memphis, July 14, '62.

Burnell, John W., D, 12th (3 Yrs.) — Killed by falling from building, July 16, '63.

303

Humble, Samuel C., F, 12th	Drowned in Wateree river, S.C., Feb. 25, '65.
Barnhisel, Abraham, I, 12th	Killed by lightning, Manchester, May 11, '65.
Moran, Dominick, C, 13th	Killed by railroad accident in Ohio.
Robbins, Richard, D, 13th	Killed by Capt. Wilson, May 3, '62.
Ruck, Christian, D, 13th	Ap'd Corp'l; killed, acc'dly, May 16, '63, Suffolk.
Tyler, George W., B, 13th (Re-organized)	Killed by explosion of shell, July 6, '64.
Littrell, Linas, Cpl., D, 13th	Killed by explosion, Ft. Fisher, Jan. 16, '65.
Furgason, George C., D, 13th	Killed by explosion, Ft. Fisher, Jan. 16, '65.
Fulk, George C., D, 13th	Killed by explosion, Ft. Fisher, Jan. 16, '65.
Hoag, Jacob F., D, 13th	Killed at Ft. Fisher, Jan. 16, '65.
Powell, Leander, D, 13th	Killed by explosion, Ft. Fisher, Jan. 16, '65.
Latterman, Adam, E, 13th	Killed by explosion, Ft. Fisher, Jan. 16, '65.
Childers, James T., A, 14th (3 Yrs.)	Drowned in Potomac, near Romney, Jan. 1, '62.
Arthur, Andrew, K, 14th	Killed by accident, Sept. 13, '61.
Schutt, Joseph, B, 15th (3 Yrs.)	Drowned, Bowling Green, March 3, '62.
Marklin, Herman, G, 15th	Drowned, Nov. 29, '61.
Drought, Solomon, K, 15th	Killed accidentally at Rich Mt'n, July 14, '61.
Coffey, Joel P., E, 16th (1 Yr.)	Killed by accident, Nov. 7, '61.
Anderson, Aaron, A, 16th (3 Yrs.)	Drowned at Helena, Ark., March 17, '63.
Neil, Jeremiah, I, 16th	Drowned at Young's Point, Jan. 23, '63.
Simmons, William S., A, 17th (3 Yrs.)	Died Dec. 26, '64; accidental wounds.
Wilson, Joseph C., A, 17th	Drowned in Tennessee River, Sept. 8, '63.
Bolden, Alfred, B, 17th	Drowned in Ocmulgee river, near Macon, June 9, '65.
Davis, James A., B, 17th	Killed, Ind'polis, Nov. 15, '64, by R.R. Acci't.
Pennington, Dennis L., Cpl., C, 17th	Veteran; drowned April 19, '64.
Devenny, Thomas, F, 17th	Killed by R.R. accident at Indianapolis.
Keeran, Patrick, F, 17th	Vet'n; drowned in Bl'k Warrior River, March 29, '65.
Evans, George L., G, 17th	Substitute, captured; lost on steamer *Sultana*, April 27, '65.
Lockman, Beam, G, 17th	Capt'd; lost on steamer *Sultana*, April 27, '65.
Hill, Hiram, D, 21st	Drowned at Baton Rouge, July 21, '65.
Taylor, Leonard O, E, 21st	Killed by Provost Guard, May 24, '65.
Ingle, John K., K, 21st	Accidentally drowned in Mobile Bay, March 15, '65.
Johnson, Timothy D., L, 21st	Drowned, Baton Rouge, Nov. 18, '63.

Smith, George W., G, 24th	Drowned, April 5, '65 in Alabama river. Also listed as Unassigned Recruit, drowned on April 15, '63.
Ballard, Jackson, I, 24th Veteran	Killed in Indiana, March 18, '64, while in pursuit of a deserter.
Bordier, Frank C., A, 25th (3 Yrs.)	Drowned at Crump's Landing, Tenn., April 12, '64.
Heatherly, David, C, 25th	Killed by accident, Aug. 3, '62.
Casper, John, C, 25th	Killed accident'y at Decatur, Ala., May 19, '64.
McIntire, Silas, D, 25th	Killed by accident, Nov. 19, '63.
Coles, Solomon, H, 25th	Drowned at Savannah, Ga., Jan. 4, '65; drafted.
Nickelson, Thomas, I, 25th	Vet.; died at Memphis, '64, of pistol shot.
Englehard, William, I, 25th	Killed, June 30, '64, accidentally.
Strong, William H., A, 26th (3 Yrs.)	Vet.; drowned, Bayous Lafourche, July 10, '64.
Hughes, Moses, D, 26th	Killed by John Campbell at Pilot Knob, May 27, '63.
Stevenson, Thomas, G, 26th	Killed, June 19, '62, accidental wounds.
Miller, Alexander, I, 1st Cav. (28th)	Killed accidentally, Sept. 10, '61.
Daugherty, Jacob, G, 29th (3 Yrs.)	Killed by R.R. at Chattanooga, May 25, '64.
Brumbarger, William, H, 29th	Killed by railroad accident, July 31, '65; substitute.

All from Terrell, *Report of the Adjutant General of the State of Indiana, 1861–1865,* 4:28, 79, 80, 83, 84, 105, 113, 117, 123, 125, 126, 131, 133, 136, 160, 163, 170, 180, 181, 197, 223, 227, 234, 242, 244, 259, 262, 264, 274, 288, 294, 302, 306, 314, 323, 338, 345, 347, 348, 349, 350, 357, 358, 361, 459, 461, 477, 479, 555, 557, 561, 564, 569, 570, 572, 581, 583, 589, 596, 603, 642, 671, 673.

Notes

Preface and Acknowledgments

1. John Keegan, *The Face of Battle* (New York: Viking Press, 1976), 15.
2. Ibid., 311–312.
3. Ibid., 312.
4. See Brian Steel Wills, *The War Hits Home: The Civil War in Southeastern Virginia* (Charlottesville: University Press of Virginia, 2001).

Introduction: "This Inglorious Taking Off"

1. Charles A. Humphreys, *Field, Camp, Hospital and Prison in the Civil War, 1863–1865* (Freeport, N.Y.: Books for Libraries Press, 1918; repr., Manchester, N.H.: Ayer Co., 1975), 218–219.
2. Quoted in Lesley J. Gordon, *A Broken Regiment: The 16th Connecticut's Civil War* (Baton Rouge: Louisiana State University Press, 2014), 126.
3. William Marvel, *The Great Task Remaining: The Third Year of Lincoln's War* (Boston: Houghton Mifflin, 2010), 215–217.
4. Garry Wills, *Lincoln at Gettysburg: The Words That Remade America* (New York: Simon & Schuster, 1992).
5. "Mavoureen, Marion, Va., APRIL 23–24, 1861," in John Preston Sheffey, *Soldier of Southwestern Virginia: The Civil War Letters of Captain John Preston Sheffey*, ed. James I. Robertson Jr. (Baton Rouge: Louisiana State University Press, 2004), 24–25.
6. Joseph Allan Frank, *With Ballot and Bayonet: The Political Socialization of American Civil War Soldiers* (Athens: University of Georgia Press, 1998), 21–22.
7. Wiley Sword, *Courage under Fire: Profiles in Bravery from the Battlefields of the Civil War* (New York: St. Martin's Press, 2007), 145.
8. "Mortality and Sickness of the United States Volunteers," *Caledonian* (St. Johnsbury, Vt.), January 30, 1863.
9. Quoted in Bell Irvin Wiley, *They Who Fought Here* (New York: Macmillan, 1959), 221.
10. Quoted in Newton T. Colby, *The Civil War Papers of Lt. Colonel Newton T. Colby, New York Infantry*, ed. William E. Hughes (Jefferson, N.C.: McFarland, 2003), 185.

11. George C. Rable, *Fredericksburg! Fredericksburg!* (Chapel Hill: University of North Carolina Press, 2002), 14.

12. Quoted in Colby, *The Civil War Papers of Lt. Colonel Newton T. Colby*, 188–190.

13. Scott Reynolds Nelson and Carol Sheriff, *A People at War: Civilians and Soldiers in America's Civil War* (New York: Oxford University Press, 2007), 123.

14. Kenneth J. Winkle, *Lincoln's Citadel: The Civil War in Washington, DC* (New York: Norton, 2013), 166–168.

15. Emory M. Thomas, *The Confederacy as a Revolutionary Experience* (Englewood Cliffs, N.J.: Prentice-Hall, 1971), 107.

16. Paul E. Steiner, *Disease in the Civil War: Natural Biological Warfare in 1861–1865* (Springfield, Ill.: C. C. Thomas, 1968).

17. James I. Robertson Jr., *Soldiers Blue and Gray* (Columbia: University of South Carolina Press, 1988), 145.

18. Bell Irvin Wiley, *The Life of Johnny Reb: The Common Soldier of the Confederacy* (Baton Rouge: Louisiana State University Press, 1943), 244.

19. Bell Irvin Wiley, *The Life of Billy Yank: The Common Soldier of the Union* (Baton Rouge: Louisiana State University Press, 1952), 124.

20. "Dear Amanda A P Hill's Division Hospital Near Richmond, Va. August 10th, 1862," in Mason Hill Fitzpatrick, *Letters to Amanda: The Civil War Letters of Mason Hill Fitzpatrick, Army of Northern Virginia*, ed. Jeffrey C. Lowe and Sam Hodges (Macon, Ga.: Mercer University Press, 1998), 23.

21. Quoted in Berry Craig, *Kentucky Confederates: Secession, Civil War, and the Jackson Purchase* (Lexington: University Press of Kentucky, 2014), 180–181.

22. Quoted in Jeffry D. Wert, *The Sword of Lincoln: The Army of the Potomac* (New York: Simon & Schuster, 2005), 91.

23. The regiments were the Sixty-Fourth and Sixty-Fifth Ohio; Gerald F. Linderman, *Embattled Courage: The Experience of Combat in the American Civil War* (New York: Free Press, 1987), 115–116.

24. "In the Field Near Front Royal, June 19, 1862," in Alvin Coe Voris, *A Citizen-Soldier's Civil War: The Letters of Brevet Major General Alvin C. Voris*, ed. Jerome Mushkat (DeKalb: Northern Illinois University Press, 2002), 64–65.

25. "Dear Wife & Chirldren, Camp Kerney, October 20, 1862," in Charles W. Sherman, *Letters to Virtue: A Civil War Journey of Courage, Faith, and Love*, ed. Ann K. Gunnin (Alpharetta, Ga.: Booklogix, 2014), 107.

26. J. R. Weist, "The Medical Department in the War," in *Sketches of War History 1861–1865: Papers Read before the Ohio Commandery of the Military Order of the Loyal Legion of the United States 1886–1888*, ed. Robert Hunter (Cincinnati: Robert Clarke, 1888; repr., Wilmington, N.C.: Broadfoot, 1991), 2:90.

27. Thomas B. Van Horne, *History of the Army of the Cumberland: Its Organization, Campaigns, and Battles Written at the Request of Major-General George H. Thomas Chiefly from His Private Military Journal and Official and Other Documents Furnished by Him*, 2 vols. and atlas (Cincinnati: Robert Clarke, 1875), 2:388, 393, 404, 414, 415, 429, 431.

28. E., "Army Correspondence, Charleston, Oct. 18, 1863," *Yorkville (S.C.) Enquirer*, October 21, 1863.

29. William Pitt Chambers, *Blood and Sacrifice: The Civil War Journal of a Confederate Soldier*, ed. Richard A. Baumgartner (Huntington, W.Va.: Blue Acorn Press, 1994), 14–15.

30. "Deaths," *New South (Port Royal, S.C.)*, May 2, 1863.

31. Carlton McCarthy, *Detailed Minutiae of Soldier Life in the Army of Northern Virginia, 1861–1865* (Richmond, Va.: C. McCarthy, 1882; repr. Lincoln: University of Nebraska Press, 1993), 45–46, 121.

32. Phillip Shaw Paludan borrowed the term coined by psychologist Robert J. Lifton, in his preface to the 2004 edition of *Victims: A True Story of the Civil War* (Knoxville: University of Tennessee Press, 2004), ix.

33. Ibid., 88.

34. Brian Steel Wills, *George Henry Thomas: As True as Steel* (Lawrence: University Press of Kansas, 2012), 242; Francis F. McKinney, *Education in Violence: The Life of George H. Thomas and the History of the Army of the Cumberland* (Detroit: Wayne State University Press, 1961), 303.

35. Tracy J. Revels, *Florida's Civil War: Terrible Sacrifices* (Macon, Ga.: Mercer University Press, 2016), 136.

36. Barton A. Myers, *Rebels against the Confederacy: North Carolina's Unionists* (New York: Cambridge University Press, 2014), 112.

37. James M. McPherson, *Battle Cry of Freedom: The Civil War Era* (New York: Oxford University Press, 1988), 854.

38. Ibid., 347n8.

39. J. David Hacker, "A Census-Based Count of the Civil War Dead," *Civil War History* 57, no. 4 (December 2011): 348.

40. James M. McPherson, "Commentary on 'A Census-Based Count of the Civil War Dead,'" *Civil War History* 57, no. 4 (December 2011): 309.

41. Quoted in Samuel Eliot Morrison, *The European Discovery of America: The Northern Voyages* A.D. *500–1600* (New York: Oxford University Press, 1971), 577.

42. "Notes on the Union and Confederate Armies," in *Battles and Leaders of the Civil War*, ed. Robert Underwood Johnson and Clarence Clough Buel (New York: Thomas Yoseloff, 1956), 4:767.

43. Joseph K. Barnes, *Medical and Surgical History of the Civil War*, 12 vols. (1870; repr., Wilmington, N.C.: Broadfoot, 1990), 1:636–648, 710–718.

44. Rhonda M. Kohl, "'This Godforsaken Town': Death and Disease at Helena, Arkansas, 1862–63," *Civil War History* 50, no. 2 (June 2004): 118.

45. W. L. Gammage, *The Camp, the Bivouac and the Battle Field. Being a History of the Fourth Arkansas Regiment, From Its First Organization Down to the Present Date. "Its Campaigns and Its Battles" with an Occasional Reference to the Current Events of the Times, Including Biographical Sketches of Its Field Officers and Others of the "Old Brigade." The Whole Interspersed Here and There with Descriptions of Scenery, Incident to Camp Life, Etc.* (Selma, Ala.: Cooper & Kimball, 1864; repr., Little Rock: Arkansas Southern Press, 1958), 139, 147, 149, 150.

46. Michael A. Cavanaugh, *6th Virginia Infantry* (Lynchburg, Va.: H. E. Howard, 1988), 76.

47. Aldo S. Perry, *Civil War Courts-Martial of North Carolina Troops* (Jefferson, N.C.: McFarland, 2012), 156.

48. Earl J. Hess, *Lee's Tar Heels: The Pettigrew-Kirkland-MacRae Brigade* (Chapel Hill: University of North Carolina Press, 2002), 337.

49. Ibid., 347.

50. Terry L. Jones, *Lee's Tigers: The Louisiana Infantry in the Army of Northern Virginia* (Baton Rouge: Louisiana State University Press, 1987), 233, 235, 236–237, 238, 240, 241, 242–243, 244, 246, 249.

51. "Appendix G Other Deaths," in Raymond J. Herek, *These Men Have Seen Hard Service: The First Michigan Sharpshooters in the Civil War* (Detroit: Wayne State University Press, 1998), 420. See also "Appendix E Sharpshooters Who Died as Prisoners of War," and "Appendix F Sharpshooters Who Died of Disease," in ibid., 413–419.

52. John L. Herberich, *Masters of the Field: The Fourth United States Cavalry in the Civil War* (Atglen, Pa.: Schiffer, 2015), 253.

53. William F. Fox, *Regimental Losses in the American Civil War, 1861–1865: A Treatise on the Extent and Nature of the Mortuary Losses in the Union Regiments, with Full and Exhaustive Statistics Compiled from the Official Records on File in the State Military Bureaus and at Washington* (Albany, N.Y.: Albany Publishing, 1889; repr., Dayton, Ohio: Press of Morningside Bookshop, 1974), 529.

54. Joseph T. Glatthaar, "The Costliness of Discrimination: Medical Care for Black Troops in the Civil War," in *Inside the Confederate Nation: Essays in Honor of Emory M. Thomas*, ed. Lesley J. Gordon and John C. Inscoe (Baton Rouge: Louisiana State University Press, 2005), 262, 264.

55. The listing includes other categories as well. Fox, *Regimental Losses in the American Civil War*, 50. Fox also broke the numbers down by regiments and states. See "Table B. Total Deaths from Disease, Accidents, and Other Causes," in ibid., 528–529.

56. Ibid., 530; "Table C. Classification of Deaths from Minor Causes," in ibid., 530–531.

57. Others perished from collateral circumstances in combat that included scalding (342) and drowning (308) during hostile actions, "Casualties in the Navy," in ibid., 537.

58. Ibid., 59–63.

59. Drew Gilpin Faust, *This Republic of Suffering: Death and the American Civil War* (New York: Knopf, 2008), xi.

60. Ibid., 261.

61. *Lincoln's White House Secretary: The Adventurous Life of William O. Stoddard*, ed. Harold Holzer (Carbondale: Southern Illinois University Press, 2007), 231.

62. Reid Mitchell, *The Vacant Chair: The Northern Soldier Leaves Home* (New York: Oxford University Press, 1993), 142–143.

63. W. H. Chamberlain, "The Skirmish Line in the Atlanta Campaign," in *The Atlanta Papers*, ed. Sydney C. Kerksis (Dayton, Ohio: Press of Morningside Bookshop, 1980), 183.

64. Reub Williams, *General Reub Williams's Memories of Civil War Times: Personal Reminiscences of Happenings That Took Place from 1861 to the Grand Review*, ed. Sally Coplen Hogan (Westminster, Md.: Heritage Books, 2006), 265.

65. Quoted from *Corning Journal (Corning, N.Y.)*, May 30, 1861, in Colby, *The Civil War Papers of Lt. Colonel Newton T. Colby*, 15.

Chapter 1. The First Fatalities

1. His remains were interred in Linwood Cemetery, in Columbus, Georgia. "Death of Rev. N. L. DeVotie," *Keowee Courier (Pickens Court House, S.C.)*, March 2, 1861.

2. Lonnie R. Speer, *Portals to Hell: Military Prisons of the Civil War* (Mechanicsburg, Pa.: Stackpole Books, 1997), 4.

3. W. A. Swanberg, *First Blood: The Story of Fort Sumter* (New York: Charles Scribner's Sons, 1957), 328.

4. Scott Sumpter Sheads and Daniel Carroll Toomey, *Baltimore during the Civil War* (Linthicum, Md.: Toomey Press, 1997), 16.

5. McPherson, *Battle Cry of Freedom*, 285.

6. Lyon Report, Saint Louis Arsenal, May 11, 1861, in U.S. Department of War, *War of the Rebellion: A Compilation of the Official Records of the Union and Confederate Armies* (Washington, D.C.: Government Printing Office, 1880–1901), Series I, 3:5 (hereafter cited as *OR*; all references are to Series I unless otherwise noted); Frost Protest, Saint Louis Arsenal, May 11, 1861, ibid., 7; William C. Winter, *The Civil War in St. Louis: A Guided Tour* (St. Louis: Missouri Historical Society Press, 1994), 34–53, 63–67; J. Thomas Scharf, *History of St. Louis City and County, from the Earliest Periods to the Present Day: Including Biographical Sketches of Representative Men* (Philadelphia: Louis H. Everts, 1883), 1:497–500, 507–508.

7. Lyon Report, Saint Louis Arsenal, May 12, 1861, *OR*, 3:9; Winter, *The Civil War in St. Louis*, 34, 52–53, 63–67.

8. Christopher Phillips, *Damned Yankee: The Life of General Nathaniel Lyon* (Columbia: University of Missouri Press, 1990), 194.

9. Winter, *The Civil War in St. Louis*, 69–70, 164, note 27; Scharf, *History of St. Louis City and County*, 1:522–524.

10. Margaret Leech, *Reveille in Washington 1860–1865* (New York: Harper & Brothers, 1941), 81–82.

11. Abraham Lincoln, "To the Father and Mother of Col. Elmer E. Ellsworth, Washington D.C. May 25, 1861, in Abraham Lincoln, *The Collected Works of Abraham Lincoln*, ed. Roy P. Basler (New Brunswick, N.J.: Rutgers University Press, 1953), 4:385–386.

12. Leech, *Reveille in Washington*, 164.

13. "Dear Father, July 18, 1861," in Colby, *The Civil War Papers of Lt. Colonel Newton T. Colby*, 28–29.

14. Quoted in Charles Carleton Coffin, *Four Years of Fighting: A Volume of Personal Observations with the Army and Navy, from First Battle of Bull Run to the Fall of Richmond* (Boston: Ticknor and Fields, 1866), 31.

15. "The First Martyr Hero," *Richmond Daily Dispatch*, May 27, 1861.

16. May 5, Sunday [1861], in Charles B. Haydon, *For Country, Cause and Leader: The Civil War Journal of Charles B. Haydon*, ed. Stephen W. Sears (New York: Ticknor & Fields, 1993), 4.

17. "Fatal Accident," *Richmond Daily Dispatch*, April 22, 1861.

18. "Powder," Norfolk, May 14, 1861, *Richmond Daily Dispatch*, May 16, 1861.

19. "A Sad Accident," *Western Democrat* (Charlotte, N.C.), May 21, 1861.

20. "Fatal Accident at the Camp of the Seventh Regiment," *National Republican* (Washington, D.C.), May 10, 1861.

21. "Fatal Accident at Camp Curtin," *Richmond Daily Dispatch*, May 20, 1861.

22. Albert O. Marshall, *Army Life. From a Soldier's Journal. Incidents, Sketches and Record of a Union Soldier's Army Life, in Camp and Field. 1861–64*, ed. Robert G. Schulz (Fayetteville: University of Arkansas Press, 2009), 20–21.

23. Richard B. McCaslin, *Tainted Breeze: The Great Hanging at Gainesville, Texas 1862* (Baton Rouge: Louisiana State University Press, 1994), 52.

24. "Collision of Railroad Cars—Men Killed and Wounded," *Richmond Daily Dispatch*, May 27, 1861.

25. "Railroad Collision—Two Volunteers Killed and Several Wounded," *Richmond Enquirer*, May 28, 1861.

26. "Casualty," *Richmond Daily Dispatch*, May 27, 1861.

27. "Dead," *Evening Star (Washington, D.C.)*, June 3, 1861.

28. "Letter from Fort Pickens," *Bradford Reporter (Towanda, Pa.)*, July 25, 1861.

29. Van Horne, *History of the Army of the Cumberland*, 2:625.

30. "On Board Steamer 'Marion,' on the Atlantic, June 6th, 1861," in Charles F. Johnson, *The Long Roll: Being a Journal of the Civil War, as Set Down during the Years 1861–1865 by Charles F. Johnson, Sometime of Hawkins Zouaves* (East Aurora, N.Y.: Roycrofters, 1911; repr., Shepherdstown, W.Va.: Carabelle Books, 1986), 16.

31. "July 19th," in Lucius W. Barber, *Army Memoirs of Lucius W. Barber, Company "D," 15th Illinois Volunteer Infantry, May 24, 1861, to Sept. 30, 1865* (Chicago: J. M. W. Jones Stationery and Printing, 1894), 19.

32. "Coroner's Inquest," *Cincinnati Daily Press*, June 4, 1861.

33. "National Theater," *Cincinnati Daily Press*, June 4, 1861.

34. Robert J. Driver Jr., *5th Virginia Cavalry* (Lynchburg, Va.: H. E. Howard, 1997), 1.

35. Jones, *Lee's Tigers*, 15–16.

36. Ibid., 17–18.

37. Webb Garrison, *Friendly Fire in the Civil War: More Than 100 True Stories of Comrade Killing Comrade* (Nashville: Rutledge Hill Press, 1999), 8.

38. Craig L. Symonds, "Land Operations in Virginia," in *Virginia at War, 1861*, ed. William C. Davis and James I. Robertson Jr. (Lexington: University Press of Kentucky, 2005), 32.

39. Pierce Report, Camp Hamilton, June 12, 1861, OR, 2:84.

40. Butler Report, Fortress Monroe, June 10, 1861, ibid., 79.

41. Butler Report, Fortress Monroe, June 16, 1861, ibid., 80.

42. "Father, Montery [Monterey], Highland Co. Va., July 15, 1861," in Irby Goodwin Scott, *Lee and Jackson's Bloody Twelfth: The Letters of Irby Goodwin Scott, First Lieutenant, Company G, Putnam Light Infantry, Twelfth Georgia Volunteer Infantry*, ed. Johnnie Perry Pearson (Knoxville: University of Tennessee Press, 2010), 10.

43. "Railroad Disaster," *Holmes County Farmer (Millersburg, Ohio)*, June 6, 1861.

44. "Fatal Accident," *Richmond Daily Dispatch*, June 8, 1861.

45. "Painful and Fatal Accident," *Richmond Daily Dispatch*, June 12, 1861.

46. "My Dear Mother, Dove Hole, Jeff Davis Rifles Camp Magnolia, Florida June 14th 1861," in William Cowper Nelson, *The Hour of Our Nation's Agony: The Civil War Letters of Lt. William Cowper Nelson of Mississippi*, ed. Jennifer W. Ford (Knoxville: University of Tennessee Press, 2007), 49, 261.

47. "Soldier Drowned," *Cincinnati Daily Press*, June 17, 1861.

48. Philip Corell, ed., *History of the Naval Brigade 99th N.Y. Volunteers Union Coast Guard, 1861–1865* (New York: Regimental Veterans Association, 1905).

49. "Fatal Accident," *New York Herald*, June 22, 1861.

50. "Sad and Fatal Accident," *Richmond Daily Dispatch*, June 29, 1861.

51. "Fatal Accident," *National Republican (Washington, D.C.)*, July 13, 1861.

52. Van Horne, *History of the Army of the Cumberland*, 2:387.

53. "Affairs at Martinsburg, Va.," *Richmond Daily Dispatch*, July 18, 1861.

54. Joseph Hopkins Twichell, *The Civil War Letters of Joseph Hopkins Twichell: A Chaplain's Story* (Athens: University of Georgia Press, 2006), 41.

55. Richard Eddy, *History of the Sixtieth Regiment of New York Volunteers, from the Commencement of Its Organization in July 1861 to Its Public Reception at Ogdensburgh as a Veteran Command, January 7th 1864* (Philadelphia: By the author, 1864; repr., Bedford, Mass.: Applewood Books), 57–60.

56. "Murder of a Soldier in Memphis, Tn.," *Richmond Daily Dispatch*, July 5, 1861.

57. Marshall, *Army Life*, 22.

58. Edward G. Longacre, *The Early Morning of War Bull Run, 1861* (Norman: University of Oklahoma Press, 2014), 325. See also William C. Davis, *Battle at Bull Run: A History of the First Major Campaign of the Civil War* (Garden City, N.Y.: Doubleday, 1977).

59. Franklin Report, Department Northeastern Virginia, July 28, 1861, OR, 2:406.

60. Sherman Report, Fort Corcoran, July 25, 1861, ibid., 369–370.

61. Davis, *Battle at Bull Run*, 204–205.

62. Edward Porter Alexander, *Fighting for the Confederacy: The Personal Recollections of General Edward Porter Alexander*, ed. Gary W. Gallagher (Chapel Hill: University of North Carolina Press, 1989), 57.

63. James I. Robertson Jr., *The Untold Civil War: Exploring the Human Side of the Civil War*, ed. Neil Kagan (Washington, D.C.: National Geographic, 2011), 36.

64. Robert K. Krick, *Civil War Weather in Virginia* (Tuscaloosa: University of Alabama Press, 2007), 29.

65. Marshall, *Army Life*, 24.

66. "July 18," in Judith Brockenbrough McGuire, *Diary of a Southern Refugee during the War, Annotated Edition*, ed. James I. Robertson Jr. (Lexington: University Press of Kentucky, 2014), 28.

67. "Explosion in the Navy Yard—Two Men Killed," *National Republican (Washington, D.C.)*, July 29, 1861. The *Evening Star* described Brown as "burnt to a crisp" by the explosion. "Terrible Explosion at the Navy Yard—Two Men Killed and two Wounded," *Evening Star (Washington, D.C.)*, July 29, 1861.

68. Winkle, *Lincoln's Citadel*, 167–168.

69. "June 25th," in John Beauchamp Jones, *A Rebel War Clerk's Diary at the Confederate States Capital*, ed. Earl Schenck Miers (New York: A. S. Barnes, 1961), 40.

Chapter 2. The Battle in Camp

1. Wiley, *Life of Johnny Reb*, 244.

2. Sword, *Courage under Fire*, 141.

3. "[May] 2d [1862]," in Dolly Lunt Burge, *The Diary of Dolly Lunt Burge 1848–1879*, ed. Christine Jacobson Carter (Athens: University of Georgia Press, 1997), 127.

4. *Lincoln's White House Secretary*, 279–280.

5. "Dear Brother and Sister, Camp Winder Richmond, Oct 14, 1861," in *The Confederacy Is on Her Way Up the Spout: Letters to South Carolina, 1861–1864*, ed. J. Roderick Heller III and Carolynn Ayres Heller (Athens: University of Georgia Press, 1992), 27–28.

6. Craig, *Kentucky Confederates*, 179.

7. Tho. E. Bramlette to General George H. Thomas, Columbia, Ky., December 23, 1861, *OR*, 7:513.

8. Quoted in Kerry A. Trask, *Fire Within: A Civil War Narrative from Wisconsin* (Kent, Ohio: Kent State University Press, 1995), 88–89.

9. Quoted in Wiley Sword, *Southern Invincibility: A History of the Confederate Heart* (New York: St. Martin's Press, 1999), 90.

10. Quoted in Rable, *Fredericksburg! Fredericksburg!*, 358.

11. "Dear Brother, Camp Banks Harpers Ferry, Thursday Aug 8," in Ambrose Henry Hayward, *Last to Leave the Field: The Life and Letters of First Sergeant Ambrose Henry Hayward, 28th Pennsylvania Volunteer Infantry*, ed. Timothy J. Orr (Knoxville: University of Tennessee Press, 2010), 31, 250n35.

12. John Gregg to W. W. Mackall, Hopkinsville, Ky., November 7, 1861, *OR*, 4:525.

13. Quoted in Peter Cozzens, *Shenandoah 1862: Stonewall Jackson's Valley Campaign* (Chapel Hill: University of North Carolina Press, 2008), 90.

14. Quoted in ibid., 95.

15. Quoted in Rable, *Fredericksburg! Fredericksburg!*, 357.

16. Quoted in Aaron Sheehan-Dean, *Why Confederates Fought: Family and Nation in Civil War Virginia* (Chapel Hill: University of North Carolina Press, 2007), 43.

17. "Dear Sister, Camp Caldwell Washington D.C. August 19th 1861," in *Dear Sister: The Civil War Letters of the Brothers Gould*, ed. Robert F. Harris and John Niflot (Westport, Conn.: Praeger, 1998), 4.

18. "Dear Sister, HEADQUARTERS Washington REGT., 3rd CAMP Caldwell Co. I Washington D.C. Sep 9th 1861," in ibid., 5, 7.

19. "Dear Sister Washington D.C. Oct 11th 1861," in ibid., 8.

20. "Dear wife November 8th Headquarters 4th Reg't. Co. I Camp Grifin 1861," in *A War of the People: Vermont Civil War Letters*, ed. Jeffrey D. Marshall (Hanover, N.H.: University Press of New England, 1999), 50.

21. "Dear Mother Camp Griffin Nov 11th [1861]," in ibid., 51.

22. "Dear Sister, Camp Wool MD Feb 7th 1862," in ibid., 13.

23. "Dear Madam," Lower Potomac Camp Wool February 26th 1862," in ibid., 14.

24. Linderman, *Embattled Courage*, 235.

25. Marshall, *Army Life*, 45.

26. "September 25, Wednesday"; "September 27, Friday"; "October 3, Thursday"; and "October 4, Friday," in *Voices from Company D: Diaries of the Greensboro Guards, Fifth Alabama Infantry Regiment, Army of Northern Virginia*, ed. G. Ward Hubbs (Athens: University of Georgia Press, 2003), 52.

27. "Wednesday Feby 19th, 1862," in Edward O. Guerrant, *Bluegrass Confederate: The Headquarters Diary of Edward O. Guerrant*, ed. William C. Davis and Meredith L. Sentor (Baton Rouge: Louisiana State University Press, 1999), 34. Guerrant referred to Gladeville, modern-day Wise, in the plural.

28. "Dear Molly, Camp near Richmond, Virginia, August 5, 1862," in *The Stilwell Letters: A Georgian in Longstreet's Corps, Army of Northern Virginia*, ed. Ronald H. Moseley (Macon, Ga.: Mercer University Press, 2002), 27.

29. "August 31st," in Chambers, *Blood and Sacrifice*, 38.

30. Samuel Summer Jr. to "Dear Parents Camp Griffin Nov 12 1861," in ibid., 53.

31. "My Dear Father, Corinth, June 20th, 1862," in Thomas Christie and William Christie, *Brother of Mine: The Civil War Letters of Thomas and William Christie*, ed. Hampton Smith (St. Paul: Minnesota Historical Society Press, 2011), 53–54.

32. "James J. Phillips, Jr., Camp Fisher, Va., Dec. 3 1861," in James J. Phillips Papers, Private Collections, North Carolina State Archives, Division of Archives and History, Raleigh.

33. "Absent sister Camp Griffin Va Dec the 22 1861," in ibid., 56.

34. December 1, 1861, in Haydon, *For Country, Cause and Leader*, 138–139.

35. Quoted in Sheehan-Dean, *Why Confederates Fought*, 104.

36. Quoted in Sword, *Southern Invincibility*, 97.

37. "Friday 28," in Sam Richards, *Sam Richards's Civil War Diary: A Chronicle of the Atlanta Home Front*, ed. Wendy Hamand Venet (Athens: University of Georgia Press, 2009), 93–94.

38. Leech, *Reveille in Washington*, 207, 232.

39. *American Citizen (Canton, Miss.)*, May 16, 1862.

40. "My dear Ellen, Camp Advance, Mechanicsville, Va., June 16th 1862," in Robert McAllister, *The Civil War Letters of General Robert McAllister*, ed. James I. Robertson Jr. (New Brunswick, N.J.: Rutgers University Press, 1965), 176.

41. "Dear Wife and Chirldren, New Orleans, June 14, 1862," in Sherman, *Letters to Virtue*, 42.

42. "James J. Phillips, Camp near Yorktown, April 26th 1862," and "Dr. James J. Phillips, Camp near Richmond, May 20, 1862," in James J. Phillips Papers.

43. Quoted in *Weep Not for Me Dear Mother*, ed. Elizabeth Whitley Roberson (Gretna, La.: Pelican Publishing, 1996), 41–42.

44. Ibid., 68.

45. "July 20 Sun. and July 22 Tues." in ibid., 131–132.

46. "Dear Brother, Camp near Harrisons Springs Va. July 30th 1862," in Henry C. Lyon, *"Desolating This Fair Country": The Civil War Diary and Letters of Lt. Henry C. Lyon, 34th New York*, ed. Emily N. Radigan (Jefferson, N.C.: McFarland, 1999), 135.

47. Hess, *Lee's Tar Heels*, 348.

48. Quoted in David Silkenat, *Moments of Despair: Suicide, Divorce, and Debt in the Civil War Era* (Chapel Hill: University of North Carolina Press, 2011), 8.

49. Rice C. Bull, *Soldiering: The Civil War Diary of Rice C. Bull, 123rd New York Volunteer Infantry*, ed. K. Jack Bauer (Novato, Calif.: Presidio Press, 1977), 24.

50. "My dear Wife, Camp in field near Stafford Court House November 20, 1862," in Daniel M. Holt, *A Surgeon's Civil War: The Letters and Diary of Daniel M. Holt, M.D.*, ed. James M. Grenier, Janet L. Coryell, and James R. Smither (Kent, Ohio: Kent State University Press, 1994), 50.

51. Quoted in Rable, *Fredericksburg! Fredericksburg!*, 14.

52. Ibid., 358.

53. "My dear Wife, Camp in field near Fredericksburg, Va. January 6th 1863," in Holt, *A Surgeon's Civil War*, 63.

54. "Wednesday 21st Jan '63," and "Friday 23d January 1863," in Guerrant, *Bluegrass Confederate*, 205, 207.

55. John D. Chapla, *50th Virginia Infantry* (Lynchburg, Va.: H. E. Howard, 1997), 155.

56. *Alexandria (Va.) Gazette*, September 11, 1863.

57. Quoted in Kohl, "'This Godforsaken Town,'" 117. Kohl found substantial rates of mortality by disease while posted in the town for the 1st Arkansas Battalion Infantry, 99

out of 145; 5th Illinois Cavalry, 76/380; 5th Kansas Cavalry, 76/221; 2nd Wisconsin Cavalry, 75/284; and 47th Indiana Infantry, 56/254; ibid.

58. Quoted in Wiley, *Life of Billy Yank,* 124.

59. "Captain V. G. McDaniel," *Weekly Register (Point Pleasant, W.Va.),* October 1, 1863.

60. John R. Lundberg, *Granbury's Texas Brigade: Diehard Western Confederates* (Baton Rouge: Louisiana State University Press, 2012), 19–20, 51.

61. Ezra J. Warner, *Generals in Blue: Lives of the Union Commanders* (Baton Rouge: Louisiana State University Press, 1964), 275.

62. Ezra J. Warner, *Generals in Gray: Lives of the Confederate Commanders* (Baton Rouge: Louisiana State University Press, 1959), 30; Michael B. Ballard, *Vicksburg: The Campaign That Opened the Mississippi* (Chapel Hill: University of North Carolina Press, 2004), 426.

63. Warner, *Generals in Blue,* 52–53. Buford received his commission as major general of volunteers as he lay dying; ibid.

64. Ibid., 570–571.

65. Ibid., 34–35.

66. Ibid., 389–390.

67. M. E. Goddard and Henry V. Partridge, *A History of Norwich, Vermont, with Portraits and Illustrations* (Hanover, N.H.: Dartmouth Press, 1905), 242–243.

68. "My Dear Father, Atlanta, Nov. 5, 1864, in Christie and Christie, *Brother of Mine,* 273.

69. "Friend Pratt, Head Quarters 23 Reg't N.Y.V., Camp McDowell, Jan. 6, 1862," in Colby, *The Civil War Papers of Lt. Colonel Newton T. Colby,* 90.

70. Fox, *Regimental Losses in the American Civil War,* 61.

71. William J. Miller, *The Training of an Army: Camp Curtain and the North's Civil War* (Shippensburg, Pa.: White Mane Publishing, 1990), 108.

72. William Fox listed Long as dying on April 18, 1862; Fox, *Regimental Losses in the American Civil War,* 61.

73. Corell, *History of the Naval Brigade.*

74. William J. K. Beaudot, *The 24th Wisconsin Infantry in the Civil War: The Biography of a Regiment* (Mechanicsburg, Pa.: Stackpole Books, 2003), 67.

75. Diane Miller Sommerville, "'A Burden Too Heavy to Bear': War Trauma, Suicide, and Confederate Soldiers," *Civil War History* 59, no. 4 (December 2013): 491.

76. Hess offered two examples of unnamed individuals who perished by their own hands at Antietam and Fredericksburg; Earl J. Hess, *The Union Soldier in Battle: Enduring the Ordeal of Combat* (Lawrence: University Press of Kansas, 1997), 90–91.

77. See Sommerville, "'A Burden Too Heavy to Bear,'" 453–491.

78. Warner, *Generals in Gray,* 57; Derek Smith, *The Gallant Dead: Union and Confederate Generals Killed in the Civil War* (Mechanicsburg, Pa.: Stackpole Books, 2005), 367.

79. "Dear Pa, Richmond, Va. December 27, 1861," in Greenlee Davidson, *Captain Greenlee Davidson, C.S.A. Diary and Letters 1851–1863,* ed. Charles W. Turner (Verona, Va.: McClure Press, 1975), 33.

80. Cavanaugh, *6th Virginia Infantry,* 127.

81. Corell, *History of the Naval Brigade.*

82. H. O. Harden, *History of the 90th Ohio Volunteer Infantry in the War of the Great Rebellion in the United States, 1861 to 1865,* ed. Scott Cameron (Kent, Ohio: Kent State University Press, 2006), 83.

83. Quoted in Kenneth W. Noe, *Reluctant Rebels: The Confederates Who Joined the Army after 1861* (Chapel Hill: University of North Carolina Press, 2010), 175.

84. Van Horne, *History of the Army of the Cumberland*, 2:387.

85. Rufus Kinsley, *Diary of a Christian Soldier: Rufus Kinsley and the Civil War*, ed. David C. Rankin (New York: Cambridge University Press, 2004), 90.

86. Williams, *General Reub Williams's Memories of Civil War Times*, 199–200.

87. "Sam to Andrew, LaGrange, Tenn./Feb. 21, 1863," in *Their Patriotic Duty: The Civil War Letters of the Evans Family of Brown County, Ohio*, ed. Robert F. Engs and Corey M. Brooks, transcriptions by Joseph Shelton Evans Jr. (New York: Fordham University Press, 2007), 107.

88. Quoted in Gordon, *A Broken Regiment*, 22.

89. "Suicide," *Camden (S.C.) Confederate*, June 5, 1863.

90. December 1, 1861, in Haydon, *For Country, Cause and Leader*, 140.

91. Warner, *Generals in Blue*, 362–363.

92. *Hillsdale (Mich.) Standard*, December 2, 1862.

93. "My dear Ellen, Wolf's Shoals Ford, Va., November 22nd 1862," in McAllister, *The Civil War Letters of General Robert McAllister*, 225. A second letter to "My dear daughter Henrietta, Wolf's Shoals Ford, Va., November 23rd 1862," repeated the explanation that Patterson "shot himself," without elaboration; in ibid.

94. "Bro Chas, Camp Near Woodstock V.A., April 5th 1862," in *A War of the People*, 73–74.

95. William D. Henderson, *41st Virginia Infantry* (Lynchburg, Va.: H. E. Howard, 1986), 94.

96. "Sunday 17h. Augst. 1862," in Guerrant, *Bluegrass Confederate*, 131.

97. Quoted in Herek, *These Men Have Seen Hard Service*, 75.

98. Halbert Eleazer Paine, *A Wisconsin Yankee in Confederate Bayou Country: The Civil War Reminiscences of a Union General Halbert Eleazer Paine*, ed. Samuel C. Hyde Jr. (Baton Rouge: Louisiana State University Press, 2009), 128.

99. "Dear Wife & Children & Parents, Berwick Bay, August 19, 1863," in Sherman, *Letters to Virtue*, 251.

100. "Dear Wife & Children, Brashear City, Berwick Bay, La., August 29, 1863," ibid., 255.

101. *Alexandria (Va.) Gazette*, January 28, 1864.

102. Eugene A. Nash, *A History of the Forty-Fourth Regiment New York Volunteer Infantry* (Chicago: R. R. Donnelley, 1911), 466.

103. Chambers, *Blood and Sacrifice*, 122–123.

104. "A Distressing Suicide," *Soldier's Journal (Rendezvous of Distribution, Va.)*, July 13, 1864.

105. Hess, *Lee's Tar Heels*, 348.

106. "Father, Montery [Monterey], Highland Co. Va. July 15, 1861," in Scott, *Lee and Jackson's Bloody Twelfth*, 10.

107. "Deaths in the Army," *Weekly Standard (Raleigh, N.C.)*, August 14, 1861.

108. "Melancholy Accident," *Richmond Daily Dispatch*, November 2, 1861.

109. Joseph Gibbs, *Three Years in the Bloody Eleventh: The Campaigns of a Pennsylvania Reserves Regiment* (University Park: Pennsylvania State University Press, 2002), 47.

110. "Monday, Feb. 10th, 1862," in Guerrant, *Bluegrass Confederate*, 29.

111. "Sunday, March 30, 1862," in Samuel McIlvaine, *By the Dim and Flaring Lamps: The Civil War Diaries of Samuel McIlvaine*, ed. Clayton E. Cramer (Monroe, N.Y.: Library Research Associates, 1990), 84.

112. Nash, *Forty-Fourth Regiment*, 240, 410.

113. "Dear Jane, Moscow, Tennessee, June 19, 1863, June 21," in *"A Punishment on the Nation": An Iowa Soldier Endures the Civil War*, ed. Brian Craig Miller (Kent, Ohio: Kent State University Press, 2012), 73.

114. "Fatal Accident," *Nashville Daily Union*, November 27, 1863.

115. "Fatal Accident," *Civilian and Telegraph (Cumberland, Md.)*, October 17, 1861.

116. "Fatal Accident," *National Republican (Washington, D.C.)*, October 24, 1862.

117. "Fatal Accident," *Evening Star (Washington, D.C.)*, October 24, 1862.

118. Van Horne, *History of the Army of the Cumberland*, 2:412.

119. Dennis W. Belcher, *The 11th Missouri Infantry in the Civil War: A History and Roster* (Jefferson, N.C.: McFarland, 2011), 14.

120. "A Soldier Drowned," *Joliet Signal (Joliet, Ill.)*, August 6, 1861.

121. *Spirit of Democracy (Woodsfield, Ohio)*, August 7, 1861; Jere, "Army Correspondence Letter from Camp Kelly, Battery Knob, Virginia, July 31st, 1861," *Spirit of Democracy (Woodsfield, Ohio)*, August 7.

122. Jere, "Army Correspondence, Letter from Camp Kelly, Grafton, Va., Aug. 9th 1861," *Spirit of Democracy (Woodsfield, Ohio)*, August 14, 1861.

123. Chapla, *50th Virginia Infantry*, 20, 160. The author speculated that Sergeant Heninger was absent from the regiment "arresting deserters" when he became the unit's "first death"; ibid., 20.

124. Corell, *History of the Naval Brigade*.

125. Kinsley, *Diary of a Christian Soldier*, 90.

126. Corell, *History of the Naval Brigade*.

127. "August 20th," in Barber, *Army Memoirs*, 77.

128. *Richmond Daily Dispatch*, July 1, 1862. The Sixth Wisconsin was under Abner Doubleday at this point.

129. "Dear Son," in Gilbert Claflin and Esther Claflin, *A Quiet Corner of the War: The Civil War Letters of Gilbert and Esther Claflin, Oconomowoc, Wisconsin, 1862–1863*, ed. Judy Cook (Madison: University of Wisconsin Press, 2013), 141 and note 4.

130. Van Horne, *History of the Army of the Cumberland*, 2:430.

131. "Tuesday Sept 1st," in William Bluffton Miller, *Fighting for Liberty and Right: The Civil War Diary of William Bluffton Miller, First Sergeant, Company K, Seventy-Fifth Indiana Volunteer Infantry*, ed. Jeffrey L. Patrick and Robert J. Willey (Knoxville: University of Tennessee Press, 2005), 136.

132. "Brownsville Texas Feby 26th 1864 Friday," in Benjamin F. McIntyre, *Federals on the Frontier: The Diary of Benjamin F. McIntyre, 1862–1864*, ed. Nannie M. Tilley (Austin: University of Texas Press, 1963), 306.

133. Myers, *Rebels against the Confederacy*, 113.

134. John M. Gould, *History of the First-Tenth-Twenty-Ninth Maine Regiment. In Service of the United States from May 3, 1861 to June 21, 1866* (Portland, Maine: Stephen Berry, 1871), 457.

135. Douglas Hale, *The Third Texas Cavalry in the Civil War* (Norman: University of Oklahoma Press, 1993), 214.

136. Robertson, *Soldiers Blue and Gray*, 100.

137. Quoted in ibid.

138. "October 27, Sunday," and "October 28, Monday," in *Voices from Company D*, 67–68.

139. "Thurs. Jan. 16th 1862," in James C. Bates, *A Texas Cavalry Officer's Civil War: The Diary and Letters of James C. Bates*, ed. Richard Lowe (Baton Rouge: Louisiana State University Press, 1999), 69.

140. *Cleveland Morning Leader*, January 4, 1862.

141. "My dear Father, On board Transport Rockland, Off Liverpool Point. Thursday Evening. April 8th 1862," in Twichell, *The Civil War Letters of Joseph Hopkins Twichell*, 108.

142. "Suffolk, Va., October 26, 1862," in Voris, *A Citizen-Soldier's Civil War*, 85.

143. Ibid., 70.

144. Lawrence Lee Hewitt, *Port Hudson: Confederate Bastion on the Mississippi* (Baton Rouge: Louisiana State University Press, 1987), 51.

145. Walter Clark, *Histories of the Several Regiments and Battalions from North Carolina in the Great War, 1861–'65* (Raleigh: E. M. Uzell, 1901; repr., Wendell, N.C.: Broadfoot, 1982), 2:170.

146. "My dear Wife, Camp Gregg, Va., Mar. 21, 1863," in William Dorsey Pender Papers, Southern Historical Society Papers, University of North Carolina, Chapel Hill; William Dorsey Pender, *The General to His Lady: The Civil War Letters of William Dorsey Pender to Fanny Pender*, ed. William W. Hassler (Chapel Hill: University of North Carolina Press, 1965), 208–209.

147. Quoted in Robertson, *Soldiers Blue and Gray*, 100.

148. "Dear Ned, Brandy Station, Va., May 1st 1864," in Twichell, *The Civil War Letters of Joseph Hopkins Twichell*, 299.

149. Quoted in Claflin and Claflin, *A Quiet Corner of the War*, 38–39n4.

150. *Alexandria (Va.) Gazette*, January 21, 1864.

151. Sam R. Watkins, *"Co. Aytch": A Side Show of the Big Show* (New York: Collier Books, 1962), 131.

152. Christopher Losson noted the incident took place on the night of April 30, 1864; Losson, *Tennessee's Forgotten Warriors: Frank Cheatham and His Confederate Division* (Knoxville: University of Tennessee Press, 1989), 135–136.

153. Fox, *Regimental Losses in the American Civil War*, 61.

154. "Friend Pratt, Head Quarters 23 Reg't N.Y.V., Camp McDowell, Jan. 6, 1862," in Colby, *The Civil War Papers of Lt. Colonel Newton T. Colby*, 90.

155. "Friend Pratt, Camp 23rd Reg't N.Y.V. Arlington Heights, Va., Aug. 24th, 1861," in ibid., 51.

156. *American Citizen (Canton, Miss.)*, May 16, 1862.

157. Henry H. Ingalls, *The Diary of Henry H. Ingalls, Sixth Regiment of Massachusetts Volunteer Militia, Company K., Suffolk, Virginia, August 31, 1862 to May 26, 1863*, ed. Giles H. Newsome (Suffolk, Va.: Robert Hardy Publications, 1986), 6.

158. Ibid., 35.

159. Ibid., 117.

160. Hale, *The Third Texas Cavalry in the Civil War*, 76.

161. Quoted in Chapla, *50th Virginia Infantry*, 104, 168.

162. "Fatal Accident," *Richmond Daily Dispatch*, January 23, 1863.

163. Myron J. Smith Jr., *The Fight for the Yazoo, August 1862–July 1864: Swamps, Forts and Fleets on Vicksburg's Northern Flank* (Jefferson, N.C.: McFarland, 2012), 232.

164. *Maysville (Ky.) Weekly Bulletin*, July 4, 1864.

165. George Newton, "Atlanta Paper No. 15 Battle of Peach Tree Creek," in *The Atlanta Papers*, ed. Sydney C. Kerksis (Dayton: Ohio: Press of Morningside Bookshop, 1980), 396–397; Valentine C. Randolph, *A Soldier's Diary: Valentine C. Randolph, 39th Illinois Regiment*, ed. David D. Roe (DeKalb: Northern Illinois University Press, 2006).

166. "Dear Folks at Home, In Camp, Saturday night. Oct. 26th 1861," in Twichell, *The Civil War Letters of Joseph Hopkins Twichell*, 76.

167. "Dear Amanda Hd. Qrs. 45th Ga. Near Petersburg, Va. Oct. 16th, 1864," in Fitzpatrick, *Letters to Amanda*, 178.

168. Francis A. Walker, *History of the Second Army Corps in the Army of the Potomac* (New York: Charles Scribner's Sons, 1886), 501.

169. William Henry King, *No Pardons to Ask, nor Apologies to Make: The Journal of William Henry King, Gray's 28th Louisiana Infantry Regiment*, ed. Gary D. Joiner, Marilyn S. Joyner, and Clifton D. Cardin (Knoxville: University of Tennessee Press, 2006), 72.

170. Ibid., 87.

Chapter 3. "The Rhythm of the Rails"

1. Gibbs, *Three Years in the Bloody Eleventh*, 46.

2. "Fatal Accident," *Richmond Daily Dispatch*, December 24, 1861.

3. Jones, *Lee's Tigers*, 15–16.

4. "Mrs. D. Callaway, Montgomery, Ala Wednesday morning Aug 6th 1862," in Joshua K. Callaway, *The Civil War Letters of Joshua K. Callaway*, ed. Judith Lee Hallock (Athens: University of Georgia Press, 1997), 47.

5. Quoted in John E. Clark Jr., *Railroads in the Civil War: The Impact of Management on Victory and Defeat* (Baton Rouge: Louisiana State University Press, 2001), 168–169.

6. C. Schurz to E. M. Stanton, Bridgeport, Ala., October 1, 1863, OR, 29, 1:181–182.

7. Joseph Hooker indorsement, October 8, 1863, ibid., 182–183.

8. "Fatal Accident," *Richmond Daily Dispatch*, January 29, 1864.

9. "Fatal Accident," *Evening Star (Washington, D.C.)*, February 5, 1864.

10. Fox, *Regimental Losses in the American Civil War*, 61.

11. Donald A. Clark, *The Notorious "Bull" Nelson: Murdered Civil War General* (Carbondale: Southern Illinois University Press, 2011), 121.

12. "Fatal Accident," *National Republican (Washington, D.C.)*, December 3, 1861.

13. "Death of a Soldier," *Daily Intelligencer (Wheeling, Va.)*, February 26, 1862.

14. John E. Divine, *8th Virginia Infantry* (Lynchburg, Va.: H. E. Howard, 1984), 18, 77.

15. "Fatal Accident," *Staunton (Va.) Spectator*, December 10, 1861; "Fatal Accident," *Richmond Daily Dispatch*, December 12, 1861.

16. "A Soldier Killed," *Daily Intelligencer (Wheeling, Va.)*, August 18, 1863.

17. "Fatal Accident," *Evening Star (Washington, D.C.)*, August 27, 1863.

18. "Benton Barracks, Mo., April 11th, 1864," in Stephen F. Flerharty, *"Jottings from Dixie": The Civil War Dispatches of Sergeant Major Stephen F. Flerharty, U.S.A.*, ed. Philip J. Reyburn and Terry L. Wilson (Baton Rouge: Louisiana State University Press, 1999), 181.

19. "Fatal Accident—A Soldier Run Over by a Train and Horribly Mangled," *Daily Ohio Statesman (Columbus)*, May 12, 1864.

20. Van Horne, *History of the Army of the Cumberland*, 2:391, 412, 414, 419, 428.

21. "Fatal Accident—Death of Major Whitehead," *Evansville (Ind.) Daily Journal*, November 13, 1863.

22. "Dear Father, Camp of the 28th Regt. Duck River Bridge Tenn Oct 12," in Hayward, *Last to Leave the Field*, 184–185.

23. "Dear Brother, Camp of the 28th Regt. Duck River Oct 14th," in ibid., 188.

24. "Fatal Accident," *Richmond Daily Dispatch*, November 27, 1863.

25. Leander Stillwell, *The Story of a Common Soldier of Army Life in the Civil War 1861–1865* (Erie, Kans.: Franklin Hudson Publishing, 1920), 107–108.

26. "Three Tuscarawas Soldiers Killed," *Ohio Democrat (Canal Dover, Ohio)*, August 14, 1863.

27. Glenna R. Schroeder-Lein, *Confederate Hospitals on the Move: Samuel L. Stout and the Army of Tennessee* (Columbia: University of South Carolina Press, 1994), 128.

28. Historian Robert Black noted that in 1860, the number of deaths dropped to 57 from the previous year's tally of 129, as rail authorities focused on safety measures; Robert C. Black III, *The Railroads of the Confederacy* (Chapel Hill: University of North Carolina Press, 1952), 32–35.

29. Kinsley, *Diary of a Christian Soldier*, 113.

30. "Camp Thibodaux, November 8, 1862," in Sherman, *Letters to Virtue*, 121.

31. Eddy, *History of the Sixtieth Regiment of New York Volunteers*, 63–64.

32. *Daily Green Mountain Freeman (Montpelier, Vt.)*, June 8, 1863.

33. *Daily Green Mountain Freeman (Montpelier, Vt.)*, June 9, 1863.

34. "Mr. James C. Fitzpatrick's Letter, Lexington, Ky., June 7, 1863," in "Interesting from Kentucky, Details of the Explosion of the Locomotive at Nicholasville—Narrow Escape of Our Correspondent—Several Lives Lost, etc., etc.," *New York Herald*, June 12, 1863.

35. "The Locomotive Explosion," *Richmond Daily Dispatch*, July 8, 1863. See also "Explosion and Loss of Life," *Abingdon Virginian*, July 17, 1863.

36. "Deaths by Railroad Accidents," *Cleveland Morning Leader*, March 16, 1863.

37. "Fatal Accident on the Virginia and Tennessee Railroad," *Richmond Daily Dispatch*, August 15, 1861.

38. "Another Railroad Disaster," *Cleveland Morning Leader*, September 19, 1861.

39. "Terrible Railroad Accident," *Cass County Republican (Dowagiac, Mich.)*, September 26, 1861.

40. "Train on the Hudson River Railroad Thrown into the Water," *National Republican (Washington, D.C.)*, March 18, 1862.

41. Chambers, *Blood and Sacrifice*, 21.

42. "Fatal Railroad Accident," *Camden (S.C.) Confederate*, May 2, 1862.

43. Larry J. Daniel, *Soldiering in the Army of Tennessee: A Portrait of Life in a Confederate Army* (Chapel Hill: University of North Carolina Press, 1991), 28.

44. "Friday 15h. Aug'st. 1862," in Guerrant, *Bluegrass Confederate*, 129.

45. Kinsley, *Diary of a Christian Soldier*, 107.

46. *Cleveland Morning Leader*, September 10, 1862.

47. Stillwell, *The Story of a Common Soldier*, 105–106.

48. "Distressing Railroad Accident," *Staunton (Va.) Spectator*, October 21, 1862.

49. "Terrible Railroad Accident," *Abingdon Virginian*, February 27, 1863.

50. S. G. Spann, "Chocktaw Indians as Confederate Soldiers," *Confederate Veteran* 13, no. 12 (December 1905): 560–561.

51. "H. W. Frillman, Three Miles from Lavergne, Tenn., Mar. 7, '63," *Nashville Daily Union*, March 10, 1863.

52. "The Late Terrible Accident on the Southern Railroad," *Staunton (Va.) Spectator*, March 10, 1863.

53. George B. Abdill, *Civil War Railroads* (Seattle, Wash.: Superior Publishing, 1961), 83.

54. "Dear Brother Wilbur, Dismounted Camp Md. Oct. 26, 1863," in *A War of the People*, 192–193.

55. "A Terrible Railroad Disaster," *Holmes County Farmer (Millersburg, Ohio)*, November 5, 1863.

56. Daniel, *Soldiering in the Army of Tennessee*, 71–72.

57. Ibid., 66.

58. "Another Railroad Accident," *Daily Ohio Statesman (Columbus)*, January 16, 1864.

59. "Local Correspondence. Chapter of Accidents . . . Johnstown, Jan. 17, 1864," *Alleghanian (Ebensburg, Pa.)*, January 21, 1864.

60. "Great Railroad Disaster," *Sun (New York)*, October 17, 1864.

61. Quoted in Ira Spar, *New Haven's Civil War Hospital: A History of Knight U.S. General Hospital, 1862–1865* (Jefferson, N.C.: McFarlane, 2014), 37.

62. Emerson Opdycke, *To Battle for God and the Right: The Civil War Letterbooks of Emerson Opdycke*, ed. Glenn V. Longacre and John E. Hass (Urbana: University of Illinois Press, 2003), 282, 283.

63. Thomas Weber, *The Northern Railroads in the Civil War, 1861–1865* (Bloomington: Indiana University Press, 1999), 44.

64. Quoted in Michael K. Shaffer, *Washington County, Virginia, in the Civil War* (Charleston, S.C.: History Press, 2012), 91.

65. *Shreveport (La.) Daily News*, September 7, 1861.

66. "The Late Terrible Accident on the Virginia and Tennessee Railroad," *New Orleans Daily Crescent*, September 11, 1861.

67. Williamson was the name given for the man who intervened to prevent other lives from being lost; "The Killed and Wounded of the Late Railroad Collision," *Richmond Enquirer*, September 17, 1861.

68. "Died of His Injuries," *Richmond Enquirer*, September 20, 1861.

69. "Fatal Railroad Accident," *Lewistown (Pa.) Gazette*, September 25, 1861.

70. John B. Gordon, *Reminiscences of the Civil War* (New York: Charles Scribner's Sons, 1905), 52.

71. Mason Whiting Tyler, *Recollections of the Civil War, with Many Original Diary Entries and Letters Written from the Seat of War, and with Annotated References*, ed. William S. Tyler (New York: G. P. Putnam's Sons, 1912), 34.

72. *Newbern (N.C.) Weekly Progress*, November 8, 1862.

73. "Accident on the Raleigh and Gaston Railroad," *Newbern (N.C.) Weekly Progress*, November 8, 1862.

74. "Railroad Collision," *Daily National Republican (Washington, D.C.)*, August 9, 1864.

75. "Railroad Accident," *Western Democrat (Charlotte, N.C.)*, May 12, 1863.

76. Clark, *Railroads in the Civil War*, 114–115.

77. "Railroad Accident," *New York Herald*, March 13, 1864.

78. Alonzo L. Brown, *History of the Fourth Regiment of Minnesota Infantry Volunteers during the Great Rebellion 1861–1865* (St. Paul, Minn.: Pioneer Press, 1892), 284.

79. "Dear uncle, Near Ramsville [Georgia], September 2nd, 1864," in *The Stilwell Letters*, 280–281.

80. "My dear Molly, Wayside Home Richmond Virginia, September 6, 1864," in ibid., 281.

81. Quoted in Black, *Railroads of the Confederacy*, 253.

82. "The Late Railway Smash-Ups in the North," *Charleston (S.C.) Daily News*, September 8, 1865.

83. Robert D. Hoffsommer, "The Wreck of the Prisoners' Train," *Civil War Times Illustrated* 3, no. 2 (May 1964): 38–39; Jack Jackson, "The Great Locomotive Wreck," *Civil War Times Illustrated* 33, no. 6 (January/February): 48–53.

84. Diana S. Berger, "The Track Is Clear to Shohola: Disaster on the Road to Elmira," *Blue and Gray Magazine* 10, no. 4 (April 1993): 26.

85. Jackson, "The Great Locomotive Wreck," 51.

86. Hoffsommer, "The Wreck of the Prisoners' Train," 39.

87. Berger, "The Track Is Clear to Shohola," 26.

88. Jackson, "The Great Locomotive Wreck," 51.

89. Quoted in Berger, "The Track Is Clear to Shohola," 26–27.

90. "Terrible Collision on the Erie Railroad," *Evening Telegraph (Philadelphia)*, July 18, 1864.

91. Hoffsommer, "The Wreck of the Prisoners' Train," 39. In another twist, apparently five of the prisoners were able to make good their escape in the confusion; ibid. Diana Berger provided a list of the guards and prisoners thought to be interred in the mass grave at Elmira. See Berger, "The Track Is Clear to Shohola," 28.

92. Quoted in John K. Derden, *The World's Largest Prison: The Story of Camp Lawton* (Macon, Ga.: Mercer University Press, 2012), 72–73.

93. *Orleans Independent Standard (Irasburgh, Vt.)*, December 2, 1864.

94. William Marvel, *Andersonville: The Last Depot* (Chapel Hill: University of North Carolina Press, 1994), 202–203.

Chapter 4. Not Fooling with Mother Nature

1. Fox, *Regimental Losses in the American Civil War*, 60.

2. Kinsley, *Diary of a Christian Soldier*, 90.

3. "Ship Island, April 11, 1862," in Paine, *A Wisconsin Yankee in Confederate Bayou Country*, 29–30.

4. Nash, *A History of the Forty-Fourth Regiment New York Volunteer Infantry*, 77, 403. See also Krick, *Civil War Weather in Virginia*, 56, who confirmed Howlett's death in this manner through his service record.

5. Krick, *Civil War Weather in Virginia*, 59.

6. "Iverson L. Graves; Camp Walker, Drury's Bluff, Va., June 16, 1862," in *A Confederate*

Marine: A Sketch of Henry Lea Graves with Excerpts from the Graves Family Correspondence, 1861–1865, ed. Richard Harwell (Tuscaloosa, Ala.: Confederate Publishing, 1963), 59.

7. "Mrs. D. Callaway, Montgomery, Ala Wednesday morning Aug 6th 1862," in Callaway, *The Civil War Letters of Joshua K. Callaway,* 47.

8. Krick, *Civil War Weather in Virginia,* 69.

9. "Father & Mother, Opelousas, around April 22, 1863," in Sherman, *Letters to Virtue,* 202.

10. "Soldier Killed by Lightning," *Dayton (Ohio) Daily Empire,* July 20, 1863.

11. Frank A. Montgomery, *Reminiscences of a Mississippian in Peace and War* (Cincinnati: Robert Clarke, 1901), 131.

12. T. W. Connelly, *History of the Seventieth Ohio Regiment, from Its Organization to Its Mustering Out* (Cincinnati, Ohio: Peake Bros., 1902; repr., La Crosse, Wis.: Brookhaven Press, 2008), 88.

13. Watkins, *"Co. Aytch,"* 84.

14. Chambers, *Blood and Sacrifice,* 59.

15. "Letters from Vicksburg, Nestor, Vicksburg, March 31, 1863," *Memphis Daily Appeal,* April 1, 1863.

16. Williams, *General Reub Williams's Memories of Civil War Times,* 100–101.

17. U. G. Owen, "Letters of a Confederate Surgeon in the Army of Tennessee to His Wife," ed. Enoch L. Mitchell, *Tennessee Historical Quarterly* 5, no. 2 (June 1946): 172.

18. Hess, *Lee's Tar Heels,* 348.

19. Van Horne, *History of the Army of the Cumberland,* 2:391.

20. John L. Collins, "Sad Story of the War," *Confederate Veteran* 6, no. 3 (March 1898): 116.

21. James A. Wright, *No More Gallant a Deed: A Civil War Memoir of the First Minnesota Volunteers,* ed. Steven J. Keillor (St. Paul: Minnesota Historical Society Press, 2001).

22. Wiley, *Life of Billy Yank,* 252–253.

23. "Railroad Accident," *Evening Star (Washington, D.C.),* August 16, 1864.

24. Rice Bull admitted that he did not witness the incident but reported what he had been "told"; Bull, *Soldiering,* 75. See also Krick, *Civil War Weather in Virginia,* 95.

25. Jones, *Lee's Tigers,* 206.

26. *Lewistown (Pa.) Gazette,* August 24, 1863.

27. Edward G. Longacre, *The Sharpshooters: A History of the Ninth New Jersey in the Civil War* (Lincoln, Neb.: Potomac Books, 2017), 253.

28. "Dear Josie, Nicholas County, Va., Miller's House, 1½ Miles North of Camp Gauley, AUG. 28, 1861," in Sheffey, *Soldier of Southwestern Virginia,* 49–50. See also Chapla, *50th Virginia Infantry,* 24.

29. William Brooke Rawle, *History of the Third Pennsylvania Cavalry, Sixtieth Regiment Pennsylvania Volunteers in the American Civil War 1861–1865* (Philadelphia: Franklin Printing, 1905), 10.

30. Robert Cowdin Report, Lower Marlborough, Md., September 12, 1861, OR, 5:597.

31. Marshall, *Army Life,* 240.

32. "Sad Disaster," *Sun (New York),* April 18, 1862.

33. Fox, *Regimental Losses in the American Civil War,* 50.

34. Ibid., 503. See also the appendix, "Massey, Wilford H., I, 8th, Drowned at Matagorda Bay, March 13, '64," 358.

35. "Dear Brother and sister, Camps on the banks of the Shannado ten miles of winchester va june the 22th 1863," in *The Confederacy Is on Her Way Up the Spout*, 99.

36. Chapla, *50th Virginia Infantry*, 55, 159.

37. "Camp at Forsyth Mo January 1863 Monday 3rd," in McIntyre, *Federals on the Frontier*, 104.

38. "1863 Camp at Forsyth Mo Sunday March 1st," in ibid., 116–117.

39. "Camp at Forsyth Mo March 1863 Monday 16th," in ibid., 124.

40. "Camp at Forsyth Mo (April 1863) Wednesday 15th," in ibid., 138.

41. B. F. Thompson, *History of the 112th Regiment of Illinois Volunteer Infantry, in the Great War of the Rebellion, 1862–1865* (Toulon, Ill.: Stalk County News Office, 1885), 37.

42. E. Tarrant, *The Wild Riders of the First Kentucky Cavalry: A History of the Regiment, in the Great War of the Rebellion 1861–1865, Telling of Its Origins and Organization; A Description of the Material of Which It Was Composed; Its Rapid and Severe Marches, Hard Service, and Fierce Conflicts on Many a Bloody Field* (Louisville, Ky.: R. H. Carothers, 1894), 159.

43. Thompson, *History of the 112th Regiment of Illinois Volunteer Infantry*, 48, 355, 364, 365, 386; Tarrant, *The Wild Riders of the First Kentucky Cavalry*, 170.

44. Thompson, *History of the 112th Regiment of Illinois Volunteer Infantry*, 71, 344.

45. "Soldier Drowned," *Staunton (Va.) Spectator*, March 3, 1863.

46. Fox, *Regimental Losses in the American Civil War*, 61.

47. Wm. W. Averell Report, *OR*, 29:1, 931.

48. Ibid., 932.

49. David Evans, *Sherman's Horsemen: Union Cavalry Operations in the Atlanta Campaign* (Bloomington: Indiana University Press, 1996), 463, 588n51. Evans listed other accounts provided by participants that set the number at between two and three men lost; ibid., 588n51.

50. "December 9, Friday," Theodore Lyman, *Meade's Army: The Private Notebooks of Lt. Col. Theodore Lyman*, ed. David W. Lowe (Kent, Ohio: Kent State University Press, 2007), 306.

51. Francis T. Sherman, *Quest for a Star: The Civil War Letters and Diaries of Colonel Francis T. Sherman of the 88th Illinois*, ed. C. Knight Aldridge (Knoxville: University of Tennessee Press, 1999), 148–149.

52. Alexander D. Betts, *Experiences of a Confederate Chaplain, 1861–1865*, ed. W. A. Betts (Sanford, N.C.: N.C. Conference Methodist Episcopal Church, South, n.d.), 16–17.

53. "November 2, Saturday," and "November 3, Sunday," in *Voices from Company D*, 70.

54. "My dear Wife, In camp near Fredericksburg Va January 6th 1863," in Holt, *A Surgeon's Civil War*, 65.

55. Wright, *No More Gallant a Deed*, 94.

56. "The Mud of Yorktown," *Cleveland Morning Leader*, May 3, 1862.

57. Jeffry D. Wert, *A Brotherhood of Valor: The Common Soldiers of the Stonewall Brigade, C.S.A. and the Iron Brigade, U.S.A.* (New York: Simon & Schuster, 1999), 204.

58. Gordon C. Rhea, *Cold Harbor: Grant and Lee May 26–June 3, 1864* (Baton Rouge: Louisiana State University Press, 2002), 39.

59. Holt, *A Surgeon's Civil War*, 12.

60. "My Dearest Mary, Camp at Jacksons Ferry Near Florence, Ala., June 18/62," in Alfred Lacey Hough, *Soldier in the West: The Civil War Letters of Alfred Lacey Hough*, ed. Robert G. Athearn (Philadelphia: University of Pennsylvania Press, 1957), 78–79.

61. "July 16th," in Barber, *Army Memoirs of Lucius W. Barber*, 73.

62. "Sam to Andrew, Memphis, Tenn./July 22, 1862," in *Their Patriotic Duty*, 50.

63. "Sam to Mary, Memphis Tenn./July 25, 1862," in ibid., 52.

64. Krick, *Civil War Weather in Virginia*, 69.

65. Quoted in Trask, *Fire Within*, 186.

66. Wright, *No More Gallant a Deed*, 274–275.

67. Quoted in *Weep Not for Me Dear Mother*, 108–109.

68. "'This Hell of Destruction': The Benjamin Thompson Memoir, Part II," *Civil War Times* 12, no. 6 (October 1973): 16.

69. Quoted in Gordon, *A Broken Regiment*, 94.

70. "The Cases of Sunstroke," *New York Herald*, August 4, 1863.

71. *Daily Green Mountain Freeman (Montpelier, Vt.)*, August 13, 1863.

72. "List of Deaths in Hospitals from July 1st to Aug. 4th," *New South (Port Royal, S.C.)*, August 8, 1863.

73. Krick, *Civil War Weather in Virginia*, 105.

74. Fox, *Regimental Losses in the American Civil War*, 61.

75. Quoted in Earl J. Hess, *The Battle of Ezra Church and the Struggle for Atlanta* (Chapel Hill: University of North Carolina Press, 2015), 106.

76. Williams, *General Reub Williams's Memories of Civil War Times*, 188.

77. Walker, *History of the Second Army Corps in the Army of the Potomac* (New York: Charles Scribner's Sons, 1886), 372. See also Krick, *Civil War Weather in Virginia*, 135.

78. Jones, *Lee's Tigers*, 36–37.

79. Ibid., 140. This soldier died on December 20, 1862.

80. "Wednesday January 22nd 1862 Camp Butler Illinois," in James A. Black, *A Civil War Diary: Written by Dr. James A. Black, First Assistant Surgeon, 49th Illinois Infantry*, ed. Benita K. Moore (Bloomington, Ind.: AuthorHouse, 2008), 27.

81. "Fatal Accident in the New York Thirty-Eighth Regiment," *New York Herald*, February 5, 1862.

82. "The Intense Cold Weather," *Weekly National Intelligencer (Washington, D.C.)*, January 14, 1864.

83. Speer, *Portals to Hell*, 121.

84. John L. Ransom, *John Ransom's Andersonville Diary* (Philadelphia: Douglas Brothers, 1883, repr., New York: Berkley Books, 1988), 8.

85. Krick, *Civil War Weather in Virginia*, 113.

86. "My dear Daughter, Camp Seminary, Va., February 21st, 1862," in McAllister, *The Civil War Letters of General Robert McAllister*, 120.

87. Krick, *Civil War Weather in Virginia*, 44.

88. "Sunday, December 7th," in *"Well Satisfied with My Position": The Civil War Journal of Spencer Bonsall*, ed. Michael A. Flannery and Katherine H. Oomens (Carbondale: Southern Illinois University Press, 2007), 64.

89. "Monday, December 8th," in ibid.

90. Benjamin Franklin Cooling, *To the Battles of Franklin and Nashville and Beyond: Stabilization and Reconstruction in Tennessee and Kentucky, 1864–1866* (Knoxville: University of Tennessee Press, 2011), 64.

91. Watkins, *"Co. Aytch,"* 38.

92. "Soldiers Frozen to Death," *Dayton (Ohio) Daily Empire*, December 8, 1862.

93. "Twelve Union Soldiers Frozen To Death," *Dayton (Ohio) Daily Empire*, December 30, 1862.

94. "My dear Ellen, Falmouth, Va., December 30th 1862," in McAllister, *The Civil War Letters of General Robert McAllister*, 250.

95. *Daily Intelligencer (Wheeling, W.Va.)*, January 5, 1864.

96. *American Citizen (Butler, Pa.)*, January 13, 1864.

97. *Evansville (Ind.) Daily Journal*, January 7, 1864.

98. The account noted that none of the men brought to the house were "expected to live" and named the individuals as "Jas Hendrickson, David Dean, George Wilson and George Havlin"; "Soldiers Frozen to Death," *Spirit of Democracy (Woodsfield, Ohio)*, January 20, 1864. William Fox added the death of "William Tyler; frozen to death near Fort Pillow, December 31, 1863"; Fox, *Regimental Losses in the American Civil War*, 61.

99. *Nashville Daily Union*, January 16, 1864.

100. "Four Soldiers Frozen to Death," *Daily Ohio Statesman (Columbus)*, January 16, 1864.

101. Lundberg, *Granbury's Texas Brigade*, 80–81.

102. "Nov. 24," in Ransom, *John Ransom's Andersonville Diary*, 7.

103. "Dec. 1," in ibid., 11.

104. Speer, *Portals to Hell*, 121.

105. "Suffering in Camp—Soldiers Frozen to Death," *Evansville (Ind.) Daily Journal*, January 5, 1864.

106. "Monday, 12 December 1864," in George Quintus Peyton, *Stonewall Jackson's Foot Cavalry Company A, 13th Virginia Infantry*, ed. Walbrook D. Swank (Shippensburg, Pa.: Burd Street Press, 2001), 150.

107. Quoted in Speer, *Portals to Hell*, 154.

108. Wiley, *Life of Johnny Reb*, 65.

109. Lee A. Wallace, *3rd Virginia* (Lynchburg, Va.: H. E. Howard, 1986), 108.

110. "Dear Sister, Camp near Vicksburg Miss June 22nd 1863," in *Dear Sister*, 89.

111. June 27, [1863], in Haydon, *For Country, Cause and Leader*, 334. Early in the next month, he recorded, "Killed a very large rattlesnake in camp"; July 5, in ibid., 336.

112. Quoted in Ballard, *Vicksburg*, 381.

113. "March 22. Sun.," in S. Millett Thompson, *Thirteenth Regiment of New Hampshire Volunteer Infantry in the War of the Rebellion 1861–1865: A Diary Covering Three Years and a Day* (Boston: Houghton, Mifflin, 1888), 120.

114. "March 27. Fri.," and "April 3. Fri.," in ibid., 121, 123.

115. "Fatal Accident," *Daily National Republican (Washington, D.C.)*, September 2, 1863.

116. W. T. Barnes, "An Incident of Kenesaw Mountain," *Confederate Veteran* 30, no. 2 (February 1922): 49.

117. Williams, *General Reub Williams's Memories of Civil War Times*, 267.

Chapter 5. Slipshod Soldiering

1. Daniel Harvey Hill was supposed to have made this point to Nathan Bedford Forrest as a way of contrasting between the men who served under him and the cavalrymen Hill

had seen perform in Virginia; John Allan Wyeth, *Life of General Nathan Bedford Forrest* (New York: Harper & Bros., 1899), 252–253. See also Hal Bridges, *Lee's Maverick General: Daniel Harvey Hill* (New York: McGraw-Hill, 1961), 219.

2. Biographer William McFeely noted, "Grant did ride exceedingly powerful and difficult horses," before describing the general's experiences with unruly mounts; William S. McFeely, *Grant: A Biography* (New York: Norton, 1981), 140–141. Lee had a mishap with Traveller but was not mounted at the time; Emory M. Thomas, *Robert E. Lee: A Biography* (New York: Norton, 1995), 255.

3. Jack Coggins, *Arms and Equipment of the Civil War* (New York: Fairfax Press, 1983), 47–48.

4. "Fatal Accident at the Government Stables," *National Republican (Washington, D.C.)*, October 7, 1861.

5. "Fatal Accident," *National Republican (Washington, D.C.)*, August 24, 1861.

6. "Fatal Accident," *Nashville Union and American*, October 13, 1861.

7. John M. Harrell, "Arkansas," in *Confederate Military History: A Library of Confederate States History Written by Distinguished Men of the South, and Edited by Clement A. Evans of Georgia*, ed. Clement A. Evans (Atlanta: Confederate Publishing, 1899), 10:298–299.

8. "Fatal Accident" and "Another," *National Republican (Washington, D.C.)*, October 23, 1861. See also "Accidental Death of Major Lewis," *New York Herald*, October 23, 1861.

9. *Local News (Alexandria, Va.)*, November 22, 1861.

10. "October 31—Pleasant," in John Mead Gould, *The Civil War Journals of John Mead Gould 1861–1866*, ed. William B. Jordan Jr. (Baltimore: Butternut and Blue, 1997), 430.

11. "November 1—Pleasant," in ibid., 430–431.

12. "Death of Col. T. L. Cooper," *Daily Constitutionalist (Augusta, Ga.)*, December 1861.

13. "Fatal Accident," *Richmond Daily Dispatch*, January 7, 1862.

14. "Fatal Accident," *Richmond Daily Dispatch*, March 10, 1862.

15. "Sunday, May 11, 1862," in *By the Dim and Flaring Lamps*, 113.

16. "Monday May 19th, 1862," in Guerrant, *Bluegrass Confederate*, 95.

17. Wright, *No More Gallant a Deed*, 174–175.

18. "March 17, 1863," in Samuel Cormany, *The Cormany Diaries: A Northern Family in the Civil War*, ed. James C. Mohr (Pittsburgh: University of Pittsburgh Press, 1982), 302.

19. "Death by Violence of a Mounted Guardsman," *New South (Port Royal, S.C.)*, August 30, 1862.

20. *Yorkville (S.C.) Enquirer*, November 26, 1862.

21. Edwin H. Rennolds, *A History of the Henry County Commands Which Served in the Confederate States Army* (Kennesaw, Ga.: Continental Book Company, 1961), 237.

22. "Fatal Result of a Hurdle Race," *Daily National Republican (Washington, D.C.)*, March 31, 1863.

23. Van Horne, *History of the Army of the Cumberland*, 2:431.

24. Marvel, *The Great Task Remaining*, 188–190.

25. "Sunday 4h, Oct. 1863," in Guerrant, *Bluegrass Confederate*, 336–337.

26. E., "Army Correspondence, Charleston, Oct. 18, 1863," *Yorkville (S.C.) Enquirer*, October 21, 1863.

27. Warner, *Generals in Blue*, 94.

28. Quoted in Timothy Egan, *The Immortal Irishman: The Irish Revolutionary Who Became an American Hero* (Boston: Houghton Mifflin Harcourt, 2016), 258.

29. Gene C. Armistead, *Horses and Mules in the Civil War: A Complete History with a Roster of More Than 700 War Horses* (Jefferson, N.C.: McFarland, 2013), 35.

30. Chambers, *Blood and Sacrifice*, 121.

31. Warner, *Generals in Blue*, 240; Smith, *The Gallant Dead*, 368.

32. "Fatal Accident," *Yorkville Enquirer*, July 3, 1862.

33. Rawle, *History of the Third Pennsylvania Cavalry*, 244.

34. "My dearest Molly, Newport News, Va. Feb. 13/'63," in Orlando Willcox, *Forgotten Valor: The Memoirs, Journals, and Civil War Letters of Orlando Willcox*, ed. Robert Garth Scott (Kent, Ohio: Kent State University Press, 1999), 417.

35. "My dearest Marie, Mouth of Antietam 25th Sept/62," in ibid., 367.

36. "My dear Father, Feb. 17/'63," in ibid., 418.

37. "My dearest Molly, Newport News Feb. 18/'63," in ibid.

38. "My dearest Molly, Newport News, Sunday Night March 1/'63," in ibid., 420.

39. Coggins, *Arms and Equipment of the Civil War*, 75.

40. Ibid., 123.

41. See, for example, Nathan Bedford Forrest at Burrow's Shop on the road toward Harrisburg, Mississippi, in Brian Steel Wills, *A Battle from the Start: The Life of Nathan Bedford Forrest* (New York: HarperCollins, 1992), 221–222.

42. Andrew J. Smith Report, Memphis, Tenn., August 5, 1864, *OR*, 39, 1:251.

43. Fox, *Regimental Losses in the American Civil War*, 59; Armistead, *Horses and Mules in the Civil War*; Thompson, *History of the 112th Regiment of Illinois Volunteer Infantry*, 344.

44. "The Nineteenth," *Western Reserve Chronicle (Warren, Ohio)*, December 18, 1861.

45. "Fatal Accident," *Richmond Daily Dispatch*, January 18, 1862.

46. "My Dear Wife, Murfreesboro, Tenn. Sept. 27th 1863," in John Bennitt, *"I Hope to Do My Country Service": The Civil War Letters of John Bennitt, M.D., Surgeon, 19th Michigan Infantry*, ed. Robert Beasecker (Detroit: Wayne State University Press, 2005), 175.

47. "Chaplain's Report, Rendezvous of Distribution, Saturday, April 16, 1864," *Soldier's Journal (Rendezvous of Distribution, Va.)*, April 20, 1864.

48. Leech, *Reveille in Washington*, 123.

49. "The Great Fire at the Government Corral Last Night," *Evening Star (Washington, D.C.)*, December 27, 1861.

50. "Friend Blake, From the Vt Cavalry Regiment Camp Harris Annapolis Md Feb 16th 1862," in *A War of the People*, 63.

51. "Steamer Herald, June 30, 1862," in Voris, *A Citizen-Soldier's Civil War*, 71.

52. Charles B. Childe, "General Butler at New Orleans, 1862," in *Sketches of War History 1861–1865: Papers Prepared for the Ohio Commandery of the Military Order of the Loyal Legion of the United States 1896–1893*, ed. W. H. Chamberlain, A. M. Van Dyke, and George A. Thayer (Cincinnati: Robert Clarke, 1903; repr., Wilmington, N.C.: Broadfoot, 1992), 5:175.

53. Krick, *Civil War Weather in Virginia*, 86.

54. "Dear Wife & Chirldren & Parents, Onboard the Cresent City, July 25, 1863," in Sherman, *Letters to Virtue*, 238.

55. "Thursday, January 22nd," in Bonsall, *"Well Satisfied with My Position,"* 81.

56. *Smoky Hill and Republican Union (Junction City, Kans.)*, August 15, 1863.

57. "Dear Jane, Helena, Arkansas, August 26, 1863," in *"A Punishment on the Nation,"* 90.

58. "Dear Jane, Helena, Arkansas, August 27, 1863," in ibid., 91.

59. "Tuesday August 25' 1863 Harkle Roads Arkansas," in Black, *A Civil War Diary*, 154.

60. "Dear Brother Wilbur, Dismounted Camp Md. Oct. 26, 1863," in *A War of the People*, 192.

61. Edward Longacre notes the general's nickname was based on his "continuing recklessness with the health of his animals." Edward G. Longacre, *From Union Stars to Top Hat: A Biography of the Extraordinary General James Harrison Wilson* (Harrisburg, Pa.: Stackpole Books, 1972), 161. Meade staffer Theodore Lyman varied the spelling: "Kill-cavalry (as scoffers call him)"; "Headquarters Army of the Potomac, February, 24, '64," in *Meade's Headquarters, 1863–1865: Letters of Colonel Theodore Lyman from the Wilderness to Appomattox*, ed. George R. Agassiz (Boston: Atlantic Monthly Press, 1922), 76, 77, 79. See also "February 29, Monday," in Lyman, *Meade's Army*, 104.

62. "A Terrible Railroad Disaster," *Holmes County Farmer (Millersburg, Ohio)*, November 5, 1863.

63. "Wednesday, 18 November 1863," in *Siege Train: The Journal of a Confederate Artilleryman in the Defense of Charleston*, ed. Warren Ripley (Columbia: University of South Carolina Press, 1986), 85.

64. "Thursday, 19 November 1863," in ibid., 85–86.

65. Quoted in Coggins, *Arms and Equipment of the Civil War*, 53.

66. Rawle, *History of the Third Pennsylvania Cavalry*, 529–532.

67. "My Dearest Mary, Head-quarters Department of the Cumberland Office Commissary of Musters Chattanooga Nov 18 1863," in Hough, *Soldier in the West*, 169.

68. "My Dearest Mary, Chattanooga Feb 6th 1864," in ibid., 177.

69. "Tuesday 19h, Apr. 1864," in Guerrant, *Bluegrass Confederate*, 403.

70. Quoted in Evans, *Sherman's Horsemen*, 464.

71. Quoted in Larry J. Daniel, *Cannoneers in Gray: The Field Artillery of the Army of Tennessee, 1861–1865* (Tuscaloosa: University of Alabama Press, 1984), 182.

72. "Murder of a Soldier," *Richmond Daily Dispatch*, October 23, 1863. Prisoners understandably did not respond with the same affection to the animal, seeing "Nero," the "huge Bavarian boar hound" that commandant George W. Alexander employed as a method of control at Castle Thunder, quite differently. See Speer, *Portals to Hell*, 94.

73. Brown, *History of the Fourth Regiment of Minnesota Infantry Volunteers*, 284.

74. "Cape Haytien Harbor Sept 1st '64," in Charles Mervine, "Jottings by the Way: A Sailor's Log 1862 to 1864," pt. 2, ed. Kent Packard, *Pennsylvania Magazine of History and Biography* 71 (July 1947): 270.

75. W. H. Tunnard, *A Southern Record: The History of the Third Regiment Louisiana Infantry. Containing a Complete Record of the Campaigns in Arkansas and Mississippi; The Battles of Oak Hills, Elk Horn, Iuka, Corinth; The Second Siege of Vicksburg, Anecdotes, Camps, Scenery, and Descriptions of the Country through Which the Regiment Marched, Etc., Etc.* (Baton Rouge: La., n.p., 1866; repr., Fayetteville: University of Arkansas Press, 1997), 44.

76. Rufus S. Dawes, "On the Right at Antietam," in *Sketches of War History 1861–1865: Papers Prepared for the Ohio Commandery of the Military Order of the Loyal Legion of the United States 1888–1890*, ed. Robert Hunter (Cincinnati: Robert Clarke, 1890; repr., Wilmington, N.C.: Broadfoot, 1991), 3:261–262.

77. Robertson, *The Untold Civil War*, 80.

78. Ibid., 81.

79. Ibid., 122.

80. James Marten, *The Children's Civil War* (Chapel Hill: University of North Carolina Press, 1998), 143.

Chapter 6. Not So Friendly Fire

1. Webb Garrison compiled a volume that covered most instances of mutinous activity, some of which led to deaths. See Webb Garrison, *Mutiny in the Civil War* (Shippensburg, Pa.: White Mane Publishing, 2001).

2. "Wednesday, February 25th," in Bonsall, *"Well Satisfied with My Position,"* 93.

3. Weist, "The Medical Department in the War," 2:93.

4. Gordon C. Rhea, *The Battles for Spotsylvania Court House and the Road to Yellow Tavern May 7–12, 1864* (Baton Rouge: Louisiana State University Press, 1997), 277.

5. "MONDAY, SEPT 30TH, 1861," in Sheffey, *Soldier of Southwestern Virginia*, 73.

6. "My Dear Brother, 3rd Cavalry Camp, Nash's Farm Thursday, November 14th, 1861," in *The Civil War Memoirs of a Virginia Cavalryman*, ed. Thomas P. Nanzig (Tuscaloosa: University of Alabama Press, 2007), 22–23; see also ibid., 231–232.

7. Jones, *Lee's Tigers*, 57.

8. "My dear Effie, Charlestown Va. Mch 9 62," in Robert Gould Shaw, *Blue-Eyed Child of Fortune: The Civil War Letters of Colonel Robert Gould Shaw*, ed. Russell Duncan (Athens: University of Georgia Press, 1992), 180.

9. "Dear Sister, Otter Island S.C. March 18th 1862," in *Dear Sister*, 15.

10. James A. Beaver Report, Headquarters Fort Drayton, Otter Island, S.C., March 15, 1862, *OR*, 53: 1–2.

11. "A Sad Accident," *Newbern (N.C.) Weekly Progress*, May 3, 1862.

12. Wright, *No More Gallant a Deed*, 190–191.

13. "August 14th, 1862," in John B. Woodward, *John B. Woodward: A Biographical Memoir*, ed. Elijah R. Kennedy (New York: De Vinne Press, 1897), 88–89.

14. "Camp 23d N.Y.V. Arlington Heights Thursday, Aug. 20th, 1861," in Colby, *The Civil War Papers of Lt. Colonel Newton T. Colby*, 47.

15. "Monday July 7th 1862 Bethel Tennessee," "Wednesday July 16th 1862 Bethel Tennessee," and "Monday August 11th 1862 Bethel Tennessee," in Black, *A Civil War Diary*, 65, 67, 73.

16. "Thursday—day," in Guerrant, *Bluegrass Confederate*, 196–197.

17. "Folly Island—May 5, 1863," in Voris, *A Citizen-Soldier's Civil War*, 119.

18. Thomas E. R. Ransom Report, Decrow's Point, Tex., January 25, 1864, *OR*, 34, 1:100; H. J. T. Dana Report, Matagorda Peninsula, January 28, 1864, ibid., 98.

19. Tunnard, *A Southern Record*, 44.

20. Quoted in Daniel, *Soldiering in the Army of Tennessee*, 166.

21. Earl J. Hess, *The Knoxville Campaign: Burnside and Longstreet in East Tennessee* (Knoxville: University of Tennessee Press, 2012), 147.

22. "June 21, Tuesday," in *Voices from Company D*, 294.

23. Quoted in Andrew S. Bledsoe, "The Destruction of the Army of Tennessee's Officer Corps at the Battle of Franklin," in *The Tennessee Campaign of 1864*, ed. Steven E. Woodworth and Charles D. Greear (Carbondale: Southern Illinois University Press, 2016), 75.

24. Wiley Sword, *Shiloh: Bloody April* (New York: William Morrow, 1974; reprinted with new introduction, Dayton, Ohio: Morningside Press, 2001), 304–307.

25. Ibid., appendix A, 465.

26. James I. Robertson Jr., *Stonewall Jackson: The Man, the Soldier, the Legend* (New York: Macmillan, 1997). Robert Krick referred to the North Carolina pickets who fired on Jackson and his party dismissively as "maladroit," suggesting they had demonstrated poor discipline or martial capabilities under the circumstances; Krick, *Civil War Weather in Virginia*, 95.

27. Gordon C. Rhea, *The Battle of the Wilderness May 5–6, 1864* (Baton Rouge: Louisiana State University Press, 1994), 370–373.

28. "Fatal Accident," *National Republican (Washington, D.C.)*, October 19, 1861.

29. Quoted in Richard Moe, *The Last Full Measure: The Life and Death of the First Minnesota Volunteers* (New York: Henry Holt, 1993), 94.

30. "Melancholy Accident.—A Soldier Shot," *Semi-Weekly Standard (Raleigh, N.C.)*, September 18, 1861.

31. "Fatal Accident," *Richmond Daily Dispatch*, December 30, 1861.

32. Cavanaugh, *6th Virginia Infantry*, 9, 99.

33. "Fatal Accident," *Richmond Daily Dispatch*, January 14, 1862.

34. "Fatal Accident from the Careless Use of Firearms," *Richmond Daily Dispatch*, October 20, 1862.

35. "Dear Bro: Camp two miles from Bealton Station (on the Alexandria R.R.) Monday, Nov. 17, 1862," in Edward King Wightman, *From Antietam to Fort Fisher: The Civil War Letters of Edward King Wightman, 1862–1865*, ed. Edward G. Longacre (Rutherford, N.J.: Fairleigh Dickinson University Press, 1985), 79.

36. S.F.F. "Camp 'Lost River' near Bowling Green, November 10, 1862," in Flerharty, *"Jottings from Dixie,"* 66.

37. Samuel H. Sprott, *Cush: A Civil War Memoir*, ed. Louis R. Smith Jr. and Andrew Quist (Livingston, Ala.: Livingston Press, 1999), 127–128. Praytor was placed under arrest but was not charged; he also died later, "but the bullet that did the fatal work in his case sped from a gun in hostile hands; ibid., 128.

38. Lorien Foote, *The Gentlemen and the Roughs: Manhood, Honor, and Violence in the Union Army* (New York: New York University Press, 2010), 69.

39. "Thursday 16h. February 1865," in Guerrant, *Bluegrass Confederate*, 643.

40. Hess, *Lee's Tar Heels*, 348.

41. "Murder of a Soldier," *Richmond Daily Dispatch*, October 7, 1862.

42. "Andrew to Sam, Home/February 15, 1863," in *Their Patriotic Duty*, 104.

43. J. R. Bowen, *Regimental History of the First New York Dragoons during Three Years of Active Service in the Great Civil War* (n.p.: by the author, 1900), 224, 377–378.

44. Eddy, *History of the Sixtieth Regiment of New York Volunteers*, 95.

45. Foote, *The Gentlemen and the Roughs*, 137–138.

46. "Sunday August 28th 1864 Holly Springs Mississippi," in Black, *A Civil War Diary*, 231.

47. "Fatal Accident," *Richmond Daily Dispatch*, January 15, 1862.

48. "Fatal Accident," *Richmond Daily Dispatch*, October 20, 1862.

49. Benjamin H. Trask, *16th Virginia Infantry* (Lynchburg, Va.: H. E. Howard, 1986), 28.

50. The author does not indicate if the soldier passed away. Quoted in Moe, *The Last Full Measure*, 94–95.

51. Nelson, *The Hour of Our Nation's Agony*, 59–60.

52. Ibid., 267.

53. William Thomas Venner, *The 7th Tennessee Infantry in the Civil War: A History and Roster* (Jefferson, N.C.: McFarland, 2013), 174, 194.

54. "Dear Brother, Camp Banks Harpers Ferry, Thursday Aug 8," in Hayward, *Last to Leave the Field*, 31.

55. Quoted in ibid., 249n34.

56. "Fatal Accident" and "Death at the Hospital," in ibid., October 8, 1861.

57. "Fatal Accident," in ibid., October 10, 1861.

58. Chapla, *50th Virginia Infantry*, 37, 174.

59. "Fatal Accident of an Officer," *National Republican (Washington, D.C.)*, November 15, 1861.

60. "Mon. Dec. 30th 1861," in Bates, *A Texas Cavalry Officer's Civil War*, 63.

61. "My Dear Rosa, Camp Hunter March 16, 1862," in William Gaston Delony Papers, Hargrett Library, University of Georgia, Athens, Ga.

62. "Dear Father, Alexandria, Va., Sunday March 9th 1862," in Twichell, *The Civil War Letters of Joseph Hopkins Twichell*, 96–98.

63. "June 30—10 A.M.," in Gould, *The Civil War Journals of John Mead Gould*, 149–150.

64. "Sunday, September 1st," in Johnson, *The Long Roll*, 45.

65. Nash, *A History of the Forty-Fourth Regiment New York Volunteer Infantry*, 240, 464. There is a slight discrepancy in the first listing, with "Mch." instead of May; ibid., 240.

66. "Fatal Accident," *Staunton (Va.) Spectator*, June 2, 1863.

67. "Killed by Accident," *Marshall County Republican (Plymouth, Ind.)*, June 25, 1863.

68. Chambers, *Blood and Sacrifice*, 64.

69. Ibid., appendix E, 238.

70. Ibid., 184.

71. "From the New-York 22d Regiment, N.G.—Campaigning in Pennsylvania—Terrific Storm—Fatal Accident from Carelessness, A Member of Co. C, Camp near Waynesboro, Pa., July 9, 1863," *New-York Daily Tribune*, July 13, 1863.

72. Chambers, *Blood and Sacrifice*, 30.

73. Driver, *5th Virginia Cavalry*, 167.

74. Lee A. Wallace Jr., *3rd Virginia Infantry* (Lynchburg, Va.: H. E. Howard, 1986), 81.

75. "Fatal Accident," *Palmetto Herald (Port Royal, S.C.)*, March 31, 1864.

76. *Alexandria (Va.) Gazette*, October 21, 1864.

77. "Dear Jane, Up the Red River, March 18, 1864," in *"A Punishment on the Nation,"* 128.

78. "Dear Jane, On Board of Steamer *Draden* near Alexandria, Louisiana, March 20, 1864," in ibid., 129.

79. Ibid., 210n26. The other man struck, Hershel I. Perrin, survived his experience; ibid., 210n27.

80. Quoted in Mark H. Dunkleman, *Brothers One and All: Esprit de Corps in a Civil War Regiment* (Baton Rouge: Louisiana State University Press, 2004), 162–163.

81. Speer, *Portals to Hell*, 166.

82. Bartlett Yancey Malone, *The Diary of Bartlett Yancey Malone*, ed. William Whatly Pierson Jr. (Chapel Hill: University of North Carolina Press, 1919), 48.

83. McCarthy, *Detailed Minutiae of Soldier Life in the Army of Northern Virginia*, 118–119.

84. Marvel, *Andersonville*, 69–71, 95–100, 141–144. The most notorious of the "raiders" was William "Willie" Collins, also nicknamed "Mosby," whose hanging was botched initially by a rotten rope before being completed successfully; ibid., 69, 143–144.

85. Speer, *Portals to Hell*, 283.

86. "Singular and Fatal Accident," *Richmond Daily Dispatch*, April 15, 1862.

87. Daniel, *Cannoneers in Gray*, 47.

88. *New York Times*, February 20, 1863.

89. Roswell H. Lamson, *Lamson of the Gettysburg: The Civil War Letters of Rosell H. Lamson, U.S. Navy*, ed. James M. McPherson and Patricia R. McPherson (New York: Oxford University Press, 1997), 77.

90. "Fatal Accident," *Smoky Hill and Republican Union (Junction City, Kans.)*, June 5, 1862.

91. "Dear Brother, Helena, Arkansas, July 16, 1863," in *"A Punishment to the Nation,"* 80–81.

92. Polk Report, Columbus, Ky., November 10, 1861, OR, 3:308–309.

93. Sam Davis Elliott, *Soldier of Tennessee: General Alexander P. Stewart and the Civil War in the West* (Baton Rouge: Louisiana State University Press, 1999), 23; Nathaniel Cheairs Hughes Jr., *The Battle of Belmont: Grant Strikes South* (Chapel Hill: University of North Carolina Press, 1991), 191. Two days later, Polk wrote his wife, "My clothes were torn to pieces, and I was literally covered with dust and fragments of the wreck"; in Joseph H. Parks, *General Leonidas Polk, C.S.A.: The Fighting Bishop* (Baton Rouge: Louisiana State University Press, 1962), 194.

94. "Fatal Accident in Kentucky," *Staunton (Va.) Spectator*, November 19, 1861.

95. "Gun Bursted—Fatal Accident," *Maryland Free Press (Hargerstown)*, December 5, 1862.

96. "The Savannah Volunteer Guards from 1858 to 1882," typescript, 92–93, in Hargrett Library, University of Georgia, Athens, Ga.

97. "Hillo Brother O Mine, Vicksburgh Bluffs in Rear Where Our Troops Are Still in Position, June 23rd 1863," in Christie and Christie, *Brother of Mine*, 143.

98. *Alexandria (Va.) Gazette*, August 29, 1863.

99. Michael V. Sheridan, "Charging with Sheridan up Missionary Ridge," in *Battles and Leaders of the Civil War*, ed. Peter Cozzens (Urbana: University of Illinois Press, 2007), 5:452.

100. Quoted in Stephen Davis, *What the Yankees Did to Us: Sherman's Bombardment and Wrecking of Atlanta* (Macon, Ga.: Mercer University Press, 2012), 165.

101. "Fatal Accident," *Richmond Daily Dispatch*, October 3, 1864.

102. N.d., in Sherman, *Letters to Virtue*, 197.

103. "Dear Wife & Chirldren, Port Hudson, June 12, 1863," ibid., 216.

104. "Dear Wife & Chirldren, Donnlsonville, July 20, 1863," ibid., 233.

105. "August 1, 1864," in *Meade's Headquarters*, 202.

106. Quoted in Herek, *These Men Have Seen Hard Service*, 279–280.

107. Letter 79 [July 10, 1863], Bright Family Papers, Wofford College Archives, Spartanburg, S.C.

108. Mary Chesnut, *Mary Chesnut's Civil War*, ed. C. Vann Woodward (New Haven, Conn.: Yale University Press, 1981), 128, 129.

109. "Lamentable Affair," *Richmond Daily Dispatch*, August 1, 1861.

110. "W.A.T. to Editors Dispatch, Richmond, Va., August 1st, 1861," in "The Late Homicide Followed by an Attempt at Murder," *Richmond Daily Dispatch*, August 2, 1861.

111. "Ellet Toland, M.D. to the Editors of the Dispatch, Camp Gregg, Vienna, Va., August 7, 1861," in "The Late Homicide at Wilson, N.C.," *Richmond Daily Dispatch*, August 10, 1861. An "Arkansas tooth-pick" was the slang name for a personal edged weapon designed especially for slashing or thrusting.

112. Foote, *The Gentlemen and the Roughs*, 83–86.

113. "Dear Brother Camp Jackson Seneca Mills MD. Oct. 16, 1861," in Lyon, *"Desolating This Fair Country,"* 44.

114. "My Dear Brother, Cavalry Camp, Young's Mill Monday, Dec. 30th, 1861," in *The Civil War Memoirs of a Virginia Cavalryman*, 24.

115. Jones, *Lee's Tigers*, 35–36.

116. "Saturday 18h. Octr. 1862," in Guerrant, *Bluegrass Confederate*, 163.

117. "Miss Sue A. Hearn, Near Chattanooga July 9th/63," in Alexander E. Spence and Thomas F. Spence, *Getting Used to Being Shot At: The Spence Family Civil War Letters*, ed. Mark K. Christ (Fayetteville: University of Arkansas Press, 2002), 68, 183–183n34.

118. *Alexandria (Va.) Gazette*, August 7, 1863.

119. Fox, *Regimental Losses in the American Civil War*, 61.

120. Foote, *The Gentlemen and the Roughs*, 135–136.

121. Webb Garrison compiled examples of such incidents in *Mutiny in the Civil War*.

122. Van Horne, *History of the Army of the Cumberland*, 2:387.

123. Robert G. Hartje, *Van Dorn: The Life and Times of a Confederate General* (Nashville: Vanderbilt University Press, 1967).

124. "May 10," in Barber, *Army Memoirs of Lucius W. Barber*, 142–143.

125. William C. Davis, *Rhett: The Turbulent Life and Times of a Fire-eater* (Columbia: University of South Carolina Press, 2001), 507.

126. Chesnut, *Mary Chesnut's Civil War*, 128.

127. Clark, *The Notorious "Bull" Nelson*, 148–152; Nathaniel Cheairs Hughes Jr. and Gordon D. Whitney, *Jefferson Davis in Blue: The Life of Sherman's Relentless Warrior* (Baton Rouge: Louisiana State University Press, 2002), 111–120.

128. The circumstances of the confrontation at Suffolk, Virginia, can be found in Wills, *The War Hits Home*, 139–141.

129. Matthew J. Graham, *The Ninth Regiment New York Volunteers (Hawkins' Zouaves): Being a History of the Regiment and Veteran Association from 1860–1900* (New York, 1900), 411–415; J. H. E. Whitney, *The Hawkins Zouaves (Ninth N.Y.V.): Their Battles and Marches* (New York, 1866), 175–177; Johnson, *The Long Roll*, 228; *New York Times*, April 16, 1863.

130. Wightman, *From Antietam to Fort Fisher*, 125.

131. Ibid.; "An Incident at Suffolk," comp. Charles L. English, George W. Griggs Manuscript, Norwich Civil War Round Table Collection, U.S. Army Military History Institute, Carlisle Barracks, Pa.

132. Johnson, *The Long Roll*, 229.

133. Wills, *The War Hits Home*, 141.

134. John Watson Morton, *The Artillery of Nathan Bedford Forrest's Cavalry* (Nashville: Publishing House of the M.E. Church, South, 1909), 101.

135. Frank H. Smith, "The Forrest-Gould Affair," *Civil War Times Illustrated* 9, no. 7 (November 1970): 32.

136. Robert Selph Henry, *"First with the Most" Forrest* (Indianapolis: Bobbs-Merrill, 1944), 162.

137. Quoted in Smith, "The Forrest-Gould Affair," 34–35; see also Henry, *"First with the Most" Forrest*, 163.

138. Wyeth, *Life of General Nathan Bedford Forrest*, 225–226.

139. Leo E. Huff, "The Last Duel in Arkansas: The Marmaduke-Walker Duel," *Arkansas Historical Quarterly* 23, no. 1 (Spring 1964): 44.

140. Foote, *The Gentlemen and the Roughs*, 59–63.

141. Warner, *Generals in Gray*, 332.

142. Lawrence Lee Hewitt, "Introduction," in *Confederate Generals in the Trans-Mississippi*, ed. Lawrence Lee Hewitt, with Arthur W. Bergeron Jr. and Thomas E. Shott (Knoxville: University of Tennessee Press, 2013), xv.

Chapter 7. "As Neere to Heaven by Sea"

1. Quoted in Morrison, *The European Discovery of America*, 577.

2. "Head Quarters 67th Reg. O.V. in the Field Below City Point, Va., July 7, 1862," in Voris, *A Citizen-Soldier's Civil War*, 72.

3. "Thursday, February 27, 1862 Louisville," in McIlvaine, *By the Dim and Flaring Lamps*, 43.

4. Bartholomew Diggins, *Sailing with Farragut: The Civil War Recollections of Bartholomew Diggins*, ed. George S. Burkhardt (Knoxville: University of Tennessee Press, 2016), xxii.

5. C. H. Davis, *Life of Charles Henry Davis, Rear Admiral, 1807–1877* (Boston: Houghton Mifflin, 1899), 236.

6. "Sam to Andrew, Paducah, Ky/March 30, 1862," in *Their Patriotic Duty*, 13.

7. McClinchy's death was listed as occurring on November 11, 1861. Van Horne, *History of the Army of the Cumberland*, 2:600, 601, 624.

8. *Memphis Daily Appeal*, December 14, 1861.

9. Longacre, *The Sharpshooters*, 34, 38–39, 74.

10. Frederick Phisterer, *New York in the War of the Rebellion* (Albany: J. B. Lyons and Co., State Printers, 1912), 306.

11. Ibid., 516, 517.

12. Rawle, *History of the Third Pennsylvania Cavalry*, 43.

13. "Deaths," *New South (Port Royal, S.C.)*, May 30, 1863.

14. "From New York," *Evansville (Ind.) Daily Journal*, November 17, 1862.

15. *Nashville Daily Union*, November 18, 1863.

16. "Dear Bro: On Board Transport Weybosset off Fort Fisher, near Wilmington, N.C., December 23 [26], 1864," in Wightman, *From Antietam to Fort Fisher*, 224–225.

17. "December 28, 1864," in ibid., 225–226.

18. William B. Cushing, *The Sea Eagle: The Civil War Memoir of Lt. Cdr. William B. Cushing*, ed. Alden R. Carter (Lanham, Md.: Rowman and Littlefield, 2009), 64.

19. Belcher, *The 11th Missouri Infantry in the Civil War*, 14.

20. *Cincinnati Daily Press*, December 21, 1861.

21. "The Savannah Volunteer Guards from 1858 to 1882," 90.

22. Warner, *Generals in Blue*, 455–456.

23. Van Horne, *History of the Army of the Cumberland*, 2:625.

24. Ibid., 619.

25. "Soldier Drowned," *Daily Evansville (Ind.) Journal*, July 25, 1862.

26. Note on rear of carte de visite, personal collection of Nicholas Picerno. See also Phisterer, *New York in the War of the Rebellion*, 513.

27. "Death of a Newspaper correspondent," *Richmond Daily Dispatch*, November 24, 1864.

28. Nash, *A History of the Forty-Fourth Regiment New York Volunteer Infantry*, 354.

29. "The Death of a Soldier," *Daily Intelligencer (Wheeling, W.Va.)*, March 28, 1864.

30. "Appendix: Muster Roll," in *A War of the People*, 328.

31. "Dear Son Feb 24th 1864 Camp Near Brandy Stashin," in ibid., 211.

32. "Monday November 28' 1864 on board Str. Spray," in Black, *A Civil War Diary*, 250.

33. Gould, *History of the First-Tenth-Twenty-Ninth Maine Regiment*, 634, 638, 639.

34. Nat Brandt, *Mr. Tubbs' Civil War* (Syracuse, N.Y.: Syracuse University Press, 1996), 186.

35. "Railroad Accident at Perryville, Md.," *Evening Star (Washington, D.C.)*, August 13, 1864.

36. Van Horne, *History of the Army of the Cumberland*, 2:407, 408, 416, 419, 425, 426.

37. W. S. Long Report, New Orleans, La., January 10, 1863, OR, 15: 209.

38. Wm. L. Burt to Banks, Inclosure No. 2, in Nathaniel P. Banks Report, New Orleans, La., January 3, 1863, ibid., 203; Chas. A. Davis Report, In Camp at Carrollton, La., January 10, 1863, ibid., 207.

39. J. M. Foltz Report, New Orleans, January 11, 1863, *Official Records of the Union and Confederate Navies in the War of the Rebellion*, Series I, 19:442 (hereafter cited as ORN).

40. John Russell Bartlett, "The 'Brooklyn' at the Passage of the Forts," in *Battles and Leaders of the Civil War Being for the Most Part Contributions by Union and Confederate Officers: Based upon "The Century" War Series*, ed. Robert Underwood Johnson and Clarence Clough Buel (New York: Thomas Yoseloff, 1956), 2:60.

41. Edward A. Butler, "Personal Experiences in the Navy, 1862–65," in *War Papers Read before the Commandery of the State of Maine Military Order of the Loyal Legion of the United States* (Portland, Maine: Lefavor-Tower, 1902; repr., Wilmington, N.C.: Broadfoot, 1992), 2:190–191.

42. Quoted in Hewitt, *Port Hudson*, 83.

43. Kevin J. Dougherty, *Ships of the Civil War 1861–1865: An Illustrated Guide to the Fighting Vessels of the Union and the Confederacy* (London: Amber Books, 2013), 152.

44. "J. W. Bell, U.S.N. U.S. Gunboat Gen. Pillow, Mound city, Feb. 8, '64," *Western Reserve Chronicle (Warren, Ohio)*, February 17, 1864.

45. "White House Ranch July 29th 1864," in McIntyre, *Federals on the Frontier*, 381.

46. "April 27," in Sherman, *Letters to Virtue*, 21.

47. "Dear Wife and Chirldren, New Orleans, June 14, 1862," ibid., 42.

48. "Dear Mother and Wife, Chirldren, Camp Parepet, New Orleans, August 10, 1862," ibid., 72–73.

49. "Dear Wife & Children, Parents, New Orleans, July 8, 1864," ibid., 308.

50. Corell, *History of the Naval Brigade*.

51. W. G. Saltonstall Report, *U.S.S. Governor Buckingham*, Off Western Bar, Wilmington, N.C., February 2, 1864, ORN, Series I, 9:436–437.

52. Steven J. Ramold, *Slaves, Sailors, Citizens: African Americans in the Union Navy* (DeKalb: Northern Illinois University Press, 2002), 89–90.

53. Stillwell, *The Story of a Common Soldier*, 230–231.

54. "Inquest," *Richmond Daily Dispatch*, January 29, 1863.

55. *Gallipolis (Ohio) Journal*, December 3, 1863; first portion reprinted in "Soldier Drowned," *Weekly Register (Point Pleasant, Va.)*, December 3, 1863.

56. Corell, *History of the Naval Brigade*.

57. J. W. Shively, "The U.S.S. 'Mississippi' at the Capture of New Orleans in 1862," in *War Papers Being Papers Read before the Commandery of the District of Columbia Military Order of the Loyal Legion of the United States 1887–1897* (1897; repr., Wilmington, N.C.: Broadfoot, 1993), 1:231. See also Craig L. Symonds, *The Civil War at Sea* (Santa Barbara, Calif.: Praeger, 2009), 107.

58. "Fatal Accident," *New South (Port Royal, S.C.)*, January 9, 1864.

59. Jno. A. Dahlgren, Flag-Steamer Philadelphia, Off Morris Island, December 9, 1863, *ORN*, 15:173.

60. *New York Times*, April 23, 1863.

61. Smith, *The Fight for the Yazoo, August 1862–July 1864*, 102.

62. "Fatal Accident," *Western Democrat (Charlotte, N.C.)*, March 18, 1862.

63. *Alexandria (Va.) Gazette*, February 17, 1863.

64. "Appalling Disaster in the Harbor," *New York Herald*, April 16, 1864. See also "Additional Details of the Shocking Catastrophe," *New York Herald*, April 17, 1864.

65. "Additional Details of the Shocking Catastrophe," *New York Herald*, April 17, 1864.

66. "The Chenango Disaster—Imperative Necessity of Reforming the System of Building the Machinery of Government Vessels," *New York Herald*, May 9, 1864.

67. *Soldier's Journal (Rendezvous of Distribution, Va.)*, January 11, 1865.

68. "The Terrible Calamity on the Lower Potomac," *Evening Star (Washington, D.C.)*, November 14, 1864. See also "Official Report of the Explosion of the United States Steamer Tulip," *Daily National Republican (Washington, D.C.)*, November 15, 1864, 2nd ed.

69. "Terrible Explosion on the Potomac," *Weekly National Intelligencer (Washington, D.C.)*, November 17, 1864.

70. Fox, *Regimental Losses in the American Civil War*, 503.

71. S. Meredith to Governor O. P. Morton, Paducah, Ky., January 27, 1864, *OR*, 49, 1:600.

72. "Steamer *Burton*, May 17, 1862," in Paine, *A Wisconsin Yankee in Confederate Bayou Country*, 64.

73. Ibid., 98. Thomas Williams died in fighting at Baton Rouge, Louisiana, on August 5, 1862, when troops under John C. Breckenridge assailed the town; Warner, *Generals in Blue*, 564.

74. "Dear Mother and Wife, Chirldren, Camp Parepet, New Orleans, August 10, 1862," in Sherman, *Letters to Virtue*, 72–73.

75. "Further Particulars of the Collision on the Potomac," *Cleveland Morning Leader*, August 18, 1862. See also John M. Taylor, "Potomac Flotilla: A Gunboat Captain's Diary," in *Raiders and Blockaders: The American Civil War Afloat*, ed. William N. Still Jr., John M. Taylor, and Norman C. Delaney (Washington, D.C.: Brassey's, 1998), 217, in which a gunboat officer discussed rescuing survivors of the wreck.

76. Clifton B. Fisk, Lebanon No. 2, Tallahatchee River, Miss., March 25, 1863, *OR*, 24, 3:144. See also Warner, *Generals in Blue*, 154–155.

77. Smith, *The Fight for the Yazoo, August 1862–July 1864*, 193.

78. David D. Porter Report, Mississippi Squadron, Flagship Black Hawk, Red River, March 9, 1864, *ORN*, Series I, 26:18.

79. Thos. O. Selfridge Report, Mississippi Squadron, Flagship Black Hawk, Red River, March 10, 1864, *ORN*, Series I, 26:19. J. F. Richardson, commander of the *General Price*, who had retired for the evening when the collision occurred, noted the exemplary behavior of his counterpart, T. O. Selfridge, as well as the loss of "George Robinson, hospital steward, and James Brennan, seaman"; J. F. Richardson Report, U.S.S. General Price, Red River, March 11, 1864, ibid.

80. Smith, *The Fight for the Yazoo, August 1862–July 1864*, 213.

81. *Smoky Hill and Republican Union (Junction City, Kans.)*, August 15, 1863.

82. "The Terrible Steamboat Disaster at Vicksburg," *Delaware Gazette (Delaware, Ohio)*, September 4, 1863.

83. *Alexandria (Va.) Gazette*, August 4, 1863.

84. "Accident," *Evening Star (Washington, D.C.)*, August 13, 1864.

85. "Fatal Accident on Board a Steamer," *Richmond Daily Dispatch*, November 22, 1861.

86. "Fatal Accident," *Evening Star (Washington, D.C.)*, June 21, 1864.

87. Quoted in Robertson, *Soldiers Blue and Gray*, 126–127.

88. "Fatal Accident," *Evening Star (Washington, D.C.)*, April 25, 1864.

89. Robert De Treville Report, Fort Moultrie, August 31, 1863, *OR*, 28, 1:706–707. See also various reports, ibid., 687–712.

90. Motte A. Pringle Report, Quartermaster's Office, Charleston, September 3, 1863, ibid., 701–702.

91. Quoted in Mark K. Ragan, *Union and Confederate Submarine Warfare in the Civil War* (Mason City, Iowa: Savas Publishing, 1999), 128. Tom Chaffin lists Frank Doyle, John Kelly, Michael Cane, Nicholas Davis, and Absolum Williams as the victims in this instance, in *The H. L. Hunley: The Secret Hope of the Confederacy* (New York: Hill and Wang, 2008), 263.

92. Quoted in Ragan, *Union and Confederate Submarine Warfare in the Civil War*, 129, and Chaffin, *The H. L. Hunley*, 141.

93. Quoted in Ragan, *Union and Confederate Submarine Warfare in the Civil War*, 145. In addition to Hunley and Thomas W. Park, Chaffin lists Henry Beard, Robert Brookbank, John Marshall, Charles McHugh, Joseph Patterson, and Charles L. Sprague as fatalities in this incident. A third crew perished when the submarine attacked and sank USS *Housatonic* on February 17, 1864; Chaffin, *The H. L. Hunley*, 263–264.

94. "Death of Major Hunt, *New York Times*, October 2, 1863. See also Ragan, *Union and Confederate Submarine Warfare in the Civil War*, 133.

95. "The Late Major Edward B. Hunt, *New York Times*, October 5, 1863.

96. Fox, *Regimental Losses in the American Civil War*, 480.

97. "Thursday, August 25, 1864," and "Friday, August 26, 1864," in Josiah Gregg, *The Diary of a Civil War Marine: Private Josiah Gregg*, ed. Wesley Moody and Adrienne Sachse (Madison, N.J.: Fairleigh Dickinson University Press, 2013), 101.

98. Quoted in Smith, *The Fight for the Yazoo, August 1862–July 1864*, 184.

99. Ibid., 187.

100. Kinsley, *Diary of a Christian Soldier*, 142.

101. "Wednesday, January 15th," in Johnson, *The Long Roll*, 85–86.

102. James M. McPherson, *War on the Waters: The Union and Confederate Navies, 1861–1865* (Chapel Hill: University of North Carolina Press, 2012), 133–134.

103. "Log of the U.S.S. Philadelphia," *ORN*, 15:170. See also Alvin C. Voris, "Charleston in the Rebellion," in *Sketches of War History 1861–1865 Papers Read before the Ohio Commandery of the Military Order of the Loyal Legion of the United States 1886–1888*, ed. Robert Hunter (Cincinnati: Robert Clarke, 1888; repr., Wilmington, N.C.: Broadfoot, 1991), 2:338.

104. Various, *ORN*, 15:161–170.

105. Jno. A. Dahlgren Report, Flag-Steamer Philadelphia, Off Morris Island December 8, 1863, ibid., 164.

106. Fox, *Regimental Losses in the American Civil War*, 507, 529.

107. Quoted in Michael J. Bennett, *Union Jacks: Yankee Sailors in the Civil War* (Chapel Hill: University of North Carolina Press, 2004), 192.

108. A. M. Pennock Report, Cairo, March 18, 1862, *ORN*, 22:695.

109. A. H. Foote Report, *U.S. Flag-Steamer Benton*, Off Island Np. 10, March 17, 1862, ibid., 694–694.

110. David D. Porter, *The Naval History of the Civil War* (New York: Sherman, 1886), 696–697.

111. Dawson Carr, *Gray Phantoms of the Cape Fear: Running the Civil War Blockade* (Winston-Salem, N.C.: John F. Blair, 1998), 189.

112. Lloyd Tilghman Report, February 12, 1862, *OR*, 7:141; Benjamin Franklin Cooling, *Forts Henry and Donelson: The Key to the Confederate Heartland* (Knoxville: University of Tennessee Press, 1987), 106.

113. "Ten Men Drowned—Heavy Firing—Thirteen of the Enemy Captured," *Wilmington (N.C.) Journal*, November 20, 1863. See also "Ten Men Drowned," *Yorkville (S.C.) Enquirer*, November 26, 1862.

114. Robertson, *The Untold Civil War*, 236; Ishbel Ross, *Rebel Rose: Life of Rose O'Neal Greenhow, Confederate Spy* (New York: Ballantine Books, 1973), 236–237.

115. Bennett, *Union Jacks*, 24.

116. Ibid., 177, 179.

117. "January 17th 63," in Charles Mervine, "Jottings by the Way: A Sailor's Log 1862 to 1864," pt. 1, ed. Kent Packard, *Pennsylvania Magazine of History and Biography* 71 (April 1947): 125.

118. "June 19th '63," in ibid., 131.

119. "September 5th 63," in ibid., 143.

120. "Roswell to Katie, USS *Nansemond* Beaufort, N.C. Oct. 15, 1863," in Lamson, *Lamson of the Gettysburg*, 139. See also "Roswell to Kate, USS *Commodore Barney* Off Sand Point, James River July 11, 1863," in ibid., 119. Strude's death is included in Phisterer, *New York in the War of the Rebellion*, 517.

121. "My Dear Father, Opposite the Mouth of the Yazoo, Jan. 26, 1863," in Christie and Christie, *Brother of Mine*, 96.

122. Bennett, *Union Jacks*, 80, 109.

123. Ibid., 108.

124. "March 25th," in Chambers, *Blood and Sacrifice*, 209.

125. S. R. Mallory, Office of Orders and Duties, C.S. Navy Department, Richmond, Va., March 17, 1864, *ORN*, 16:462.

126. B. F. Sands Report, *U.S.S. Fort Jackson*, Off Galveston, Tex., May 24, 1865, ibid., 22:197.

127. William N. Still Jr., "The Confederate Tar," in *Raiders and Blockaders: The American Civil War Afloat*, ed. William N. Still Jr., John M. Taylor, and Norman C. Delaney (Washington, D.C.: Brassey's, 1998), 97.

128. Craig L. Symonds, *Lincoln and His Admirals: Abraham Lincoln, the U.S. Navy, and the Civil War* (New York: Oxford University Press, 2008), 238–239.

129. John M. Coski, *Capital Navy: The Men, Ships and Operations of the James River Squadron* (Campbell, Calif.: Savas Woodbury, 1996), 168.

130. Ramold, *Slaves, Sailors, Citizens*, 174.

131. Stephen D. Trenchard Report, *U.S.S. Rhode Island*, Hampton Roads, Va., September 6, 1862, *ORN*, Series I, 27:459.

132. Edward Conroy Report, U.S. Supply Steamer Union, New York June 30, 1864, ibid., 593.

133. "Dear Mother, At Sea Friday, July 8th 1864," in "Yellow Fever on the Blockade of the Indian River: A Tragedy of 1864," *Florida Historical Quarterly* 21, no. 4 (April 1943): 352.

134. "Off Indian River, Sunday, Aug. 7th, 1864," in ibid., 353.

135. "Wednesday, Aug. 10," in ibid., 355.

136. "Dear Brother, Indian River Saturday, Aug. 13/64," in ibid., 356.

137. Ibid., 356–357; *ORN*, Series I, 17:748, 749.

138. Smith, *The Fight for the Yazoo, August 1862–July 1864*, 244.

139. Quoted in Bennett, *Union Jacks*, 76.

140. Coski, *Capital Navy*, 214; Raphael Semmes, "Admiral on Horseback: The Diary of Brigadier General Raphael Semmes, February–May 1865," ed. W. Stanley Hoole, *Alabama Review* 28 (April 1975): 134–136.

141. Gordon, *A Broken Regiment*, 185–186, 332.

142. Quoted in ibid., 186.

143. Gene Eric Salecker, *Disaster on the Mississippi: The Sultana Explosion, April 27, 1865* (Annapolis, Md.: Naval Institute Press, 1996), 206, 216.

144. Tom Chaffin, *Sea of Gray: The Around-the-World Odyssey of the Confederate Raider Shenandoah* (New York: Hill and Wang, 2006), 284.

145. Ibid., 301.

146. Quoted in ibid., 305.

147. Ibid., 341–343.

Chapter 8. Industrial and Storage Mishaps

1. Clayton E. Jewett, *Texas in the Confederacy: An Experiment in Nation Building* (Columbia: University of Missouri Press, 2002), 165–172.

2. Emory M. Thomas, *The Confederate State of Richmond: A Biography of the Capital* (Austin: University of Texas Press, 1971), 112.

3. J. Matthew Gallman and L. Stanley Engerman, "The Civil War Economy: A Modern

View," in J. Matthew Gallman, *Northerners at War: Reflections on the Civil War Home Front* (Kent, Ohio: Kent State University Press, 2010), 111.

4. Nelson and Sheriff, *A People at War*, 243–244.

5. Drew Gilpin Faust, *Mothers of Invention: Women of the Slaveholding South in the American Civil War* (Chapel Hill: University of North Carolina Press, 1996), 89–90.

6. "Percussion Caps," *National Republican (Washington, D.C.)*, October 18, 1861.

7. "Fatal Accident," *Cincinnati Daily Press*, November 7, 1861. The *Richmond Daily Dispatch* picked up the story and printed it November 15, 1861, as "Fatal Accident in Philadelphia."

8. *Local News (Alexandria, Va.)*, November 9, 1861.

9. Sallie Putnam, *Richmond during the War; Four Years of Personal Observation. By a Richmond Lady* (New York: G. W. Carleton, 1867), 82–83.

10. "Terrible Explosion in Philadelphia," *New York Herald*, March 30, 1862.

11. "Terrible Explosion at Jackson's Pyrotechnic Factory, Philadelphia," *National Republican (Washington, D.C.)*, March 31, 1862.

12. "Explosion of the Pyrotechnic Factory," *Daily Green Mountain Freeman (Montpelier, Vt.)*, March 31, 1862.

13. "Accident," *Memphis Daily Appeal*, May 28, 1862.

14. "Explosion of a Cartridge Factory," *Daily National Republican (Washington, D.C.)*, June 3, 1863.

15. "Horrible Explosion and Loss of Life at Pittsburgh," *Daily Evansville (Ind.) Journal*, September 19, 1862.

16. "Frightful Catastrophe," *Western Democrat (Charlotte, N.C.)*, September 30, 1862.

17. *Daily Dayton (Ohio) Express*, October 18, 1862.

18. *Semi-Weekly Standard (Raleigh, N.C.)*, November 11, 1862.

19. "Dreadful Calamity," *Staunton (Va.) Spectator*, November 11, 1862. See also *Semi-Weekly Standard (Raleigh, N.C.)*, November 11, 1862.

20. *New-York Daily Tribune*, January 28, 1863. *Daily National Republican (Washington, D.C.)*, January 30, 1863, reported the death of "one man" as well.

21. *Alexandria (Va.) Gazette*, January 31, 1863.

22. *Alexandria (Va.) Gazette*, February 2, 1863.

23. "Explosion at the Arsenal," *Raftsman's Journal (Clearfield, Pa.)*, February 11, 1863.

24. "March 13th, [1863]," in Jones, *A Rebel War Clerk's Diary*, 175.

25. "March 15th," in McGuire, *Diary of a Southern Refugee during the War*, 147.

26. Putnam, *Richmond during the War*, 83.

27. David L. Burton, "Richmond's Great Homefront Disaster: Friday the 13th," *Civil War Times* 21, no. 6 (October 1982): 38.

28. "March 14th," in Turner Vaughn, "Diary of Turner Vaughan Co. 'C' 4th, Alabama Regiment, C.S.A. Commenced March 4th, 1863 and Ending February 12th, 1864," *Alabama Historical Quarterly* 18, no. 4 (Winter 1956): 575.

29. "Terrible Explosion," *Abingdon Virginian*, March 20, 1863. On the same day the *Athens (Tenn.) Post* provided a brief notice that set the dead at thirty. See also "The Late Explosion at Richmond," *Camden (S.C.) Confederate*, March 20, 1863.

30. "Saturday March 21 [1863]," in Josiah Gorgas, *The Journals of Josiah Gorgas, 1857–1878*, ed. Sarah Woolfolk Wiggins (Tuscaloosa: University of Alabama Press, 1995), 57. See also Thomas, *The Confederate State of Richmond*, 117.

31. Burton, "The Victims," in "Richmond's Great Homefront Disaster," 41.

32. "Terrible Accident—Explosion of a Powder Mill," *Wilmington (N.C.) Journal*, May 28, 1863.

33. Clarence L. Mohr, *On the Threshold of Freedom: Masters and Slaves in Civil War Georgia* (Athens: University of Georgia Press, 1986), 178, 342.

34. Alfred Bellard, *Gone for a Soldier: The Civil War Memoirs of Private Alfred Bellard*, ed. David Herbert Donald (Boston: Little, Brown, 1975), 265.

35. "Terrible Accident," *Western Democrat (Charlotte, N.C.)*, May 26, 1863. Raleigh's *Semi-Weekly Standard* reprinted the essence of the story in its edition of May 29, 1863.

36. "A Calamity," *Camden (S.C.) Confederate*, June 5, 1863.

37. "Explosion of a Cartridge Factory," *Evening Star (Washington, D.C.)*, June 3, 1863.

38. *Alexandria (Va.) Gazette*, June 6, 1863.

39. *Alexandria (Va.) Gazette*, August 17, 1863.

40. "Explosion," *Evansville (Ind.) Daily Journal*, October 6, 1863.

41. "The Late Accident at Springfield," *Dayton (Ohio) Daily Empire*, March 21, 1864.

42. *Soldier's Journal (Rendezvous of Distribution, Va.)*, March 23, 1864.

43. "Another Victim," *Burlington (Vt.) Free Press*, April 8, 1864.

44. Geo. W. Rains, *History of the Confederate Powder Works* (Augusta, Ga.: Chronicle and Constitutionalist Print, 1882), 21.

45. "Fatal Accident," *Richmond Daily Dispatch*, May 6, 1864.

46. "Explosion in a Percussion Cap Manufactory—One Man Killed," *New York Herald*, May 12, 1864.

47. "Frightful Explosion at the Arsenal," *Evening Star (Washington, D.C.)*, June 17, 1864.

48. Edwin M. Stanton to Major Benton, War Department, June 19, 1864, reprinted in *Evening Star (Washington, D.C.)*, June 21, 1864.

49. "The Victims of the Arsenal Explosion," *New York Herald*, June 20, 1864. See also *Alexandria (Va.) Gazette*, June 21, 1864.

50. "Navy Yard—Fatal Accident," *Evening Star (Washington, D.C.)*, February 22, 1865.

51. "Fatal Accident," *Daily National Republican (Washington, D.C.)*, July 31, 1863. See also "Fatal Accident at the Arsenal," *Evening Star (Washington, D.C.)*, July 31, 1863.

52. "Terrible Catastrophe," *Daily Evansville (Ind.) Journal*, August 27, 1863.

53. "The Terrible Steamboat Disaster at Vicksburg," *Delaware Gazette (Delaware, Ohio)*, September 4, 1863.

54. "Dear Brother, Vicksburgh Mississippi, Agust 20th 1863," in Christie and Christie, *Brother of Mine*, 166–167.

55. J. C. Van Duzer to General Garfield, Battle Creek, September 30, 1863—3 P.M., OR, 30, 3:947.

56. R. F. Smith to Major-General Rosecrans, Bridgeport, October 1, 1863, ibid., 4:19.

57. Grant to Halleck, City Point, August 9, 1864,—11:45 A.M., ibid., 42, 2:94–95. Grant followed with a list of casualties from the affair; Grant to Halleck, City Point, Va., August 11, 1864, ibid., 112.

58. Ella S. Rayburn, "Sabotage at City Point," *Civil War Times Illustrated* 22, no. 2 (April 1983): 30–31. William Fox recorded the death of John Edleman, of Company C, Eightieth New York, "killed by explosion of ammunition, August 8, 1864, at City Point, Va."; Fox, *Regimental Losses in the American Civil War*, 61.

59. "August 9, 1864," in *Meade's Headquarters*, 210.

60. John Maxwell Report, Richmond, December 16, 1864, OR, 42, 1:955.

61. Rayburn, "Sabotage at City Point," 32–33.

62. Harold S. Wilson, *Confederate Industry: Manufacturers and Quartermasters in the Civil War* (Jackson: University Press of Mississippi, 2002), 216.

63. "Further Particulars of the Terrible Explosion at Fort Lyon," *Evening Star (Washington, D.C.)*, June 10, 1863. This version set the explosion at 2:15 P.M.

64. "Fort Lyon, Near Alexandria, Blown Up!," *Weekly National Intelligencer (Washington, D.C.)*, June 11, 1863.

65. "The Terrific Explosion at Fort Lyon," *Alexandria (Va.) Gazette*, June 12, 1863.

66. Jno. P. Slough Report, Alexandria, Va., June 9, 1863, OR, 27, 2:871.

67. G. A. De Russy Report, Alexandria, Va., June 9, 1863—8 P.M., ibid.

68. Thompson, *History of the 112th Regiment of Illinois Volunteer Infantry*, 386, 401.

69. "Tuesday, 15 Sept. 1863," in *Siege Train*, 40.

70. *Big Blue Union (Marysville, Kans.)*, November 5, 1864.

71. Rod Gragg, *Confederate Goliath: The Battle of Fort Fisher* (New York: HarperCollins, 1991), 233–234.

72. William Lamb, "The Defense of Fort Fisher," in *Battles and Leaders Being for the Most Part Contributions by Union and Confederate Officers: Based upon "The Century" War Series*, ed. Robert Underwood Johnson and Clarence Clough Buel (New York: Thomas Yoseloff, 1956), 4:654.

73. Alfred H. Terry Report, Fort Fisher, N.C., January 20, 1865, OR, 46, 1:401.

74. Phisterer, *New York in the War of the Rebellion*, 136.

75. "Roswell to Kate, New York, Jan. 19, 1865," in Lamson, *Lamson of the Gettysburg*, 226.

76. "Proceedings of a Court of Inquiry constituted to examine into the cause of the explosion of the powder magazine, Fort Fisher, N.C., January 20, 1865," OR, 46, 1:425–431.

77. "February 19th. Sunday," in Emma LeConte, *When the World Ended: The Diary of Emma LeConte*, ed. Earl Schenck Miers (New York: Oxford University Press, 1957), 54–55.

78. William T. Sherman, *Memoirs of General William T. Sherman* (New York: Charles L. Webster, 1892), 2:288.

79. James Harrison Wilson, *Under the Old Flag: Recollections of Military Operations in the War for the Union, the Spanish War, the Boxer Rebellion, etc.* (New York: D. Appleton, 1912); Longacre, *From Union Stars to Top Hat*, 209, 215; Brian Steel Wills, "The Confederate Sun Sets on Selma: Nathan Bedford Forrest and the Defense of Alabama in 1865," in *The Yellowhammer War: The Civil War and Reconstruction in Alabama*, ed. Kenneth W. Noe (Tuscaloosa: University of Alabama Press, 2013), 71–89.

80. Williams, *General Reub Williams's Memories of Civil War Times*, 247–248.

Chapter 9. Collateral Casualties

1. Hugo Slim, *Killing Civilians: Method, Madness, and Morality in War* (New York: Columbia University Press, 2008), 1–3.

2. Quoted in Christopher Phillips, "The Hard-Line War: The Ideological Basis of Irregular Warfare in the Western Border States," in *The Civil War Guerrilla: Unfolding the*

Black Flag in History, Memory, and Myth, ed. Joseph M. Beilein Jr. and Matthew C. Hulbert (Lexington: University Press of Kentucky, 2015), 27.

3. Quoted in Robert L. Kerby, *Kirby Smith's Confederacy: The Trans-Mississippi South, 1863–1865* (New York: Columbia University Press, 1972), 89.

4. John C. Inscoe and Gordon B. McKinney, *The Heart of Confederate Appalachia: Western North Carolina in the Civil War* (Chapel Hill: University of North Carolina Press, 2000), 238–240.

5. Paludan, *Victims*.

6. Mark Grimsley, *The Hard Hand of War: Union Military Policy toward Southern Civilians 1861–1865* (New York: Cambridge University Press, 1995).

7. Halleck to Sherman, Washington, September 28, 1864, OR, 39, 2:503.

8. Grimsley, *The Hard Hand of War*, 167, 183.

9. Jewett, *Texas in the Confederacy*, 94, 97–98, 111.

10. Stanley S. McGowen, *Horse Sweat and Powder Smoke: The First Texas Cavalry in the Civil War* (College Station: Texas A&M University Press, 1999), 31–32.

11. Revels, *Florida's Civil War*, 14, 28, 33–46, 119, 136.

12. "January 8th," in McGuire, *Diary of a Southern Refugee during the War*, 135. Her niece was Harriet Keene; ibid., 303.

13. Thomas G. Dyer, *Secret Yankees: The Union Circle in Confederate Atlanta* (Baltimore: Johns Hopkins University Press, 1999), 136.

14. "Dear wife November 8th Headquarters 4th Reg't. Co. I Camp Grifin 1861," in *A War of People*, 50.

15. "Fort Brown Texas July 2d 1864 Saturday," in McIntyre, *Federals on the Frontier*, 364.

16. McGowen, *Horse Sweat and Powder Smoke*, 65–73.

17. McCaslin, *Tainted Breeze*, 53.

18. Ibid.

19. Victoria E. Bynum, *The Free State of Jones: Mississippi's Longest Civil War* (Chapel Hill: University of North Carolina Press, 2001). In addition to Jones County, Timothy Smith also discussed Honey Island as a deserter refuge; Timothy B. Smith, *Mississippi in the Civil War: The Home Front* (Jackson: University Press of Mississippi, 2010), 138–142.

20. Polk to Cooper, Demopolis, Ala., March 3, 1864, OR, 32, 3:580–581.

21. Polk Report, Demopolis, March 17, 1864, ibid., 1:499.

22. See note to David Davis, "Washington July 2, 1864," in Lincoln, *The Collected Works of Abraham Lincoln*, 7:421–422. See also Samuel H. Treat, "Washington July 2, 1864," in ibid., 422–423.

23. Mitchell Report, Mattoon, Ill., April 8, 1864, OR, 32, 1:633–635. Mitchell included a list of the dead from the incident: "Killed—Maj. Shuball York, Fifty-fourth Illinois Infantry; Privates Oliver Sallee and James Goodrich, Company C, and John Neer and Alfred Swim, Company G, Fifty-fourth Illinois Infantry; Private William G. Hart, Sixty-second Illinois Infantry; John Jenkins, citizen (loyal); Nelson Wells, citizen (sheriff's party); John Cooper, citizen (sheriff's party)." See also Hosmer Report, Washington D.C., July 26, 1864, ibid., 635–643.

24. Heintzelman Report, Columbus, Ohio, March 29, 1864, ibid., 629.

25. "Dear Sister Hannah, Camp near Hustonville, KY May 18th 1863," in *Dear Sister*, 81.

26. "Dear Wife & Chirldren, Camp Berwick Bay, March 3, 1863," in Sherman, *Letters to Virtue*, 183.

27. S. G. Hicks Report, Paducah, Ky., February 29, 1864, *OR*, 32, 1:417.

28. Brian D. McKnight, *Contested Borderland: The Civil War in Appalachian Kentucky and Virginia* (Lexington: University Press of Kentucky, 2006), 1, 193.

29. Ibid., 122–123. The individual, whom Brian McKnight termed understandably "a remarkable woman," survived her wounds, although the family later had to leave their home.

30. "General Orders, No. 59, Lexington, Ky., July 16, 1864," *OR*, 39, 2:174.

31. Burbridge to Hugh Ewing, Lexington, Ky., July 25, 1864, ibid., 203.

32. Dyer, *Secret Yankees*, 102–104.

33. Stephen W. Sears, *Landscape Turned Red: The Battle of Antietam* (New York: Ticknor & Fields, 1983), 285; Ted Alexander, "Destruction, Disease, and Death: The Battle of Antietam and the Sharpsburg Civilians," *Civil War Regiments* 6, no. 2 (1998): 160.

34. Although popularly known as "Jennie," she signed her name Ginnie, according to historian Stephen Sears, who also noted, "Ginnie Wade would be the only civilian killed during the battle"; Stephen W. Sears, *Gettysburg* (Boston: Houghton Mifflin, 2003), 391, 578n15.

35. Alexander, "Destruction, Disease, and Death," 157–159.

36. Quoted in Craig, *Kentucky Confederates*, 166.

37. Quoted in Cozzens, *Shenandoah 1862*, 105.

38. Marvel, *The Great Task Remaining*, 259.

39. Quoted in ibid.

40. "My Dear Friend, Gayoso House, Memphis, Tenn., October 4, Midnight. [1863]," in William T. Sherman, *Sherman's Civil War: Selected Correspondence of William T. Sherman, 1860–1865*, ed. Brooks D. Simpson and Jean V. Berlin (Chapel Hill: University of North Carolina Press, 1999), 551–552.

41. "Dearest Ellen, Gayoso Memphis Oct. 6 [1863] 7 A.M.," in ibid., 552.

42. "Dearest Ellen, Memphis Oct. 10, 1863," in ibid., 556.

43. David Herbert Donald, *Lincoln* (New York: Simon and Schuster, 1995).

44. William C. Davis, *Jefferson Davis: The Man and His Hour, A Biography* (New York: HarperCollins, 1991), 551–553; see also "May 2d [1864]," in Jones, *A Rebel War Clerk's Diary*, 365.

45. Davis, *Jefferson Davis*, 553; September 18th, [1864], in Jones, *A Rebel War Clerk's Diary*, 422.

46. "Dear Mother Sisters and Brothers Williamsport Md June 7, 1862," in *A War of the People*, 81.

47. Quoted in Cozzens, *Shenandoah 1862*, 368–369.

48. Quoted in Bennett, *Union Jacks*, 204–205.

49. Quoted in McGowen, *Horse Sweat and Powder Smoke*, 104.

50. McKnight, *Contested Borderland*, 165.

51. Moe, *The Last Full Measure*, 80.

52. "Resulted Fatality," *Daily National Republican* (Washington, D.C.), November 23, 1863.

53. "From Charlottesville," *Richmond Daily Dispatch*, November 12, 1861.

54. "Lamentable Accident," *Western Democrat* (Charlotte, N.C.), June 9, 1863.

55. "My dear Wife, In Camp near Fredericksburg, Va., January 12th, 1863," in Holt, *A Surgeon's Civil War*, 66.

56. Marten, *The Children's Civil War*, 111.

57. Wills, *The War Hits Home*, 142–143; O. Kermit Hobbs Jr., *Storm over Suffolk: The Years 1861–1865* (Suffolk, Va.: Suffolk Nansemond Historical Society, 1979), 19–20; Stephen A. Cormier, *The Siege of Suffolk: The Forgotten Campaign, April 11–May 4, 1863* (Lynchburg, Va.: H. E. Howard, 1989), 218–221.

58. *History of the Eleventh Pennsylvania Cavalry, Together with a Complete Roster of the Regiment and Regimental Officers* (Philadelphia: Franklin Printing, 1902), 66.

59. "My dear Ellen, Alexandria, Va., April 13th, 1862," in *The Civil War Letters of General Robert McAllister*, 133.

60. "Accident on the Raleigh and Gaston Railroad," *Newbern (N.C.) Weekly Progress*, November 8, 1862.

61. Silkenat, *Moments of Despair*, 59.

62. Brown, *History of the Fourth Regiment of Minnesota Infantry Volunteers*, 284.

63. Henderson, *41st Virginia Infantry*, 102.

64. *Alexandria (Va.) Gazette*, May 7, 1863.

65. Williams, *General Reub Williams's Memories of Civil War Times*, 82.

66. "Sunday, March 15," in Robert Patrick, *Reluctant Rebel: The Secret Diary of Robert Patrick*, ed. F. Jay Taylor (Baton Rouge: Louisiana State University Press, 1959), 105.

67. "Dear Brother, Before Vicksburgh, June the 6th 1863," in Christie and Christie, *Brother of Mine*, 136–137.

68. Ibid., 369.

69. Ballard, *Vicksburg*, 47, 387, 416.

70. Terrence J. Winschel, *Triumph and Defeat: The Vicksburg Campaign* (Mason City, Iowa: Savas Publishing, 1999), 152.

71. Quoted in ibid.

72. Quoted in ibid.

73. Ballard, *Vicksburg*, 385.

74. "Fatal Accident at Shelby," *Cleveland Morning Leader*, July 10, 1863.

75. Henry Bryan Report, Charleston, January 6, 1864, *OR*, 28, 1:682–684.

76. Alfred Rhett Report, Charleston, January 1, 1864, ibid., 685.

77. E., "Army Correspondence, Charleston, Oct. 18, 1863," *Yorkville (S.C.) Enquirer*, October 21, 1863.

78. Marten, *The Children's Civil War*, 111.

79. *New South (Port Royal, S.C.)*, October 24, 1863.

80. "Fatal Accident," *Richmond Daily Dispatch*, July 7, 1864.

81. Hewitt, *Port Hudson*, 80.

82. *Smoky Hill and Republican Union (Junction City, Kans.)*, August 15, 1863.

83. Hess, *The Knoxville Campaign*, 7.

84. Ibid., 73, 205; Robert Tracy McKenzie, *Lincolnites and Rebels: A Divided Town in the American Civil War* (Oxford: Oxford University Press, 2006), 175.

85. E. Tarrant, *The Wild Riders of the First Kentucky Cavalry*, 212.

86. "February 3d," in Barber, *Army Memoirs of Lucius W. Barber*, 133–134.

87. Walker, *History of the Second Army Corps*, 500–501.

88. *Civilian and Telegraph (Cumberland, Md.)*, June 2, 1864.

89. Ira Berlin, Joseph P. Reidy, and Leslie S. Rowland, eds., *Freedom: A Documentary History of Emancipation, 1861–1867* (Cambridge: Cambridge University Press, 1982), series 2, 367–386, 411–431, esp. 418.

90. Revels, *Florida's Civil War*, 87.

91. "General Orders, No. 99, Washington, April 24, 1863," OR, Series III, 3:147–164. For these examples, see 158.

92. Craig, *Kentucky Confederates*, 225–226.

93. Quoted in Stephen Z. Starr, *The Union Cavalry in the East: From Gettysburg to Appomattox* (Baton Rouge: Louisiana State University Press, 1981), 2:172.

94. Virgil Carrington Jones, *Eight Hours before Richmond* (New York: Henry Holt, 1957), 46–47, 74; Duane Schultz, *The Dahlgren Affair: Terror and Conspiracy in the Civil War* (New York: Norton, 1998), 118–120; Emory M. Thomas, "The Kilpatrick-Dahlgren Raid, Part II," *Civil War Times Illustrated* 17, no. 4 (April 1978): 26–27.

95. John C. Babcock to Dear Colonel, OR, 33:221.

96. Jones, *Eight Hours before Richmond*, 74; Schultz, *The Dahlgren Affair*, 119–120; Thomas, "The Kilpatrick-Dahlgren Raid, Part II," 26–27; "Murder of Their Negro Guide by the Raiders," OR, 33:221.

97. Quoted in Craig, *Kentucky Confederates*, 206–207.

98. Hughes and Whitney, *Jefferson Davis in Blue*, 305–314.

99. Jacqueline Jones, *Saving Savannah: The City and the Civil War* (New York: Vintage Books, 2009), 202.

100. Sherman to Halleck, In the Field, Savannah, January 12, 1865, OR, 47, 2:36. Sherman added that he had no reports from the generals that "Wheeler killed [even] one of them"; ibid.

101. Cooling, *To the Battles of Franklin and Nashville and Beyond*, 209; Van R. Willard, *With the Third Wisconsin Badgers: The Living Experience of the Civil War through the Journals of Van R. Willard*, ed. Steven S. Raab (Mechanicsburg, Pa.: Stackpole Books, 1994), 239.

102. Davis, *What the Yankees Did to Us*, 248.

103. Ibid., 108–110, 188–191.

104. Quoted in ibid., 151–158. See also "Sunday 7," in Richards, *Sam Richards's Civil War Diary*, 230, for a brief reference.

105. A. Wilson Greene, *Civil War Petersburg: Confederate City in the Crucible of War* (Charlottesville: University of Virginia Press, 2006), 315n4.

106. Ibid., 191–192.

107. Ibid., 200, 211.

108. Marvel, *The Great Task Remaining*, 165–171; Iver Berstein, *The New York City Draft Riots: Their Significance for American Society and Politics in the Age of the Civil War* (New York: Oxford University Press, 1990).

109. Wool to Stanton, New York, N.Y., July 15, 1863, OR, 27, 2:876; Wool to Stanton, New York, July 16, 1863—1 A.M., ibid.; Wool to Stanton, New York City, July 20, 1863, ibid., 878.

110. Wool to Stanton, New York City, July 20, 1863, ibid., 882.

111. Jones, *Saving Savannah*, 222. Jones set the number of deaths at "less than a dozen"; ibid.

112. "Terrible Conflagration in Savannah," *Alleghanian (Ebensburg, Pa.)*, February 9, 1865.

113. H. K. Thatcher Report, May 28, 1865, ORN, 22:199.

114. E. Simpson Report, May 26, 1865, ibid., 200.

115. Alfred Fredberg to C. T. Christensen, Mobile, May 26, 1865, OR, 49, 2:912–913.

116. Wm. S. Beebe in James Totten Report, Mobile, Ala., May 25, 1865, ibid., 1:565–566.

117. Jas. G. Patton Report, Mobile, Ala., May 25, 1865, ibid., 566–567. Several subsequent newspaper accounts referenced arrests of suspicious individuals. See, for example, "Cause of the Explosion at Mobile," *Daily Ohio Statesman (Columbus)*, June 13, 1865.

118. E. R. S. Canby to J. A. Rawlins, New Orleans, May 26, 1865, OR, 49, 2:911. See also G. Granger to Canby, Mobile, May 25, 1865, ibid., 907.

119. E. R. S. Canby to Granger, New Orleans, [May] 26, 1865, ibid., 914.

120. "The Mobile Explosion," *New York Herald*, June 10, 1865.

121. "The Late Explosion, Mobile, Ala., June 4, 1865," *New York Herald*, June 17, 1865. Even as this reporting was occurring, a smaller event involving exploding ordnance and resulting in deaths occurred in Chattanooga, Tennessee, on the evening of June 9, 1865. See, for example, "Explosion at Chattanooga," *Daily Intelligencer (Wheeling, W.Va.)*, June 12, 1865; "Explosion and Fire at Chattanooga," *Daily Ohio Statesman (Columbus)*, June 13, 1865.

122. "The Savannah Volunteer Guards from 1858 to 1882," 214, 241.

123. Patrick A. Schroeder, *More Myths about Lee's Surrender* (Farmville, Va.: Farmville Printing, 1995), 9.

124. Walter J. Fraser Jr., *Charleston! Charleston! The History of a Southern City* (Columbia: University of South Carolina Press, 1989), 268–269.

Chapter 10. Not Cheating the Hangman

1. John Keegan, *A History of Warfare* (New York: Knopf, 1993), 382.

2. Wiley, *They Who Fought Here*, 175.

3. Ibid., 182.

4. Fox, *Regimental Losses in the American Civil War*, 61.

5. "Died of His Injuries," *Daily Exchange (Baltimore)*, August 5, 1861.

6. B. F. Schulz, "Lieut. A. H. Vaughn, Killed in the War," *Confederate Veteran* 8, no. 12 (December 1900): 518.

7. Quoted in Bates, *A Texas Cavalry Officer's Civil War*, 7–8.

8. Jones, *Lee's Tigers*, 41–42.

9. Alfred Horatio Belo, *Memoirs of Alfred Horatio Belo: Reminiscences of a North Carolina Volunteer*, ed. Stuart Wright (Gaithersburg, Md.: Old Soldier Books, n.d.), 10–11.

10. Richard Taylor, *Destruction and Reconstruction* (New York: D. Appleton, 1879), 25.

11. *Local News (Alexandria, Va.)*, December 12, 1861.

12. "Dear Wife, Father and Mother, New Orleans, May 6th 1862," in Sherman, *Letters to Virtue*, 30.

13. "Dear Father, Head Quarters Post Commander Indianapolis, Ind., April 5th, 1864," in Colby, *The Civil War Papers of Lt. Colonel Newton T. Colby*, 253.

14. December 1, 1861, in Haydon, *For Country, Cause and Leader*, 138–139.

15. Leech, *Reveille in Washington*, 123–124.

16. McCaslin, *Tainted Breeze*, 50.

17. "Dear Father, In Camp—Lower Potomac. Feb. 9th 1862," in Twichell, *The Civil War Letters of Joseph Hopkins Twichell*, 93.

18. Corell, *History of the Naval Brigade*.

19. Marten, *The Children's Civil War*, 111.

20. Quoted in Corell, *History of the Naval Brigade*, addenda, 21.

21. Horatio J. Sprague, Consulate of the United States of America, Gibraltar, October 18, 1862, *ORN*, 1:508–509.

22. "Local," *Alexandria (Va.) Gazette*, November 17, 1862.

23. "Homicide," *Nashville Daily Union*, January 11, 1863.

24. Bradley R. Clampitt, *Occupied Vicksburg* (Baton Rouge: Louisiana State University Press, 2016), 157–158.

25. "General Orders, No. 7, Vicksburg, Miss., May 18, 1864," *OR*, 39, 2:38.

26. Clampitt, *Occupied Vicksburg*, 162–163.

27. Quoted in Cavanaugh, *6th Virginia Infantry*, 9.

28. Ibid., 29, 80.

29. Ibid., 117.

30. Perry, *Civil War Courts-Martial of North Carolina Troops*, 156.

31. "Thursday 15th May, 1862," in Guerrant, *Bluegrass Confederate*, 84.

32. "Not a Deserter," *Richmond Daily Dispatch*, August 12, 1862.

33. "Dear Bro: Camp on the Rappahannock River 2 miles from Falmouth opposite Fredericksburg, Va. Thursday, Nov. 20, 1862," in Wightman, *From Antietam to Fort Fisher*, 83.

34. "Fatal Shooting Case," *Maryland Free Press (Hagerstown)*, December 5, 1862.

35. "Proceedings in the Courts," *Richmond Daily Dispatch*, November 26, 1862.

36. "From Petersburg, Murder of a Soldier," *Richmond Daily Dispatch*, March 13, 1862.

37. "Murder in the Rebel Army," *Daily National Republican (Washington, D.C.)*, June 3, 1862.

38. McKnight, *Contested Borderland*, 123–124.

39. Harden, *History of the 90th Ohio Volunteer Infantry*, 83.

40. "Foul Play," *Sunbury (Pa.) American*, March 26, 1864.

41. "Early's Movements a Mystery—A Cavalry Fight—A Negro Soldier Killed by a Lieutenant," *Daily Ohio Statesman (Columbus)*, August 8, 1864.

42. "Thursday, 23," in Elizabeth Curtis Wallace, *Glencoe Diary: The War-time Journal of Elizabeth Curtis Wallace*, ed. Eleanor P. Cross and Charles B. Cross Jr. (Chesapeake, Va.: Norfolk Historical Society, 1968), 50; "Murder of a Vermonter," *Orleans Independent Standard (Irasburgh, Vt.)*, August 7, 1863; A. E. Bovay to Dix, Norfolk, Va., July 11, 1863, *OR*, Series II, 6:106; J. L. Holt Report, Washington, August 19, 1863, ibid., 216–218.

43. Lincoln to Foster, Washington, D.C., October 17, 1863, in Lincoln, *The Collected Works of Abraham Lincoln*, 6:522; the letter is listed in *OR*, Series II, 6:426, as October 27.

44. J. G. Foster to Halleck, Fort Monroe, Va., October 23, 1863—11:20 A.M., *OR*, 29, 2:370.

45. James A. Greer, U.S.S. Benton, Off Natchez, August 25, 1863, *ORN*, 25:384.

46. *Alexandria (Va.) Gazette*, September 8, 1863.

47. Foote, *The Gentlemen and the Roughs*, 145–146.

48. "Tuesday 24h, May 1864," in Guerrant, *Bluegrass Confederate*, 449.

49. *Alexandria (Va.) Gazette*, October 1, 1862.

50. Corell, *History of the Naval Brigade*.

51. Quoted in Walter T. Durham, *Reluctant Partners: Nashville and the Union, 1863–1865* (Knoxville: University of Tennessee Press, 2008), 40.

52. Ibid., 150.

53. "Murder of a Soldier," *Richmond Daily Dispatch*, October 23, 1863.

54. Speer, *Portals to Hell*, 94.

55. Ibid., 81, 83, 145.

56. "Fatal Accident," *Richmond Daily Dispatch*, August 25, 1862.

57. *Report of the Adjutant General of the State of Indiana* (Indianapolis: Samuel M. Douglass, 1866), 4:595–596.

58. Quoted in Coski, *Capital Navy*, 183.

59. *Alexandria (Va.) Gazette*, October 25, 1864.

60. Fox, *Regimental Losses in the American Civil War*, 60.

61. "Progressing," *Tri-Weekly Herald (Newberry, S.C.)*, April 1, 1865.

62. Coski, *Capital Navy*, 183.

63. "Murder of a Sailor," *Richmond Daily Dispatch*, February 17, 1864.

64. Bellard, *Gone for a Soldier*, 264.

65. The literature is extensive concerning outcomes that involved the deaths of men after combat, tinged with racial and sectional animus. See, for example, Brian Steel Wills, *The River Was Dyed with Blood: Nathan Bedford Forrest and Fort Pillow* (Norman: University of Oklahoma Press, 2014); George S. Burkhardt, *Confederate Rage, Yankee Wrath: No Quarter in the Civil War* (Carbondale: Southern Illinois University Press, 2007); *Black Flag over Dixie: Racial Atrocities and Reprisals in the Civil War*, ed. Gregory J. W. Urwin (Carbondale: Southern Illinois University Press, 2004).

66. The versions of events vary, but Jeffry Wert captured them from the perspectives of both Mosby and Custer; Jeffry D. Wert, *Custer: The Controversial Life of George Armstrong Custer* (New York: Simon & Schuster, 1996), 185–185; and Jeffry D. Wert, *Mosby's Rangers* (New York: Simon & Schuster, 1990), 214–218. See also James A. Ramage, *Gray Ghost: The Life of John Singleton Mosby* (Lexington: University Press of Kentucky, 1999), 199–200.

67. Quoted in Craig, *Kentucky Confederates*, 270–271.

68. Henry A. Chambers, *Diary of Captain Henry A. Chambers*, ed. T. H. Pearce (Wendell, N.C.: Broadfoot's Bookmark, 1983), 178.

69. W. J. McMurray, *History of the Twentieth Regiment Volunteer Infantry, C.S.A.* (Nashville: Publication Committee, 1905; repr., Nashville: Elder's Bookstore, 1976), 144.

70. Leech, *Reveille in Washington*, 111.

71. Mark A. Weitz, *More Damning Than Slaughter: Desertion in the Confederate Army* (Lincoln: University of Nebraska Press, 2005), 287.

72. Bonsall, *"Well Satisfied with My Position,"* 109–110.

73. Ibid., 114. See Bonsall's remarks, "Monday, January 26th," and "March 4th, Wednesday," in ibid., 86–87, 97.

74. Quoted in John J. Hennessy, *Return to Bull Run: The Campaign and Battle of Second Manassas* (New York: Simon & Schuster, 1993), 55–56, 484n51.

75. "Wife & Chirldren, Camp Parapet, New Orleans, August 30, 1862," in Sherman, *Letters to Virtue*, 82.

76. "Dear Father, In Camp—Lower Potomac. Feb. 9th 1862," in Twichell, *The Civil War Letters of Joseph Hopkins Twichell*, 93.

77. "Mother & Sister, Pine Bluff, Ark Mar, 22, 1863," in Noe, *Reluctant Rebels*, 180.

78. "March 12th 1862," in Cyrena Bailey Stone Diary, 1864, Hargrett Library, University of Georgia, Athens, Ga.

79. "My Dear wife, Near Rapidan Station, Va., Sept. 28th, 1863," in Joseph J. Hoyle, *"Deliver Us from This Cruel War": The Civil War Letters of Lieutenant Joseph J. Hoyle, 55th North Carolina Infantry*, ed. Jeffrey M. Girvan (Jefferson, N.C.: McFarland, 2010), 144.

80. "Dear Cousin Headquarters 11th Regt. P.R.V.C. Camp near Rappahannock Station, Va. Sunday Morning Aug 30th 1863," in Bright Family Papers, Wofford College Archives, Spartanburg, SC.

81. See, for example, Weitz, *More Damning Than Slaughter*, 56–85.

82. Ibid., 44–45.

83. Harden, *History of the 90th Ohio Volunteer Infantry*, 84.

84. Shaw to "Dearest Mother, St. Helena's Island, S.C. June 28th 1863," in Shaw, *Blue-Eyed Child of Fortune*, 362–363.

85. Trask, *16th Virginia Infantry*, 28, 125.

86. Ibid., 28, 78.

87. "My dear Ellen & family, Hatcher's Run, Va., February 16th 1865," in McAllister, *The Civil War Letters of General Robert McAllister*, 587.

88. "Mr. President, Hd Qrs Army N. Va. 13th April 1864," in Robert E. Lee, *Lee's Dispatches: Unpublished Letters of General Robert E. Lee, C.S.A., to Jefferson Davis and the War Department of the Confederate States of America, 1862–1865, from the Private Collection of Wymberley Jones de Renne, of Wormsloe, Georgia*, ed. Douglas Southall Freeman (New York: G. P. Putnam's Sons, 1915), 155–158.

89. "Tuesday 21, Mar 1865" and "General Orders No. 13, Head Quarters Giltner's Brig. Jonesville, Va. 21, Mar. '65," in ibid., 663–664.

90. "Friday 24, Mar: 1865," in ibid., 666–667.

91. *Daily Confederate (Raleigh, N.C.)*, December 3, 1864.

92. Chapla, *50th Virginia Infantry*, 165.

93. McKnight, *Contested Borderland*, 166.

94. Bynum, *The Free State of Jones*, 105.

95. Quoted in ibid., 112.

96. "James Hamilton to Col. T. M. Jack, Office Controlling Quartermaster Tax in Kind for Mississippi and East Louisiana, Columbus, Miss., March 31, 1864," OR, 32, 3:727.

97. James Lile Lemon, *Feed Them the Steel! Being, the Wartime Recollections of Captain James Lile Lemon Co. A, 18th Georgia Infantry, C.S.A.*, ed. Mark H. Lemon (n.p., 2013), 17.

98. "Terrible Accident in Nashville," *Dollar Weekly Bulletin (Maysville, Ky.)*, October 8, 1863.

99. "Fatal Accident," *Daily Confederate (Raleigh, N.C.)*, December 3, 1864.

100. McPherson, *Battle Cry of Freedom*, 797. McPherson noted that Salisbury's 34 percent mortality rate compared to Andersonville's 29. The North's highest facility in this respect was Elmira, New York, at 24 percent; ibid.

101. "Fatal Accident," *Daily Confederate (Raleigh, N.C.)*, December 3, 1864.

102. A. H. Potten to Col. W. Wallace, Office of Military Prisons, Camp Chase, Ohio, January 17, 1864, OR, Series II, 6:855.

103. Inclosure No. 1 and No. 2, Jno. S. Larkin to Capt. Ralph Hunt, Headquarters Exchange Barracks, Nashville, Tenn., December 5, 1862, ibid., 650–651.

104. Quoted in Driver, *5th Virginia Cavalry*, 140.

105. J. J. Burroughs to Seddon, Saltville, March 28, 1864, OR, Series II, 6:1109–1110.

106. Ro. Ould, Second indorsement, April 5, 1864, ibid., 1110.

107. See various communications, *OR*, II, 6:1097–1104; quotation from Third Indorsement, Washington, March 31, 1864, ibid., 1103.

108. Marvel, *Andersonville*, 50.

109. Ibid., 287n58.

110. Quoted in Chapla, *50th Virginia Infantry*, 107,168.

111. "Sunday, June 12th," in Charles Mattocks, *"Unspoiled Heart": The Journal of Charles Mattocks of the 17th Maine*, ed. Philip N. Racine (Knoxville: University of Tennessee Press, 1994), 155–156n59, 348–350.

112. "Friday, June 17th," in ibid., 156.

113. "Oct.," in ibid., 228.

114. James E. Fales, *Prison Life of Lieut. James M. Fales*, ed. George N. Bliss (Providence, R.I.: N. Bangs, Williams and Co., 1882), 49–50.

115. "Fatal Accident," *Richmond Daily Dispatch*, December 31, 1864.

116. "Nov 7th 1863," in John Dooley, *John Dooley's Civil War: An Irish American's Journey in the First Virginia Infantry Regiment*, ed. Robert Emmett Curran (Knoxville: University of Tennessee Press, 2012), 220–221.

117. "23rd [Feb. 1864]," in ibid., 247–248.

118. *Confederate Soldiers, Sailors and Civilians Who Died as Prisoners of War at Camp Douglas, Chicago, Ill., 1862–1865* (Kalamazoo, Mich.: Edgar Gray Publications, n.d.), introduction.

119. Michael Horigan, *Elmira: Death Camp of the North* (Mechanicsburg, Pa.: Stackpole Books, 2002), 179–180.

120. These numbers represent a highlighted and selected portion of the returns from May 1862 to November 1865 rather than the comprehensive listing that appears in the OR. "Abstract from monthly returns of the principal U.S. military prisons," *OR*, Series II, 8:986–1002. July–November 1865, continued in ibid., 1003–1004.

121. Speer, *Portals to Hell*, xiv.

122. Gordon, *A Broken Regiment*, 180–181.

123. Quoted in ibid., 181.

124. Brian D. McKnight, *Confederate Outlaw: Champ Ferguson and the Civil War in Appalachia* (Baton Rouge: Louisiana State University Press, 2011).

125. Warner, *Generals in Gray*, 340–341; Arch Fredric Blakey, *General John H. Winder, C.S.A.* (Gainesville: University of Florida Press, 1990).

126. Blakey, *General John H. Winder, C.S.A.*, 201.

127. Ibid.; Smith, *The Gallant Dead*, 369.

Conclusion: "There Is No Glory in It"

1. McGowen, *Horse Sweat and Powder Smoke*, 95.

2. Linderman, *Embattled Courage*, 116.

3. Sword, *Courage under Fire*, 145.

4. "Mobile, Alabama, Saturday, March 26, 1864," in Patrick, *Reluctant Rebel*, 138.

5. "A Friend," "Obituary of Capt. Henry F. Spahr," *Abingdon Virginian*, April 17, 1863.

6. "My Dear Father, Vicksburg, Aug. 6, 1863," in Christie and Christie, *Brother of Mine*, 161.

7. See, for example, Eric T. Dean, *Shook over Hell: Post-traumatic Stress, Vietnam, and the Civil War* (Cambridge, Mass.: Harvard University Press, 1997).

8. Longacre, *The Sharpshooters*, 134–135, 140.

9. "White House Ranch July 29th 1864," in McIntyre, *Federals on the Frontier*, 381.

10. "Sat. 8" and "Sunday 16," in Richards, *Sam Richards's Civil War Diary*, 191, 192.

Bibliography

Primary Sources

Hargrett Library, University of Georgia, Athens, Ga.
    William Gaston Delony Papers.
    "The Savannah Volunteer Guards from 1858 to 1882." Typescript.
    Cyrena Bailey Stone Diary. 1864.
North Carolina State Archives, Division of Archives and History, Private Collections,
    Raleigh.
    James J. Phillips Papers.
Southern Historical Society Papers, University of North Carolina, Chapel Hill.
    William Dorsey Pender Papers.
U.S. Army Military History Institute, Carlisle Barracks, Pa.
    George W. Griggs Manuscript, Norwich Civil War Round Table Collection.
Wofford College Archives, Spartanburg, S.C.
    Bright Family Papers.

Newspapers
Abingdon Virginian
Alexandria (Va.) Gazette
Alleghanian (Ebensburg, Pa.)
American Citizen (Butler, Pa.)
American Citizen (Canton, Miss.)
Athens (Tenn.) Post
Big Blue Union (Marysville, Kans.)
Bradford Reporter (Towanda, Pa.)
Burlington (Vt.) Free Press
Caledonian (St. Johnsbury, Vt.)
Camden (S.C.) Confederate
Cass County Republican (Dowagiac, Mich.)
Charleston (S.C.) Daily News
Cincinnati Daily Press
Civilian and Telegraph (Cumberland, Md.)
Cleveland Morning Leader

Daily Confederate (Raleigh, N.C.)
Daily Constitutionalist (Augusta, Ga.)
Daily Dayton (Ohio) Express
Daily Evansville (Ind.) Journal
Daily Exchange (Baltimore)
Daily Green Mountain Freeman (Montpelier, Vt.)
Daily Intelligencer (Wheeling, W.Va.)
Daily National Republican (Washington, D.C.)
Daily Ohio Statesman (Columbus)
Dayton (Ohio) Daily Empire
Delaware Gazette (Delaware, Ohio)
Dollar Weekly Bulletin (Maysville, Ky.)
Evansville (Ind.) Daily Journal
Evening Star (Washington, D.C.)
Evening Telegraph (Philadelphia)
Gallipolis (Ohio) Journal
Hillsdale (Mich.) Standard
Holmes County Farmer (Millersburg, Ohio)
Joliet Signal (Joliet, Ill.)
Keowee Courier (Pickens Court House, S.C.)
Lewistown (Pa.) Gazette
Local News (Alexandria, Va.)
Marshall County Republican (Plymouth, Ind.)
Maryland Free Press (Hagerstown)
Maysville (Ky.) Weekly Bulletin
Memphis Daily Appeal
Nashville Daily Union
Nashville Union and American
National Republican (Washington, D.C.)
Newbern (N.C.) Weekly Progress
New Orleans Daily Crescent
New South (Port Royal, S.C.)
New-York Daily Tribune
New York Herald
New York Times
Ohio Democrat (Canal Dover, Ohio)
Orleans Independent Standard (Irasburgh, Vt.)
Palmetto Herald (Port Royal, S.C.)
Raftsman's Journal (Clearfield, Pa.)
Richmond Daily Dispatch
Richmond Enquirer
Semi-Weekly Standard (Raleigh, N.C.)
Shreveport (La.) Daily News
Smoky Hill and Republican Union (Junction City, Kans.)
Soldier's Journal (Rendezvous of Distribution, Va.)
Spirit of Democracy (Woodsfield, Ohio)

Staunton (Va.) Spectator
Sun (New York)
Sunbury (Pa.) American
Tri-Weekly Herald (Newberry, S.C.)
Weekly National Intelligencer (Washington, D.C.)
Weekly Register (Point Pleasant, W.Va.)
Weekly Standard (Raleigh, N.C.)
Western Democrat (Charlotte, N.C.)
Western Reserve Chronicle (Warren, Ohio)
Wilmington (N.C.) Journal
Yorkville (S.C.) Enquirer

Books

Alexander, Edward Porter. *Fighting for the Confederacy: The Personal Recollections of General Edward Porter Alexander.* Edited by Gary W. Gallagher. Chapel Hill: University of North Carolina Press, 1989.

Barber, Lucius W. *Army Memoirs of Lucius W. Barber, Company "D," 15th Illinois Volunteer Infantry, May 24, 1861, to Sept. 30, 1865.* Chicago: J. M. W. Jones Stationery and Printing, 1894.

Barnes, Joseph K. *Medical and Surgical History of the Civil War.* 12 vols. 1870. Reprint, Wilmington, N.C.: Broadfoot, 1990.

Bates, James C. *A Texas Cavalry Officer's Civil War: The Diary and Letters of James C. Bates.* Edited by Richard Lowe. Baton Rouge: Louisiana State University Press, 1999.

Bellard, Alfred. *Gone for a Soldier: The Civil War Memoirs of Private Alfred Bellard.* Edited by David Herbert Donald. Boston: Little, Brown, 1975.

Belo, Alfred Horatio. *Memoirs of Alfred Horatio Belo: Reminiscences of a North Carolina Volunteer.* Edited by Stuart Wright. Gaithersburg, Md.: Old Soldier Books, n.d.

Bennitt, John. *"I Hope to Do My Country Service": The Civil War Letters of John Bennitt, M.D., Surgeon, 19th Michigan Infantry.* Edited by Robert Beasecker. Detroit: Wayne State University Press, 2005.

Berlin, Ira, Joseph P. Reidy, and Leslie S. Rowland, eds. *Freedom: A Documentary History of Emancipation, 1861–1867.* Series 2. Cambridge: Cambridge University Press, 1982.

Betts, Alexander D. *Experiences of a Confederate Chaplain, 1861–186.* Edited by W. A. Betts. Sanford, N.C.: N.C. Conference Methodist Episcopal Church, South, n.d.

Black, James A. *A Civil War Diary: Written by Dr. James A. Black, First Assistant Surgeon, 49th Illinois Infantry.* Edited by Benita K. Moore. Bloomington, Ind.: AuthorHouse, 2008.

Bonsall, Spencer. *"Well Satisfied with My Position": The Civil War Journal of Spencer Bonsall.* Edited by Michael A. Flannery and Katherine H. Oomens. Carbondale: Southern Illinois University Press, 2007.

Bull, Rice C. *Soldiering: The Civil War Diary of Rice C. Bull, 123rd New York Volunteer Infantry.* Edited by K. Jack Bauer. Novato, Calif.: Presidio Press, 1977.

Burge, Dolly Lunt. *The Diary of Dolly Lunt Burge 1848–1879.* Edited by Christine Jacobson Carter. Athens: University of Georgia Press, 1997.

Callaway, Joshua K. *The Civil War Letters of Joshua K. Callaway.* Edited by Judith Lee Hallock. Athens: University of Georgia Press, 1997.

Chambers, Henry A. *Diary of Captain Henry A. Chambers*. Edited by T. H. Pearce. Wendell, N.C.: Broadfoot's Bookmark, 1983.

Chambers, William Pitt. *Blood and Sacrifice: The Civil War Journal of a Confederate Soldier*. Edited by Richard A. Baumgartner. Huntington, W.Va.: Blue Acorn Press, 1994.

Chesnut, Mary. *Mary Chesnut's Civil War*. Edited by C. Vann Woodward. New Haven, Conn.: Yale University Press, 1981.

Christie, Thomas, and William Christie. *Brother of Mine: The Civil War Letters of Thomas and William Christie*. Edited by Hampton Smith. St. Paul: Minnesota Historical Society Press, 2011.

The Civil War Memoirs of a Virginia Cavalryman. Edited by Thomas P. Nanzig. Tuscaloosa: University of Alabama Press, 2007.

Claflin, Gilbert, and Esther Claflin. *A Quiet Corner of the War: The Civil War Letters of Gilbert and Esther Claflin, Oconomowoc, Wisconsin, 1862–1863*. Edited by Judy Cook. Madison: University of Wisconsin Press, 2013.

Coffin, Charles Carleton. *Four Years of Fighting: A Volume of Personal Observations with the Army and Navy, from First Battle of Bull Run to the Fall of Richmond*. Boston: Ticknor and Fields, 1866.

Colby, Newton T. *The Civil War Papers of Lt. Colonel Newton T. Colby, New York Infantry*. Edited by William E. Hughes. Jefferson, N.C.: McFarland, 2003.

The Confederacy Is on Her Way Up the Spout: Letters to South Carolina, 1861–1864. Edited by J. Roderick Heller III and Carolynn Ayres Heller. Athens: University of Georgia Press, 1992.

A Confederate Marine: A Sketch of Henry Lea Graves with Excerpts from the Graves Family Correspondence, 1861–1865. Edited by Richard Harwell. Tuscaloosa, Ala.: Confederate Publishing, 1963.

Connelly, T. W. *History of the Seventieth Ohio Regiment, from Its Organization to Its Mustering Out*. Cincinnati, Ohio: Peake Bros. 1902. Reprint, La Crosse, Wis.: Brookhaven Press, 2008.

Cormany, Samuel. *The Cormany Diaries: A Northern Family in the Civil War*. Edited by James C. Mohr. Pittsburgh: University of Pittsburgh Press, 1982.

Cushing, William B. *The Sea Eagle: The Civil War Memoir of Lt. Cdr. William B. Cushing*. Edited by Alden R. Carter. Lanham, Md.: Rowman and Littlefield, 2009.

Davidson, Greenlee. *Captain Greenlee Davidson, C.S.A. Diary and Letters 1851–1863*. Edited by Charles W. Turner. Verona, Va.: McClure Press, 1975.

Dear Sister: The Civil War Letters of the Brothers Gould. Edited by Robert F. Harris and John Niflot. Westport, Conn.: Praeger, 1998.

Diggins, Bartholomew. *Sailing with Farragut: The Civil War Recollections of Bartholomew Diggins*. Edited by George S. Burkhardt. Knoxville: University of Tennessee Press, 2016.

Dooley, John. *John Dooley's Civil War: An Irish American's Journey in the First Virginia Infantry Regiment*. Edited by Robert Emmett Curran. Knoxville: University of Tennessee Press, 2012.

Fales, James E. *Prison Life of Lieut. James M. Fales*. Edited by George N. Bliss. Providence, R.I.: N. Bangs, Williams and Co., 1882.

Fitzpatrick, Mason Hill. *Letters to Amanda: The Civil War Letters of Mason Hill Fitzpatrick, Army of Northern Virginia*. Edited by Jeffrey C. Lowe and Sam Hodges. Macon, Ga.: Mercer University Press, 1998.

Flerharty, Stephen F. *"Jottings from Dixie": The Civil War Dispatches of Sergeant Major Stephen F. Flerharty, U.S.A.* Edited by Philip J. Reyburn and Terry L. Wilson. Baton Rouge: Louisiana State University Press, 1999.

Gordon, John B. *Reminiscences of the Civil War*. New York: Charles Scribner's Sons, 1905.

Gorgas, Josiah. *The Journals of Josiah Gorgas, 1857–1878*. Edited by Sarah Woolfolk Wiggins. Tuscaloosa: University of Alabama Press, 1995.

Gould, John Mead. *The Civil War Journals of John Mead Gould 1861–1866*. Edited by William B. Jordan Jr. Baltimore: Butternut and Blue, 1997.

Gregg, Josiah. *The Diary of a Civil War Marine: Private Josiah Gregg*. Edited by Wesley Moody and Adrienne Sachse. Madison, N.J.: Fairleigh Dickinson University Press, 2013.

Guerrant, Edward O. *Bluegrass Confederate: The Headquarters Diary of Edward O. Guerrant*. Edited by William C. Davis and Meredith L. Sentor. Baton Rouge: Louisiana State University Press, 1999.

Haydon, Charles B. *For Country, Cause and Leader: The Civil War Journal of Charles B. Haydon*. Edited by Stephen W. Sears. New York: Ticknor & Fields, 1993.

Hayward, Ambrose Henry. *Last to Leave the Field: The Life and Letters of First Sergeant Ambrose Henry Hayward, 28th Pennsylvania Volunteer Infantry*. Edited by Timothy J. Orr. Knoxville: University of Tennessee Press, 2010.

Holt, Daniel M. *A Surgeon's Civil War: The Letters and Diary of Daniel M. Holt, M.D.* Edited by James M. Grenier, Janet L. Coryell, and James R. Smither. Kent, Ohio: Kent State University Press, 1994.

Horigan, Michael. *Elmira: Death Camp of the North*. Mechanicsburg, Pa.: Stackpole Books, 2002.

Hough, Alfred Lacey. *Soldier in the West: The Civil War Letters of Alfred Lacey Hough*. Edited by Robert G. Athearn. Philadelphia: University of Pennsylvania Press, 1957.

Hoyle, Joseph J. *"Deliver Us from This Cruel War": The Civil War Letters of Lieutenant Joseph J. Hoyle, 55th North Carolina Infantry*. Edited by Jeffrey M. Girvan. Jefferson, N.C.: McFarland, 2010.

Humphreys, Charles A. *Field, Camp, Hospital and Prison in the Civil War, 1863–1865*. Freeport, N.Y.: Books for Libraries Press, 1918. Reprint, Manchester, N.H.: Ayer Co., 1975.

Ingalls, Henry H. *The Diary of Henry H. Ingalls, Sixth Regiment of Massachusetts Volunteer Militia, Company K., Suffolk, Virginia, August 31, 1862 to May 26, 1863*. Edited by Giles H. Newsome. Suffolk, Va.: Robert Hardy Publications, 1986.

Johnson, Charles F. *The Long Roll: Being a Journal of the Civil War as Set Down during the Years 1861–1865 by Charles F. Johnson, Sometime of Hawkins Zouaves*. East Aurora, N.Y.: Roycrofters, 1911. Reprint, Shepherdstown, W.Va.: Carabelle Books, 1986.

Jones, John Beauchamp. *A Rebel War Clerk's Diary at the Confederate States Capital*. Edited by Earl Schenck Miers. New York: A. S. Barnes, 1961.

King, William Henry. *No Pardons to Ask, nor Apologies to Make: The Journal of William Henry King, Gray's 28th Louisiana Infantry Regiment*. Edited by Gary D. Joiner, Marilyn S. Joyner, and Clifton D. Cardin. Knoxville: University of Tennessee Press, 2006.

Kinsley, Rufus. *Diary of a Christian Soldier: Rufus Kinsley and the Civil War*. Edited by David C. Rankin. New York: Cambridge University Press, 2004.

Lamson, Roswell H. *Lamson of the Gettysburg: The Civil War Letters of Lieutenant Roswell H. Lamson, U.S. Navy*. Edited by James M. McPherson and Patricia R. McPherson. New York: Oxford University Press, 1997.

LeConte, Emma. *When the World Ended: The Diary of Emma LeConte.* Edited by Earl Schenck Miers. New York: Oxford University Press, 1957.

Lee, Robert E. *Lee's Dispatches: Unpublished Letters of General Robert E. Lee, C.S.A., to Jefferson Davis and the War Department of the Confederate States of America, 1862–1865, from the Private Collection of Wymberley Jones de Renne, of Wormsloe, Georgia.* Edited by Douglas Southall Freeman. New York: G. P. Putnam's Sons, 1915.

Lemon, James Lile. *Feed Them the Steel! Being, the Wartime Recollections of Captain James Lile Lemon Co. A, 18th Georgia Infantry, C.S.A.* Edited by Mark H. Lemon. N.p., 2013.

Lincoln, Abraham. *The Collected Works of Abraham Lincoln.* 11 vols. Edited by Roy P. Basler. New Brunswick, N.J.: Rutgers University Press, 1953.

Lincoln's White House Secretary: The Adventurous Life of William O. Stoddard. Edited by Harold Holzer. Carbondale: Southern Illinois University Press, 2007.

Lyman, Theodore. *Meade's Army: The Private Notebooks of Lt. Col. Theodore Lyman.* Edited by David W. Lowe. Kent, Ohio: Kent State University Press, 2007.

Lyon, Henry C. *"Desolating This Fair Country": The Civil War Diary and Letters of Lt. Henry C. Lyon, 34th New York.* Edited by Emily N. Radigan. Jefferson, N.C.: McFarland, 1999.

Malone, Bartlett Yancey. *The Diary of Bartlett Yancey Malone.* Edited by William Whatly Pierson Jr. Chapel Hill: University of North Carolina Press, 1919.

Marshall, Albert O. *Army Life. From a Soldier's Journal. Incidents, Sketches and Record of a Union Soldier's Army Life, in Camp and Field. 1861–64.* Edited by Robert G. Schulz. Fayetteville: University of Arkansas Press, 2009.

Mattocks, Charles. *"Unspoiled Heart": The Journal of Charles Mattocks of the 17th Maine.* Edited by Philip N. Racine. Knoxville: University of Tennessee Press, 1994.

McAllister, Robert. *The Civil War Letters of General Robert McAllister.* Edited by James I. Robertson Jr. New Brunswick, N.J.: Rutgers University Press, 1965.

McCarthy, Carlton. *Detailed Minutiae of Soldier Life in the Army of Northern Virginia, 1861–1865.* Richmond, Va.: C. McCarthy, 1882. Reprint, Lincoln, University of Nebraska Press, 1993.

McGuire, Judith Brockenbrough. *Diary of a Southern Refugee during the War, Annotated Edition.* Edited by James I. Robertson Jr. Lexington: University Press of Kentucky, 2014.

McIlvaine, Samuel. *By the Dim and Flaring Lamps: The Civil War Diaries of Samuel McIlvaine.* Edited by Clayton E. Cramer. Monroe, N.Y.: Library Research Associates, 1990.

McIntyre, Benjamin F. *Federals on the Frontier: The Diary of Benjamin F. McIntyre, 1862–1864.* Edited by Nannie M. Tilley. Austin: University of Texas Press, 1963.

McMurray, W. J. *History of the Twentieth Regiment Volunteer Infantry, C.S.A.* Nashville: Publication Committee, 1905. Reprint, Nashville: Elder's Bookstore, 1976.

Meade's Headquarters, 1863–1865: Letters of Colonel Theodore Lyman from the Wilderness to Appomattox. Edited by George R. Agassiz. Boston: Atlantic Monthly Press, 1922.

Miller, William Bluffton. *Fighting for Liberty and Right: The Civil War Diary of William Bluffton Miller, First Sergeant, Company K, Seventy-Fifth Indiana Volunteer Infantry.* Edited by Jeffrey L. Patrick and Robert J. Willey. Knoxville: University of Tennessee Press, 2005.

Montgomery, Frank A. *Reminiscences of a Mississippian in Peace and War.* Cincinnati: Robert Clarke, 1901.

Morton, John Watson. *The Artillery of Nathan Bedford Forrest's Cavalry.* Nashville: Publishing House of the M.E. Church, South, 1909.

Nelson, William Cowper. *The Hour of Our Nation's Agony: The Civil War Letters of Lt.*

William Cowper Nelson of Mississippi. Edited by Jennifer W. Ford. Knoxville: University of Tennessee Press, 2007.

Opdycke, Emerson. *To Battle for God and the Right: The Civil War Letterbooks of Emerson Opdycke.* Edited by Glenn V. Longacre and John E. Hass. Urbana: University of Illinois Press, 2003.

Paine, Halbert Eleazer. *A Wisconsin Yankee in Confederate Bayou Country: The Civil War Reminiscences of a Union General Halbert Eleazer Paine.* Edited by Samuel C. Hyde Jr. Baton Rouge: Louisiana State University Press, 2009.

Patrick, Robert. *Reluctant Rebel: The Secret Diary of Robert Patrick.* Edited by F. Jay Taylor. Baton Rouge: Louisiana State University Press, 1959.

Pender, William Dorsey. *The General to His Lady: The Civil War Letters of William Dorsey Pender to Fanny Pender.* Edited by William W. Hassler. Chapel Hill: University of North Carolina Press, 1965.

Peyton, George Quintus. *Stonewall Jackson's Foot Cavalry Company A, 13th Virginia Infantry.* Edited by Walbrook D. Swank. Shippensburg, Pa.: Burd Street Press, 2001.

Porter, David D. *The Naval History of the Civil War.* New York: Sherman, 1886.

"A Punishment on the Nation": An Iowa Soldier Endures the Civil War. Edited by Brian Craig Miller. Kent, Ohio: Kent State University Press, 2012.

Putnam, Sallie. *Richmond during the War; Four Years of Personal Observation. By a Richmond Lady.* New York: G. W. Carleton, 1867.

Rains, Geo. W. *History of the Confederate Powder Works.* Augusta, Ga.: Chronicle and Constitutionalist Print, 1882.

Randolph, Valentine C. *A Soldier's Diary: Valentine C. Randolph, 39th Illinois Regiment.* Edited by David D. Roe. DeKalb: Northern Illinois University Press, 2006.

Ransom, John L. *John Ransom's Andersonville Diary.* Philadelphia: Douglas Brothers, 1883. Reprint, New York: Berkley Books, 1988.

Rawle, William Brooke. *History of the Third Pennsylvania Cavalry, Sixtieth Regiment Pennsylvania Volunteers in the American Civil War 1861–1865.* Philadelphia: Franklin Printing, 1905.

Report of the Adjutant General of the State of Indiana. Indianapolis: Samuel M. Douglass, 1866.

Richards, Sam. *Sam Richards's Civil War Diary: A Chronicle of the Atlanta Home Front.* Edited by Wendy Hamand Venet. Athens: University of Georgia Press, 2009.

Scott, Irby Goodwin. *Lee and Jackson's Bloody Twelfth: The Letters of Irby Goodwin Scott, First Lieutenant, Company G, Putnam Light Infantry, Twelfth Georgia Volunteer Infantry.* Edited by Johnnie Perry Pearson. Knoxville: University of Tennessee Press, 2010.

Shaw, Robert Gould. *Blue-Eyed Child of Fortune: The Civil War Letters of Colonel Robert Gould Shaw.* Edited by Russell Duncan. Athens: University of Georgia Press, 1992.

Sheffey, John Preston. *Soldier of Southwestern Virginia: The Civil War Letters of Captain John Preston Sheffey.* Edited by James I. Robertson Jr. Baton Rouge: Louisiana State University Press, 2004.

Sherman, Charles W. *Letters to Virtue: A Civil War Journey of Courage, Faith, and Love.* Edited by Ann K. Gunnin. Alpharetta, Ga.: Booklogix, 2014.

Sherman, Francis T. *Quest for a Star: The Civil War Letters and Diaries of Colonel Francis T. Sherman of the 88th Illinois.* Edited by C. Knight Aldridge. Knoxville: University of Tennessee Press, 1999.

Sherman, William T. *Memoirs of General William T. Sherman*. New York: Charles L. Webster, 1892.

———. *Sherman's Civil War: Selected Correspondence of William T. Sherman, 1860–1865*. Edited by Brooks D. Simpson and Jean V. Berlin. Chapel Hill: University of North Carolina Press, 1999.

Siege Train: The Journal of a Confederate Artilleryman in the Defense of Charleston. Edited by Warren Ripley. Columbia: University of South Carolina Press, 1986.

Spence, Alexander E., and Thomas F. Spence. *Getting Used to Being Shot At: The Spence Family Civil War Letters*. Edited by Mark K. Christ. Fayetteville: University of Arkansas Press, 2002.

Sprott, Samuel H. *Cush: A Civil War Memoir*. Edited by Louis R. Smith Jr. and Andrew Quist. Livingston, Ala.: Livingston Press, 1999.

Stillwell, Leander. *The Story of a Common Soldier of Army Life in the Civil War 1861–1865*. Erie, Kans.: Franklin Hudson Publishing, 1920.

The Stilwell Letters: A Georgian in Longstreet's Corps, Army of Northern Virginia. Edited by Ronald H. Moseley. Macon, Ga.: Mercer University Press, 2002.

Tarrant, E. *The Wild Riders of the First Kentucky Cavalry: A History of the Regiment, in the Great War of the Rebellion 1861–1865, Telling of Its Origins and Organization; A Description of the Material of Which It Was Composed; Its Rapid and Severe Marches, Hard Service, and Fierce Conflicts on Many a Bloody Field*. Louisville, Ky.: R. H. Carothers, 1894.

Taylor, Richard. *Destruction and Reconstruction*. New York: D. Appleton, 1879.

Terrell, William Henry Harrison. *Report of the Adjutant General of the State of Indiana, 1861–1865. Containing Rosters of Enlisted Men of Indiana Regiments Numbered from the Sixth to the Twenty-Ninth Inclusive*. Indianapolis: Samuel M. Douglass, 1866.

Their Patriotic Duty: The Civil War Letters of the Evans Family of Brown County, Ohio. Edited by Robert F. Engs and Corey M. Brooks. Transcriptions by Joseph Shelton Evans Jr. New York: Fordham University Press, 2007.

Thompson, B. F. *History of the 112th Regiment of Illinois Volunteer Infantry, in the Great War of the Rebellion, 1862–1865*. Toulon, Ill.: Stalk County News Office, 1885.

Thompson, S. Millett. *Thirteenth Regiment of New Hampshire Volunteer Infantry in the War of the Rebellion 1861–1865: A Diary Covering Three Years and a Day*. Boston: Houghton, Mifflin, 1888.

Tunnard, W. H. *A Southern Record: The History of the Third Regiment Louisiana Infantry. Containing a Complete Record of the Campaigns in Arkansas and Mississippi; The Battles of Oak Hills, Elk Horn, Iuka, Corinth; The Second Siege of Vicksburg, Anecdotes, Camps, Scenery, and Descriptions of the Country through Which the Regiment Marched, Etc., Etc.* Baton Rouge: La., n.p. 1866. Reprint, Fayetteville: University of Arkansas Press, 1997.

Twichell, Joseph Hopkins. *The Civil War Letters of Joseph Hopkins Twichell: A Chaplain's Story*. Athens: University of Georgia Press, 2006.

Tyler, Mason Whiting. *Recollections of the Civil War, with Many Original Diary Entries and Letters Written from the Seat of War, and with Annotated References*. Edited by William S. Tyler. New York: G. P. Putnam's Sons, 1912.

U.S. Department of War. *The War of the Rebellion: A Compilation of the Official Records of the Union and Confederate Armies*. 70 vols. in 127 serials and index. Washington, D.C.: U.S. Government Printing Office, 1880–1901.

U.S. Naval War Records Office. *Official Records of the Union and Confederate Navies in the War of the Rebellion*. 30 vols. Washington, D.C.: U.S. Government Printing Office, 1894–1922.

Voices from Company D: Diaries of the Greensboro Guards, Fifth Alabama Infantry Regiment, Army of Northern Virginia. Edited by G. Ward Hubbs. Athens: University of Georgia Press, 2003.

Voris, Alvin Coe. *A Citizen-Soldier's Civil War: The Letters of Brevet Major General Alvin C. Voris*. Edited by Jerome Mushkat. DeKalb: Northern Illinois University Press, 2002.

Wallace, Elizabeth Curtis. *Glencoe Diary: The War-time Journal of Elizabeth Curtis Wallace*. Edited by Eleanor P. Cross and Charles B. Cross Jr. Chesapeake, Va.: Norfolk Historical Society, 1968.

A War of the People: Vermont Civil War Letters. Edited by Jeffrey D. Marshall. Hanover, N.H.: University Press of New England, 1999.

Watkins, Sam R. *"Co. Aytch": A Side Show of the Big Show*. New York: Collier Books, 1962.

Weep Not for Me Dear Mother. Edited by Elizabeth Whitley Roberson. Gretna, La.: Pelican Publishing, 1996.

Wightman, Edward King. *From Antietam to Fort Fisher: The Civil War Letters of Edward King Wightman, 1862–1865*. Edited by Edward G. Longacre. Rutherford, N.J.: Fairleigh Dickinson University Press, 1985.

Willard, Van R. *With the Third Wisconsin Badgers: The Living Experience of the Civil War through the Journals of Van R. Willard*. Edited by Steven S. Raab. Mechanicsburg, Pa.: Stackpole Books, 1994.

Willcox, Orlando. *Forgotten Valor: The Memoirs, Journals, and Civil War Letters of Orlando Willcox*. Edited by Robert Garth Scott. Kent, Ohio: Kent State University Press, 1999.

Williams, Reub. *General Reub Williams's Memories of Civil War Times: Personal Reminiscences of Happenings That Took Place from 1861 to the Grand Review*. Edited by Sally Coplen Hogan. Westminster, Md.: Heritage Books, 2006.

Wilson, James Harrison. *Under the Old Flag: Recollections of Military Operations in the War for the Union, the Spanish War, the Boxer Rebellion, etc*. 2 vols. New York: D. Appleton, 1912.

Woodward, John B. *John B. Woodward: A Biographical Memoir*. Edited by Elijah R. Kennedy. New York: De Vinne Press, 1897.

Wright, James A. *No More Gallant a Deed: A Civil War Memoir of the First Minnesota Volunteers*. Edited by Steven J. Keillor. St. Paul: Minnesota Historical Society Press, 2001.

Articles

Barnes, W. T. "An Incident of Kenesaw Mountain." *Confederate Veteran* 30, no. 2 (February 1922): 48–49.

Bartlett, John Russell. "The 'Brooklyn' at the Passage of the Forts." In *Battles and Leaders of the Civil War Being for the Most Part Contributions by Union and Confederate Officers: Based upon "The Century" War Series*, edited by Robert Underwood Johnson and Clarence Clough Buel, 2:56–69. New York: Thomas Yoseloff, 1956.

Butler, Edward A. "Personal Experiences in the Navy, 1862–65." In *War Papers Read before the Commandery of the State of Maine, Military Order of the Loyal Legion of the United States*, 2:184–200. Portland, Maine: Lefavor-Tower, 1902. Reprint, Wilmington, N.C.: Broadfoot, 1992.

Chamberlain, W. H. "The Skirmish Line in the Atlanta Campaign." In *The Atlanta Papers*, edited by Sydney C. Kerksis, 182–196. Dayton, Ohio: Press of Morningside Bookshop, 1980.

Childe, Charles B. "General Butler at New Orleans, 1862." In *Sketches of War History 1861–1865: Papers Prepared for the Ohio Commandery of the Military Order of the Loyal Legion of the United States 1896–1903*, edited by W. H. Chamberlain, A. M. Van Dyke, and George A. Thayer, 5:175–198. Cincinnati: Robert Clarke, 1903. Reprint, Wilmington, N.C.: Broadfoot, 1992.

Collins, John L. "Sad Story of the War." *Confederate Veteran* 6, no. 3 (March 1898): 116.

Dawes, Rufus S. "On the Right at Antietam." In *Sketches of War History 1861–1865: Papers Prepared for the Ohio Commandery of the Military Order of the Loyal Legion of the United States 1888–1890*, edited by Robert Hunter, 3:252–263. Cincinnati: Robert Clarke, 1890. Reprint, Wilmington, N.C.: Broadfoot, 1991.

Harrell, John M. "Arkansas." In *Confederate Military History: A Library of Confederate States History Written by Distinguished Men of the South, and Edited by Clement A. Evans of Georgia.* Edited by Clement A. Evans. 19 vols. Atlanta: Confederate Publishing, 1899.

Lamb, William. "The Defense of Fort Fisher." In *Battles and Leaders of the Civil War, Being for the Most Part Contributions by Union and Confederate Officers: Based upon "The Century" War Series*, edited by Robert Underwood Johnson and Clarence Clough Buel, 4:642–654. New York: Thomas Yoseloff, 1956.

Mervine, Charles. "Jottings by the Way: A Sailor's Log 1862 to 1864." Pts. 1 and 2, edited by Kent Packard. *Pennsylvania Magazine of History and Biography* 71 (April 1947): 125; (July 1947): 270.

Newton, George. "Atlanta Paper No. 15 Battle of Peach Tree Creek." In *The Atlanta Papers*, edited by Sydney C. Kerksis, 391–408. Dayton: Ohio: Press of Morningside Bookshop, 1980.

"Notes on the Union and Confederate Armies." In *Battles and Leaders of the Civil War*, edited by Robert Underwood Johnson and Clarence Clough Buel, 4:767. New York: Thomas Yoseloff, 1956.

Owen, U. G. "Letters of a Confederate Surgeon in the Army of Tennessee to His Wife." Edited by Enoch L. Mitchell. *Tennessee Historical Quarterly* 5, no. 2 (June 1946): 142–181.

Schulz, B. F. "Lieut. A. H. Vaughn, Killed in the War." *Confederate Veteran* 8, no. 12 (December 1900): 518.

Semmes, Raphael. "Admiral on Horseback: The Diary of Brigadier General Raphael Semmes, February–May 1865." Edited by W. Stanley Hoole. *Alabama Review* 28 (April 1975): 129–150.

Sheridan, Michael V. "Charging with Sheridan up Missionary Ridge." In *Battles and Leaders of the Civil War*, edited by Peter Cozzens, 5:452. Urbana: University of Illinois Press, 2007.

Shively, J. W. "The U.S.S. 'Mississippi' at the Capture of New Orleans in 1862." In *War Papers Being Papers Read before the Commandery of the District of Columbia Military Order of the Loyal Legion of the United States 1887–1897*, 1:226–245. 1897. Reprint, Wilmington, N.C.: Broadfoot, 1993.

Smith, Frank H. "The Forrest-Gould Affair." *Civil War Times Illustrated* 9, no. 7 (November 1970): 32–37.

Spann, S. G. "Chocktaw Indians as Confederate Soldiers." *Confederate Veteran* 13, no. 12 (December 1905): 560–561.

Taylor, John M. "Potomac Flotilla: A Gunboat Captain's Diary." In *Raiders and Blockaders: The American Civil War Afloat*, edited by William N. Still Jr., John M. Taylor, and Norman C. Delaney, 214–223. Washington, D.C.: Brassey's, 1998.

Van Nest, John F. "Yellow Fever on the Blockade of the Indian River: A Tragedy of 1864." *Florida Historical Quarterly* 21, no. 4 (April 1943): 352–357.

Vaughan, Turner. "Diary of Turner Vaughan Co. 'C' 4th, Alabama Regiment, C.S.A. Commenced March 4th, 1863 and Ending February 12th, 1864." *Alabama Historical Quarterly* 18, no. 4 (Winter 1956): 573–601.

Voris, Alvin C. "Charleston in the Rebellion." In *Sketches of War History 1861–1865: Papers Read before the Ohio Commandery of the Military Order of the Loyal Legion of the United States 1886–1888*, edited by Robert Hunter, 2:293–341. Cincinnati: Robert Clarke, 1888. Reprint, Wilmington, N.C.: Broadfoot, 1991.

Weist, J. R. "The Medical Department in the War." In *Sketches of War History 1861–1865: Papers Read before the Ohio Commandery of the Military Order of the Loyal Legion of the United States 1886–1888*, edited by Robert Hunter, 2:71–95. Cincinnati: Robert Clarke, 1888. Reprint, Wilmington, N.C.: Broadfoot, 1991.

Secondary Sources

Books

Abdill, George B. *Civil War Railroads*. Seattle, Wash.: Superior Publishing, 1961.

Armistead, Gene C. *Horses and Mules in the Civil War: A Complete History with a Roster of More Than 700 War Horses*. Jefferson, N.C.: McFarland, 2013.

Ballard, Michael B. *Vicksburg: The Campaign That Opened the Mississippi*. Chapel Hill: University of North Carolina Press, 2004.

Beaudot, William J. K. *The 24th Wisconsin Infantry in the Civil War: The Biography of a Regiment*. Mechanicsburg, Pa.: Stackpole Books, 2003.

Belcher, Dennis W. *The 11th Missouri Infantry in the Civil War: A History and Roster*. Jefferson, N.C.: McFarland, 2011.

Bennett, Michael J. *Union Jacks: Yankee Sailors in the Civil War*. Chapel Hill: University of North Carolina Press, 2004.

Berstein, Iver. *The New York City Draft Riots: Their Significance for American Society and Politics in the Age of the Civil War*. New York: Oxford University Press, 1990.

Black, Robert C., III. *The Railroads of the Confederacy*. Chapel Hill: University of North Carolina Press, 1952.

Black Flag over Dixie: Racial Atrocities and Reprisals in the Civil War. Edited by Gregory J. W. Urwin. Carbondale: Southern Illinois University Press, 2004.

Blakey, Arch Fredric. *General John H. Winder, C.S.A.* Gainesville: University of Florida Press, 1990.

Bonds, Russell S. *War Like a Thunderbolt: The Battle and Burning of Atlanta*. Yardley, Pa.: Westholme Publishing, 2009.

Bowen, J. R. *Regimental History of the First New York Dragoons during Three Years of Active Service in the Great Civil War*. N.p.: by the author, 1900.

Brandt, Nat. *Mr. Tubbs' Civil War.* Syracuse, N.Y.: Syracuse University Press, 1996.

Bridges, Hal. *Lee's Maverick General: Daniel Harvey Hill.* New York: McGraw-Hill, 1961.

Brown, Alonzo L. *History of the Fourth Regiment of Minnesota Infantry Volunteers during the Great Rebellion 1861–1865.* St. Paul, Minn.: Pioneer Press, 1892.

Burkhardt, George S. *Confederate Rage, Yankee Wrath: No Quarter in the Civil War.* Carbondale: Southern Illinois University Press, 2007.

Bynum, Victoria E. *The Free State of Jones: Mississippi's Longest Civil War.* Chapel Hill: University of North Carolina Press, 2001.

Carr, Dawson. *Gray Phantoms of the Cape Fear: Running the Civil War Blockade.* Winston-Salem, N.C.: John F. Blair, 1998.

Cavanaugh, Michael A. *6th Virginia Infantry.* Lynchburg, Va.: H. E. Howard, 1988.

Chaffin, Tom. *The H. L. Hunley: The Secret Hope of the Confederacy.* New York: Hill and Wang, 2008.

———. *Sea of Gray: The Around-the-World Odyssey of the Confederate Raider Shenandoah.* New York: Hill and Wang, 2006.

Chapla, John D. *50th Virginia Infantry.* Lynchburg, Va.: H. E. Howard, 1997.

Clampitt, Bradley R. *Occupied Vicksburg.* Baton Rouge: Louisiana State University Press, 2016.

Clark, Donald A. *The Notorious "Bull" Nelson: Murdered Civil War General.* Carbondale: Southern Illinois University Press, 2011.

Clark, John E., Jr. *Railroads in the Civil War: The Impact of Management on Victory and Defeat.* Baton Rouge: Louisiana State University Press, 2001.

Clark, Walter. *Histories of the Several Regiments and Battalions from North Carolina in the Great War, 1861–'65.* 5 vols. Raleigh: E. M. Uzell, 1901. Reprint, Wendell, N.C.: Broadfoot, 1982.

Coggins, Jack. *Arms and Equipment of the Civil War.* New York: Fairfax Press, 1983.

Confederate Soldiers, Sailors and Civilians Who Died as Prisoners of War at Camp Douglas, Chicago, Ill., 1862–1865. Kalamazoo, Mich.: Edgar Gray Publications, n.d.

Cooling, Benjamin Franklin. *Forts Henry and Donelson: The Key to the Confederate Heartland.* Knoxville: University of Tennessee Press, 1987.

———. *To the Battles of Franklin and Nashville and Beyond: Stabilization and Reconstruction in Tennessee and Kentucky, 1864–1866.* Knoxville: University of Tennessee Press, 2011.

Corell, Philip, ed. *History of the Naval Brigade 99th N.Y. Volunteers Union Coast Guard, 1861–1865.* New York: Regimental Veterans Association, 1905.

Cormier, Stephen A. *The Siege of Suffolk: The Forgotten Campaign, April 11–May 4, 1863.* Lynchburg, Va.: H. E. Howard, 1989.

Coski, John M. *Capital Navy: The Men, Ships and Operations of the James River Squadron.* Campbell, Calif.: Savas Woodbury, 1996.

Cozzens, Peter. *Shenandoah 1862: Stonewall Jackson's Valley Campaign.* Chapel Hill: University of North Carolina Press, 2008.

Craig, Berry. *Kentucky Confederates: Secession, Civil War, and the Jackson Purchase.* Lexington: University Press of Kentucky, 2014.

Daniel, Larry J. *Cannoneers in Gray: The Field Artillery of the Army of Tennessee, 1861–1865.* Tuscaloosa: University of Alabama Press, 1984.

———. *Soldiering in the Army of Tennessee: A Portrait of Life in a Confederate Army.* Chapel Hill: University of North Carolina Press, 1991.

Davis, C. H. *Life of Charles Henry Davis, Rear Admiral, 1807–1877*. Boston: Houghton Mifflin, 1899.

Davis, Stephen. *What the Yankees Did to Us: Sherman's Bombardment and Wrecking of Atlanta*. Macon, Ga.: Mercer University Press, 2012.

Davis, William C. *Battle at Bull Run: A History of the First Major Campaign of the Civil War*. Garden City, N.Y.: Doubleday, 1977.

———. *Jefferson Davis: The Man and His Hour, A Biography*. New York: HarperCollins, 1991.

———. *Rhett: The Turbulent Life and Times of a Fire-eater*. Columbia: University of South Carolina Press, 2001.

Dean, Eric T. *Shook over Hell: Post-traumatic Stress, Vietnam, and the Civil War*. Cambridge, Mass.: Harvard University Press, 1997.

Derden, John K. *The World's Largest Prison: The Story of Camp Lawton*. Macon, Ga.: Mercer University Press, 2012.

Divine, John E. *8th Virginia Cavalry*. Lynchburg, Va.: H. E. Howard, 1984.

Donald, David Herbert. *Lincoln*. New York: Simon and Schuster, 1995.

Dougherty, Kevin J. *Ships of the Civil War 1861–1865: An Illustrated Guide to the Fighting Vessels of the Union and the Confederacy*. London: Amber Books, 2013.

Driver, Robert J., Jr. *5th Virginia Cavalry*. Lynchburg, Va.: H. E. Howard, 1997.

Dunkleman, Mark H. *Brothers One and All: Esprit de Corps in a Civil War Regiment*. Baton Rouge: Louisiana State University Press, 2004.

Durham, Walter T. *Reluctant Partners: Nashville and the Union, 1863–1865*. Knoxville: University of Tennessee Press, 2008.

Dyer, Thomas G. *Secret Yankees: The Union Circle in Confederate Atlanta*. Baltimore: Johns Hopkins University Press, 1999.

Eddy, Richard. *History of the Sixtieth Regiment of New York Volunteers, from the Commencement of Its Organization in July 1861 to Its Public Reception at Ogdensburgh as a Veteran Command, January 7th 1864*. Philadelphia: By the author, 1864. Reprint, Bedford, Mass.: Applewood Books.

Egan, Timothy. *The Immortal Irishman: The Irish Revolutionary Who Became an American Hero*. Boston: Houghton Mifflin Harcourt, 2016.

Elliott, Sam Davis. *Soldier of Tennessee: General Alexander P. Stewart and the Civil War in the West*. Baton Rouge: Louisiana State University Press, 1999.

Evans, David. *Sherman's Horsemen: Union Cavalry Operations in the Atlanta Campaign*. Bloomington: Indiana University Press, 1996.

Faust, Drew Gilpin. *Mothers of Invention: Women of the Slaveholding South in the American Civil War*. Chapel Hill: University of North Carolina Press, 1996.

———. *This Republic of Suffering: Death and the American Civil War*. New York: Knopf, 2008.

Foote, Lorien. *The Gentlemen and the Roughs: Manhood, Honor, and Violence in the Union Army*. New York: New York University Press, 2010.

Fox, William F. *Regimental Losses in the American Civil War, 1861–1865: A Treatise on the Extent and Nature of the Mortuary Losses in the Union Regiments, with Full and Exhaustive Statistics Compiled from the Official Records on File in the State Military Bureaus and at Washington*. Albany, N.Y.: Albany Publishing, 1889. Reprint, Dayton, Ohio: Press of Morningside Bookshop, 1974.

Frank, Joseph Allan. *With Ballot and Bayonet: The Political Socialization of American Civil War Soldiers*. Athens: University of Georgia Press, 1998.

Fraser, Walter J., Jr. *Charleston! Charleston! The History of a Southern City*. Columbia: University of South Carolina Press, 1989.

Gammage, W. L. *The Camp, the Bivouac and the Battle Field. Being a History of the Fourth Arkansas Regiment, From Its First Organization Down to the Present Date. "Its Campaigns and Its Battles" with an Occasional Reference to the Current Events of the Times, Including Biographical Sketches of Its Field Officers and Others of the "Old Brigade." The Whole Interspersed Here and There with Descriptions of Scenery, Incident to Camp Life, Etc.* Selma, Ala.: Cooper & Kimball, 1864. Reprint, Little Rock: Arkansas Southern Press, 1958.

Garrison, Webb. *Friendly Fire in the Civil War: More Than 100 True Stories of Comrade Killing Comrade*. Nashville: Rutledge Hill Press, 1999.

———. *Mutiny in the Civil War*. Shippensburg, Pa.: White Mane Publishing, 2001.

Gibbs, Joseph. *Three Years in the Bloody Eleventh: The Campaigns of a Pennsylvania Reserves Regiment*. University Park: Pennsylvania State University Press, 2002.

Goddard, M. E., and Henry V. Partridge. *A History of Norwich, Vermont, with Portraits and Illustrations*. Hanover, N.H.: Dartmouth Press, 1905.

Gordon, Lesley J. *A Broken Regiment: The 16th Connecticut's Civil War*. Baton Rouge: Louisiana State University Press, 2014.

Gould, John M. *History of the First-Tenth-Twenty-Ninth Maine Regiment. In Service of the United States from May 3, 1861 to June 21, 1866*. Portland, Maine: Stephen Berry, 1871.

Gragg, Rod. *Confederate Goliath: The Battle of Fort Fisher*. New York: HarperCollins, 1991.

Graham, Matthew J. *The Ninth Regiment New York Volunteers (Hawkins' Zouaves): Being a History of the Regiment and Veteran Association from 1860-1900*. New York, 1900.

Greene, A. Wilson. *Civil War Petersburg: Confederate City in the Crucible of War*. Charlottesville: University of Virginia Press, 2006.

Grimsley, Mark. *The Hard Hand of War: Union Military Policy toward Southern Civilians 1861–1865*. New York: Cambridge University Press, 1995.

Hale, Douglas. *The Third Texas Cavalry in the Civil War*. Norman: University of Oklahoma Press, 1993.

Harden, H. O. *History of the 90th Ohio Volunteer Infantry in the War of the Great Rebellion in the United States, 1861 to 1865*. Edited by Scott Cameron. Kent, Ohio: Kent State University Press, 2006.

Hartje, Robert G. *Van Dorn: The Life and Times of a Confederate General*. Nashville: Vanderbilt University Press, 1967.

Henderson, William D. *41st Virginia Infantry*. Lynchburg, Va.: H. E. Howard, 1986.

Hennessy, John J. *Return to Bull Run: The Campaign and Battle of Second Manassas*. New York: Simon & Schuster, 1993.

Henry, Robert Selph. *"First with the Most" Forrest*. Indianapolis: Bobbs-Merrill, 1944.

Herberich, John L. *Masters of the Field: The Fourth United States Cavalry in the Civil War*. Atglen, Pa.: Schiffer, 2015.

Herek, Raymond J. *These Men Have Seen Hard Service: The First Michigan Sharpshooters in the Civil War*. Detroit: Wayne State University Press, 1998.

Hess, Earl J. *The Battle of Ezra Church and the Struggle for Atlanta*. Chapel Hill: University of North Carolina Press, 2015.

————. *The Knoxville Campaign: Burnside and Longstreet in East Tennessee.* Knoxville: University of Tennessee Press, 2012.

————. *Lee's Tar Heels: The Pettigrew-Kirkland-MacRae Brigade.* Chapel Hill: University of North Carolina Press, 2002.

————. *The Union Soldier in Battle: Enduring the Ordeal of Combat.* Lawrence: University Press of Kansas, 1997.

Hewitt, Lawrence Lee. *Port Hudson: Confederate Bastion on the Mississippi.* Baton Rouge: Louisiana State University Press, 1987.

History of the Eleventh Pennsylvania Cavalry, Together with a Complete Roster of the Regiment and Regimental Officers. Philadelphia: Franklin Printing, 1902.

Hobbs, O. Kermit, Jr. *Storm Over Suffolk: The Years 1861–1865.* Suffolk, Va.: Suffolk Nansemond Historical Society, 1979.

Hughes, Nathaniel Cheairs, Jr. *The Battle of Belmont: Grant Strikes South.* Chapel Hill: University of North Carolina Press, 1991.

Hughes, Nathaniel Cheairs, Jr., and Gordon D. Whitney. *Jefferson Davis in Blue: The Life of Sherman's Relentless Warrior.* Baton Rouge: Louisiana State University Press, 2002.

Inscoe, John C., and Gordon B. McKinney. *The Heart of Confederate Appalachia: Western North Carolina in the Civil War.* Chapel Hill: University of North Carolina Press, 2000.

Jewett, Clayton E. *Texas in the Confederacy: An Experiment in Nation Building.* Columbia: University of Missouri Press, 2002.

Jones, Jacqueline. *Saving Savannah: The City and the Civil War.* New York: Vintage Books, 2009.

Jones, Terry L. *Lee's Tigers: The Louisiana Infantry in the Army of Northern Virginia.* Baton Rouge: Louisiana State University Press, 1987.

Jones, Virgil Carrington. *Eight Hours before Richmond.* New York: Henry Holt, 1957.

Keegan, John. *The Face of Battle.* New York: Viking Press, 1976.

————. *A History of Warfare.* New York: Knopf, 1993.

Kerby, Robert L. *Kirby Smith's Confederacy: The Trans-Mississippi South, 1863–1865.* New York: Columbia University Press, 1972.

Krick, Robert K. *Civil War Weather in Virginia.* Tuscaloosa: University of Alabama Press, 2007.

Leech, Margaret. *Reveille in Washington 1860–1865.* New York: Harper & Brothers, 1941.

Linderman, Gerald F. *Embattled Courage: The Experience of Combat in the American Civil War.* New York: Free Press, 1987.

Livermore, Thomas L. *Numbers and Losses in the Civil War in America, 1861–65.* Boston: Houghton Mifflin, 1900.

Longacre, Edward G. *The Early Morning of War Bull Run, 1861.* Norman: University of Oklahoma Press, 2014.

————. *From Union Stars to Top Hat: A Biography of the Extraordinary General James Harrison Wilson.* Harrisburg, Pa.: Stackpole Books, 1972.

————. *The Sharpshooters: A History of the Ninth New Jersey in the Civil War.* Lincoln, Neb.: Potomac Books, 2017.

Losson, Christopher. *Tennessee's Forgotten Warriors: Frank Cheatham and His Confederate Division.* Knoxville: University of Tennessee Press, 1989.

Lundberg, John R. *Granbury's Texas Brigade: Diehard Western Confederates.* Baton Rouge: Louisiana State University Press, 2012.

Marten, James. *The Children's Civil War*. Chapel Hill: University of North Carolina Press, 1998.

Marvel, William. *Andersonville: The Last Depot*. Chapel Hill: University of North Carolina Press, 1994.

———. *The Great Task Remaining: The Third Year of Lincoln's War*. Boston: Houghton Mifflin, 2010.

McCaslin, Richard B. *Tainted Breeze: The Great Hanging at Gainesville, Texas 1862*. Baton Rouge: Louisiana State University Press, 1994.

McFeely, William S. *Grant: A Biography*. New York: Norton, 1981.

McGowen, Stanley S. *Horse Sweat and Powder Smoke: The First Texas Cavalry in the Civil War*. College Station: Texas A&M University Press, 1999.

McKenzie, Robert Tracy. *Lincolnites and Rebels: A Divided Town in the American Civil War*. Oxford: Oxford University Press, 2006.

McKinney, Francis F. *Education in Violence: The Life of George H. Thomas and the History of the Army of the Cumberland*. Detroit: Wayne State University Press, 1961.

McKnight, Brian D. *Confederate Outlaw: Champ Ferguson and the Civil War in Appalachia*. Baton Rouge: Louisiana State University Press, 2011.

———. *Contested Borderland: The Civil War in Appalachian Kentucky and Virginia*. Lexington: University Press of Kentucky, 2006.

McNally, Margaret Cheney, and Frances L. Niles. *Norwich*. Charleston, S.C.: Arcadia, 1998.

McPherson, James M. *Battle Cry of Freedom: The Civil War Era*. New York: Oxford University Press, 1988.

———. *War on the Waters: The Union and Confederate Navies, 1861–1865*. Chapel Hill: University of North Carolina Press, 2012.

Miller, William J. *The Training of an Army: Camp Curtain and the North's Civil War*. Shippensburg, Pa.: White Mane Publishing, 1990.

Mitchell, Reid. *Civil War Soldiers: Their Expectations and Their Experiences*. New York: Viking Press, 1988.

———. *The Vacant Chair: The Northern Soldier Leaves Home*. New York: Oxford University Press, 1993.

Moe, Richard. *The Last Full Measure: The Life and Death of the First Minnesota Volunteers*. New York: Henry Holt, 1993.

Mohr, Clarence L. *On the Threshold of Freedom: Masters and Slaves in Civil War Georgia*. Athens: University of Georgia Press, 1986.

Morrison, Samuel Eliot. *The European Discovery of America: The Northern Voyages* A.D. *500–1600*. New York: Oxford University Press, 1971.

Myers, Barton A. *Rebels against the Confederacy: North Carolina's Unionists*. New York: Cambridge University Press, 2014.

Nash, Eugene A. *A History of the Forty-Fourth Regiment New York Volunteer Infantry*. Chicago: R. R. Donnelley, 1911.

Nelson, Scott Reynolds, and Carol Sheriff. *A People at War: Civilians and Soldiers in America's Civil War*. New York: Oxford University Press, 2007.

Noe, Kenneth W. *Reluctant Rebels: The Confederates Who Joined the Army after 1861*. Chapel Hill: University of North Carolina Press, 2010.

Paludan, Phillip Shaw. *Victims: A True Story of the Civil War*. Knoxville: University of Tennessee Press, 1984.

Parks, Joseph H. *General Leonidas Polk, C.S.A.: The Fighting Bishop*. Baton Rouge: Louisiana State University Press, 1962.

Perry, Aldo S. *Civil War Courts-Martial of North Carolina Troops*. Jefferson, N.C.: McFarlane, 2012.

Phillips, Christopher. *Damned Yankee: The Life of General Nathaniel Lyon*. Columbia: University of Missouri Press, 1990.

Phisterer, Frederick. *New York in the War of the Rebellion*. Albany: J. B. Lyons and Co., State Printers, 1912.

———. *Statistical Record of the Armies of the United States*. New York: Charles Scribner's Sons, 1883.

Rable, George C. *Fredericksburg! Fredericksburg!* Chapel Hill: University of North Carolina Press, 2002.

Ragan, Mark K. *Union and Confederate Submarine Warfare in the Civil War*. Mason City, Iowa: Savas Publishing, 1999.

Ramage, James A. *Gray Ghost: The Life of John Singleton Mosby*. Lexington: University Press of Kentucky, 1999.

Ramold, Steven J. *Slaves, Sailors, Citizens: African Americans in the Union Navy*. DeKalb: Northern Illinois University Press, 2002.

Rennolds, Edwin H. *A History of the Henry County Commands Which Served in the Confederate States Army*. Kennesaw, Ga.: Continental Book Company, 1961.

Revels, Tracy J. *Florida's Civil War: Terrible Sacrifices*. Macon, Ga.: Mercer University Press, 2016.

Rhea, Gordon C. *The Battle of the Wilderness May 5–6, 1864*. Baton Rouge: Louisiana State University Press, 1994.

———. *The Battles for Spotsylvania Court House and the Road to Yellow Tavern May 7–12, 1864*. Baton Rouge: Louisiana State University Press, 1997.

———. *Cold Harbor: Grant and Lee May 26–June 3, 1864*. Baton Rouge: Louisiana State University Press, 2002.

Robertson, James I., Jr. *Soldiers Blue and Gray*. Columbia: University of South Carolina Press, 1988.

———. *Stonewall Jackson: The Man, the Soldier, the Legend*. New York: Macmillan, 1997.

———. *The Untold Civil War: Exploring the Human Side of the Civil War*. Edited by Neil Kagan. Washington, D.C.: National Geographic, 2011.

Ross, Ishbel. *Rebel Rose: Life of Rose O'Neal Greenhow, Confederate Spy*. New York: Ballantine Books, 1973.

Salecker, Gene Eric. *Disaster on the Mississippi: The Sultana Explosion, April 27, 1865*. Annapolis, Md.: Naval Institute Press, 1996.

Scharf, J. Thomas. *History of St. Louis City and County, from the Earliest Periods to the Present Day: Including Biographical Sketches of Representative Men*. Philadelphia: Louis H. Everts, 1883.

Schroeder, Patrick A. *More Myths about Lee's Surrender*. Farmville, Va.: Farmville Printing, 1995.

Schroeder-Lein, Glenna R. *Confederate Hospitals on the Move: Samuel L. Stout and the Army of Tennessee*. Columbia: University of South Carolina Press, 1994.

Schultz, Duane. *The Dahlgren Affair: Terror and Conspiracy in the Civil War*. New York: Norton, 1998.

Sears, Stephen W. *Gettysburg*. Boston: Houghton Mifflin, 2003.

———. *Landscape Turned Red: The Battle of Antietam*. New York: Ticknor & Fields, 1983.

Shaffer, Michael K. *Washington County, Virginia, in the Civil War*. Charleston, S.C.: History Press, 2012.

Sheads, Scott Sumpter, and Daniel Carroll Toomey. *Baltimore during the Civil War*. Linthicum, Md.: Toomey Press, 1997.

Sheehan-Dean, Aaron. *Why Confederates Fought: Family and Nation in Civil War Virginia*. Chapel Hill: University of North Carolina Press, 2007.

Silkenat, David. *Moments of Despair: Suicide, Divorce, and Debt in the Civil War Era*. Chapel Hill: University of North Carolina Press, 2011.

Slim, Hugo. *Killing Civilians: Method, Madness, and Morality in War*. New York: Columbia University Press, 2008.

Smith, Derek. *The Gallant Dead: Union and Confederate Generals Killed in the Civil War*. Mechanicsburg, Pa.: Stackpole Books, 2005.

Smith, Myron, J. *The Fight for the Yazoo, August 1862–July 1864: Swamps, Forts and Fleets on Vicksburg's Northern Flank*. Jefferson, N.C.: McFarland, 2012.

Smith, Timothy B. *Mississippi in the Civil War: The Home Front*. Jackson: University Press of Mississippi, 2010.

Spar, Ira. *New Haven's Civil War Hospital: A History of Knight U.S. General Hospital, 1862–1865*. Jefferson, N.C.: McFarlane, 2014.

Speer, Lonnie R. *Portals to Hell: Military Prisons of the Civil War*. Mechanicsburg, Pa.: Stackpole Books, 1997.

Starr, Stephen Z. *The Union Cavalry in the East: From Gettysburg to Appomattox*. 3 vols. Baton Rouge: Louisiana State University Press, 1979–1985.

Steiner, Paul E. *Disease in the Civil War: Natural Biological Warfare in 1861–1865*. Springfield, Ill.: C. C. Thomas, 1968.

Swanberg, W. A. *First Blood: The Story of Fort Sumter*. New York: Charles Scribner's Sons, 1957.

Sword, Wiley. *Courage under Fire: Profiles in Bravery from the Battlefields of the Civil War*. New York: St. Martin's Press, 2007.

———. *Shiloh: Bloody April*. New York: William Morrow, 1974. Reprinted, with new introduction. Dayton, Ohio: Morningside Press, 2001.

———. *Southern Invincibility: A History of the Confederate Heart*. New York: St. Martin's Press, 1999.

Symonds, Craig L. *The Civil War at Sea*. Santa Barbara, Calif.: Praeger, 2009.

———. *Lincoln and His Admirals: Abraham Lincoln, the U.S. Navy, and the Civil War*. New York: Oxford University Press, 2008.

Thomas, Emory M. *The Confederacy as a Revolutionary Experience*. Englewood Cliffs, N.J.: Prentice-Hall, 1971.

———. *The Confederate State of Richmond: A Biography of the Capital*. Austin: University of Texas Press, 1971.

———. *Robert E. Lee: A Biography*. New York: Norton, 1995.

Trask, Benjamin H. *16th Virginia Infantry*. Lynchburg, Va.: H. E. Howard, 1986.

Trask, Kerry A. *Fire Within: A Civil War Narrative from Wisconsin*. Kent, Ohio: Kent State University Press, 1995.

Van Horne, Thomas B. *History of the Army of the Cumberland: Its Organization, Campaigns, and Battles Written at the Request of Major-General George H. Thomas Chiefly from His Private Military Journal and Official and Other Documents Furnished by Him.* 2 vols. and atlas. Cincinnati: Robert Clarke, 1875.

Venner, William Thomas. *The 7th Tennessee Infantry in the Civil War: A History and Roster.* Jefferson, N.C.: McFarland, 2013.

Walker, Francis A. *History of the Second Army Corps in the Army of the Potomac.* New York: Charles Scribner's Sons, 1886.

Wallace, Lee A., Jr. *3rd Virginia Infantry.* Lynchburg, Va.: H. E. Howard, 1986.

Warner, Ezra J. *Generals in Blue: Lives of the Union Commanders.* Baton Rouge: Louisiana State University Press, 1964.

———. *Generals in Gray: Lives of the Confederate Commanders.* Baton Rouge: Louisiana State University Press, 1959.

Weber, Thomas. *The Northern Railroads in the Civil War, 1861–1865.* Bloomington: Indiana University Press, 1999.

Weitz, Mark A. *More Damning Than Slaughter: Desertion in the Confederate Army.* Lincoln: University of Nebraska Press, 2005.

Wert, Jeffry D. *A Brotherhood of Valor: The Common Soldiers of the Stonewall Brigade, C.S.A. and the Iron Brigade, U.S.A.* New York: Simon & Schuster, 1999.

———. *Custer: The Controversial Life of George Armstrong Custer.* New York: Simon & Schuster, 1996.

———. *Mosby's Rangers.* New York: Simon & Schuster, 1990.

———. *The Sword of Lincoln: The Army of the Potomac.* New York: Simon & Schuster, 2005.

Whitney, J. H. E. *The Hawkins Zouaves (Ninth N.Y.V.): Their Battles and Marches.* New York, 1866.

Wiley, Bell Irvin. *The Life of Billy Yank: The Common Soldier of the Union.* Baton Rouge: Louisiana State University Press, 1952.

———. *The Life of Johnny Reb: The Common Soldier of the Confederacy.* Baton Rouge: Louisiana State University Press, 1943.

———. *They Who Fought Here.* New York: Macmillan, 1959.

Wills, Brian Steel. *A Battle from the Start: The Life of Nathan Bedford Forrest.* New York: HarperCollins, 1992.

———. *Confederate General William Dorsey Pender: The Hope of Glory.* Baton Rouge: Louisiana State University Press, 2011.

———. *George Henry Thomas: As True as Steel.* Lawrence: University Press of Kansas, 2012.

———. *The River Was Dyed with Blood: Nathan Bedford Forrest and Fort Pillow.* Norman: University of Oklahoma Press, 2014.

———. *The War Hits Home: The Civil War in Southeastern Virginia.* Charlottesville: University Press of Virginia, 2001.

Wills, Garry. *Lincoln at Gettysburg: The Words That Remade America.* New York: Simon & Schuster, 1992.

Wilson, Harold S. *Confederate Industry: Manufacturers and Quartermasters in the Civil War.* Jackson: University Press of Mississippi, 2002.

Winkle, Kenneth J. *Lincoln's Citadel: The Civil War in Washington, DC.* New York: Norton, 2013.

Winschel, Terence J. *Triumph and Defeat: The Vicksburg Campaign*. Mason City, Iowa: Savas Publishing, 1999.

Winter, William C. *The Civil War in St. Louis: A Guided Tour*. St. Louis: Missouri Historical Society Press, 1994.

Wyeth, John Allan. *Life of General Nathan Bedford Forrest*. New York: Harper & Bros., 1899.

Articles

Alexander, Ted. "Destruction, Disease, and Death: The Battle of Antietam and the Sharpsburg Civilians." *Civil War Regiments* 6, no. 2 (1998): 142–173.

Berger, Diana S. "The Track Is Clear to Shohola: Disaster on the Road to Elmira." *Blue and Gray Magazine* 10, no. 4 (April 1993): 24–28.

Bledsoe, Andrew S. "The Destruction of the Army of Tennessee's Officer Corps at the Battle of Franklin." In *The Tennessee Campaign of 1864*, edited by Steven E. Woodworth and Charles D. Greear, 66–80. Carbondale: Southern Illinois University Press, 2016.

Burton, David L. "Richmond's Great Homefront Disaster: Friday the 13th." *Civil War Times* 21, no. 6 (October 1982): 36–41.

Gallman, J. Matthew, and Stanley L. Engerman. "The Civil War Economy: A Modern View." In J. Matthew Gallman, *Northerners at War: Reflections on the Civil War Home Front*, 87–119. Kent, Ohio: Kent State University Press, 2010.

Glatthaar, Joseph T. "The Costliness of Discrimination: Medical Care for Black Troops in the Civil War." In *Inside the Confederate Nation: Essays in Honor of Emory M. Thomas*, edited by Lesley J. Gordon and John C. Inscoe, 251–271. Baton Rouge: Louisiana State University Press, 2005.

Hacker, J. David. "A Census-Based Count of the Civil War Dead." *Civil War History* 57, no. 4 (December 2011): 307–348.

Hewitt, Lawrence Lee. "Introduction." In *Confederate Generals in the Trans-Mississippi*, edited by Lawrence Lee Hewitt, with Arthur W. Bergeron Jr. and Thomas E. Shott. Knoxville: University of Tennessee Press, 2013.

Hoffsommer, Robert D. "The Wreck of the Prisoners' Train." *Civil War Times Illustrated* 3, no. 2 (May 1964): 38–39.

Huff, Leo E. "The Last Duel in Arkansas: The Marmaduke-Walker Duel." *Arkansas Historical Quarterly* 23, no. 1 (Spring 1964): 36–49.

Jackson, Jack. "The Great Locomotive Wreck." *Civil War Times Illustrated* 33, no. 6 (January/February): 48–53.

Kohl, Rhonda M. "'This Godforsaken Town': Death and Disease at Helena, Arkansas, 1862–63." *Civil War History* 50, no. 2 (June 2004): 109–144.

Phillips, Christopher. "The Hard-Line War: The Ideological Basis of Irregular Warfare in the Western Border States." In *The Civil War Guerrilla: Unfolding the Black Flag in History, Memory, and Myth*, edited by Joseph M. Beilein Jr. and Matthew C. Hulbert, 13–41. Lexington: University Press of Kentucky, 2015.

Rayburn, Ella S. "Sabotage at City Point." *Civil War Times Illustrated* 22, no. 2 (April 1983): 30–31.

Sommerville, Diane Miller, "'A Burden Too Heavy to Bear': War Trauma, Suicide, and Confederate Soldiers," *Civil War History* 59, no. 4 (December 2013): 453–491.

Still, William N., Jr. "The Confederate Tar." In *Raiders and Blockaders: The American Civil*

War Afloat, edited by William N. Still Jr., John M. Taylor, and Norman C. Delaney, 80–99. Washington, D.C.: Brassey's, 1998.

Symonds, Craig L. "Land Operations in Virginia." In *Virginia at War, 1861,* edited by William C. Davis and James I. Robertson Jr., 27–44. Lexington: University Press of Kentucky, 2005.

"'This Hell of Destruction': The Benjamin Thompson Memoir, Part II." *Civil War Times* 12, no. 6 (October 1973): 13–23.

Thomas, Emory M. "The Kilpatrick-Dahlgren Raid, Part II." *Civil War Times Illustrated* 17, no. 4 (April 1978): 26–33.

Wills, Brian Steel. "The Confederate Sun Sets on Selma: Nathan Bedford Forrest and the Defense of Alabama in 1865." In *The Yellowhammer War: The Civil War and Reconstruction in Alabama,* edited by Kenneth W. Noe, 71–89. Tuscaloosa: University of Alabama Press, 2013.

Index